HARDPRESS.NET
HOME OF HARD-TO-FIND BOOKS

The Knickerbocker
by Charles Fenno Hoffman

Address:
HardPress
8345 NW 66TH ST #2561
MIAMI FL 33166-2626
USA
Email: info@hardpress.net

THE

Knickerbocker,

OR

NEW-YORK MONTHLY MAGAZINE

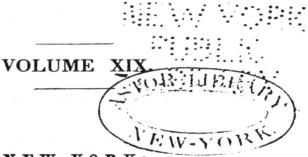

VOLUME XIX.

NEW-YORK:

PUBLISHED BY JOHN BISCO, 121 FULTON STREET.

1842.

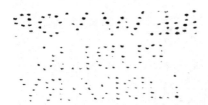

INDEX.

THE KNICKERBOCKER.

Vol. XIX.   JANUARY, 1842.   No. 1.

PARALLEL BETWEEN BONAPARTE AND WELLINGTON.

BY AN AMERICAN.

THE early part of the nineteenth century beheld military fame carried to a higher point perhaps than any other period since the earth was formed. The French revolution taking place the latter part of the eighteenth century, seemed to prepare the way for torrents of blood; for revolutions, and heart-stirring events and changes, which shook the nations of Europe as with an earthquake. Distinguished military captains made their appearance in rapid succession. Doumourier and Pichegru astonished the world by the rapidity of their conquests and the splendor of their achievements. So high was their renown in arms, that other aspirants for glory in war had little hopes of reaching, much less of surpassing and eclipsing it.

But subsequently their names were almost forgotten in the noise which that of BONAPARTE raised through the world, carrying with it dismay to the nations bordering on France. Their splendid exploits were soon overshadowed by the dazzling glory which accompanied his footsteps. He rose rapidly through all the grades of military honor, till he became General, Field-Marshal, First Consul, Consul for three years, Consul for life, and finally Emperor of the French. His battles were numerous, (and his victories for a long time kept pace with them,) and his conquests great and surprising. His power accumulated rapidly, and threatened the subjugation of all Europe. Great Britain alone, separated from France by the Straits of Dover, and protected by her wooden walls, escaped his inroads, and her soil the tracks of 'the Grand Army.' Although long menaced by immense preparations on the opposite coast, and the hostile array of 'the army of invasion,' the shores and cliffs of 'those famed Islanders,' as he termed the English, were never visited by his eagles, and felt not the feet of his standard-bearers. He was much chagrinned that he could not gain the ascendancy over that nation, and bring this ancient enemy, and sometimes the conqueror of France, submissive to his feet. It was an object which lay near his heart, and which, being effected, would have placed him on the very pinnacle of glory. This he kept in mind in all his campaigns on the Continent; and he was constantly augmenting his navy at home, intending to dispute with his antagonist the dominion of the ocean. Having the control of Spain, and uniting her navy with that of France, he was elated with the expectation of soon riding triumphant also on the water, and thus gaining the object so dear to him.

It was a critical moment for Great Britain. Neutral nations, particularly the United States, looked with deep interest and trembling solicitude at the issue, fearing it might be Old England's last struggle. But her favorite son, the hero of the Nile, was the instrument in rescuing his country from this perilous state; falling himself, to use the language of Collingwood, 'in the arms of Victory.' The combined fleet was discomfited; and Nelson's victory off Trafalgar was thenceforth the most splendid in the annals of naval engagements.

About this time another favorite son was making his appearance on the theatre of action, and was destined to run a successful and glorious career on the land. It was Sir ARTHUR WELLESLEY, since the DUKE OF WELLINGTON. Subsequent events called him to measure swords with Napoleon himself.

After several years' service in India, with distinguished credit as a general officer, he went to Portugal, and long tried the manœuvres and policy of war with Massena, one of Bonaparte's most favorite field-marshals. In Spain he spent several years, alternately in defensive and offensive war with some of the ablest generals of France, Jourdan, Marmont, Suchet, and Soult. Many a hard-fought battle and illustrious victory was sustained and won by him. The Peninsular campaigns formed the scene of his principal military labors. He pursued Marshal Soult into the southern part of France; and near Bayonne and Toulouse fought several bloody battles; one or two even after Bonaparte had capitulated in Paris, and before the news had reached the frontiers.

After Bonaparte's escape from Elba, Wellington again took the field; and the long and arduous struggle, in which most of the nations of Europe had been involved, was finally settled at Waterloo. The star of Wellington was ascendant, and Napoleon was compelled to relinquish, like Hannibal, the fond hope of entering the capital of his steadfast enemy. He has since died at St. Helena; and Wellington survives at the age of seventy years. Their mighty exploits are before the world, and the palm of generalship, compared with most if not all other captains, is to be awarded them.

But to weigh in the balance of justice and equity their military qualifications and deeds; to draw the line of demarkation between their respective claims, and show which has the precedence, is a difficult task. Perhaps it is premature yet to attempt it. Sufficient time may not have yet elapsed since they were in the field of competition, to do it with candor and impartiality. The prejudices of partisanship and national jealousies may not have sufficiently subsided, and the blindness of favoritism removed.

But on this side of the Atlantic we have been little more than spectators in this great drama of European nations. We viewed it with emotions somewhat resembling those with which we read history, and look at similar acts in the past nations of the world. In doing this, we incline, perhaps unavoidably, to one side. Taking all things into consideration, we think, and it is undoubtedly true, that one of the parties in these great national struggles has the greater claims to our approbation and sympathy. In the feats of generalship, the plan of campaigns, and the execution, in reducing fortresses, and fortified towns; in selecting sites for encampments, and the ground to await an attack, and for the battle-field; in conducting the operations of the conflict; the use made of victory, and the manner of retreat, we cannot avoid forming our opinions of different leaders. ' Nor would it be strange if we should at times manifest bias and partiality in forming these opinions. But so far from the scene of action, and after a lapse of more than a quarter of a century since the actors retired from the field, we are surely in not much more danger of undue prepossessions than in reading the history of Rome and Carthage, and in drawing a comparison between Cæsar and Hannibal.

In running a parallel between Bonaparte and Wellington, it will be only as military captains, and their characters in the profession of arms; and not in the rank sustained by them, as Emperor of the French, and the Duke of Wellington, a subject of the Sovereign of Great Britain.

In their early choice and fondness of military life, there was a resemblance in them. They early chose arms as a profession. Thus Bonaparte, while a lad, said to the youth who had rescued him from a watery grave, ' I am not now in a situation to reward you; but my *sword* may earn me the means of doing it at some future period.' Wellington, a school-boy, turned his attention to military studies; and arrived at manhood, chose the army as his department for life. Being offered a seat in Parliament, he accepted it only on condition of returning to his profession of arms when he chose, and opportunity presented. They both rose regularly through the grades of distinction in the army, from the lowest to the highest.

Bonaparte was distinguished for his rapid movements. He prided himself much on surprising his enemy, and taking him unprepared. Indeed this was a leading trait in his military character; and places him in this respect above all other leaders, ancient or modern. As he generally engaged in offensive wars, making conquests and subjugating kings and emperors to his control, the choice of time and manner in making his attacks was with him. He made his preparations with celerity and little noise; without exciting the suspicion, and often without the knowledge, of his opponent. He had the address to make his enemies believe that he was for peace, or at any rate without intention of immediate hostilities; and thus lull them into a false security. Such was his adroitness in this part of military tactics, that it was difficult and almost impossible for those watching his movements to conjecture in what direction he would begin his march, or where would fall the first blow. In this way he often foiled the plans of the most skilful leaders, and secured great advantages to himself. The march of his armies was so sudden and rapid, and the first onset so impetuous, that consternation and confusion were produced in the ranks of the enemy before they were aware of the cause. This was his favorite policy through life, and was pursued by him in his very last campaign. The short time he spent in Paris after his escape from Elba was diligently though quietly improved in collecting and equipping, to use the words of Marshal Ney, 'one of the best-appointed armies in the world.' This army was marched with incredible celerity into the heart of Belgium; and before the Allied forces were concentrated, Blucher was attacked with great spirit and defeated; and the van-guard of the English army driven back. So sudden and silent was his advance, and so unguarded against this his usual stratagem were his enemies, that many of the English officers were at a ball in Brussels when the report of cannon announced his arrival in the vicinity.

Wellington was distinguished for cool, determined, unyielding resistance. In this very important qualification in a general he was perhaps unrivalled. It is indeed true that his great antagonist was not so often called to the exercise of this military endowment. Opportunities however of displaying it could not be wanting to him in the great variety of circumstances in which his military career placed him. Nor is it said that he was deficient, but that he was not so distinguished in this respect as Wellington. The latter was cautious and wary before risking battle; but having engaged in it, it seemed to be his fixed purpose to keep his ground. Thus in Portugal he disputed the ground inch by inch, so to speak, with Massena. The greatest firmness and perseverance marked his conduct in that celebrated campaign, and indeed throughout the war of the Peninsula. These countries had been nominally conquered, but not subdued and won over in cordial reconciliation to the terms of the conqueror. Its strong-holds were occupied by the invader's troops; but the people were divided, or rather most of them were in a state of revolt from his authority. The army of Wellington was made up in part of undisciplined and inexperienced Spanish and Portuguese soldiers. With these and his own soldiers he had to meet Bonaparte's lieutenant and his most experienced troops, with a charge from him that Spain *must* be made to respect his authority.

In such circumstances, he found need of the highest military talents, but especially the faculty of resisting and turning back accumulated difficulties. He was endowed with the right qualifications. For several years he there sustained the cause of those invaded nations, resisting attack after attack with cool and deliberate fortitude and perseverance. By long encountering and overcoming their enemy, he won the confidence of the Spanish nation, and by persevering efforts was enabled to force him to quit their territories. This military trait, that of unflinching resistance, he communicated more or less to his soldiers. It was displayed in a striking manner by both at the battle of Waterloo. So unmoved were the troops at the reiterated assaults upon them, that Bonaparte could not suppress his admiration, who said to Soult, 'They will yield at last.' 'No, Sire,' said he, 'they prefer being cut down.' To the request made him twice from the same regiment to send them help, he returned answer that he had none to send; they must with him maintain their ground to the last. They did it. If the wish said to have been expressed by him toward the close of the battle, that 'night or Blucher would come,' was evidence of the critical state of the battle, and of the pressure of difficulties on his mind, it manifested also his purpose of dying on the field rather than yield it to the enemy.

The secret of Bonaparte's great success in the former part of his career was the want of union among the allied powers, and the consternation inspired by his sudden onset. It is difficult to bring separate and independent nations to act with the union and celerity of a single one. Jealousies and clashing interests more or less prevail, and prevent concentrated and united effort. This was the case with the several confederacies to counteract his increasing menacing power. Each nation had its own armies and officers and mode of operation; and each waited for the other to go forward and take the lead, watchfully guarding against doing in advance more than its share. A want of understanding between them existed, and they pursued a different and contrary policy; some of them prompt and efficient in their measures and movements; others dilatory and embarrassing. Bonaparte took advantage of this state of things; and no man knew better how to do this. Making good use of the natural impetuosity of the French, and even increasing it by his own example of enthusiastic ardor and rapid motion, he defeated in detail the armies of his opponents. Choosing his own time and manner of striking the first blow, he threw into disorder their operations, and disconcerted their plans before they were brought to maturity.

In attack also his policy was to make the onset as impressive and tremendous as possible; thus carrying dismay into the heart of his antagonist: the first opposing army being discomfited, weakened the confidence of the next, till dispirited they were all in succession overcome, and he was deemed invincible. But experience at length convinced the allies of the necessity of more united action. Their own safety required it. Making a common cause in earnest against their wary adversary, they learned to meet him on more equal terms. They began to gain confidence, and to question his invincibility. His celerity and ardor were met in a similar way; and his impetuous assaults with determined resistance, till the tide of success turned, and victory changed sides.

The success of Wellington seemed the result of skill and constancy, and comprehensive foresight. It was not owing to the coincidence of favorable circumstances. This he did not enjoy. The very *name* of his antagonist was a terror to nations; and he was surrounded by numerous field-marshals and generals, skilful and experienced, and with veteran troops in abundance. He had at command exhaustless resources; the wealth and power of almost all continental Europe. Spain and Portugal, the principal seat of Wellington's military operations, were in an unsettled state, and had been more or less overrun by the French. The number of British troops with him was comparatively small. He could not have effected what he did in the Peninsula without consummate military talents. He had to make soldiers from raw recruits, organize a provisional government, and resist the persevering encroachments of a vigilant and powerful enemy; and this he did for a series of years in succession. He fought several very severe and bloody battles with distinguished success; and by siege and storm gained possession of several towns as well fortified and garrisoned as any in Europe. He finally compelled Bonaparte's lieutenant with his armies to quit the country. It is impossible that such advantages should have been the effect of ordinary skill in conducting the operations of war. There must have been the highest mental resources in the leader who under such circumstances devised and executed plans so varied, extensive, and effective. It may, it is apprehended, be safely said, that the peninsular campaigns were more distinguished for high military science and foresight, and minute and circumspect calculation, than any since the French revolution. It was so on both sides. It was a war of mental resources and policy; of marches and countermarches; of resolute, fixed purpose; of patient and cool deliberation. The judgment and comprehensive perspicacity of Wellington shone conspicuous, and gained him in this respect the first place among military chieftains, not excepting his great competitor at Waterloo. In effecting the glorious events of that period, he owed less to physical force than to the resources of his own mind.

Bonaparte was hasty in forming the plans of his campaigns, and sometimes failed in executing them. Action, rapid movement, display, and the ardor of enterprise, and of making a strong first impression, were so characteristic of that extraordinary man, that he was hurried into measures without due consideration and reflection. Steadily intent on the object to be attained, and dazzled with the glory of its achievement, he sometimes overlooked intermediate and minor steps, and yet steps necessary to enable him to reach it. Less cautious in removing interposing obstacles than prudence required, he was led beyond the bounds of reason and moderation. Thus he failed in his expedition to Egypt; lost his fleet at the mouth of the Nile; and his army by disasters and sickness was dissipated; and he returned almost alone, gaining little or no honor to himself, and procuring no benefit or glory to France. Such was the Russian campaign. Glory fixed his mind; and the thought of wintering in the ancient capital of the Czars inspired him with an enthusiasm which seemed to render him inattentive to the voice of prudence and the warnings of experience. Did he make his calculations for the various casualties and uncertainties of war? Why did he commence this expedition so late in the season? Did he secure his way for a safe return, if necessity should compel him to retreat? Did he maturely weigh the consequences of a defeat in a Russian winter climate? If he had been circumspect and deliberate in all his calculations, would his powerful and well-appointed army have been so nearly annihilated amid the dreary desolations of a northern winter?

Thus he seemed not so much desirous of securing what he had gained, as of making new conquests; not content with the glory and advantages acquired by his great victories, he sought to gather fresh and still more glittering laurels. The glory of rising from the condition of an ordinary citizen of Corsica to the throne of France was not sufficient. He seemed to aim at nothing less than the diadem and monarchy of Europe. But he neglected to secure his acquisitions as he went forward. Much that seemed accomplished was so only in appearance, and cost him much trouble in retracing once and again his steps. Even after the current of adversity was setting strongly against him, and experience ought to have made him more cautious, opportunity remained to have secured to himself and family the crown of France. But '*cedere nescii ;*' he could not brook the thought of being baffled in his purposes, much less of descending from the eminence which he had already reached. He seemed governed by the determination of either gaining or losing all. Neglecting to make sure his steps as he advanced, and deaf to the voice of friends and counsellors, and the lessons of experience, he *lost all.*

Wellington was deliberate and circumspect in forming his plans, and rarely failed in their execution. His position was indeed more often defensive, and therefore not admitting so much choice and latitude in measures of operation. But it does not hence follow that equal military knowledge and art are not necessary. In offensive war the leader is his own rule of action ; and can make his own selection in the points of attack, and vary his plans according to circumstances. But he that acts on the defensive has not only to guard his own posts from being surprised and taken, but to read in his movements the purpose of his adversary, and govern himself accordingly. He had the faculty to do this ; to comprehend the policy and intentions of his enemy before they were developed, and successfully to counteract them. He rarely failed in his manœuvres to accomplish his design. Guarded and deliberate in his movements, and securing every advantage as he gained it, he advanced, if slowly at first, yet safely, and with certainty. Thus advancing from one position to another, and guarding his acquisitions, he in time became the assailant, particularly in Spain. Marshal Soult he foiled in attempting to get in his rear, and brought him to battle near Pamplona after thirty-six hours of rapid and parallel marching of the two armies, in which Wellington proved himself not deficient in celerity of movements and operations ; a policy in which Bonaparte so much excelled. In the last struggle at Waterloo, the plan of campaign on the part of Wellington was successfully executed. If he retreated a few leagues before the battle took place, it was that he might have the coöperation of Blucher and the Prussian army. He secured to the very last his positions as he advanced, and rose to the highest elevation. If he rose gradually, he had no falls, no eclipses. His was the light and glory of the unclouded ascending sun.

Bonaparte had the control of ample means of carrying into effect all his warlike schemes. He had converted France into one great magazine of war ; and having only to make known his will, men, money, weapons, and military stores came to him in abundance. His system of recruiting his army by annual conscription placed at his disposal the flower of the male population of France. All these means of carrying forward wars of conquests and usurpation were under his immediate call and direction. They came to him with the velocity and despatch so characteristic of himself. Such means in such hands might not be expected to remain inactive. Idolized as he was by the enthusiastic and warlike French, little less was to be apprehended than that the car of war would be rolled over the neighboring nations. But that he should so arrest the gaze of the world by the overwhelming progress of his arms; that the centre of Europe should feel his footsteps, and the walls of most of her capitals be shaken by his cannon, and their gates opened to his triumphant entrance, was matter of reality rather than apprehension. That the coast of Africa should witness his prowess at the head of his army, and the snows of Moscow be tinged with the blood of his battles, were things little thought of till they were transactions. States, and kingdoms, and empires were overrun by his victorious armies; and the terms of holding their crowns and territories were dictated by him to kings and emperors. He broke once and again the combined power of Europe; dissolving the confederacies against him, defeating in detail and scattering their armies, before they could come to the succor one of the other. These things are proof of what a great and ambitious mind, with exhaustless means at command, can do under favorable circumstances.

Here one is reminded that Napoleon resembled Alexander more perhaps than any other ancient conqueror. They were both at the head of warlike nations; and selected from a boundless source, and controlled, their own means. Their conquests were alike great and extraordinary; and their progress rapid and irresistible.

But Wellington, like Hannibal, had to make the best use he could of the means placed in his hands. His appointment as general and field-marshal was from his king. His army and province were assigned him, and the plan of operations in a measure marked out to him. He was accountable to his sovereign for his measures and for the use made of the means intrusted to his care. As the Hanno faction in the senate of Carthage sought to cast a shade over the exploits and victories of Hannibal, and prevent supplies being sent him, ridiculing his despatches; so the opposition in parliament were for a time clamorous for his recall. They denounced the war of the Peninsula as impolitic, and endeavored to discredit and underrate the merits of him to whom it was intrusted.

So far then as generalship is to be estimated by the extent and splendor of military achievements, the difference in the means and circumstances of the two is to be taken into consideration. If in Bonaparte was seen more of the 'pomp and circumstance of war,' does it follow that Wellington could not have exhibited as much in a similar situation, and under the same incentives? But the preparations, plans, and demonstrations of Napoleon were on a scale more magnificent. Be it so. His means, opportunities, and incentives were proportionally and comparatively greater. Before the precedence is in this way to be conceded to Bonaparte, it is to be shown that he would have been what he was in the circumstances of Wellington; and that the latter could not have achieved what the former did, had he possessed his means. But it would be less difficult to make it evident that Wellington *might* have done what Bonaparte did, had he been in his place, than it would to satisfy military men that the latter *could*, in the same circumstances, have effected what was done by the former.

The number of their battles and victories is inconclusive in favor of either. So is their magnitude. Bonaparte may have been engaged in more battles, and those on a larger scale. His field of action was more extended; and his, and the armies opposed to him, were often very great.

Nor were the battles fought by Wellington few, or of minor importance. Spain, Portugal, and France and Belgium, witnessed not a few conflicts of his arms. Some of these also were battles to all intent of the first class, in numbers, extent and duration. Such were those of Talavera, Vittoria, Salamanca, Pamplona, Bayonne and Toulouse. If these may not compare in extent and importance with those of Austerlitz, Eulau, Tilsit, Marengo, and Borodino, surely that of Waterloo claims the precedence. If not in the number of men, yet in their discipline and conduct; in the extent of the ground occupied; the martial science displayed; the presence of mind manifested; in the repeated and desperate onsets; the unflinching resistance; in the carnage both of the slain and wounded; in the decisiveness of its issue, and in the consequences which followed, the battle of Waterloo stands unrivalled perhaps on the records of time.

If uniform success in pitched battles is evidence of martial talents in a leader, Wellington has in this respect the advantage. Of him it may be said, as it was of Cæsar, that he never lost a battle. This is no ordinary fortune in a general called to the trial of skill and constancy so often as he was, and in such circumstances. Meeting repeatedly in the fields of manœuvre and battle the very best of Bonaparte's marshals with some of his bravest troops, he gained the ascendancy uniformly; and in the first and only interview with their great master and exemplar, victory still stood by him. But it was a field contested in a manner worthy the teacher of such pupils; and memorable will be the spot where two such champions met, and spent the long eighteenth of June in the trial of martial skill and prowess.

The battles of Wellington were also decisive victories; not *drawn*, nor doubtful; leaving no room for his opponent to claim the mastery. Bonaparte lost the important battle of Liepsic decisively; and at Borodino and Dresden and other places, the palm of victory was denied him by his antagonists. If he often succeeded on occasions of the highest importance, on others equally momentous he failed. The success of Wellington was uniform; not that of faultless mediocrity, but often of incomparable judgment and comprehensive discernment, particularly at Waterloo.

In mistakes and errors committed, Wellington perhaps will not suffer in the comparison. He indeed detected one in himself, which perhaps might not otherwise have been brought against him; but for which he could hardly forgive himself. He had posted a guard in the farm-house of La Haye Sainte. In front of this the carnage became terrible; and the men enclosed in it had expended their ammunition. To supply them in front was impossible, because access was cut off by the enemy. In the rear, it might have been done, but it did not occur to him in season.   For this it is said he blamed himself when the battle was ended, and ever after.

Bonaparte is charged by Marshal Ney with committing a great mistake in suffering Marshal Grouchy with thirty thousand men to remain unengaged in the battle of Waterloo.   He was indeed sent to watch the movements of Blucher ; but he failed in throwing any obstacles in the way of his approach.   But the first object of Napoleon, said Ney, should have been the destruction of the English army.   He ought then, irrespective of the Prussians, to have concentrated his forces for the accomplishment of that object.   The addition of that corps of thirty thousand he supposes might have turned the fortune of the day in his favor.   The opinion of this distinguished officer that this was a military oversight in his great master will probably be sustained by competent judges.   It has already been said that the Russian campaign was commenced too late in the season ; and the disasters attending it prove that he misjudged in the time of commencing and the manner of prosecuting that stupendous undertaking.   He seemed not to have taken into consideration the possible and probable casualties attending it, nor made provision for failure and defeat.   If he intended by his Egyptian expedition to prepare the way to attack Great Britain in her East-India possessions, he failed in his purpose.   It is difficult to imagine how he should have committed such an error, and in that way aimed at an object so hopeless.   The miscalculation cost him a fine army and fleet ; a solitary frigate being left to bear him back to France.

In following up success and making good use of victory both were distinguished.   Bonaparte especially in this part of military tactics was conspicuous ; and with characteristic speed suffered not his enemy to forget the impression of the first blow before the second was applied. He gave him little opportunity to rally and recover from the disorder and consternation into which his first impetuous and often unexpected attack had thrown him.   He lost nothing by delay, and suffered not the ardor of his troops to cool by inaction.   The danger was on the other side ; that of being carried too far, and not seasonably setting bounds to his ambition.

As Wellington's position was more often defensive, the opportunities of exhibiting this trait of military character were not so many.   The numerous fortified towns in Spain enabled his enemy, though defeated and crippled in the field, to take shelter behind walls and ancient bulwarks.   In this way his retreat was more slow ; and the work of exterminating him from the country more arduous.   But after the conflict in Belgium, his pursuit of the French was rapid ; and a few days brought him to the gates of Paris.   The terms of capitulation were immediately signed, and Bonaparte became a prisoner.

The precedence of skill and adroitness in reducing fortified towns clearly belongs to Wellington.   Places thought impregnable yielded to his indefatigable assiduity, and to his military science in planning measures of besieging places and in planting the instruments of battering down or scaling walls.   He applied with great judgment and foresight the physical force at his command, and committed important and perilous services to tried officers and men.   The operations of regular sieges, requiring time and untiring perseverance; of resisting sorties, and of storming at critical moments redoubts and fenced cities, were conducted by him with singular success.   He watched at the same time the movements of the enemy in the field ; was ready to give him battle there ; and lost no opportunity of compelling and hastening his retreat.   This is one very important part of military qualifications in a general ; and the taking of Ciudad Rodrigo, Badajos, St. Sebastian, and other strong places, will remain monuments of Wellington's superior talents in this kind of warfare.

The skill of Bonaparte was not often exhibited in this way, and he has left no striking exemplification of his ability to bring to capitulation cities and garrisons, requiring regular and protracted circumvallation.   If he had the requisite qualifications, his ardent, impetuous temperament, and his love of field exploits, and of quick movements, precluded the exercise.   In discipline and in gaining the confidence and affection of their troops, both excelled.   Certainly with regard to order and subordination and martial appearance both the English and French armies at that time took the precedence of all other nations. This was owing to the personal inspection and superintendence of these remarkable men.   Wellington manifested less enthusiastic ardor in marshalling his men, but more skill and exactness in his evolutions.   If he was less frequently out in disguise at midnight, to try the faithfulness of his guards and sentinels, he was more regular in seeing personally that every thing was right and safe at the hour of rest, and at the early dawn.   If his soldiers did not so often salute him with huzzas, they stood by him to the last.

Bonaparte's faculty in securing the affections of his followers was wonderful ; several of his officers and attendants accompanying him into exile with the most affecting fidelity and devotedness.   Wellington enjoyed the confidence of his officers, who united with him in counsel on occasions of critical emergency.   In the battle of Waterloo his infantry often opened and closed upon him as he rode in; intercepting with their bayonets the pursuing cavalry of the enemy ; *enshielding* him, as it were, in their hearts and affections.   If Bonaparte was more enthusiastically hailed by his men, Wellington was not less steadfastly adhered to in the trying, perilous moment.   If the Imperial Guards obeyed with alacrity his last call, and went to the final onset crying ' Vive l'Empereur !'   Old England's Cold-Stream Guards stood fast by their leader, with warm hearts and strong arms ; and with levelled steel returned the charge, carrying before them the chillness of death and dismay.

In battle Wellington was generally on horse-back, and usually in front of his army, watching every movement of the enemy, and sending directions and messages to different points by his aids.   He was pre-eminent for presence of mind, deliberation, and fortitude; and when necessary, for exposing himself to imminent danger; quick in devising expedients to meet sudden emergencies, and in discerning and seizing the favorable moment to avail himself of any advantage to be gained by the errors of his opponents, and to secure the battle in his favor.   In his last battle these traits were wonderfully manifested.   His station in front of his army by a tree, which was thence named 'the Wellington Tree,' marked and scathed with balls, was as animating to his men as it was full of danger to himself. His resisting the request of his troops, time and again, to be led to the charge; and persuading them to keep their ground against the furious onsets of the enemy for nearly ten hours; and then ordering a charge, on his part, at the very right time, are evidences of his coolness and eagle-eyed discernment through all the events of that memorable day.

Bonaparte was equally tranquil during battle; gave orders with the utmost precision; and was a stranger to fear in the most perilous circumstances. His advancing with the standard to the bridge of Lodi, in the face of artillery, was an instance of memorable bravery. On many other occasions amid the din of arms he displayed the greatest self-possession and readiness of mind. He turned to good account every incident that could be made to bear in his favor. This was his general demeanor in battle. But at Waterloo he seemed, like Pompey at Pharsalia, to have been too confident of success. He relied more than usual on his marshals. His confidence was indeed well placed. They exerted all their skill in his behalf. Being informed by a prisoner that Wellington commanded the English army, 'It is well,' said he, 'but it will not avail.' He seemed far from apprehending such a result. He rode in his carriage, less conspicuous and exposed to danger than usual. It is difficult to account for his position and demeanor at this battle, but on the ground of being in little doubt of success. Highly respecting, as is evident from his words above, the character of Wellington as an officer, yet his estimate was too low of his military talents. This false measure of him by Bonaparte has probably led many others into the same error. His wounded honor and false pride prevented him subsequently from doing justice to his great and successful competitor.

Here one cannot but regret that these two men could not have had, like Hannibal and Scipio, a personal interview, attended by their officers; and in their tents conversed on the art of war and the chances of battle. Their estimate of each other might have been more correct, and Bonaparte might have found motives in the plain, unassuming deportment and martial accomplishments of the Irish hero, to have soothed his disappointment for the laurels lost at Waterloo. He might have seen that the game had been played by no ordinary hand; and if sides had changed and made him what his antagonist is, of all generals, ancient or modern, to him would have fallen the first place.

Wellington lives to enjoy the glory of his victories. The honors and rewards of his sovereign and his grateful country have been showered upon him in richest profusion. The highest honor at the disposal of the crown has been conferred upon him, and the office of Prime Minister has been given and offered him several times. In Belgium he sustains the title of Prince of Waterloo; and estates and annuities have been settled upon him accordingly. These and many other similar things being taken into consideration, the Conqueror of Napoleon occupies a position the most enviable of all military captains. Nelson fell in the conflict, and lived only to hear the shouts of victory. Wolfe fell on the walls of Quebec, living only to see the banners of his king floating on the Heights of Abraham. Hannibal, pursued by his implacable enemy, was driven to suicide; and the dead body of Pompey was thrown dishonored on the shores of Egypt. Alexander, in the height of his glory died of excess, an ignominious death; and Cæsar fell as a tyrant by the hands of his countrymen in the senate chamber of Rome. But Wellington lived to see the disturber of nations and the threatener of his country dethroned and powerless, and a military cordon encircling France for the safety and peace of Europe. Having been instrumental in raising the military renown of his country to the very summit of glory, he has for a quarter of a century since enjoyed the satisfaction of beholding her unrivalled prosperity, the smiles of Providence giving her a sovereign bearing a *name* corresponding with her standing among the nations of the earth. He and his country occupy a perilous eminence. They have yet to see how it will go with them in future. As death is the test of individual success or failure, so time is the test of national prosperity or adversity. How important that the individual so favored should become ' a soldier of the cross,' and a follower of ' the Prince of Peace,' and the kingdom thus distinguished cleave to that ' righteousness which exalteth a nation ! '

The Prince of Waterloo has lived to witness the fall of the French Emperor before the King of Terrors, the universal conqueror. He has seen this vanquisher of kings and emperors on the bed of death calling for his military dress, his sword, his boots and spurs, with which to meet the Last Enemy; a melancholy spectacle of the weakness of the strongest — of ' the ruling passion strong in death.' He has beheld the ashes of that mighty man translated from their lowly bed in the wastes of the sea, where for twenty years they had been ' a mark for all who sailed along the watery ways,' to the cemetery of the French kings; the six-fold coffin borne in sacred procession amid military parades, and the shadows of departed human greatness and glory !

Such is the singular position occupied by the Duke of Wellington; and if his head be not giddy with the elevation, farther proof is afforded of his military endowments — *moderation in success.* He has borne with unaffected modesty and self-denial the trials and temptations of *prosperity,* that rock on which so many promising beginnings have been fatally terminated. Victory did not intoxicate him; and his despatches, even after the battle of Waterloo, far from wearing the appearance of boasting and self-gratulation, exhibit the plainness of ordinary business communications, and unaffected sorrow in view of the price at which such advantages had been gained. How different the bulletins of ' the Grand Army ! ' With characteristic brevity they were indeed penned; but with ostentation also, and somewhat of boastful exaggeration.

Nor does Bonaparte gain in the comparison of the effects produced on their minds by great success. He was too much elated, and flattered himself that Fortune had chosen him as her favorite son for life. He was rendered vain by such singular prosperity; presumptuous in his expectations; rash and precipitate in his conduct and measures. But he bore adversity with unyielding constancy. He did not make a good use of his first disasters, by securing what was clearly left within his grasp. His exile however to St. Helena was endured with heroic fortitude and self-denial. The reverse was great, and almost unexampled, resembling that of Hannibal perhaps more than that of any other great captain. Rome, so to speak, could never sleep in safety while the Carthaginian general was alive and at large. They required Carthage to give him up to them; and by their incessant pursuit of him he was made a vagabond. To relieve them from the fear of his name he submitted to the frequent custom of the age, and swallowed poison rather than fall a prisoner into their hands. Europe felt unsafe while Napoleon was unrestrained, and demanded of France the keeping of his person, for the common safety. He surrendered himself into the hands of his most persevering enemy; and the councils of Europe awarded him his destiny. He rose superior to the temptation and weakness of suicide, and here the comparison ends. He exhibited the consummate resolution of looking steadily in the face degradation and exile.

But this eclipse of his glory and his disastrous end excite deep interest in his behalf, and perhaps partiality in judging of his character as a military man. That such a precipitate fall, such a termination of his days on a rock in the midst of the ocean, and the removal, 'with the pomp and circumstance of war,' of his coffin after a lapse of almost twenty years, should excite great sympathy for him, is natural. Such catastrophes stir the master passions of the soul, and call forth the strongest interest in behalf of the leading actors in them. Fiction strives in vain to reach such realities. The youthful reader of ancient history in following Hannibal over the Alps; reading the account of his great and decisive victories; of his encircling Rome itself; and of his being recalled to Africa after remaining in Italy seventeen years; compelled to give up all his sanguine hopes; and as he went, turning his eyes for the last time on her pleasant valleys and fruitful fields, blaming gods and men as the cause of his bitter disappointment, has been known to be more deeply affected than in the reading of any tale of fictitious suffering. The exit of Bonaparte furnishes another page in this world's history of intense sympathy. As time smooths over his footsteps, and wears out the blood that marked his course, the *circumstances* attending it will probably be made to extenuate his faults and magnify his virtues as a general and as a man. In weighing the claims of these men, this natural bias, created by the last acts in the drama, before the curtain dropped, should be counteracted. Their claims to preëminence in military fame should be decided by their counsels and deeds in war and in battle, and in the use made of victory. An attempt has been made to show what these were comparatively, in the foregoing pages. Napoleon is to be highly commended for the manner in which he sustained his reverses in the end. But the sympathy and partiality which these reverses are apt to excite in the mind of the *spectators*, should not be allowed to prejudice the claims of Wellington as an officer, or cast a shade over his exploits. The defeat of Bonaparte at Waterloo was not the result of any unfairness on the part of Wellington. The failure of the former should not therefore, through commiseration, be placed on a level with the success of the latter. It is more glorious in a leader so to conduct the operations of war as not to need commiseration, than it is to rely on it as a foil to the triumph of his competitor.

To the hardships of a soldier's life both were habituated. The habits of Wellington were more regular and systematic; and his life is represented as a model of military character. Bred in the midst of luxury, amply furnished with the means of ease and indulgence, he has been distinguished for the Roman virtues of abstinence and energy; of enduring fatigue and labor, watchfulness and privation. Scorning effeminacy, he seemed ambitious to inure himself to the most laborious exercises and to the simplest mode of living; and so formed a hardihood of character as honorable as it is singular in the self-indulgence and excess which surrounded him. His field-bed it is said was so narrow as not to admit of his turning in it; and being asked what he did when he wanted to turn himself, he replied, ' It is then time to turn out.' Not long since a sudden illness alarmed his friends; when it was found that it was faintness only, from spending a day in the toils of hunting, having taken no other sustenance save a crust of bread in the morning. Even now, having past more than seventy winters, report says, he has the appearance of being no more than forty-five years of age. Such traits in one so familiar with luxurious modes of living and examples of indolence and excess are admirable. They are such as are needed in military leaders; and by way of example have a powerful influence on subordinate officers, and on a whole army. In this way it might be expected that his troops would be, what they proved, preëminently efficient. He seems not to have suffered himself to be seduced by the deceitful charms of prosperity and victory. The regimen of the army and field; the habits of early rising, of action, and of abstinence, accompany him in his retired employments and civil avocations. In short, this energetic, indomitable spirit he succeeded in' infusing more or less into his fellow officers and into the army. A band of noble marshals and generals were formed under his eye, by his example, counsel, and encouragement. The names of Beresford, Hill, Anglesea, Proctor, Packenham and others, will long be illustrious in the annals of military fame, and reflect praise on their chief. Theirs will probably be the age of Old England's greatest military fame on land; the period of ' her martial airs' reaching their highest note, as that of Nelson when the ocean felt the loudest roar of her cannon. Surely it should be enough of glory and honor in this way. It becomes her now to cast anchor, and make fast her present position. She should now hold out to the nations the olive-branch; cultivating the arts of peace, and extending the reign of Immanuel; sending out her favorite sons, heralds of glad tidings, ' on the earth peace, and good will toward men.'

Bonaparte was well schooled in the toils and labors of the camp, and capable of enduring much hardship. His long continued marches, and joining the enemy in battle, days in succession, as he sometimes did, could not have been endured, unless his physical energies had been great and well trained by exercise. As his life was made up of extremes, so in his habits and personal endurance were seen great contrasts. Abstinence and indulgence, vigilance and supineness, great exertion and consequent inertness, were alternately exhibited by him. Of heat and cold, hunger and thirst, he was patient; but occasionally indulged in the pleasures of the table and the excesses of Paris. To counteract the effect of inaction he would sometimes mount his horse and ride at once seventy or one hundred miles. Again, after great effort and much fatigue, his room and couch witnessed his slumbers, rest, and dreams, sixty or eighty hours in succession. ' *Nil fuit unquam sic impar sibi.*'

Such are the comparative merits of these military leaders, in the estimation of the writer, who, a spectator, has attentively noticed their career. An uninterested one he could not be, for their deeds were of such a character, the results of their battles and victories so extensive and momentous, that he has been deeply interested in the pages of the world's records which their exploits have furnished. The above regards only the military character of these men. It pretends not to be their biography, nor a history of their campaigns. The writer's object has been to place them in juxta-position as leaders of armies and conductors of battles, and as victors or vanquished. He has felt the delicacy of the task. The name of Napoleon is imposing. It seems to have taken possession of the world's mind as synonymous with the sublime of military glory. To doubt his supremacy in every thing pertaining to the science of war, the managing of battles, and the concerns of camps, was not only to find one's self in the minority, but almost alone. But the time had come, it was thought, to look at him as a fellow mortal; and no longer under the bias of first impressions. It is time to separate appearances from realities; to be no longer dazzled by the effulgence of light by which he has concealed his progress, but to measure his deeds and manner of doing them by the standard of military excellence. That his claims are great, has been granted; and in some particulars greatest; but inferior as a whole to him who conquered him on the soil of Belgium. It seems not to occur to those who claim the first place for Bonaparte in every thing pertaining to war, that the higher they raise him the more they elevate his conqueror. But it is said the victory was very nearly won by Bonaparte, and that Wellington narrowly missed a defeat. For this very reason the victory was more glorious, and proof of the highest military qualifications. Bonaparte and his marshals and his troops exerted all their energies of body and mind. They were fairly met on the part of the English and their associates, and counteracted. The result was clear and decisive.

Blucher indeed came up opportunely to witness the defeat and to pursue the flying enemy. His appearance strengthened the courage and resolution of Wellington and his men, enabling them to move on the French in offensive operations. But he took little or no part in the battle itself. That had been fought. Bonaparte turned not his attention for a moment from the English army, but directed his whole power against it, to force it to give way. Being baffled in their repeated charges for ten or eleven hours, his troops had become dispirited, and ready to give up the ground, when the Prussians made their appearance. The grand charge along the whole line by the English army, which decided the contest, was made very soon after the flag of Blucher came in sight. His presence was indeed the decisive moment for making that movement, and the activity of the Prussians rendered the defeat more signal, and the victory complete and glorious.

In moral courage, as far as it goes to make up military character, both have shown themselves distinguished. If courage is meeting danger without fear, the ground of the distinction between natural and moral may not seem obvious; for the incurring of popular disapprobation and odium in the discharge of conscious duty is meeting and disregarding danger. It is indeed often the peril of character and standing; jeoparding the reputation which one has previously acquired. But something more than this is sometimes brought into jeopardy by inflexible adherence to justice and equity. Even personal safety is not unfrequently hazarded; and the courage to face it differs little from that which duty calls into exercise on the field of battle. ' *Quid times, Cæsarem vehis ?* ' the question of Cæsar to the fearful pilot in the storm, ' Why do you fear? you are carrying Cæsar ! ' is always cited as an example of moral courage and the sentimental sublime. But how it differs from presence of mind and self-possession in the midst of personal danger in battle, or in any other circumstances, it is difficult to see. The same invisible agency overrules our chances of safety in the raging battle as in those of the storm. If Cæsar's presence was the ground of confidence to the pilot amid the dashing of the waves, why not to the soldier by his side in the clashing of arms and carnage of battle? Why should the one be an example of moral and the other of natural courage? Was he less intrepid at Pharsalia than on the water in the storm? Was he in the latter case more secure from human casualties than in the former?

But there are those who trembled not at the thunder of cannon in battle array, who have fallen before the blasting influence of popular frowns. This cannot be said however of either Bonaparte or Wellington. We have seen in what a noble manner the former sustained his reverses. If he had not uttered now and then complaints of the manner of his treatment while a prisoner; if he had not sometimes lamented the loneliness of his condition, and indulged in invidious remarks on some of his opponents in battle, his would have been a matchless example of moral courage and sublimity. Even for this he had the authority of Achilles, mourning under circumstances of far less magnitude the loss of the fair Briseis by the hand of Agamemnon, and of the booty awarded him by the Greeks.

Wellington incurred and met popular odium in the trial of Queen Caroline. Something more than moral courage was called forth by the indignation of the populace for the part he took in that affair ; for he was sometimes beset and almost dismounted and made the victim of a mob in going to and from the House of Lords. But he met and overcame the formidable array of popular frenzy with characteristic energy and perseverance : ' *Virum justum, et propositi tenæm.*' He would sometimes stop, it is said, and divert himself with the caricatures of him exhibited in the windows of the print-shops in London, as insensible to them as the statue of Achilles itself. On several other occasions he found opportunity to exercise this trait of character. As Prime Minister, he matured and accomplished several important measures, particularly the Irish Catholic Emancipation Bill, which evinced his possession in the highest degree of moral courage. Many acts of his, and incidents in his life, have shown him able to rise superior to popular disapprobation; a lesson not easy to learn by one who had been so long a favorite of the public. But the popular current has since turned, and is flowing calmly but strongly in his favor, promising serenity to his remaining stage in life's journey. H. B.

PAST HAPPINESS.

BY CLARENCE HERBERT.

How many happy hours
In Memory's wide wastes unnoted lie,
Or faintly cherished, like neglected flowers
Exhale their sweets and die !

O'er youth's clear sunny sky
On life's chill winds the clouds of care will roll,
Yet one bright memory ever dear will lie
Resplendent in my soul.

Brightly the glad earth shone
'Neath the all-glorious heaven on that proud morn ;
The bursting leaf, the wild birds' thrilling tone,
Songs of glad life, breeze-borne :

And odors many a throng,
Joyed in the May-beams on the earth's warm breast,
And tuned in unison with Nature's song,
Our souls found peace and rest.

Far on the rippling bay
The light gleamed tremulous mid the winding shores,
Glanced on the sails, low stooping on their way,
And sparkled on the oars.

Thus on the hill's steep side
Resting, we watched the shores, the sails, the isles,
While the bright morn o'er Narraganset's tide
Lavished her pomp and smiles.

Love hallowed that bright hour ;
Above the beauty of the isle, the glow
Of the warm earth, its spirit-thrilling power
Gave the soul's founts to flow.

Sweet was the song of birds,
The whispering breeze, the sheen of the broad river ;
Dear was Spring's music, but thy murmured words
Dearer than all — than ever !

Ne'er from the Lesbian steep,
From Dorian shore, or sacred Delian grove,
Gazed maid more graceful o'er the Ægean deep,
Entranced with purer love.

No maid of other climes,
Orient or Grecian, nor the glorious throng
Who won from bards of other lands and times
Their passion-burst of song:

Wore brighter form than thine;
Our own land's matchless beauty shone in thee,
The heart, the soul, the mind, the grace divine —
The spirit of the free!

THE COUNTRY DOCTOR:

AN AUTOBIOGRAPHY: WRITTEN AT THE REQUEST OF GLAUBER SAULTZ, M. D.

CHAPTER EIGHT.

'WHAT a beautiful boy!' exclaimed Mr. Waller, who had accompanied me in the old vehicle; and as he said this, he involuntarily seized the reins, and we halted abruptly, (Codger always halts abruptly on the slightest hint,) under the projecting shadows of an ancient elm. Mr. Waller had scarcely left his apartments for a month, and experiencing that pleasing languor which accompanies returning health, was in a frame of mind to be delighted with the beauty of external objects, and with every influence of the glorious day, with its sun-light and its music. When the invalid lifts up his head from the couch of dangerous illness, how delicious are the first revisitings of health! The grave with its thick darkness is receding from him, and the dark valley of the shadow of death. The heart which was almost cold throbs again with its mysterious and mighty pulses; the ear is awake to earth's intricate harmonies; the eye opens as from a deep sleep, and the illumined earth breaks in upon it — a gay and moving panorama. What a luxury is there in the west breeze, as it comes wooing the pale cheek! How intoxicating the perfume of flowers! What rapture in the voice of the birds! But sweeter than all tune are the accents of kindness to the affectionate heart. It is worth lying on a sick couch, with its fever and delirium, its days of anguish and nights of weariness; it is worth encountering pain and despondency, and the dismal phantoms which hover around the grave, to wake up from this into a new being, a new world of light and beauty, where all things greet you with a welcoming smile, and you hear but the voice of gladness. *It is only not Heaven.*

The ride had been long and pleasant. We had been sauntering over hill and dale; at one time stopping to pluck a flower, at another to admire the 'garniture of fields.' Then we came upon a romantic spot where the rocks and stones were thrown together in a wild chaos, and we were caught in the pleasing intricacies of a dell or ravine in the woods, where like lost children we could have rambled until the setting sun, without a wish to be extricated. There was a charming coolness and solitude about the circuitous path, which was thickly overshadowed and grotto-like. The water came tumbling down a precipitous place, where an old tenement was perched amid the rocks and woods, and a ghostly miller looked silently down from his eyrie on the little water-wheel and the dark pool below. Here were many pine-trees, which they say sound musically when the wind sweeps through them, some shooting upward to an enormous height like vast excrescences of barrenness, others uptorn by the blast with their roots high in air, thrown across the chasm in contrast with yon aërial bridge of the spider's web, across which the stray sun-beams glide on their passage. Here were to be found at once the germ and the maturity of greatness; the acorn toyed with by the dainty squirrel, the tender sapling and the giant oak; while prostrate on the ground lay the vast trunk, the relic of a former age, given up to decay, its inmost heart consumed, but mummy-like preserving the outward form and semblance of itself. Lichen and green mosses grew over it, and flowerets which once bloomed like pigmies at its roots, while vines and parasitic plants, whose ambition was to clamber up and be hid among its leaves, revelled around it in gay luxuriance, and blossomed and smiled over its melancholy remains.

How different is the city's solitude from that of groves, and how desolate are you when you ramble a stranger in the crowded mart! And of the thousands who pass by you in eager haste, none know you, care for you, or possess hearts which beat responsive with your own! But the fields, the woods, the rocks, the streams are your companions, and you go nowhere that you do not meet with friends. Not a leaf falls, not a rain-drop sparkles in the sun, not a blade of grass waves in the breeze, not a ripple stirs the lake, not a floweret blooms at your feet, not a bird sings on the spray, that each does not contribute to the pervading sympathy which animates all nature, and with eloquent implorings beseeches you to look up to the Maker of all things — GOD.

Some fondly talk of the sweet security of streets; and it might form a study which the heart of a cynic would delight in, to gaze at the unsocial company of those who throng in thoroughfares, to read the full outlines of history and character depicted in the flash of many faces, as the suddenness of the intense lightning instantly reveals on the dark night the landscape in its minutest details; the trees, the rocks, the river, the bridge. The multitudes of those who go forth on the genial morning on their own errands of gayety or sorrow; the joyous bridegroom stepping forth to support his young bride to the chariot, and hastening to the Gothic aisle, there in its solemn light to pronounce the vow upon earth recorded in heaven; the old man borne away to his dusty sepulchre, whose cold, dead heart, reckoning back through many a prosperous day, once fluttered as wildly on *his* bridal morning; the pilgrim with white locks trembling solitary among the erect men of another age, his dim eye and narrow vision yet mistaking the distance of his goal, and who is crowding gigantic schemes into life's little interval, as he walks on the pathway where the tombs of his contemporaries throw their long shadows athwart his feet; the youth girding himself for the long race, and enchanted with the oak-leaf crown of victory; the strong man hastening on with resolute energy and concentrating the powers of his soul to gain the gold which perisheth; the rich rolling in gilded carriages, and envying the peace which wealth cannot procure; the poor creature of shame or poverty wistfully gazing with cold, wan eye; the beggar with outstretched hand silently supplicating for alms; the child of gay heart and few summers, whose firmament is undimmed with clouds, and whose earth is undefiled with graves; the maiden for whose blush the emulating palette has no colors, the life blood gushing up from a pure heart, the heavenly Madonna face upturned from earth to gaze upon the blue sky; the countenance where all the passions have driven in their chariots, and left their marks in wrinklings, contortions and frowns; the unbound criminal who longs for the clanking chains, and whose heart burns to confide the murderer's secret to the world; the unhappy wretch rushing to the river's brink, to be arrested in the fatal plunge by a voice, a word, some heavenly interposition which bids him still to hope; these and a thousand others pass you by, and leave you melancholy and alone. And still the crowd sweeps onward, and the hum goes up. The city's hum is but the turmoil of earth; the fields resound with the music of heaven. Every aspiration meets with its response, every voice its echo, every confiding breast with sympathy; and you cannot choose but join in the *Te Deum* which swells the grateful heart, when the simplest flower in the valley looks upward in the bright sunlight toward heaven.

Oh! there is in the great and wide fields a philosophy never dreamed of in the deepest speculations; a learning not found in the most erudite books; a poetry which surpasses the artifice of numbers; a music which excels the transports of the lyre; an eloquence which defies the wealth of words; an harmonious beauty which leads you into a sweet captivity, and fills up the soul to its utmost capacity with a pure delight. Here is a revelation which tells as clearly as the written word of the benign God, which is acknowledged in all objects in nature; in the sun at noon-tide, in the profound darkness or stars of night. No speech, no language; their voice is not heard; but their line is gone out through all the earth, and their words to the end of the world.

Thus musing, (and a Country Doctor is sure to muse and moralize in his long solitary rambles,) we emerged from that romantic dell, and breaking the charm of silence, struck upon a new path-way. We saw the waters of the Sound on the left gleaming in the sun, and the beautiful model of a steam-boat, with gay streamers flying, gliding on her course as if animated by a soul to guide her motions, and with a swift ease which can be compared only to the gracefulness of the living form. Ah! how different the sunny prospect, and the gently rippling waves, and the serene heavens, from that moonless wintry night when from yonder promontory I looked afar over the scene, and saw an ill-fated vessel wrapt in fire and the flames shooting luridly toward the sky, and took refuge from the bitter cold and from the dreadful scene in that cottage on the hill! There all was cheerfulness and peace.

The winds cried piteously about its eaves, but cheerily the fire blazed upon the hearth, while the widow read from the Ancient Book, lifting up an involuntary prayer for a son who was dear to her; and blessed ignorance! she did not know that he was suffocating at that moment in the wintry waves. But *I* knew how sad a spectacle was enacting there, and gazed silently at the embers on the hearth. The morrow came and brought no healing on its wings; but when the winter's ices had all vanished, and the spring-time arrived again, and the last relic which appertained to him who was lost was yielded up to these shores, the BOOK OF LIFE which had been given him to be his companion was found imperishable, and, emblem of happy significance! the victim's name was discovered upon its opening page, clearly written therein.

'I knew one,' said Mr. Waller, 'who witnessed that conflagration, and perished in it. Wild, joyous, of bright talents and an intense ambition, he bounded at once upon his career with a courage which no obstacles could oppose. For him there were fascinations which the world proffers not to all. He pictured the future in the brightest hues; its objects were of the true *coleur de rose*. See, here are the last words which he wrote to me before he met his fate: 'Pardon me, my friend; I may speak too confidently; my heart is full of emotions, and the race is not to the swift. I have to work out my own destiny, and I set about it with no craven heart. Fear me not. I know what my friends, my country, the world expects of me. I shall not sit down in sloth or idleness; I shall not prove recreant to the trusts committed to my charge. I know what it is in me to effect; I know what I *will* do, so help me God! Pride, honor, manfulness, self-respect, all urge me on, to enter the great contest; to fight the battle, to win the crown. To-morrow — it is no matter; you shall hear from me yet again. Farewell!'

'And there was a player,' said I, 'among the number of those who perished. On the night before he died he was the favorite of a gay theatre; applauded to the echo; his very shadow the signal for a tumult of approbation and delight: and when the play was over, and he stepped forward in his player's garments almost into the midst of the eager, approving crowd, to receive the laurels he had earned, he made a well-timed speech: 'My friends,' said he, 'I am grateful. It is rumored that I shall not return here any more. I hope this may not be prophetic. Nothing can be farther from my intentions. I hope to see you soon again.' And so saying, he passed before the curtain, and never appeared again on any stage. And I knew a youth who perished in the same disaster; sanguine, gay-hearted, who had scarcely yet dreamed of death. Do you see yon country-seat with Greek portico and observatory? Only three nights before he died I saw him dancing in the lighted rooms. It was a festal occasion, a birth-day night. There were many happy children and bright faces. He admired and basked in the light of *one*. And this is the way of the world. There be those who say 'How beautiful!' to the roses of a banquet, who shall never live to lament them dead. For them the cypress is prepared, and all the melancholy flowers which we strew upon the grave. Ah! how infinitely removed, and yet at how short a remove, is life from death, and how nearly do the waters of bitterness spring up from the very fountains of joy!* It is well that the dark future is hidden from us, and that we may be happy in the bright present. But could we look around upon the glad company, and know that the innocence which is so pure, and the wit so bright, and the laughter so hilarious, must on the morrow die, we should never know happiness any more. There are friendships so pure and loves so sweet that we despair at the death which threatens them, and perish in the graves where they are buried with our hopes.'

From such casual remarks we gradually slid into other topics, and coming on a great battle-ground, spoke of the men of the Revolution, and the scenes in which so much costly blood was spilled, and regretted the necessity of arms, and desired the happy age when they should yield to the toga of peace. Then we discoursed of the progress of the arts, and the charms of literature, whose peaceful triumphs are better than the tyrant's blood-bought crowns.

We were now arrived at a pleasing seclusion, and as already mentioned, beguiled to pause awhile under the covert of an old tree. A cottage in the French style stood not far from the road, and a child of four years was playing before the door on the green-sward. He was attended by a faithful domestic, and ever and anon ran to throw himself with a passionate joy into the arms of an old man who sat near, and whose hairs were as white as snow; speaking all the while in the French tongue, whose idiomatic graces lose nothing when falling from infantile lips. He was of a soft and tender beauty, as if fallen from the skies. How his mild eyes beamed with light, attempered by long lashes! — and his cheeks somewhat pale, and pure brow, and auburn hair falling over his shoulders, fitted him for caresses. What a spectacle is a child! Happy, passionless, innocent, uncontaminated, belonging at the same time to earth and heaven; sporting gaily in the golden age of his young years. He is born into a garden of Eden, where the flowers bloom and the birds sing, and there is yet no TEMPTER. Turmoils and anxieties there are none, and the terrible phantom of death cannot dispel the smiles which flit over the face of him sleeping. If there be clouds, they soon let the sunshine through them, and so his tears are but the forerunners of smiles and laughter; and if he has any grief it soon vanisheth away :

νέα γὰρ φροντὶς οὐκ ἀλγεῖν φιλεῖ. — ΕΥΡΙΠ.

What man of ordinary guiltiness can look upon an innocent child, thus playing among flowers, without a thought of what he once was, and without shedding tears of vain regret for what he may never be again? Mr. Waller was thus affected. 'Do you know the history of the old Frenchman?' said he.

'I should be glad to hear it,' replied I.

'It is short, and without plot to recommend it.'

'Perhaps I shall like it the better on that account.'

'It is well,' said he, throwing himself back in the old vehicle, and

---

* Medio de fonte leporum surgit amari aliquid quod in ipsis floribus angat. — LUC.

then in his sentimental way, making much out of little, told me these few facts as nearly as I remember them:

That little building with wings and conservatories and gardens so artfully disposed, once had its counterpart in a stately château and grounds on the banks of the Seine. There is not a nook or turret or casement of the latter which is not represented in yonder miniature mansion; and so all the walks, flower-beds and pretty embellishments are but copies of a true original. Thus it is that the exile dying to his country, remembers the beloved Argos where he was born.

During the reign of faction and terror in France, when the elements of society appeared to be stirred up from the very dregs, and the state had become ripe for a revolution which brought the poor monarch Louis *Seize* to the block, among the many brave, noble, gallant, thrown from day to day into gloomy prisons to await their doom, or like the prisoner of the Bastile to become squalid and forgotten in the revolutions of the state, was that venerable man who has just clasped yon beautiful child in his arms. You saw how aged he looked, and how comely were his gray hairs mixed up with the beautiful tresses of the child.

At that time he was in the vigor of age, and full of manly beauty. Birth and talents fitted him for a prominent place, and he had already fallen under the eye of Robespierre, and his name graced the lists of proscription which like those of Sylla were doomed to fill the city with cries and mourning. But he had hitherto remained firm at his post. He was willing to die with, to die for, but not to forsake or survive his country.

One day he sat solitary in his prison. It was the approach of evening, when the last rays of light were struggling through the bars, and the sounds of the city became dull. Imaginations come up thick, fast, almost oppressively at such a time, even to the happy; how much more so to the prisoner of hope! He had dropped the book which he had been reading (it was a volume of Montesquieu) from his hand, and became lost in reverie. He remembered the past, and among its happy scenes sought refuge and consolation. The future he had been wont to picture, that boundless prospect, so full of enchanting sights, but now how circumscribed! Then he steeled his soul to the worst of terrors, and was prepared to welcome death. At that moment he listened attentively, and caught the fall of footsteps without in the paved corridor. It might be the approach of the turnkey bringing the death-summons for the morrow. The heavy bolt shot with a noise which caused him to start nervously, the door moved slowly on its hinges, and in an instant he beheld — not the gaoler's gaunt form, but dimly revealed by the declining day, a woman's majestic figure. 'Marianne!' exclaimed the father, stretching out his fond arms; 'can it be? How unexpected this meeting! How have you gained access here? Bless thee, my child, this is not the time or place for thee! Retreat immediately. Tarry not here. Make haste! Let me bid you farewell — for ever!'

'Not so, my father. I came hither without attendant; I cannot go forth without you. Ask me not who effected this entrance. I did it — gold did it. I have seen the gaoler. He was the old porter at

Neuilly. A great sacrifice is preparing. Bertrand, Montreville, Villeneuve, a score of others, you too, are destined for the morrow. The way is prepared; there is no obstacle. Fly, Sire; emigrate to another land.'

It was very dark within the walls of the prison, but not too dark to veil the moral beauty of the scene. Love, danger, filial piety, parental fondness, all powerfully appealed. The royalist embraced his child, and they passed silently down the gloomy stair-case, got beyond the sentinels, ascended the carriage, crossed the Pont-Neuf, and in two hours reached the old château. It was a beautiful summer night. There was confusion and bustle in the castle for many hours. Caskets and jewels were collected hastily, and whatever precious things could be removed with ease. A sad and solemn preparation was preparing for the morrow. Fields and groves and hereditary trees, which we love as dearly as dearest relatives or truest friends, were to be relinquished, it might be for ever. And there was a sadder farewell. Marianne walked in the garden — not alone. She was accompanied by one, young, ardent, of whom all the world spake well, and whom she *loved;* and he implored her with a tender eloquence, in vain. Two affections struggled in the same heart, whereof the noblest was victorious. It was the noblest because less tinctured with self. So she withdrew from him her hand, and dismissed him from her presence, to cherish him in her heart of hearts for ever. VARENNES disappeared among the trees, and she never saw him again.

When the gray light of the morning dawned they were awakened by the sounding of a huntsman's horn, which was the signal to be ready. Marianne hastened to the library. Her father had just impressed his seal on the last package. He seized her hand and gazed wistfully in her face, which was bright and cheerful.

'Varennes!' murmured he, inquiringly.

'Say nothing, I entreat you. I have bidden him farewell.'

'Nay, you must not, shall not accompany me; you shall remain, protected by our friends. I will go alone upon this voyage. In more tranquil times we shall meet again on this spot, and be happy.'

But neither commands nor entreaties can prevail against a woman's strong resolution. They entered the cabriolet amid the tears of the menials, and in an instant more were upon the road. When they had arrived at a spot whence it was possible to catch a last glimpse of the château through the trees, Marianne commanded the carriage to halt a moment, that she might take a final look, satisfied with which, she gave directions to proceed upon the journey, and leaning upon her parent's breast shed a torrent of tears.

The white sails of the brig were already flapping in the breeze, and they embarked on the voyage. Propitious gales wafted them on. When the shores of dear France were fading away from the sight, Marianne gazed eagerly toward the land, as she had taken a last look at the château. She felt a presentiment that she should never visit it any more. Deep sadness and melancholy stole over her when she thought of those whom she had left behind; (among them Varennes was not forgotten;) and a host of emotions came up over the soul almost to overwhelm it. This was but a momentary weakness and defection. A better courage animated her breast and inspired her with new resolutions, when she beheld the form of one approaching her whom she loved more than any in the world. It was her father.

To him she would devote her whole life; sharing in his prosperity, alleviating his adversity, watching him in sickness, and tenderly regarding him when growing old. And for this she looked for none other reward than the approval of her own heart, the smiles of Heaven. And Heaven always smiles upon such noble conduct. The admiration of the world never inspired it, and cannot bestow upon it its just deserts. The strong mind of the virtuous hath rich resources within itself, and can draw much from its own deep and pure affections. How much soever the visible sun is absent from the heavens, there is a light which shineth in the soul, and it shineth more and more unto the perfect day.

A few years glided by, and yonder château appeared among the trees. It had been selected as a refuge and a home; and it was happy and beautiful, but it owed every thing to HER hand. She touched nothing that it did not exhibit the attractive graces of a pure taste. Without her, not a plant sprang up in the gay paterre, or a single flower in all the wilderness of sweets. If she planted any thing, though it were a tender, fragile exotic, it acknowledged the hand which fostered it, and flourished. For trees and plants and dumb animals have sensitive natures, and are susceptible of kindness; and nothing died beneath her affectionate care. It was her idea to make the new place image forth the old. It was its pretty diminutive. Arbors and grottoes and sweet alcoves were reduced upon the scale, and all things copied with a tenacious memory. Rose-trees and eglantines bloomed in their own places, and wherever she had planted a vine, there grew one, only with richer clusters and of a warmer hue, at the ancient château. It was a garden without thorns; a seclusion which Shenstone might have admired; and having rendered the place what it was by her own taste, it became the abode of kindness and hospitality. Hers was a fixed character; a resolute energy, a religious devotion. She founded the little chapel with gilded cross on the hill. At the matin-hour and at vespers she was unfailing as the gray-haired priest. There was not a poor or decrepit person within miles who did not regard her as an angel of mercy. She was the almoner of a bounty which giving never seemed to impoverish, and which imparted to the slightest boon a more than intrinsic value. Gold given from the reluctant hand is but despised dross, though it may save from starving; but a cup of water from the merciful imparts a shock of pleasure to the frame

> 'More exquisite than when nectarian juice
> Renews the life of joy in happiest hours.'

Marianne had been once beautiful; she was still stately and majestic. Her father listened to her voice as to that of a charmer. She filled up his whole house. She was instead of home, friends, country, and made the days of his exile sweet. With such a companion there is no exile. The very desert becomes an oasis, refreshed, verdant, and blooming as the rose.   She was passionately devoted to music and the arts, and the mistress of a harp, sometimes mournful.   She was the admired of all the exiles.   When the old Frenchmen came to her father's house to partake of his welcome and hospitality, to ramble with dog and gun in his woodlands, to talk of the old dynasty, to drink his wine of the ancient vintage, and forget their griefs, she presided at his table in such a manner as to leave nothing desired by the guests Think not that all this is but a kind of the beautiful ideal without reality or truth.   Are there not many who have beheld such excellence, and yet can testify how rare it is on earth?   The path of such is as the beautiful path of the just.   They scatter joy and gladness around them; relieving the dry places which were else fruitless; making the earth pleasant, and imaging in their faces the benign happiness of the better clime to which they shall be transplanted.   Even so the waves of a fair river which lave the fairer shore, adding luxury to the verdure and beauty to the scene, shall one day be absorbed into the summer sky, and form a part of that heaven which they so gloriously reflect.

It was a mild day at the end of the uncertain, stormy month of March.   The violets which struggle first upward from the snow in our severe clime shed a faint perfume beneath the windows, and the blue-bird heralding the new spring sang on the leafless tree.   Untrue prophets!   The winter was not yet past.   It was usually a busy season of the year at the château, when the lady of the mansion was wont to order the gardener to clear away the old leaves, and prune the vines, and prepare for the happy summer.   At present she lay ill (none sus-pected how ill) in her chamber.   But the poor, the aged, the many pensioners of her bounty were continually coming to inquire after her health, and went away with anxious faces.   Toward evening a deeper gloom rested over the house.   The old man bending down with his white locks was weeping hopelessly over his daughter's couch.   The menial looking out beheld a carriage before the door, and the name of VARENNES was on his lips.   'Faithful Jerome!' exclaimed the latter, springing into the hall, and almost embracing him: 'How fares the Marquis and his lovely daughter?'

But the ancient domestic, being almost choked with tears, could only articulate to his eager inquiries, and with a faltering voice, 'MA-RIANNE IS DEAD!'

CHAPTER NINE.

'AND what of the boy?' said I, when Mr. Waller had got through with the little French story.

'He is the old man's grand-child, whose mother died in France.   He inherits her beauty, and is therefore the more loved.   You observe yon white shaft in the garden.   When it shall be inscribed with another name, and there are two graves in the small enclosure, Jerome will be intrusted to carry him back to France.   That time cannot be far dis-tant, for his grand-sire's head is whitened with the snows of many winters, and the companions of his exile are all dead.   Then I foresee that this pleasant place will lapse into melancholy ruin, or it will be invaded by others who will innovate on beauties which they have not planned and enjoy the fruits which they have not planted. Gee-up Codger ! — the sun is getting warm.'

PERHAPS it was a month after this, perhaps less, that the Country Doctor was securely smoking a long pipe in his sanctum, involved in smoke, and thinking about nothing in particular, when he was hastily sent for. It may be remarked that disturbances of this kind were sure to come either when he was smoking a pipe or eating his dinner, or falling into a pleasant sleep. Hence it is that country doctors always have more philosophy and of a better kind than any other class of men. They rely less upon certainties, and are regulated by a rigid penance and self-denial. If they sit down for very weariness, it may be only to rise up again at the bidding of any one; they know how to dispense with a substantial meal whose provocative incense makes the deprivation most trying; and they emerge from the oriental splendor of dreams to visit the abodes of squalid poverty ; and in return for this they receive the unkind rebukes of the ignorant and ungrateful. After all, where can those whose business is with the world look for their reward but in the conscious rectitude of the heart within, and in the right pulsations of that little monitor?

'But who is it that wants me now? Is it Cuff, or Bill, or Burks, or the blind ostler, or who?'

'Doctor, go to the French gentleman's ; the little boy is ill.'

'Oh! — indeed ; I am grieved to hear it ; but not very ill, I hope?'

The old domestic's eyes filled with tears. He bowed, said nothing, turned upon his heel, and went out.

'I will follow his steps,' said I, 'immediately,' rising up, and letting my pipe fall in the hurry to be gone. Where are my hat and whip and gloves? All things are sure to be mislaid when one most wants them. Who has taken my spectacles off the shelf?'

'They're on your head, you foolish man!'

'I thank you, Madam. I am in haste. Do not expect me home to dinner.' So saying, I went out, and taking the reins from the hand of Flummery, drove away. 'I feel an unwonted interest in this boy,' said I ; 'perhaps the reason is, that I was so much impressed with his beauty on first seeing him. Probably he is but slightly ailing, and I shall arrive to find him engaged in his usual sports. If the slightest accident happens to such idols, how is a whole household thrown into alarm!'

'Indulging in such reflections, I arrived at last before the door. Passing through the library, (it was well furnished with books,) I ascended into an upper chamber, where I saw the old French exile supporting in his arms and watching with a tender solicitude the same beautiful boy whom I had before seen playing on the green. What a contrast! — the veteran oak of four-score stormy winters, the blooming plant of a few peaceful summers; and which was destined first to droop and die? I looked at the boy's flushed cheeks and felt his quick fluttering pulse, as he reclined on the old man's breast. He was languidly turning over a *porte-feiulle* of water-colored paintings, exquisitely tinted, (the artist's hand was cold!) and these he at last put from him, too ill to regard them any more. A painful expression came over his countenance, as he turned his head away and would not be entertained.

'Ah! how ill he is!' said the old French gentleman; 'Jami never refused to be delighted with pictures before. The fever must abate soon. He *has* a fever, has he not, Doctor?'

'Yes, said I, 'it is *scarlatina.*'

Terrible disease! There are those who hear the name with as much equanimity as the mention of a deadly pestilence or plague. How many houses that used to be gladdened by the voices and merriment and carnival pleasures of children are rendered desolate by it! And when the Christmas and New Year come again, which would also bring them, a joyful company, around the sacred hearth, their places are all empty, and the broken-hearted sit there in silence and tears, while the Patron Saint once so ardently expected turns away his aërial chariot, and goes to deposit his gifts in the midst of happier homes! I know many families in town and country to whom this malignant disease has not spared one out of the group of children who were the delight of fond parents, and the hopes of their house. In its character and developement it is such as too frequently to disappoint the predictions of medical skill; ever running into new stages, at one moment giving hopes of recovery, at the next putting on malignant symptoms, and at last, when least expected, resulting in death.

'Is the child in any danger?' said the old man, relinquishing him into the arms of the attendant; 'he has not complained much until to-day.'

'He has scarlet-fever, and in its milder form there is little to apprehend.'

'Thank God for that! Watch him closely, Doctor. He is a very dear boy. He prevents my gray hairs from going down in sorrow to the grave.'

'Jerome!' exclaimed the boy, rousing up a little from his listlessness, and speaking in the French tongue; 'good Jerome, give me the musical box.'

'Ha!' said the old man, smiling for pleasure, 'better! better! The fever will soon abate; his cheeks are already less flushed.' So they wound up the box, and placed it in his hands, and it played the *Ranz des Vaches.*

'Pretty tune!' exclaimed Jerome, looking into his face; 'we will make it play again.' But a change came over him, and he put it away peevishly, and was querulous for something else.

'I think,' said I, 'he had better be put into bed.'

'Certainly. Wheel out the crib;' and in a moment the nurse brought out from the next apartment a notable piece of furniture, of dark mahogany, and of rare workmanship.

'It is an ancient relic, Doctor, an heir-loom in the family. I slept in it when a child, and some brave generals and renowned men of France have slumbered there, I assure you. Jerome, put the boy in it; he will rest better.'

I could not help scrutinizing the venerable crib, and such a singular train of associations stole upon me, connected with the fortunes of those who had once occupied it, and in reflecting how much more peaceful were their infantile slumbers than the feverish dreams of their after life, that it would be foolish to put down my thoughts; and when I awoke from the reverie, it was time to administer the medicines and come away.

I HAVE said that there was little to apprehend from the milder and more benign form of the disease. But it came in its most malignant shape; and I find in my diary, after the lapse of a few days, the short record of the child's death.

I recollect it quite well. Perhaps there were some incidents which impressed it more deeply on my mind. How cutting is it to witness the pangs and agonies of a dying child, when he looks around so supplicatingly on those who have been accustomed to gratify his slightest will, but looks in vain for succor; and when at last conscious of the approach of death he gathers up his little resources and takes a touching farewell of the world! It melts the stoutest soul to pity, and calls up tears difficult to be staunched. It is a triumph which is sublime in the brave man.

It was toward the close of a beautiful day in autumn, and the reapers were mowing down the hay on the lawn. Within, the Reaper of Death was putting in his sickle. So thought I, as I looked first out of the window and then upon the countenance of the beautiful child. It wore an expression of intense pain. but how patient, how innocent, how infantile! Who would not become a vicarious sufferer in these cases, if it were possible for such pangs to be transferred! There were many toys scattered about the room which were soon to be gathered together and locked up in some little depository. Alas! who would be left in that house to discover such a magazine in after years, and to bedew each fond memento! For such incidents *do* happen in families; and they call forth many a secret gush of old sorrow, and that hopeless pining for the dead for which we have no word, but which the Latins denominate *desiderium.* The books with pictures which used to afford so much delight, all thumbed and dog-leaved and tattered; the box of games, the Christmas presents, the sword, the gun, the trumpet, the drum, the gay plume — look at the cheeks of the mother, and say whether the tear is less sacred because it rolls in silence!

There was a toy-horse upon the bed. The child threw out his wasted arm, drew it toward him a few inches with a wistful look, and then let go the string. But he drew his grandfather down to him, throwing his arms about his neck, and seeing a tear which had filled up the wrinkle on his face, (it was the last from a once full fountain!) he wiped it away, kissed him with parched lips, and articulated with French accent, 'ADIEU!'

'It is too much!' said the old man, pressing his hands upon his heart and sinking into a chair. Then he rose up and went out of the room.

'Jerome,' murmured the child, looking wildly.

'Hasten, hasten, Jerome! — he is calling you.'

But when the faithful domestic came up, the child was speechless; and in a few moments after he was dead.

Ah! how beautiful is that sleep which is without dreams by night, and from which there is no waking in the morning! I stood over him, and as the golden light streamed through the casement and lay upon his auburn locks and on his pure brow, I thought within myself, 'How dainty a potentate is Death; and seeing that his realms are only darkness and his food the worm, what need has he to quench the light of the young, or to deck 'his kingdom with the beautiful? When there are such multitudes who would willingly throw themselves into his arms, and hail him as a boon friend, why does he exact the company of those who shrink from him as the KING of TERRORS? Why does he despise the decrepit, the aged, and the unhappy, and take with him the beautiful child, the young virgin, and the youth of promise? To these, the air which they breathe is luxury, and they pine not yet for the peaceful rest of the tomb. These are not questions for the heart to suggest, for the lips to express, or for man to answer. But this we know, that neither animated rooms nor gay assemblies, nor the living world itself, contain so much of what was once wit and beauty, and passion and glory, as thy still, cold sanctuary, oh Grave!

Such reflections stole upon me; and going home and sitting down in the undisturbed solitude of my chamber, I composed these few lines:

T O   A   D E A D   C H I L D.

OH! brightest dream and fairest form
 My vision ever knew!
Thou art melted from my sight away
 As heaven absorbs the dew.

Closed are those lips that cannot speak,
 And the dull eye is dead;
The rose is banished from thy cheek,
 The dimpling smile is fled.

Thy little feet no more on earth
 Shall ramble midst its sweets,
But kiss the flowers of heavenly birth,
 Or tread the golden streets.

Oh! in yon high ethereal isles
 By ancient patriarchs trod,
Thy brow is radiant with the smiles
 And sunshine of its GOD.

For thee, so destitute of sin,
 So passionless, my boy!
The task was light to enter in,
 And claim the promised joy.

Oh! for the spirit of a child,
 A mould of purer clay,
To burst its bands with rapture wild,
 And rise to endless day!

THE TAKING OF BASING HOUSE.

DEFENDED BY THE MARQUIS OF WINCHESTER AGAINST A DETACHMENT OF THE PARLIAMENTARY FORCE
UNDER CROMWELL.

BY A NEW CONTRIBUTOR.

THE court-yard of old Basing rings with many an arméd heel,
And on the ear comes sharp and clear the clink of martial steel;
And in the hall and from the wall it is a goodly sight
To see the dauntless cavaliers all harnessed for the fight;
For loyal hearts are beating there, and vaulted arches ring
With the brave old English war-cry, 'For GOD and for our King!'

But ere that gallant heart-acclaim is hushed within the hall,
A herald's trumpet summons forth the chieftain to the wall:
'Say wherefore flaunts yon banner upon the wings of pride,
And wherefore gleams the hostile sword at each Malignant's side?
Unbar old Basing's massive gates, ungird the threatening sword,
Nor dare with rebel force dispute the legions of the Lord!'

'Hence to the crop-eared knaves and say yon banner's every fold
Bears 'Aimez Loyauté' emblazed in characters of gold;
If farther speech the churls would have, we'll answer them right soon
From mouth of clamorous culverin and fiery musketoon;
Ho! soldier! blow thy bugle-blast, and with no stinted breath
Hurl back into the traitor's teeth defiance to the death!'

Lo! who is he that strides yon tent with fierce and moody eye,
As herald's voice recounteth o'er stern Winchester's reply?
Why gnaws he thus his nether lip as if to hold confined
Bold thoughts of high aggrandizement that haunt his troubled mind?
And wherefore clenches he so fast his broad and heavy hand,
As if he kingly sceptre held, or baton of command?

The swart and burly OLIVER, who grasps his ready sword,
And cries aloud: 'Here's work for those who battle for the Lord!
Awake, arise! gird well your loins, ye chosen men of might,
He calls whose glory ye have seen in visions of the night.
To horse ere dawn! for when the sun shall sink beneath the flood,
His rays will catch a redder glow from off a field of blood!'

A thousand told of men as bold as e'er of woman born,
With psalm and prayer and solemn air watch anxiously the dawn:
They gaze in sadness on the sun, for who can surely say
The blesséd beam that greets them now is not his farewell ray?
And every pulse beats hurriedly, and busy thoughts are rife,
For none are there to prophesy the issue of the strife.

The lady Helen with her lord sate waiting for the day,
And ever as her tear-drops came he kissed those tears away:
'Ho! warder! tell us of the night!' cried many a gallant peer,
And 'warder, tell us of the night!' cried many a cavalier:
And worthy master Fuller, in his sable garments dight,
Throwing back his study-window, asked the tidings of the night.

'God sain ye, noble masters!' the ancient soldier said,
And leaning on his partisan, he slowly shook his head;
I have peered into the darkness till mine eyes are dim, I trow,
Yet as mine ears are not grown dull, methinks I hear them now;
Now, as the morning sun comes up, and with his golden fire
Is gilding hill and tree-top, and the chapel's lofty spire.

'Not with war's gorgeous blazonry of banner, trump and drum,
But like a gathering thunder-cloud the grim enthusiasts come.
All solemnly and silently they are looming on their way,
With a stern and gloomy bearing, and an ominous array.
I should take them for a spectral host from the charnel of the dead,
Were it not for the low ceaseless hum and heavy martial tread.

'Ah well I know stout OLIVER, and well have cause to know,
For never saw I man before dealt such a fearful blow:
I saw him at red Naseby, and my heart was troubled sore,
And I lay beneath his horse's feet at bloody Marston-moor,
Where, as the smith his hammer plies, plied he his arm in fight,
With a stately and a solemn stroke, and a resistless might.'

Uprose the lady Helen, and a silken scarf took she,
Where woven by her own fair hands shone 'Aimez Loyaute!'
She girded it about her lord and buckled on his spur,
And thus she spake with faltering tongue to princely Winchester:
'I do not bid thee, good my lord, be backward in the strife,
But oh! a woman's love still pleads, be chary of thy life!'

'Look from thy lattice, gentle Nell,' the fearless warrior said,
'And where the combat presses most thou 'lt find thy silken braid:
Foul scorn it were if he whom thou hast guerdon'd with thy love,
In such a cause 'gainst such a foe a recreant should prove!
Houseless and landless I may be, but never blush of shame
Shall mantle o'er thy pale pure brow at mention of my name.'

At morn the lofty fortress frowned in grandeur on the foe,
Noon saw its walls, all rent and torn, heaped in the fosse below;
And still the work goes on amain, with strong unfaltering arm,
And taunt and jeer from cavalier are answered by a psalm;
Till stroke on stroke the strong chain broke, and with a thundering sound
The broad and ponderous draw-bridge falls, loud crashing to the ground!

'Smite down the sons of Belial!' those iron foemen cry;
'For church and king, and woman's love!' the bristling walls reply.
As waters which their barriers burst impetuous roll along,
So from the gates the cavaliers pour forth upon the throng;
And ever where the scarf is seen, amid the bloodiest press,
There 's a lifted hand and a gleaming brand, and a sturdy foe the less!

But bootless is the fierce assault of chivalrous emprize,
For OLIVER is bearing down, and whoso dares him, dies!
Amid the thickest of the fray his crimson blade hath shone,
And though there 's blood upon his brow, that blood is not his own.
From right to left his weapon falls, nor falleth it in vain,
For men can trace his gory path by gazing on the slain.

'Hosannah to the Lord!' he cries, 'the victory is won!
But not by us, by HIM alone the good work hath been done;
Lo! prideful Winchester at bay, like lion in his lair,
With corslet hacked and scarf all torn, and wild dishevelled hair:
He yields, he yields! — not unto us the glory of this day,
But unto HIM whose name hath been our buckler in the fray!'

NOTES OF LIFE IN HAYTI.

BY AN AMERICAN.

NUMBER THREE.

THE cultivator of the North, where Christophe reigned, has the reputation of being more industrious than his brethren in the other districts. His black Majesty saw that they were disposed to give up all habits of labor, and counteracted such effects by the most arbitrary tyranny. The terror of his name was as effectual as the whip of the overseer; and they have accordingly preserved in some degree a taste for work. Not that the indolent are left entirely to their own free will, for there are various laws not only to promote but to enforce labor. Every country negro for example is obliged to live on his own land, or 'to take the act,' by which he binds himself to work upon a certain estate for a term of years; and any vagabonds who are found in the country without any visible means of subsistence are sent to prison. Often too, when the towns show an unusual number of idlers, a proclamation is issued by the commandant of the same, ordering them to betake themselves to their several places of abode. And there are other measures still more effectual to enforce labor; to compel people, in other words, to drive the wolf from their own doors. There resides within given limits a personage called the 'rural officer,' who has the supervision of the neighboring country, who visits the farms, and notes neglected land. Where the ground is found bearing too flagrant proofs of lazy occupants, they are marched off 'sans ceremonie' to gaol. Then a file of soldiers is seen marching into town, having in their midst a posse of men and women, ragged and half starved, coming from a rich piece of land overgrown with weeds and thickets, the coffee-trees overrun and choked up with worthless vines. Nothing prevents this wilderness from being made to blossom like the rose but the inveterate sloth of the shameless and sturdy occupants.

If it is asked how there can be any lazy people in such a country, the answer is, that the standard of industry is too low. The occasional punishment of individuals has doubtless some good effect as an example; but a good estate, having any thing like the comforts which a man with the aid of his family *might* command, is seldom seen. The number of whites residing in the Island is probably less than five hundred, (the population being not less than five hundred thousand,) and the deaths of whites in the different ports probably exceeds this number annually. There are not more than fifteen or twenty Americans residing in the whole length and breadth of the land; and of American merchants it is believed there is not one. An edict was issued a few years since, that no foreigner should henceforth be allowed to take a license as a merchant, excepting those already in trade, who could continue business by petitioning the President for permission, at the beginning of each year, which permission he promptly granted.

The writer of this article was for some time the only American merchant in the Island, holding the right to do business in his own name, and paying therefor an annual tax of six hundred dollars. Having left the country, there is not now a single individual of his countrymen possessing this privilege; and the very large trade which we have with the Island has passed into the hands of native merchants. But not only are there no American merchants; there is no consul or other representative of the United States to protect her seamen and the interests of her citizens. At the same time the above regulation was promulgated, another was put forth, to the effect that no foreign consul or commercial agent should be recognized by government, unless he was the bearer of a letter from his own government to President Boyer. This stroke of policy was aimed directly at the United States, or rather it was beating Old Nick round the stump; since they well knew that our government would not notice the new law, and our consuls would immediately die a natural death, as far as the exercise of their functions was concerned.

To the foreigner landing upon these shores, or elsewhere within the tropics, the sun appears to have very nearly the same power at all seasons of the year; and one feels a constant anxiety more or less intense, until he is taken in hand by the acclimating fever. His chance then for life depends very much upon his habits, his constitution, and his medical attendance. If he survives the attack, he is ready to tread the soil like a native. With a broad Panama on his head he braves the scorching sun at every hour of the day; he enjoys the sea-breeze as it pours its refreshing streams through his apartments; and when it dies away he waits, cool and patient, for the land-wind which comes, as regular as night, fresh from the mountains. He no longer worries over every meal he eats, anxious and alarmed lest something which he has taken may be feverish and unwholesome food. His first glance in the morning is not at the glass to ascertain if his complexion has altered since the previous day. He no longer shrinks from a delicious morceau, fearing lest his enemy may lurk there; and he no longer shudders when a case of sickness or death is mentioned. But if he dies — ah! *then* there is the unattended hearse, the friendless funeral; and he lies unwept and forgotten in the stranger's grave.

There came to reside among us a French merchant, who received from his friends a large business. So thriving was he, that he sent all the way to Bordeaux for his brother. The latter soon arrived and proved a valuable acquisition to our little circle. Good tempered and gentlemanlike, and understanding perfectly the ' *savoir vivre*,' he became at once a general favorite. After a residence of six or seven years it was agreed that Antoine, the younger, should return to France, to make arrangements for a more extensive trade. The ship was in the harbor which was to bear him to his native city, and he was making his preparations in the highest spirits, waiting for the voyage, and longing with a Frenchman's enthusiasm once more to see his own dear France. The anchor was a-peak, the sails were loosed, and the good ship was ready 'like a greyhound in the slips' to bound away. The boat was sent for the passenger; he was feverish and could not embark; she waited for him until the next day; but he grew worse, and the ship went to sea. In one week, instead of being on his way *home*, he was in the silent grave-yard. His brother, who had been esteemed a hard unfeeling man, took his death deeply to heart. He lost his interest in every thing; his appetite failed him; and the strong man took to his bed, and in one month died of a broken heart, and was laid by the side of his brother. The visiter may find the grave-stones of Joseph and Antoine Savona side by side in that secluded cemetery. And yet this is perhaps the healthiest spot in the West Indies. Deaths among the foreign seamen are extremely rare, having averaged not more than one in three years, for the last nine! I never knew a case of yellow fever to occur; while Port-au-Prince, a hundred miles distant, has been the grave of tens of thousands slain by this fell destroyer.

The coast from Jeremie to Port-au-Prince presents a great variety of mountain scenery; and for two-thirds of the distance the voyager has the smooth 'bight of Leogane' to sail through, protected by the Island of Gonaives, which extends along the seaward side. Along this coast lay the district ruled by one of the five great Caciques, whom Columbus found when he dropped among them 'from the skies.' This was the territory of Xaragua. 'The Spaniards (who had formed a colony at the other extremity of the Island) had heard,' says IRVING, 'many accounts of the soft and delightful region of Xaragua, in one part of which some of the Indian traditions placed their Elysian fields. They had heard much also of the beauty and urbanity of the inhabitants. The mode of their reception was calculated to confirm their favorable prepossessions. About this time messengers arrived from Behechio, cacique of Xaragua, informing him that he had large quantities of cotton and other articles in which his tribute was to be paid, ready for delivery. The Adelantado, the brother of Columbus, immediately summoned a numerous train, who gladly set forth with him to revisit this fruitful and happy region. They were again received with songs, and dances, etc.' · · · · 'The accounts of Xaragua give a picture of savage life in its perfection of indolent ease and untasked enjoyment. The troubles which distracted the other parts of devoted Hayti had not yet reached the inhabitants of this pleasant region. Living among beautiful and fruitful groves, on the borders of a sea which appeared forever tranquil and unvexed by storms; having few wants, and those readily supplied, they appeared emancipated from the common lot of labor, and to pass their lives in one uninterrupted holiday. When the Spaniards regarded the fertility and sweetness of this country, the gentleness of its people and the beauty of its women, they pronounced it a perfect paradise.'

The writer, for many years a resident in Xaragua, bears his testimony to the fidelity of these accounts, so far as soil, scenery and climate are concerned.

Hills of every shape, sometimes throwing up a wall five hundred feet above his head, appear about to oppose the traveller's progress, while the tall trees waving over the brink seem as if they might lose their balance and come crashing down upon his path. As he winds round the base, a broad amphitheatre spreads out before him, formed by a series of hills sweeping round and up, in vast waves of verdure. Here, his horse treads upon a soft grassy carpet, where the ear cannot detect his footfall; and from the summit of this hill the blue ocean bursts upon the view, and apparently a stone cast from the hand would fall upon the beach below, though it is several miles distant. Here groves of the palmetto wave their crackling limbs; there the huge mahogany stands, the monarch of the woods. Now, as you pass under the lofty 'Monbin,' you crush at every step its fragrant and refreshing fruit. Here, you wind up a path so serpentine that you may converse with your companions who are higher up though they are two miles in advance by the road. There you may follow a river road, and completely change your prospect every hundred rods; there, you may follow another, and be compelled to ford its crystal waters thirty times in a less number of miles. Here a stream rushes through the defiles of the hills with the velocity of a torrent; there another flows gently along over snow-white pebbles. Here you pass through forests whose tall trees are so enveloped with vines running to their tops, that not a leaf of their own nor a particle of the trunk are visible. Now, the waves of the ocean lave your horse's feet as you ride along the beach, and anon you are climbing a hill where the steep sides and the thick growing trees contract the broad view of the minute previous into a few feet of pathway, and the light of noon is changed to the twilight of evening.

But where are now 'the gentle people' who lived on these fruits, and bathed in these rivers, and roamed over these hills, and were happy for unknown ages in this unknown world? They are gone, like the Iroquois, the Hurons, and the Delawares; yet *not* like them; for while these fell manfully, disputing the right of the intruders, and died like warriors, the mild children of Hayti were worn out with unaccustomed labor, and hunted to death, hardly striking a blow in defence of their beautiful homes! Two short centuries have passed, and their existence is like a dream. And who is the successor of the exterminated race? Is it the greedy Spaniard raving for gold? — or *his* supplanter, the proud Frenchman, smiling and satisfied, as he gazes upon the rich coffee-groves and cane-fields with which his enterprise had covered the soil? It is none of these. Another people, a stranger to them all, transplanted from their own distant homes, not by their own wills or their own wants, but to serve the wills and the wants of alien masters, are now the uncontrolled lords of the soil which their slavish hands had tilled. What romance, what tale that wiled away the 'nights' of the Arabian Caliph, is stranger than this romance of the red race and the black? The one unfitted by his wild education to breathe the same air with the white intruder upon his soil, and so to perish; the other brought from a distant quarter of the globe, humble and strong and easy, kisses the rod, until the day of change comes, and then, where the red AMERICAN perished, the AFRICAN overpowers the EUROPEAN, and rules triumphant over a land bathed in the blood of all!

To wile away a heavy hour, I was wont to stroll to a neighboring hill, where a broad expanse of ocean was spread out, and far on the distant horizon was seen the faint outline of mountains in Cuba and at

Cape Nicholai Mole. Part of the town swept around the base of the hill, and in full view lay the market-place and parade-ground; and as the different guard-stations were relieved, the roll of the drum came clear and sharp up the hill, reminding us that no display of guns and drums and bayonets was required in our own favored land. Many a sad and many a happy hour have we passed there. Sad, when the ocean gave no sign of long-expected tidings from home, throwing back upon our hearts the bitter feeling of 'hope deferred;' cheerful, joyous, when the good glass defined the white speck on the far distant horizon to be the square topsail of a foreign and probably of an American vessel! And then we were wont to sit down in the pleasant shade and watch her for hours as she grew taller and taller upon the waters, until at last the welcome emblem floated from the mast-head, and crowned our hopes with full fruition.

The summit of this hill was covered with the ruins of the mansion of the 'Commandant de la Place' of the ancient régime. The arches of the cellars, a rabbit warren, and other apartments of the basement remained, but not another vestige of the building itself, excepting the steps in front. The gardens extended round on every side, and were divided into sections or plots of some sixty or eighty feet square by solid masonry four feet high; and these walls are perfect. Many fruit trees still wave their golden boughs over these grounds, and the fragrant jasmines still 'waste their sweetness on the desert air.' The thoughts naturally reverted to the builders and occupants of this pleasant spot; to the fair children of France who assembled in this shady grove to hold pleasant converse; to read the last romance from Paris; to tune the light guitar, and to enjoy the view and the breezes of ocean. From the tall topmasts in the harbor below the lily-white flag of the Bourbons constantly greeted their sight; and as the warm thoughts of *home* arose, they would turn to the distant horizon, and gaze as if their vision could pierce through the thousand leagues which lay between them and their own or their fathers' birth-place. Is this mere fancy? Answer, emigrant or traveller, on whatever shore your alien feet have trod!

And thus they passed their days amid gardens and groves, and flowers and fountains; the busy town at their feet, with its paraphernalia of trade, was to them a volume which they did not seek to open; for these favorites of fortune were the children of colonial officers or of wealthy planters, and nothing but rank or riches found their way within the magic circle in which they moved. What gay banquets had been held beneath that roof! How had the tables groaned beneath the rich viands served in massive plate! How obsequious had been the slaves stationed behind each guest to change the varying courses and serve the sparkling wine! And where were now those guests? Though little more than a quarter of a century had passed, most if not all of them had paid the debt of nature; and if there were any survivors of the revolutionary horrors, they were far away, seeking consolation for their losses in the vain hope of restitution to their former grandeur. And where were the obsequious slaves? Many of them still lived. The old couple in yonder hovel were of the number. Victors in the struggle, they lived still in sight of their old home, and the magnificence of their master's establishment is freshly remembered. Question them; their answers are vague and unsatisfactory. There is too much crime involved in such recollections. They would that a Lethe might pour its streams over the land and wash out the remembrance of the past, and the danger of future retribution! The negro of Hayti loves not to dwell upon by-gone days!

On my last visit 'to the hill,' in 1840, the flowers once so carefully nurtured still survived the neglect of an age, and were yet blooming around the broken steps and gate-way, and the guava and mango and orange bore their fruit in the deserted gardens: but the only charm of the spot, the melancholy one of loneliness, was destroyed. A squalid band of beggars and cripples had taken up their dismal abode in the arched cellars, from whence, as the bats flew in at dawn, they sallied forth, to begin with the day another struggle with famine and disease. The following anecdote will illustrate the aversion which the Haytien has to recur to past events. A Frenchman travelling in the island stopped at the house of an old negro, who for his zeal in revolutionary times had been raised to the rank of colonel. A plentiful repast of rice, fowls, bananas, etc., was set before the hungry Gascon, who did ample justice thereto. Turning over the heavy silver fork in his hand, he read a name engraved in large letters which he recognized as that of a rich planter who had lived in these parts. With vast indiscretion, our white man pursued his examination to the other spoons and forks upon the table, of which there was made quite a display, and found upon all, in large letters, as was the fashion with the ostentatious planter, the name of D'ORVILLE at full length. Aware that it was a ticklish question, but bursting with curiosity, he bearded the lion in his den, and cried out: 'Why, Colonel where did you get all this plate, which I perceive belonged to the family of D'Orville?' The Colonel laying down the banana which he was discussing with the knife and fork of Dame Nature, fixed his guest (and that guest a Frenchman) with a steady gaze, and without any outward sign of discomposure, answered quietly : '*Mangez mangé ou, blanc, et pas mélez corps ou dans z'affaires qui pas gardé ou,*' which means : 'Eat your victuals, white man, and don't ask questions about things which don't concern you.' The inquisitive guest afterward had his curiosity satisfied, by ascertaining that he had eaten his dinner on the D'Orville estate, and that the Colonel had been one of the D'Orville slaves! But the blacks are sometimes, nay often, much attached to the families of their old masters; bringing them presents from the country, living with them as servants, and taking an interest in all their concerns. This feeling is seen more commonly in the women. I refer to their *colored* owners, and not to the whites. None of the latter ever venture themselves upon the island.

There was one expression which the negroes bestowed upon each other occasionally, which I could not for a long time interpret. This was 'Negre-maitre.' Did it mean that the person addressed was a 'master negro' or negro 'par excellence?' From the vanity of the race, I thought this likely; but at last I ascertained the true meaning, which is ' master's negro.' So the next time I heard it I knew that *the two had belonged to the same master*, and that they gave each other the affectionate title of 'master's niggers.' Great respect is paid to a difference of age. The boy of six years addressing the boy of ten, or the youth of sixteen accosting the man of twenty-five, is always expected to fit a handle to his senior's name. Among friends and intimates it is 'frere' or 'cousin,' or 'compere.' Thus, Jaques speaking to his elder, Pierre, says 'brother Pierre,' or 'cousin Pierre,' though there be no consanguinity between them. It is a singular mark of respect, always expected and always paid to a difference in age. When there are two of the same name, they call each other 'Tokai.'   St. Croix.

A THOUGHT OF THE PILGRIMS.

BY MRS. MARY E. HEWITT.

How beauteous in the morning light,
　All glittering in her pride,
Tri-mountain from her ancient height
　Looks down upon the tide !
The fond wind woos her from the sea,
And the wave clasps her lovingly
　As bridegroom clasps his bride.

And out across the waters dark,
　Careering on their way,
Comes many a gallant home-bound bark,
　Swift dashing o'er the bay.
Their canvass hath the morning gales,
The sunlight gilds their swelling sails,
　And flashes on the spray.

Not thus toward fair New-England's coast,
　With eager-hearted crew,
The Pilgrim-freighted, tempest-tost,
　And lonely Mayflower drew !
There was no hand outstretched to bless,
No welcome from the wilderness
　To cheer her hardy few.

But onward drave the wintry clouds
　Athwart the darkening sky,
And hoarsely through the stiffening shrouds
　The wind swept stormily ;
While shrilly from the beetling rock
That seemed the billows' force to mock,
　Broke forth the sea-gull's cry.

God's blessing on their memories !
　Those sturdy ones and bold,
Who girt their hearts in righteousness,
　Like martyr-men of old ;

And mid oppression, sternly sought
To hold the sacred boon of Thought
  In freedom uncontrolled.

They left the old ancestral hall,
  The creed they might not own;
They left home, kindred, fortune, all —
  Left glory and renown;
For what to them was pride of birth,
Or what to them were pomps of earth,
  Who sought a heavenly crown?

Strong armed in faith they crossed the flood;
  Here, mid the forest fair,
With axe and mattock, from the wood
  They laid broad pastures bare;
And with their plough-shares turned the plain,
And planted fields of yellow grain,
  And built their dwellings there.

The Pilgrim Sires! How from the night
  Of centuries dim and vast,
It comes o'er every hill and height,
  That watch-word from the past!
And old men's pulses quicker bound,
And young hearts leap to hear the sound,
  As at the trumpet's blast!

And though the Pilgrims' day hath set,
  Its glorious light remains;
Its beam refulgent lingers yet
  O'er all New-England's plains.
Dear land! — how, doomed from thee to part,
The blood that warmed the Pilgrims' heart
  Swells proudly in my veins!

Blest right of consanguinity
  (And who shall me despoil?)
I claim with thy bold yeomanry,
  Thy stalwart sons of toil.
Brave shoots of that good Pilgrim stock
Whose strong roots clasp old Plymouth's rock,
  And widely vein the soil.

Go to the islands of the sea,
  Wherever man may dare,
Wherever pagan bows the knee,
  Or christian bends in prayer;
To every shore that skirts the main,
Wherever keel on strand hath lain,
  New-England's sons are there!

Toil they for wealth on distant coast,
  Roam they from sea to sea,
Still doth each bosom proudly boast
  Its birth-place 'mong the free!
Or seek they fame on glory's track,
Their hearts, like mine, turn ever back,
  New-England! unto thee.

A PIC-NIC.

BY THE AUTHOR OF 'THE AMERICAN IN PARIS,' 'FAMILIAR LETTERS FROM LONDON,' ETC.

A PLEASANT morning three months ago, a gentleman was seen bending his way through Chestnut-street, then veering off for the north-western regions of the city; conducting a lad of about six years with the right hand, and carrying on the left arm a basket — a couple of claret-bottles just exhibiting their slender necks over its margin. He had on a green coat, a white hat, unmentionables of a blue lilac, and a snowy dimity vest reflected the azure hues of its lining upon his cheeks. His form was robust, complexion rosy, and a volume of fair straight hair hung like the scutched flax upon his broad shoulders. The boy was tight belted in a blouse, and stuck out at the tail like a funnel. His face had the oval form of an egg, the bigger end down, and his pair of little eyes were blinking in their sockets in the anticipation of a day of pleasure. At the same time was seen, about fifty paces distant, a lady gradually dropping into the rear as she approached Chestnut-street, apparently not wishing to be noticed upon a polite promenade as appertaining to so scurvy a caravan. A gauze of attenuated and transparent meshes concealed her bosom as a mist; otherwise she was habited richly in silks, a little awry perhaps from some irregularity in the folds of her petticoat; but in natural beauty she exceeded the common endowments of her sex. Her eyes were gray like Minerva's and Bonaparte's, and her hair of a glossy brown gathered itself into ten thousand spontaneous curls upon eye-brows gracefully arched. Her nose was straight as the arrow, and her upper lip the exact image of Cupid's bow. In other respects her style was the luxuriant — in fashionable phrase, *embonpoint;* that is, her shapes were founded on facts; facts authentic, historical, demonstrable as geometry; and not indebted for contours and developements to the villanous ingenuity of Madame Cantello and ' her successors ; ' reminding the writer of this memoir of his more primitive days, and his uncottoned sweet-hearts of the Juniata.

Such was Mrs. Stripe, for so the lady was named, as I have since discovered; she having been united in second marriage with Mr. Richard Stripe, school-master of the classical department. It had been her husband's pleasure, to which after some opposition and the usual entreaties she had consented, to spend the first day of May, it being a holiday, his wife's birth-day, and the sweetest day of spring, in mounting declivities, walking in the solitude of valleys, listening to the warbling of birds, in a *pic-nic* with his ' soul's dearest half' and little Chip, (her son by the former marriage,) and other innocent recreations of the country ; and upon this errand they had set out just as the sun was peering over the vertex of Beck's shot-tower in Southwark. From the events of this day, its mishaps and enjoyments, with some casual adventures, and the usual number of digressions and conversations, I have made up, dear Editor, the subject of the present communication. For the convenience of readers who may not like to take the whole at once, it is divided as you will see into chapters, as follows.

CHAPTER FIRST.

THE WALK UPON CHESTNUT-STREET

—— 'Where alone our fashionable fair
Can form some slight acquaintance with fresh air.'

'YOUR servant!' said with great affability Mr. Bustleton. 'How is the wife and the little ones? — how is all the family?' And he passed on like Pontius when he asked 'what was truth,' without waiting an answer. A man of business — a note to pay at three — quick! He was out of sight; and Dick's bow wasted itself in empty air just opposite the United States' Bank, and he walked on, musing upon the fragility of banks and wooden pavements, till he reached Fifth-street. How beautiful are these English lindens! If but continued from river to river, Chestnut had been the queen of streets, and this alone had honored and beautified the city — at the expense only of pushing the lower section fifty yards upon Southwark. Here Mr. Cade, Mr. Straw, Mr. Kettle, the scene-shifters, the patriots, the politicians, and all those who, at a moment's warning, are ready to die for their country, were huddled under the shade; and Dick read the city, county, and state offices in large caligraphic letters overhead; the *Mayor's, Recorder's, Prothonotary's, Commissioners.'* 'Happy republic!' thought he, 'that stands in spite of the rats that are nibbling its timbers; *suapte vi stat;'* and he stood still awhile, the right foot in advance. Lawyers with green bags, one carrying briefs, another his breeches to the tailor, were going in and out.

Dick had been cast in a suit lately, and hated all lawyers; so he set to cursing them in the dead languages — the Latin is so expressive! He called them '*Fori tintinnabula,*' cow-bells of the court; '*Accepitres auri;'* '*Pecuniarum hamiolæ;'* '*Harpagones Curiæ;'* '*Rabulæ forenses, qui licitum latrocinium exercent;'* '*Damnifici linguis, nisi funibus argenteis vincias.'* Paid to talk, paid to hold their tongues; sowing law-suits, reaping fees. Equity, it occurred to him, must be, by the rule of opposites, from *equus,* a horse, for she do n't ride — '*Lacrymosa mora claudicans;'* and then he hobbled on, moved by the classic sounds, through the midst of that public hedge of constables, sheriffs, politicians and pick-pockets, embroidering the front of the old State-house, and the numerous pot-houses on the right, where sits apart, in great enjoyment of his mug of ale and his Virginia or Oronoco, the 'loafer,' watching the smoke as it curls slowly to the heaven of his divan, without knowing the existence of such things upon the earth; 'on diviner things intent;' and then he quoted what he thought the finest of Virgil's lines:

' Sic tandem Euboicis Cumarum illabitur oris : '

fancying he saw the vessel scud through the briny surge; and he arrived in a fast walk at the theatre. What a huddle of fashionables in grim moustaches, waiters, cab-drivers, and blackguards, about the hotels! Strange! how many of our republican youth pique themselves upon this kind of gentility! The crowd thickens here toward five, when you will see them pick their teeth with an air of contented satisfaction, as if they had dined.

Heavens! the exquisite creature! Who can she be! Such a girl, in French and even English customs, would venture upon this street only with her *bonne* or grandmother; our republican walks out, as you see, in all her independent and unguarded loveliness, not afraid of the Decemvirs. Dick made none of these reflections; I made them for him, which is the same thing; but he read over the play-bill, and out hopped, in his imagination, Fanny Elssler, undressed to the quick, skipping, flitting, pirouetting, sommersetting; and he stood, a leg at full stretch in the rear, and arms in a swimming posture; then, cased in her Cracovienne panoply, she rattled her castanets, and Dick snapped his fingers and cut a caper. The basket dropped, and Chip fell in the gutter.

‘ Hold your tongue, you little botheration ! ’
‘ I ’ll tell mother ! — so I will ! ’
‘ Tell the d — l ! Who cares ? ’
A silk gown rustled by, and Dick quailed. It was however not Mrs. Stripe, and he breathed again.

It was a Miss and Mister of the fashionable cut, who passing in front discovered, she her waist squeezed to an isthmus between two continents, and he an inch of snowy cambric peeping from his pocket, and a bud and two leaves, twined by the fingers of the Graces, at his buttonhole. ‘ Pon honor, Me-e-m · · · ’ But here an equipage, screaming on its axle-tree, with two stately negroes in the rear, and at six feet from the wheels two pot-bellied nags, looking like two rats in the family-way, drew up at the ‘ Washington.’ ‘ A great senator from the ‘ Old Dominion ! ’ ’ Every body stared, and Dick, with the basket and Chip, stared ; and three omnibusses and two funerals intervening, the street was choked up, and a part only of the conversation reached Mr. Stripe’s ears.

· · · ‘ Seen much ? ’ said the lady — casting an eye upon the play-bill, then on the beau — ‘ much of Miss Elssler ? ’

‘ Yes, Mem, a good deal. She was supremely beautiful last night in the Sylphide, was she not ? I say last night, for I believe you —— ’

‘ Ye — yes, Sir · · · on the second tier ! ’ (And she honored the young gentleman with a blush.) · · · Pa took a box up ’ · · · Think of modest sixteen, that scarce can garter up its own stockings in America, looking on, before company, at Fanny’s · · · gymnastics ! And the blush died away just opposite Godey’s.

‘ You have access, Mem, to the ‘ Lady’s Book ? ’ It is published here.’

The lady assented.

‘ May I ask you, Mem, have you not read the ‘ Land far Away,’ by ‘ Flora of Pheladelphy ? ’ And a delightful little tract by ‘ Amelia of

Louisville!' · · · 'Wonder who she is?' Then he thought the writings of the modern Magazines superior to Addison's, generally speaking. Many of them were indeed equal to the most ornate and elaborate compositions of antiquity. He could point out for example, in the last-named production, a description of the most irresistible pathos. Here he changed the bud and two leaves to another button-hole, being just over the place where young gentlemen put their hands upon their hearts, and continued:

'May I ask also, Miss Grace, being on the subject of letters, have you not perhaps read a work recently issued from the British press, entitled 'Flowers of Loveliness?' Eminently beautiful!'

'Very!' said Miss Grace; and then she eyed her beautiful self, reflected in one of Mrs. Tyndale's China pots. (Tea-pots.)

Here dropped in an acquaintance, with whiskers that scorched the sun: who doffed his hat, and making a bow with appropriate jut, stood bending his affability toward the lady; to which she, her head a little upon one shoulder, and with a sort of dyingness of expression, replied. A person calling himself Smith, or some such a name, at the same time took Dick by the button-hole, and all came to a stand. Little Chip, who in the back-ground stood grinning upward like a small steel-trap, had his share in the general effect. Smith descanted upon the passing world. He is soured with mankind, and glad of an opportunity of railing at them, whatever be the medium of communication. Mrs. Stripe, who had just stepped into Charles Martel's, that great perfumer of the Merovingian race, to · · · was to be waited for.

'That personage on the empty side of the street, so stately, was a year ago rich: he had wit then to be retailed about town, and men set their judgments by his, as their watches by the regulator; watched as he escaped through the back-door the crowd of friends, to obtain a bow, and went home and told their wives and children. But alas! how many bad speculations have fallen upon our great houses since a twelve-month! The money's gone; now, as you see, he walks incommoded by no friendly importunities. The swallows have migrated.

'That old lady? I knew her a fashionable *belle*. As she passed, hats kissed the pavement, and heads turned easily on their hinges. How light, how airy her step! scarce it made a dent upon the down; so halt and tottering now! She coquetted, flirted, played, sang, fluttered in the quadrille, languished in the waltz. Pretty accomplishments enough, Mr. Stripe, at seventeen; but ladies, especially American ladies, are not always seventeen!

'The young gentleman in ringlets? He is of the sea; troubled a good deal with woman being enamoured of him. A plague on being too handsome! · · · Foppery requires a population thick-settled and refined. How expect it, your Yankees squatting at the rate of eighty-seven to a square mile?

'Those are spirited horses; the equipage tasteful; does infinite honor to the coach-maker. The owner is rich to a million; trading on three ideas; with just arithmetic enough to keep the nick-sticks of his baker. He dines sumptuously, and has the fashionable diseases. He thinks his gout is hereditary; his wife's mother had it before him.

'This one is rich of his father's knavery. ' Happy the son whose father goes to h — l!' I forget who made this profane speech. But he gives sumptuous suppers and brings out the wine fuzzed and cobwebbed from the innermost cellar. Who dares say he is not the completest gentleman of the town?

'Stand aside! It is orator Puff. He delivers speeches, and makes the democracy laugh at the town-meetings. He is a useful man in politics, who gets others together in squads. Cato said long ago it was easier to drive the whole flock than a single sheep. He is useful also who has the knack of conferring greatness on others. The American plan is, you know, a great man being wanting, to get him up for the occasion, as the French *modistes* get up a woman into fashionable shapes. They want only the legs and arms of the right length.

' Your opinion of this pair of pretty girls ; good samples of the American *belle*. Complexion delicate, figure dainty, air graceful, and street dress fit for Milton's or Ariosto's Paradise, or Armidas' gardens. Was the gem made to sparkle and the worm to spin, and the sex not designed to be decked?

'The next in view is a man of first respectability. He puts out his money on good security, is regular at prayers ; loves heaven for the respectability it confers. He expresses himself cautiously, and with the most enigmatic grace imaginable, on all subjects upon which public opinion is undecided ; nor is he content with mere domestic authority. He has his opinions by the Great Western, and his wife her frocks *via* Havre. Take care to have your opinions in the fashion, Mr. Stripe ; you can get them ready made, as other articles of dress ; with this difference only, that the coat is not accommodated to the wearer, but the wearer to the coat.

' Alas, human Greatness! Her household gods are shattered ; her hearth · · · a · · · '

Suddenly the Signior Charivari ground an air of Mozart upon his organ, which cut off a fine philosophical sentiment somewhere about the middle. Dick brightened into a fine frenzy, and little Chip jumped out of his shoes at the monkey in regimentals, and left moralizing Smith to reflect upon the difference between monkeys and philosophers. The strain at length died away, and the world again passed by. The rumbling and ponderous omnibus and clattering cab, rattling and bumping high upon the rough ribs of Chestnut-street, passed on ; and Mr. Webster, and the aquatic Prince de Joinville, and ' Black Sall' with a prisoner for the ' Lock-Up,' and Fanny Elssler, who capered last night to fifteen hundred at her benefit; and Mrs. Wood, who tuned her throat to Bellini's Norma at five hundred a night ; and Mr. Praymore, laden with ten years' Greek, awaiting ' a call ' of five hundred per annum ; and Mrs. Stripe came out aromatic from Charles Martel's perfumery. Dick again, with his basket and Chip, delivering himself to his solitary reflections, and walking now fast and now slow ; now presenting his august visage to the firmament, and now his eyes downward in leaden community with the ground ; journeyed onward.

Not to disturb him, we will go back a few steps, if the reader please, to Mrs. Stripe, who had been overtaken at the outset by Mr. Ketchup, the interesting foreigner, just arrived in the city.   He designs to make a book upon our manners, and had just stepped out this fine morning to see upon Chestnut-street,

> 'That microcosm on stilts,
> Y'clept the great world;'

and he overtook Mrs. Stripe.

'My heavens! I was just saying to myself, 'Who is this elegant woman alone upon the walk?' I am not surprised · · · ·'

'Oh, Sir!'

'Word of honor! · · · If you will allow me, I will go before the mayor and swear you are the prettiest woman (and there are some delicious ones) upon Chestnut-street.'

'Oh! · · · ·'

Then other compliments succeeded, which called the lady a shepherdess, a turtle-dove, the nymph Egeria, the Queen of Jove, or any other goddess that came uppermost, for a whole square; ending in a general conversation, of which a part only was audible for the noise; the rest for the gods.

'Husbands! I have little sympathy with them any where, and least of all here. I resolved in the outset to hold no intercourse with them. They are unusually cunning, speculating, and unrefined; indeed the only gentlemen I have met in America are the Cherokees. · · · But I assure you, (tenderly to Mrs. Snipe,) I take a very cordial interest in their better halves. (*Bitter*, he would like to have said, but did not.) Your Chestnut-street is looking gay and beautiful to-day. I am fond of elegant streets. There is an utility as well as delight in them. One feels for the time being a genteel disgust at low life. If shabby, one shrinks instinctively into some less elegant resort. It is a feeling natural even to the lower animals. The peacock, they say, in moulting time hides and waits in secret till his plumage is restored. Do you not like them too?'

'Peacocks! I can't say I do. If there was nothing but me and them in the world, I guess the world would soon come to an end!' Mrs. Stripe looked beautiful; nonsense could not spoil her.

Here followed descriptions of fine European streets; of promenades in Regent-street in the long English twilight; of the Boulevard Italien and ices at Tortoni's; and what every one knows of the beautiful French gardens; of the 'King's,' so wild and romantic; the Luxembourg, so serene and philosophic; of the Tuilleries so gay and elegant; and so unceremonious and so unburdened of all etiquette, the Champs Elysées. Pity William Penn could not have spared a hundred or two of acres! But it would have been a prodigal waste of his State of Pennsylvania!

Mrs. Stripe said she had read all about the 'Place Louis McKinsy,' or some such a name,* last night in the Magazine, and the 'Obstacle of Luxor.'

---

* Miss STRIPE should have consulted Mrs. RAMSBOTTOM's Letters.   It was the 'Place Louis QUINSY,' named after a French King who died of a sore-throat!' — ED. KNICKERBOCKER.

' A capital engraving this, Ma'am. Let us see. A scripture-piece, I think. Joseph and his · · · Eh?'

' Joseph and the Pharisees. Yes, I guess it is,' replied Mrs. Stripe; but she could not say for certain; ' she had n't much bibolical learning.'

' But only look, Sir, at this statute, with the fiddle! What a queer crooked man it is! Did you ever see! *Peggi!* · · · what do you call him? · · ·

' *Tickets for Norma?* ' ' Suppose we go, Ma'am?' (sings) ' *Do I not prove thee, how much I love thee?* ' ' *Perish lonely, and bless thee with my latest breath!* ' ' *Oh dread reflection!* ' and Mrs. Stripe looked into the mirror.

' Seen it, I suppose?'

' Yes. It 's quite equal they say to any thing in the old countries.' And now she hugged the gentleman's arm closely. Mrs. Stripe is of an affectionate turn of mind, when she takes a liking; I mean that tender, purring kind of affection which rubs itself against you. He, intent with a glass examining prints of hounds and whippers-in at Melton, bending forward and one leg retro-ceding to preserve the equilibrium, while a little rogue, hawking news, pulls out slyly his snowy handkerchief. ' *Pheladelphy Paul Pry!* '

' Get out! you little noisy vagabond! It is known, Ma'am, in London that these hawkers, getting while young into vagrant habits, become unsettled as gypsies, and as disqualified for honest pursuits. This little chap will at last steal, I have no doubt. Do n't you think so, Ma'am?'

Mrs. Stripe with great presence of mind, and a reasonable concern for the morals of the community, replied : ' Yes!'

And then the walk was resumed. ' About Norma. I ask your pardon. The scenery and choruses are well enough. The mere mechanical part is easily attainable in all countries; but the combination of musical talent of all kinds in the Parisian and London theatres · · · · '

' Oh, it must be nice!'

' Mrs. Wood and her husband · · · · '

' As for me, I do n't like her a bit. She gets into such stormy fits about nothing; she 's so fussy; she 's so · · · so obstetrical.'

' And then the Italian orchestra! every instrument so balanced, each to its nicest proportion, to the infinitesimal of a note. And the fulness and variety of vocal talent! One hears, indeed, Mrs. Wood with pleasure; but in a comparison with Grisi, Malibran, and the rest, who would think of Mrs. Wood? And how to match Lablache as bass, in any country? He is a cataract of voice, putting to silence the fury of a hundred instruments; and then the silver-wired voice of Tambourini, like the chiming of distant bells! As for Rubini, Madam, there is no object of comparison. I consider him as *unique.* '

' Oh dear!' said the lady.

' But we have not taken ices together. Indeed I wo'n't suffer a refusal.'

' But my husband · · · He wo'n't know · · · · '

' All the better!'

'Oh, Sir, he'll be so angry! · · · '
'One look of that sweet face will please him again.'
'Oh dear! you have put me in such a flustration! I feel quite historical!'
'The ices will restore us. Here they are. Mrs. Parkinson would have taken it very ill · · · This is vanilla; this, lemon. (They eat.)
'It must be confessed you are the prettiest woman in this new world. England, alas! I bid thee adieu. I shall see thee no more; nor friends, nor native home!'
'Why, what does make you look so sad, Sir? What makes you say so?'
'While I was yet a child, Madam, a prophetic old woman, the nurse, said, putting her hand upon my head: 'This boy will not fall a victim to the cholic, or the measles, or the whooping-cough. He will not die of drowning, or hanging, or any of the natural accidents of humanity. Some pretty woman ——' And here she paused; she meant some pretty woman of Chestnut-street; 'will bring him to an end.' Madam, I see my destinies are about to be accomplished.'
Two drops stood glistening in Mrs. Stripe's large gray eyes, and the spoon rested in the untasted cream. Mrs. Stripe's bump of benevolence was large. She pitied the unhappy English gentleman from her heart; she hoped no ill would befall him; she was sorry he had ever seen her. · · · And then they took a glass of maraschino.
They walked now pensively at the side of each other, for a square and more, without saying a word; Mrs. Stripe just stealing a glance at Mr. Ketchup, and Mr. Ketchup at Mrs. Stripe. A sigh now and then struggling into being was smothered by modesty; till at length Mr. Ketchup opened his mouth with the following remarkable words:
'Madam! · · · '
Mrs. Stripe looked up tenderly, and again they fell into the same speechless eloquence of looks; and it was not till their sensations began to flow in a shallower current that they recovered that noisy faculty we denominate speech. This occurred about the corner of Eleventh-street.
'One could not long object to the 'splendid misery' of living in one of these sumptuous palaces.'
Mrs. Stripe only replied, 'they were the most costive houses in the city.'
All at once Mr. Ketchup recollected he had an engagement. 'Bless me! How time gallops away in your company, Madam! At four I will see you again.'
'The rock overlooking the dam. Do n't forget, Sir.'
'In the mean time, dear Stripe!' and he held her by the hand —'a little corner of your heart! However little, I will think it much. Good bye! All the rural divinities watch over you till four. Good bye!'
'I declare, these foreigners, they are *so* polite! He's the completest gentleman!' Again he kissed the ends of his fingers a hundred yards off, and the corner of Twelfth-street rudely interposed between Mrs.

Stripe and Mr. Ketchup. The latter just stopped a moment to make an entry in his memorandum book:

'*American Women.* — Prettiest in the world; but ungrammatical. Mrs. Malaprop, etc. · · · faithful · · · want of temptation. Husbands · · · notes to pay · · · unexpert. Women more easily · · · etc., etc.

Meanwhile Mr. Richard Stripe, who had walked on wrapped up in his meditations, was seen looking over his left shoulder several times, and finally waking up to the terrifying certainty that Mrs. Stripe was missing. He stared, hesitated, stopped; then ran half a mile to the west, thinking she had gone ahead, and then as far east, dragging Little Chip, *non æquis passibus;* when he discovered Madam issuing from Parkinson's, accompanied, as the reader is aware, and in a more than usual glow from the warmth of her feelings and the maraschino. He resumed his walk, not without certain conjugal apprehensions at seeing the stranger's gallant attentions to his wife; and he jerked up his legs under the excitement of his feelings and walked quicker.* But just as he had whipped his rage up into a fury, he stumbled luckily upon a woman begging, with a baby, her little stock in trade, and let off the stream of his ill-humor upon her: 'Get out of the way! you bundle of rags, fit only to set up a paper-mill! What business have you with children, not able to maintain them?' (He gave her slily a shilling.) And then he relapsed into reflection. There is something sedative and purifying in the exercise of the charitable affections. 'Strange! that women are more prolific the more they are poor, as if beggars were a provision of nature! They breed the more they are beaten. They cuff the wenches in Georgia · · · If it had been a man, not a penny would he have gotten from me; (or *got;* both are good grammar.) But these women, even in their rags, have I know not what power over us. D — n them! But I am resolved (he stopped, and then walked on) that no woman shall rule me! There's Mrs. Klink, who brought her husband so much money, and has such a name for faithfulness and housekeeping, and all that, and stays always at home; stays to scold her husband and beat the children, and has no more domestic virtues all the while than a cuckoo. If she was *my* wife, by —! I'd shake her out of her · · ·'

The truth is, when alone, Dick really felt the most magnanimous dispositions, and worked himself often into fits of desperate resolution. At these times he would fight duels, rout armies, save ladies from ruin, and do a hundred other things that were impracticable. He would make a fist under Mrs. Stripe's nose; chafe the tigress in its den; pluck the grave justice from the bench and wring his beard; he would bend down Christ-Church steeple to the earth with his little finger.

'By the Lord,' he exclaimed, 'I'd shake her out of her petticoats!' Then he gave a convulsive jerk to little Chip, (of Chippendale,) who screamed aloud; and perceiving the mother at his heels, he felt a chill run through his blood. 'Come along, Chippy! What a sweet little boy it is! We shall have a fine day, love, for our pic-nic.'

---

* Not by a man's skull only are the mental affections distinguished, but also by the calves of his legs. *Nota bene:* The same remark is made by the historian of Cataline.

'Fine days have furnished many a fool's head with conversation,' replied the dame. 'Let me see you dare to drag that child again in that manner! Come, my pet, *I'll* protect you;' and she kissed away the tears from the blubbering boy. 'He may dupe a novice; but your mother is not to be noosed by such a shallow simpleton. He has been used to taking woodcock upon his Blue Mountains. I wonder, since he was so quick in learning rudeness from the bear, he had not learned a little cunning from the fox.'

Dick, who could have borne any thing else but a slur upon the Blue Mountains, rallying his forces by an extraordinary effort, replied: 'There are people born at the Blue Mountains old enough, I guess, to be their own masters.'

'People who are their own masters have often fools for their scholars.'

'No more a fool · · · '

'Hold your tongue! · · · Ah, Mr. Cunningham, how do you do? We are just going over, my love and I, and our dear little boy, upon the hill to spend the day. It is a delightful little spot as there is about the city; a great deal of shade, fine turpentine walks, and the beautifullest perpendicular declivities that overhang the dam · · · '

'A quarter each,' said the driver, which Madam, the purse-bearer on such occasions, having paid, they disappeared in one of the new cabs rapidly toward Fair Mount. But this brings me to the end of my first chapter.

STANZAS.

My love dwells not in a lofty dome,
  Nor flaunts in the garb of pride,
But sweet is her low and happy home
  By the murmuring streamlet's side;
Where the earliest flowers of the merry spring
  Ope their mild eyes to the sun,
And the wandering birds first rest their wing,
  Their home of the summer won.

Nor storied race nor wealth hath flung
  Their magic around her name;
The simple songs her bard has sung,
  And his love, are her only fame;
Nor the diamond's gleam nor the lures of art
  O'er my graceful maiden shine,
For the priceless love of her warm true heart
  Do I thrill to call her mine!

The wine-cup's flash mid the reveller's din
  For her has never gleamed,
For the few she loves, who love again,
  Hath her gentle beauty beamed :
Others may bend to haughtier charms,
  To wealth or lofty line,
They are naught, when my trustful maiden's arms
  Press her faithful heart to mine!

C. H.

TORRIJOS AND HIS COMPANIONS.

AN AUTHENTIC SKETCH.

IT will probably be recollected by some of my readers, and particularly by those who feel an interest in the stirring events that have so strongly marked Spanish history for the last quarter of a century, that toward the close of the year 1831, the Count TORRIJOS, together with a party composed of forty-eight Spaniards and a young Irishman by the name of Boyd, who had for some time previously made their rendezvous at Gibraltar, deceived by MORENO, the then Goveror-General of Malaga, left the former port, for the purpose of effecting a landing in Spain, revolutionizing the country, and declaring the constitution of 1812.

The late king, Ferdinand the Seventh, through his spies, had sometime previously obtained an intimation of their intention, and instantly concerted measures to ensnare them. Moreno, in his youth, had been the school-fellow and familiar friend of the devoted Torrijos. The king being aware of this circumstance, and knowing the abject and mercenary character of the man, communicated to him his plans for the capture of this little band of patriots, and as may be supposed found a ready coadjutor. Moreno entered into a friendly correspondence with Torrijos, gained his confidence, became apparently a party to all his plans, and after a time gave him to understand that every thing was ready for his landing; that several of the regiments of royal troops then stationed at Malaga were ready to receive them as brothers in the good cause, the moment they should effect a landing on the soil of Spain; and finally fixed upon a day, when a certain regiment should be waiting their disembarkment at Fuengerola, a little fishing town on the coast, about five leagues from Malaga.

The plan was effective. The regiment was in waiting; the little band landed in the full confidence of friendship; and the next half hour saw them chained together in pairs, and marching in silence toward that city which they had expected to enter in triumph, as the liberators of their country.

On their arrival they were crowded into a convent; an extraordinary express despatched to Madrid with the intelligence of their capture; and at midnight of the sixth day, a solitary horseman arrived at the residence of the governor, bearing a despatch from the king, characteristic of that weak despot. It was in these words: ' *Let the traitors be shot within twenty-four hours after the receipt of this decree !* '

The morning sun ushered in Sunday the eleventh day of December, 1831; and the tragic event which followed, as well as the gallant bearing of this little band of heroes previous to their exit, is well described in the following translation of a letter from one of the confessors, a Spanish priest, to his father, immediately after, and discovered by the writer of this communication among the papers of the late consul of the United States at Malaga.

'MY DEAR AND BELOVED FATHER:

Health and the Grace of God!'

'I SUPPOSE you will by this time have received both my letters which I forwarded by the last mail. Their contents should have been included in one, had the express arrived at an earlier hour from Madrid; but as it did not reach Malaga until between the hours of three and four o'clock, P. M., on Saturday, my first letter of the same date had been already sent to the post-office.

'It is now my intention to give you a circumstantial account of what took place in the execution of the royal order with respect to Torrijos and his followers. The express from Madrid, as I have already mentioned, reached Malaga between the hours of three and four o'clock, on Saturday afternoon, bringing the positive order of the King our Lord, that Torrijos and all his companions should be prepared for death, and the sentence put in execution without the smallest loss of time. The General, governor of this city, took the most prompt measures to carry into effect the order of the king, and in consequence had Torrijos taken from the barracks in which he had been confined, and conducted in a carriage to the Convent of Carmelite Friars, the refectory of which was destined to be the condemned cell of all his party.

'After the removal of Torrijos, his companions, forty-eight in number, were taken from their several dungeons in which they had been placed, and loaded with heavy irons, marched to the same convent, where their general, Count José Maria Torrijos, had been placed. At about the hour of seven o'clock, P. M., all the culprits were assembled in the refectory of the convent, where there had previously met a number of reverend Fathers, composed of friars from different orders, and some secular priests.

'One of the priests thus addressed himself to Torrijos : 'I suppose you know for what purpose we are here?' To which he replied : 'I do not, but think I cannot be mistaken in my conjecture;' for he had not been informed why he had been removed to the convent. The reverend Fathers then commenced exhorting him and his companions to receive with christian resignation the sentence of the king, which condemned them all to death within a few hours, requesting at the same time that Torrijos would make choice among all the ministers of the Almighty, of the person he might wish to assist him in his preparation for death. Torrijos replied that for that purpose all ministers of the Almighty were equally reverenced by him, so that he who would undertake the charge had only to offer himself; and the reverend Father of our order, Friar Jerome of Ardales, remained with him. He asked Torrijos if he entertained any doubts or had any difficulty in respect to the most holy mysteries of the Catholic religion ? To which he replied without hesitation, that he was by the grace of God a Roman Catholic, and never had entertained the smallest doubt with respect to all and every thing which the Holy Catholic church proposed to his belief, whatever his errors might have been as a weak mortal in other respects.

'He made his confession without the slightest repugnance ; and after receiving absolution arose from his knees, and with some difficulty, on account of the weight of his irons, walked down the centre of the spacious refectory, and having addressed himself in particular to some of his companions, spoke to them all in an audible voice, saying : ' Brave comrades! The moment has now arrived in which we are called upon to look Death firmly in the face. In a few hours all will be at an end as regards us, so far as mortality is concerned ; and we shall then be placed beyond the power of the weak revenge of man to add to our bodily sufferings. Let me then beseech you to banish from your brave bosoms every earthly thought, and prepare to receive like christian heroes that glorious fate which awaits us ; for what can be so glorious for man, as in some degree to imitate the Saviour of mankind, in suffering with meekness and resignation the tortures of an ignominious death ? But death can only destroy our bodily existence ; our souls, being immortal, must exist for all eternity ; and our holy faith teaches us to believe that there is an eternity of bliss in store for those who die innocent.'

' All Torrijos' companions listened with the greatest attention to his exhortation, and replied to it in the most enthusiastic terms of fervor. The General then addressed himself in particular to one of the prisoners who had been Minister of War at the time of the Spanish constitution ; and afterward to another, of the name of Flores Calderon, who had been one of the members of the Cortes at that time, and said to them : 'The chief regret that oppresses my heart at this moment is, that these brave fellows' lives should be sacrificed, who have committed no other crime than that of permitting themselves to be persuaded by us to participate in our illusion, and offering to take a part in an expedition into which the world will some day know how treacherously we were enticed and basely betrayed.'

' They all confessed as good Catholics that night, and received absolution, except one, an Englishman, who said as he was not a Roman Catholic, he had nothing to do with the spiritual fathers or ministers of our holy religion ; adding, that for his part he had always endeavored to adore the Almighty with a pure heart, and to avoid all such crimes as could give rise to remorse of conscience, and as his was free from scruples, he relied too firmly on the mercy of God to feel alarmed at the approach of death. This person had lent fifty-five thousand dollars to Torrijos.

' All these poor creatures passed the night cheerfully, some occupied in writing to their wives, others to their families. They all gave up to their confessors such money as they had contrived to conceal on their persons, some ordering it to be remitted to their families, and others directing it to be laid out in masses for their souls ; and one in particular gave to his confessor four thousand rials, to be invested in the purchase of wax-lights, for the purpose of illuminating the blessed sacrament. Several of them subscribed different sums, to be paid to the soldiers employed to shoot them.

' The convent bell at last announced the approach of the aurora of the holy Sabbath, and of the hour for the bloody sacrifice. The victims again repeated their confessions, and with the gentleness of lambs and firm composure of martyrs, awaited the first signal in fervent prayer, still assisted by their spiritual directors.

'At exactly half-past ten o'clock on Sunday morning, twenty-five of the prisoners had their irons taken off, and being pinioned, were taken under a strong military escort down to the sea beach, at about the distance of a musket-shot from the convent, shackled together in the following order :   First, Golfin, who, as already mentioned, was Minister of War at the time of the Constitution, followed by Count Torrijos ; after him the English gentleman ; then Flores Calderon, one of the famous deputies of the Cortes ; next an artillery officer by the name of Pinto, who had been named Captain-General by Torrijos ; then another Englishman who was a Catholic, followed by a Spanish officer who had been one of the most determined chiefs of the late conspiracy at Cadiz, and some other deputies and chiefs, amounting in all to the before-mentioned number.

'When they reached the beach, they were blind-folded, and being placed in a line on their knees, there was a terrible discharge of musketry fired among them, by which they were all either killed or wounded, except the English gentleman, who did not receive the slightest injury, but was soon despatched by the subsequent shots, a number of which it was necessary to fire, as the greatest part of the victims had only been wounded by the first discharge.   Ten police-carts were in waiting to carry off the bodies to the place of interment, five of which were loaded with them, only leaving that of the English gentleman, which had been claimed by the English consul, and escorted by a party of lancers, drove off to the burial place, situated at the other extremity of Malaga.

'It was now necessary to bring some cart-loads of gravel to cover the great quantity of blood which remained on the ground, in consequence of the repeated wounds received by the principal part of these unfortunate men.   This arranged, the remaining twenty-four were brought from the convent, shackled as the former, to the same spot, where they experienced the like fate.

'I must not omit to mention, that all these unhappy men embraced affectionately their confessors before they knelt down, and Flores Calderon in particular called to his fellow collegian, Father Peter, who was a townsman of his, and said in a firm voice : 'Come, my dear countryman, and receive my last embrace!   God be with you !'

'Thus had they all ceased to exist before the hour of one o'clock, having had only fourteen hours granted them to prepare for death. Thousands of persons flocked to the place of burial, where a large trench had been dug to receive their bodies ; and such was the general curiosity to see the corpse of Torrijos, that it was not thrown into the ditch for some time.   The body of the Englishman, which remained on the beach, was removed in one of the English consul's carriages, in which his son, the vice-consul, went in person, carrying with him the English colors, in which the body of his noble countryman was shrouded.   On arriving at the consul's house, the body was laid out in great state until the evening of the following day, Monday, when it was taken to the English burial-ground, and interred, according to the rites of their religion, the ceremonies being performed by the consul.

New York, December, 1841.   G. B.

BALBOA ON THE ANDES.

God of the boundless universe!
   Our hearts gush forth to Thee,
Who built this noble mountain,
   And who filled yon glorious sea!
High is the peak whereon we stand,
   Chainless those waters are;
And our hearts, O God of Nature!
   Are loftier, freer far.

Thou art the shield that sheltered us
   From death in many a form;
The tropic's heat, its deluge-flood,
   The hurricane — the storm;
The rushing river's headlong rage,
   The forest and the fen;
From many a secret ambush,
   Where lurked the wild red men.

Death comes to us in thousand shapes;
   It floats upon the gale;
It climbs with us the mountain,
   And with us threads the vale.
'Tis tangled in the thicket's depths,
   'Tis wafted on the waves;
And the broad and smooth savannah
   Is printed with our graves.

Yet heed we not these troubles now;
   They cheaply buy the bliss
The Genoese long labored for —
   A moment such as this.
There, there it rolls! the long-sought sea,
   The ocean of the west:
No keel hath yet been wedded
   To its pure and virgin breast!

Where were ye born, ye fragrant winds
   That on my warm brow play?
Come ye from unknown countries?
   From India or Cathay?
What undiscovered shores may spread
   Beyond that rolling deep:
What sisterhood of islands
   May on its bosom sleep!

For whom we braved these perils all,
   Of midnight and of noon;
Faithful as yonder billows
   Are loyal to the moon;
We claim supreme dominion here,
   The mountain and the main;
We claim them for our sovereign,
   For Ferdinand of Spain!

THE QUOD CORRESPONDENCE.

The Attorney.

CHAPTER XII.

A FEW nights after the occurrences narrated in the last chapter, Lucy was sitting alone in the drawing-room. Since the lawyer's visit, a strong feeling of misgiving was working its way into her very life. Her cheek grew hollow and thin, and her eye larger, deeper, and more dazzling. She was restless and uneasy. Sometimes she started from her seat, and hurriedly paced the room; sometimes she wandered about the house, apparently without an object. At others, she endeavored to cheer up the girl who had been so kind to her; but there was something so mournful, so despairing in her manner, and in the tones that seemed to well from a broken heart, that it made Miss Crawford even more sad than before; and after an effort of this kind, she would often sink into gloomy silence, and remain so for hours. Even the servants noticed her altered appearance, and hinted darkly to each other that 'there was a screw loose somewhere,' and that ' all was not as it should be' with her.

Her imagination was teeming with fears and suspicions respecting her husband, that made her sick at heart. She tried to keep them out, but they *would* intrude. She fancied him hand-cuffed, a felon, dragged through the streets, with a crowd following at his heels, hooting and pointing at him, with hisses, groans, and execrations. The number seemed to increase, the more she thought of it. They came from all quarters, in multitudes that had no end; until all about him, house-tops, windows, steps and side-walks were swarming with a countless throng of faces. Then the scene changed to a court of justice, and he was arraigned there for trial. It was crowded from floor to ceiling; but all were against him. Every eye burned with fury; every tongue uttered a menace. None pitied him — not one! And there he was, shrinking and crouching before the eye of the multitude, and looking imploringly at her, to help him — and she could not! And at the bottom of all was that will. She pressed back her hair, and gazed eagerly around the room. She would have sworn that she heard his voice; but it was all fancy. She trimmed the lights, and drew nearer the fire, for she was very lonely.

The door-bell rang. The servant crept slowly through the entry, and spoke to some one. Then he came to the room-door; opened it, and thrusting in his head, said there was a man asking for some one, and he guessed it must be her, and wanted to know if he should let him in.

Lucy nodded; and a moment after a heavy step sounded in the entry, and a large man entered. He was dressed in a rough great-coat, with a broad-brimmed hat drawn down over his eyes, so that together with the dimness of the light it completely concealed his face. He walked to the middle of the room, looked irresolutely about him, then went to where the light shone full in his face, took off his hat, and stood still without speaking.

The girl watched him without a word, until he raised his hat, and then said sadly, and with more of disappointment than surprise in her tone :

'So, it's you, Jack Phillips?'

'Yes, Lucy,' replied the young man, gravely: 'I came here, I scarcely know why. I went to your house and found you gone; and George either could n't or would n't tell where you were. I've searched for you, all over; and by the merest chance saw you here as I was passing. I was afraid you might be in want, or trouble, and I could n't bear the thought of that But you seem quite comfortable,' said he, looking about the richly-furnished room.

'Yes, for a time I am,' said Lucy. 'The young lady who lives here has been very kind to me. But I shall soon be where I can earn my own bread. With a will, Jack, there's always a way; and I will earn an honest living, if I work my fingers to the bone!'

Phillips looked at her and shook his head; for he saw how thin her face was, how dark, and deep, and glowing were her eyes; and he observed the bright and feverish glow of her cheek; and a foreboding came across him, that her hour of toil was drawing to its close.

'But can't I help you in any way, Lucy?' inquired he earnestly. 'You know I would slave like a dog to do it. I need n't tell you that.'

The girl approached him, and laying her hand on his arm, and sinking her voice, said : 'Jack, I have something on my mind that has been wearing away my life by inches. I wanted to speak to some one about it, but I was afraid. I could n't trust it with *them*,' said she, pointing as if to those in the other part of the house, 'and least of all to *her* — the young lady, I mean — but I 'll tell *you*.' She looked about her, as if fearful of being overheard, and spoke almost in a whisper :

'You must n't breathe it to a soul. I need n't go over the difficulties between George and myself. You've seen a good deal,' said she, half choking in the effort to conceal her agitation, 'though you have n't seen all. You must n't come here again. It will be the worse for me if you do. It's no freak,' said she, quickly, observing an expression as of pain that crossed his face; 'but it was all about you we quarrelled. He had suspicions of me, which I never dreamed of. They were hard to bear; but he was in earnest in them; and you were the man he was jealous of.'

'Me!' exclaimed Phillips, 'and did he tell *you* this?'

'Yes, he did,' replied Lucy, earnestly, 'and in such a way that I hope I may rest in my coffin before I hear him speak so again.' The tears gushed to her eyes, but she dashed them off, and went on. 'I only speak of this, that you may know why I will not see you again. You are the truest friend I ever had; but I will not lay myself open to suspicion; nor shall there be even the shadow of a cause for slander. George was mad, I believe, or he would not have struck me. He was bad enough, often, but he never did *that* till then. I wish it had killed me at once!'

Phillips scarcely breathed as he listened. Every feature of his face was bloodless, and his lips were firmly set together. The girl went on without noticing it.

'Some one was at the bottom of all this, and there's one whom I suspect — a man named Bolton. From the time George first fell in with him, all has gone wrong. He has grown poor, and his disposition become changed. He never goes to the office of that man but he leaves it worse than he went. I've heard things about him too, that make my blood run cold. They're always here,' said she, pressing her hand on her forehead, and I can't get rid of them. He came here two nights since, with a will which was to strip Miss Crawford of every thing in the world, and give it to himself. It was signed by her father; and there were two witnesses — George Wilkins and William Higgs,' said she, in a low tone. 'They saw him sign it, and will swear to it, I'm told.'

She paused and pressed her hand painfully on her side; and Phillips could hear distinctly the rapid pulsation of her heart. 'Yes; that's what they are to do. They are to swear to *that*,' continued she, trembling as she spoke; 'but there's something worse than all that. *Neither of them ever saw him sign it.* As true as I stand here, they did not!'

'Good God!' exclaimed Phillips.

'It's true! before the God of heaven it's true! I say it — I, the wife of one of them. I know it, and I could prove it!' exclaimed the girl, wildly. 'Perhaps I ought to; for the young lady saved my life, and the very bread I eat is hers. It almost chokes me when I think of *him*. But Jack, when I married him, I swore before God to love, honor, and cherish him; to stand by him, when all others deserted him; and come what will, I cannot betray him now. Hear me out,' said she, holding up her hand to prevent him from interrupting her. 'Hear me out, while I *can* speak — God only knows how long it will be. Now, you must do this for my sake,' said she, speaking so rapidly that he could scarcely understand her, and grasping his arm with a force which was even painful: 'You must seek him out; track him from street to street, from house to house: no matter where or in what places it leads you; you must follow him up as if your very life depended on it; you must not give up till you find him. Tell him all you know. Tell him that Mr. Crawford's will has been forged; that his name is signed to it as a witness; that there is one who can prove that will to be forged, and will; aye *will* — say *that*. That may have some weight, if nothing else will. If that fails, keep him away; shut him up, drag him off — any thing; *any* thing! — only do not let him have that heavy sin on his soul. The bare thought of what may happen to him is killing me. There is a weight *here*,' said she, laying her hand on her heart, 'that is dragging me down to the grave. I have spoken openly to you; more so perhaps than I ought; but you are my only friend now. You may be able to save him when I cannot, though God knows, I would drop down dead on this very spot if I could! There, now go; you've heard all. Learn what you can, and let me know. Don't come yourself; but write. I cannot tell you what to do, or how to set about it. In that you must judge for yourself: but you *must not fail!* There, go, go!' said she, half pushing him to the door; 'make haste, and I will thank you to the last day of my life, and on my bended knees I will bless you and pray for you!'

Phillips hesitated for a moment, and then said:

'Well Lucy, for your sake I will see what I can do: but d — n him! I think the State-prison the best place for him!' exclaimed he, clenching his fist; 'if I had him here, I'd break every bone in his infernal carcass!'

Having thus given vent to his anger, he went through the entry and out of the door, without even looking back. He set out determined to find Wilkins; to discover how he was connected with the lawyer in this transaction; and if the fears of his wife were just, either by persuasion or menace to keep him from implicating himself more deeply. If he failed in this, he intended to go directly to the lawyer, discover to him what he knew, and then to threaten him with disgrace and punishment if he persisted in his attempt to establish the will. But all this depended on the fact of its being a forgery. He had no proof of that, except the bare word of a poor, half-distracted girl. Yet he believed her without hesitation, and did not scruple to act upon her words as if they were established beyond a doubt.

'She sha'n't say she has n't one friend, while *I* live!' muttered he, as he went through the street. 'Poor Lucy! God help her! she might have got a wiser head but not a more willing heart. Yes, poor dear broken-hearted little Lucy!' exclaimed he, the tears filling his eyes as he spoke, 'I'm afraid it's your last wish. I am indeed; but I'll do it. I'll find him; I'll stand between him and harm, as *you* would have done; and if he resists persuasion, by G — d! I'll thrash him within an inch of his life!'

He knew not where to look for Wilkins; but as the most probable place, directed his steps to his dwelling. When he came to it, it was dark and seemed deserted. He went to the door of the room and knocked. There was no answer save the ringing echo of his own blows. He then called his name.

'What yer kickin' up such a rumpus about?' growled a savage voice from a door at the head of the stairs, leading to the second story. At the same time, a rough head, garnished with a red beard of several days' growth, and bandaged across one eye, was thrust out, while the remaining eye, which was ominously bruised, by the assistance of a sickly candle was brought to bear upon Phillips.

'What yer want?'

'Where's Wilkins?' demanded he; 'I want him.'

'You *do*, do yer? — well, look for him. I thought the house was a-fire;' and the head and candle were withdrawn simultaneously; and the door slammed to. Phillips thought it worse than useless to prosecute his inquiries in this quarter, and accordingly left, and went straight to one of those houses which he knew Wilkins was in the habit of frequenting. But wherever he went, his inquiries were fruitless. At some places he had not been for more than a week; at others, the time was even longer; and at none had he stopped within the last two or three days. From all that he could ascertain, Phillips thought it doubtful whether he had been at any of his old haunts since the night he had parted with him. One or two had met him in the streets within a day or two, but he appeared so savage and morose that they pretended not to notice him, and passed without greeting him. They all spoke of him as gaunt, haggard, with wasted and sunken cheeks, like one who had been on the verge of the grave. Farther than this, Phillips could learn nothing; and he now determined to see Higgs (who from Lucy's account was also linked with him) and the lawyer.

He had little difficulty in ascertaining where Higgs was. In fact there were few places where he was not. A dozen were mentioned in a breath where he had been seen that day. The last person however had left him at Quagley's within an hour. He was greatly improved in appearance; having as he said inherited a considerable amount of property from a relative recently dead. Phillips did not wait to hear the end of the man's surmises as to where his wealth came from and how much it was, and which were as correct as the surmises of a man who knows nothing about a matter generally are, but left him and proceeded to 'Quagley's Retreat.' He soon came in sight of the flaring light, with its red letters, pointing it out as the place to which that gentleman retreated, but whether when tipsy or pursued by creditors is a matter of some surmise.

Without pausing to knock, Phillips opened the door and walked in. He was unnoticed by all except the stunted marker, who stared at him until he had firmly established him in his mind's eye; and then betook himself to the duties of his office.

Higgs was sitting on a settee in one corner of the room; but so much changed in attire, that Phillips did not at first recognize him. His whole dress was new, and surprisingly well chosen; plain, neat, with no attempt at show. In his hand he held a glass of some kind of liquor, with which he refreshed himself during the intervals of a very confidential conversation which he was holding with Mr. Quagley. It must have been strange as well as confidential, for Mr. Quagley was completely overcome either by the information which was entering his head, or the liquor which had entered his stomach. He nodded wisely, and blinked at Mr. Higgs as if an idea was kindling in his head, and would soon break out into a blaze; but it smouldered away in smoke, and left nothing but mist. He shook his head, but it was empty; so he took to his liquor in sad silence.

As soon as Phillips saw Higgs, he went up to him. 'I scarcely knew you,' said he.

'That's strange. Most folks are just beginning to know me; now that I'm in luck's way,' replied Higgs, gently raising his glass to his lips, and sipping some of its contents.

'Then the story's true about your fortune?' said Phillips.

'Ya – as. I've suddenly stept into a small fortin. A respectable elderly gentleman has been keeping it for me these twenty years,' said he, crossing his legs deliberately, holding his tumbler to the light, and ogling its contents. 'He died t' other day; a fine old boy he was, that elderly gentleman; a distant branch of my family. I'll sport a crape for him, when my hat grows shabby. Mr. Quagley, a rum-and-water — stiff.'

'Certainly,' said Mr. Quagley, bowing low; for his civility had redoubled within the last few days.

'Stop!' said Phillips, abruptly; 'you've had enough already. I've that on hand which needs a clear head. I've been looking for you these two hours; so come along.'

'I'm in great demand since the death of my elderly relative,' remarked Mr. Higgs, placidly, and without moving; 'but what's all this about? Where am I to go? — what for? — and would n't to-morrow do as well?'

'No, it wo'n't,' replied Phillips. 'You'll learn the rest soon enough; come!'

There was something in the stern peremptory manner of the young man, that impressed Higgs, in spite of himself; so he rose, and stretching himself, said:

'Well, if I must, I suppose I must. Mr. Quagley, you may let that order for a rum-and-water stand over till to-morrow; or perhaps late this evening.'

Mr. Quagley bowed low, and laid his hand where his heart should have been — on his stomach.

'Now go on,' said Higgs.

Phillips led the way into the street; but before they had gone many steps, Higgs came to his side, and laying by his usual careless manner, said:

'Now then, before I move another step, I must know where I am going, and for what. I did n't insist on it there,' said he, pointing toward the place they had just left, 'because there are things which are best known only to two, and this might have been one; but now I must know more.'

'This is no place to reveal what I have to say,' replied Phillips, bluntly. 'It's a matter of little consequence to me, but of much to you. You'd better come on. I'm only going to my rooms. They're not far off, and there'll be none but ourselves. For your sake, I want no listeners.'

'Go on!' said Higgs: 'but the interest you take in me seems to have come on you d — d sudden!'

Nothing farther was said until they had crossed the Bowery, and reached one of the streets which led down to the East river. At the door of a neat wooden building Phillips knocked. It was opened by a girl who seemed to know him, and who, in reply to an inquiry of his, informed him that every body was out except herself. Making a gesture to Higgs to follow him, he led the way to a room in the second story, plainly but comfortably furnished, with a cheerful fire burning on the hearth. A small shelf of books stood in one corner; a clock ticked on the mantel-piece; a few pictures were hung on the walls, and every thing wore an air of snugness and comfort.

Phillips placed a chair for Higgs, who had not uttered a word since those last mentioned. Higgs sat down, and Phillips shutting the room door, drew another chair, took a seat facing him, and so near that their knees nearly touched.

Still Higgs did not speak; but looked at him as if he waited for him
to go on.

'I will come to the point at once,' said Phillips.

'Do!' replied Higgs.

Phillips got up; trimmed the lamp which stood on the table, and as
if by accident, drew it so that its light fell full in the face of his guest.

'First, I want a piece of information,' said he. 'Where's Wilkins?'

'I don't know,' answered Higgs, laconically, and weighing every
question before he spoke.

'When did you see him last?'

'I don't remember.'

'Nor where?'

'No.'

'Can't you tell me where I can find him?' inquired Phillips, earnestly. 'It was principally on his account I wanted you. It will be
worse both for you and him, if I don't find him soon. Worse than he
and you dream of.'

'If that's all you want,' said Higgs, coldly, 'you might have asked
it in the street. I could have told you there, as much as I've told you
here.'

'That was *not* all,' replied Phillips. 'You shall hear the rest at
once. A few days ago a gentleman in this city died, leaving a large
property, and an only daughter, who would by law have inherited it. A
day or two after the death of that gentleman, a lawyer called at the
house of that daughter and claimed the property as his, and declared
that girl penniless. He brought with him a will to support his claim;
a will signed by the gentleman, giving his property to that lawyer, and
stripping his daughter of all she had. This will was witnessed by two
men, who are to swear that they saw it signed by that gentleman. The
names of those two men are George Wilkins and William Higgs; the
lawyer, Reuben Bolton. Perhaps you understand now what I want,
and why I could n't speak out in the street.'

Phillips watched the face of his listener with intense anxiety; but
not a muscle moved; not the slightest alteration took place in look or
color; and when he paused, Higgs gazed in the fire, as if in deep
thought. At last he said quietly, without replying to Phillips' last
words: 'yes, I remember something of the kind; Wilkins and I happened to be in Bolton's office, when an old man was making his will,
and he asked us to witness it. I forget the old fellow's name. It was
Crawley or Crawman, or some such name. I did n't know till now
what he 'd done with his cash. It was d——d hard to cut the girl off in
that way;' and again Higgs gazed in the fire in deep thought.

'Then he did sign it!' exclaimed Phillips, starting to his feet. 'To
be sure he did,' replied Higgs; 'I saw him.'

'And it is n't forged?' demanded Phillips, speaking with the greatest
rapidity.

'Forged!' exclaimed Higgs: 'if it's forged, he forged it himself.
Why, who *says* it is?'

'One who is willing to swear to it, and will. Those are the very

words that person used to me, at the same time begging me to use
every means to prevent the witnesses from endeavoring to establish it,
as detection and punishment were certain.'

'Did that person know the young lady — what's her name?' asked
Higgs, calmly.

'Miss Crawford.'

'Ah! Crawford! that's it; that was the old man's name. Was that
person acquainted with Miss Crawford?'

'Yes.'

'Perhaps a friend of hers?' suggested Higgs, in the same quiet
manner.

'I know she was,' replied Phillips. 'Well, what of it?'

'Pshaw! don't you see it all?' exclaimed he, rising from his chair.
'It's a trick of the girl to prevent our appearing to prove that will.
She would scare us. What a fool!'

The red blood rushed into Phillips' face. He knew little of law, and
the thing seemed plausible. Could he have been duped, and by Lucy?
Lucy had been deceived herself; he was sure of it. The whole conduct of Higgs had been quiet and self-possessed. There had been none
of the embarrassment attendant on detected guilt; and especially of
guilt which involved so severe a punishment. He was convinced that
the feelings of the girl had been worked on by the arts of Miss Crawford, until they had led her astray. But how to undeceive her!

''That Miss Crawford's a deep one,' said Higgs, after a pause of
some duration. 'How the devil could she find out that you knew us,
and set you to work at us?'

'That was easy. There happened to be a person in the house
who knew all three of us. She accidentally learned the names of the
witnesses, knew me, and asked me to see you and Wilkins. Why she
thinks it forged, is more than I can tell.'

'Who was she?' inquired Higgs.

'No matter who,' replied Phillips; 'I am not bound to secrecy, but
I shall keep her name to myself.'

Higgs nodded acquiescence; and after humming a low tune to himself for a few moments, asked if he had any thing farther to say; and
receiving an answer in the negative, he wished him good night, and
withdrew.

CHAPTER XIII.

It was a bright sunlight afternoon; and the golden sunbeams came
flooding in the windows of the attorney's office, forcing their glad light
through the dingy panes, and over tables, books and walls. It was a
rich warm sunshine, such as cheers the heart. Thousands of little
motes, the very dust of the earth, were revelling in its beams; rising
and falling, dancing, whirling hither and thither, up and down; sporting like things glad of life. The old room had a cheerful look that
was not natural to it. The very spiders that had nestled in its crevices
for months, startled at the strong light, stole off to dark corners, and
doubling themselves into knots, seemed to wonder what was to come

next. High in the heavens rode that sun, and over all came its glorious rays, shining in crack and cranny; over ruined house-tops and in damp, dark court-yards, brightening the homes of the wretched, and gilding the graves of the dead. How many were revelling in its beams! The rich and the poor; the sick and the healthful; the strong and the feeble. It was a glad sun to each; and it shone alike on all. Gold could not buy it; poverty could not exclude it. It is one of God's gifts, of which he allows no monopoly. It is to cheer the path of all, and to serve too often for fire and raiment for the poor.

It doubtless had its effect upon the attorney's clerk, who was lolling out at one of the windows, regaling himself with a prospect of two brick walls, and a distant view of a dead tree, which formed the background of a narrow alley. He seemed uncommonly merry, and not a little inclined to mischief. He ran his eye up and down the stone-wall opposite; examined the dead tree; but nothing offered worthy of attention. He then rose, and deliberately threw several pieces of coal over unknown house-tops, whose jagged chimneys frowned upon the yard, in the hope that the jingling of broken glass might follow as an indication that this onslaught upon some unseen window had been successful. Being disappointed in this, and having caught sight of a small baby in a distant window, he was in the act of producing several violent contortions of countenance, for the desirable purpose of reducing the said baby to tears, when he was called to himself by a sharp application from behind, which felt as if it might have come from a foot. The clerk jerked in his head to see who had favored him with this abrupt summons.

'Oh! you are at home, my bu'ster, are you? I thought I'd knock and inquire.'

This speech came from a stunted boy with a square mouth, who was leaning leisurely against the back of a chair. A small cap was stuck jauntily on the side of his head, and one hand was resting on his hip, the other being fully occupied in holding in the slack of his trousers, which, owing to his having been busily engaged in other matters, had got considerably the start of him in size.

'Where's the Boss?' said he, after pausing a moment to enjoy the surprise of the clerk. 'I want him.'

'Hats off is manners; caps off is manners too,' replied Tom quietly, saluting the side of the boy's head with a small ruler, which sent the cap to the far end of the office.

The stunted marker was too much accustomed to scuffles and blows, not to be prepared for all emergencies of that nature; and the clerk was too much delighted at the prospect of a recreation of any kind to care much in what shape it came. So after describing several circles around each other, brandishing their fists and elbows in the various attitudes recognized by standard authorities, by way of showing their science, at it they went, rough-and-tumble, over the floor, upsetting chairs, desks and tables; scattering papers and bringing down clouds of dust which had slept undisturbed for years. While the battle was at its height a man's step in the lower passage caught the ear of both boys.

'By thunder! it's the Boss!' cried the clerk; 'jump up quick; put the chairs up, while I fix the papers and tables. Bustle! bustle!'

The apprehension of the clerk was one in which the boy fully sympathized. The battle ceased instantly, and by dint of the united efforts of the two the office had resumed its usual appearance. The clerk was reading violently, and the stunted marker, though somewhat heated, was modestly sitting on a chair in one corner, with his cap resting on his knees, when the door opened, and Bolton walked in.

When he saw the boy he stopped and looked at him, as much as to ask what he wanted, for few people called there without an object.

The boy understood the look, and recovering something of his usual effrontery, asked, though without rising from his chair:

'Are you the Governor? 'cos if you are, I've got somethin' for you. If you a'rn't, I'll wait till he comes.'

'My name is Bolton, if you want me,' replied the Attorney, eyeing him with some surprise.

The boy took off his cap and felt in the lining, from beneath which he drew a letter.

'Reuben Bolton, Esquire, Lawyer at Law, etc., etc.,' said he, reading the superscription. 'Is that you?'

'Yes.'

'Very well; then you can take it,' said he, reaching it out from where he sat. 'It came from a gen'leman, named Higgs; and he wants an answer; so just be spry in reading it, will you? 'cos I'm in a hurry.'

Having thus delivered himself, the boy thrust a thumb in each pocket of his jacket, and commenced whistling with a shrillness that caused the attorney, after a vain attempt to look him into silence, to hurry in the back room and shut the door.

No sooner was the door shut than the clerk turned to the boy with an approving grin, and asked:

'What's your name?'

'Charles Draddy, Esquire,' responded the other, breaking off his tune only to answer, and then resuming it as vehemently as ever.

'Well, you *are* a great one, you are,' said Tom, strengthening his remarks with an encouraging nod: 'There a'rn't many would a-dared to have whistled at *him*, as you did. He's a snorter when he's riz.'

'Pshaw!' replied the stunted marker; 'he ar'n't nothin', he ar'n't; but if you could only see Dick White when he's tight up; or Lankey Jim, arter four cock-tails, and a rum-and-water, quite weak — that's all; only see *them*, and you would n't even look at the chops of that 'ere 'spectable gen'leman in the other room. My eyes! he ain't nothin' to *them*. Oh! no. Git eöut!'

Having thus given vent to his admiration of the two gentlemen just mentioned, he resumed his whistling, from which no observation of the clerk could induce him to desist, and who could obtain no other reply to all his questions than a nod, a wink, or a shrug of the shoulders.

In a short time Bolton opened the door and beckoned the boy to come in.

'Do you know Mr. Higgs?'

The boy nodded.

'Well?'

'Do n't I?' said the boy. 'I *guess* I do.'

'When will you see him?'

'When I go back. He 's waiting where I come from.'

Bolton drew out his watch, looked at the hour, put it back in his pocket, took up a piece of paper as if to write; then threw it down, and said :

'Tell him to be here in two hours; that 's all. Go.'

Notwithstanding the boy's natural effrontery there was something in the stern, peremptory manner of the lawyer so different from what he had been accustomed to, that he shut the door, and left the office without remark; unless a jerk, with which he favored the hair of the clerk as he went out, might be viewed in the light of a passing observation. Having got in the entry, he gave vent to one or two unearthly yells, went through the intricacies of a dance somewhat between a Scotch reel and a nautical horn-pipe, delivered himself of one or two other frivolities of an extraordinary nature, and then quietly walked down stairs and took the shortest route to 'Quagley's Retreat,' where he expected to find Mr. Higgs.

No sooner was the boy gone than Bolton took up the note and read it again. It was paradoxical enough, and worded with the elegance peculiar to the gentleman who wrote it. It ran thus :

'DEAR SIR : I 'm afraid your cake 's dough. I think we are smoked. If we are, we 're dished too, and there 's an end of it. But perhaps it was only a fetch, and I 'm hallooing before I 'm hurt. If so, all he got out out of me wo n't increase his wisdom much. I want to *see* you. When can I? Send me word by the bearer.

'WILLIAM HIGGS.'

Unintelligible as this was, it was sufficient to drive the blood from the cheek of the lawyer. 'Another blow too, on the back of what came to-day!' muttered he. 'Can it be that I am to fail now! I, who have hatched so much mischief, threaded so many dangers? — I, that have walked firmly where other men trembled; who never feared man nor God nor law? — *I* to fail now!'

He looked suspiciously about him, as if the very walls might tell tales. Could they have spoken he might well have feared; for many a dark plot, many a scene of sorrow and of sin would they have disclosed. Men would have been astounded to think that a single individual, flesh and blood like themselves, could have worked so much harm. Men who had once been rich crept away from there beggars; and females who, glad and unsuspecting of heart, had accidentally fallen in his way, had gradually grown poorer and poorer, until stripped of every thing, in very desperation they became outcasts, without hope, and beyond redemption. Ruin, starvation, crime and death followed in the wake of that single man, like jackals on the track of a beast of prey. But he had long since become callous. He had dealt so long in crime that he thought the rest of the world like himself; that to plot, to deceive, and to beggar was the aim of all.

Within two hours after the departure of the boy Higgs made his appearance. Nodding familiarly to the clerk, whom he had never seen before, he went to the door of the back-room, opened it, went in, and closed it after him.

The Attorney pointed to a chair as he entered, and no sooner was he seated than he took up his note and handed it to him.

'What does it mean?' demanded he.   'It's a riddle I can't solve.'

'Is the young gentleman in the outer office in your confidence,' inquired Mr. Higgs, in reply to the question.   'He ain't in mine, and I don't want him to be.'

Bolton got up and spoke a few words to Tom, who nodded, and taking up his hat, went out.

'He's gone for an hour at least,' said he, returning and seating himself.   'Now about the letter.'   Higgs could be as concise and clear as any one when he thought fit; and he now gave an account of his interview with Phillips, detailing the conversation word for word.

The Attorney listened without a single remark or a single question. The statement was so full yet concise, so plain and straight-forward, that it left nothing untold; and Bolton for the first time knew the man he had to deal with, and the cause of the implicit confidence with which Wilkins had recommended him and appeared to feel in his abilities.

'That's all,' said Higgs, as he finished.   'If I talked an hour I could tell no more.'

Saying this, he leaned back in the chair, and folding his arms, watched the countenance of the lawyer with a keen inquisitive eye.

'Did he give you no hint who this woman was?'

Higgs shook his head.

'Have you no suspicions?'

'None.'

'Can it be a trick of this girl's to drive us off? If so, it is flimsy enough.   This Phillips might have lied too.'

Higgs shook his head.   'Phillips wo'n't lie.   I know *that* much. When he's wrong, it's because he's deceived himself.   All of us may be at times.   If this is a trick, *he* do n't know it.'

'Then Mr. Higgs,' said Bolton, in a low, calm voice, which contrasted strongly with the excited manner in which he had hitherto spoken, and becoming pale and red in the same instant: 'Wilkins must have betrayed us.'

Higgs did not answer for some time.   Then he said: 'I do n't believe it.   He's not the man to blow on a comrade.   He gets strange freaks, and is as mad as a bedlamite at times, I think; but never mad enough for that.   He knows *me* too well,' said he, sternly.   And again the attorney saw in his face that cold, savage expression which had once before made his flesh creep.   'No, no; no fear of that.   But I'm puzzled, I must confess.'   There was a dead pause, in which these two confederates sat looking each other in the eyes.

'You understand the law,' said Higgs at last; 'I do n't.   Let me hear the will; perhaps I may think of something which do n't strike you.'

Bolton got the will, and sitting down, read it from beginning to end.

'That's all right in law, is it?' demanded Higgs.

Bolton nodded.

'Cuts her off without a copper?'

'She 'll have nothing.'

'Then how can she *law* it? Law is n't made for poor people.'

'Perhaps she has friends who will stand by her.'

''T'ain't the way of the world. They stand by people who are going into fortins, not out of 'em,' said Higgs. He took up a roll of paper and commenced drumming with it on the table, while the attorney, usually so shrewd and ready, stood in front of him with his eyes fixed on his face, as if he expected to find in his cold unmoved features some indication of the thoughts at work in his brain.

'Illegitimate, illegitimate,' muttered he. 'That I suppose is all gammon.'

Bolton looked at him with a sharp, cautious, irresolute eye, but did not answer.

'That 's enough; need n't say a word more,' said Higgs, reading the glance. 'I suspected as much. Another little item in the general bill. But I do n't see the use of it. Suppose she *is* a bastard? What then? How does it help you?'

'A natural child can't inherit.'

'Well, suppose *she* can't? Can *you?*'

'No, not without the will,' replied Bolton. 'But once prove to her that she cannot gain, even though I do not, and there will be no object in her contesting the matter. There 's no other next of kin, for she was the only relative he had on earth. If I proved her illegitimacy I would then pretend to feel for her desolate situation, and make her a present of ten thousand or so; that would effectually keep her quiet; for she would know that by proving I had no right to her father's property she would also prove I had no right to the money which I had so generously handed over to her.'

'There 's a good deal in that,' said Higgs, rubbing his hands as if he fully appreciated the merits of the scheme. 'But can you convince her? Some women are awful incredulous; and if you can't keep her quiet, can you satisfy the doubts of those who 'll try it?'

The Attorney clenched his fist and struck it on the table with a force that made it rattle; his eyes flashed; and as Higgs looked in them he fancied that he could see through them deep into his very brain, which seemed on fire too, as he answered:

'No! I cannot. From what that besotted old fool her father let drop while he lived, about the private manner in which he was married, and about the death of those who saw it, and about his having lost the certificate; with none to thwart me but a silly girl, I felt as if houses, lands, and gold were in my grasp. For months I 've had my eye on the traces of those who witnessed the marriage; made inquiries in every direction; and felt sure that they were in their graves; ay, dead and crumbled to dust. On that supposition I set to work; drew up that will; waited till the old man died; went with it to the girl; advanced my claim, and boldly asserted her illegitimacy. To-day! to-day!' exclaimed he, gasping as he spoke, and shaking both hands over his head like a man in a frenzy; 'this very day, when I am committed beyond redemption; when I have unmasked myself, and there is no retreat; one of these very witnesses springs up, as if from hell itself; seeks me out; says he hears that I have been looking for him, and would be glad to know what I want! I could have killed him! — I could have murdered him on the spot!'

He strode rapidly up and down the room, muttering to himself and clenching his hands together, as if he had the object of his wrath in his grasp, and were strangling him on the spot. Passions fierce as a whirlwind had got the better of him, and it was some time before he could master them. When he did, he paused opposite Higgs, with a face as pale as that of the dead, but said not a word.

'Was the witness old or young?' at length inquired Higgs.

'Old enough to have been in his grave years ago. He tottered as he came through the entry, and was sick and ghastly, as if he had just started from his coffin to cross me.'

Higgs rested his head on his hand, and then asked in a quiet voice: 'What's the punishment if we trip up?'

'Ten years' hard labor, at least,' replied Bolton; 'at least that. Curse him! — curse him!'

Higgs again rested his head on his hand, and mused.

'Was he sickly? — very sickly?' inquired he, in the same low tone. 'Did he look as if he'd *go* soon?'

'He might at any moment.'

'Perhaps he will,' said Higgs; 'perhaps he will.'

He reached out his hand, took the Attorney by the collar, drew him down to him, and whispered in his ear: 'I *know* he will; *don't you?*'

Bolton started up, glared at him, drew back farther and farther; his face became ghastly white; his heart beat till it could be heard; then the burning blood came dashing through his veins, over head, temples, face, and darting through his brain like liquid fire.

'No, no! not *that!*' gasped he. 'No, I cannot — I cannot! I can stand imprisonment, if it comes to that; but I can't die!'

'Well, have it your own way,' replied Higgs, carelessly. 'I've no taste for it myself. I've never dabbled in things of the kind, and as a general rule would as lief not; but when the state-prison ogles a fellow in the face, it's different. We must think of something else.'

Bolton was completely unnerved. There was something in the cold indifferent manner in which his confederate suggested murder that made his very heart thrill with fear. Higgs however did not follow up his suggestion, but asked:

'What's the old man's fortune?'

'About two hundred thousand,' replied Bolton.

'Ph — w! Is the girl married?'

'No.'

'Good looking?'

'Very.'

'Got an eye on any one?' inquired Higgs.

'Not that I know of.'

'Have you a lovely wife or an interesting family?'

'No, none.'

'Then by G — d!' exclaimed Higgs, starting to his feet, 'I have it! You must marry her yourself! *That* will settle it. You must saddle yourself with a wife; get the cash, and hush up all difficulties. She'll snap at the chance of marrying you. You'll both gain your end, and this awkward little matter will never come to light. I don't pretend to be squeamish, but for my part I'd rather it should n't.'

Bolton folded his arms, and stood for some moments looking in the fire, in deep thought. At last he said: 'It's plausible; and the girl's not amiss; but it's too late. The time's too short.'

'Pshaw!' exclaimed Higgs; 'what do you want of time? Go at once, this very day; before she speaks to any one about this will; and before she has published you to all the world as a scoundrel. She could n't marry you after that. It ain't a courtship; it's a bargain; although neither of you says so. She takes you to save her money; you take her to get it without a law-suit. Both of you understand it, although mum's the word between you. That's it! that's it!' And Mr. Higgs in the excess of his joy, gave vent to a loud shout, and actually danced a gentle hornpipe around the office.

'By G — d! I'll try it!' exclaimed Bolton.'

'To be sure you will!' said Higgs; 'of course you will! Be about it at once. It's 'most dark; that's better than day-light if you should happen to change color. If you agree on the spot it'll settle the question of by-blow with the other. Be oily with her. Women like a greasy tongue; but go it strong and marry her at once — to-night if you can. It's astonishing how a marriage will hush up various awkward little matters. Where does she live?'

Bolton mentioned the place.

'I'll be there to hear your luck,' said Higgs, taking his hat. 'Good bye!'

'Stop!' said the Attorney, who was not so sanguine as his companion; 'where's Wilkins? I have n't seen him since we last met here.'

'I met him once. He's a queer one. He looked as if he would eat me when I spoke of his wife, and walked off without even answering me.'

'Bring him along. I expect to fail; and we might as well be prepared for what's to be done next.'

Higgs assented; and having already bade him good-bye, walked off without repeating the ceremony.

EPIGRAM.

' 'Hermocrates' nose' say not, for you err;
The greater to the less, when you refer:
But if correctly you would speak, why please
Always to say, 'Nose's Hermocrates!'   M.

MY GRANDFATHER'S PORT-FOLIO.

NUMBER ONE.

I HAVE an indistinct recollection of having taken a journey of some fifty miles with my father, when I was about four years old, to visit my grandfather, who had been for nearly half a century the minister of a large parish in the goodly town of P——.   He was a tall and vener-able-looking old man ; with a mild but brilliant eye, and a voice so sweet that it won my confidence at once, and drew me to his buckled knee — to which, patting it with his hand, he beckoned me — as if it were a familiar seat.   There must have been something peculiarly bland and attractive in his address, or the awe which his enormous wig inspired would not so easily have been subdued.

With the exception of these peculiarities of his person, together with his golden-headed cane, which during the week we spent under his roof often served me for a horse, and his large library of books and manuscripts, ornamenting three sides of the low but spacious apart-ment that served him for both study and eating-room, all the circum-stances of that early visit have so far faded from my memory that the attempt to recall them is fruitless.   Along with the good and the bad of his ever-memorable generation my grandfather has long ago gone to his account ; so long indeed, that when lately I made a pious pilgrim-age to his grave, I found the tall stone by which the affectionate care of his Parishioners had designated it already well-nigh covered with moss.

His manuscripts however are his monument to me.   In them his nobler part survives ; and I recur to them with reverence, as if the spirit were still acting in the impressions which it has left of its charac-ter and its processes upon their pages.   Among these there is a large bundle of miscellaneous papers, written evidently for his own eye only, in which are recorded the impressions made by passing events, by the books which he read or studied, and the characters of the persons about him ; moreover, some of the most important trains of thought which passed through his mind, and his reflections upon such subjects as chiefly interested him.   It has often occurred to me that some of these papers might without injustice to his intentions and perhaps in some degree to the benefit and amusement of such persons as may be induced to read them, be brought into the light in this day of general illumination.   If therefore, Mr. EDITOR, you are not overburdened with articles for your Magazine — now, when every third man is an Elihu, ' full of matter ' and forced to speak that he may ' refresh *him-self*,' whatever may be the effect of his utterances upon all the rest of the world — you are at liberty to make use of such of the contents of ' My Grandfather's Port-folio ' as may to your discretion seem worthy.

The old gentleman appears to have been peculiarly fond of studying and analyzing the characters of those whom it was his province to oversee and influence. He has left some thirty or forty descriptions of prominent individuals in his parish; which, whatever other merit they may possess, are evidently so true to the life, that they appear like a gallery of moral portraits, in which one can easily see the distinct images of the originals, as if they were alive before him, and not persons of a buried generation; subject to his inspection and not merely pictured to his imagination. Will you give to your readers the following specimens? The date of the manuscript, it may be well to state for the sake of the curious, is 1771.

THE THREE DEACONS.

DEACON D.

My right hand man. He was in office at my settlement; and even then I thought him old, so grave was he, so staid, so measured his words and his steps. He had kept the church records from the date of my predecessor's death; with a pastor's watchfulness had looked after the flock when without a Shepherd, and had been to the parish meanwhile what both weight and pendulum are to the clock. I am sure that I could never have kept matters in trim without him. He is the axis of the church — the immovable centre of parish affairs. Let things go as they will, Deacon D. remains ever the same. In excited times he is imperturbable. When all the reeds among us — of which there are many — quiver violently, and even the old stems shake, his trunk of oak never vibrates. In times of lukewarmness and spiritual drought, the even measure of his zeal knows no diminution. Let the weather be what it may, the tenant of our pulpit can always look down upon one attentive and constant listener, and the eyes of the congregation see before them a model of gravity and veneration. There is not a youth in the town who does not stand in awe of him; nor a sinner of them all whose heart does not quail as he approaches. I am not myself always at ease in his presence; for if there be any flaw in my dutifulness, Conscience always paints it in the Deacon's eye.

That he attaches the highest importance to his office, and is determined to 'purchase to himself a good degree' by using it well, is a matter concerning which no one who sees him for half an hour can entertain a doubt. He is every where and every inch a Deacon. He dresses like a deacon, walks as a deacon, talks like a deacon, smiles like a deacon, (for he never laughs,) eats like a deacon; and all these and every other function of life he discharges like nothing else under the sun. Strange that he is never off his guard — never forgets himself! But so it is. The people say that he was *a Deacon born;* that even from his cradle there has been an air about him that clearly marked him for his future office; that when he was a boy, his playfellows prophetically nicknamed him, while he accepted the *soubriquet* with something more than Mosaic meekness; that from his first appearance in the Church, it has been noticed that the direction of his glances fell a little beneath the pulpit, to the level of his venerable predecessor's head, to which the palsy had given in the eyes of the children a very ominous shake; that never did one of those indispensables of the Church pass him in the streets, without receiving his profoundest salute, being scanned from head to foot, and leaving him still looking after his 'retiring glory'* in a fit of deep musing, as if he were studying into all the arcana of the profession, and settling deeply in his mind the stern proprieties of deaconhood; and that as soon as a vacancy occurred in the office, the eyes, not of the church only, but of every member of the parish, turned simultaneously toward him.

These rumors account so well for the phenomenon of his rare consistency, that I have never thought it worth my while to investigate their authority.

In short, he is a very Saint. In him is our spiritual continuance; and so long as his soul is held in life, the Church of P—— is safe. I dare not look beyond the day when he shall go to stand in his celestial lot. So strongly do I rely upon him, that I would not undertake to answer for what we should be without him. May the Good Lord spare him to the Church and to me! Amen.

DEACON Q.

CAN a plump, round, ruddy man ever be noted for gravity? He who *must* eat and drink bountifully, and open his mouth wide, and display therein two even rows of brilliant teeth, that make one's eyes glisten good humoredly only to look at them; whose portly sides hang loose, awaiting to be shaken, and needing the exercise of laughter that it would be cruel to deny them; whose pulses must play strong and quick to circulate the life-blood through such an expanse and conglomeration of flesh; whose voice must come out loud and clear; whose capacious chest heaves lustily and gaily with every breath he draws; whose foot treads firmly and quickly, as if motion were a delight; whose whole animal functions are carried on with a zest; to whom mere existence is a rich enjoyment; upon whose brain no black vapors settle; who looks through two clear twinkling eyes upon a world that has never treated him otherwise than well? I think not. I am sure that I never could find it in my heart to wish he could — even though a man so constituted were my own Deacon. And such he is.

Deacon Q. is certainly the most charming specimen that the annals of New-England's churches can afford, of the perfect blending of piety with good nature, of reverence with hilarity, of conscientiousness with comfort. Religion in him is grafted upon the healthy stock of a perfectly sane and happy nature, and the fruit of the union is beyond measure beautiful and rich. A large and sound heart, overflowing with generous impulses and benevolent sympathies, sanctified, harmonized and elevated, but not in the least degree checked nor stunted by

---

* THUS my worthy theological professor early taught me to render the sublime and significant Hebrew phrase which is somewhat unhandsomely translated in Exodus xxxiii., 23.

Christian principle, cannot but be an object of admiration in the sight of every man who is not either a bigot or a misanthrope. Such men ought to be now and then, to show us how good is God, and to cast gleams of sunshine upon a gloomy and repining world. His face is a Thanksgiving Sermon every day in the year. And I verily believe that where Deacon D. by his gravity has brought one sinner to think on his ways, and turn with contrition to the Lord, Deacon Q. by his genial smile and his perpetual cheerfulness has won the feet of a score toward the altar of God — his exceeding joy. It is a comfort to see him on a communion-day carry along the aisle the consecrated emblems of love and peace : distributing them on the one side and the other, with the sweet countenance of an Angel, and an expression which seems to say, ' The blessing of Him I love be with you ! ' And then when he puts them to his own lips, to observe the tears of gratitude and affection fall upon them, ' an offering worthy Heaven,' and which my own eye has often moistened to see.

I look for his coming on a Sunday night to my fireside as the choicest refreshment after the day's fatigue ; and as for my wife and children, they are sure to mope and nod and become positively stupid if he does not appear. There is not a child in the parish that he does not know, or with whom he has not had some mirthful encounter ; nor an old lady or a young that cannot tell you what ' excellent company ' he is.

He is invariably my attendant at Councils and Ordinations, and on every occasion when the presence of our Church is asked ; and not a rood of the road for miles around has not echoed to his ringing laugh as we have journeyed along in his broad old chaise. He knows all my habits and my heart ; for all that official dignity which I find it usually so convenient to wear falls off of itself the instant we are alone with each other.

If there is difficulty in the parish, he comes in like the morning light upon my despondency. If there is any pleasant news to tell, he is ever the bearer of the tidings. If there is a breach to be healed, he is the peace-maker. If there is poverty to be relieved, he is the almoner. If there is death in a house, he is the best comforter. If there is a wedding, he must be in attendance to give his blessing. If there is an extra religious service, he must come and sing. If there is a meeting of friends, his presence makes the circle and the joy complete.

In one word I love him, and we all love him. God bless the good soul !

DEACON T.

THE last man that I became acquainted with in our parish ; and even now I am by no means sure that I can say I know him. Not that he is in the least degree hypocritical, but so quiet, taciturn, and reserved. Tall even to deformity, homely to a proverb, spare as the leanest of Adam's descendants, graver even than Deacon D., though of a gravity far less forward and impressive, he seems to vanish as you approach, like a spectral shadow, and the nearer you draw to him the more intangible and elusive does he become. He may be seen day after day treading in the same paths, from his house to his counting-room and from his store to his house, with strides of the same longitude — with which no living man could keep in step, even if he felt, as no one does, desirous of being long in his company — looking neither to the right hand nor to the left, but with his eyelids straight before him, exchanging 'good-morrow' with but few, never looking at a child, never in haste, never struck by a sudden thought, dreading nothing so much as to be noticed, and expending no more breath in words than is absolutely necessary for the commonest purposes of life.

His visits to the parsonage are periodical, and not more frequent than the season's changes; and when he pays them, its inmates as well as himself breathe always more freely when they are over. For he sits upright and stiff, as far from the true line of our little circle as he can get; never hazards a remark of his own; escapes with a monosyllabic answer when a still more simple sign of attention will not suffice; and seems waiting only for the old family clock to give him a hint that the hour of his release has come.

Of course, he is far from being a favorite in the town. Yet he is a meek and blameless man. I have heard it whispered, indeed, that as a creditor he is somewhat too hard; as a man of business, as sharp as (on the right side of dishonesty) a conscientious man can be; and saving, to a limit too closely bordering upon Mammon-worship for a virtuous mind. But this I believe to be scandal. He is prudent, laborious, frugal; and so was his father before him, and thus he has made himself at length the richest man in the town. But if any man among us is scrupulously honest, it is Deacon T.; though I *have* often wished and even prayed that his integrity might receive a larger infusion of benevolence, and his iron justice be softened by the glowing heat of Christian love. But for all this, I do not know that I have any thing to charge against him, or that at heart he may not be a charitable man. In word, certainly, I have never known him to offend against the golden rule. If we never hear from him the grateful tones of kindness, neither does he open his lips to accents of bitterness : and sometimes I am induced to think, that perhaps, down in the silence of his heart, sentiments of peace and good-will make music to the ear of Heaven, and merciful judgments upon all men are meted to them in liberal measure. Indeed I have heard of several timely and generous donations being conveyed very stealthily to the unfortunate and the poor, which I have made up my mind must be traced back to him : and once or twice, I remember, when he has heard me mention cases of extreme want, without appearing at the time to be moved, or joining in the general expression of sympathy, that, as I have met him soon after in private, his hand has fumbled in his pocket and awkwardly thrust into mine a truly generous sum; while he has merely whispered the name of the distressed individuals I had previously designated, and without a syllable added, walked away.

At the judgment of the Great Day I expect there will be revelations of his character which will strike his townsmen with surprise. Would to God that all those who are now enjoying the praise of men might meet that time of solemn scrutiny as creditably as he !

I HAVE spent many an hour in weighing these three characters one against another♦ That of Deacon T. in my balances is ever the lightest. But, between the other two, the scales to this day have not settled. Great are the virtues and the uses of both. Great are the good influences which both have exerted upon myself. Deacon D. is the rock on which I stand. Deacon Q. the bosom upon which I lean. From the former comes the strength and discipline of virtue. From the latter the inspiration of love and hope.

But, I know not how it is, as I grow older, and reflect more upon life and its Author, the character of the latter preponderates more and more. Love and Joy! Love and Joy! These are the most precious fruits of the Spirit; the offering of sweetest savour to the Giver of every perfect gift. And these are the rarest found. As for my own faith and love, I feel that they dwell too much with sadness. The example of Deacon Q. ever, like a fresh burst of sunbeams from the Light that is full of Glory, makes every better sentiment of my nature glow, and my piety become more *filial*, as if I had 'seen the Father.' He speaks to me as in the words of the Shepherd to the Ancient Saint of visionary memory — which words, in my first manhood, when the perhaps needful shadows of despondency came over my spirit, (then first learning to doubt and think,) to temper its excessive gayety and chasten its wild enthusiasm, like a blessed revelation direct from Heaven; and from that day have been ever fresh in my memory. 'Remove from thyself *sadness*, nor give pain to the Holy Spirit, which dwelleth within thee. For the Spirit of the Lord which is given thee cannot endure to be tormented by its possessor. Wherefore clothe thyself with cheerfulness, which has *always* favor with the Lord. For every cheerful man does well, and has a true and keen relish of those things which are good. But the gloomy does always wickedly. First, because he grieveth the Holy Spirit, which dwelleth in a happy nature. And again, because he maketh not acknowledgment unto the Lord for former mercies. Moreover, the prayer of a sad man has no elasticity to rise up to the altar of God. And, I said unto my Shepherd, 'Sir, why has not the prayer of a sad man virtue to come up to God?' 'Because,' said he, 'that sadness weigheth down his affections. For as wine when it is mingled with vinegar keeps not its delicious flavor, so sadness being mixed with the Holy Spirit takes the living sweetness from his prayers. Wherefore cleanse thyself from sadness which is evil, and the Holy Spirit shall dwell within thy heart. And all others, as many as shall lay aside despondency and put on cheerfulness, shall live unto God.' *

.   .   .   .   .

Upon the whole, sure never a minister was blessed with three better deacons than mine. But they are growing gray — they are growing gray! Ah me! and so am I. The goal is near. May we all finish our course with joy, and be found at last with the Lord, to behold and to share his glory!

---

* Shepherd of Hormas.

LITERARY NOTICES.

RESEARCHES AND CONJECTURES RESPECTING THE LOVE, MADNESS, AND IMPRISONMENT OF TORQUATO TASSO. By RICHARD HENRY WILDE In two vols. 12mo. New-York: A. V. BLAKE.

It will not require our humble aid to assist in securing for these volumes a wide and general perusal. Attention has already been called in these pages, and by far abler pens than our own, to many of the interesting themes which abound in the work before us, for the early sheets of which we should not omit to state we are indebted to the publishers. The last number of the 'New-York Review' has also especially awakened a fresh interest in these 'Researches' by a succinct account of the great Italian poet's birth and parentage; the contradictory stories of his loves; an account of his various wanderings, and of the Alberti Manuscripts, and their first perusal, as originally described in the KNICKERBOCKER, in a letter written from Florence at the time. Before proceeding to quote a few passages of interest from a chapter of the 'Researches' touching the causes of Tasso's real or pretended madness and the true reasons of his imprisonment, we shall avail ourselves of the labors of our quarterly contemporary, in presenting a brief synopsis of the previous history of the poet.

'TORQUATO TASSO, whose epic all christendom, except Great Britain, ranks next to Virgil's, was born in Sorrento, a village on the Bay of Naples, on the eleventh of March, 1544. His father Bernardo, himself a poet of no small merit, descended from a long line of illustrious ancestors in Bergamo. His mother, Portia Rossi, was a noble Neapolitan lady, whose beauty, virtues and misfortunes, have been celebrated by her husband and her son, in language so full of truth and tenderness that it is impossible to read it unmoved. Tasso's father was confidential secretary to the Prince of Salerno, chief of the Neapolitan aristocracy, who were at enmity with the Spanish viceroy, Toledo. The political intrigues in which this nobleman became involved, drew down upon himself and his followers a sentence of attainder. Bernardo Tasso, like the rest, was banished, and his property confiscated. His young and lovely wife, prevented by the interference of her relations from sharing the exile of her husband, shut herself up in a convent, where she died prematurely of grief, and her brothers possessed themselves of her property, which they withheld from her children. Torquato in his boyhood was thus deprived of home and fortune. His earliest instruction he received under the paternal roof; afterward in the school of the Jesuits at Naples, and two years before his mother's death his father sent for him to Rome, and thence transferred him to Pesara, where he became the companion of Francesco Maria della Rovere, afterward Duke of Urbino. From Pesara he was removed to Padua, his education being continued under able masters, by whose lessons he profited so well as to be soon remarkable for his proficiency not only in the learning, but in the exercises and accomplishments of the time. In obedience to the wishes of his father he began the study of the civil and canon law, but his heart and his leisure were given to the muses, and the fame won by his

Rinaldo, composed at seventeen, induced Bernardo to abandon all thoughts of opposing his son's inclinations.

'Love increased young Tasso's devotion to poetry, and Laura Seperara, as we learn from Rosini, received the homage of his verse. Cardinal Louis of Este, brother of Duke Alphonso Second, became his patron, under whose protection Torquato came to Ferrara in 1565. His reception was flattering. The court of Alphonso was a splendid one, of which the princesses, his sisters, a few years older than Tasso, were the most distinguished ornaments. Lucretia and Leonora both favored the young poet, and between the latter and himself there sprung up, it is alleged, a romantic affection, whose mysteries, not yet thoroughly penetrated, literary curiosity is still eagerly investigating. On the one hand, it is contended that this passion was serious, mutual, and the source of all Tasso's persecutions and misfortunes. On the other, it is utterly denied, or held to be merely poetical and Platonic, and his imprisonment is attempted to be otherwise accounted for. Whether the poet subsequently lost his senses, or only affected madness, is another open question of great interest : and if the perusal of some of his own letters leaves us with a strong impression that he labored under strange illusions, our curiosity to ascertain the true character of a malady consistent with such extraordinary powers of composition as he exhibited, is rather increased than diminished ; ' and that curiosity, let us add, will in a good measure be satisfied, by the facts and conclusions of our author, to which we shall now invite the attention of the reader. After a rapid but perspicuous sketch of the different opinions of Tasso's biographers touching his loves, madness, and imprisonment, and a glimpse into the chaos of ' doubt, obscurity, and despair' which Mr. Wilde was compelled to explore, he proceeds :

"It were inexcusable to be of no opinion, where there is such an endless variety of choice. That of the author, if not already guessed, w ll most probably be no secret before the end of his pages. He is far more anxious, however, not to mislead his readers, than to impress upon them any fixed belief." . . . "The question whether Tasso was really insane or not, is that which lies at the bottom of all the rest. If he was mad, his treatment requires no other explanation, though, considered in a medical or moral point of view, it may have been neither judicious nor humane. If his reason was unimpaired, some other sufficient cause for his long and rigorous imprisonment must be found. The two subjects are so closely interwoven in the proofs to be submitted, that it is impossible to separate them ; but the reader, bearing in mind the alternatives, will have gained one vantage-ground of truth, as soon as he shall be able to determine whether the poet was shut up in the hospital of the poor and the insane, for cure or from vengeance. According to the former supposition there is no longer any mystery ; according to the latter, one obstacle to its elucidation is removed.

"There are some points on which all Tasso's biographers are agreed, a concurrence that could not well be avoided, since it is founded on the authority of his own letters. Among these are, the difficulties he encountered in the publication of his Jerusalem ; his vexation at the objections to it ; his trouble of mind from religious doubts ; the interception of his correspondence ; his desire to leave the Duke's service ; his vacillation about accepting or refusing the place of historiographer ; the opening of his apartments by false keys, and the examination of his papers ; the treachery of Madalò ; the combat ; his enemy's flight ; his own melancholy ; his fear of being poisoned, and suspicions of every one.

"It is evident enough, that love, envy, jealousy, and superstition, conspired to torment him, and these are surely sufficient evils. Yet what ground have we for excluding the statement of Manso, who tells us, in addition, that ' a friend with whom he had every thing in common, even to his very thoughts, and from whom he had not altogether concealed the secret of his loves · · · whatever may have been the cause, revealed some of the mysteries of his passion.' There was no such passion, and, consequently, no such confidante, say Black and Serassi. In the first they are clearly wrong by the poet's own showing ; and upon the same authority it may be affirmed, that, beside the Countess Livia D'Arco, there was a confidante.

"This is the beginning of one of his sonnets :

"Since he, our once true messenger, no more,
Our mutual sighs and our affections dear,
Will bear — or our sweet strifes and quarrels hear,
And subtly judge — as once he heard and bore —
Rebel to love — cruel to us — from fear —
Lost by the winds on air, I must deplore
My tender words, and deep in my heart's core
Its lofty secrets shut from mortal ear ! ''

"That Tasso was surrounded by treachery of every kind is undeniable ; and the hardship of his position was increased by the impossibility of retiring from, or maintaining it. Its dangers and vexations, and the little reward that attended his labors, made him desirous of exchanging servitude at Ferrara for liberty in Rome, and his friend Scipio Gonzaga sought to draw him into the service of the Medici. The bitter hatred and jealousy existing between the courts of Florence and Ferrara, would, of course, render such a step on Tasso's part exceedingly offensive to Alphonso. In those days, a change of masters was a kind of treason, and in corresponding with Gonzaga, in March, 1575, from Padua, he begs him not to mention it in his letters to Ferrara, as their falling into other hands might be of evil consequence. As early as May, 1575, he apprehended that his correspondence was intercepted. In June of the same year he went to Bologna, either to subject his Jerusalem to the censure of an inquisitor, or to consult him on some religious doubts, which he had incautiously let drop in the carelessness of friendly intercourse, and which he feared had been denounced to the holy office. He had been warned by the Duchess of Urbino that he was watched, and she cautioned him against his projected journey to Rome. 'The Duke,' says he, in one of his letters, 'has gone to the country, and left me here, *invitus invitam*, at the request of the Duchess of Urbino, who is taking the waters, and requires amusement. I read my book to her, and we are many hours a day entirely alone. I told her of my intention to go to Rome in October, which she disapproves. She thinks I ought not to leave Ferrara before my work is published, unless to go with her to Pesaro, because every other journey will be suspicious and odious. She mentioned a circumstance to me which shows that I am very closely watched, so let Scalabrino cease to confide in his opinions,' etc.

"We have seen that copies of his sonnet to the Countess of Scandia got out, he knew not how, unless by magic. It appears that he doubted the fidelity of his servants, by whom he feared his private papers were stolen, and sought to procure a faithful domestic from Urbino, or the neighboring mountains. The earnestness with which this request was urged, in two letters to the Marquis del Monte, and the minute directions given, show the importance he attached to it.

"Serassi distinctly admits the existence of a conspiracy to ruin Tasso's literary reputation, of which Montecatino, Giraldini, and others, were the heads, and Madalò an instrument.

"The quarrel of Tasso with the latter, is related both by Manso and Serassi, but with some difference of circumstances. The latter says nothing about love secrets, and represents the blow to have been given in the court, not the hall of the ducal palace, and to have been succeeded by a casual rencontre in the public square, not a regular duel.

"Tasso had solicited the place of historiographer, made vacant by the death of Pigna. He anticipated a refusal, but it was given to him. Regretting his acceptance, and becoming aware that in writing of the times of Leo and of Clement, he must offend either the Duke of Ferrara or the Medici, to whom he thought himself obliged, he wished to resign, yet repented of his resolution shortly after it was taken.

"He had subjected his Jerusalem to the revision of several friends, who wearied him with doubts and objections, and to comply, as far as he could, with their opinions, and give as little room as possible for the interference of the inquisition, he had resolved, at one time, to cancel some of the most beautiful parts of his poem, and among them the episode of Olindo and Sofronia. There was too much love in it, said some of his censors, and one of the fathers of the holy office desired it should be fitted for the lecture of monks and nuns, rather than ladies and cavaliers.

"He himself confesses having entertained serious doubts, not merely of the truth of many dogmas of the catholic church, but of some of the leading doctrines of Christianity. To these circumstances, excluding all belief in his love for Leonora, Black attributes the madness of Tasso and Serassi his melancholy.

"Yet the objections to his Jerusalem, greatly insisted on by both, though he frequently complains of their absurdity, and the trouble they gave him, do not seem to have seriously affected his spirits, at least before the middle of the year 1576; and the grave and temperate tone of his reply to the Crusca, in 1585, has nothing of the character of a poet stung to frenzy by his critics. At the time of his departure for Modena, he jokes with *Scalabrino*, crying 'plague on the pedants!' and relying confidently on the predictions of an astrologer who had cast his nativity without knowing him, expects honors, and fortune, and long life. He recounts with complacency the distinction he enjoys, the court paid to him, and from the indications of the stars, anticipates great benefits from ladies. The fulfilment of these omens seemed indeed to have commenced. 'I had yesterday,' he continues, 'a long letter from the Duchess of Urbino, in which she offers to employ in my behalf whatever influence she has with her brother, although I had not requested it. Madam Leonora told me to-day, without the least occasion, that heretofore her means were limited, but now being more at ease, by reason of her mother's fortune, she would assist me. I have not asked, nor will ask, nor remind, either them or the Duke. But I shall be pleased with any marks of their favor, and accept them willingly.' This whole letter is full of hope, and mirth, and confidence, so short is the space of time which divides the summit of fortune from the depths of misery.

"Even after his return from Modena, and the discovery that a packet coming to him from Scalabrino had been confided to a faithless messenger, he mixes some drollery with his anger. 'My laughter does not reach beyond the throat, and if the Duke had not given me a cask of excellent wine, I would spit gall and aloes.'

"It is still more remarkable, that the first mention of Madalò's treachery, which occurs in a letter dated a few days afterward, is made without passion : 'The accomplice of the treason is Madalò, and to render good for evil, I shall procure him letters of favor from some princes.'

"When the circumstance is again mentioned, in the letter already quoted, respecting his canzone :

"'O chosen with the graces and the loves,'"

it is still without any violent indignation : 'I have discovered,' he merely says, 'a hundred treasons of Brunello.' The identity of Madalò and Brunello will appear hereafter.

"Tasso's own account of his quarrel with the former is found in his letter to Orazio Caproni, dated the tenth of October, 1576 :

"'My absence from Ferrara, and my troubles, have prevented me from examining three of your letters, one of some pages, inviting me to a long discussion. To reply, beginning with the last, the subject of which is most important to me, I assure you that I entered into this quarrel involuntarily, not from anger or impetuosity, but forced by my honor, and provoked by the lie most insolently and impertinently given to me, and repeated. And as I engaged in it against my will, I will endeavor to get out of it as soon as possible, but to extricate myself with all honor and satisfaction. Being thus far superior to my adversary, not only in the justice of my cause, but in what has passed between us, I having struck him, as an honorable man, and he me, as a traitor, who added to his treason the baseness of a sudden flight, I might, after making known the circumstances, agree to an accommodation, were he my equal. But as there is between us much difference of blood, and, I will add, of every other quality, if it ever comes to that, I will show to the world how much he is my inferior there also. And if other considerations than such as concerned him or his brothers, had not restrained me, he should have been taught it, instead of going about boasting that he had - - - etc. - - - - * But as this quarrel of mine is complicated with a thousand other intrigues, I must act coolly. I do not wonder that he dares to show a written statement, for what may not be expected from such a wretch, but I should wonder if he were not what he is. Both the blow I gave him, and his base attempt to assassinate me, took place, not by night, nor in a desert, but in open day, in the court, and in the public square, and all Ferrara knows, that when I struck him I was alone, and unarmed, and he did nothing to resent it. Afterward, however, he came, accompanied by many, and set upon me behind my back, but fled almost before he touched me. All this is known here, and will soon, I trust, be known to all Italy, since he will be proceeded against as he deserves. He told you no lie, Sir, when he said he had seen a great number of your letters; for, beside those I showed him, he contrived, by his own industry, to see others, having caused a false key to be made for the box where I keep my papers. But enough of this infamous wretch, to whom the shelter afforded by Signore Cortile will not, I am persuaded, be very agreeable to the Duke.'

"Some farther circumstances concerning this quarrel, are mentioned in a letter written about the same period to SCIPIO GONZAGA:

"'For some days past I have not left my room, except once to visit the DUCHESS and once Madam LEONORA. Nothing more being said about my affair, I began to think it had blown over, but yesterday evening I was invited in the name of his highness to accompany him to LOPARE, where he goes to-day with very few attendants. This morning, also, CRISPO, privy counsellor of his highness and chief minister of justice, summoned me, and repeated some kind and honorable expression of my Lord Duke, publicly made to show his affection and esteem for me, which have been confirmed to me by many others. He then added, that I must not wonder if the case had gone on slowly, for that was done purposely, with the hope of laying hands on the culprits; but now that he knew they were out of the state, he was commissioned by the Duke to proceed with extraordinary rigor. Of his highness's commission, I am certain: the rest I believe. I have written thus in detail that you may see my affair is in good train. I will hereafter inform you of what passes between the Duke and myself. . . . Tell Signore Luca that the doctor, his neighbor, is as great a knave as fool; he wishes to become the successor of Madalò, but I shall make short work with him. The friend, of old suspected, whose letter I sent you some months since, is without doubt false, and I have ascertained it most clearly, by a subtle device. Now let Signore Luca say I am too suspicious. I must tell you one of the feats of BRUNELLO. When I went from home, he used to ask me for the key of my rooms, pretending to want them in some of his love affairs, and I lent it to him, locking up, however, the chamber containing my books and papers, in which there was a box where, beside my own compositions, I kept most of your letters and Signor Luca's, especially those touching our political discussions. Conversing afterward with him and with others about my poem, which they had never seen, I heard them make some of the same objections urged by Signor Barga, and this made me suspicious, particularly as I knew them to be men not apt to hit upon such things of themselves. Sounding about to clear up this suspicion, I heard at last, from a servant of Count LOUIS MONTECUCCOLI, my neighbor, that when I was in MODENA this Lent, he saw BRUNELLO enter my rooms by night with a lock-smith. I took so much pains that I found the smith, who confessed to me he had been to court to open a chamber, the key of which the owner had lost. You can infer the rest. This is one of his frauds, and there are others as petty, but some, I think, of more importance, though I cannot be certain. I am glad that I destroyed all your letters and those of M. Luca, in which there was any thing too freely said about those particulars of Sperone. Nothing farther occurs to me, but that, with all affection, I kiss your hands.'

"SERASSI says, his utmost diligence did not enable him to find out who this *Brunello* was; and BLACK, if he pursued the like search, met with the like fortune. It is plain, however, that he and MADALÒ are the same person. The same acts are imputed to each, and, unless we suppose TASSO's rooms to have been twice opened with false keys, by different individuals, a supposition manifestly irrational, the identity of *Madalò* and *Brunello* is made manifest by contrasting the two letters. By this, one step at least is gained, for MADALÒ, unquestionably, was no imaginary personage. All agree in admitting his reality, and yet to this moment it is not very certain who he was.

"MANSO's manner of relating the foregoing circumstances is as follows:

"'TASSO, while residing at the court of ALPHONSO, had contracted a strict friendship with a gentleman of Ferrara who frequented the Ducal palace, distinguished, as he thought, above all others for purity of blood and nobility of manners, with whom he had every thing in common; even to his very thoughts, and from whom he had not entirely concealed the secret of his loves. This friend, whatever may have been the cause, whether malevolence of disposition or incontinence of tongue, repeated some of the particulars, and, being taxed by Torquato, neither gave any reasonable excuse, exhibited any penitence, nor offered to repair his fault, so that TASSO, greatly and justly incensed, struck him in the face, in the very hall of the ducal palace. The latter, not daring to draw arms in such a place, quietly departed, but immediately sent Torquato a defiance to meet him outside the gate of *San Lionardo*. The challenge being accepted, they began a fierce encounter, when three brothers of the traitor

---

* Thus published by SERASSI. The original, formerly in the Albano library, disappeared during the invasion of the French. It has since been found, like other plunder of Italy, in a library at Montpellier. But in it also the mysterious black is found. Probably it is not the very letter sent to Capponi, but a copy kept by Tasso, written in his own hand.

joined him, against all whom TASSO gallantly defended himself until the noise attracted persons to the spot, and the assailants fled.'

" SERASSI well remarks on the improbability that TASSO would have been favored by the Duke, after this quarrel, if it had originated from the revelation of the poet's passion for his sister. It is by no means clear, however, that the whole truth reached the Duke at once, if it ever reached him. MANSO does not say the secret of TASSO's love had been confided, but that it had not been altogether concealed ; and SERASSI would have more fully entitled himself to our confidence if he had not attempted to deny altogether the existence of this passion.

" The poet's melancholy, and fears, and flight, are attributed, by his noble friend and biographer, to the suspicion that his attachment had become known to ALPHONSO, and that the latter did not believe it to be altogether of the Platonic cast which the Marquis himself insists it was. MANSO adds, that the Duke ought not to have taken it in bad part ' on account of that ample and general license, conceded as a special privilege to men eminent for science, whose desires affect only the beauties of the soul as philosophers, and nourish themselves speculatively upon abstractions, whatever they may write as poets.' · · · 'Nevertheless, the secret having been revealed, and touching a person of the ducal family, it was natural enough for him to suspect that ALPHONSO, if he paid more attention to the malignant suggestions of his enemies than the innocence of his intentions, might be roused to great indignation, and perhaps inflict on him severe punishment. And, so firmly did this imagination fix itself in the mind of TASSO, already affected by the death of his father, the loss of his fortune, the objections to his poem, and his constitutional melancholy, that he could never divest himself of it, but for the rest of his life continued in perpetual fear and trouble, and from that cause did many of those things for which he was thought mad.'

" There is no room to doubt that the poet had suffered from some act of treachery which deeply and painfully preyed upon his spirits. He wrote two sonnets on this subject ; one of which deserves to be quoted, because it is too natural and pathetic to be a work of fancy :

" 'TO AN UNGRATEFUL FRIEND.

FORTUNE's worst shafts could ne'er have reached me more,
Nor ENVY's poisoned fangs. By both assailed.
In innocence of soul completely mailed,
I scorned the hate whose power to wound was o'er ;
When THOU — whom in my heart of hearts I wore,
And as my rock of refuge often sought —
Turned on myself the very arms I wrought,
And HEAVEN beheld — and suffered what I bore !
O ! holy FAITH ! O ! LOVE ! bow all thy laws
Are mocked and scorned — I throw my shield away,
Conquered by fraud. · · · Go ! seek thy fact's applause,
TRAITOR ! yet still half mourned — with fond delay · · ·
The hand, not blow, is of my tears the cause,
And more thy guilt than my own pain I weigh !' ''

" BLACK and SERASSI suppose the treason of MADALÒ referred solely to the poetical letters of TASSO and his friends, and attribute the impression it made on him to the aid thus given from his own papers to the detractors of his Jerusalem. The shaft that went to his heart was feathered from his own wing ; and this, considering the acute sensibility to criticism imputed to him, they deem quite sufficient to account for a melancholy which reached or passed the verge of madness.

" But TASSO himself says, that beside the letters of Gonzaga and Scalabrino, the box contained ' other compositions ;' and afterward mentions, that he thinks ' there were frauds of more importance, though he cannot be certain.'

" MANSO may be wrong, therefore, in attributing the quarrel exclusively to the revelation of some particulars of TASSO's love. Yet, as there was something which it deeply concerned him to conceal, there must have been, under such circumstances, an apprehension that it had been discovered. A visit of eleven days which he made about this period to LEONORA, at Consandoli, is attributed by SERASSI to the Princess's desire of diverting his melancholy. But if some of his productions, not destined to see the light, began to be circulated, the subject of their conferences must have had a deeper and more painful interest." .

These extracts, which, copious as they are, we could yet desire to extend, will afford the reader some idea of the faithful researches of our author. We should add, that his reference to authorities is minute and universal, and that his frequent felicitous translations from the Italian of his renowned subject are in all cases accompanied by their original. We hoped to have found room for some of the many touching supplications, memorials, and justificatory pieces, intended by TASSO to facilitate his release from imprisonment, and some account of the state of his mind in the latter years of his confinement, where he exhibits numerous and serious marks of veritable madness; but for these, and many matters of cognate interest, we must refer the reader to the ' Researches ' at large, which we again cordially commend to a wide public acceptance.

THE POEMS OF JOHN G. C. BRAINARD. A NEW AND AUTHENTIC COLLECTION, WITH AN ORIGINAL MEMOIR OF HIS LIFE. In one volume. pp. 191. Hartford, (Conn.): EDWARD HOPKINS.

THE cordial thanks of the public are due to the publisher of this beautiful volume. It has long been a desideratum in our literature, and we welcome it with heart-felt satisfaction, not less for the many admirable poems which it contains, and which have made the writer affectionately known to his countrymen, than for the excellent memoir of the bard, and the appreciating critique upon his writings, with which the volume opens. BRAINARD was a gentle-hearted, affectionate young man, of the most generous nature and the finest sensibility; greatly beloved by all who knew him, and eminently formed for society and the enjoyment of its innocent festivities and delights; notwithstanding the retiring modesty and the keen sensitiveness by which he was distinguished. And although subject to an occasional melancholy, that in his poems assumes a touching tenderness, there was yet a quiet sportiveness and humor about him, which arose often into wit of a keen and brilliant character, and which rendered him a highly agreeable companion. 'His poetry,' it is well observed by his biographer, 'is the expression of clear and quiet thought. The image is brought out with distinctness, and there is no effort to make it dazzling and impressive.' In simple pathos, in felicitous humor, and in variety and appropriateness of manner, BRAINARD is preëminent. He recommends himself also to his countrymen as a truly *American* poet. His topics, his imagery, his illustrations, are mostly of native growth. There is a raciness about them which bespeaks their indigenous originality. Moreover, his writings are free from all vicious or infidel taint. 'It is safe,' says his biographer, 'to the healthfulness, purity, and peace of the heart, to read his productions. A strain of humor, of merriment, may occasionally relax the muscles of the face; but no licentious or maddening thoughts are suggested by the pictures of his Muse. Generally a serious though correct view is taken of human life and its great interests, and the reader frequently encounters a sweet religious sentiment.' BRAINARD died young, of that *utterly incurable disease*, consumption; and in the triumphs of christian faith ascended to the GOD whom he loved, and the works of whose almighty hand he had so often and so fervently sung.

We commence our extracts with a passage or two from the poem on Connecticut River, parts of which will forcibly remind the reader of GOLDSMITH:

"THE young oak greets thee at the water's edge,
Wet by the wave, though anchored in the ledge.
'T is there the otter dives, the beaver feeds,
Where pensive oziers dip their willow weeds,
And there the wild-cat purrs amid her brood,
And trains them in the silvan solitude,
To watch the squirrel's leap, or mark the mink
Paddling the water by the quiet brink;
Or to out-gaze the gray owl in the dark,
Or hear the young fox practicing to bark.

"Thou didst not shake, thou didst not shrink when late
The mountain-top shut down its ponderous gate,
Tumbling its tree-grown ruins to thy side,
An avalanche of acres at a slide.
Nor dost thou stay, when winter's coldest breath
Howls through the woods and sweeps along the heath;
One mighty sigh relieves thy icy breast,
And wakes thee from the calmness of thy rest.

"Down sweeps the torrent ice; it may not stay
By rock or bridge, in narrow or in bay;
Swift, swifter to the heaving sea it goes,
And leaves thee dimpling in thy sweet repose.
Yet as the unharmed swallow skims his way,
And lightly drops his pinions in thy spray,
So the swift sail shall seek thy inland seas,
And swell and whiten in thy purer breeze,
New paddles dip thy waters, and strange oars
Feather thy waves and touch thy noble shores.

"Thy *noble* shores! where the tall steeple shines,
At mid-day, higher than thy mountain pines,
Where the white school-house with its daily drill
Of sun-burnt children, smiles upon the hill,
Where the neat village grows upon the eye
Decked forth in nature's sweet simplicity;
Where hard-won competence, the farmer's wealth,
Gains merit, honour, and gives labor health;
Where Goldsmith's self might send his exiled band
To find a new 'Sweet Auburn' in our land.

" What Art can execute, or Taste devise,
Decks thy fair course and gladdens in thine eyes ;
As broader sweep the bendings of thy stream,
To meet the southern sun's more constant beam.
Here cities rise, and sea-washed Commerce hails
Thy shores and winds with all her flapping sails,
From Tropic isles, or from the torrid main,
Where grows the grape, or sprouts the sugar-
    cane,
Or from the haunts where the striped haddock
    play,
By each cold northern bank and frozen bay.
Here safe returned from every stormy sea,
Waves the striped flag, the mantle of the free ;
That star-lit flag, by all the breezes curled
Of yon vast deep whose waters grasp the world !

" In what Arcadian, what Utopian ground
Are warmer hearts or manlier feelings found ;
More hospitable welcome, or more zeal
To make the curious 'tarrying' stranger feel
That, next to home, here best may he abide,
To rest and cheer him by the chimney-side ;

Drink the hale farmer's cider, as he hears
From the gray dame the tales of other years.
Cracking his shag-barks, as the aged crone
(Mixing the true and doubtful into one)
Tells how the Indian scalped the helpless child,
And bore its shrieking mother to the wild,
Butchered the father hastening to his home,
Seeking his cottage — finding but his tomb.
How drums, and flags, and troops were seen on
    high,
Wheeling and charging in the northern sky ;
And that she knew what these wild tokens meant,
When to the Old French War her husband went.
How, by the thunder-blasted tree, was hid
The golden spoils of far-famed Robert Kidd ;
And then the chubby grand-child wants to know
About the ghosts and witches long ago,
That haunted the old swamp.

                  " The clock strikes ten ;
The prayer is said, nor unforgotten then
The stranger in their gates. A decent rule
Of elders in thy puritanic school."

. We gave some months since 'The Captain' who ran his schooner afoul of a Methodist meeting-house in Long-Island Sound. The sly turn of the following is something akin to the dry humor of that admirable sketch :

THE ROBBER.

Two large bags containing newspapers were stolen from the boot behind a mail coach between New Brunswick and Bridge-
town. The straps securing the bags in the boot were cut, and nothing else injured or removed therefrom. The letter mails
are always carried in the front boot of the coach, under the driver's feet, and therefore cannot be so easily approached.

" The moon hangs lightly on yon western hill ;
And now it gives a parting look, like one
Who sadly leaves the guilty. You and I
Must watch, when all is dark, and steal along
By these lone trees, and wait for plunder. Hush !
I hear the coming of some luckless wheel,
Bearing we know not what ; perhaps the wealth
Torn from the needy, to be hoarded up
By those who only count it ; and perhaps
The spendthrift's losses, or the gambler's gains,
The thriving merchant's rich remittances,
Or the small trifle some poor serving girl
Sends to her poorer parents. But come on !
Be cautious. There — 't is done ; and now away,
With breath drawn in, and noiseless step, to seek
The darkness that befits so dark a deed.

Now strike your light. Ye powers that look
    upon us !

What have we here ? Whigs, Sentinels, Gazettes,
Heralds, and Posts, and Couriers ; Mercuries,
Recorders, Advertisers, and Intelligencers —
Advocates and Auroras ! There, what 's that !
That 's — a Price Current.

                  ' I do venerate
The man who rolls the smooth and silky sheet
Upon the well cut copper. I respect
The worthier names of those who sign bank bills ;
And, though no literary man, I love
To read their short and pithy sentences.
But I hate types, and printers — and the gang
Of editors and scribblers. Their remarks,
Essays, songs, paragraphs, and prophecies,
I utterly detest. And these, particularly,
Are just the meanest and most rascally
'Stale and unprofitable' publications
I ever read in my life ! "

Although there is not a great deal of *poetry* in the conclusion of the above, yet it illustrates a *truth* which will be less unwelcome to the reader than it was to the mail-robbers. The annexed lines 'To a young Friend learning to play the Flute' partake of the same playful spirit :

" There 's a wild harp, which unconfined by rule
Of science, varies with the varying air,
And sympathizes with the free-born wind ;
Swelling, when'er the tempest swells, or sad
When the soft western-breeze in moans goes down,
And sighs, and dies away. 'T is sweet to mark
Its tone, and listen in some musing mood
To its strange cadence. Be your music such,
And let it die at sundown, if you please."

We are reluctantly compelled to omit several passages which we had indicated to the printer ; and among them a long extract from ' An Occurrence on board a Brig,' a most forcible and pathetic picture ; contenting ourselves with a pleasant sketch of those of the gentler sex who (in contradistinction to the heartless votaries of fashion) ' love a rainy day : '

> " She loves a rainy day who sweeps the hearth,
> And threads the busy needle, or applies
> The scissors to the torn or threadbare sleeve ;
> Who blesses God that she has friends and home ;
> Who, in the pelting of the storm, will think
> Of some poor neighbor that she can befriend ;
> Who trims the lamp at night, and reads aloud
> To a young brother tales he loves to hear ;
> Or ventures cheerfully abroad, to watch
> The bedside of some sick and suffering friend,
> Administering that best of medicine,
> Kindness and tender care, and cheering hope ;
> Such are not sad, e'en on a rainy day."

An unfinished pencil-sketch of BRAINARD, by WENTWORTH, the only portrait ever taken of the poet, and a fac-simile of his hand-writing accompany the volume.

THE NEUTRAL FRENCH: OR THE EXILES OF NOVA SCOTIA. BY MRS. WILLIAMS, Author of ' Religion at Home,' ' Revolutionary Biography,' etc. Providence, R. I.: CRANSTON AND COMPANY.

WE have heretofore borne our tribute to the simple yet forcible style of Mrs. WILLIAMS' writings ; and are glad to find in the volume before us additional examples of this great literary merit. The traditionary tale to which the book is mainly devoted is told in the writer's best manner. As a story proper, it can scarcely fail to interest and instruct the reader ; and its *American* tendency, its fervent spirit of liberty, we are sure will find many warm admirers. Mrs. WILLIAMS has embodied the history of a people long since extinct as a nation, although found still in scattered fragments in parts of the British North-American provinces, in the ' disputed territory,' and sometimes incorporated with the Indian tribes — the Acadians, or Neutral French, who were expelled by the English from New Scotland, or Nova Scotia, in open violation of numerous protective treaties. We perceive the fruits of untiring industry on the part of our author, in the large amount of historical facts with which she has preceded, and which she intersperses throughout, her narrative ; and we ask, with confidence in the result of our recommendation, that the reader will seek out and peruse this melancholy story of the Neutral exiles. The following ' palpable hit ' from the introduction is worthy the attention of the cheap philanthropists from the other side of the water, who abuse us so lustily for an evil which their own country assisted to entail upon us. Mrs. WILLIAMS has been speaking of the Indians, and of their removal to the west by the American Government, where they are permitted to govern themselves in their respective tribes, but where all are yet protected by the Republic :

" And for all this, shall we be accused of barbarity ? And by those, too, who have driven an innocent, confiding, and unoffending people into banishment, stripped of their property without remuneration ; separated wantonly from each other, driven among a strange people, lighted from their native shores by the blaze of their own dwellings, and left unsuccored and unprovided for, either to perish with want or be relieved by the charities of strangers ? We think for one that the charge, though baseless in itself, would come better from some other quarter.

" ' But,' say my English readers, ' there are your slaves.' True, and who made them slaves in the first place ? Who entailed this curse upon our land, and taught us we could not do without it ? Who resisted the remonstrances of the people of Virginia, and other colonies, not to impose them upon the white population, and continue to inundate them by fresh importations, many, many years since ? "

EDITOR'S TABLE.

'ANOTHER YEAR!'— We thought to have sat down to an easy task, dear reader, in invoking for you the joyous associations of this festive season. But emotions which we would not intrude upon the happy, press heavily upon the heart; remembrances of that 'dark backward and abysm of time' in which have been swallowed up affections that can know no renewal on earth, and mutual ties that can never bind again:

> 'The burning thoughts of hours of old
> Run molten in sad Memory's mould;
> And will not cool
> Until the heart itself be cold
> In Lethe's pool.'

Let the words then of one whom we all loved, who has gone hence to be here no more, and with whom 'time is ended,' fall upon reflecting hearts; tempering the reckless enjoyments of the gay present with thoughts of a solemn future. 'We are standing (so he wrote) once more at that fairy vestibule which opens rich perchance with hope, and bright to expectation, upon another twelvemonth; a coming lapse of time, that like a swell of the ocean tossing with its fellows, heaves onward to the land of Death and silence. We gaze around for a moment from the point where we stand, and as the events of the past come thronging to our minds, the griefs or the raptures that have been commended to us in the annual span, as yet hardly closed, again move the soul and heart, to animate or subdue. From the transports that are gone, there rises, like a strangely-pleasant odor from autumnal fields, the antepast of coming enjoyment; while from the sorrows we have borne, there breathe the voices of Resignation, and the warnings of Experience. We bethink us of imaginings that time has dissolved, of visions unrealized; and as we gather contentment from surveying the mingled web that has been given us, we seem to ask but the power to bear, without undue depression or elateness, the lot that is to come. We desire not the eye of the seer, or the spell of the horoscope:

> 'We stand between the meeting years,
> The coming and the past,
> And question of the future year,
> Wilt thou be like the last?'

And if we look aright, we are not *over*-joyed at the jocund day which seems to sit in misty brightness upon the delectable scenes of that distance whose enchantments are born of remoteness, and only dazzle when afar. Comparing our years in the mass, we find them all wearing the same shade and garniture, save that as they increase they shorten: the tide of existence acquires additional momentum as it rolls; and the land-marks that we pass on the receding shores, admonish us, by the rapidity with which they disappear, that our days are few at the longest, and checkered at the best. Time himself teacheth a thousand homilies. His warning finger points to the lessons of other years. There is a voice and a tablet of morality in the rush of his pinions and the flashing of his sythe. Insatiate and mysterious husbandman of mortality, he fells the young and the beautiful, and lays them 'green in earth.' Hopes, joys, and aspirations are the bubbles dissolved by his breath, the play-things of his will. He goes onward, and Death, his gloomy pursuivant, strikes down host after host for his ever-yawning garner. The Past becomes one vast sepulchre, or rather one wide plain where the innumerable armies of the dead are encamped, in stations which centuries have made, waiting to rise at the voice of the Archangel and the trump of God.

'From the general havoc made by Time and Death through the world from year to year, it is natural to turn to the ravages which they create in our own social circles. Since the morning of the last, many a true heart has been smitten into silence, and placed in the dust; many a child, many a parent, has poured the sigh of regret; many a brother and sister been laid side by side; and the places that knew them will know them no more. There are vacant chairs around the saddened hearth, and added monuments in the cemetery. Fair faces and fond bosoms that have met before in annual festivals, around the evening blaze of home, are now faded and still. The knell has been sounded; the requiem sung.

'But let us not approach such a subject with darkened spirits, for it is one that has little gloom to the reflecting mind. In seeing many around us yield to the common lot, we grow familiar with the truth, that this is not our continual abiding city; that 'our days only become considerable, like petty sums, by minute accumulations, where numerous fractions make up but small round numbers; so that our years of a span long make but one little finger.' What good deed is not suggested by these considerations? What appeals do they not furnish, for the suppression of those wranglings and storms of ill-feeling, which disturb the fountains of life and cause them to flow with bitter waters? Seeing that we are all stewards of a day, and that none has immunity from death, is it not a duty to lay aside those baser passions which so easily beset the heart and sow our way with thorns? — to be just and generous, forgiving and kind? It is only to the selfish, that the prospect of Age is wearisome or Death unwelcome. Wrapt up in visions of their own advancement or pleasure, they approach that wide and mighty gate of Time which swings outward into Eternity; and as they mingle in the dense and countless throngs pressing thitherward, their wailings arise like funeral murmurs. *They have lived without doing good to their day and generation;* and so, having existed without kindness, they are lost without grief. · · · The sweet charities of life are many. They spring up like flowers in its walks at every turn. Open-hearted benevolence, the forgiveness of injuries, the crucifixion of ignoble desires, the amendment of errors, these should be the main objects of our lives, and the burden of our resolves at the dawn of the year. Then, though the sun of our decline should ' make but right declensions and set in winter arches,' yet we shall be calm in our souls, when we are bidden to lie down in the dust, and make our beds in ashes! Then, whether we are called in the morning or noon or the twilight of life, to repose in the grave, we are ready to rest. We can look back with tranquillity upon the works of our span, and with unshrinking vision gaze onward to that era when years shall be ended and Time no more!'

THE 'PRINCE DE JOINVILLE BALL' AT BOSTON. — We are indebted to a friend who flitted hence to the 'American Athens' on the occasion of the late Ball to the PRINCE DE JOINVILLE, for a brief yet graphic sketch of that memorable fête, which it is conceded, we believe, has never been surpassed, if it has been approached, on this continent. 'I was especially struck,' says our correspondent, 'with *one* thing; the ball was in all respects thoroughly *social*, and this constituted one of its most delightful features. There were no exclusive 'cliques' nor 'sets;' but the richest, the proudest, the most magnificently attired, were to be seen partaking the common enjoyment with the humble, the modest, and the plainly-dressed. As for the decorations of the Hall, it is not too much to say that they were what even a Frenchman might term '*grand*.' I doubt whether the 'Old Cradle' was ever before so be-wreathed, festooned, and canopied with the insignia of France intermingled and blended with our own glorious stars and stripes. For a time I assure you my imagination was quite bewildered with the multitude and variety of attractions, under the blaze of a thousand lights. Let me attempt to give you a little idea of the external scene. The names of the Royal Family of France, of our beloved WASHINGTON and LAFAYETTE, were panelled under the east gallery in bold, brilliant characters, and 'THE PRINCE DE JOINVILLE' filled the eye along the western wall. The front of the rostrum was decorated with the insignia of the Legion of Honor and the Arms of France, supported on each side by those of the United States and Massachusetts. Over these, at the head of the hall, was a beautiful miniature representation of the frigates La Belle Poule and La Cassard. The positions for the quadrilles and cotillons were defined by ornamental devices on the floor, which were executed with much taste. There was a flash of joy lighted up in the faces of the great assembly, especially of the fairer portion, when at about eight o'clock the bugle 'rang loud and clear,' to call up the first set of cotillons. These rapidly succeeded each other, until the arrival of the distinguished guest. It was near ten o'clock when he entered the hall, preceded by the Chief Marshal, Lieutenant-Colonel TRAIN and his Aids, accompanied by his suite, and JAMES READ, Esq., Chairman of the Committee of Arrangements. They were met by His Honor the Mayor, and escorted to the head of the hall, where upon the *dais* or raised platform the Prince was introduced to many eminent citizens of Boston; among them, the Hon. BENJAMIN RUSSELL, an old friend of LOUIS PHILLIPPE during his sojourn in this country many years since. The venerable old gentleman gave the Prince a hearty welcome, who seemed delighted with his conversation, and treated him, I was pleased to see, with marked attention. His Highness presently led out the lady of the Mayor in the dance. At about twelve o'clock, to the inspiring music of the 'Marseilles Hymn' — which echoed along the lofty ceiling of 'Old Faneuil' and filled the vast hall with a volume of eloquent sound, every tone of which did honor alike to the composer and to KENDALL's band — the Prince with the assemblage moved through the covered and decorated *tunnel* that connects Faneuil and Quincy Halls, to the Rotunda of the latter, where a sumptuous entertainment, embracing all that was rich and rare in potables and edibles, and in amplest abundance, was provided and admirably served. The Prince's position was directly opposite the entrance, where he could not fail to be 'the observed of all observers.' He is a tall, good-looking young man, with dark hair, moustaches, and whiskers. His complexion is olive, his face oval, and his eyes dark. On the whole, I thought him very prepossessing. He was certainly very affable to all who were near him at the table, and was sufficiently conversable with his three or four partners in the dance.

Indeed, he seemed fully to appreciate the distinguished attentions which he received. He was dressed in a plain naval-blue coat, close-buttoned to the chin, with blue pantaloons. He sported two epaulettes, wore the riband and star of the Legion of Honor, and carried an elegant sword in his hand.

'It may perhaps be invidious to particularize in such an assemblage of grace and beauty, but I cannot forbear. I had nearly lost my heart with Miss G——, a brilliant creature, in a white tunic not unlike Amy Robsart in the Waverly Picture Gallery; the superbly-dressed and very distinguished and accomplished Mrs. O——; with Miss S——, a young Scottish Venus; and Mrs. B——, in a charming bodice of crimson velvet; but I was presently *startled* by the Countess Vespucci, whose regal bearing and brilliant beauty won many 'a corner' in the bosoms of the bachelors present; not one of whom, had they been at that moment members of congress, but would have granted her 'a little corner of land' any where in the United States. She has the form and stature of a Diana. Her dress was a robe of dark crimson velvet, with close bodice; a beautiful Grecian cap, trimmed with gold-lace, upon her head, from which her long black hair, in two-braided folds, gracefully descended over her shoulders. I had scarcely filled my heart with *her* presence, when two lovely creatures, in light-blue muslin, over white satin, with a sylph in virgin white, glided gracefully by, and changed at once the whole current of my thoughts. And so it chanced with all susceptible beaux on that memorable night. The man who 'knew his own mind' for ten minutes at a time, was a fortunate wight.'

Thus far our correspondent. He must permit us to add our own impressions of the Prince, whom we have had the pleasure to encounter on one or two occasions, so that between our reports, the distant reader may draw his or her fancy-sketch. He appeared to us a pleasant but plain-featured man of about thirty; a little *courbé*; the forehead in no wise remarkable in height or developement; with a redundance of beard, moustaches, and whiskers; and his manner, so far from being easy or graceful, seemed to indicate a sort of person who would rather be on board his ship and at sea, than partaking the burdensome honors which have been poured upon him without stint, since his last arrival among us. All agree indeed in according to the Prince great simplicity of manner and of character. A friend has mentioned to us an anecdote touching upon this point, which we shall venture to cite here. During a former visit to this country, our distinguished stranger sojourned for a few days at Cincinnati, stopping with his limited *suite* at the inn of a Mr. C——, a plain-spoken, jolly Boniface, who cared little for rank or nobility, beyond the 'custom' they might bring him. The Prince was very fond of fowling; and his 'right-hand man' (young Las Cassas, if we remember rightly,) borrowed the landlord's rifle for his use. He met with such success with the weapon that he directed M. Las Cassas to purchase it at any price for his occasional use in his farther western travel. The morning the distinguished party were to leave, our Boniface encountered the Prince in the hall: 'Oh, look a-here!' said he; 'about that 'ere rifle. You may think may-be that I 've walked into you 'bout a feet in chargin' you seventy-five dollars for that we'pon; but t'ain't so. I was 'tached to it, for it never missed in *my* hands nor my son Tim's; and I tell you what 't is, Mr. Johnny-ville, if you do n't think, now, when you come along back this way, that that rifle 's really *wuth* seventy-five dollars, *I 'll take it off* your hands! Now that 's fair, I 'm sure!' The Prince was in high good humor with the incident; and has often reverted to it since, while the honest host is frequently heard to say: 'I *thought* he 'd keep her! There ain't such a rifle west o' the Alleganies!'

NAPOLEON AND WELLINGTON. — The reader's attention will be forcibly attracted to the article which opens the present number. The writer has discarded the *prestige* of a great name, and recorded his impressions of BONAPARTE in an evident spirit of candor and impartiality. Whatever diversity of opinion may exist as to the correctness of the conclusions at which he arrives, all will admit that he brings to his task a mind thoroughly conversant with his subject, and a christian love of peace, which cannot be too highly commended. He would say with the poet, and the friends of humanity every where will join in the aspiration :

> ' The cause of Truth and Human weal
>   Oh, God above !
>   Transfer it from the sword's appeal
>   To peace and love ! '

We are indebted for the following to the obliging friend who translated for our last issue the ' Story of the Chevalier de Beauvoir.' Such sketches from life (and how many thousands of similar scenes did NAPOLEON cause !) go far toward lessening the pity one feels in contemplating the fallen Emperor throned on his prison-rock :

> ——— ' banished forlorn,
> Like a limb from his country cast bleeding and torn.'

It seems like the gradual but certain retributive justice of an avenging Heaven.

THE CONSCRIPT.

—

TRANSLATED FOR THE KNICKERBOCKER FROM THE FRENCH OF M. DE BALZAC.

—

IN 1813, at the time the last levies were made by NAPOLEON, and which the prefects enforced with a rigor which contributed perhaps to the first downfall of the empire, the son of a poor farmer in the environs of a city which shall be nameless, refused to serve in the Imperial Army, and fled his home.

The first summons executed, rigorous measures were put in force against the father and mother. At length the prefect, tired of seeing the affair protracted, one morning summoned the father before him. The peasant presented himself at the prefecture, and there the secretary first, then the prefect himself, endeavored by words of persuasion to convert to the imperial faith the father of the delinquent, and to discover through him the retreat where his son had concealed himself. They entirely failed, however ; such was the system of denial in which the peasantry enclosed themselves, with the instinct of the oyster which defies all attacks against its hard shell. From persuasions the prefect and his secretary passed to threats.

' We will *force* you to find your son ! ' said the secretary.

' I should like to find him very much, my lord,' replied the peasant.

' I must have him, dead or alive ! ' cried the prefect, putting an end to the discussion.

The father returned in despair to his house ; for in truth he did not know where his son was. He foresaw what would be his fate. In fact the following day he saw early in the morning, while on the way to his field, the high cap of a gen-d'arme who came galloping along the hedges, and whom the prefect had sent to lodge with him until the delinquent should be found. He was obliged to feed and clothe him, and provide sustenance for his horse. The poor peasant soon expended the little sum which he had laid up by the strictest economy : then he sold the gold cross and silver ear-rings of his wife ; her locket and clothes ; then his field, and at last his house.

Before the sale of the house and the little plat of land attached to it, there was a terrible dispute between the husband and wife ; he having charged her with knowing where her son had concealed himself. The gen-d'arme was obliged to interfere ; for the peasant, maddened with rage, had taken up his " sabot " to throw at the head of his wife.

From that day the gen-d'arme, pitying these unfortunate people, sent his horse to graze on the road and the commons near by. Some neighbors joined together to furnish him provender and straw ; the most part of the time he bought meat for himself, and endeavored to assist in providing for the support of the miserable family. The peasant threatened to hang himself.

At length one day, when wood was required to cook the dinner for the gen-d'arme, the father of the delinquent went early in the morning to a neighboring forest to gather the dead branches which had fallen from the trees. At night on his return he saw in a ditch near some houses a whitish mass, and going up to it, recognized the body of his son. He had died of famine ; and between his teeth was the last herb which he had been trying to eat.

The peasant threw the body over his shoulders, and without showing it to any one, and without saying a word, carried it three leagues. On arriving at the prefecture, he inquired for the prefect, and learning that he was at a ball, he waited for his return. When he came home at two o'clock in the morning, he found the peasant at his door.

'You wanted my son, Monsieur le Prefect ; there he is !'

He threw the dead body at his feet, and fled.

He and his wife now beg their bread.

———

IT somehow always chances, that in reading of NAPOLEON we cannot help calling to mind the striking picture drawn by Rev. ROBERT HALL of the career of the all-conquering Captain. It even occurred to us the other evening, while sitting entranced with the superb spectacle of 'Napoleon' now performing to crowded audiences at the Bowery Theatre. The following is a brief extract : 'Recollect for a moment,' says he, ' his invasion of Egypt, a country which had never given him the slightest provocation ; a country so remote from the scene of his crimes, that it probably did not know there was such a man in existence ; (happy ignorance, could it have lasted !) but while he was looking around him like a vulture perched on an eminence, for objects on which he might gratify his insatiable thirst of rapine, he no sooner beheld the defenceless condition of that unhappy country, than he alighted upon it in a moment. In vain did it struggle, flap its wings, and rend the air with its shrieks : the cruel enemy, deaf to its cries, had infixed his talons, and was busy in sucking its blood, when the interference of a superior power forced him to relinquish his prey, and betake himself to flight. He saw nothing in the simple manners and blood-bought liberties of the Swiss to engage his forbearance ; nothing in proclaiming himself a Mahommedan to revolt his conscience ; nothing in the condition of defenceless prisoners to excite his pity ; nor in that of the companions of his warfare, sick and wounded in a foreign land, to prevent him from despatching them by poison.' These and other the like scenes *relieve* the excess of brightness which circles around the fame of BONAPARTE.

———

BOOKS FOR THE YOUNG. — Messrs. MUNROE AND FRANCIS, Boston, and Mr. C. S. FRANCIS, New-York, are doing good service to the rising generation in the various entertaining and instructive books for young persons which they frequently put forth. Three of these are now before us : the time-honored favorite, ' Robin Hood and his Merry Foresters ; ' ' Farewell Tales by Mrs. HOFLAND,' both illustrated by numerous cuts ; and ' PAUL PRESTON's Gymnastics, or Sports for Youth : a Legacy to support the Health and Long Life of his Young Friends. The illustrative engravings in this little volume are, as the reader will perceive, of an order altogether unique. Take the annexed exercise for example :

Observe the *chiar-'oscuro*, ' the breadth and depth, the universal light and shade, the general perspective,' and in short the artistical *oneness* of the entire picture ! The style is immense !

'OLD PUT.' AT THE BAR' AGAIN. — The accusers and advocates in the case of GENERAL PUTNAM *vs.* THE UNITED STATES' PUBLIC are on the increase, as we have abundant evidence in diverse communications upon the theme which have of late accumulated on our hands. In the mean time, we await the promised paper of our correspondent, who writes us : 'The article on PUTNAM is not concluded. I am disappointed in the receipt of some affidavits I had expected from Connecticut ; but a delay of a month or two can make but little difference.' We have been requested to copy a series of labored and clumsily-written articles from an eastern journal, composing a crude and passionate miscellany in relation to Gen. PUTNAM and other matters, and abounding in adscititious invective and labored abuse of our original correspondent. We respectfully decline the proffered favor ; but at the same time, the friends of Gen. PUTNAM may rest assured that the defence of that officer will be committed to an abler writer, who will deal with the *statements* of our contributor, instead of occupying our pages with remarks — which are sufficiently ill-natured and would be satirical perhaps with more force — concerning his *motives.*   An article published in the 'North-American Review' some twenty years ago, and attributed, we think without sufficient authority, certainly without internal evidence, to Hon. DANIEL WEBSTER, has recently been revived, as an answer to the charges in our August number. A new correspondent has sent us a long reply to this review, and urgently solicited its publication in the present number. But we reserve it for consideration in connexion with the forth-coming defence, from the pen of a correspondent to whom we have already alluded. The writer informs us that the review had its origin at a time of high political excitement, in which Gen. DEARBORN was a prominent party ; that he himself was a warm opponent of Gen. DEARBORN ; but he is compelled to add, that in relation to his pamphlet concerning the Battle of Bunker's Hill, 'if ever a man wrote as if his hand and mouth were on the Bible, and who considered nothing so sacred and holy as truth, *he* did ; and notwithstanding every effort made to contradict him, not an officer in the action, nor any one else who attained to a known and respectable standing in after life, has been found to weaken or disprove his statements.' We have neither present space nor leisure to indicate the topics of our correspondent's article ; but thus much we may mention. The witnesses introduced into the review are examined, and their testimony contrasted ; and it is due to the cause of truth to say, that their *separate* testimony completely nullifies the *general* tendency of their representations. Our correspondent cites the late Col. SAMUEL L. KNAPP, then residing in Boston, to prove that at this exciting political period 'any and every one who would come forward and swear that they saw Gen. PUTNAM in the memorable action, was paid the same sum for his travel and attendance, as a member of the legislature ;' and it is this testimony which he analyzes. 'PRESCOTT and STARK,' adds the writer, and he sustains his assertion by *proofs,* 'from the day of the battle to the day of their respective deaths, made and often repeated the charges of Gen. DEARBORN against Gen. PUTNAM, and in the most public manner.'   In relation to a remark in the review, that 'Col. PRESCOTT and Gen. PUTNAM kept up a friendly correspondence during their lives,' he interposes a *flat denial,* and challenges the reviewer (and if he be Mr. WEBSTER, he says, he is well acquainted with the children of both) to produce 'a single friendly letter in corroboration of this unfounded declaration.' He alludes to the remarks in a late lecture of Mr. SPARKS, in relation to Gen. PUTNAM, concerning whom he spoke in general terms as 'a brave man,' whom WASHINGTON honored with his confidence and applause ;

but we are furnished, on the other hand, with *numerous* authentic extracts from WASHINGTON's letters, (in addition to two or three already quoted in these pages,) which may not have met the eye of our respected and eminent historian, and which are of a directly *opposite* tendency. Moreover, the proofs are thickening upon us, from some of the most distinguished citizens of this State, that Gen. PUTNAM's extraordinary popularity at length subsided into an entirely different sentiment on the part of the people; and some of the reasons for this change in public opinion we are confident will shake the faith even of 'true believers.' There are two parties to this controversy. We verily believe that the one is not more thoroughly AMERICAN than the other; and we have no doubt, moreover, that *the truth* lies between the two extremes. If on the one hand Gen. PUTNAM was not a coward, on the other he has borne honors which were clearly not his own, but which have been tacitly rendered him by a great republic, tired of war and 'rejoicing in the beams of peace.' With certain doubts strengthened and others removed by the discussion which has been awakened, we stand an honest and a *disinterested* umpire before the public, seeking only THE TRUTH, without fear or favor, and determined to promulgate it, which side soever the scales may preponderate.

GOSSIP WITH READERS AND CORRESPONDENTS. — We say *No*, at once, to 'PHILO-FRANKLIN,' and very willingly take hold of the dilemma's *horn* with which he thought to gore us. Our correspondent is *too* matter-of-fact, and errs on the other side of CARLYLE. We think of an illustrative example at this moment:

> ''Tis morn, but scarce yon level sun
> Can pierce the war-cloud, rolling dun,
> Where furious Frank and fiery Hun
>   Shout in their sulph'rous canopy!'

Will 'PHILO-FRANKLIN' contend that there would have been more poetry in this sublime-obscure scene, if the sun had shone full upon the awful picture? 'Guess not!' · · · '*An English Churchman*' has called our attention to the counter-statements of Mr. LESTER, in his '*Glory and Shame of England*' and those of the good BISHOP MEADE, of Virginia, both of whom have recently returned from the mother country. Mr. LESTER describes, in exaggerated phrase, the parish poor as neglected by the ministers of the Church; as dying without the consolations of religion, etc., while BISHOP MEADE remarked, especially, that the poor filled the isles of the English churches; and that they were looked after and cared for in the parishes with a solicitude almost paternal. The impression would seem to be general, that Mr. LESTER is very far from being accurate in many of his sketches and statements. · · · There is evidence of decided talent in the '*Tale of Florence*,' but the *class* of composition is not to our taste; and the writer will be surprised perhaps to learn that the 'little piece which he throws in as a make-weight' is accepted, while the more elaborate favor is declined. There is a scene in the opening of the second chapter which really reminds us of a burlesque passage in 'The Heroine:'

'All was dark. The hurricane howled, the wet rain fell, and the thunder rolled in an awful and Ossianly manner.

'On a beetling rock, lashed by the Gulf of Salerno, stood Il Castello di Grimgothico.

'My lads, are your carbines charged, and your sabres sharpened?' cried Stilletto.

'If they ai'n't, we might load our carbines with this hail, and sharpen our sabres against this north wind!' cried Poignardini.

'At that moment the bell of Grimgothico tolled one. The sound vibrated through the long corridors, the spiral stair-cases, the suites of tapestried apartments, and the ears of the personage who now has the honor to address you.'

The '*Thoughts on American Transcendentalism*' (which will appear) remind us of a discovery we have recently made, in a perusal of the *Apocrypha*; namely, that the writers of those 'books' were the first Transcendentalists. Take the annexed passage for example from 'The Wisdom of Solomon.' It has much of the vagueness and all the characteristic beauty of the 'inner light' style of the present day: 'For wisdom, which is the worker of all things, taught me: for in her is an understanding spirit; holy, one, manifold, subtil, lively, clear, undefiled, plain, not subject to hurt; loving the thing that is good, quick, which cannot be letted, ready to do good; kind to man, steadfast, sure, free from care, having all power, overseeing all things, and going through all understanding; pure, and most subtil spirits. For Wisdom is more moving than any motion; she passeth and goeth through all things by reason of her pureness. *For she is the breath of the power of God, and a pure influence flowing from the glory of the Almighty*; therefore can no defiled thing fall into her. For she is the brightness of the everlasting light, the unspotted mirror of the power of God, and the image of His goodness. And being but one, she can do all things: and remaining in herself she maketh all things new: *and in all ages entering into holy souls, she maketh them friends of God and prophets.* For God loveth none but him that dwelleth with Wisdom. For she is more beautiful than the sun, and above all the order of stars: *being compared with the light she is found before it.* For after this cometh night; but Vice shall not prevail against Wisdom.' · · · It is due to Mr. J. H. INGRAHAM, (whose authorship of '*Lafitte, or the Pirate of the Gulf*' was questioned, on the authority of a correspondent, in the 'Gossip' of our last number,) to state that he explicitly denies the charge. Mr. INGRAHAM has been furnished with the name of our correspondent, who holds himself responsible for the accuracy of his statements. · · · The annual dinner of the '*Saint Nicholas Society*,' celebrated on the 6th ultimo at the American Hotel, was one of the most spirited and numerously-attended festivals of our good patron Saint which we have had for years. The launch of the noble ship 'Saint Nicholas' a few hours before, (and her admirable re-launch by Mr. VAN BUREN in a most felicitous speech in the evening;) the presence of several distinguished guests, among them Lord MORPETH and Col. CLIVE, from the other side of the 'great waters' — the former of whom made one of the best and most appropriate addresses on the occasion — and the general hilarity of the scene, from beginning to end, altogether rendered *this* annual event one to be proëminently remembered. We are sorry to be compelled to dismiss a matter-full theme in so few and insufficient words; but the tyranny of space is despotic. · · · Among new articles filed for insertion are: 'An Apology for Authors,' by a favorite contributor; 'Granada and the Alhambra;' 'The Polygon Papers,' Number Four; 'English Etymology;' 'Edward Alford and his Play-fellow;' 'My Grandfather's Port-folio,' Number Two; 'The Pic-Nic: The Ride in the Cab,' Number Two. The annexed were received at too late an hour for examination: 'Captain WILDING's Verses about a Brook,' by SIMEON SILVERPEN, and 'American Novelists, a Critical Essay.' · · · Several publications of interest or value, and among them CHANDLER's Criminal Trials, and 'Kabosa, or the Warriors of the West,' reached us at too late an hour for any other notice than this hurried announcement of their reception.

'THE MECHANIC,' a volume from the pen of Miss FRANCES HARRIET WHIPPLE, of Rhode-Island, escaped our notice until it was too late to render it adequate consideration in the present number. But we ask the attention of our readers to the preface :

" IT may be objected that the incidents, characters, and modes of life, embodied in the accompanying Narrative, range too far above the common lot, to come within the sphere of POPULAR TALES; that they are, in short, deficient, in not giving the just medium picture of common life; that they ought to be brought down more upon a level with the habits and tastes of the common people. To this I reply: We have, already, done enough of *bringing down*; let us now begin to LIFT UP — to ELEVATE our fellow men! In fine, if those who are called levellers, would stop *levelling down* and begin to LEVEL UP! — if, instead of attempting to bring down the higher orders of society, they would aim at elevating the low, if they would preach at the corners of the streets and by the fire-side, through all our high-ways and through all our bye-ways, the great doctrine of the dignity, the divinity of human nature — a dignity, a divinity, which the contact of no outward circumstance could possibly either degrade or exalt, a great change would begin to be wrought; and this, undoubtedly, would lead to a clearer perception of the spirit, and a carrying out of the principle, which was in the mind of Jesus. Is the diamond less a diamond because accident has cast it among flint or pebble-stones? Is it more a diamond, if set in the finest gold? Is not the gem one? are not its beauty and its value one, wherever or however it may be set? When these doctrines are generally preached, and embodied in practice, every man will begin to feel himself, and TO BE — A MAN; and feeling and being this, however high or however low he may be in a worldly point of view, he will regard his fellow men as equals, and brethren, all walking in different paths, it may be — all pursuing different avocations; yet each bearing on his brow the visible signet of Jehovah, which confirms THE NOBILITY OF A GODLIKE NATURE — each invested with a mission to his race, for the faithful discharge of which he is accountable to all future generations. When this spirit comes to be diffused, the rich man will cease to be arrogant, and the poor man will forget to be servile; for will not each feel himself equally a MAN? And where upon the face of the wide earth could be found a higher dignity? "

The benevolent and catholic spirit of this preface will be a sufficient recommendation of the work to the attention of our readers.

LITERARY RECORD.

VALUABLE BOOKS. — We are indebted at a late hour to the New-York publishers, Messrs. LOCK-WOOD AND SMITH, No. 34 Bowery, for copies of several very valuable works, which we have barely room to mention, leaving the rest to the reader's general confidence in our commendations : ' BOTTA's History of the War of the Independence of the United States, translated from the Italian by GEORGE ALEXANDER OTIS, Esq.,' in two handsome volumes, with engravings ; ' PITKIN's Statistics of the United States,' embracing banks, manufactures, internal trade, improvements, revenues, expenditures, etc., accompanied by numerous tables ; ' DANA's Mineralogy,' a standard work, and one of a high order of excellence, illustrated by very numerous wood-cuts ; and ' BAKEWELL's Geology,' to which the same commendation may with equal force be applied. The same house publish President DAY's ' Inquiry respecting the Self-determining Power of the Will, or Contingent Volition,' and that distin-guished writer's ' Examination of President EDWARDS' ' Inquiry on the Freedom of the Will.' Both works have attracted much attention among theologians and others. An excellent reprint of WORDS-WORTH's Poems, ' the first complete from the last London edition,' accompanied the foregoing works, all of which will readily command the favor they deserve, from the scientific, the religious, the literary and the general reader. Mr. LOCKWOOD, the senior member of this firm, an obliging and gentleman-like person, will be remembered as long connected with the house of Messrs. WILEY AND PUTNAM. An earnest this, that the trusts committed to his hands in the matter of foreign books, prints, fancy station-ery, etc., will be faithfully and promptly discharged. We have pleasure in commending this new estab-lishment to the favor of our citizens residing in the vicinity of the busy thoroughfare in which it is situated.

' GOULD's UNIVERSAL INDEX.' — We have received from Mr. M. T. C. GOULD, the distinguished ste-nographer, a copy of a work which in the hands of *every body* will be of the greatest service. It is entitled ' GOULD's Universal Index, and Every Body's Own Book,' with directions for saving time, acquiring knowledge, and having it at command through life, by means of an appropriate alphabetical and numerical Key ; designed for the use of schools and colleges in the United States ; for professional men, lovers of literature and science, politicians, men of business, and for all who think with FRANK-LIN that time is money, that a penny saved is worth two earned ; or with SOLOMON, that knowledge is better than fine gold, and wisdom better than rubies. Mr. GOULD numbers among his subscribers all the most eminent men of the nation, who have expressed the most unqualified approbation of the plan. It deserves the amplest success.

MOTHERWELL's POEMS. — We have in a handsome volume from the press of Mr. WILLIAM D. TICKNOR, Boston, the narrative and lyrical poems of WILLIAM MOTHERWELL, whose ' Jeanie Morri-son ' and ' My Heart is like to rend, Willie ' have been felt to the remotest corners of this western world. By reason of the scarcity of the only edition ever published, the larger part of MOTHERWELL's poems are known to but few. ' Varied in style and subject,' says the editor of the present volume, ' the author seems always at home and at ease ; whether he sings of love or battle, he is equally in spirit : his poetry is the same full stream, whether it flow quietly amid myrtle-groves or foam along a battle-field, bearing upon its bosom a Norseman's fleet.' There are fifty-four poems in the collection, embracing among them all of the writer's more renowned effusions. A brief memoir of the poet is embodied in the preface.

LANMAN's HISTORY OF MICHIGAN forms No. 139 of HARPER's Family Library. The author's design, which we think he has well carried out in execution, was to present to the reader, in a brief and popular form, a view of the principal events connected with the history, progress, and present condition of Michigan, condensed from the larger work prepared by the author under the sanction of a law of that State. Such a work, embracing a great variety of particulars relating to the early settle-ment and subsequent growth of the West, cannot fail to be both useful and interesting. The rapid advance of the vast territory bordering on the lakes, in population and wealth, is the best commentary on the nature and effects of our free institutions, and offers a political phenomenon well worthy of being studied.

COLMAN'S 'ANTIQUITIES.' — A review of COLMAN'S 'Antiquities of the Christian Church,' reprinted from the 'Banner of the Cross,' has been sent us from Philadelphia by an esteemed friend. The reviewer we think establishes the fact that the 'Antiquities' are wholly worthless as a book of reference, or guide to the scholar and antiquary. He shows by the exposition of numerous glaring errors, that no scholar can rely upon the accuracy of the volume, and that no student can derive from it a correct and faithful view of the Church and her customs in ancient days. The reviewer fortifies his positions with ample authorities, indicating great familiarity with his theme; and though he uses a trenchant critical blade, he tempers justice with courtesy. We commend this little pamphlet, wherever accessible, to our readers.

LOCKHART'S SPANISH BALLADS. — We alluded in our last to an illuminated London edition of LOCKHART'S Historical and Romantic Ballads of Spain; and we are glad now to be enabled to call the reader's attention to an American edition of the same work, from the house of Messrs. WILEY AND PUTNAM, accompanied by all the notes, and an admirable introductory 'Essay on the origin, antiquity, character, and influence of the Ancient Ballads of Spain, and an Analytical Account, with Specimens, of the Romance of the Cid.' The execution of the volume does great credit to the press of Mr. WILLIAM OSBORN. It is in this respect scarcely surpassed by the superb London edition of MURRAY. Of the ballads themselves it is quite unnecessary to speak. Several translations of BRYANT and LOCKHART have already made their merits widely known in America.

ANTHON'S 'LATIN PROSODY AND METRE.' — Professor ANTHON, as we gather from the preface of the present work, prepared several years ago a Treatise on Latin Prosody and Metre, which met with no unfavorable reception, and proved a useful guide to the young prosodian. This volume having been for some time completely out of print, the author has been induced to write a new work on the subject: one that may not only be more worthy of his increased experience as an instructor, but may furnish also more detailed information on various points that were necessarily omitted in the previous treatise. The young scholar will find in it every thing that may be needed by him, not only at the commencement but also throughout the several stages of his academic career. The Brothers HARPER are the publishers.

POEMS BY 'FLACCUS.' — We are right well pleased to find on our table, in one of the neatest and most tasteful volumes of the season, a collection of the several poetical series which have appeared from time to time in the KNICKERBOCKER, under the general title of 'Passaic: a Group of Poems touching that River;' together with other 'Musings,' which became widely and most favorably known to the public through the 'New-York American.' Wholly aside from the partiality which we feel for an old and popular correspondent, we have an affection for much of the '*heart-poësis*' of 'FLACCUS;' and sure we are that our readers share our impressions in this regard. We commend the volume confidently to the warm hearts and good tastes of the public.

BELZONI'S TRAVELS IN EGYPT. — We have been entertained and instructed by a little volume recently from the press of Mr. C. S. FRANCIS, Broadway, and one of the books in his 'Library of Instructive Amusement.' It is a new edition, revised and enlarged, of 'The Fruits of Enterprise exhibited in the Adventures of BELZONI in Egypt and Nubia; with an account of his discoveries in the Pyramids, among the ruins of cities, and in the ancient tombs.' The volume is presented upon a large, clear type, and is illustrated with very numerous pictures, in the old-fashioned clearly-traced style of engraving.

JOAN OF ARC. — We have from the press of the Messrs. APPLETON a very handsome medium-sized volume, embellished with twenty-four plates, containing the interesting story of the brave Joan of Arc, with a history of the causes which reduced France to its dreadful condition at the period when Joan appeared at Chinon to rouse up the indolent and despairing French monarch, and impart fresh energy to his soldiers and subjects. The work is pleasingly written, well executed upon a large type, and its embellishments are in the first class of wood-engravings.

THE KNICKERBOCKER.

VOL. XIX.   FEBRUARY, 1842.   No. 2.

AN APOLOGY FOR AUTHORS.

To young people of lively and romantic imaginations there is nothing so fascinating as the stage and those who tread it. Before the world has shed over them its chilling influence, and opened to their trustful minds its mortifying truths, they never believe that the hero of to-night may be the gambler or the sot of to-morrow; still less that the graceful Viola or the tender Juliet who sighs and weeps in satin and diamonds, may be found at certain seasons quarrelling in the green-room like a tigress, or slip-shod and uncombed, conning her well-thumbed lesson in the den of a slattern. They know indeed that these people are not exactly the beings whose sentiments delight them, yet they cherish the grateful illusion that they must be at least souls of similar tone, or they could not give so movingly the touching thoughts of Ion or of Julia. They do not suppose a 'vocalist' to be eternally singing, or a 'tragedian' to sleep in his buskins; but it never enters their heads that these idols of their evening worship can at other times condescend to be mere mortals like themselves, or — sadly unlike any thing so innocent. The moment the mystery is unfolded, the illusion vanishes. The veil was the charm. The fitness of the actor for the 'genteel comedy' in which he made so shining a figure often becomes more than doubtful when he attempts to play a corresponding part in real life; and he appears even more vulgar and common-place than he would have done if we had seen him only in his own natural position and character. We are disappointed, and wish we had never been tempted to peep behind the scenes.

I am far from intending to institute any thing like a parallel between actors and authors; yet it has struck me that there is a degree of similarity in the feeling of disappointment which has so often been experienced on a near view of the one and the other. Nothing can be more natural than the desire to enjoy the society of authors whose writings have pleased us. If the actor attracts the young, not less surely does the favorite author excite a feeling of interest in maturer minds. We love the intelligent and suggestive companion of our quiet hours. We rank him among our benefactors, and we long for a nearer acquaintance. His person, his voice, his every-day habits and ordinary sentiments acquire a certain kind of importance, and for this reason those biographies which let us most completely into these minutiæ have ever been esteemed the most precious. We have read the man in his book, however unconscious he may have been that he was writing himself down. 'As a man thinketh, so is he.' No man can write a book without letting his real self peep out, whatever be the style he chooses to assume, or the sentiments he endeavors to adopt for the time. The reader catches glimpses of his face behind a mask. He sees enough to excite curiosity, but not enough to satisfy it. He finds a chord of sympathy, and feels his heart stir with its vibrations. He discovers that some one thinks as he does; loves what he loves; prizes what he most values; has acquired what he most admires and covets. He seeks the writer with a feeling of ready-made intimacy; he is a friend before he is an acquaintance; and he goes, with his heart in his hand, to find another heart which he knows to be congenial.

He meets — what? A being whose exterior probably resembles any thing rather than the graceful mental image; and who, considering his visiter as a mere stranger, and knowing nothing of the invisible chain so prized by the other, chills him with indifference, or repels him by the aid of an icy shield which he has been forced to adopt as a defence against intrusive impertinence. Wounded self-love, heightened by a feeling nearly akin to disappointed affection, transforms at once to gall the loving sympathy of the disciple, and he retires to add another atom to the mountain of testimony that authors are agreeable only on paper.

Once and again has it been my own fortune to encounter in broad daylight and to behold with my bodily eyes that mysterious and dream-colored entity, an author; a personage whose imposing *eidolon* had long tenanted one of the most garnished chambers of my inmost heart. I had pictured this favorite of nature enjoying even in this envious world a sort of apotheösis. Fame blew her sweet-voiced trump before him; Beauty watched for his glance; Wisdom hung on his words; Fortune poured her treasures at his feet; while far in the mighty distance a countless posterity flung high its shadowy arms at the mention of his name.

I saw, as I have said, an author bodily. I surrendered myself to the belief that this was indeed the original of the picture my imagination had drawn. I approached with awe, almost with trembling; but the bright dream faded as I drew nigh. My idol was of clay; a mere man — a very man; man with all the extra foibles and failings which are avoided by the discreeter part of the species. He was a self-worshipper — an egotist — a boaster; as cold to the claims of others as he was tenacious of his own. He was opinionated, he was morose, he was testy; and alas! even envious. I turned away, heart-sick. I forgot to ascertain his real merits, the points in which he was acknowledged to excel his fellow men. My disappointment was as unreasonable as my expectations had been unwarranted.

Why should an author have fewer faults than other men? Why should he not rather have more? He is in the first place a peculiarly sensitive being; as little fitted to encounter with dignity the hard rubs of this struggling world as to endure with patience its severer ills. The coldness of a friend or the fickleness of fortune, instead of rousing his spirits, discourages and depresses him; leaving him more than ever at the mercy of any of those accidents of life which afford to men of a different temperament the best opportunities for distinction. He has adopted a profession in which there is no invariable standard of excellence. His pretensions are to be decided upon not by one or two, but by ten thousand judges; a majority of whom must concur in his favor before he can assume the position to which self-love assures him he is undoubtedly entitled. This fluctuation of hope is strikingly unfavorable to that equable and placid mental condition which is a pre-requisite for the enjoyment of society.

The habits of an author are indeed almost inevitably anti-social. This world is for some wise reason so ordered, that the good, and charming, and intelligent people in it are distributed very impartially; a little leaven only being allowed in each portion of the mass. No society, however fortunately collocated, possesses any great number of highly cultivated minds; and it certainly falls to the lot of many who are capable of relishing the most refined intellectual tone, to pass through life with scarce an opportunity of tasting this choicest earthly bliss. 'Whoever,' says Curran, 'succeeds in attaining the splendid heights of intellect, will be doomed to find himself in a region nearly uninhabited.' Authors are not rich men; they are not men who choose their position; they are rather, even to a proverb, the sport of fortune. In the narrow round to which Fate usually confines them, they can hope to meet but few minds competent to shed light into theirs, or to increase their brightness by collision. Is it then surprising that they should fall into the error of preferring the converse of books to that of men? That the study, with its loaded shelves and its shaded lamp, should prove more attractive than the mixed concourse, where a small amount of talent suffices for an unmeasured flow of words, and where the recluse, listless and uninterested, is unable to afford his quota of pleasure, and soon learns to feel himself *de trop?*

'Reading maketh a full man, writing an exact man, conference a ready man,' says Lord Bacon; and truly the habit of seclusion unfits a man more and more for doing himself justice in conversation. 'If he confer little, he had need have a present wit,' or he must with all his reading prove but a poor auxiliary in the social circle.

This same accident of poverty which naturally belongs to authors, since their pursuit is seldom that of money, has many attendant ills. It subjects them to a thousand vexatious hinderances and interruptions which try their tempers and pervert their views of our common nature and condition.

Every author worthy of the name has at intervals what he himself denominates moments of inspiration, though others may give them the more humble character of periods of mental excitement. Call them what we may, they are inestimable. To be interrupted at these critical points of time by any thing whatsoever; to be brought back to cold reality just as the fervid glow promises a torrent of liquid gold, or of thoughts and words infinitely more precious; this would seem enough. But to be dragged down to earth to pay a tradesman's bill out of an empty purse, or to indite, 'as per order,' a penny-a-line paragraph to save the faithful companion who is to partake the triumph from starving *ad interim;* what, short of madness, could be surprising? And who can doubt that this sketch has been often realized? Of the great Butler, 'all that can be told with any certainty is that he was poor.' Dryden *contracted to furnish* ten thousand verses to a book-seller. The laborious orientalist Ockley confesses that in his agonizing efforts to finish his History of the Saracens, he was forced to take advantage of the slumber of his cares, and that his only quiet time was while he was in prison for debt. Were these the men for parlor converse? Ceaseless anxiety on the subject of the mere materials for decent subsistence is no promoter of gayety. 'Sweet colloquial pleasures' are not the soothers of 'penury.'

Nobody has ever complained that Sir Walter Scott was incommunicative, or Mr. Rogers reserved and morose. In these and similar cases of happy exception to the general rule, we are enabled to perceive what the pursuits of literature can effect for human happiness; and these eminently favored individuals have evinced their grateful sense of their advantages by an enlarged and diffusive benevolence of soul united with a corresponding amenity of manners. May their number increase! As to self-esteem, that most pardonable yet least pardoned foible of minds of all calibres, how can an author be expected to eradicate it? Repress it he must, and doubtless does, even where the protuberance is most prodigious to the observer. We see the excrescence, but

> ' We know na' what 's resisted.'

Authors are always praised and flattered by some circle or coterie, high or low. This is natural and kind. It arises from a spontaneous benevolence — an impulsive generosity, which leads people to give that which costs them little or nothing to one who will appreciate it extravagantly. A dearth in this quarter would save the press many a groan. No man would write a second time if nobody praised the first effort. Praise serves instead of the divine afflatus which in our day revisits the earth only at rare intervals. It is the vital air of the true author :

> ' A simple race — they spend their toil
> For the vain tribute of a smile ; '

and it would be churlish indeed to deny them so cheap a recompense. Now not more surely does the imponderable gas lift the silken balloon from the level of those who have helped to inflate it, than does this same easy praise puff up the recipient, and inspire him with an idea that an exalted place is his natural right. Then we point at the cords which keep him among us, and laugh cruelly at his aspiring thoughts.

But perhaps the inflating power has been insufficient, and the balloon, after hovering and hovering, in uneasy suspense, at length falls to the ground, a mere bag. When an author's fate corresponds with this — and there are some to whom the figure applies most lamentably — we berate him for being testy. Who would not be? At best, the appetite for praise is insatiable. The higher the zest, the more does the over-stimulated sense require ; and when the acmé is reached, the desire is still unquenched. This makes egotists; and we, who

> 'Build him a pedestal and say 'Stand there,
> And be our admiration and our praise,' '

are the first to be disgusted with the legitimate result of our own efforts.

What dare I say in extenuation of that proneness to envy which is so often held up to our detestation in that dreadful dissecting-theatre which we call Literary Biography? When the quivering heart of the author is exposed with professional coolness to the gazing multitude, we are pointed to the dark plague-spot on its surface which tells that it sickened at the success of another, and we turn away shuddering from the sight.

But here again we must recollect that literary merit is reducible to no unerring and universal test. It is a matter referred to taste and fancy, and these must often seem to an author to be governed by mere caprice, partiality, interest, or malice. He has staked his all upon a single throw, and he is maddened by seeing the prize which he had considered his own, snatched by one whose pretensions appear to his blinded eyes as nothing. He believes indeed that posterity will do him justice, but he cannot wait for posterity. He is forbidden the open expression of his anguish, and it consumes his heart in silence, or bursts forth in words or actions of which he is himself ashamed.

Let us judge him mercifully. If 'every author would his brother kill,' the punishment comes with the offence, and is renewed and redoubled afterward. Pope and Addison poisoned their own springs of happiness while they lived; and when they were dead, Johnson wrote their biography.

But we are straying a little from our subject, which relates rather to the excuses to be made when authors prove less agreeable than their writings. Some have been accused of reserving for the public the good things which rise spontaneously to the lips in the hilarious flow of intimate conversation. This can only be true of those whose necessities are such as to demand the most rigid economy of all the means of life; and this form of economy must be of all others the most painful and odious to a man of genius; so that we should rather commiserate than censure one who would be more liberal if he dared.

Among the complaints sometimes adduced against popular writers, is their inaccessibility, and also a certain coldness and cautiousness of expression, which bespeaks distrust and suspicion. For this fault, where it exists, it is probable the true cause must be sought in the conduct of such people as the cavillers themselves. If an author has been taught by vexatious experience that a certain portion of those who seek his society are watching for his sayings in order to report them, either for the gratification of a very common kind of vanity, or still worse, from a more sordid motive, what marvel that he should be chary of his words, or that he should require very ample letters of credit ere he admit strangers to the sacred fire-side?

May we not conclude then, that we expect too much from authors; that we do not enough consider their trials and temptations; that we make less than the proper allowance for their peculiarities of temperament, and overlook too often their points of especial and exclusive merit?

If the literary character fell always into hands as generous as those of the elder D'Israeli, the sensitive heart of the man of genius might be at rest as to his posthumous estimation. There is one author at least who seems to have forgotten his own claims tò no unenviable place in the republic of letters, in his zeal to show in its full lustre the splendor of departed genius; while he casts the veil of a most fraternal charity over the 'follies of the wise' — the frailties inseparable from humanity, however exalted.

Women are seldom authors by profession, and we have not therefore considered them as requiring any defence on the score of having merged the social in the literary character. The side-blows which have been aimed at those who have ventured occasionally to snatch the pen have scarcely been such as needed warding off. The beautiful and witty Lady Mary Wortley is indeed said to have 'infested' the table of Lord Oxford; but she was considered a pest not because she was a *bas-bleu*, but because she would persist in tormenting Pope, who wished to sink the poet in the lover. Of Madame de Staël it has been observed that her sincere earnestness of soul was such that she cherished a boundless sympathy for the most insignificant of her race. Byron said of her that she not only had never ridiculed any one, but that he did not believe she had ever even thought any one ridiculous. Her character as a woman was as worthy of all love, as were her literary achievements of all admiration. And we must believe, from universal testimony, that the female writers who have adorned England within the last age have sought rather to become the most estimable than the most brilliant of their sex. Nearer than this we must not come; and here we close our remarks for the present.

SONNET.

ON THE DEATH OF A BROTHER AT A DISTANCE.

BROTHER! we parted on an autumn day:
    Fair was the sky, and bright the sun-beams fell,
As the good ship went gliding down the bay,
    Upon whose deck we bade our last farewell.
Our LAST farewell! Ah! little did I think,
    When hands were grasped and tears were dropping free,
That thus should sever our fraternal link,
    And twenty years' communion cease to be!
Soft fall, ye dews! — gild bright, ye morning beams!
    The tufted hillock where my brother lies;
Though distant far, I'll visit it in dreams,
    And to the south-wind give my mournful sighs!
Methinks e'en now he's standing by my side;
    I turn to grasp — lo! DEATH our hands divide.

New-York, December, 1841.   HENRY A. BUCKINGHAM.

THE FIFTH OF MAY.

TRANSLATED FROM THE ITALIAN OF MANZONI, BY WILLIAM PETER.

Σιδηρόφρων τε κά κ πίτρας ειργασμένος
Οστις, Προμηθεῦ, σδίσιν ου ξυνασχαλᾷ
Μοχθυις.— Æschyl. Prom. vinct 242.

He was!—now motionless and lone,
  All hushed life's latest sighs,
That mighty breath forever flown,
  The unconscious Ruin lies;
And earth, as desolate and chill,
Earth, awe-struck at the tale, is still;
   Mute, musing o'er the last sad hour
    Of the portentous Man,
   Nor knows when mind of equal power
    Shall flame in Glory's van;
When mortal step, so vast, so dread,
Shall thunder o'er her blood-stained bed!

Him, high-enthroned in sovereign state,
  I saw, nor woke the strain;
When, by vicissitude of fate,
  He fell, rose, sank again,
Though thousand voices rang around,
Mine joined not in the empty sound:
   No dastard outrage on these lips,
    No breath of servile praise;
   Now, in that mighty Sun's eclipse,
    My virgin voice I raise,
And twine around his distant tomb
A wreath, which yet perchance may bloom.

From Alp to Pyramid, from far
  Manzanar to the Rhine,
We heard the thunder-crash of War,
  We saw his lightnings shine!
On, on they burst, from sea to sea,
From Tanais to Sicily.
   Was this true glory? Future Time
    Will say; meanwhile in dim
   Suspense before that Power sublime
    We bow, who willed in him
To stamp a trace more vast, more grand,
Of His own all-creative hand.

The trembling and tempestuous thrill
  Of thought, of purpose high,
The anxious heart, th' unbending will,
  That burned to rule or die,
And grasped and held a power, a scope
Not Folly's self had dared to hope;
   All this he proved; and glory bright,
    Enhanced by perils past,
   The strife, the victory, the flight,
    And exile sad, at last;
Twice prostrate, in the dust o'erthrown,
And twice exalted to a throne.

He NAMED HIMSELF!—in death-like gloom,
 Against each other armed,
To him, expectant of their doom,
 Two Ages turn—alarmed;
He saw, judged, spake his sovereign will,
And at the mandate both were still!
 He VANISHED!—on a lonely Isle,
  In languor closed his days,
 A mark for Envy's baleful smile,
  For Pity's softest lays;
For inextinguishable Hate,
And Love, triumphant over Fate!

As on the shipwrecked wretch's head
 The o'erwhelming billow weighs,
From which but now, with arms outspread,
 And wandering, wistful gaze,
He vainly strove, while heaved on high,
Some far-off headland to descry;
 Thus on that Soul the gathering shade
  Of sad reflection fell;
 Alas! how often he essayed
  His own vast tale to tell;
While on the eternal page, unmanned,
Down sank his listless hand!

And oh! how oft when pensive day
 Was lingering in the west,—
Downcast those eyes of lightning-ray,
 Arms folded on his breast,—
He stood, while memory of the past
Its quivering flashes round him cast:
 Again, in glory's day revealed,
  He saw his eagles fly;
 The waving plume, the tented field,
  The squadrons rushing by;
Warriors, that heard but to obey—
Monarchs, who crouched beneath his sway!

Mid pangs like these, against despair
 The breathless Spirit strove,
Fast-sinking; but a hand was there,
 In pity, from above;
Wafting him to a purer clime,
And leading him, through paths sublime,
 That cloudless hopes inspire,
To prize eternal, which exceeds
 The bosom's fond desire,
Where glory round his noontide played—
Now but silence and a shade!

Lovely, beneficent, divine,
 To noblest triumphs prone,
Do thou, O Faith! with joy benign
 Inscribe upon his stone,
That never eminence more proud
To the Last Enemy has bowed.
 True to his merits as his faults,
  Be hushed all harsher zeal;
 The God who prostrates and exalts,
  Who wounds, but loves to heal,
That pitying God was there to shed
A solace on his lonely bed!

WHAT IS MAN: A SONNET.

BY S. D. DAKIN.

MAN's spirit is a vapor, pressed to earth,
While on it Doubt and Error darkly lie ;
But with the light quick seeks the upper sky,
Pleased to regain the regions of its birth ;
Suspended for a while 'twixt earth and heaven,
And bathing in the light its God bestows,
From the pure depths where its bright essence glows,
It sees new beauty to the round earth given,
E'en by the very distance it has gained ;
And shining from that height in glory's crown,
It scorns not earth, that once its brightness stained,
But sheds the dews of love and pity down,
Refreshing all her plains, in gloomiest night,
And winning followers, by the morning light.

THE PIC-NIC.

CHAPTER SECOND.

THE STRIPES' RIDE IN A CAB.

'Sunt quos curriculo.'

DICK was by habit and principle a peripatetic. He hated all kinds of vehicles, and notably the new cabs. He hated rail-roads also, and sat railing at them, looking out at one window, and his wife at the other, upon the retreating Broad-street. 'The poetry of travelling,' said he, ' is gone. Domesticity is gone. Our people, restless enough already, are now totally unsettled; as erratic as the Arabs. The adventure too of travelling is reduced to the simple bursting of a boiler. Steam has set its foot upon pastoral life as effectually as gunpowder upon chivalry.' He wondered if the world would grow happier by all these facilities — going to Boston in two days instead of two weeks; and then he wondered if hens were happier since they have found out the way of hatching chickens by steam ; when bob went his head against the side of the cab, and rebounded by a violent repercussion against Mrs. Stripe's bump of combativeness. The window was fractured, the lady's bonnet smashed, and her temper ruffled. A rude push from his fair moïety followed, and a storm of reproaches ; to all which Dick submitted patiently, saying nothing of the bit of glass that stuck into his *os sincipitis.*

There is no keeping down the ascendency of the petticoats. Solomon, as great a clerk as any of us about women, has said as much. Indeed I have never read or heard of any one married man, whatever his pretensions to independence, who was not in some way or other subject to this sway; unless perhaps Adam, and he only before the fall. I am aware that Peter Martyr and St. Christopher hold different opinions on this point; but the latter seems to me to be in the right, who saith that Eve, being formed of her husband's uppermost rib, commenced in some sort her authority before she was born. What signify the salique laws? In France, where they exist in greatest rigor, woman's authority is supreme. What signify any human laws? She rules by divine right.

Nor does the sceptre of this gynocratic empire extend only upon husbands. States are as subject to it as individuals; even our republic, which is as hen-pecked as any of the old countries of Europe. Happily!— for what has thrown upon the sternness of our republicanism so many of the gentle graces of life; what but woman has reclaimed this country itself from the barbarism of its aboriginal inhabitants; planted these sumptuous dwellings upon a spot where but a century and a half ago the panther screamed and the wolf suckled her whelps, and covered with superb navies this lordly river, that a little beyond the life of one of our transitory species rolled its tide through the lone and silent wilderness? America! thou bright occidental star, now rivalling with the radiance of thy name the splendor of the ancient world, but for a woman * thou hadst yet slept in the great repository of things unknown upon the earth!

I do not repine. There is as much pleasure in obedience as command. I love a wife who governs. I mean with somewhat a limited monarchy, like that spoken of by Juliet, who would let her husband ' hop a little from her hand,' and then with a silken thread pull him back again. However, Mrs. Stripe was so beautiful that even her tyranny was agreeable. There was a *je ne sais quoi* about her that so fascinated Dick — something like that charm which snakes exercise upon toads — that he would sit and gaze upon the smooth alabaster and rich mantling red of her complexion, for the live-long day, and not even conceive a wish to get his feet loose from the connubial trap in which he had been caught; and she had by degrees gained such a mastery over his meek and uxorious disposition, that he now obeyed her almost instinctively. He did indeed once — it was in a fit of excessive impatience — kick Mrs. Stripe's slippers, which lay on the floor, she not being present; but his conscience smiting him, he took them up after a little while and laid them side by side of each other in a corner.

It is at least two miles from Broad-street and Chestnut to Fair Mount. To relieve a little the tedium of the ride, I will relate to you, gentle reader, by what accidents Mr. and Mrs. Stripe, in whom by this time you must have felt some interest, were joined in holy wedlock. I knew Mr. Stripe well, being of the same county, and therefore

---

* Isabella.

qualified in this respect to be his biographer. We used to eat together out of the same dish, love the same girl, and were whipped together at the same school; our noses were frosted together; we often ran to get ahead of the moon, and against the wind, trying to spit in our own faces. It is perhaps known to most of my readers that some years ago General Jackson made a tour to the eastern states of this great republic, and that on his way thither he fell in with Philadelphia, into which city he made a *grand entrée.* I remember the very time. It was of a summer's morning — I forget the year. We went out, five hundred in a squad, to meet him upon the Delaware; and as he passed by, smoking his pipe, seated on a chair with one leg mounted upon the knee of the other, we crowded to the margin of the steam-boat for a nearer view: the boat tilted, and the water came upon deck; we rushed to the other side, and the boat tilted again; and we kept running and screaming from one side to the other, to the imminent hazard of our lives, till at length our captain, a man grave by his piety, and ripe in age and experience, stood upon the middle of the deck, and said: 'D — n your souls! if you do n't stop in the middle of the boat you will be drowned, every devil of you!' And then seizing the younger population by the petticoats, he compelled them to stand. General Jackson took the pipe out of his mouth, and the equilibrium was restored. I have established it as a rule of prudence ever since this occurrence, that in emergencies we should avoid extremes; and that safety is somewhere about the middle.

The General landed at the navy-yard, and bestriding a mettlesome steed in waiting, proceeded onward, with the city at his heels. He had a commanding brow, a lank Kentucky face; and his hair, white and stiff, stood bristled upward like ramrods. The horse too was gray, 'but not with age,' and he pranced, and reared, and bounded sometimes; but the General stuck to him as if a part of the same animal. He rode bare-head, bowing incontinently, now on this side, now on that; the multitude pouring around him like the noise of many waters, and greeting him with shouts — inextinguishable shouts, which I despair of making any one accustomed only to the ordinary noise comprehend. Some of you may perhaps have heard Wellington's musketry on the 'Day of Waterloo,' on Hyde Park, and can conceive ten thousand explosions concentrated into one general and uninterrupted crack, an hour long. Several birds which flew over are reported on this occasion to have fallen down dead. The newspapers had announced this grand *entrée* two weeks before, and invited us to turn out and be overjoyed; and we were overjoyed, just as the newspapers had predicted.

It is perhaps also known to my readers that congress once voted us to be 'the most enlightened people upon the earth;' and so we are. We do n't go quite so high up as some of the old countries into the transcendant branches: but as for all that learning most necessary to life, such as religion and morals, and political economy, and the whole science of politics, and also arithmetic, it is universally diffused among this people; above all, in Pennsylvania — excepting about two-thirds of them, who 'can't read only but Dutch.' Now it is not to be wondered at that some rays of this universal illumination should have penetrated the obscurity of the Tuscarora Mountain; where, scutching flax, hoeing potatoes and planting cabbages, lived old Mrs. Stripe.

One Saturday evening, as Dick sat reading the ' Pennsylvanian,' (for it goes every where,) the advertisement above alluded to fell under his notice; and as he read it over, a thought like inspiration struck old Mrs. Stripe; and what do you think it was? It was to ' send Dick down to Pheladelphy to see the world and General Jackson.' The truth is, she suspected Dick, in addition to his other merits, of being very brave, and secretly hoped he might one day perhaps be made a general himself; and there was no knowing how soon the republic might have need of his services. We had to be sure more than we wanted of territory, yet she knew that was no reason for not quarrelling about boundaries. Beside, she foresaw that we might take up some British subject, too big a coward to kill any one, and hang him for a murderer. We were a very spirited nation, she said, and a very slight puff would blow open the temple of Janus. Not that Dick had ever shown any great stomach for fighting himself, but he had had a great-grandfather, of the maternal branch, who had been killed at Quebec, with Montgomery; a man of such extraordinary bravery that he not only made great havoc of the English while living, but actually ran about fighting for a minute or two after he had been shot fourteen times through the heart. (See Sparks's Revolution.)

It was resolved therefore that Dick should set out; and the old gentleman brought forth a leathern bag containing, in fi'ppeny bits, about fifty dollars, which had been accumulating for a series of years, and handed it over to Mrs. Stripe to defray the expenses of the journey; with indeed some reluctance, for he had destined it, after reaching the necessary amount, to the purchase of a horse; but his philosophy was, not to allow the slightest opposition to his better half; and they had discussed the matter together. Man and wife, he said, were a couple of instruments designed to play together, and should be tuned to the same key; vessels bound on the same voyage, and should sail on the same tack. A man, he said proverbially, who would have a mule without fault, should not keep any; and he must sail obliquely who would overcome a torrent. It was by these observances that, beside furnishing a wholesome example to his son Dick, he had avoided all those matrimonial broils which so often imbitter life in the purest fountain of human felicity.

We contemplate with very different feelings a journey at a remote time and at the hour of separation from the domestic ties. The sad day arrived, and Richard bade his friends and sweethearts farewell; and last of all, mingling his tears with theirs, took leave of his affectionate parents. Alas, human improvidence! Little did they know, as they pressed their darling boy to their bosoms, that it was a separation for eternity! Little did the fond mother think, that for the last time she felt the warm pressure of his lips; and the poor father, as he gave way to the holy feelings of parental affection, and stretched his eyes after the retiring vehicle, that he had caught his last earthly glimpse of Richard Stripe!

Rivulets and refreshing shades; loves and gambols of the village, farewell !   The hills of Tuscarora, the Blacklog and Blue mountain receded from the view, and became gradually level with the plain; and Richard, on the second evening after his departure, was set down, as if by enchantment, in Philadelphia — the city being all bustle and parade of preparation for the ensuing magnificent fête — without any more memorable occurrence than mistaking the Susquehanna for the ocean, an upset in the stage under side of four ladies, trunks and other baggage, and finally being awakened at Lancaster by the watchman's cry of ' *Twelve o'clock !* ' which he mistook for some dreadful alarm; sitting in consequence upon the bed-side the long night, after hurrying on his clothes, ruminating upon what noise had thus robbed him of his sleep and so defamed music of its harmony.   He had heard the panther scream and the wolves howl upon the Alleghany, but sounds such as these had not yet pierced his ears.   Sleep therefore fled his eye-lids, and a thousand apparitions haunted his brain till morning.

Richard, as I said, was set down from the stage in Market-street, and by the guidance of a fellow traveller lodged for the first night at the widow Snap's boarding-house, Sansom-street, one of the prettiest retirements of the city.   It is perhaps known to most of my readers that to the lower chambers upon the south side of this street is commodiously appended a wide piazza-roof, extending to the extremity of the row or square.   The air was hot; and our stranger, used to inhale the fresh mountain breeze, feeling something like suffocation, threw wide the windows, and admitted the still hotter atmosphere of the city; then prostrating himself upon his bed, snored loudly toward heaven. But on his desolate home that night no god of sleep poured the oblivious balm.   Retiring to rest, Mrs. Stripe heard a mournful shriek, like the wailings of a troubled spirit; a screech-owl hooted from a neighboring tree ; the watch-dog howled melancholy; and the night winds sighed along the hollow shores of the Juniata.   Now hardly had the night clomb half way in the heavens, when one of those ordinary members of a civilized community vulgarly called a thief mounted upon the roof, and directing the ' noiseless tenor of his way ' to Dick's chamber, removed, in the way of his business, the whole of Richard's apparel, partly from his trunk and partly from the back of a chair in the proximity of the windows, while the owner slept, ' unconscious of the theft.' His whole wardrobe was actually stolen, not excepting that department of it which lay nearest his heart; for to look spruce next morning at the General's *entrée*, he had taken the precaution to sleep without his shirt.

As soon as the bright day had poured its light upon his eye-lids, he arose, full of life and animation.   But judge of the alarm that was gradually communicated to his feelings on learning the extent of his misfortunes ; that his fine ruffled-shirt, cotton hose, new pantaloons, shoes, trunk — in fine the whole stock of his habiliments — were missing ; and imagine how he paced the floor of his chamber in agony, looking earnestly through the window to catch a glance of the thief; then recoiling from the prying eyes of Hetty and Kitty, laughing aloud from the opposite garret of Walnut-street at his distresses !   For two whole hours he remained in this state of nakedness and discomfort, a prey to the most melancholy reflections ; one while devising expedients of escape, and then bursting out into bitter lamentations; and finally, smothering his face in his pillow, he relieved himself with a flood of tears.

A gentle rap was at length heard at the door. It was Mrs. Snap, who hailed him with the usual salutation of 'Breakfast!' Richard arose and advanced cautiously toward the door, where standing with intro-verted knees and pendant arms, he explained through the key-hole as well as he could the condition of his affairs, in a tremulous and inar-ticulate voice, often smothered by his feelings beyond the power of utterance. To add to the infelicity of his situation there was not in the house any male servant to act as ambassador between the two parties; and it was not till after long hesitation that he yielded to the entreaties, and finally the orders, of his landlady to open the door; and no sooner had the key turned upon its grooves than he was again buried in his downy refuge, with not less precipitation than one of those frightened Greeks who returned into the belly of the Trojan horse; and the lady entered.

I pass over in silence this interview; remarking only a similar situa-tion described by Homer, of Ulysses and the fair princess Nausica, to which the readers of this Magazine are respectfully referred. Dick's leathern purse, containing about fifty dollars, having been the preceding evening laid with his watch upon a table, both these articles had escaped the furious grasp of his nocturnal visiter. It was therefore agreed that a suit ready made should be procured; which by the assi-duity of his hostess was accomplished forthwith; and Richard, to his own astonishment, was presented to the company in the parlor, in less than fifty minutes from that time, braced in the panoply of a man; a celerity of execution of which the experience of his native village could have furnished him with no example.

The attention and sympathy of the guests, especially of the ladies, who had been apprised of his misfortunes, were now turned upon him, and the success of his *début* at the breakfast-table was complete. The rich blood, from the agitation of the morning, glowed in his cheek with more than usual ruddiness; and the rustic honesty and candor of his disposition stood out in bright relief upon his countenance, as they were graven there by the hand of their great Author; and that which was not least in the appurtenance of good looks was the suitableness of his new dress. It was contrived to set his person off to the greatest advantage, and cut in the latest fashion by the French tailor Scipio, Second-street; an individual who has conferred more merit upon vari-ous members of this community than any nine men in it of any other profession; and who for the excellent breeches he has cut out is as much entitled to the appellation of the 'Great Scipio' as his name-sake of antiquity for cutting men's throats. All pitied the young vil-lager — all admired him; but especially the devoted Mrs. Snap:

'Explore mentem nequit, ardescitque tuendo.'

She presented herself in her most magnificent attire, as his escort into the city, conducting him through all the mazes of the procession by day and the illumination by night: at all which his eyes were dazzled, his ears ravished, and all his fine senses feasted with delight.

But the love of Mrs. Snap was in the mean time kindled into an inextinguishable flame; and day after day passed away without respite to her passion. She would begin often to speak, and the unfinished sentence expired upon her tongue. Often, her market-basket on her arm, she would wander frantic through the city, forgetting that the hour of dinner was past; as the wounded deer wanders through the vast forest, the deadly arrow of the huntsman still clinging to its side. As Dick related his youthful achievements — how he arrested the sly trout with the spear, or pursued the rabbit to its hollow tree — she would hang upon his lips, and wish that Heaven had made her such a — hunter of rabbits. And when Night had thrown its mantle on the Day, she would sit either alone in her chamber, or press her solitary pillow. Then she seemed to herself to go unaccompanied upon a long journey, or to be abandoned upon a desert island. Thus the reputation of her house was neglected; the cat sipped the cream, and the beef-steak took fire upon the gridiron.

There was a merry fellow who supped at Plato's three thousand years ago; and the conversation turning upon love and choice of wives, he said: ' He had learnt from a very ancient tradition that men had been originally created male and female; each individual being provided with a duplicate set of limbs, and performing his locomotive functions with a kind of rotatory movement, as a wheel; that he became in consequence so excessively insolent that Jupiter, indignant, split him in two; and since that time that each half runs about the world in quest of its other half: if the two congenital halves meet, they are a very loving couple; otherwise they are subject to a miserable, scolding, peevish, and uncongenial matrimony. The search he said was rendered difficult, for the reason that one man alighting upon a half that did not belong to him, another did necessarily the same, till the whole affair was thrown into irretrievable confusion.' But here I am moralizing as if the day stood still. All that is necessary for you to know farther, dear reader, is that Richard Stripe, Esq. is irrevocably married to Mrs. Snap; that turning the Latin he had acquired from the village clergyman to account, he kept a school and his wife the house, till his father's decease, which has given him possession of an independent fortune, and leisure for pic-nics and other matrimonial recreations. An episode, saith Aristotle, may be happily used to relieve the monotony of a narrative; but if long, it may retard its progress. I hope you find this the proper length. We return to Mr. and Mrs. Stripe, whom we left pouting in a cab, full tilt toward Fair-Mount.

For a mile or so Mrs. Stripe was gruff and snappish, but relented by degrees. The lively green of spring opening on the view communicated a pleasurable feeling; as they approached the country there was a delicious freshness and healthiness in the air; except in the suburbs it was now and then a little miasmatic. And after all, there is something joyous in the bumping up and down of a cab that disposes to good-humor. It makes little girls giggle; it would have made Mrs. Stripe laugh out, but for her husband's presence. Also he had transferred a bouquet of daisies from his own to Chip's button-hole, picked off a feather from her frock, and performed other such tender offices as might propitiate her displeasure. Good humor was Mrs. Stripe's best aspect, and she admitted his attentions with a smile, as she alighted amidst the crowd standing about the stairs leading up to the great basin. It threw a new charm upon her features, and gave the lookers-on a favorable presumption of Dick's conjugal felicity.

MOUNTING THE STAIRS.

'Whereto the climber upward turns his face.'—SHAKSPERE.

THE ascent by these stairs is very steep and long, and gives quite a fair chance to a lady going up and down of showing her address — also her ankles; and to encourage innocent little vanities of this kind, a number of amateurs are seen standing underneath and patiently gazing upward, like so many astronomers. The number of the fair who mount daily by these stairs is wonderful; the reason, some think, of calling the place Fair-Mount. (See Osmond's Etymology.) Mrs. Stripe was puzzled. She had a very pretty pair of *papooshes* at home, of muslin, crimped at the extremities; and though used to wear these emblems of domestic authority in common, she had left them off to-day by reason of the heat; and how to get up the stairs in her present untrousered condition! While she stood irresolute, Dick ventured a little Latin: *Fas mihi conspecta loqui;* and he translated it thus: 'My love, Mrs. Trusscot, the Frenchwoman, garters her · · · '

The dark eye-brows of Mrs. Stripe clashed together in a frown that froze Dick into instant silence. He was yet a novice in the genteel world, and knew not how much more chaste ears are than eyes in a refined state of society. For example, he would *talk* of Fanny Elssler's garters over the knee as innocently as other people would *look* at them. But Mrs. Stripe was of better breeding, being brought up in the city. Indeed she was particular in this. She would never allow little Chip, when she found out the etymology of the word, to say *mamma*. The truth is, Mrs. Stripe's ankles (I regret to say it of one so unexceptionable in all other respects) were not of an exhibitive species; therefore the indelicacy of such displays seemed to her the more flagrant. Indeed it was a remark of Dick's, (which he kept to himself,) that those who were running so without scruple up and down the stairs were of very perfect forms, generally speaking; differing it is true in some fundamental points from the genuine English style, but nearer in his conception to the atticism and concinnity of the elegant Greeks, who were his models — *artium exempla.* He had a little plaster image of the Venus Calipygeia, which stood up on the mantel-piece of his study, in open vindication of the American forms against English authority. Mrs. Stripe's resolution was at length taken. Casting therefore upon a youth who stood close by a deprecating look, which made him retrograde three steps, and directing Dick to cover her rear, as far as he could, himself and the basket with little Chip, she ran straight up, knees at

right angles, two steps at a stretch, and stood tip-toe on the utmost
round ; escaping thus the prying eyes of impudent curiosity.

F A I R - M O U N T .

WHEN it has pleased the poetic fancy of men to paint human Happiness, they have placed her usually in a valley.   I suspect the nymph to
be a native of the mountains.   It is a pleasant sight, a city at one's
feet ; it is pleasant to be above so many of the grovelling species.   One
breathes a purer air, and feels proud of his nearer intimacy with the
angels.   Mrs. Stripe stood still in contemplation of the vast and beautiful prospect ; the immense city ; the lordly Delaware and its navies ;
the villages of Hamilton and Mantua spread upon the landscape ; and
the Schuylkill so transparent* that its top and bottom seemed but one ;
and beyond, a hundred little hills lying affectionately at the side of each
other, and lifting up their faces toward heaven.   And Lemon-Hill ! · · ·
Thou luxury of the rich ! — thou resting-place of the disconsolate !
Thou art bare and desolate now.   Thy shrubs, sweeter than Araby,
have withered.   Thy old castle stands a bleak solitary tenement, and
thy giant oak stretches forth its arms, a leafless skeleton.   Alas ! thou
hast fallen under the *cui-bono* clutches of a joint-stock company, and
thy lemons and palmettos under the hammer of the auctioneer !   Sweet
Lemon-Hill !   I knew thee in thy palmy days ; in the rosy spring ; in
the scorching canicule, when sweet-briar, ivy, and honey-suckle crept
around thy cottages ; in the hazy skies of the Indian-summer, when the
sere leaf, loosened from its branch, came slowly fluttering toward the
ground !   I have brushed the dew of morning from the mullen's vel-
vety leaf ; wandered under shelter of the 'Syrian heats' through the
cool shades, and from a loop-hole looked out upon the low and skulking city ; or sat at eve by the lonely Schuylkill, the murmuring water-
fall underneath, while the owl hooted over head, and the wild and wailing whip-poor-will brought on the night.   He is fit for any other havoc
who with dry eyes could decree this destruction.   Nature had not put
a grain of ideality into his bumpless occiput.   So fare thee well ! sweet
Lemon Hill !   Farewell to thy lakes and silver-fish ; to thy woodlands
and dimpled hills ; to thy

> —— 'delicati colli
> Chiace aque, ambrose ripe, et pratti molli.'

The Girard College stands proudly on its eminence.   The neighboring houses seem to crouch with humility in its presence — itself the
ornament of a city.   Whoever refuses his admiration, or connives not
at the violent breach of trust by which it was reared, alas! he has not
visited the Ægean shore nor stood upon the Acropolis.   There, where
the wretch sits solitary at his penance, the Penitentiary, instead of
cowering in shame, rears its head impudently ; and the 'House of
Refuge,' low skulking in a corner, where perverse youth is hardened or
reclaimed, covers its acres.   The cotted hills rise up toward the west,

---

* When filtered.

and huts and cows and trees seem painted on the opposite sky. Toward the east the easy citizens take the air upon distant roads. Now a coach whirls by, enveloped in its dust; a rider, his horse pushed to the utmost acceleration of his speed, devours the road, or mounted six inches over his saddle, churns the air in his stirrups, trotting melancholy. Church-bells are chiming in the distance, cow-bells are dingling on the commons; a funeral jogs slowly on toward Laurel Hill; and an old horse, worn to his ribs, is turned out to starve by hard-hearted man. All these objects presented themselves successively to the vivid and fresh admiration of Mrs. Stripe.

But Richard, no lover of rural images, mounted a terrace and looked down upon the city. He admired, for want of steeples, the shot-tower, and he admired the chimneys that stood up smoking so sociably at the side of one another; then seeing the ten thousand streets and alleys choked up with human beings, and contemplating their busy and impatient ardor silently; their hastening, crowding, and jostling each other; stretching out his neck, he proclaimed to the utmost extent of his vociferation, making a funnel of his two hands:

> —— 'O cives! cives!
> Quærenda pecunia premiem et virtus post nummos!'

And little Chip, in the mean time, spiritualized by the lively air and rural liberty, ran about chattering like a *blatherskite*, as they say in the simple Doric of the country; and there was a general flow of good humor. Mrs. Stripe, as she looked around upon the enchanting scenes, felt all the springs of enjoyment opened in her heart — and she felt a little hungry.

THE DINNER.

The valley intervening between Fair-Mount and Lemon-Hill was soon traversed by the little party; and at the side of a piney thicket which served for a screen, having the dam at her feet and the romantic scenery which skirts the right bank of the river in perspective, down sat Mrs. Stripe on a bed of moss; and the bed of moss seemed joyous at being sat upon by so fair a lady. The basket was now unpacked, and the rich bounties of Ceres spread upon their mother earth: ham, cold eggs, fresh butter, and little loaves almost jumping from the plate with lightness; and under the ministration of Mrs. Stripe's rosy fingers, rosy as Aurora's, the cork leaped from the bottle. To Mrs. Stripe's fancy these were rare and unappreciable delicacies. Her taste was yet undebauched by the adulteries of art, and she lived in blissful ignorance of Monsieur Ude and Jean de Caréme. Pity! that sinful, vexatious knowledge should have got into the paradise of woman! She espied suddenly at only ten paces a man reclining in an idylic attitude upon a rock, with a book, apparently wrapped in his meditations. He was unobserved by any other eyes but the pretty gray eyes of Mrs. Stripe. She thought no more of eating; though women have a capacity for this branch equal to the other sex. 'What's the matter, my love? You look pale!' said the husband. And little Chip, who was not yet helped, looked with a kind of canine expression of countenance upon his mother and then upon the knife which stood still in a rosy and delicate rump of cold mutton. But it was discovered that an essential ingredient of the repast was wanting — and Mrs. Stripe was very dry. (A long pause.)

'And so you sit there, your two feet in one sock! Why do n't you hasten to the tavern there below, and have some brought?'

And Richard vanished, disappearing round the brow of the hill, in quest of the liquid element for which Mrs. Stripe thirsted; for which cities have surrendered, and kings have been made slaves.

It was a fairy spot. Flora's prettiest buds were unbuttoned by the Spring. Just overhead a leaf was flirting with a zephyr. A squirrel was sitting on a limb munching a nut. The winds played wantonly with Mrs. Stripe's tresses, dishevelled her frock of the pure multicaulis, and rippled the surface of the wizard stream; and as the strange gentleman seated himself by her, all the heaven of her beauty was lighted up to a glow. Her bonnet hung upon a branch, and a single curl, loosened from its fastnesses, lay upon the lily of her bosom, rising and sinking, as a light feather upon a billow. The rules of high breeding require a lady always to speak first on such emergencies. It would not be quite civil in a gentleman to be less smothered by his emotions than she. Though words cost Mrs. Stripe no more on common occasions than to the brook its babbling, on this could she not utter a monosyllable. At length, stretching out her hands, she said in a low soft voice, soft as Love's first whisper, as the breeze on beds of flowers, as the murmurings of the waters when they meet at midnight; she said:

'What book? · · · '

To which the gentleman, in the same subdued and tremulous accent, replied:

'Childe Harold!'

Mrs. Stripe then read silently, eyeing occasionally the gentleman, then hummingly:

'The long file of her dead doges!'

'What careless wretches these printers are! A pretty way of spelling *dogs!*'

These English are facetious and clever when set a-going, but it is troublesome to break their 'confounded ice.' Mr. Ketchup had now kissed little Chip and stuck a johnny-jump-up in his cap. 'The sweet little fellow! — so like his mother!' And the conversation was kindled.

'What a romantic little wood! I will stroll here often with a book. In just such a spot Myrtillus died of love of the Nine Sisters.'

'Oh the wretch! He should have been prosecuted for bigamy!'

Here he related to her a pathetic tale, a legend of the place, at which Mrs. Stripe wept, and laid her head upon his shoulder, and Chip wept in sympathy with his mother, and put his head upon the gentleman's knee. I will perhaps tell it to you one of these days, Mr. KNICKERBOCKER; if I do it will make you cry too. And now they had nearly finished the dinner, and the second bottle was uncorked, when Richard glided softly and unnoticed behind the hedge, in time to hear a part of the interesting conversation.

'The truth is, dear Stripe, it is not enough that a woman be amiable and beautiful; there must be in her husband the taste and understanding to appreciate such qualities; and to judge by Mr. Stripe's expression · · ·'

'Expression! Did you ever hear of the expression of a wig-block?'

'He appears to me not likely to discover any thing else in a wife than the common properties of matter — length, breadth, and thickness.'

'Nor is this all, Captain; you see how long he stays at the tavern. (A little wine, if you please.) I fear he is getting habits of intemperance; and the tears started in Mrs. Stripe's eyes as she set down her glass. The conversation now grew more confidential, and by degrees they sat closer and closer; till some how or other the winds seemed to hold their breath! Some how or other their lips came together in a kiss! Mrs. Stripe, half forced, half consenting, half pleased, half affrighted, shrunk back; and oh horror! Richard Stripe stood before her! He uttered not a word. His teeth and fists were clenched and his whole frame seemed convulsed with an agony of passion: and then he turned with a scowl, as a cloud that threatens a hurricane, upon the English captain, who recoiled and assumed an attitude of defence. 'I am not going to knock you down,' said Richard; 'do n't be afraid! I never knocked any one down except once. It was when I was at school, a boy.'

'You then were fool enough,' interrupted his spouse, who by this time had recovered from her fright, 'to believe that you had stolen across that rustling wood and placed yourself behind that hedge so dexterously without being seen! — with your cat-like watch, which you learnt no doubt from your countrymen the Mohawks! You thought I suppose we had our eyes in our pockets. Sir, it was to punish the baseness of such conduct that this gentleman and I contrived to · · · say aloud what best might ruffle your spirits; and it seems we succeeded. But let me tell you, Sir, such behavior would deserve another chastisement. Why do n't you speak to the gentleman? Captain Ketchup, Mr. Stripe.'

Dick was confused, and ashamed of his misconduct; and mustering the entire stock of his affability tried to salute courteously his guest; but his eyes falling upon the fragments of the dinner and empty bottles, he felt the smile die upon his lips. He accepted however the stranger's hand, and with a very rueful expression of countenance made his apology — for being in the right.

The rain began suddenly to pour down with the rapidity of a May shower. The boys and girls ran helter-skelter over the hills, with their fragrant treasures, to seek shelter in the neighboring houses and villages; and our little party of the pine-hedge made haste to imitate their example. Richard immediately busied himself in collecting the plates, knives, empty bottles, and fragments of the dinner; but rising from the recumbent posture this duty required, he found himself with Chip and the basket, alone; the lady and the stranger having vanished from sight.

'Speluncam Dido, dux et Trojanus eandow.'

He therefore commenced forthwith the pursuit, dragging the little

urchin by the hand; but after many circuitous windings to no purpose, he returned to the spot whence he had set out; and there mounting a tree, stretched his eyes over the forest in all directions; little Chip standing beneath, his knees and chin near together, and looking like a drowned rat.   Maternal affection had in the mean time brought hither the mother, who finding her son, and embracing him in her arms, again disappeared with her cavalier unobserved.   Richard descended. · · ·
Who will attempt to describe the nature of his feelings on this occasion! He wished to run to all points of the compass at once, and stood still in motionless irresolution.   At length he set out to each of the cardinal points in succession, filling the groves of Lemon-Hill with lamentable invocations.   The storm increased, and the heavens darkened almost to night under the scowl of the lowering elements.   The thunder rattled along the flanks of Henry Pratt's garden, and bellowed in the hollow valleys, and the earth shook to the antipodes.   Yet not the less did the wretched man run to and fro, and with the name of the lost child fatigue the echoes of the mountains; *Chip!* the hills, *Chip!* the vales, and *Chip!* the sympathizing streams rebound.

How to revisit the fire-side of Mrs. Stripe!   How alas! to approach the inexorable woman!   At the very thought he was seized with a nervous agitation; and his knees like those knees spoken of in Holy Writ smote upon each other.   Then becoming frantic, he tore his hair; and at last, entirely overcome by his feelings and the vexations of the day, he burst into tears; and prostrating himself upon the earth, poured out his soul in loud sobs and lamentations.

By this explosion of feeling the exacerbation of his grief was in some measure assuaged.   It was the sobbings of the abated storm. · · · But I have now reached the last chapter of my narrative.

THE RETURN.

—

' Pluit tota nocte, redeunt spectacula mane.'

—

DARKNESS had now risen out of the west; the stars again twinkled in their spheres; and the village cock counted the night-watches to his feathery dames; and Richard Stripe pursued his way toward the city. He was now to appear before Mrs. Stripe, to render her an account of the melancholy loss of her son!   He summoned his reflections, and endeavored to acquire a proper tone of mind for the emergency.   ' Let a man,' said he, ' show at least the temper of his manhood, and if he must die, let him not die without a battle.'   But as he came near his own dwelling he felt these valorous dispositions die away within him. A religious horror came upon his countenance, and he shook like a leaf. He approached home with almost inaudible footsteps and suppressed respiration, and placed his bent knee upon the marble, where the accents of his redoubtable partner for life fell like the cold north upon his heart. He was startled, and would have shrunk in terror from the door; but he lingered yet awhile, with an ear pressed closely to the key-hole, in the faint hope that he might perhaps catch the voice of the unfortunate Chip. That voice which had so often molested his repose by day and by night ; which so often he had deprecated in secret curses ; he would have given the world to hear now, in its most aggravated discord. Alas! it was (and he thought for the first time) silent! Not a note floating upon the air! The little urchin, unconscious of his father's agony, was wrapped in innocent slumbers upon his couch.

Richard returned again to the street, where he passed and repassed his own door, a prey to the bitterest afflictions ; his hands now clenched in anguish upon his brow, and now, to the astonishment of the passer-by, bursting into exclamations of distress. 'Chip! Chip! Would that I could have died for thee!' Thrice he had taken the knocker, resolved to announce his arrival, and thrice his paternal hands had failed to execute their office.

As he stood with limbs paralyzed in motionless gaze, he was suddenly accosted by a woman who rushed precipitately from an adjoining alley : 'For Heaven's sake, hold this infant till I run across the street for the doctor! His father is dying! Alas! Sir, he will die, without the help of the doctor!'

Richard instinctively held out his arms, and found the infant pressed upon his benevolent bosom. The woman immediately vanished from his sight, running with the utmost speed ; and for aught any one knows is running yet — for she has never since come back!

Richard looked with tenderness upon the sleeping babe, pressing it to his bosom. He pitied its dying father — he pitied its mother. Then he looked again upon the interesting creature ; indulging sometimes, as he walked up and down, in a silent wish that he had had himself such a son. Thus a considerable time passed away, and he continued to cradle the little human being in his arms. At length he was seen to turn his eyes frequently toward the opposite side of the street, and his features gradually assumed an expression of surprise. This was however soon removed by a scrap of paper which he accidentally perceived pinned upon the child's bosom, and which being read over by the light of the street-lamp, informed him that Richard Stripe was the sole proprietor and disposer of the infant. At this moment the little creature awakening, began to evince its displeasure at the open air and bad nursing, by the most clamorous outcries. A crowd, in an instant, composed chiefly of his neighbors and intimate acquaintances, gathered about. The child still continued its obstreperous squalling ; and Dick, sensible of the ludicrous predicament in which he stood, was covered with confusion. At this moment his own door flying open, to escape the interrogatives or sneers of the mob, he rushed into the parlor, and found himself suddenly in the presence of Mrs. Stripe, holding out the child!

He stood like one who had seen the snaky head of Medusa. No one who looked upon that petitionary and apologetic face will forget its expression ever. Not a muscle, not a limb but had lost the faculty of motion. But in despair I must leave the rest to the imagination of my readers. Perhaps some one of them may have seen the condemned wretch look upward upon the gibbet from which he is about to be suspended!

THE ANTIQUITY OF FREEDOM.

BY WILLIAM CULLEM BRYANT.

HERE are old trees, tall oaks and gnarléd pines
That stream with gray-green mosses ; here the ground
Was never trenched by spade, and flowers spring up
Unsown and die ungathered.   It is sweet
To linger here, among the flitting birds
And leaping squirrels, wandering brooks, and winds
That shake the leaves, and scatter as they pass
A fragrance from the cedars thickly set
With pale blue berries.   In these peaceful shades —
Peaceful, unpruned, immeasurably old —
My thoughts go up the long dim path of years,
Back to the earliest days of liberty.

Oh FREEDOM ! thou art not, as poets dream,
A fair young girl, with light and delicate limbs,
And wavy tresses gushing from the cap
With which the Roman master crowned his slave,
When he took off the gyves.   A bearded man,
Armed to the teeth, art thou ; one mailéd hand
Grasps the broad shield, and one the sword ; thy brow,
Glorious in beauty though it be, is scarred
With tokens of old wars ; thy massive limbs
Are strong with struggling.   Power at thee has launched
His bolts, and with his lightnings smitten thee :
They could not quench the life thou hast from heaven.
Merciless Power has dug thy dungeon deep,
And his swart armorers, by a thousand fires,
Have forged thy chain ; yet while he deems thee bound,
The links are shivered, and the prison walls
Fall outward : terribly thou springest forth,
As springs the flame above a burning pile,
And shoutest to the nations, who return
Thy shoutings, while the pale oppressor flies.

Thy birth-right was not given by human hands :
Thou wert twin-born with man.   In pleasant fields,
While yet our race was few, thou sat'st with him,
To tend the quiet flock and watch the stars,
And teach the reed to utter simple airs.
Thou by his side amid the tangled wood
Didst war upon the panther and the wolf,
Thine only foes ; and thou with him didst draw
The earliest furrows on the mountain side,
Soft with the Deluge.   Tyranny himself,
Thy enemy, although of reverend look,
Hoary with many years, and far obeyed,
Is later born than thou ; and as he meets
The grave defiance of thine elder eye,
The usurper trembles in his fastnesses.

Thou shalt wax stronger with the lapse of years,
But he shall fade into a feebler age :
Feebler, yet subtler ; he shall weave his snares,
And spring them on thy careless steps, and clap

His withered hands, and from their ambush call
His hordes to fall upon thee.   He shall send
Quaint maskers, forms of fair and gallant mien,
To catch thy gaze, and uttering graceful words
To charm thy ear; while his sly imps, by stealth,
Twine round thee threads of steel, light thread on thread,
That grow to fetters; or bind down thy arms
With chains concealed in chaplets.   Oh! not yet
May'st thou unbrace thy corslet, or lay by
Thy sword, nor yet, O Freedom! close thy lids
In slumber; for thine enemy never sleeps,
And thou must watch and combat, till the day
Of the new earth and heaven.   But would'st thou rest
Awhile from tumult and from treachery,
These old and friendly solitudes invite
Thy visit.   They, while yet the forest trees
Were young upon the unviolated earth,
And yet the moss-stains on the rock were new,
Beheld thy glorious childhood, and rejoiced.

GRENADA AND THE ALHAMBRA.

BY REV. GEORGE B. CHEEVER.

You have done me the kindness, Mr. EDITOR, to request for publication some of my notes on Grenada and the Alhambra.   My materials are very simple; but inasmuch as the route we took is not one beaten into powder by travellers, simplicity itself may have something of the charm of novelty.   Our journey to Grenada was undertaken in the latter part of the month of March, though had it been possible, we would rather have deferred it till the sweeter month of May.   Do not however connect the season in your mind with the dreary storms of that wintry month in New-England, for though we were unfortunately in the rainy fortnight of the Andalusian spring, yet the earth was putting on her green dress, and the wheat was in the tender blade.

The first thing to be attended to was our passport, which is requisite even in passing from one city to another; and the next our mode of conveyance, for which we concluded to apply to an honest old fellow who lives near the cathedral, and keeps a complement of carriages and mules, hiring himself out with them as the driver.   A rude sign over the door of his livery establishment proclaims his avocation in the following terms: *Aqui vive Bautiste, alquila coches para todos partes:* ' Here lives Battiste, who lets coaches for all parts.'   We were received by the furious barking of the dogs at the door, but the old dame his wife soon unbarred the portal, and in the absence of her good man showed us the array of equipages to which our choice for the journey must be restricted, and promised that Battiste should come to us as soon as he returned, and propose his terms.   The old fellow demanded thirty dollars for his vehicle and mules, and a certain sum per day while he should remain at Grenada; a bargain to which he contrived to add in his own favor, when we came to settle with him on our return, a number of francs as a gift, imploring us to remember his wife and children, and the increase of his family.

Behold us then, at six o'clock in the morning, on our way from the city of Malaga to Grenada. Our carriage was just such an one as I remember to have seen depicted in the frontispiece of old books; a square, antique and rather aristocratic-looking vehicle, on four wheels, with seats for four passengers. It was drawn by three mules, or animals of a breed between the horse and the mule, with rather less than the usual proportion of bells and tassels, while the harness had nothing to boast save that it was in no respect deficient as to clumsiness. Our muleteer, Battiste, was a good-natured native Andalusian, (though, if I remember rightly, we were afterward told that he was born in Genoa,) with a spice of humor in his composition, and all the stubborn patience requisite for driving his mules at the rate of a little more than three miles an hour. He was attended by a shaggy little dog, who had evidently travelled the road before, and knew where his master's stopping places were, for he made up to the *ventas* with the air of an animal very much at home. We had calculated on reaching Grenada in two days, a distance of about eighty miles, but it began to rain as soon as we started, and continued at intervals through all the journey; so that the road soon became very much worse than usual. Until this week there had been scarcely a day's rain for several months, and this was the season for the half year's supply.

During the first day our route lay through a succession of mountains covered with vineyards, the road winding among them in such a manner that the city of Malaga and the Mediterranean continued visible at intervals nearly all the day. The first town we came to was Colmenar, a collection of white walls clustered thick together, with a church and convent in a commanding and picturesque situation. The region between this and Malaga seems as if it had been formed by nature for the express purpose of the cultivation of the vine; nor was there any thing else to be seen than the dark vine-stocks against the soft brown soil, save here and there a plantation of olives. The region is an undulating sea of mountains, from the highest ascent of which the prospect west and north, landward, and south and east toward the Mediterranean, is exciting for its extent and grandeur. In the road and region from Malaga to Grenada there are three divisions; the vine-region, from Malaga to Colmenar, a region of rocky mountains and pasturage intermingled; from Colmenar to Loxa; and the great Vega of Grenada and the Xenil, from Loxa to the Moorish city. From the commencement of the rocky region the mountain ridges rise on both sides, very similar in their appearance to the rock of Gibraltar, piled up sometimes in savage grandeur, approaching and retreating, with most noble commanding views of the country for many miles. Through all this region you travel onward as through a depopulated state, or a territory from which you might suppose its inhabitants had just fled in the terror of some sudden invasion. Only here and there at very distant intervals is the eye gladdened by the picture of the dwelling by the road-side, and only here and there can a village be distinguished in the distance. When such a thing is seen, the traveller is struck with its close and fortress-like appearance, without any straggling dwellings separate from its walls or in its outskirts. No indications in the increasing population of the country give you notice when you are near a town, and you come upon it directly from the open, unfenced, uncultivated heath. Herds of sheep and goats and droves of black swine straggle along here and there under the care of two or three herdsmen, and now and then a band of peasants are seen at work in the cultivation of the soil. Bands of muleteers with well-laden *borricos*, and at intervals two or three armed horsemen or a solitary *calesa*, or a line of enormous *galeros*, or baggage-wagons, meet and pass you, the peasants generally greeting you with a touch of the hat and a ' *Va usted con Dios,*' which is the most common salutation, and means literally ' Go with God.'

From Colmenar we proceeded on our winding way till at about six o'clock in the evening we stopped for the night at a *venta*, or *posada*, built like a fort among the mountains. We were glad to reach it, whatever it might be, for we had dined in the coach from our little hamper of provisions; and the poor mules were much more glad, for Battiste had driven from six o'clock in the morning without stopping at all, even to give them water. Twelve mortal hours they had toiled among the mountains, without resting either to eat or drink, and this I suppose is a favorable specimen of the manner in which the Spanish peasants treat their beasts of burden; for Battiste would not whip his horses, whereas the whole race of mules and borricos may almost be said to live upon blows.

The venta was built, as I have said, in the manner of a fort or castle, with but one entrance into the open court, through which Battiste drove the coach, as it was raining, almost into the kitchen. This in a Spanish venta is the grand hall of entrance and departure, cooking and conversation, eating and drinking. The guests come in one after the other and seat themselves around the fire kindled on the floor at one end of the apartment, and the process of cooking is carried on at the same fire, or over furnaces in a dresser at the side of it. Our party was greatly increased in the evening by the arrival of the galeros from Grenada, loaded with men, women and children. A motley group was collected around the burning embers, and a villanous looking peasant thrummed the guitar, some of the girls of the inn singing an accompaniment by snatches. By and by a wild ferocious looking squad of peasants collected round a table and began to circulate their liquor, offering it according to their custom to us, and drinking so freely and getting so noisy that we feared a savage quarrel. The conversation in these inns is generally of the grossest description.

As for our sleeping arrangements, we were ushered into a naked room having one grated window without glass, but a shutter on the inside, which served partially to exclude the damp air, into which our Maritornes dragged a pair of light mattresses, with a quantum of dirty blankets, all of which were spread upon the brick floor, the luxury of a bedstead being quite unattainable. Thus we slept; and before our early departure in the morning we were regaled with a small cup of chocolate so thick as to be more of the consistency of a boiled custard than a fluid, but very delicious to the taste, and several slices of bread fried in oil.   The chocolate is a sort of universal stirrup-cup in Spain, before a morning's ride upon a journey; indeed it is so rich as to be of itself almost sufficient for a man's breakfast.   It is said there is a sumptuary law in Spain that all chocolate sold at the inns shall be made so thick that the spoon shall stand upright in it.   If there be such a law, it must have been the friars that made it.

Our second day's ride carried us through a region very different from the vine-clad hills among which we had been thus far winding. About half a mile from our venta we passed on our right a little village called Alfernate, situated in a very picturesque manner at the foot of a rough gray rocky mountain, with a lovely green meadow stretched out beneath it.   A church tower added interest to the picture.   For some distance we rode through a series of bare rocky mountains, looking like the Grand Monadnock in Massachusetts, relieved at intervals by a beautiful extent of rich land, covered with grain in the green blade, or an olive plantation, most grateful to the eye amidst such a barrenness of trees.   The interesting city of Loxa — interesting for its historical recollections and the strength and extreme picturesqueness of its situation — lay next in our route.   It was once a Moorish city, governed by a brave and fiery warrior, and garrisoned as nobly; and the history of its battles and sieges occupies an interesting page in the story of the conquest of Grenada.   Hanging in a rocky defile above the commencement of the rich vega of Grenada, it was considered with its strong fortress as the key of that kingdom.   Lovely indeed was the appearance of the valley of the Xeuil opening upon us beneath the city, and beautiful the view of the ancient church and fortress as we entered its environs!   The whole place is built over rugged mountain declivities, and the streets themselves look like battlemented terraces hewn out of the rock.   The road descends from a high point into the city, and in the first view which you have of it, the fortress and the principal church seem to occupy the two sides of a deep ragged rocky ravine, along which the street seems winding into the heart of the city. From the top of the fortress the view is truly exciting, for its variety and extent, its mingled boldness and beauty.   On the east continues to rise high above the city the enormous mountain ridge, in the craggy defile of which, adown its base, the buildings are clustered like the cope-stones of a tower.   On the west is the deep valley of the Xeuil, with a bridge crossing the river, a green wooded alameda on the other side, and a part of the city spreading over the meadow, with an extensive convent at the base of the mountain ridge beyond.   South and west the valley of the Xeuil continues its windings among the intersecting ranges of the mountains, and the eye roams across their summits through one of those far-distant, clear-tinted, gorgeous perspectives, that seem like openings into infinity.   On the north you follow the valley of the Xeuil where it opens into the commencement of the vega of Grenada.

Coming into Loxa *from* that city, the view is in some respects equally striking.   There are two roads, the carriage-road below, along the border of the river, and a narrower road far up the side of the mountain. I chose the latter, and walked the circuit of an immense craggy curvature in the mountain, gazing down its precipitous walls upon the busy scene of women washing clothes at a mountain stream far below me, and descended into the city through a street of mountain fastnesses on the north. I enjoyed the lonely and wild walk at some little risk of being robbed, but met with nothing more terrific than a few shepherd boys and haggard old women. Through the open doors of houses in the city it was easy to see that they were all abundantly supplied with images of the Virgin, and paintings identified with the Catholic faith. We entered the church, with whose picturesque aspect we had been so much struck externally, and found it as squalid and gloomy within as it was attractive from a distance without. The worshippers also gazed at us with a strange inimical sort of scrutiny, that seemed to say, ' You are heretics, and we should like to burn you ; ' or as Giant Grim in Pilgrim's Progress, when he could not come at Great Heart's company to hurt them, ' You will never mend till more of you are burnt.' The appearance of an ' Inglese ' in a church at Loxa was however so strange an occurrence that the inhabitants might be pardoned even if they had looked aghast at the spectacle.

Our posada at Loxa was of the same character with the last near Alfernate, but somewhat more comfortable, being on the side of a mountain. The stable, kitchen and court-yard were all in one, but the mistress of the inn was a neat and fine looking woman, with a number of healthy, rosy children. We ordered a dish of *miças* for dinner, and simple as it was, being neither more nor less than a sort of fried pudding made out of the rich Andalusian bread mingled with shreds of meat and dressed with oil, to me it was the only palatable thing they cooked for us. From this place we rode through the mud and rain about a league and a half to the next venta, where we spent the night. They called it by way of eminence *La Venta Nueva*, or ' The New Sun,' and it seemed to be regarded as a model of *ventaical* grandeur. It was a great oblong square, the ground floor of which constituted one immense apartment, occupied at once as a stable and a kitchen. The kitchen portion was separated partly from the rest by a wall running as far as the staircase, over which an ascent was obtained into the region of the *quartos*, or sleeping apartments, and being thus ensconced in one corner of the long building, afforded quite a retirement from the stalls of the beasts. Here the parties of travellers collect to warm themselves, surrounding the same fire over which the cook is frying, boiling and stewing in huge shallow pans the savory mixtures for the many guests. Returning from Grenada, we found at this inn a cavalcade of eight or nine *galeras* and coaches within the great court-yard, and our hearts began to sink within us at the prospect that every quarto, or sleeping cell, must have been taken up long before our arrival. This was not the case, though the venta that night was very much crowded, and exhibited a most lively and stirring scene, of a character at once motley and picturesque. Among other comers whom we met were Don Lopez Pinta, the late governor of Malaga, and a liberal canon of the Cathedral and governor of the bishop's palace, both of them men of uncommon liberality and intelligence, and proceeding on their way northward through Grenada toward Madrid, as members of the new assembly of the Cortes. They were escorted by a party of Spanish soldiers, and altogether there was a great stir in the inn. The care of every thing seemed to devolve upon the women, the landlord keeping quite aloof from the bustle; so much so that even the bills were paid to the mistress. Tables were set here and there, and the different parties fell to with fingers or wooden spoons as fast as their messes were provided, tables being also ranged along the doors of the quartos in the second story.

After eating comes the business of sleeping, which is despatched much in the same way. Some stretch themselves in their cloaks before the fire, others in the corners under the canopy of the huge gaping chimney, others upon chairs or benches, and others among the borricos and horses. These were feeding in immense numbers, ranged along in double rows side by side the whole length of the venta; and with plenty of straw to lie upon, seemed to be champing their provender with a grateful sense of comfort, to which the human inmates of the inn must have been quite strangers.

The third day of our journey, a little before we came upon the great Vega of Grenada, we passed a solitary guard-house, where a guard is stationed to protect the way from banditti. An armed man issued from the hovel and made up to us, looking more like a robber than any thing else; and I confess that at first, not knowing the purpose of the building, I thought the fellow might be going to make a demand upon our purses. I was walking along beside the coach, and heard Battiste tell the soldier that we expected to return that way on Monday or Tuesday of next week; a speech which we regarded as a very gratuitous piece of information, and one which would be very likely to lead to a robbery on our return, at any rate. However we both passed and repassed in safety, though when we got back to Malaga a sagacious old Spaniard told us that he would not on any account have returned the same way after so suspicious a circumstance. The third day of our journey back, three wild-looking armed men hailed us from a thicket on a bank above the road-side, and we paid them for the privilege of passing unmolested, under the name of a gratuity for their vigilance in guarding the road from banditti! This was something like the *black-mail* paid by the government to the banditti above Madrid for the privilege of running the mail diligence unmolested. These people may be guards and they may be robbers, but they are very likely to be both together.

We came speedily upon the Vega of Grenada, and continued in it almost the whole day, with the city and the snow-crowned mountains of the Sierra Nevada in full view at the end. We passed through the village of Larcha, at the southern borders of the Vega, and the half-ruined city of Santa Fé, at several leagues distance from Grenada, built by Ferdinand when besieging the Moorish capital. It is now one of the most miserable looking places to be found in the kingdom. But nothing can be more beautiful than the perspective of the scene, passing toward Grenada; the immense plains over which we were slowly travelling, surrounded and hemmed in by mountains retreating gradually into the sky, stretching out before us at so great a distance; the city of Grenada with its white dwellings and gray majestic towers rising up the base of the mountain declivity at the farthest end; and the glittering sierra shooting their snowy summits into the blue sky directly above. The effect of the changing light and shade thrown in bright and dark masses upon the city and the mountains was extremely grand; and as the sun broke out upon the rising city and the towers of the Alhambra embosomed in trees, I thought it one of the most glorious spectacles I had ever witnessed. It was full in our view for several hours, increasing in distinctness as we advanced, the Vega too increasing in loveliness. As we neared the city, the plain became one vast carpet of luxuriant green, whose tints in the slanting sun-light were beyond measure beautiful and refreshing to the eye.

I declare to you that the splendor of the region is so great, that if Milton had ever been known to have visited it, one would feel assured that it must have been from this earthly type that he drew his description of the sun setting against the gate of Paradise:

> ' Meanwhile, in utmost longitude, where heaven
> With earth and ocean meets, the setting sun
> Slowly descended; and with right aspéct
> Against the eastern gate of Paradise
> Levelled his evening rays: it was a rock
> Of alabaster, piled up to the clouds,
> Conspicuous far; winding with one ascent
> Accessible from earth, one entrance high:
> The rest was craggy cliff, that overhung
> Still as it rose, impossible to climb.'

I walked for hours, absorbed in the multitude of melancholy, romantic, and most interesting associations connected with the sight of this beautiful region and the picturesque and noble city before me. The towers of the Alhambra rise far above the rest of the city, and are certainly as magnificent in the distant perspective as they are in their own interior splendor. The slow pace at which Battiste permitted his mules to drag the carriage allowed us to walk at leisure on the high banks by the road-side, with our gaze directed steadfastly toward the city and the snow-covered mountains above it. It was so beautiful, that toward evening on a sunny day, with the golden rays from the west streaming over its towers and pinnacles and flashing on the mountains of snow as they ascend into the blue sky right above the palaces, an imagination like that of Milton or the author of the Pilgrim's Progress might indeed have read in it a type of the splendors of the Celestial City. And in truth we were advancing through a region and toward a city in which its inhabitants dwelt as in an earthly paradise, and which they filled with the most luxuriant and magnificent productions of industry and art. They made it renowned through the world for science, and crowned it with palaces that seemed but a realization of the brightest creations of their oriental tales. They lived in it with a character of bravery, generosity, and devotion more worthy of the spot and more in keeping with its natural romantic magnificence than that exhibited by any other people. The towers which they reared and the halls in which they rested, attest to this day the greatness of their conceptions, and the extraordinary mixture of luxury, energy and religious veneration in their minds. Would that they had remained to this day the industrious inhabitants and lords of their beloved kingdom and city! not indeed as Mussulmen, but as christians; that they had been left to enjoy the influences of a benevolent and not a bigoted christianity; to retain possession of a place to which their bold romantic genius seemed so admirably fitted, and which their united industry and refinement would not have suffered to pass into degradation and decay. What an interesting spectacle it would have been, had this splendid palace continued the abode of an unbroken line of Moorish kings and princes, and had they with the fiery people whom they governed become penetrated with the regenerating influences of the gospel of Christ! But this is a dream of the fancy, musing over its own vain wishes. They were driven from their beloved country, treated not even with the favor of conquered enemies, but banished, burned, and exterminated by the fierceness of bigotry and the fires of the inquisition from the land they had covered with beauty; and a race degraded by the bondage of civil and religious despotism occupy their places. The fiery, generous, industrious Moor is succeeded by the bigoted, lazy, priest-ridden Spaniard, and the land itself has almost forgotten its natural richness. Alas! alas! for the melancholy change!

But oh! how bright will be the dawning of christianity upon this lovely region! When this luxuriant vega, these plains, that might well be called a vale of paradise, begirt with those magnificent ranges of mountains, shall be redeemed from the darkness that now covers them, and lighted with the meridian splendor of the Sun of Righteousness; when they shall be consecrated to the spiritual worship of that God, of whose wisdom and goodness they are such bright types and memorials; when they shall be filled with smiling villages and cities prosperous in the arts of peace, whose inhabitants shall be enlightened and ennobled by the truth that makes all men free, and on whose employments and manners, arts, palaces and temples, shall be inscribed in living reality, HOLINESS TO THE LORD:

> —— ' When that blest day arrives,
> When they, whose choice or lot it is to dwell
> In crowded cities, without fear shall live,
> Studious of mutual benefit ; and he
> Whom morning wakes among sweet dews and flowers,
> Be happy in himself. The law of Faith,
> Working through Love, such conquest it shall gain,
> Such triumph over sin and guilt achieve.
> Almighty Lord! thy farther grace impart,
> And with that help the wonder shall be seen
> Fulfilled, the hope accomplished, and thy praise
> Be sung with transport and exceeding joy!'   WORDSWORTH.

THE PAST: A FRAGMENT.

How wild and dim this life appears!
  One long, deep, heavy sigh,
When o'er our eyes, half clothed in tears,
The images of former years
  Are faintly glimmering by;
And still forgotten while they go,
As on the sea-beach wave on wave
  Dissolves at once in snow!

STANZAS.

I.

Sleepest, Lady?　I am waking,
　　Thinking still of thee,
Looking at the images
　　In my mind that be,
Worshipping the images
　　Fancy forms of thee.

II.

Lovely images it maketh,
　　Pleasant as the day;
But though Fancy pleaseth me,
　　Something seems to say,
'Thou, the dear Original,
　　Fairer art than they.'

Cambridge, Dec., 1841.

III.

Still thy voice is gently sounding,
　　Falling on my ear
Like the brook's soft summer voice,
　　Singing low and clear;
I have loved to hear thy voice
　　While none else was near!

IV.

Speaking with thine eyes so holy,
　　Thou dost say: 'Above,
Where the blessed angels dwell,
　　Every one doth love;
Imitate the spirits good
　　In the worlds above.'

　　　　　　　　　　　　　　　　f.

THE WIDOWER BEWITCHED.

A SCENE OF REAL LIFE.

It is quite unnecessary to account for the publication of the following apparently confidential letter: it is enough to say that it came into my hands in a very strange manner; and its contents being of a serious nature, I thought it best, after consulting with a judicious friend, to send it to the 'OLD KNICK,' as I knew of no way of forwarding it to its destination direct.

Swampville, January 1, 1842.　　　　　　　　　　　　HARRY FRANCO.

TO MARY IN HEAVEN.

MY DEAR MARY:　I cannot say my lost one, because I know that you are in heaven, and it is I that am lost and not you.　But, my dear Departed!　Alas, that I should live to call you so; and alas! that I should call you so and live!　But we know ourselves as little as others know us; indeed we do not know ourselves so well; because in judging of others we are influenced by the whole conduct of their lives; and as men never alter, we know that what they will do at one time they will do at another, under the same circumstances; but in judging of ourselves we reason from the feelings of the moment.　Thus when stunned with the awful announcement, just twelve months ago this very hour, that the Angel of Death had caught you in his arms, I threw myself upon your stiffening form, which never until then had refused to return my embrace, and swore in my heart that henceforth, if doomed to live, I would live only for you; that I would die to the world and its blandishments, and never would pollute my heart by allowing the thought of another to usurp the throne where you had reigned supreme; forgetting that I had before made many solemn vows and had broken them all. Yet I was sincere, dear Mary; I was true and honest; and your parting spirit, still cognizant, as I fondly thought, of earthly things, bore up to heaven the vows I had uttered in my heart. But ——

What a horrible word is this ' But!' What a sure prelude to disappointed hopes! How many a pale cheek and beating heart has the bare utterance of it caused; how many knees have faltered, how many eyes have been dimmed at the mere sight of it; how suddenly Hope withers at its sound, and Expectation stands on tip-toe to learn what it half announces! If it were possible for your gentle spirit to feel with earthly feelings you could not suspect the truths to which this word is a preface. But as I know you would have forgiven me when here, let my offence have been what it might, you will not forgive me less now that you are in heaven where my vileness cannot mar the happiness that you enjoy. Therefore I will confess all. But before I relate the events which have occurred since you were taken from me, let me once more call to mind the sad occurrence that hurried you away; that my own conduct may appear to me in its true light, without palliation or excuse. I would recall again the story of our love, but that I could not bear.

We had been married just two years; two moments you called them; and yet they should have been heavy years to you, for you had been turned from your father's door for marrying me, and had exchanged the elegances of a happy home for privations and hardships of which you could not have dreamed, until they fell to your lot. I was forced to leave you to go on a business errand to the South. How I cursed my slender income which compelled me to go! And how gently you rebuked me and instilled new hopes in me, until as the time of our parting drew nigh your faltering voice told too plainly that you needed the consolation that you were endeavoring to afford me. At last we parted — neither able to say farewell. I know not what forebodings filled your mind, but for myself I was strangely oppressed with the conviction that I should never return; and it was the agonizing thought that you would be left alone in the world without a protector, that caused my unhappiness; for my stay was not to be long, and the prospect of seeing you again would have alleviated the pain of our parting.

I had scarcely arrived at the place of my destination, when one of those fatal epidemics peculiar to the South broke out, and threatened to sweep off all who were not inured to the climate by a long residence. Frightful and exaggerated accounts of the ravages of the distemper reached you at the same time with the news of my arrival, and filled you with the most gloomy apprehension. I knew what effect such reports would have upon you, and I endeavored by frequently writing to inform you of my health, to soothe your fears. At last, having escaped the contagion unharmed, I set sail for home with a light heart. What a vision of delight danced before my eyes when I thought of meeting you! But we had to contend with foul weather and head winds; and our voyage was prolonged to an unusual length. Fool that I was! I forgot the kind Providence that had kept me unharmed in the midst of pestilence, and now murmured at the little delay that kept me from you!

But my punishment was in store. If the time passed wearily with me, oh! how sadly it passed with you! You suffered a daily and hourly agony in watching for my return, the intensity of which I can only know from its fatal termination. You had watched so fondly and so long, with such unceasing anxiety and such singleness of affection, that when at last they brought you intelligence of my safe arrival, and assured you that in an hour you would see me, the sudden realizing of your hopes and the dissipation of all the cruel fears that beset you proved too much for your slender frame, and you sunk under the happy reverse. The excess of your joy and the wild tumult of your exultations had destroyed you. And now, dear Mary! I live, and know that you died for me. And now, I live —— But I will not anticipate. It will come too soon, though it comes last.

With fond haste I hurried to your apartment, little dreaming of the sad greeting that awaited my coming. You were surrounded by strange people, and a stream of blood was gushing from your mouth. Oh! what a sea of blood it seemed to me, drowning in its red waves all that was dear to me in life! It was in vain that kind and sympathizing friends crowded around me. I could not be comforted. How idle were their gentle words! They could not restore you to life; of what worth then were they to me? Even your old father, your implacable father, who had refused to see you when living, for my sake, now knelt at my feet and begged my forgiveness; he bathed my hands with his tears and kissed me because I had been loved by you; you, whom he turned from his door. Strange! that Death, which makes no change in the departed, should so change the living! The world erects a monument to-day over the man to whom it refused a shelter but yesterday. Your father begged my forgiveness for his cruelty to you, and for your sake I forgave him. Why should I not? *You* would have done so.

Your poor old Aunt Keziah, who had so often dandled you upon her knee, and who loved you with a mother's love, came to find consolation, if haply she might, from mingling her tears with mine. Poor simple affectionate soul, how dearly she loved you! — and with true womanly affection forgot her own grief in remembering the proprieties that were due to one she loved. Her over-solicitude for your poor remains distressed me. They were most dear to me because they had been the habitation of your better part; but to her your lifeless body was yourself. She was most anxious about the place of your burial; to me it did not matter. Let your remains be buried where they might, it would be a holy place to me.

'Shall we not bury her in the Concordance?' said Aunt Keziah; ''t is a lovely spot; so full of green trees and flowers; and then it's so quiet and so genteel!'

'It matters not,' I replied, 'if it only be in a quiet spot, where I can sit and weep without being gazed at. But the place you named I never heard of before. Where is it?'

'O, she means the Commentary,' said another old lady; 'do n't you, Aunty?'

'Yes, yes; I did mean the Commentary,' said Aunty; 'the Greenwood Commentary, of course. But my poor head is turned. Ah! it is a dreadful thing not to call things by their right names in these days.'

Whether or not Aunty had discovered a knowing look in any one present, and wanted to upbraid him with the superior civilization of the gentlemen of the old school, who would allow things to be miscalled with impunity, I do not know; but she continued to play upon that one string for some time.

'Well, well,' continued Aunty, 'we must all die, whether we read the Bible or the dictionary. Ah! it matters but little, if the heart is only right, how wrong the head may be. Yes, yes; we must all go when our time comes, learning or not. Learning wo'n't save us, nor dictionaries, but the Bible will. Well! ah!—the Greenwood Commentary. That's it I suppose. Yes. It's a dreadful thing not to know the right names. Well, learning wo'n't save a poor soul from dying. Money we can leave behind us for others, but learning we can neither take with us nor leave behind. But it's a dreadful thing not to be learned. Ah! well; yes, the Commentary—the Green-wood Commentary, that's it I suppose.'

And here grief stopped the utterance of poor Aunty. Kind-hearted, womanly soul! She now lies in the very spot where she was so anxious for your remains to be placed. She bequeathed her little fortune, which you know would have been yours, to the church of which she had been a member, upon the condition that the vestry should have her grave freshly sodded every spring. Tidy soul! But some of her graceless nephews disputed the validity of her will upon the ground of insanity, alledging in proof the terms of her bequest, which to my perception was the strongest evidence that she could have given of her perfect soundness of mind. They went to law, the nephews and the church, quite in a christian spirit, contending for a small sum of money; a very edifying spectacle to world's-people, who rather like such things themselves, and would take vast comfort in the thought that the church sanctioned their likings. But it is impossible to tell in whose favor the law would have decided, for the suit was just about coming to trial, after having been put off three times at the instigation of the defendants, and having missed one term from the illness of the judge, when the bank broke in which Aunty's fortune was invested, and the parties withdrew their suits, each paying their own costs, which I have been told was no trifle. And poor Aunty's grave to this day has never been sodded once. Alas, for human calculations! The tidy old creature left this world with the pleasing consciousness that a neatly-trimmed hillock of green turf would always be lying upon her breast. What a lesson for those who place their affection upon earthly objects—and their money in banks!

. . . . . .

After they had borne you away, and I sat weeping in the fading twilight, some of the neighbors remained to offer such aid as they could render to one in my sad condition. Among them there was one who spoke to me in so sweet a tone that I could not but look up and thank her for the interest she took in my behalf; for I knew it was rather for your sake than mine; and so she declared it was; and this pleased me

so well that I half fancied she resembled you.   Perhaps she was neither
so youthful nor so delicate in her beauty; my eyes were blurred, and I
was not disposed to be critical.   She said she had loved you, and I
almost loved her for it.   When she was about to leave, I could not but
see her to the door and ask her to return the next day, for it was a sad
pleasure to me even to see those who had known you and loved you.
She came the next day, and I thought the resemblance to you was
stronger than before.   She stayed long, was very kind, and said a
thousand things in your praise.   She told me how well you had loved
me, and she thought that I was the most miserable of men.

But to spare myself the recital of events that would give pain to both,
if you were capable of pain, I will confess in brief that she awakened
a thought in my mind that one who bore so strong a resemblance to you
in her person might not be altogether objectionable as a companion.
It was but the shadow of a thought, dear Mary! — it just floated tran-
siently through my mind, and left no mark behind : — just as we see a
black cloud sometimes flit through a bright blue sky, without leaving
scarce a remembrance that it had existed.   But my fair neighbor called
again, and all her talk was still of your virtues.   She did not remain as
long as she had before, and when I pressed her to stay she,reminded
me that the world was censorious, and told me that a proper regard for
her character would not allow her to repeat her visit.   She was sorry;
but having discharged her duty to the memory of her friend, by attending to my wants and trying to soothe my grief, she must now be content
to sympathize with me in silence and apart.   But before we parted for the
last time on this side the grave, for she did not suppose that we should
ever meet again, she begged that I would give her one little lock of
your hair.   How could I refuse this gentle request? I could not.
Indeed it was grateful to my feelings to grant it; but as I wore your
lock of hair next my heart, I could not grant it then; so I promised to
bring the ringlet to her.   Believe me, dear Mary! it was for your sake!
It was because I could never tire of hearing her speak in your praise;
and I knew she would never tire of hearing me speak of you.   For
what other reason could I have been induced to see her?   It was so
gratifying to my feelings to hear her speak of you, that at last I became
uneasy and dejected unless I was in her presence.

At first I gave her the lock of hair which I had worn next to my
heart; then I gave her your miniature, the same that you gave to me;
next the little trinkets that you used to wear, some of which were
presents from me before our marriage; and at last I gave her my hand,
just one month after I had seen your still beauteous form shut up in the
tomb; but in so doing I thought I was paying a tribute to your worth.

Dear Mary! will you believe it?   Since that time your name has
been a forbidden word!   I only whisper it when I am alone.   The
trinkets that you used to wear, and which I prized so dearly, have been
exchanged for others; your miniature and the lock of hair have both
strangely disappeared, and whenever I ask for them I am answered with
a flood of tears.   I have even been reproached with loving you too well;
and once she insinuated that you never did deserve my esteem ; and
more cruel than all, that your beauty never had an existence except in

my imagination. Once I asked her to walk with me to the place of your burial. A fainting-fit was the consequence. I have been careful not to make the request a second time. These fainting-fits are shocking affairs. But they cannot be altogether avoided; for whenever I am detained at my business she accuses me of 'walking among the tombs,' a subject that is sure to bring them on. Dear Mary! I strive all I can to make no allusion to you in her hearing; but little words will sometimes escape from my mouth that recall you to her mind; and then for some unexplained reason her fainting-fits begin. She wanted me to promise her that I would not marry again if she should die, and I took a solemn oath that I would not. And this oath, dear Mary! I know I shall never break. *One* promise at least I will keep.

You remember your Uncle Ned, who used always to be singing 'What is a woman like?' He would sometimes answer his chant in a low mellow voice: 'A woman is a riddle.' I have often thought of Uncle Ned during the past year.

Dear Mary! I have been the father of a little angel, who lived just long enough to bless me with a fond look from her soft blue eyes, and then she died. I have bent over her little form, and have wept as I wept for you. I would have called her Mary, but I dared not. I know she will go where you have gone, for all pure and gentle beings must live together; and you will know that she is mine, and she will nestle in your bosom, and you will love her for my sake. The last kiss upon her cheek was mine.

I have penned this letter in a fond dream. I will cheat my senses. The harsh realities of the things around me shall not break my gentle delusion. I rave, but am quiet. I will fold this letter and put it in her little hands, crossed as though in sleep upon her breast. You will not get it I know, but I will think you do.

Dear Mary! farewell!

THE LESSONS OF ILLNESS.

FROM AN UNPUBLISHED POEM.

O couch! O feverish couch of pain!
Thou tamer of proud hearts! How vain
With thy unwearied strength to strive,
And hour by hour refuse to give
Thy wasting fires life's energies,
And all, save that which never dies!
He, who hath lain in thy embrace,
Laid to thy breast his burning face,
And shrunk beneath thy stifling breath,
And felt each moment nearest death,
(Though Reason still retained her throne
And viewed no empire but her own,)
He yet hath wished, the struggle o'er,
He were asleep — to wake no more!

But when the soul hath lost the helm,
And wandereth o'er a trackless realm;
The deep of the eternal mind,
Now lulled to calm, now torn with wind,
And still by terror's phantoms haunted,
Oh! *then* that lonely voyager, daunted;
As visions of strange worlds are seen,
And things and forms of fearful mien,
Would in its fear and wild despair
Fly from the wreck, it knows not where,
Did Reason yield one transient ray
To guide its trembling flight away!

THE POLYGON PAPERS.

NUMBER FOUR.

From boyhood I have always taken great delight in fables parables and allegories. Almost my earliest remembrance of intellectual pleasure is of that arising from the perusal in Webster's Spelling Book of the fable of the Fox, the Swallow, and the Flies. As I could not penetrate the moral drift of the tale, it arrayed itself to my eyes in all the interest of undoubted fact. I pictured to myself the very spot where the tragedy occurred; I felt a personal gratitude to the Swallow for the benevolence of his wishes; and sympathized with the sufferer himself in his hopelessness of escape from the pitiless phlebotomists which tormented him. In reading the chronicles of the ancient Hebrews, so varied, so romantic, so affecting, my attention was enchained by Jotham's fable of the trees — the earliest allegory on record. The touching parables of our Saviour, couched as they are in language of the utmost plainness, based on the familiar principles of our daily life, and bearing in themselves a moral which 'he who runs may read,' were more alluring than the most high-wrought narrative, and more instructive than the most labored sermon. The divine Redeemer in these artless emblematic tales brings down his godlike faculties to the level of children, and adapts his heavenly teachings to the capacity of the meanest of our race. How beautifully through the veil of harmless fiction beam the features of symbolic truth!

Passing from the sacred records to the volumes of worldly wisdom, I can scarce express the quiet pleasure with which, when in the vestibule of the classic temple, I studied the exquisite little paintings of animal life left us by the Phrygian bondman, the immortal Æsop. I stopped not then nor will I linger now to inquire with Bentley, whether the fables reputed as Æsopic áre the genuine productions of the slave of Xanthus, the freedman of Iadmon and the courtier of King Crœsus. It is sufficiently evident from their unadorned conciseness that they had their origin in high antiquity, before men had learned to write so elegantly that they were forced to annex a postscript to explain their meaning. Language in those blessed days interpreted itself as it went, and it was not thought necessary to tag a moral to the end of the fable for fear the allusion might be mistaken. This refinement was reserved for Phædrus, the Roman freedman, who copied and diluted his Grecian prototype, as most subsequent fabulists have imitated and weakened them both. The praise of great elegance and simplicity cannot be denied to Phædrus ; but his groups of brutes have not the life-like strength of the Greek. They are somewhat overcharged, and we always see the figure of the painter himself in one corner of the picture. Therefore they are less pleasing than the Æsopian fables, and almost the only passage I remember is the beautiful tribute to the memory of his model :

> ' Æsopo ingentem statuam posuere Attici,
> Servumque collocârunt æternâ in basi,
> Patere honoris scirent ut cuncti viam,
> Nec generi tribui, sed virtuti gloriam.'

I was charmed to discover in the Viri Romæ the practical power of the little fable of 'The Stomach and the Limbs,' by a well-timed rehearsal of which Menenius Agrippa brought back the disaffected populace of Rome from beyond the Anio, and restored them to concord with the trembling fathers. And at a subsequent period I was scarce more pleased with any thing in the pages of the captivating Livy, whether speech or battle, than in finding a grave historian confirm that triumph of a homely apologue over the passions of an infuriate and senseless mob.

I know not whence the charm of these compositions arises, unless it be from their expressing so much sound sense under the careless form of fiction, and at the same time by their verisimilitude gratifying our love of imitation. When we hear characteristic truths from the mouth of Reynard or Bruin, we at once gain the profit of instruction and the pleasure derived from the contemplation of resemblances, and those teachings come to us in a more agreeable and impressive manner than they would from the lips of Plutarch or Bacon.

Then too there is the charm of seeing the brute creation gifted with human intelligence, and even inanimate existences endowed with our own beloved life. We love to be creators, though it be but infancy. We love to extend the realms of reason and vitality beyond the narrow bounds prescribed to them by nature ; and this explains the universal prevalence of personification among the poets, or rather among all mankind ; for all mankind are poets, so far as they are men. Living and moving and sentient beings ourselves, we can hardly sympathize intimately with any thing unless we consider it as possessed of life and sense and motion. Therefore Grief calls upon the trees to weep, and Joy bids the mountains clap their hands and sing. Therefore Superstition peoples the woods and the mountains with hosts of bodiless rovers, and Guilt enlivens the solitude of deserts, and illuminates the darkness of midnight with myriads of all-seeing eyes. Therefore Poetry inspires into each frail flower an airy spirit, ennobles even the insensible rock with a living essence, and sees the green earth smile an eloquent answer to the smiling heavens. And therefore Truth delivers her lowly lessons in the language of beasts and birds, and the self-deceiving reader is ashamed not to acknowledge and practice what even the brutes admit.

Among the moderns may be found many very fine apologues, bearing however the same relation to the ancient fables that modern literature in general bears to the classic — that is, inferior in simplicity and terseness, but superior in subtlety and polish. The Russians appear to have a particular genius in this line, and Bowring's translations exhibit some master-pieces. The English Gay and the French La Fontaine maintain the first rank as fabulists in their respective nations, though the latter is far superior to the former in wit, drollery and nature. But I think none of the moderns have composed fables with more skill and beauty than the Italians. Their language, so copious in diminutive and amplificative expressions; their language, so polished and so delicate:

> —— ' a soft Latin,
> Which melts like kisses from a female mouth,
> And sounds as if each word were writ on satin,'

seems peculiarly adapted to the simplicity of fable. I have indeed a ponderous effort in this kind; no less than an epic poem in twenty-six cantos, composed by Giambattista Casti, entitled ' Gli Animali Parlanti,' and displaying a great deal of learning and acuteness, with not a little even of poetic genius. The author under cover of an ingenious and well-sustained narrative of the events which occurred in the animal kingdom under the reign of Lion the I., and during the minority of Lion the II., under the regency of the queen-mother, showers the arrows of his satire on kings and sycophants, and shadows forth an outline, half tearful half ludicrous, of the tragi-comic history of man. There appear upon the stage all the marvellous animals imagined by the poets; the hybrid griffin, the many-headed hydra, and that unique self-resurrectionist, the semi-millennial phœnix. There are the mammoths whose bones lie bleaching on the Siberian steppes; and there the leviathan,

> —— ' which God of all his works
> Created hugest that swim the ocean stream : '

there all the pre-Adamitic monsters now imbedded in the strata of the earth or stared at in the cabinets of fossilists; there all that ' tumbled round the globe' in the unwieldy ark of Noah; and there all the tribes extinguished before or since the Deluge by their own mutual ferocity or by the cruelty of man. All are decorated with their appropriate robes; all enact their respective parts; and all in the intrigues of state or the walks of plebeian life exhibit their instinctive qualities — the stupid or the subtile, the cowardly or the courageous.

Among the fabulists however, properly so called, the most simple and elegant are Bertola and Pignotti. Some of the apologues of the latter strike me as particularly fine and natural; and I here present one of them, translated as literally as was compatible with ease and spirit. If I have but partially succeeded in transfusing into English the quiet humor and exquisite *naïveté* of the original, I may well felicitate myself. I need hardly say that it is not intended by the translator, any more than it was by the author, as an attack on religion in general, or a slur upon any church in particular, but merely as a humorous hit at those who make devotion a mask for self-indulgence.

THE HERMIT RAT.

I.

On winter evenings oft my good old granny,
 Plying her swift wheel by the faggot's blaze,
Upon my thirsty ear would pour full many
 A strange and curious tale of other days ;
Spinning them out with such a pleasing grace,
I sat a statue, rooted to my place.

II.

Now would she tell how, crazed with martial glory,
 The frogs and mice in ardent battle strove ;
Then of the wolf and crafty fox some story,
 And then what happened in the reign of Jove ;
When imps and demons, goblins, elves and fays
Gambolled and frisked along the mountain ways.

III.

Once, as the flattened heap of glowing embers
 Threw a red light upon her withered frame,
The boy besought her, as he now remembers,
 With many a dulcet and endearing name,
To tell some story of that golden time
When birds and beasts conversed in prose or rhyme.

IV.

After much previous coughing and some spitting,
 She ope'd her toothless jaws, and thus she said :
'There was an aged Rat, who thought it fitting
 In saintly cell to hide his hoary head,
And far withdrawn from earth's polluted ways,
Devote to Heaven the remnant of his days.

V.

'Our hermit chose a very odorous cloister—
 The centre of an old Parmesian cheese,
Where safe and silent as the shell-girt oyster,
 He passed his moments in religious ease ;
And since Heaven hates the indolent, forsooth !
With zeal he exercised his pious tooth.

VI.

'In fact, attracted by the grateful savor,
 He never ceased to *prey* — upon the cheese !
And (so does Heaven distinguish by its favor
 Those who as he did *labor* on their *knees*)
He grew as fat and round, and sleek and cheery
As the intendant of a monastéry.

VII.

'Meanwhile a pining, life-consuming famine,
  With lean, sharp visage, stalked across the earth,
And the poor rats, their maws with saw-dust cramming,
  Now pined in tears, now danced in maniac mirth;
While, scouring all their haunts by night and day,
Whom famine left Grimalkin bore away.

VIII.

'The rats then all convened in public meeting,
  And *vivâ voce*, chose a deputation,
Who, bag in hand, to all the kind repeating
  Their woful state, should beg a small donation.
They visited the monk, and humbly prayed
The godly father to bestow his aid.

IX.

' 'My dearest children, I have closed the portals
  Of my pure breast against all worldly cares,
And I have nothing to bestow on mortals
  Save my advice, my blessing, and my prayers.
Come not to me, when smarting 'neath the rod
Of earthly sorrows — seek the grace of God.

X.

' 'Praying and fasting, where should *I* have treasure,
  A starving sinner by this naked wall?
Go ask of God, in his most gracious pleasure,
  For those kind crums which from his mercy fall.'
This said, with many benedictions, smirks, and graces,
He kindly shut the door to in their faces.'

XI.

'Well my dear Granny,' said I then, loud laughing,
  'Your hermit rat must be our Father Paschal,
Who prays and fasts, meanwhile the red wine quaffing,
  Bought by indulgence from some sinning rascal;
Whose plumpness says he never knew by trial
The theme of all his sermons — self-denial!'

XII.

'Hush! hush! dear grand-son!' said my good grand-mother;
  'How dare you thus inveigh against a friar?
He who speaks evil of a holy brother,
  Will scorch for years in purgatorial fire:
Oh! wicked age, when even the fair and young
Give lawless license to an impious tongue!

XIII.

'Speak with due reverence of our 'alma mater,'
  The Holy Church, and view her priests with dread;'
And then she mumbled o'er her 'noster pater,'
  While I withdrew me to my little bed;
Thinking 't would be as well my prate to cease,
And leave Fra Paschal and his wine in peace.   POLYGON.

MY GRAND-FATHER'S PORT-FOLIO.

NUMBER TWO.

MY grand-father was evidently a man of a gentle and affectionate heart. In all his manuscripts I do not remember to have met with one uncharitable sentiment or one harsh word. There is some reason to believe that an undue tenderness of disposition was the weak point in his character. I have heard my father say that he very rarely punished his children, and never without tears; that he was habitually indulgent and easy to be entreated, and that his pity for the guilty wreathed the point of his rebukes and blunted the edge of his censures. If this *were* his weakness, and if the infirmity, transmitted down to the third generation, had been all concentrated in the character of the unworthy descendant who is now reverently unloosing the seals of his private papers, this inheritor of the good man's foible could not find it in his heart to cherish against him a single reproachful feeling. For it has been the lot of the grand-child to find so much uncongeniality, whether in reality or appearance, in the composition of the many; so much indifference, coldness and formality, at least in manner; so much polished hardness, rejecting the delicate feelers which gentle natures with a modest hopefulness throw out around them, and so many sharp thorns hedging the paths of the young and innocent-hearted, as they sally out in frolicsome confidence from the covert of home; that he would far rather covet than shun a weakness that, being opposite to the prevailing fault, may perchance afford a slight refreshment to those who are seeking for sympathy, and yield a balm for the wounds which neglect and abuse have made.

But far be it from me to uncover the moral nakedness of my venerable progenitor. Not for this do I draw aside the veil which his instinctive delicacy spread before the lucubrations of his private hours; but rather to bring into the light reflections and observations which, whatever element of weakness may mingle with them, I would fain hope may do some good to others, as they have not been I trust altogether without service to myself.

The paper, Mr. EDITOR, of which I now send you a copy, contains nothing so occasional to the close of the last century as to confine its applicability to the men of a buried generation. Had I written it myself it could not more accurately describe what I have often seen and felt. And if it should chance that any of your readers should detect in its portraitures a likeness of his own manners or of those of any of his neighbors, I must shelter myself from the rising suspicion that the originals are now alive, by representing myself to him in the guise of the artless and grave-looking boy in a favorite picture; clothed in spectacles and wig, long waist-coat, and hat of immense brim; working with my grand-father's implements, and having no other agency than merely to give life and motion to the cast-off materials of a good man who has long since ceased from his earthly labors. And that I may give a conspicuous evidence of the scrupulousness which it is my purpose to use in separating what belongs to the old gentleman from that which is the work of his descendant, I will take this opportunity to remark, that the manuscripts themselves are in the original destitute of *titles.* Of these therefore I confess to the authorship.

SALUTATIONS.

I HAVE just returned from my usual morning ramble. I went forth fresh from sweet slumbers, and feeling in every pulse the exhilarating influence of the south-west wind, the clear air and the gay sun-shine. All nature seemed to bid me 'good morning,' and every familiar scene to welcome me abroad; the trees to wave their graceful salutations; the birds to hail my coming; and even puss, dozing at the warm cottage window, and Rover on the green bank before his master's door, to nod kindly at me as I passed along. The little children running to and fro on mamma's morning errands; the rosy milk-maids as they went and came with their shining pails; the tidy matrons cooling their glowing cheeks at the open door-way, or, with clean aprons flung over their heads, stooping at the wood-pile or the well-side; the sturdy ploughmen harnessing their teams for the field; the early shop-boy whistling as he fastened back his shutters or scattered the dust of yesterday with his broom; the cows ruminating in the barn-yards; the horses looking wisely over the fences; the crowned protectors of the poultry-yard flapping their wings and responding to one another from post to post; the old buildings, wet by last night's shower, sending up their fragrant incense to the rising sun — *all things,* animate and inanimate, seemed to express good will to the light-hearted pedestrian who had an eye and an ear for their kindly salutations. But more than all the rest, those good honest creatures, who met their pastor with unaffected delight, and paused for his morning benediction. My face was in a perpetual twinkle of good-nature; my head nodding in every direction like the plume of a bride receiving congratulations: my right hand continually extended, to return some rough or gentle pressure or to pat some glossy head; my lips overflowing with 'good morrows.'

While I was in this humor, I came suddenly at a turn in the street upon a parishioner who, to judge from his appearance, was angry with Providence for having made all his creatures happy, and had come out into the paradise that was smiling around him with the spiteful purpose of doing his best to spoil the divine arrangement. There was a scornful curl on his lip, a straitened haughtiness in his air and a moody misanthropy in his whole demeanor, that Satan himself might have been glad to borrow for *his* morning walk.

Our meeting was sudden, and although I knew the man well enough, had I had time for a second thought, to have spared myself the misery of casting before him the pearls of my sympathy only that they might be trampled under his feet, yet instinctively I stopped, and giving him a most cordial greeting, reached forth a hand that had never been weary in doing him good. A cold and supercilious nod, and a muttered word of recognition that had more the tone of·a curse than a blessing, were all the response I received; and he went striding on as if he had shaken off a dog.

Chagrined, surprised, shocked, I could not move, nor do any thing but gaze upon his retreating form. I know not how long I remained in this awkward position; but it was long enough to have all my happiness dissipated, and for a dreary change to come over the glad humor of the morning. No effort that I could make availed to shake off the chilling influence of that unfortunate meeting. I reasoned with myself: 'It is after all but a single cold-hearted individual in a countless multitude of the good-natured and the kind. It is his way. It indicated no particular dislike or disesteem for myself. I am sure there is no word or deed of mine that can have stirred his ire against me. It is folly and weakness to be put out of humor by a single wolfish howl amidst these choruses of sweet congratulations. Look at the trees, the corn-fields, the children; listen to the birds; walk briskly on, whistle a cheerful air, and forget this slight rebuff of a poor man whom nobody loves.'

But in vain. A feeling of bitterness remained. A dull weight lay upon my heart. I turned and walked home; while a cloud seemed to have settled over all the beautiful landscape. Well then, as a last resort, let me sit down in my quiet study; lock the door against all the world, surround myself with the moral presence of those worthies of other days who have ministered to my dejection a thousand times, and wrapt my *soul* in a peaceful world, far away from the petty troubles of the present scene; here let me sit down and *write* this annoyance away, by writing myself into a better and wiser mood.

It is evident that few persons are accustomed to reflect upon the importance of attention to the *common civilities* of life with that seriousness which the subject deserves; or to feel how much of human happiness depends upon the manner in which the courtesies of our daily intercourse are discharged. Or I should rather say, that very few cherish toward their fellow-creatures that real interest and brotherly kindness, which would cause them to attend to these matters, even *without* express reflection and purposed self-discipline.

Better salutatory phrases and better signs for expressing all that men ought to feel toward each other could not be invented than those which are already in use. The inclination of the head, the pressure of the hand, the more tender embrace of kindred and intimate friends, and the vocabulary of civilities and good will, are enough; are full of significance; are all that we could desire, to sweeten, harmonize and adorn social intercourse. All that is needed in order that they may accomplish their beautiful and beneficent purpose is, that a new and liberal supply of genuine emotion should be infused into them; that they should be redeemed from the character of being mere compliments, matters of policy and show, forms and formulas of polished society; that they should be no more regarded as having their foundation in the arbitrary appointment of fashion and etiquette, but as springing out of the very nature of man; not as accomplishments to be learned of the dancing-

master and in courts, but as solid personal graces, to be cultivated
from a sense of duty, and as the beautiful fruits of brotherly love ; and
that they should least of all be looked upon as common-place and
indifferent matters, but rather as being full of importance; signs of
what is due of deference, respect and love between man and man ;
essential to the harmony and happiness of social life.

There is a beautiful significance in the salutatory phrases and customs of almost every nation, especially of those of the oriental family.
They plainly indicate that the rules of true politeness are written by the
finger of God upon the human heart.   They prove that the sentiment
of respect for man is an original element of our nature.   They express
exactly what all ought to feel in their intercourse with one another :
though as used by sophisticated characters and in an artificial state of
society they come to mean much more than he who employs them
intends to express.   The Hebrew salutation, 'The Lord be with you,'
and the customary response, ' The Lord bless *you ;*'   The Turkish, ' May
God be gracious to you,' and the answer, ' May God be with *you ;*'
the Arabian, accompanied with the emphatic gesture of the hand upon
the heart, ' Peace be with you,' and the rejoinder, ' With *you* be peace ;'
when they were for the first time used by fresh and true natures, represented as nearly as language and gesture could portray the genuine
feelings of friends and brethren ; and at the same time had a reverential
regard to the Deity ; acknowledging him as the author of all good, and
recognizing him as listening with a benignant ear to the mutual inter-
cessions of his children.   And in like manner our English ' How do
ye ? ' was at first an earnest and tender inquiry, whose interested
author willingly tarried for a precise reply.   The hand was not extended
to grasp a neighbor's except the heart went with it.   And the parting
valediction, ' Good by,' God be with you, or good bide you, took not
the form of a prayer without a simultaneous spiritual intercession.

Moreover, these kindly and emphatic greetings are not only the dictate of nature, but also of our benevolent religion.   Indeed it is the
spirit of christianity alone which gives a clear interpretation of the
common civilities of life, and an essential dignity and value to the small
charities of social intercourse.   For this it is which throws a strong
and full light upon the worth of the individual soul ; teaching us to
look through all the external distinctions which separate man from man ;
to forget the worldly-magnified differences of cultivation, station and
wealth, and to regard every human being, no matter what his garb or
his complexion, or how rude soever his manners and his speech, as a
child of God, a fellow traveller to eternity, a *brother ;* entitled to a full
share of the sympathy and attention of all who compose the great family
of mankind.

When I look at Jesus himself, in his intercourse with individuals and
families ; picture to myself *his* demeanor, and consider the sense of all
his precepts of conduct and feeling as they apply to social intercourse ;
when I call to mind the manner of Paul in his memorable letters ; how
careful he always was to communicate friendly salutations and affectionate messages to all and each of his friends ; filling up a large space,
even when writing upon the gravest subjects, with an enumeration of

the names of whole households to whom he desired his kind remembrances; when I observe the spirit and example of these great masters of christian ethics, I cannot ask for a more convincing and beautiful evidence that our celestial faith is instinct with the very spirit of courtesy and politeness, and tends no less to give sweetness and grace to the ordinary civilities of social intercourse, than to sanctify the moral nature and elevate the soul to the disposition of the angels.

But nothing can make me feel so deeply the importance and excellent uses of heart-felt salutations and valedictions, as the remembrance of their inimitable exemplification in the manners of my oldest friend and class-mate, Doctor H. I feel the inspiriting influence of his smile while I write his name. Thank Heaven, that my pen has at length conjured up his image! — that the necromancy of writing has brought him before me, with a potent medicine in that warm right hand to cure the malady of humor contracted in this morning's stroll! Now, gruff Major of the scornful brow! your chilling shadow passes off from my heart. I would laugh at a hundred gruff majors with Doctor H. in my eye. A thousand misanthropes, scowling in a mass upon their soft, mellow-hearted pastor, should not cast me down, if only *his* beaming face could look upon me as it does at this instant. Who never saw him has yet to see the most perfect image God has set up, in this generation, of a whole-hearted man. How much significance and kindness are manifested in his nod and smile of recognition! How much emphasis in the pressure of his hand! How much genuine affection and interest in his kind inquiries and good wishes for you and yours! What an atmosphere of ease and happiness is irresistibly diffused from about him! How instantly and delightfully does every one whom he meets feel that he is in the presence of a sympathizing brother! The man does not live whose nature is so peculiar that it could find any antagonism in his. How gently are the channels of your own best and sweetest emotions unstopped at his touch! How pleasant are the gates and walls of his dwelling! How graceful and lovely is his pathway in the streets! And yet all the while he says nothing more, and does nothing different from almost any other well-bred man that you meet. But then he says and does nothing *of course;* nothing of formality and ceremony; but every thing of the heart and of a redundant good will.

Who can calculate how much real uneasiness and misery that gruff Major will produce in our little town to-day, as he goes out to his business or his pleasure, careless, neglectful, haughty to all whom he meets in the streets! For myself, if God give me grace to do no more good in any single day of my life than merely to walk forth and smile, and speak kindly and nod sympathetically and heedfully upon every acquaintance I may chance to meet, this at least I will do faithfully and of the heart; and then I am sure that I can rest upon my nightly couch or my last pillow and feel that I have not lived in vain.

We are all fellow travellers for a few days in this vast time-chariot, the world; brothers and sisters, tabernacling for a little while under the same magnificent tent. We need each other's least word of cheer, least passing look of kindness. Each has infinite need of sweet charities from all the rest, and each should task himself to render them abundantly to all. And who can look out upon the emblems of nature that environ our journey and not perceive how pregnant they are with suggestions to brotherly love; while an invisible but closely-drawn chain binds together each creature and image of the material world! The ocean lends to the clouds and the clouds repay to the springing fields. The stars reciprocate their light and keep time in their majestic dance; the regal sun himself reaches down to greet and raise from the clod the humblest lily of the field; and the obscurest floweret in the valley unfolds its modest beauty to the 'eye of day.' The remotest and mightiest globe pays homage to the minutest pebble of the beach; and no existing thing is so mean as to be rejected from the embrace of the most gigantic member of the majestic company of the worlds. Thus the heavens and the earth and the waters all read to us unceasingly their code of brotherly kindness, of true politeness and respectful intercommunion, with an eloquence and beauty that no Chesterfield can borrow or comprehend.

But of what use are all these magnificent emblems to my unfortunate parishioner, who has cost me more heaviness of heart this morning than I am sure he could comprehend, if he were to read what I have been writing? Of the same use forsooth as the sermons and prayers of the last twenty years. Alas! for all our moralizing, say I, when only those feel it for whom it is *not* intended. But if preaching wo'n't conquer my gruff Major, I have hit upon an instrument that shall. I will not have my morning walks imbittered, bright days clouded, and the happiness of half the town destroyed by that one hard man, without another attempt to mend his disposition. He shall have a meeting with the Doctor! Here in my study shall they come together! I will have them appointed on some committee with myself; I will protract the business; I will multiply our sessions; if need be, I will carry on the artifice for years. And then, my redoubtable Major, we shall see — we shall see! God help his poor minister! You shall be something more of a saint in your salutations before you make your bow to Death!

MIND vs. INSTINCT.

Proud man alone, of all that lives
In ocean, earth, or air, derives
Light from his fellows; man alone
By tracing backward, marches on.

O'er all that has been, retrospects,
And hence on all that is, reflects;
And where success or failure steers,
A beacon or a pharos rears.

Keen to one point, beyond it blind,
Could Instinct *here* compete with Mind,
Some change had marked the spider's loom,
Bee's fragrant cell, or beaver's room.

Then might the ape be taught to swell
And feed the flame he loves so well;
Or India's ant to shun the bank
Where all his van by millions sank.

For Instinct is as one that sees
The hour-hand trace its slow degrees,
But ne'er can tell the time of day
By such a circumscribed survey.

But Man his firm foundation lays
On past experience, and surveys
His sons advancing in their might,
Like Time, through darkness as through light!

TO MY BOY IN HEAVEN.

WRITTEN ON THE ANNIVERSARY OF HIS DEATH, SEPTEMBER 19, 1841.

BY MRS. R. S. NICHOLS.

I.

I GAZED upon thee!   Was it rigid Death
  That sate enthroned upon thine icy brow?
Ah no! methought I saw the living breath
  Of life expand thy heaving breast but now:
He sleeps!   Tread softly — wake him not!   How bright
  These dreams of Heaven upon his spirit fall!
They fold it slumbering 'neath their wings of light,
  And bear it up to Heaven's high festival —
The festival of dreams — where spirits hold
  Their deep communings, when the seraph Sleep
Spreads his encircling wings, and seeks to fold
  Earth to repose, and calm the hearts that weep.

II.

It was a fearful dream!   Methought ye said
  That he, *my boy*, was of the earth no more!
That all the sentinels of life had fled,
  And that pale Death their portals guarded o'er.
Ye deemed that I should weep; but not a tear
  Burst from the frozen founts where they were pent,
Though dark foreboding thought and bitter fear
  Rushed to my heart, and bade my soul lament!
He is not dead! — he sleeps!   He could not die,
  So loved, so beautiful!   If Death should bear
His spirit hence, e'en to his native sky,
  My voice would pierce the inner temples there!

III.

He is not dead!   Ah! how my spirit mocks
  The vain delusion!   Can I look on this,
And doubt whose hand each charmed vein now locks?
  I dare not claim what Death hath sealed as his!
And thus I gave thee, ARTHUR, to the tomb,
  And saw the brow oft pillowed next my heart
Laid down amid the dust and darkling gloom,
  To be, alas! too soon of dust a part!
I saw them heap the earth about thy form,
  And press the light turf o'er thy peaceful breast,
Then leave thee to the cold and brooding worm,
  As some young dove in a deserted nest.

IV.

I gazed: it was the autumn's golden light
  That flung bright shadows o'er thy new-made home;
While through the trees that waved in colors bright,
  I heard the low sweet winds thy dirges moan!
And there was *One* looked with me on that scene,
  Who bade me know our bitter loss thy gain:

But ah! his cheek was pale as thine, I ween,
  And from his eyes the hot tears fell like rain.
That eve, while gazing on the midnight sky,
  One bright new star looked out from its lone sphere;
We knew no name to call the stranger by,
  So gave it thine, and deemed that thou wert near.

v.

The Autumn passed. How desolate was earth!
  How froze the lucid veins upon her brow!
While oft the spectre-winds now wandered forth
  Like unseen spirits, treading sad and slow;
Dark, hoary Winter came with piercing breath,
  And gave to Earth a passionless embrace:
Ah me! 't was as the lip of white-browed Death
  Had kissed with fondness some beloved face:
The dazzling snow-wreath garlanded thy tomb,
  While each pale star, effulgent as the day,
Led forth its glittering beams amid the gloom,
  And dimpled Earth, where this white splendor lay.

iv.

I left thee; wooed to that rich southern clime
  Where glows the orange and where blooms the rose;
The land of passion, where the brow of Time
  Dims not, but with renewéd splendor glows;
The joyous Spring on her triumphal car
  Rode through the land in beauty and in light,
And on the young south wind flung wide and far
  The odour of her flowers—her spirit's young delight!
I rested not, though all was bright and green,
  For still I heard thy gentle voice's moan;
My spirit leaped the darkling space between,
  And knelt, all breathless, by thy twilight home!

vii.

One year hath flown—one little circling year,
  A dim, faint shadow of the wing of Time;
Nor hath mine eye forgot the secret tear,
  Or heart to weave the sad and mournful rhyme:
I stand beside thee; and I quickly trace
  The loving hand that hath been busy here:
Who gave such beauty to thy dwelling-place,
  And bade the fresh green grass wave lightly there?
My heart is full, nor can I say farewell,
  E'en to thy gentle shade, O spirit bright!
Without one prayer for him who wove the spell
  Of loveliness, where all was rayless night.

viii.

Not unremembered then thy narrow home,
  Within the city of the voiceless dead;
For hither oft a kindred form would roam,
  And place fresh turf above thy fair young head.
I stand beside thee!—and again the dreams
  Of olden time rise up before my view,
And lulling sounds, like to the voice of streams,
  Float o'er my soul, soft as the morning dew!
Could prayers or tears of mine but win thee now
  From thy high walk around the starry thrones,
So selfish this, my tears would cease to flow,
  My voice refuse to falter forth the tones.

Cincinnati, (Ohio.)

FLÉANCE: A DOMESTIC STORY.

BY THE AUTHOR OF 'THE COUNTRY DOCTOR.'

CHAPTER FIRST.

'MERCIFUL Heavens! how the guns boom! Every report tells of destruction and death. The bombardment has commenced; and if the enemy take the town, their next step will be here; and if disposed to be unmerciful,' exclaimed the youth, pausing and looking tearfully at the couch of his dying mother, 'what will become of us, already too much afflicted? There! again and again! How the panes rattle, and the whole house is jarred! Those cruel sounds will disturb her slumbers after the restless night. Draw the curtains closer around her, Mary. But I suppose it will be all in vain.' And the youth bent his head to the pillow, and kissed his mother's brow.

An aged woman sat in an antique chair by the bed-side. She was tall and stately. A certain bloom which must have been very bright upon her young cheeks had never faded away, and there was that serene composure and grace in her mien which make up a beautiful, admired old age. Hers was a serenity springing not from the perpetual absence of sorrow, or from having ever dwelt in some vale of quiet loveliness, but from an energy which had risen triumphant over the most poignant griefs, and a cheering faith which looked beyond the grave. 'My child,' said she, clasping the hand of the agitated boy, 'never let despair fasten on so young a heart. If you tremble and weep on the first threshold of life, how can you breast the mighty griefs and conflicts of the world? Learn even thus early in the hour of darkness to hope for the glimmerings of light. Though your father be dead in his country's cause, and she, poor sufferer! your only parent on earth, in God's good pleasure may soon die, learn to look up with me, and to say confidingly, 'OUR FATHER WHO ART IN HEAVEN!'

Tears and smiles gleamed at that same moment from the uplifted eyes of the aged woman, and she looked as if she had caught the very spirit which makes the angels happy. And then with a fine eloquence, which consisted rather in aspect and expression, and in the mournful scene, than in any words which can be committed to our page, she proceeded, holding the boy's hand still in her own: 'Let God be your refuge from this time, my son; and whenever troubles come you shall not flee to him in vain. You shall be shielded from those which are too heavy to be borne, by the merciful hand of Him who tempers the wind to the shorn lamb, and you shall go forth to battle with the world with a strength not your own. Look at me, Fléance. Am not I three-score years old and ten, and have I ever despaired? I have seen nearly all who were dear to me and who set out with me in the journey of life one by one fall away from my side, until I am left almost alone and unsupported except by HIM. I have beheld my fondest hopes all perish, and I live but to acknowledge God's goodness, and to enjoy his benefits, and yield a willing submission to his providences; and cheerfully will I abide, while I have one to love in the world, and while with these feeble arms I can sustain one drooping head.   Listen to me, Fleance, and let me say now'what I may not have so good an opportunity again of saying.   Should your mother die ——'

The boy looked up and trembled as with an ague.   'Say not so!' said he.   'It cannot be; at least not yet—not yet!   She has been better for a week past.'

'All things are possible with God, my son; let us ever hope the best. But whenever such an event may come, you will be left alone to guard your sister; she is your only one.   I need not implore you to cherish and defend her.   Your own kind heart prompts you to do all that. But should I too die, and the aged must expect to die soon, there are truths which you must diligently instil into her young mind, and teach her to read that blessed Book which my poor dim eyes would have delighted to teach before they were closed for ever.'

The boy's countenance sparkled with an unwonted intelligence, and stretching forth his hand involuntarily to that sacred Book which lay near, silently indicated by his looks a promise which carried with it the force and solemnity of an oath.   Then dashing the tears from his eyes he ran to seek his young sister in the garden, whither she had just gone.   She was playing among the flowers, wildly beautiful as they. Taking her by the hand he led her back into the melancholy apartment from which she had escaped, and made her contemplate the faded form of her parent.   'She is her mother's image,' whispered the aged woman, 'her image to the very life.   The same speaking lineaments, the same auburn ringlets, the same soft large eyes.'

The child gazed about her unconsciously, awed into silence, but unable to appreciate the emotions which agitated their hearts.   With the exception of the dreadful sound of the distant cannon, and the ticking of a watch, and the hard respiration of the sleeper, a hushed stillness prevailed.   At last some women who were neighbors came into the room to inquire how the sick person did.   They looked ominously at her, whispered among themselves, and then shook their heads. 'I have just been told,' said one, 'of a remedy which has done wonders in consumption.'

'Consumption!' exclaimed the youth, looking up in consternation, and struck with the matter-of-fact air of the speaker.   The dame went on to say:

'The tea of liverwort has been known to cure the most desperate cases, if one can put any faith in what is told one.   It is true our poor neighbor was not so far gone as this dear lady, but he was wonderfully ill.   No one would have believed that he could live a month.   He was wasted away to a shadow.   He had hectic fever, night-sweats, and a cough that was painful to listen to; and he was getting worse, until some one told him to take the tea of liverwort, and he did so night and morning, and now he is a hale man, and ascribes his life to it.   Depend upon it, it is a great remedy in consumption.'

'Liverwort!' exclaimed the boy, starting from his seat with eager pleasure; ‘then I know where it may be found, and I will go instantly to obtain it.   It grows in the woods where Mary and I used to gather wild strawberries in June.   Spare me a little while, grand-mother.   The sun is three hours high, and I will gather a goodly parcel before he goes down.’

‘Do not stay long, my love.   Do not be absent after night-fall.’

The youth went to the door, then came back a moment, drew the curtains of the bed, and looked upon his mother’s face.   It was calm and peaceful, but the cheeks how sunken!   At times a transient smile would flit over it, as if some pleasant image were suggested, or as if she were anticipating those happy scenes which could not be won without a struggle — the last struggle of death.   He gazed long and ardently; then he took a little basket upon his arm and went out.

CHAPTER SECOND.

As he left the cottage (it was the cottage where he had been born) he murmured to himself, as he cast a hasty glance about its portals, that all things wore an air of neglect.   The vines wandered about wildly, the rose-trees drooped to the earth, and seemed to lament the hand which had ceased to care for them of late.   Neatness and trim embellishments speak of life and taste and happiness and hope.   But around the household where Death hovers and threatens to be present with his dark wing, flowers and all that is beautiful in the fields as well as the blue skies above them are nugatory and vain.   The time may indeed come again when we may merrily keep tune with the birds of spring-time, or with the reaper as he binds the sheaves of harvest; but we have no heart to enjoy the bloom or to gather the flowers which spring up in the valley of tears.   Nevertheless, the youth stretched forth his hand instinctively, and grasping a handful of half-blown roses which grew from a single stalk, placed them in the crown of his hat as he hastened forth upon his filial errand.   He took a solitary path which led to the neighboring woods.   He had just turned an angle of it, when a young woman met him from a near cottage.   She might have been a year older than himself, and he stopped to converse with her a moment; and the conversation was with the easy familiarity of those who from their childhood had been friends.   ‘The good news has already reached us,’ said she, brightening in all her features; ‘the enemy have been repulsed.’

‘The enemy!’ exclaimed the youth, reflecting back the same sudden joy, and holding the girl’s hand; ‘I seem at this moment to have none upon earth.’

A crimson hue flashed over her cheeks and then receded as suddenly.   A winning story had been told without words.   Minutes winged their flight; but hours would have seemed as minutes.   At last the youth reproached himself for tarrying so long, and hurried on without revealing to her his errand.   He could not help glancing backward once; he saw her retreating form, and smiled.   She was one whom having once seen one might well look back upon, and by virtue of that second glance the heart would take her image indelibly; and if she were never seen again, it would be an ERA in that HEART's HISTORY. He walked with quicker step and with a better spirit. He felt happier than before. The gloom of external things had in a measure vanished, and they appeared in all their natural pleasantness, and his heart swelled with a calm courage, and his destiny seemed more clear. Thus it is that a beautiful compensation is visible in God's severe providence; and when one affection is blasted or buried, there springs up a newer, sweeter one, sometimes from its very grave.

The youth went into the woods and began to search diligently and not without success for the plant which he had heard spoken of. He knew it by its pale flower, not unlike the violet. He pictured to himself its healing qualities, and he put the plants into the little basket with a firm confidence that they might bring back the hue of health to his mother's cheek and happiness to his home. And certainly a simpler cause than a slender flower has sometimes been sufficient to avert the shafts of death. He was very happy in this occupation, and labored until his back was weary, when perceiving that the sun was nearly down, and remembering his promise, he directed his footsteps toward home. He had proceeded a short distance, when he stopped to refresh the plants at a pure spring which bubbled up on the edge of the wood.

As he was engaged in this way, reclining idly on the turf, he was attracted by a sudden noise, and looking behind him saw four men of a rude aspect, who were unknown to him. He was not alarmed, except at the suddenness of their presence, apprehending nothing. But in an instant, before he could make any resistance or utter any cry, his mouth was closed, his arms were tightly pinioned, and he was dragged by a lonely path down to the water's edge. The ruffians then placed him in a boat which lay ready, manned the oars, and pulled rapidly from the shore. Twilight concealed the deed. He had been hurried away by a press-gang.

CHAPTER THIRD.

WHEN the evening was far advanced, and he did not return home, surprise and alarm seized on the unhappy household. What ulterior object could have detained him? He was too well acquainted with the thoroughfares to have lost his path in the woods or ignorantly to have strayed to a distance. The neighboring people were kind, and participated in the apprehension. They took lanterns and commenced a vigilant search; but they saw nothing except the flare of the lights as they streamed over chasm and ravine and rivulet, relieving the intense darkness. They stopped at intervals, making the woods ring with their shouts; the only response which they received was the echo of their own voices. The next day they renewed the search with the same success, but they found the basket filled with liverwort by the spring; and unable to trace his footsteps, they returned, and said that he must have strayed to the river and been drowned.

The night which came on was indeed gloomy in the chamber of the dying. A storm which had been long brewing burst upon the earth with relentless fury. The large, heavy drops dashed against the panes of glass, and the heavens were incessantly lit up with sharp lightning. If the wanderer indeed lived and was in the woods, which at that time were thick and inextricable, and extended for many miles in that vicinity, what but divine power could preserve him without food or shelter through the inclement night! A child had been once bewildered in these same woods, and they were unable to discover its hiding-place, though sometimes near enough to listen to its feeble cries, until at last it was found by chance on a winter's day, lying on the ground, with berries in its hand, naked and starved and frozen.

The aged woman sat by the bed-side rocking to and fro, or with her head bent down upon her hands in agony. But her spirit was absorbed in prayer to the Father who ordereth all things in his providence; and pausing not to inquire why the innocent were afflicted, or to deprecate His rod, she begged only for sustenance, and that all things might work together for good. And it is the prayer of such which bringeth peace to the spirit, and causeth it to be lifted heavenward above the vapors of the low earth, as the fragile plant beaten down with storms looks up to salute the sun-god. When she arose from the conflict she exhibited the same serene composure which had so long glowed upon her visage, as if it came from some perpetual source. Yet not unconsonant, a tear of pure pity stole from her eye. She noticed the small basket containing the healing plants, remembering by whose hand they had been plucked, and resolving to try their virtue, singled out a few, and placed them over the fire to be boiled. But the last tribute of an affection so touchingly bestowed was vain. The sick woman arousing, demanded impatiently her absent son. They invented some tale, which little satisfied her mind, that he had gone to a distance to obtain efficacious medicines, and would soon return.

The storm howled without. At midnight, when the taper burned dimly on the hearth, and the little Mary slept in her couch as soundly and as sweetly as if there were no troubles either within or without, and only the watchers were up, a flash, a crash, blinding, appalling, burst on the very roof, and a sulphureous vapor filled the house; and rising above the winds and pelting rain without, a cry struck upon the startled ear, 'FIRE, FIRE, FIRE!' The alarm spread far and wide, and a crowd assembled, gazing astonished at the rare spectacle. The flames spread upward and burst out in every quarter, and whirled round, and irretrievably wrapt the whole house; and in the deep confusion, forth from the crackling rafters and the ashes of a once happy home a litter was hastily borne to the nearest house which offered shelter; and there many steps were passing in and out, and strange faces gazed on the dying.

It was a scene of wonder, confusion, terror. No master-spirit directed the agitated people; and on the first moment when the houseless family could reflect with calmness, they discovered that the little Mary was missing. Painful suspense reigned in their bosoms, and a messenger hastened to bring tidings; but at that moment a rough kind rustic brought in the frightened child, and she clung trembling to the neck of her old relative.   An ejaculation, a burst of thanksgiving came from the lips of the latter.   Then she consigned the child to the arms of another, and turned to watch with attentive eye a fearful paroxysm of the mother.   Merciful Heavens ! one other such, and she would cease to live.   But her spirit yet lingered a little around earth, although full plumed for heaven ; and willing to impart with her lips the last kiss, and to breathe the last farewell, she murmured passionately, though with a faltering voice : 'MY SON ! MY SON !— WHERE IS MY SON !'

<hr>

CHAPTER FOURTH.

HE was far away over the wide, wide sea.   When he had been so ruthlessly torn from his home on the evening when he had gone forth on such a worthy errand, as soon as he had recovered a little from his surprise, he became conscious by the plashing of oars and the sound of the water on the keel that he was in the hands of sea-faring men ; but whither borne or for what purpose he could form no conjecture. Not a word was exchanged among the ruffian gang, but they pulled hard at the oars, and toward the river's mouth.   In an hour or more they came under the dark shadows of a ship's deck, and forcing the youth to ascend a steep ladder, instantly ushered him upon scenes which were to him those of a new life.   When he knew that the sails were set, and felt himself borne swiftly away, he could not tell whither, he supplicated and wept in agony, surprise, and rage.   It was all futile.   The breeze blew freshly, and when the morning dawned he was far from the home of his childhood and from the friends of his youth.   As he looked in the direction of the dim shores, and endeavored to recall the events of the night, he could hardly trust the evidence of his senses as to what had really happened, for all appeared like a dream.   As however the full reality burst upon his mind, he was ready to die with the most violent paroxysms of grief.

Days passed over him, and he learned to submit to the hard necessity of such a cruel bondage, yielding a silent, sullen obedience, and jeered at by the rude companions of his life.   He went mechanically about his allotted tasks, wrapt in a sort of oblivion, except when a memory of the past flashing over his mind drove him to the very brink of madness.   One day he had ascended to the mast-head, and as far as his eye could reach looked over the vast magnificent sea.   It was calm and silent, and not a sail was to be descried over all the boundless expanse.   Weary and sick at heart, he sought for some token of his childhood's home ; and as he drew forth the withered roses whose fragrance was not all gone, by them he pledged himself that he never would forget his lost friends.   Then the circumstances of his departure recurring to him, and how he had been robbed of his mother's parting blessing, and that he might never return to his native village again, but for the intervention of some good genius, he would have leaped into the sea.   As he lay in his hammock, and ventured to reflect at all, the same madness and despair possessed him ; and in a transport he stretched forth his hand to grasp an instrument of death, and his heart encouraged him to commit the great crime; but a torrent of tears coming instantly to his relief removed the weight which oppressed him; and remembering at that moment the admonitions last given by one whom he had loved, and whom he never expected to behold again, he lifted up his swollen eyes and exclaimed, 'OUR FATHER WHO ART IN HEAVEN!'

CHAPTER FIFTH.

THEN he fell into a tranquil repose. Wandering back to the untroubled scenes of his life, he was on the firm land, listening to the song of the birds, and to the murmuring of streams, and to the music of his native fields. The errand on which he had gone had proved successful, and there was a magical virtue in the plants he had gathered, which had restored the lost bloom to his mother's cheeks; and he saw one radiant with beauty, whose love could never change, but was reserved for him to make his life happy. All this was a sweet dream. But it did not make the morning wretched which scattered its brief illusion, but imparted a firmer courage, and seemed a welcome assurance of that which was to be. Thus Hope like a sweet singer follows us wherever we go upon earth; and though she may not deceive our vigilant hours, she leads the unguarded mind gently captive in dreams. Once as the youth looked abroad from his station, with only the sea around him and the heaven above him, as the hart panteth for the water brooks so his soul desired the word of God.

Nor was the wish which might have been considered a silent prayer unheard or ungranted. A comrade was committed solemnly to the deep. He obtained one relic found among his treasures, and on the title-page of the book was engraven 'HOLY BIBLE.' Had he left his own home a willing wanderer, such would have been the last and best gift which with the kiss of parting affection would have been bestowed; and it is hard and it is perilous to go far, far away on the long weary journeys of adventure or ambition, without this only chart, to guide to a protected haven, or to bring back the erring footsteps to the paths of innocence and peace. Weary, dejected, spirit-stricken, the youth found golden promises and a certain solace in God's Book. He made it his companion (for he found none other) at morning and at noon, and at midnight; in sunshine and in storm and in battle; and it shared his safety; and when the ship struck a coral-reef, he swam with it in triumph to the desert shore.

Years rolled over him, and the contact of the rude world had wrought its transforming influence on his character. He had armed his soul with a stern strength and resolution, and for the imbecility of youth he had exchanged the vigor and energy of manhood. During the long interval he had no tidings or missives from the home which he had never ceased to remember with tears and sadness. At last with emotions which cannot be defined (for so much of pain and doubt was mingled with a sense of pleasure) he found himself wafted toward the very haven whence he had set out. Here in terror and agony and compulsion he had commenced his wanderings, and he could not tell what termination they might now have. He had found his country, but he knew not where to look for his home.

Nevertheless with a bounding throb he leaped upon his native shore, and leaving the busy mart, directed his swift steps by a well-remembered path into the fields. The sun was sinking low in the sky, and the summer air was sweet; and instead of the rustling of cordage and the beating of waves he heard the evening carol of the birds. How sweet the transition from the dreary immensity of ocean to the verdant limits of fields and groves! Oh! who can know, save he whose heart has sprung toward the sea, and bounded like a bird in triumph over the waste of waters, what rapture it is to visit the land once more, to witness the sweet round of the seasons, to behold the verdure of fields, the foliage of trees, and the beauty of flowers; to listen to the lowing of herds upon the hills, to the noisy gladness of the running rill, to the murmur of winds through the solemn groves, and to suspend the votive chaplet in the temple where he offers up his prayers! As he advanced upon his path, every step seemed to awaken old images, and the whole train of associations which connects the present with the past; ever bringing before him some spot remembered by romantic reveries, pleasant adventures, holiday rambles or fond partings; and familiar faces glanced by him without the well-known recognition of other years; for he was unrevealed to all by reason of a changed aspect, and durst not make any inquiries, but chose to remain a little longer in suspense.

Presently he knew by the dense monuments which were seen at a distance that he was approaching the village place of graves; and beyond it he saw through the trees the spire of a small church glittering in the last rays of the sun. Here slumbered the generations of those who were once the life of yonder hamlet. A path led transversely over the spot, and it was the daily thoroughfare of those who hoped, and many with a religious trust, at one day to partake of its quiet rest. When he approached the spot sacred to the repose of those whom he had loved, he wavered and stood still, and averted his eyes and trembled. His boyish feelings returned and impetuously swayed his whole soul. As one who gazes upon a dark seal, and puts it away from him unbroken, and anticipates all, he hesitated to read the first intelligence from HOME. When at last he looked toward the scene he saw an additional white stone, but only *one*, marking the place of another grave. Many reasonings passed through his mind; he was in doubt and perplexity to whom it should belong. Bending over it by the dim light of day, he deciphered the inscription. He was standing over his mother's grave. He remained there a little while, and the tears which fell from his eyes were very silent. Then he directed his steps to the cottage, and seeing nothing but a pile of stones and ashes, and some charred timbers, he sat down wearied on a large stone which used to be the old threshold.

Two young women were drawing water from the well. It was one of ancient construction. An upright trunk of an old tree stood near the spring, and where its first branches had once jutted forth a horizontal beam was pivoted, loaded at one extremity, and so the water-buckets attached to the other were easily drawn up. He longed to taste the waters ; and rising from where he sat, and begging of them a little to alleviate his thirst, he found them sparkling and sweet as they were wont to be. Oh! many a time had he drunk of them and been refreshed, and many a time had he looked down upon them in boyhood to see his image, and many a time had he bathed his brow in them when weary, and many a time had he given them to the way-faring man who asked for them, and that too with a spirit which makes a cup of water doubly prized. And now, while he eagerly quaffed them again, his eyes acknowledged the matchless beauty of her who gave the boon ; and as he restored the cup with no ungracious air, he inquired if those who once dwelt there with the exception of her who slumbered in the church-yard still lived, and they answered YES, and they pointed to a cottage dimly seen among the trees.

When he turned away and left them, following the directions which had been given, they whispered eagerly together for a moment, and then one of them leaving her companion sought her own home, and wildly rushed into its doors ; and when inquired of by those who could not comprehend her hurried air, she could only laugh and weep alternately.

CHAPTER SIXTH.

WHEN the returned wanderer had followed the direction of the maidens, he came in a few moments to a secluded habitation, and hovered around it in the dusk of the evening, retreating frequently from the threshold, and not knowing how to make his presence known. At last he knocked gently at the door, and a voice which he should have recognized bade him enter. He obeyed the summons, and sat down as a stranger would in the house which afforded him a casual welcome ; but his heart told him that he had found a secure resting-place ; whence, after so many storms, he need not depart again upon his troublesome journey.

Ah! how like a pleasant picture was the scene which he beheld! The old clock telling the flight of time in the corner ; the old Bible lying open on the polished stand ; an aged woman, blind and bent down by infirmities, listening attentively, while a beautiful child, whose ringlets fell away luxuriantly from her brow, read to her out of that book. The guest composing himself, would have affected a short concealment, but unrestrained affection wears an ill disguise. For the aged woman arose when he spoke, and her sightless eyes appeared again to beam with pleasure ; and as she took his hand in her own, she said that strange music greeted her ears, for the voice she listened to sounded marvellously like that of *her boy.* So as one detected in an unworthy act he confessed all, and joyfully wept in her embrace. Then she asked him whence he came, and he replied from over the sea.

It takes few words and but a little time to tell the story whose plot and incidents and stirring events up to its dénouement have filled up the weary interval of many years. And when we compute the total amount of all which we have done and suffered, how doth it dwindle down to a small reckoning. We toil and bustle, and struggle and labor through many a day — and one page suffices to declare the whole! How happily the moments flew beneath the humble roof in listening to the mutual story! And the youth found that prayers had never ceased to ascend for him from one faithful heart, and perchance they had reached Heaven, and were answered at the very moment when he would have despaired. Thus it is that one rushes in some passionate hour to the crisis of his fate, and trembles, while in another clime the taper burns in the obscure chamber, and the prayer goes up which lets loose the guardian angel to stay the guilty hand.

Rumor, which is ever busy, flew over the little neighborhood, and groups of the aged and the young waited not for a better opportunity to gaze upon the lost found. Kindly intrusive, they mingled their tears, and embraces, and exclamations, and eager questions, with those of the small household, and could with difficulty believe the truth. The young man missed indeed the greeting of some who would have given him no less warm a welcome; for it is to be hoped that they had gone whither there is no such thing as partings. But he pressed alone, beneath the holy light of even, the hand which had given him the water to drink at the spring; and that night, beneath the trysting-willow, he kissed the brow which for so many waning moons had been gathering paleness.

A year passed over from the date of these events, and then another aspect presented itself in the youth's dream of life. The church-going bell sounded solemnly, and the long procession winding through the green lanes and alleys paused at the ready-made grave, and ashes were committed to ashes again, and dust to dust. We acknowledge the just debt of nature when the old depart, and brush away the tears which are as bright and sparkling as for the young, not to recur to them again. As well might we weep when the glorious sun sinks down in the sky at evening, or when any glowing light is quenched in darkness, or when flowers having finished their beautiful career drop their petals to the earth, or when the leaves wither and die at autumn, or when the wheat-crop is mowed down by the sickle, golden and fully ripe. And it is better for them, after having smiled with those who have smiled and wept with those who have wept, and passed through all life's checkered scenes and acquitted them of all its duties, and borne all its trials and heroically contended with its powers of evil, to lie down and sleep with patient waiting in the grave!

When the youth returned from paying the last tribute to the old, and passed by his native cottage, he saw it still in ruins, and resolved to rescue the place from long neglect. So ere long he ordered the rubbish to be cleared away, and a new cottage arose from the ashes, and became the abode of hospitality. And its precincts were as sweet and as verdant as ever, and the neglected plants took root and flourished again; and bright faces gathered around the hearth; while, equal to any fortune, he who had been so severely schooled in the past learned not to despair of the future; but burying all his griefs and forgetting all his sorrows in the bosom of his young WIFE, he experienced once more, and with tears of gratitude, WHAT IT IS TO BE HAPPY.

S T A N Z A S .

'LOOK NOT THOU UPON THE WINE WHEN IT IS RED.'

BY WILLIAM FITZ PALMER.

I.

O soft sleep the hills in their sunny repose
In the lands of the South, where the vine gaily grows ;
And blithesome the hearts of the vintagers be
In the grape-purpled vales of the isles of the sea !

II.

And fair is the wine when its splendor is poured
From silver and gold round the festival board,
Where the magic of music awakes in its power,
And wit gilds the fast-falling sands of the hour.

III.

Yet lift not the wine-cup, though pleasure may swim
Mid the bubbles that flash round its roseate brim ;
For dark in the depths of the fountains below
Are the sirens that lurk by the vortex of wo !

IV.

They have lured the gay spirit of Childhood astray,
While it dreamed not of wiles on its radiant way,
And the soft cheek of Beauty they 've paled in its bloom,
And quenched her bright eyes in the damps of the tomb !

V.

They have torn the live wreath from the brow of the Brave,
And changed his proud heart to the heart of the slave ;
And e'en the fair fame of the good and the just
With the gray hairs of age they have trampled in dust.

VI.

Then lift not the wine-cup, though pleasure may swim
Like an angel of light round its roseate brim ;
For dark in the depths of the fountains below
Are the sirens that lurk by the vortex of wo !

TIME'S CHANGES.

Time's telescope more wonderful appears
    E'en than his sythe, and deeper truths conveys ;
His tube prospective lengthens days to years —
    Reversed, our years it shortens into days !

Then ponder well the substance and the sum
    Of what, unscanned, a contradiction seems ;
Valued aright, compared with time to come,
    Time past is but the wealth of him that dreams.

THE MYSTERIOUS LAKE.

A SOUTHERN SKETCH: FROM THE NOTE-BOOK OF A CLERGYMAN.

NUMBER TWO.

SOME time ago, when I sent you Mr. EDITOR an account of that mysterious spring, THE WAKULLAH, I promised as you will remember farther particulars of this wonderful land in which my lot is cast. In performance of that promise I think of nothing which will interest you more than our near neighbor LAKE JACKSON, which I shall prove to be as self-willed and unreasonable a body of water for a lake as the Whigs fancy they have proved its illustrious namesake to have been as a president and a man.

Three years ago it was a beautiful sheet of water, extending north and south a distance of about seven miles, and varying in width from one to two. Its shores were uneven; sometimes rising abruptly to the height of forty or fifty feet, and sometimes running in a gentle slope from the water's edge to a considerable distance; but always they were beautiful. The sturdy live oak was there, casting its branches out with perfect *abandon;* looking as brave and free as the noble ship itself of which it some day will form a part. The grand magnolia was there, the monarch of the southern grove, to which the oak succumbs as the stout and serviceable yeoman bends to his slight but handsome and accomplished lord. These with the countless other trees which this climate produces, tied together with festoons of wild vines, and draped with long gray moss, made its shores a resort for all who loved the beautiful in nature. Nor was art entirely wanting. At an early period after the occupation of the country the neighboring planters, availing themselves of the many beautiful situations which its banks presented, built their houses on the high bluffs that overlooked the lake, and cultivated the grounds in falling gardens down to the water's edge. Two at least of these establishments would in all respects compare favorably with many in older countries; and in hospitality and good cheer they are certainly no where to be surpassed.

You have perceived that in all this description I have been speaking in the *past tense;* and you will ask, 'Why adopt this mode of telling your story?' You shall hear.

Two years ago the dwellers on the lake were startled to observe a strong current setting from all directions toward one or two particular spots. The waters were all greatly agitated, and strong eddies were observed to be working where the currents met. The level of the water rapidly subsided several feet, then suddenly remained stationary for a few hours, and then fell again as the same mysterious currents set in afresh from every side. This continued until the whole lake, with the exception of a few deep places here and there, was drained; and the poor fishes and other swimming and crawling things that 'do business in great waters' lay floundering in the mud, at the mercy of animals of the other element, chiefly men and hogs. But there were many who went there not for fish but to find out what had produced so great a revolution. This they easily discovered. The strong currents had ploughed broad furrows in the sand, and following them they found their termination in deep chasms and crevices in the rocky bottom of the lake, but which were too narrow and irregular to be satisfactorily examined.

Here then was the explanation: tired of the sunlight and glitter of this upper world, it had broken the crust and inundated Symmes's hole; or weary of the name it bore on earth, or disgusted with the injustice its namesake encountered among men, it had gone down to Radamanthus and to Minos for their opinion.

I was not there at the time, and cannot say for certain. It was some months after the event that I found time to ride out with one who once was a bold dragoon, but who now sleeps, alas! where he can never again hear his bugle's call. A merry ride we had; but sad am I, poor G ——— ! to think even of its joyousness, when I remember all that has happened to thee since.

But for the ride. The Captain mounted on a vicious little black, and I upon a powerful and well-conditioned roan; and followed by a couple of attendants, we started for the runaway lake. Our intentions were chiefly scientific; but to be ready for every emergency we each of us shouldered a double-barrelled fowling-piece heavily loaded with buckshot, and had plenty more of the *matériel* stuffed in flasks in our pockets, or slung in pouches over our shoulders.

The first view of the lake, as we emerged from the skirt of woods, was very fine — a vast sea of waving grass. Water could not have yielded more readily to the influences of the breeze than did the long and feathery herbage which spread for miles before us. Wave after wave rolled up grandly to the shores, making long sweeps and broad furrows where the wind played freely, and petted into dimples and eddies as they rounded the headlands, and were met by opposing currents.

But we did not stand long to look. There was a stronger attraction in the clouds of game which from time to time were floating over the lake from one feeding-ground to another; and we plunged into the long grass, riding till we got within gunshot of the nearest pond, and then proceeding more cautiously on foot, that we might not alarm our quick-sighted prey.

'There!' exclaimed the Captain, in a nervous whisper, 'what a fine chance! Why did you not shoot?'

I gave him no cause, you may rest assured, for a second similar remark, for as he afterward laughingly said, 'I let nothing escape my *aim*;' impossible distances never daunted me; all I wanted was to see the bird, and bang went my gun, and away flew the shot, describing harmless parabolas in the air. The consequence was, that before my companion had done any thing my shot was all gone; and not caring to burn powder to no purpose, nor to shorten his sport by borrowing his ammunition, I left the field and wandered off in search of the chasms of which I had heard so much.

I soon came to one of the gullies which traverse the bed of the lake. It was perfectly dry, but it was easy to tell from the appearance of the sand which way the waters had run; and walking down an imperceptible slope, a few hundred paces brought me to a kind of basin, in the farther side of which I saw the subterraneous opening. I could make nothing of it. I might as well have tried to study the constitution of the human brain by looking into the orifice of the external ear. For about a foot there was a stratum of sand mixed with a rich loam, but then came the rough and jagged edges of crumbling limestone; and these were so irregular, and were so lapped one above another, that nothing more could be seen than six or seven feet below the surface.

The irregular shape of this aperture suggested to my mind the reason why the waters, as I mentioned above, suddenly ceased to flow. The fish and rubbish of all kinds which were carried down might easily have choked up the entrance, and for a time at least have obstructed the passage altogether. But why the waters should run away at all, or where they ran to, I found nothing to help me decide; nor has any one whom I have asked been able to tell. It is the general opinion here that the lake has committed this same freak at least once before, although none of the present generation remember any thing about it. A stump of a pine tree, which must have taken at least forty years to grow, is found in one of the lowest parts of the bed of the lake; and it is not too much to argue from this circumstance, that for so long a period, a great while ago, the place was bare of water. Beside this, I have been told that some Indian pans were found near one of the chasms, as if it had in old times been a camping-ground or spring. But it is probable enough, without any proof except what is found in the nature of the strata of which this part of the earth is composed. After we got below the soil we came to a bed of 'rotten limestone,' which goes down nobody knows how deep. We have tried to get through it once or twice, in the attempts we have made at Artesian wells; and at once at least in the capitol-yard we got down several hundred feet; but it was a hopeless undertaking. We bro e our augers, and our wise legislators have to content themselves with surface water instead of drinking it fresh from the antipodes.

Well, this vast body of limestone is nothing but a petrified honey-comb, and there are chambers enough in it to hold all the water that was ever drunk in by the deserts of Zahara: of course therefore the only thing that is necessary when we desire to empty our lakes is to cut a hole in the bottom, and they sink. This unsoundness in our physical construction had the effect of frightening from among us a worthy immigrant from either the Granite or the Key-stone state. Finding no spring in his immediate neighborhood, his first care after 'squatting' on a desirable piece of the public domain, was to dig a well. He and his son John and his boy Jim in a few days got pretty well down into the bowels of the earth, and hoped that one day's labor more would furnish them with a purer and cooler draught than they could get from the Branch, near half a mile away. Such were their attempts at night; for they had heard the sound of water, and a few more strokes they were certain would cut the vein and bring its volume into their well. But to their dismay they found next morning that the bottom of their well had fallen out, and a heavy current was moving lazily along and gradually undermining the ground on which they stood. It did not take them long to harness up their oxen, to throw their skins and kettles into their carts, and to ' be movin'.' They were assured that hundreds of years might elapse before the earth would cave, but it was to no purpose; and I should not be surprised to hear that they are planting corn and roasting potatoes very near the place from which they originally came. But I am running away from my lake.

After satisfying my curiosity, I bethought myself of returning to the gallant Captain, and as the sun was nearly down, of setting our faces homeward. But it is an old experience that the descent to Avernus is an easier thing than to retrace your steps, and my fate was classical. To follow my footsteps in the sand was an easy thing enough; but when I came to the place where I entered the gully, there was the 'opus' and the 'labor.' All around me and two feet above me I saw interminable fields of grass; and my passage through had left no more trace than that of the birds I had been seeking had done upon the air. 'Whichever way I turned' was grass; and to continue the burlesque upon the hero, who is quite *àpropos* to subterraneous thoughts, I could have confessed ' myself am grass,' if it would at all have helped me out of the difficulty. I travelled on, not knowing whether I was right or wrong, occasionally firing off my powder and shouting always until I was completely tired out; and then I laid down upon an arm-full of the said grass and rested.

How long I should have remained there I do not know; but fortunately sportsmen came within hail, and in answer to my appeal, pointed out where the Captain and the horses were. I took the direction, and watching the sun, hurried to them. I had been going precisely wrong for more than a mile, and but for the sportsmen I should have been compelled to spend the night upon the lake. A short ride brought us to B——, where we had a comfortable dinner by candle-light, and then a long dark ride carried two tired people home. The next day the servant brought to us, nicely cleaned, the brant the Captain had bagged; but when I asked him for the snipe that I had shot, he declared they were only kildees!

Between you and me, Mr. EDITOR, Tom ate those snipe himself!

Tallahassee, (Florida,) January, 1842.			Yours,			L.

WISDOM: A LACONIC.

Nor men nor days unborn, untold,
Shall ever witness Wisdom old;
For she alone, refreshed by time,
Still marches onward to her prime;
Doomed, like the lines herself can teach,
T' approach it never — never reach.

ENGLAND'S MERRIER DAY.

BY W. H. CARPENTER.

COME listen all who proudly speak our brave old English tongue,
And all whom WILLIAM SHAKSPERE is a household god among;
Young giants of the western world, of goodly Saxon strain,
Dull doubters from the land of France, grave pilgrims from Almaigne:
Ho! Merchant leave thy galleons, well-freighted though they be,
And dusky Labor cease thy toil, and give an ear to me;
Pale dame in splendid solitude, brown knitter in the sun,
And merry damsel light of lip, yet coyly wooed and won;
And stately maiden brideward bound, with dark imperial eye,
And love-lorn girl with golden hair, and ever-frequent sigh —
Come each, come all, and gather round, and hearken to a lay
Of England's Court and England's Queen in England's merrier day!

The summer sun looks brightly down from blue unclouded skies,
O'er princely London gaily decked in maskers' changeful guise;
For all around and every where is seen a gorgeous store
Of glittering silver tissues, and silks embroidered o'er;
And every where and all around rare tapestry is seen,
With emblems and devices of flowers and branches green:
The city gates are garlanded, the conduits run with wine,
And banners kiss the wanton air along the lengthened line.

The wealthy burgher treads the street with consequential pride,
And in French hood and farthingale the matron walks beside;
The wild apprentice, club in hand, is laughing loud and long,
The Euphuist with dainty phrase is mincing through the throng;
The sinewy craftsman sallies forth, clad in his best array,
The Temple student swaggers by, and quotes the newest play:
The fierce Alsatian struggles up from dark and loathely lair,
To mix once more with honest men, and breathe the purer air.

And far and near the crowd appear, as wave on wave they come,
To the music of the city bells, to trumpet-blast and drum;
A motley tide of human life, of ribald and of sage,
From lisping child to sturdy youth, from manhood to old age;
From all the wolds of Essex, from the fertile lands of Kent,
The country squire and husbandman with earnest speed are bent;
And from old Surrey's lofty hills they pour in thousands down,
To swell the veins and arteries of famous London Town!

From head to heel in buff and steel, with gonfalon and lance,
A hundred horse from Charing-Cross with steady step advance;
Next ride three hundred gentlemen, the goodliest of our Isle,
With flaunting plume and silken scarf, and velvet of three pile;
The lord and knight, all richly dight, of loyal heart and bold,
The housings of whose matchless steeds are shining cloth of gold;
The ladies of high lineage, and in their midst is seen
On a gentle milk-white palfrey our own right royal Queen!

Now bursts one loud heart-cheering shout from all th' assembled throng,
As if the mighty multitude spake with a single tongue:

'Huzza! God bless our dear Queen Bess!' uprose from Temple-Bar,
And all the street, from strand to Fleet, caught up the loud huzza;
St. Pauls repeats the welcome, and with a right good will
It echoes and reëchoes from the May-pole on Cornhill;
It speaks in thunder from the Tower — in thunder and in flames,
And waves in silent gracefulness from all the ships of Thames!

Now spur me on! — the Queen has gone to where old Eltham's pile
Uprears its head and looks on Kent, the garden of our Isle.
What ho! thou gray-haired seneschal, thy robes of office don,
A courier nears with breathless speed the palace of King John;
The soldier from the watch-tower a noble train hath spied,
A noble train with tightened rein, and hitherward they ride;
And by her milk-white palfrey, and by her lofty mein,
And by her regal bearing, full well he knows the Queen!

Of tables groaning 'neath the weight of ever-bounteous cheer,
Of how was chased the livelong day the noble fallow deer;
Of hawking sports by river side, by field or bosky dell,
Of minstrel's song and jongleur's art, it skills not us to tell;
So pass we these, and shaking off sweet music's dearer thrall,
Tread with the chosen of the land the fair-proportioned hall:
The roof with dainty carvings is quaintly fretted o'er,
And storied arras hang around, and rushes strew the floor;
The lattice pane with curious stain subdues the light of day,
And tempers all within the hall with soft and doubtful ray.

'Room for the Queen!' and followed close by gentleman and dame,
All towering in her pride of place, the gracious maiden came:
The haughty Essex curls his lip, and scarce inclines his head,
While Cecil bends his fawning knee, like courtier duly bred;
And Raleigh feigns to shade his eyes, as if so great a blaze
Of glory round the presence shone, he feared to trust his gaze;
Whereon her Grace right coyly smiles, with most demure surprise,
And all the woman at her heart glows in her sparkling eyes.

But seeing Burleigh's awful frown, a light laugh laughéd she,
As thrice he shook his solemn sconce with owl-like gravity;
Then turning to Southampton, she bade him forth and seek
His friend the poet-player, with whom she willed to speak:
And all the court drew slowly back, and formed a glittering ring,
And WILLIAM SHAKSPERE knelt before proud England's woman-king!
No pompous terror bound his brow, no azure braid his knee,
And yet there never lived through time a mightier man than he;
From charnel bed upsprang the dead, his bidding to fulfil,
And sprites of air as bond-slaves were obedient to his will.

'Rise, Master SHAKSPERE,' said the Queen; 'our play-mates sadly moan
That thou should'st take their baser coin and stamp it as thine own;
Nay, answer not, for such a charge a worthy one we hold,
Which by a cunning alchemy transmutes their lead to gold;
We do commend the loyal vein in which thy plays are writ,
And marvel not our lieges find thou hast a proper wit;
For never saw we merrier knave than that same craven wight,
The burly Sir John Falstaff, young Harry's guardian knight;
Could'st thou but set him wooing, man, rare sport methinks 't would prove;'
And SHAKSPERE said: 'So please you, the portly Knight shall love.'
Retiring then, with fluent pen and joyful heart he strives,
And hence the pleasant comedy of Windsor's Merry Wives.

THE QUOD CORRESPONDENCE.

The Attorney.

CHAPTER XIV.

EARLY the next morning there was a violent ring at the door of Miss Crawford's house, and a letter was left for Lucy. It came from Phillips, informing her that he had seen Higgs, and was sure that she was mistaken in supposing the will to be a forgery; and begging to see her, that he might tell her all he had heard. He would not come without her consent. And that was all. She read it through, folded it up, and placed it in her bosom. She knew that Phillips was deceived, and there seemed no hope left.

'*He* has given out too!' said she, in a low, broken voice. 'God help me! for George has no one left now but me.'

She went up to her own room, drew a chair to the table, and clasping her hands together, leaned her head upon them, and endeavored to think. Thoughts came fast and troubled enough; but they gradually settled down into one strong and intense purpose, that of seeking him out, wherever he might be; of bearing with every thing, and of never giving up till she found him.

She rose up, took down her hat and shawl, and prepared to go out. She spent a few moments at her toilette; added one or two ornaments which Wilkins had given her long before, and which she always wore. There was little indeed to arrange; for her well-worn dress, faded and mended in many places, and miserably thin for the season, showed that she was one of the 'very poor;' and God knows they have little to do with ornament. But she remembered that Wilkins had once been proud of her beauty; and she was not willing to believe that that time had passed for ever. Whatever he had fancied or praised in happier hours, she thought of now: and Hope whispered that when he saw her he might think of old times, might ask her to come back to their snug old home, and say he regretted the past, and beg her to forgive and forget it. How her heart leaped at the thought! How the mild patient face beneath that old bonnet brightened! And as she stole down the stairs there was a smile on her cheek, and a feeling of happiness in her heart that seemed like the dawning of brighter days. She was a long way off from where they lived; but she hurried on. She felt stronger than she had been for weeks, and her step was lighter. If the thought of a chilling reception sometimes crossed her, she chased it away. If she could but see him; free him from the influence of that dreaded man, and know that he was safe; even then, if he drove her from him, she would lay her down amid her withered hopes, and die without a murmur, for there would be nothing left to live for; and perhaps when she was dead and in her grave, and out of his way, he would think kindly of her as he had once done; and although she would not know it or care for it then, still there was a sad pleasure in the thought.

But Fate has a strange way of interfering with the plans of all. It takes its courses of mingled storm and sunshine; thwarting the best devised projects; blighting hopes; bringing happiness where all was despair; crushing bright hearts to the very dust; but onward, forever onward; never pausing, never resting; carrying plotting, scheming, restless, rebellious man in its giant arms.

At the very time that Lucy was standing in her little room, thinking only of him, Wilkins was pacing up and down the walk in front of his house, in a mood which, had she seen it, would have scattered her day-dreams to the winds. Up and down that walk he went, casting fierce glances along the street, and muttering to himself. So gaunt and thin had he become; his beard long; his eyes sunken, and glowing like two globes of fire deep in his head; and his whole frame wasted, as if the spirit were too strong for the body, that his wife would scarcely have recognized him.

Presently a cart drove around the corner and stopped in front of his house. Wilkins strode up to the man, and shaking his fist in his face, said:

'Is this what you call hurrying? I spoke to you more than an hour ago; and did n't you say you 'd come right off?'

The man looked at him for some time, as if in doubt what to make of him; then he took off his cap, drew out a cotton handkerchief, wiped his face very hard, after which he rolled the handkerchief in a ball, flung it back in his cap, put his cap on by a dexterous jerk at its leathern front, and muttered something about his horse not being fed, and he had waited for that.'

'D — n you and your horse too!' muttered Wilkins; 'nobody 's in a hurry now but me — nobody but me; and every thing is driving, push-ing, tearing at me all at once. Come on now, will you?' said he to the carter, who having jumped off his cart, stood staring at him, and wondering what sort of a customer he had picked up. 'Jam your wheel against the curb-stone, so as to load without trouble. There; now come along.'

He turned to the house, followed by the man, half sullen and half intimidated at his savage temper. Wilkins walked straight to the door of his room; and finding it locked, without uttering a single word or searching for the key, dashed it open with his foot. He thrust his hands in his pockets, strode to the middle of the room, and seating himself on the table, commenced gazing about him, whistling, and swinging his feet to and fro, without speaking. The cartman stopped just inside of the door, waiting for orders. 'What am I to take?' he at length inquired.

Wilkins looked at him as if he had forgotten he was there, and won-dered what he wanted. Then he sprang across the room, seized a chair and flung it violently down in front of him.

'Take *that* — and *that* — and *that!*' shouted he, dragging forward article after article, and crowding them toward him as if he would have pushed them over his very body. 'There 's your work. Be about it, will you?'

The man seized the things, and hurried them into the street, glad to get out of the room. He went out and came back several times, until he had taken all that had been pointed out. Then he paused, and asked what was to go next.

'Every thing! every thing!' exclaimed Wilkins. 'I'll make a home for her; a home such as those have who pray to God night and day to kill them! Take every thing; beds, table, chairs — *all.* Do n't leave a stick or a rag, or a coal of fire to keep her from freezing.'

The cart-man dragged the heavy table across the floor.

'Out with it!' shouted Wilkins, pushing it along. 'You 're as weak as a child.'

He shoved it into the entry, and then returned to the room. The cup-board happened to catch his eye, and he jerked the doors violently open. A bottle half full of brandy stood on the shelf. He took it down, emptied its contents into a cup, and drank them off as if they had been water.

'Brandy 's nothing, now-a-days. All *here,*' said he, thumping his fist against his breast, 'is so hot and burning, that every thing feels cool now. What!' cried he, seeing the man again entering the room, 'you want more, do you? More — always more! That 's right — that 's right!'

The liquor seemed to have maddened him. He sprang on the bed; dragged it to the floor; dashed with it into the street, and flung it on the cart. He muttered as he went, 'that if she did come back, she should find an empty house;' and as he thought of that, he laughed and shouted and swore, rushing around the room, seizing different movables, and casting them into the street; nor did he desist until not a thing was left. The cartman shrank from his savage eye; for of all the men he had ever dealt with, Wilkins was the most ungovernable. He obeyed every gesture, and did not pause until there was nothing more to be done.

''There — now go!' said Wilkins. 'Take them away: sell them for whatever they 'll bring — no matter what; and fetch the money where I told you.'

The man went out of the room, mounted his cart, and drove off. Wilkins stood at the window watching him until he turned a corner, and then he went round the room, examining every part of it, cup-boards, fire-place, window-sills, even the walls, to see if any thing was left; but the harpies of the law could not have swept cleaner.

· 'Now let her come!' said he, exultingly. 'All 's ready for her. Let her come, I say; and she 'll find her home what she wanted to make mine. Ha! ha! She *would* run away, would she! Ha! ha! ha!' And he paced up and down the apartment, waving his hands over his head with a kind of fiendish glee, and laughing until the room rang again. After a while, he leaned carelessly against the walls, and said in a musing tone:

'Nothing left! nothing left! I 've done my work well! All empty! all empty!' He kept repeating these words at longer and longer intervals, until gradually and almost imperceptibly a change came over his countenance. It grew stern, and more dark and gloomy, as he said:

'Well, old room, good by! It'll be a long time before I see you again. I feel sad at leaving you, for I feel like a ship without an anchor. God knows where I'm going now! I'm cut adrift, and am floating on to where all seems black. Well, you are not what you used to be when *she* was here — and we had plenty — and she loved me. She *did* love me, poor Lucy! God bless her! And I — I loved her! But she went off — yes, she went off! — she went off!'

He kept muttering these words to himself, and gazing vacantly about him, and at last he sauntered into the street and strolled off.

How little a space there is between sorrow and joy! How our very fate depends on the turning of a straw! Had Wilkins remained in that room but five minutes longer what a change might have taken place in his lot! For not that time had elapsed, when there was a knock at the door, so faint and trembling that it seemed scarcely to touch it. It came again and again. The door opened, and a face, pale and thin but exceedingly beautiful, looked in, and gazed timidly about the deserted room. Then a female entered hesitatingly, as if she feared a rough welcome; and Lucy found herself once more in what had been her home. And this was the end of all her dreams! Here her hopes crumbled to dust. She had nerved herself to encounter every thing but this; cold looks, hard words, even ill usage; but not this desolation.

The room appeared to have grown time-worn and ruined, even in a day. It looked as if years had passed over it since she was there last. The windows were dim and dust-covered, and the hearth black and cold, as if there had been no fire there for months. Now that their common home was gone, a gulf seemed to have started up between her and her husband which separated them for ever. All that had ever passed in that room sprang up in her mind as vividly as if it were even now before her. It was one of those waking dreams, so full of sadness, in which the voice of the past comes sighing in the *ear*, conjuring up phantoms of scenes and things long forgotten, and touching chords in the human heart that seemed unstrung for ever. Things which she had never heeded she thought of now. She recollected the position of each article in the room. Here had stood the table — there the old broken chair — there an old chest. They were mere pieces of furniture, miserable and old; yet they were part of her home; and it made her very sad to think that they were gone. She recollected the many happy hours she had spent in that room; their many wants too, as they became poor; how she had concealed them from her husband; how he had scolded her for it; and at the same time caught her to his bosom and called her his dear little wife. How cheerful the old room was then! and how gay he was! and how merrily he used to laugh at its inconveniences, and say it was a poor place, but they would have a better some day. Could this cold, dreary chamber, with its broken and dismantled walls, be *that* room! Could the man who had struck her to the earth be George!'

While she was standing there, an old woman hobbled down stairs with a pail in her hand. She had lived for a long time in one of the upper rooms, and was very poor and almost double with age. Lucy called her by name. She stopped, set her pail down on the floor, and leaned on a stick which she carried to help her as she went.

'Ah child! is it you?' She always called her child, for she seemed so in comparison with her. 'It's a long day since I see you; and so you're going away, are you? More's the pity; for now I'll have no one to sit by me the long nights when I git the agy; nor to give me my doctor stuff; nor to speak, as if there was some one to care for an old soul like me. As for *them*,' said she, giving an indignant fling of the elbow in the direction of the second floor: 'they'd see me die under their very eyes, and would n't stir a finger to help it. Out on them! I say,' and she knocked her cane violently on the floor; 'out on them! for a selfish, good-for-nothing, thieving pack, as they are!' And again the stick came in contact with the floor, in a succession of short venomous knocks.

'And so you've moved away?' continued she in the same whining tone in which she had first spoken; 'and where are you going?'

Lucy shook her head, and said she did n't know; she said she had been away for a few days, and was not aware that her husband intended to leave there; that she had come back and found every thing gone. 'Perhaps *she* could tell where he was.'

'No, no!' said the old dame, drawing in her shrivelled lips, and shaking her head so long that she seemed to have forgotten it was customary not to continue the motion for ever: 'no, no! he never speaks to the likes of me. He comes in and he goes out without so much as a 'Good day, Martha! how's your rheumatis, or your cold, or your corns?' No, no; none of the little attentions as are so gratifying to old ladies like me. *He* tell me! He comes in; slam goes the door, lock goes the key; and then he walks, and walks, and walks all night long; and then when morning comes, slam goes the door, snap goes the key, and off he goes for the day. *He* tell me! He was here half an hour ago a-loading a cart with things; and I went in, and went a-purpose; he did n't say a word but once, and then he called me a d —— d old woman, and told me to get out of the way or he'd break my neck. He *do* it! I'd like to catch him at it!'

The mere idea of his performing a feat of that kind caused her to burst into a strain of vituperation which easily accounted for the little attention which she received at the hands of most of her neighbors; as it required a pretty stout head and no very sensitive ears to remain in her neighborhood when she was fairly under way.

Lucy, finding there was nothing to be gained from the old woman, whose key was becoming more and more shrill every instant, went to several of the neighbors; but they could tell her nothing more than she had learned already. One or two confirmed the old woman's story, but knew nothing more. The room had been shut up for some time, and Wilkins had not been there in the day-time. One man had observed him one cold morning some time since standing on tip-toe at his window and looking in. He remained but a short time, and had not been seen by him since.

There was nothing left now but to seek him among his comrades. His wife's cheeks burned with shame as she thought of the low haunts of vice which he had of late frequented; and for a short time that feeling mingled with fear was so strong that it almost made her shrink from her purpose. But she thought of what he had once been to her, and all her old affection gushed up at the idea of the fate which would be his if she failed to see and warn him.

Drawing her bonnet so as to hide her face, and disguising herself as well as she could, (for she well knew there were many places in this dark labyrinth of souls called ' the city,' where her beauty would bring any thing but protection,) and with a shrinking yet hopeful heart she set out.

Hour after hour fled by as she searched in vain. At some places she received information which urged her on with renewed hope; at others she was mistaken for one of those females whom God made and man blighted; and only subjected herself to the ribald taunts and sneers which are so liberally showered upon the wretched and broken-hearted. Through places that might make a bold spirit quail, that poor girl bent her steps; for as her husband's money grew low he became desperate, and associated with those even more reckless than himself; men whom suffering had driven to crime, and crime to despair.

It was late in the day, and hope was nearly dead. She was walking wearily toward a house in a dark narrow street which she had never heard of before. She had inquired the direction of several persons, who looked strangely at her when she did so, but gave her the information she required. It was the last place to which she had been directed, and in spite of all her misgiving thither she went.

It was a tall old building, which seemed going to pieces from age. The bricks had toppled down from the chimneys; the floors sagged; the mortar had been beaten by the weather from between the bricks; and the stone-work of the doors and windows was cracked by time and exposure. The windows were old and broken, and patched and stuffed in many places. Altogether it was a wreck, and stood in a neighborhood rank with vice and suffering. Opening from the street was a door with its lintel so cracked and crumbling that it threatened to come down on the heads of all who entered, and rendering it a matter of no small labor to open or shut it.

At this door Lucy knocked. All was silent, although but a moment before she had heard the sound of voices, as if a large number of people were within.

She knocked again, and was more successful; for two voices, apparently engaged in consultation as to the propriety of admitting her, reached her ear. Then by dint of several violent jerks the door was opened, and a man looked out. After surveying her from head to foot he told her to walk in. Lucy obeyed, stepping just inside the door.

It was a small room, and about as old and ruinous as the rest of the building. In the centre of it was a wooden table with two bottles on it, several dirty tumblers, a large piece of cheese, and part of a loaf of bread. Although she had heard the sound of many voices before she knocked, there was but one other man in the room; and he was sitting by the fire with his hands thrust in the pockets of his great-coat, smoking an unusually long and black cigar. He had a fur-cap drawn

over his eyes, and was contemplating a small stump of wood with
intense abstraction.

The person who admitted her was short and square-built, with a
wolfish eye, and a large swelling throat, which looked as if it hankered
for a halter.   When he had ushered her in, and after contemplating her
with evident admiration, he said, with a slight distortion of the face,
intended to be insinuating :

' Well, sweet-heart, which of us do you want ? '

Lucy shrunk from his bold glance, and hurriedly told him that she
was looking for Mr. Wilkins, and had been directed there to find him.

' Oh, it 's *him* you want, then ? ' said he, with a leer.   ' He *does* come
here sometimes, but he is n't here now.'   Turning to the man at the
fire : ' I say, Bill,' said be, thrusting his tongue in his cheek, and
jerking his thumb over his shoulder, ' she wants Wilkins.'

' She *does*, does she ? ' replied the other, removing his cigar from his
mouth, and gently tipping the ashes from its end with the point of his
little finger, as he spat upon the floor ; ' there 's a good *many* that does,
'specially the state-prison.   Who is she ? '

' Some gal or other — *I* do n't know her,' replied the other, looking
over his shoulder, and again scrutinizing the girl · from head to foot.
' Not so bad, n'ither.'

' It 's a blasted shame in George to cut and run, and leave her !   It
is n't honorable, it is n't ! ' said the man with the cigar, raising one foot
after the other to a shelf considerably higher than his head : after
which he put his cigar in his mouth and smoked violently for some
moments.   There was something in his appearance and even in his
crude notions of honor which caused Lucy to draw toward him as if
for protection from his sinister-looking companion.

' How long have you known Wilkins ? ' inquired he, speaking
through his teeth, which were tightly closed to prevent the cigar from
falling out ; and with his face screwed in a complication of wrinkles to
enable him to see through the smoke which eddied about it.   ' Young
women do n't know exactly, of course ; but how long — about ——— ? '

' A long time,' replied she timidly : ' I 'm his wife.'

' His wife ! ' exclaimed the man, dropping his feet to the floor,
jerking his cigar from his mouth, blowing out a furious cloud of smoke,
and starting up.   ' Married to him by a parson ? — all sound, tight and
reg'lar ? '

Lucy replied in the affirmative.

' Then what the devil brings you here ?   Tell me that !   Get out of
this place as fast as you can !   Come along.'

As he spoke, he flung his cigar in the fire, buttoned his coat to the
chin, and taking her by the arm, led her into the street.

' Are you taking me where I 'll find my husband ? '

' No ! ' replied the man bluntly ; ' I 'm taking you out of this neighborhood.   This is no place for you.'

Without waiting for her reply, he placed her arm in his, and led her
on until they came to a broad thoroughfare.   Here he stopped.

' Now, my good woman, take a friend's advice.   When a man has
made up his mind to go to the devil, *let* him ; for go he will, in spite of

you. Your husband has done that, and you 'd better not cross him.
Above all, do n't look for him in such holes as that you 've just left ;
and as you value your life do n't mention that you 've been there.   All
I can tell about Wilkins is that he has n't been at any of his old
places for a week or more.   If I was you I 'd go to the police and
inquire.   Perhaps he 's cleaned a house ; stopped an old gentleman ;
robbed a mail, or something of that kind ; and while you are wearing
your little soul out, he 's stowed away snug and comfortable at the
expense of the State, with a man to wait on him and shut the door
arter him to keep the cold out.'

Having thus delivered his opinion, he perpetrated an indescribable
contortion intended for a bow, and diving round a corner instantly disappeared.

Although his parting advice was that of one well acquainted with the
world, or at all events with that portion of it with which he mingled, it
had little weight with Lucy.   For all she remembered or thought of was,
that Wilkins was gone ; all trace of him was lost, and all hope with it.

The sun was glowing brightly when she set out in the morning.   It
gradually ascended the sky and journeyed to the west.   The shadows
of the buildings which had been thrown in sharp outline in the street
began to creep up the opposite houses ; then the walls became dark,
and the sun shone only on the tall chimney tops.   As it sank gradually
down, the streets became dim and gray ; some of the narrow ones were
dark already ; and the last thing that reflected its light was a distant
spire whose golden ball gleamed in the sky like a globe of fire.   At
last that too became less and less bright, until it disappeared and night
set in.

Lucy's strength failed as her hopes faded, and with a weary step she
sought her new home.

<hr />

CHAPTER XV.

MAN does not become a fiend at once.   He does not burst into the
world with a panoply of crime about him ; with a heart of stone ; a
conscience seared, feelings dead, and affections withered at the root.
These are the work of years ; the result of long and bitter struggle.
Every noble feeling, every warm impulse ; all that is great and good
and glorious in the human soul battles to the last, before it yields its
purity ; and when they are crushed, and sunk, never again to rise, the
victor has won a barren wreath.   He bears marks and brands, stamped
upon heart and feature, never to leave them while life lasts.   His
triumph and curse go hand in hand ; for when the heart loses its freshness, every hope grows dim, and has a shadowy fear hanging like a pall
over it.

The Attorney had passed the fiery ordeal, and came out of it callous
to crime, but with a heart teeming with its own vague fears.   Tormented by a thousand suspicions and forebodings of ill, he was in little
mood for the business he had to perform.   He never drew near that
girl, or even thought of her, without a creeping, cowering sensation of
guilt and shame.   He had experienced the same feeling in other instan-

ces; but it was rare, and never stepped between him and his victim. With his eye fixed on his object, diverging neither to the right nor left, he pursued his course. This was the strong feature of his character. Obstacles never daunted him. Distrust, suspicion, and disgrace thickened around him, but never turned him from his path. There were times indeed when rumors of himself came to his ears that made his heart fail and his eyes grow dim; when he sank his head in his hands, and thought of the past, and looking back to early days, longed to be a boy again. Yet none knew it but himself; and to the world he was always the same.

He had reached a stage of his game where it became complicated. Each move involved so many consequences, connected with what had already been done, and what was yet to be done, that it required a degree of cold, quiet calculation, which at that particular time he felt little able to give. He saw at a glance the full advantage of Higg's suggestion; but it came so suddenly, and required such immediate action, that he had not time to ponder, and scheme, and brood over it, as was his habit; and in no easy frame of mind he set out for Miss Crawford's house.

Just at the gray, dusky hour, when Lucy turned with weary steps and drooping spirits to seek her home, the Attorney skulked out of his den. He walked slowly along the street, with his head bent down on his chest; his hand thrust in the breast of his coat, where his fingers worked convulsively, and his eyes fixed on the ground. If he occasionally raised his head, and gazed up at the pale stars which were beginning to flicker in the twilight, or the gray moon as it floated through the sky, it was not of them that he thought. Sometimes he paused, and stood perfectly still, as if he had forgotten whither he was going; and then hurried rapidly on for a short distance, and again fell into his old pace. He kept on, in lonely by-streets, where he thought there would be few to interrupt him, or to read his gathered brow and anxious eye.

For a long time none heeded him; for every man had his own little world in his thoughts; and if a straggler glanced at him as he went by, he might have dwelt for a moment on the care-worn face on which his eye had just rested, and then forgot it.

At last a crippled beggar stopped him and whined forth a supplication for charity. The Attorney thrust his hand in his pocket and gave him a small coin, scarcely conscious of what he did.

'Ha! that's something,' muttered the beggar; 'something's better than nothing — nothing is better than starving.'

Startled at this strange exclamation, Bolton turned to look at the man more narrowly; and as he did so, the light of a street-lamp fell strongly in his face.

'Ha! ha!' shouted the man, looking in the wan face of the Attorney. 'That's better than all! The lawyer disgorges — the lawyer Bolton.'

'Who are you, in the name of Heaven!' demanded Bolton, drawing back from his startling companion.

'Who am I?' repeated the beggar; 'who am I? And you to ask that! I am Tom, the beggar: I *was* Mr. Thomas Nikols once; that was before I knew you. Now I'm only the beggar. Shall I tell you how Thomas Nikols became what you see him? *Shall* I?' shouted he, thrusting his face almost against that of the lawyer, and laughing with a kind of devilish glee.

'No, no; not now!' exclaimed the Attorney, with something like a shudder, and he hurried off. Long after he was out of sight, there stood the cripple looking after him, and making the still street ring with his loud mocking laugh.

'They all haunt me now!' said Bolton, drawing in his breath with a gasp as he paused to rest. 'More than ever before. They crowd round me; and to-day, from morning till night, they've been about me. Let them come! They'll not scare me from my prey. Do I not know that they are dreams — dreams? How my heart beats!' He placed his hand on his heart, and felt its wild, irregular throbbing; and for an instant a sickening sensation of fear came over him; and the idea shot athwart his mind that its pulsations were unnaturally strong; some vital chord might snap, and he fall dead on the spot. For that single instant his terror amounted to agony; but that subsided, and he went on; although until he reached his place of destination, this was the uppermost thought in his mind.

When he reached the house, he stood and contemplated it as it rose a huge black mass against the sky, without form or outline, looking as if in that spot the very darkness had been embodied and concentrated. There was no light burning. The windows were shut and dark. Every thing about it looked so chilling, and silent, and church-like, and Death had been at work there so recently, that it seemed as if the grim phantom still lingered in the precincts. No one was stirring in the neighborhood, for it was an out-of-the-way street. The Attorney held his breath, in hopes of hearing some one approaching; but the barking of a dog a great way off, and the rumbling of vehicles in the distant streets, were all that broke the silence.

Feelings hitherto unknown began to creep through his mind; and a deep, thrilling presentiment of coming evil hung round him like a shadow. Suddenly, uttering a loud, taunting laugh, and a curse at his own folly, he sprang up the steps and rang the bell until the house echoed. This broke the spell, and he was again the cold, crafty man that he had always been.

He inquired of the servant who came to the door, if Miss Crawford was at home, and on being answered in the affirmative, without waiting to be announced, he walked directly to the room and entered. All trace of indecision had disappeared. He was perfectly collected; his cheek was a little pale, but his eye was bright and clear, and his manner confident and unconstrained; and he prepared to play his game with his usual coolness.

Miss Crawford was sitting at a table, with her face half turned from him, so that she did not observe him as he entered. She was very pale, and there were traces of tears on her cheek. A book was lying on the table, with a glove in it, as if she had been reading, but her eyes were then fixed on the floor. Bolton gazed at her without speaking.

'I can see the old man in her eye;' thought he, 'but she's worse;

she's suspicious. He was not. Fine words go far with most of them. Will they with her? We'll see. I'll trim to the breeze. I'll make the offer; but she must at the same time see that there is no choice, except to marry or starve.'

His train of thought was interrupted by the girl herself, who happening to look up, caught sight of him, and instantly rose, her eyes flashing and her cheeks coloring at the recollection of his last visit.

'May I ask to what I am indebted for this visit?' For an instant Bolton quailed before the keen, scornful eye of that single girl, who stood before him strong only in the consciousness of her wrongs; but it was only for an instant; and he answered calmly:

'I come here to see Miss Crawford on matters of much interest, both to her and to myself.'

Seeing that he paused, as if he expected an answer, the girl said coldly: 'State your business briefly. From what I know and have heard of you, I care not how soon our interview ends.'

'If I were not traduced,' said the lawyer, speaking gravely, and weighing every word before he uttered it, 'I should be more fortunate than hundreds who are better than myself. I am fully aware that many foul slanders are in circulation respecting me; and I now feel them the more deeply, that they have reached your ears, and you believe them.'

Miss Crawford made no reply, although he evidently paused for that purpose.

'May I not at least be allowed the opportunity of clearing my character, by learning what has been said against it?' said he earnestly.

'I make no charges, and wish to hear no justification,' replied the girl firmly. 'Let me know the nature of your business at once, or I shall retire without it.'

From this abrupt answer there was no appeal; and Bolton said in the same calm manner that he had hitherto adopted: 'Since you wish it, I'll waive all farther allusion to these idle tales, which a breath might scatter, and come at once to the object of my visit, which refers principally to yourself, as connected with your father's will.'

Miss Crawford became exceedingly pale, and her fingers grasped the top of a chair convulsively.

'You need say no more,' said she; 'I understand all the rest. You would tell me that this house is yours; that I am an intruder on your bounty; that the possessions of which you defrauded me are no longer mine; that my father's house, in which I have lived from infancy, is no longer a home for me; that I must go from it, what you have made me — a beggar. You see, Mr. Bolton, the thoughts of some people are written in their faces, and can be read.'

Bolton bit his lip; and his cheek flushed slightly; but there was nothing else to indicate emotion on his part, as he said: 'I am deeply grieved that you interpret my thoughts so harshly. Had you heard the offer I came to make, whether it be agreeable or not, you will at least acquit me of selfishness; and if you accept it, it will settle this whole matter much to my satisfaction, and I shall only be too happy if it is to yours.'

'And the offer is — what?' inquired she, without the slightest abatement of the coldness of her manner.

'That you should share the fortune with me,' replied Bolton.

'I thought so. If I will give you a portion of my fortune, you will leave me the rest.'

Bolton's face wore a soft smile, but it was a dangerous one, as he answered : .

'I am particularly unfortunate in not being understood.'

'Was not such your meaning, Sir?' said Miss Crawford, keeping her eye fastened on his, and watching every sign of equivocation or guilt; 'your language was plain enough.'

Distrust and anger were written in every feature as she spoke. Bolton saw that there were prejudices which he had not the time to overcome; and he felt that he was watched by one whose intellect was naturally keen, and whose faculties were sharpened by fear and suspicion. So he determined to appeal at once to her interests.

'Such was *not* my meaning,' said he, in a decided tone. 'And it is time that we came to a full and clear understanding of it, without farther waste of words. When I offered to share your father's property with you, it was by making you my wife. On these terms, and on these alone the wealth which your father has made *mine*, will become yours, and at your disposal.'

'Now, at least, I understand you, Sir,' said she, drawing herself up; while every feature of her beautiful face seemed gleaming with anger and contempt : 'you would buy my silence; for the sake of my fortune, you would take the encumbrance of its lawful owner. You would be magnanimous, and make the beggar your wife! No Sir!' said she, speaking with an earnestness that astonished him; 'not until every appeal that the law allows has been made, will I yield possession of one single thing. From court to court I will contest that will as a forgery; and until expelled from hence, I will maintain my hold. Should I fail, I would starve in the streets before my name should be changed for yours. Begone, Sir! Until the law gives you this house, you have no business here.'

'Resist if you will,' said the Attorney, still retaining full command of his temper; 'but you will repent it. You will expose to the world the stain upon your family, which otherwise would be known to but few. You will tarnish the fame of her who gave you birth, and will cast a shade upon the memory of the gray-headed old man who has just gone to his grave.'

''T is false!' exclaimed the girl, now fairly aroused; ''t is you who disgrace them, yourself, and human nature. I *will* make this matter public. The truth shall come out at last, and prove *them* unsullied; and brand *you* for the black-hearted man that the world now suspects you to be. You cannot frighten me from my purpose. If I fail, I shall only have done my duty; if I succeed, I will have justice measured out, of which you shall have a full share.'

'You speak confidently; but you do n't know what law is,' said Bolton, coldly.

'I know what it is meant to be. It is intended to shield the weak from the strong; the injured from the oppressor; to right the wronged; to keep down injustice and crime. That's what it 's *meant* for; but there are those who disgrace it as much as they disgrace the image of the great God which they bear.'

The Attorney had remained cool until now; but now he fairly shook with passion, as he answered in a quick, stifled voice:

'It is *my* turn now. I have made a fair and honorable proposal to you. I have offered to share the fortune which you father gave me, with one whom I know he loved; not from fear of what you or the law could do; not from love of you, but from gratitude to him. I am frank, you see. You have scouted my offer; insulted me, and claimed the law of the land. That law you shall have, to your cost. Drag this matter from court to court, and from court to court I'll follow it; and when it is decided, what the law allows you, you shall have; but not one tittle more; not the tenth part of a cent, if you were begging your bread; not one crust to keep the soul in your body! Now you understand me!'

'It would be devilish strange if she did n't,' said a stern voice behind him. At the same time a heavy hand was placed on his shoulder. ' So the devil has dropped his mask?' Bolton turned and found himself face to face with a young man of four or five and twenty, whose manner plainly showed that he had overheard a part of the conversation. Before the Attorney had time to collect his thoughts, the other said:

'Are you going out of the house? or will you wait until you are thrust out like a dog?'

'By what right?' demanded the lawyer.

'No matter,' interrupted the stranger. ' *You* are not the person to question that.'

Bolton measured him with his eye. He was slight, but tall and muscular, and might prove an unpleasant antagonist. The lawyer was no coward, where his life was not immediately concerned; but there was nothing to be gained by a scuffle; and that was a thing which he never at any time lost sight of. So he said:

'I did not come here to raise a riot over the grave of my friend, or to break in upon the grief of his daughter by outrages or violence that would disgrace a midnight brawl.'

'Your last words to Miss Crawford were certainly expressive of very great consideration for the daughter,' said the stranger, with a slight sneer. ' I have told you to quit this house; and now you *must*, without farther parley.' As he spoke, he led him to the door, but using no violence. He opened it and pointed to the entry.

Every feature of the lawyer's livid face was distorted by the scowl which settled on it, as he turned and fixed his eye on him; and shaking his thin finger, he uttered the words:

' *I'll remember you!* '

'I do n't doubt it,' replied the young man; and he slammed the door in his face.

Bolton strode through the entry, banged the street-door after him, and sprang down the steps into the street.

Nearly the whole time that he had been in the house his confederates, Higgs and Wilkins, had been loitering about it. No sooner was he come out than they joined him.

Mr. Higgs was considerably elated; possibly by the fineness of the night, although it is not unlikely that several visits which he had paid to a small tavern three streets off might have had something to do with it. Wilkins, on the other hand, was the same sullen savage that he had been for some time past.   When he joined the Attorney he did not utter a syllable; but stalked silently at his side; noticing him no more than if he had been a mile off.

'Well, old boy;' said Mr. Higgs, speaking a little slowly, and somewhat thick: 'when is it to be?'

'Never!' answered the Attorney, abruptly.

Mr. Higgs stared at him solemnly.

'I beg pardon, Mr. Bolton,' said he; 'but did you make use of the word *never?*'

'I did.'

'Speak out, man, will you?' said Wilkins, in a harsh voice: 'what have you done?   We must know some day, so tell us at once; what luck?'

'D — n her! none! This blasted will must be proved. She rejected me; scouted me; all but cursed me. I bore it as long as I could, then I threatened; and by —— she defied me; and vowed she would not quit the house till forced by law.'

'A young woman of mettle,' ejaculated Mr. Higgs.

The Attorney did not notice him, but went on. 'She has a fellow leagued with her; a young slip as fierce and proud as herself. He looked as if he only wanted an excuse to take me by the throat. Ha! ha!' muttered he, between his teeth, shaking his hand at the empty air, and striding along, so that it was no easy matter for his companions to keep pace with him.

'Did you place your hand emphatically on your heart, so?' asked Mr. Higgs, steadying himself in front of the excited lawyer; and after several attempts, laying his hand on the spot designated, 'and try to come the insinuating over her? It's wonderful how they swallow that — them women.'

'Then there's trouble in the wind,' said Wilkins, bluntly.

'She'll fight to the last.   Then there's this boy, too; a lover, I suppose.   Let him look to himself!   He has crossed me; and few do that without repenting it.'

'That's true!' muttered Wilkins; 'but,' continued he, in so low a tone that the lawyer could not understand him; 'there's a day of reckoning, when our score will be settled.'

He said nothing more, but dropped behind his companions; for he had observed a dark figure following them, keeping in the obscure parts of the street, but always having them in full view. He stopped to watch it, until they were at some distance off, when the person suddenly darted forward. It was a female, with her face so closely muffled that he could not see it; but a hand touched his arm, and a voice that thrilled through his very heart said:

'George, can I speak one word with you?'

Wilkins gasped for breath, and staggered against a wall, as powerless as a child.   He could not speak.

'George, dear George, for God's sake let me have a few words with you!' said the same low, supplicating voice. She took his hand, which shook violently, in both of her's. 'You will George, will you not?'

'Holla! what are you about? Come on, will you? We're waiting for you,' shouted Higgs.

'Do n't go! do n't go, George!' exclaimed the girl, earnestly; 'do hear me — *do*, before it's too late!'

The man hesitated; but at that moment both Higgs and Bolton turned back and began to come toward him. He drew himself up, unclasped the fingers which were twined round his own, and flung the hand from him:

'Begone!' exclaimed he.

'No, George, I will not! Hear me but this once; give me but five minutes, and I will never trouble you again.'

Wilkins bent his mouth to her ear, and said in a hoarse whisper:

'You know how we parted last. If you follow me, we'll part so again.'

The girl shrank from him, and her husband strode off without once looking back.

THE WARRIOR LOVER.

BY J. M. ORDWOH, ESQ.

I've roamed over mountain,
　　I've plunged the dark wave,
I've bled on the battle-field,
　　Where fell fast the brave;
I've parched in the tropics,
　　Nor strove to be free;
I've chilled 'neath the polar-star,
　　Maiden for thee!

Dark deserts I've traversed —
　　Dark, rugged and drear;
Through burning sands struggled,
　　Nor felt toil or fear,
And dost thou then love me,
　　All scarred though I be?
My fair form was mangled,
　　Dear maiden! for thee.

Sweet hope! thou'rt fulfilled!
　　These smiles are my joy;
And hearts in such sunshine
　　Can know no alloy!
Though we roam by the river
　　Or sit by the sea,
My life and its hopes, love!
　　Centre in thee!

LITERARY NOTICES.

HISTORY OF NAPOLEON'S EXPEDITION TO RUSSIA, in 1812. BY GENERAL COUNT PHILIP DE SEGUR. HARPERS' Family Library: Volumes 141–2. pp. 662.

THE combined energies and horrors of war, it is well assumed by the publishers of these intensely interesting volumes, were never perhaps so frightfully exhibited as in the memorable Russian campaign, of which they are the subject. If in some instances we read of armies more numerous, never was there one in all respects so formidable as that with which the French emperor marched to the invasion of the country of the Czars. Amounting to nearly half a million of men, it was composed for the most part of veteran soldiers long accustomed to victory; its officers, from the field-marshal to the subaltern, had been thoroughly trained in the school of war; and it was led on by a chief whose name alone carried dismay to his enemies. And yet this mighty host, seemingly invincible by human means, was discomfitted, scattered, and destroyed; conquered, not by its enemies, but by the avenging elements that were armed against it. 'Nothing,' says the American editor, 'can more effectually dissipate every illusion of military glory than the perusal of this dreadful narrative; nothing more strikingly manifest the folly as well as wickedness of that unhallowed ambition which seeks aggrandizement by deeds of aggression and blood.' Well may it be termed a '*dreadful* narrative.' We have read many accounts of this disastrous campaign, but do not remember ever to have encountered, save perhaps in 'Russia as it was in 1812,' from the pen of a German writer, so vivid a description of its sanguinary incidents as is contained in the narrative of Count SEGUR. He but depicts to his readers 'that which he saw, and part of which he was;' yet in concluding his task, he calls upon his brave comrades to bear their testimony to the truth of his sad picture; and adds that in their eyes and hearts, full of great remembrances, its colors will appear pale and dim. We make a single extract, including as least revolting in its yet sufficiently sad details a sketch of the *beginning* of the distresses which attended the retreat of the but late 'Grand Army' through Russia:

"The army marched enveloped in a chilling mist. This mist became thicker, and presently a blinding storm of snow descended upon it. It seemed as if the sky itself were falling, and uniting with the earth and our enemies to complete our destruction. All objects rapidly changed their appearance, becoming utterly confounded, and not to be recognized any more: we proceeded without knowing where we were, without perceiving the point to which we were bound; every thing was converted into an obstacle to stop our progress. While we were struggling with the tempest of wind and snow, the latter, driven by the storm, lodged and accumulated in every hollow, concealing unknown abysses, which perfidiously opened beneath our feet. There the soldiers were ingulfed, and the weakest, resigning themselves to their fate, found their grave in these treacherous pits.

"Those who followed turned aside; but the tempest, driving into their faces the snow that was descending from the sky and that which it raised from the earth, seemed resolved to arrest their farther progress. The Russian winter, in this new form, attacked them at every point; it penetrated through their light garments and their rent and worn-out shoes. Their wet clothes froze to their bodies: an icy envelope encased them, and stiffened all their limbs. A piercing and violent wind almost prevented respiration; and seizing their breath the moment it was exhaled, converted it into icicles, which hung from their beards all about their mouths.

"The miserable creatures still crawled shivering along, till the snow gathering in balls on the soles of their shoes, or a fragment of some broken article, a branch of a tree, or the body of one of their comrades, encountered in the way, caused them to stumble and fall. There their groans were unheeded; the snow soon covered them; slight hillocks marked the spots where they lay: there was their only grave. The road, like a cemetery, was thickly studded with these elevations; the most intrepid and the most indifferent were affected; they passed quickly on with averted looks. But before them and around them there was nothing but snow; this immense and dismal uniformity extended farther than the eye could reach; the imagination was astounded: it seemed a vast winding-sheet which Nature had thrown over the army. The only objects not enveloped by it were some gloomy pines, trees of the tombs, with their funereal verdure and their gigantic and motionless trunks completing the solemnity of a general mourning, and of an army dying amid nature already dead."

Let us ask with CARLYLE, had these poor sufferers *themselves*, and the still more unfortunate victims who survived them, any quarrel with the antagonist forces against whom they were sent forth, through the insatiate ambition and relentless cruelty of *one* man? Busy as the devil is, not the smallest! They fell, whole hecatombs, a sacrifice to an unhallowed lust of conquest. But we would not pursue the melancholy retrospect. The great result which this campaign precipitated taught the belligerent nations that

—— 'too long at clash of arms amid her bowers
And pools of blood, the Earth had stood aghast;'

and though there have not been wanting pens, from that time to the present, to almost deify NAPOLEON; to pronounce, as does MANZONI in preceding pages, his spirit 'lovely, beneficent, divine,' and prone to noblest triumphs; yet how has legitimate public sentiment changed! No one can read the work before us without being struck with the indecision, recklessness, and even despair, which BONAPARTE exhibited in this his most memorable invasion. It was on rising from a perusal of these volumes, that we encountered the following passage from the papers of ' a Philosopher,' a professor, at the time of which he writes, in the University of Leipsic. Like the narrative of Count SEGUR, it is the testimony of an eye-witness:

"At length the day dawned on which the great Napoleon himself was expected to honor Leipsic with his presence. He did not appear however until three days after the time appointed; and meanwhile the chief authorities of the town were moved about from place to place, and kept almost continually on their feet. We had indeed a most weary time of it during these three days. At length the great man arrived, and gave us an audience in the King of Saxony's palace in the market-place. Here the domineering character of the man displayed itself most conspicuously. He came burning with wrath against the university, and almost the first words he uttered were: 'Where are the deputies of the university?' My colleagues and myself immediately came forward, when he overwhelmed us with a torrent of invective, on account of some students who had enlisted in the corps of Luckow's volunteers, as if the students had been school-boys who could not take a single step without the permission of the Senatus Academicus. He then turned to the mercantile authorities, and demanded ' How many millionaires have you in Leipsic?' (he alluded to francs, but those interrogated thought that he meant dollars;) and when it was answered him that there was not one, he clapped his hand upon his pocket with a sarcastic leer, as much as to say: 'I'll find out a method to make them render up their coin.' Avarice and the lust of dominion seemed to be the only passion of his soul.

"When the audience was at an end, and Napoleon was departing, one of my colleagues ventured to step forward to address him. The Emperor started back, apparently doubtful what the intentions of my friend might be. For so timorous was this great man grown, that he lived in the constant dread of assassination; and when I was at Königsberg, I remember his once leaping out of a boat in the middle of the Pregel, and making for the shore, because he had observed a movement among the crowd upon the opposite bank of the river, and imagined that an attempt was about to be made upon his precious life. But on the present occasion, when he discovered that the professor had no dagger in his bosom, and merely wished to mollify the tiger with a few civil words, he grinned scornfully in his face, and then turned his back upon him. And this was the great man who had made the world his footstool, and whom all the nations worshipped as a perfect god! To me he appeared to be nothing but a drill-sergeant, who had a certain knack of railing the rabble into obedience to his will. Neither in his demeanor nor in his language was there the smallest trace of dignity or grace. Terror was his only talisman.

"The Colossus was now tottering on his pedestal, but he had not yet fallen. He collected his strength for one last desperate effort, and assembled all his forces in the neighborhood of Leipsic. My house was in the outskirts of the town, and commanded a prospect of a large portion of the battle-field. Cannon-balls and hand-grenades flew around us on all sides, and many peaceful inhabitants were struck dead in the streets. The hot tide of battle then set in upon the city itself, and raged furiously within its narrow precincts. But the brave Allies were at length victorious, and before night-fall I had the satisfaction of witnessing from my windows the flight of the discomfitted foe. And what a flight it was! Pell-mell they went — neck and heels, by scores, into the ditches which intercepted their ignominious retreat. Napoleon himself escaped by blowing up a bridge in his rear, and thereby consigning to death or captivity many of his devoted train. Did I not burn with the desire that my hand had been then upon his throat! '*Voici*,' I would have shouted, '*voici, scélérat! le Recteur de l'université de Leipsic qui vous avez si maltraité!*' The retreat of several thousand Frenchmen was cut off by the waters of the Elster. They surrendered at discretion to a company of Prussian jagers: and when I saw them marched, with their general at their head, between a double-colonnade formed by the allied troops, my mind recurred with great satisfaction to the *furcæ Caudinæ* and the *sub jugum mitti* of Roman warfare."

BALLADS AND OTHER POEMS. By HENRY WADSWORTH LONGFELLOW, author of 'Voices of the Night,' 'Hyperion,' etc. In one volume. pp. 132. Cambridge : JOHN OWEN.

IT is but a little while ago since we had the pleasure to announce the *fifth* edition of the 'Voices of the Night;' and we hailed the fact as an evidence that the love of true poetry, the poetry of the heart and the affections, had taken so general and deep a root among us. The beautiful volume before us we are sure will share the fate of its immediate predecessor. It will be widely read, admired, and treasured up. The book opens with the 'Saga of the Skeleton in Armor,' which appeared originally in the KNICKERBOCKER, and is followed by 'The Wreck of the Hesperus,' a poem of great power, and abounding in felicitous language and forcible illustration. We cannot yield much admiration for so common-place a couplet as

'The skipper he stood beside the helm,
  With his pipe in his mouth;'

although it may serve as a foil to such graphic lines as the following :

'Colder and louder blew the wind,
  A gale from the Northeast ;
*The snow fell hissing in the brine,
  And the billows frothed like yeast.*'

The skipper's little daughter bears him company, who trembles at the gale and the angry sea, and is lashed by her father to the mast. A sublime picture ensues of the struggling vessel, the fog-bell and the dim 'light of the light-house' on the distant coast ; the lifeless skipper, all stiff and stark, lashed to the helm, while

'The lantern gleams through the gleaming snow
  On his fixed and glassy eyes!'

Mr. LONGFELLOW well understands the force of our simple vernacular expressions. Observe the following :

'And ever the fitful gusts between,
  A sound came from the land ;
It was the sound of the *trampling surf*
  On the rocks and the hard sea-sand.'

. . . . .

'She struck where the white and fleecy waves
  Looked soft as *carded wool* ;
But the cruel rocks, they gored her side
  Like the horns of an angry bull.'

Many of the later poems in this collection we had pencilled for insertion; but the eager public, and those who serve it oftenest with literary delicacies, have generally anticipated us; so that we content ourselves with calling the attention of our readers to the volume itself, and especially to 'The Children of the Lord's Supper,' from the Swedish of Bishop TEGNER, and the admirable and picturesque sketch of the manners and customs of rural life in Sweden, to be found in the introduction. It is in the *form* of prose, but is in reality 'unmitigated poetry.'

LECTURES ON MODERN HISTORY: from the Irruption of the Northern Nations to the Close of the American Revolution. By WILLIAM SMYTH, Professor of Modern History in the University of Cambridge, (England.) In two volumes. pp. 935. Cambridge: JOHN OWEN.

Mr. SPARKS, our distinguished historian, in introducing the first American from the second London edition of this valuable work, informs us that its author has been eminently successful in removing the numerous obstacles which have hitherto so greatly embarrassed the student of history. He teaches his readers how to read history for themselves; shows them the path, and furnishes them the best lights for pursuing it; enables them to form a just estimate of the principal authors, and to bring forward in bold relief those prominent parts of history to which their attention should chiefly be directed. His plan is broad and comprehensive, and such as could not have been so faithfully carried out, without a critical examination of a large number of authors, and close and patient meditation upon the contents of their works. His method is perspicuous, and well suited to the end he has in view. He selects certain periods of history, and groups together the great events in each; investigating their relation to each other in the order of cause and effect, and their results on the civilized and political condition of states and communities; preserving as he advances an easy and natural transition from one period to another. The author has treated the subject of the American Revolution with so much candor, and such perfect freedom from party feelings and national prejudice, that Mr. SPARKS expresses a doubt whether any American writer can claim on this score a higher degree of confidence. He has drawn from original fountains, consulted public documents; and has examined the American side with no less diligence than the English. 'In short,' says Mr. SPARKS, 'it would be difficult to find any treatise on the American Revolution from which so much can be learned, or so accurate an estimate of the merits of both sides of the question can be formed.' A work like this, distinguished in its externals by the characteristic care of the publisher, must needs find a ready acceptance at the hands of the American public.

WEALTH AND WORTH, OR WHICH MAKES THE MAN? In one volume, 16mo. New-York: HARPER AND BROTHERS.

SUCH is the admirable title of an admirable little book which we could wish were in the hands of every young American reader and every American father and mother. In its salutary teachings, and in the interest which attaches to it as a narrative, it forcibly reminds us of kindred works by Miss SEDGWICK. In these days of English republications, when much that is unsuited in its character to our republican institutions finds its way every where among us, a work like this, which shows in a manner the most forcible and attractive the superiority of moral and intellectual worth over factitious position or money, is especially refreshing. We are glad to perceive that this little book is the first of a series. We shall look for the accomplishment of a national good among our rising generation, through the instrumentality of lessons so clearly portrayed and felicitously enforced. The volume is of a neat, convenient form, and otherwise executed with taste.

THE JACQUERIE: A NOVEL. By G. P. R. JAMES. In two volumes, 12mo. New-York: HARPER AND BROTHERS.

WE should like, were such a thing possible, to lift the cover from the brain of Mr. JAMES, and to be able to survey amid its vexed convolutions the *disjecta membra* of the scores of unborn novels that must be simmering in a ' dome of thought ' which has hitherto proved so prolific of historical tales. We say ' *must* be,' because it is scarcely possible, judging from the fecundity which he exhibits, that Mr. JAMES should have less than three or four works in his mind at the same moment ; making his head a sort of literary cauldron, replete with material 'slab and good,' and ready for combination at the shortest notice from his publishers. We must not be understood, however, as depreciating the great merits of Mr. JAMES as an historical novelist. His is not altogether a fatal facility ; for the least elaborate and finished of his performances are never unreadable ; they even rarely fail to be in a high degree what novel-readers term 'exciting' and 'thrilling.' Mr. BUNN, speaking of FORREST's appearance at Drury-Lane Theatre, observes, that he had not heard him repeat three lines of his part, at his first reading in the green-room, before he foresaw his eventual triumph ; and he thus judged, he says, from the *energy* of his manner. This is one great secret of Mr. JAMES' success. In his pictures of human character and passions our author has often won all suffrages. His plots at the same time are not always of the clearest, nor are the incidents and hair-breadth-'scapes of his principal personages always on the side of a reasonable credulity ; and yet nearly all his works are entertaining, and to most readers intensely *interesting*. As we have before remarked, his individuality, phrenologically speaking, cannot be large. He is in our judgment a great mannerist. Let the reader run over in his mind the prominent characters of Mr. JAMES' novels, from ' Philip Augustus ' down to the present, and observe the *sameness* of certain heroes and heroines, and mainly also of his style. This is a great fault ; and it is this limited range which we fear will ere long consign many of our author's works to Time's wallet for oblivion. In the volumes under notice, the reader will be especially impressed with the vivid description which is given of the well-known revolt of the French peasantry in the fourteenth century, when their king was imprisoned in England, and their unhappy country was rent with civil feuds and drenched with fraternal blood. But for a picture of some of the most important events and personages of this chivalric and memorable era, we must refer the reader to 'The Jacquerie ' itself, with the assurance that they will find it amply to reward perusal. It is no small correlative praise of their attractive qualities to say, that the demand for the works of Mr. JAMES is as great as at any previous period.

EDITOR'S TABLE.

THE COUNTRY-WOMEN OF NEW-ENGLAND. — A correspondent in New-England, who professes to have burning at his heart the welfare of the beautiful country girls by whom he is surrounded, has sent us a communication, from which we shall venture to select a few passages for the benefit of our fair readers in all sections of Yankee-land. 'The young women of the country towns of New-England,' he writes, 'are much more eager to adopt the city fashion of dress, than to bend their thoughts to the garniture of the mind; and hence they are becoming more and more tinged with that compound of silliness and affectation which always arises from an attempt to ape where one cannot imitate. Mammoth tournours, suffocating corsets, and low-cut dresses, find their way to our most retired country towns within a month after they have arrived from Paris, while the standard *literature* of the day is unthought of and neglected. I once knew a young lady of excellent natural sense, quick in learning, and of acute perceptions, the marvel indeed of the whole village, by reason of her acquaintance with general literature, who asked me if COOPER wrote 'Ivanhoe;' adding, that of all the fictitious works she had ever read she considered 'The Solitary' the best! Such persons present a fair mark for the arrows of ridicule; and we accordingly find that almost every tale-writer has tried his hand at the bow. Now this is hardly just. There may be rare exceptions; yet in nine cases out of ten, the defect may be traced to a *wrong education*. The usual course of instruction for a female in the country is nearly as follows: At an early age she is sent to the district school, or perhaps if there be one, to the village academy. Here she is initiated into the common branches of English study, and here nearly all her knowledge, which may be termed literary, is acquired. At the age of sixteen or seventeen, she is sent to some boarding-school for a term or two, and then — her *education* is 'finished!' In the mean time however, while the daughter is at home, she is taught the domestic 'sciences;' but of reading, to acquire general information, little is thought. The long evenings of winter, which might be spent so profitably by the aid of books, are either wasted in idle conversation, or occupied in unnecessary labor. · · · But Woman did not come into the world simply to be given in marriage. She has higher and nobler aims; the cultivation of the intellect, the improvement of herself, and the benefit of others. I would not have our young women despise domestic duties, nor neglect them to cultivate literature. Their sphere in life is domestic: but let parents, while they teach their daughters the domestic arts, also imbue their minds with a taste for reading; and this taste once formed will be a permanent source of after enjoyment. If a young girl on arriving at years of discretion shall find her mental education neglected, her taste vanished or vitiated, why should she sit down and mope over lost time, and waste the precious hours of her youth in idle lamentation?

> 'Lose this day loitering, 't will be the same story
> To-morrow, and the next more dilatory;
> The indecision brings its own delays,
> And days are lost, lamenting o'er lost days.
> Are you in earnest? Seize this very minute!
> What you can do, or *dream* you can, begin it;
> Boldness has genius, power, and magic in it!
> Only engage, and then the mind grows heated;
> *Begin it*; and the work will be completed.'

Almost all families, even of moderate means, are provided with a small library, which though not perhaps very judiciously chosen, may yet contain many things worthy to be read. I would not have all sorts of reading piled upon the memory at once. *Legere non multa, sed multum*, 'read not many, but much,' is an excellent motto. History should claim the earliest attention. It may at first seem dry and uninteresting, especially to one previously accustomed to light reading; but that mind which cannot enjoy with a deep pleasure the works of such writers as ROBERTSON, GIBBON, and our own IRVING, can neither be very deep nor very susceptible. The labor of sowing may be great, but the crop will yield a plentiful and rich reward. ROLLIN'S great work is on the shelves of almost every library; and although as a translation it will necessarily be more dry than an original English work, yet by an attentive perusal, the great object, the acquisition of knowledge, may be accomplished. In modern history, the 'Decline and Fall of the Roman Empire' by GIBBON, the Life of Charles V. by Dr. ROBERTSON, and of Columbus by IRVING, will aid the tyro more perhaps than more elaborate works. History should be the ground-work; and next to it I conceive should come poetry; not the jargon of brain-struck fools, but the offspring of *genius*, like that of SHAKSPERE and MILTON. Poetry seems to be especially fitted for the mind of youth. It supplies the place of romance in the imagination, and does more toward cultivating a vivid fancy and correct taste than any other department of literature. 'With the young of both ages,' says WORDSWORTH, 'poetry is like love, a passion; but far much the greater part of those who have been proud of its power over their minds, a necessity of breaking the pleasing bondage arises, or it relaxes of itself; the thoughts being occupied in domestic cares, or the time engrossed by business.' If this be true, there is much greater reason that during that portion of life in which poetry *can* prevail over the mind, it should be cultivated. 'It is the duty of the great poet to spiritualize humanity,' says an able writer in the New-York Review. He might have added, what indeed his language implies, 'this the great poet accomplishes.' · · · Thus far our fair New-England readers are indebted to the desultory advice of our right-judging correspondent. But lest his exposé of the ignorance of one of their number should excite mortification, we must inform them that even fashionable city damsels are often caught tripping in literary matters. One of our most distingué belles at Saratoga last season is reported to have said, in reply to an inquiry whether she had ever seen CRABBE's 'Tales:' 'Never! I did n't know that crabs *had* tails!' And we have heard of another, who at one of our fancy-balls regretted that she had not appeared as 'Rebecca' in Ivanhoe, but that she had fancied a *Quaker* dress would not become her! Can New-England match such stupidity? 'Guess not!'

'THE IMMORTAL WASHINGTON.' — One of the most amusing things we have encountered for many a long day is an article in the December issue of BLACK-WOOD'S Magazine upon our unhappy United States. The writer, from an excess of sympathy with a congenial spirit and fellow-countryman, then on his trial at Utica for a crime of which he falsely confessed himself guilty, waxes particularly wroth, and evinces as much irritability as if he had just been indulging in a pro-longed practice of the 'Caledonian violin.' But *ubi dolor ibi digitus;* 'one must *needs* scratch where it itches;' and something is certainly to be pardoned to a Sawney who trembles for the fate of a kindred ass in the rough hands of a Republic that never so much as said 'By your leave' to Great Britain, before they took him in hand and dealt with him 'as the law directs.' Setting aside the laughable blus-ter and bravado about the bravery of our transatlantic neighbors and the cowardice of the Americans, (of which Great-Britain had once a little pleasant experience, when she reasoned after the manner of the lad who desired to be 'parted' from a disagreeable antagonist, 'Part us! part us! Two of you hold him! — *one* can hold me!') we come to a passage which is really worth quoting, for the freshness, in fact the *oneness* of the highly-important opinion which it embodies. Mr. MAX-WELL, a young Scottish gentleman of character and talent, whom we had the pleasure to meet while in this country, in a book of travels which he published on his return home, alludes to 'the immortal WASHINGTON's head-quarters at Cam-bridge,' and adds, that he beheld the place with almost as much interest as he had done that of NAPOLEON at Point Brique, near Boulogne. Upon which our doughty champion of Scotch toryism — the smallest possible imitation, by the way, of the imposing English article — pronounces as followeth: 'We shall have no quarrel with any man for expressing his sentiments, if he has taken any trouble to form them. But the epithet 'immortal' applied to WASHINGTON is not put in any other sense than as it may be applied to any other successful culprit. If ever man was a rebel, that man was GEORGE WASHINGTON. We are not going to fight that con-troversy now; but if an oath of allegiance was ever worth a straw, it is impossible to reconcile WASHINGTON's conduct with honor. He was undoubtedly a very able man, and a very successful one; but that he had the right on his side, that he was justified in his revolt, or that he was any thing beyond the slave of an uncon-scientious ambition in his own person, and the instrument of a corrupt and unprin-cipled revolt in that of others, facts give the most unanswerable testimony. He was 'immortal' in no other sense than any lucky transgressor is immortal.' Now 'these be very cruel words,' yet they are even more harmless than malignant; and we only place them on record here to warn American readers against assum-ing for a moment that they speak the sentiments of Scotland or England, or any respectable portion of the inhabitants of either. England's opinion of WASHING-TON is well expressed by one of her most distinguished scholars, in the University of Cambridge, Professor SMYTH, whose admirable work is elsewhere noticed in these pages. 'To the historian,' says he, 'there are few characters that appear so little to have shared the common frailties and imperfections of human nature as that of WASHINGTON. Let it be considered what it is to have the management of a revolution, and afterward the maintenance of order. Where is the man that in the history of our race has ever succeeded in attempting successively the one or the other? Not on a small scale, a petty state in Italy, or among a horde of barbarians; but in an enlightened age, when it is not easy for one man to rise superior to another, and in the eyes of mankind:

> ———— 'A kingdom for a stage,
> And monarchs to behold the swelling scene.'

The plaudits of his country were continually sounding in his ears, yet neither the judgment nor the virtues of the man were ever disturbed. Armies were led to the field with all the enterprise of a hero, and then dismissed with all the equanimity of a philosopher. Power was accepted, was exercised, was resigned, precisely at the moment and in the way that duty and patriotism directed. Whatever was the difficulty, the trial, the temptation, or the danger, there stood the soldier and the citizen, eternally the same, without fear and without reproach; and there was the man who was not only at all times virtuous, but at all times wise.' · · · 'As a ruler of mankind, he may be proposed as a model. Deeply impressed with the original rights of human nature, he never forgot that the end and meaning and aim of all just government was the happiness of the people, and he never exercised authority till he had first taken care to put himself clearly in the right. His candor, his patience, his justice, were unexampled; and this, though *naturally* he was not patient—much otherwise, highly irritable. He therefore deliberated well, and placed his subject in every point of view before he decided; and his understanding being correct, he was thus rendered, by the nature of his faculties, his strength of mind, and his principles, the man of all others to whom the interests of his fellow creatures might with most confidence be intrusted; that is, *he was the first of the rulers of mankind.*' · · · Now *such* is the opinion of enlightened England of the character of Washington, as expressed by some of her most eminent men, and by the greatest of her later poets. For says Byron, in his Ode to Napoleon:

> 'Where may the wearied eye repose,
>   When gazing on the great;
> Where neither guilty glory glows,
>   Nor despicable hate?
> Yes! *one*—the first, the last, the best—
> The Cincinnatus of the West,
>   Whom Envy dared not hate,
> Bequeathed the name of Washington,
> To make man blush there was *but* one!'

Inman's Portrait of Fanny Elssler, one of the most graceful and beautiful efforts of that fine artist's pencil, and withal a most perfect likeness, has been reproduced on stone by Heideman. The engraving is in the best style of the lithographic art, is of the same size as the painting, and is remarkable moreover as embodying many finer touches of the original, which have hitherto been deemed inaccessible to this species of engraving. It is a beautiful picture, and a cheap, being afforded at the low price of five dollars. 'The Artist's Dream,' a fine picture by Comegys, selected by the Apollo Association for their second annual engraving, has recently been finished in mezzo-tint by Sartain of Philadelphia, in his accustomed style of excellence. The artist has fallen asleep, and a long procession of ancient masters of the pencil pass in review before his dreaming eye. The likeness of each is correctly preserved, and the accessories are few and well conceived. It is painful to think that the intellect of the painter is now itself but a dream. He is an inmate of one of our lunatic-asylums.

'REVIEW OF UNPUBLISHED WORKS.'— Under this head a late London Magazine has been showing up the stupidity of the large and costly English Annuals which are indebted to the nobility exclusively for their contents. The 'unpublished work' in this instance is 'The Topaz;' and its embossed boards, splendid engravings, and gilded edges set forth the lucubrations of the DUKE OF WELLINGTON, LORD VINCENT FLUTINGHAM, Sir E. L. CHEVELEY, etc., with capital imitations of LOCKHART's Spanish Ballads, the pen-and-ink author of 'Jack Sheppard,' the overdone sea-tales of the day, etc. The 'D. of W.'s' sonnet is thus introduced :

'Deep as our obligations are to the many noble and literary characters who have enriched the pages of THE TOPAZ by their contributions, we feel assured that we reflect no discredit upon any of them when we state our candid and impartial opinion, that the splendid Military and Patriotic Sonnet which we have now the good fortune to present to our readers will be regarded by all competent judges as the brightest and most original gem that has ever appeared in this or in any other miscellany. Motives of delicacy which our readers will at once appreciate have prevented us from disclosing, in its full blaze of European celebrity, the name of The Illustrious Individual who has selected us as the medium of conveying his military opinions, clothed in the 'sounding robes' of verse, to a gratified world. Still we feel assured that there are none so dull of apprehension as not at once to perceive, from the terseness of the composition, the boldness of its character, its laconic simplicity, and its martial determination, that it could have emanated only from one honored pen, which has been wielded almost as successfully as his sword, and with at least as much despatch, by the greatest captain of the age.

> HALT! Shoulder arms! Recover! As you were!
> Right wheel! Eyes left! Attention! Stand at ease!
> O Britain! O my country! Words like these
> Have made thy name a terror and a fear
> To all the nations. Witness Ebro's banks,
> Assaye, Toulouse, Nivelle, and Waterloo,
> Where the grim despot muttered, ' *Sauve qui peut!* '
> And Ney fled darkling. Silence in the ranks!
> Inspired by these, amidst the iron crash
> Of armies in the centre of his troop
> The soldier stands — immovable, not rash —
> Until the forces of the foemen droop ;
> Then knocks the Frenchmen to eternal smash,
> Pounding them into mummy. Shoulder, hoop!'

In the following admirable imitation, a hero of the 'Jack Sheppard' school is awaiting his jailer, that he may knock him down with a stone tied up in a stocking. The extract partakes of the *genius* of Mr. AINSWORTH :

'He seated himself upon the bed, and deliberately pulling up the indispensable garment which covered his left leg, proceeded to undo the fastening that held up his stocking, which, at the period of which we write, was called a garter. Throwing it aside with a hasty impatience, he pulled off his stocking by turning it over at the top, and then drawing it toward the heel inside out. This done, he once more poised the stone in his hand, and surveyed it with a fond yet anxious glance. This was the work of a moment. The next it was rolling down the inside of the stocking, and only paused when it had reached the toe and found itself unable to proceed farther. This was all that Hagart desired ; and now he had to think of some means of fastening the stone in its place. He tore a few threads from his bed-cover, twisted them into a cord, fastened it round the stocking above the stone, and tied a knot upon it.' . . . 'The key turned in the lock — the bolt fell. Slowly and heavily the door grated on its hinges, for it had not been oiled for three years and two months. David is behind it. In his hand he holds the stocking — the stocking with the stone. Thrice has he raised it, and prepared to bring it down upon the jailer's head. But that unsuspecting myrmidon of a sanguinary law had been seized at the threshold with a sudden fit of coughing, which delayed his entrance for some time, and thrice David's hand descended to its former place, its purpose unaccomplished. At last the pulmonary impediment was removed, and Rusty Rob advanced. 'Tumble up, my kiddy!' he exclaimed, as he stepped beyond the door. Another moment, and he was stretched lifeless and bleeding on the floor. Hagart's aim was a sure one. The stone, and the centrifugal action caused by the intervention of the stocking, made it descend with terrific force.'

Here ensue some lines from a poem by 'Sir E. L. CHEVELEY,' which we take to mean Mr. BULWER. The contrasts are somewhat striking :

> 'Hark! where from yonder grove the nightingale
> Pours out the passion of her fiery heart,
> Trilling her notes all up and down the scale,
> Like Grisi in some very touching part:

While the grave owl, that in yon abbey sits,
    Mid ruins smouldering in immortal smash,
Throws in a casual hoot, that counterfeits
    The contra-basso of the old LABLACHE.

'In this calm nook, sequestered from the strife
    Of eager bailiff and tormenting dun,
The hum and humbug of our human life
    Unheard, unfelt, afar from us shall run :
No friends that on us for our dinners doat,
    Are here — no scandal-mongers darkly sly ;
No smooth tuft-hunters, to cram down our throat
    Warm protestations, that are all my eye.'

After perusing the foregoing, the reader will be at no loss to hear the reviewer
exclaim, on completing his task : 'The 'TOPAZ' is no common Annual, but the
quintessence of all possible Annuals for this or any other year. Such delicious
absurdity ! — such charming twattle ! Illustrations so exquisitely insipid ! Romance so harrowing in its extravagance ! Poetry so touching in its inanity ! Contributors of such celebrity ! Heavens ! After we had skimmed it through, we felt
as if we had been shut up in our bed-room and dieted on water-gruel for a month ! '

'HINTS TO AUTHORS.' — We have already made our readers acquainted with a
series of papers under this title, which ever and anon enrich the pages of BLACK-
WOOD'S Magazine. The fine satire and the quaintness of the style are alike irresistible. The last number is upon ' *The Epistolary*,' and proceeds, as we judge
from the felicitous introduction, from the pen which sketched the essay upon
'Murder considered as one of the Fine Arts,' heretofore quoted in the KNICKER-
BOCKER. We annex the opening :

'SOME people have a horror of house-breakers. A great strong fellow in a fustian-jacket, with a
piece of crape over his face and a pistol in his hand, is certainly a disagreeable visiter to a quiet
country gentleman in the middle of a dark night in December; the hoarse whisper, conveying a delicate allusion to your money-bags or your life, is far from a pleasing method of carrying on a conversation ; and therefore, without descending to any more minute particulars, or pluming myself on my
personal immunity from such visitations on the score of having no house, I agree at once that a house-
breaker is a detestable character, and worthy of all condemnation. A murderer, also, I am not prepared to vindicate ; for though instances may occur — such as in the case of annuitants and superannu-
ated relations — where murder becomes a virtue if not a duty, still, on the whole, it cannot be
defended on its own merits. A knife forced into the stomach of an elderly gentleman in a half sleepy
state after a bottle of old port ; a razor drawn across a beautiful bar-maid's throat ; or a bullet scientifically inserted through the ear-hole of the deaf old lady engaged in secreting her half-year's divi-
dends in a black trunk in the garret ; are disagreeable objects of contemplation to the philanthropic
mind ; and I therefore at once coincide in the fervent execration in which a murderer is held by every
person I have ever conversed with on the subject, except some students of anatomy and two or three
popular authors of the convulsive school. But there is another miscreant for whom I have no commiseration ; a wretch, compared with whose atrocities house-breaking becomes meritorious, and murder innocent ; before whose negro-like blackness — to borrow the language of CHARLES PHILLIPS,
the darkness of annihilation becomes white as snow ; whose benediction is a curse ; whose breath is
a pestilence ; whose name is a hell ; over whose sunless memory shall settle the conflagration of a
fury, and whose soul shall shudder beneath the appalling convulsions of a fathomless doom for ever !
After this description, need I say that I mean a scoundrel who neglects to pre-pay the post ? — a fellow
who, to make the paltry saving of a penny, forces his correspondent to an outlay of two-pence ? You
will also uniformly find that the unpaid letter is of a most disagreeable nature in other respects ; that
it twits you with a deficiency in memory — whereas you have vainly flattered yourself that you have
an excellent recollection ; that it dwells particularly on the ancient date of your habiliments — whereas
you have deluded yourself with the belief that your clothes were nearly new ; and finally, that it glar-
ingly protrudes before your eyes the total sum to which a column or two of smaller figures amounts,
as if your education had been so grossly neglected that you could not run up a simple sum in addition.
But no sum in addition, whether simple or compound, will the unconscionable rascal allow you to run
up ; and therefore you have no resource but either to refuse all unpaid letters or to change your name,
and take lodgings in a different street. The latter process admits a man, even in his life-time, to the
enjoyment of a little posthumous fame, and enables him to arrive at the unbiassed judgment of an impartial posterity. I remember when I was the Honorable Reginald Finsborough, in a dark complexion
and splendid apartments in Sackville Street, being very much delighted with the astonishing reputation I had acquired in the name of Captain Sidney Fitzherbert de York, with light-brown hair, thin
mustaches, and a suite of rooms in the Albany. All my jocular efforts to amuse my mercantile friends,
by leaving them in the outer passage while I slipped down by the front window ; all my philanthropic

endeavors to inculcate on them the virtues of patience and resignation; all my self-denying ordinances which compelled me to dismantle the apartments which I considered too handsomely furnished, and dispose of mirrors and chandeliers to the highest bidders — all were kept in fond record by the various tradesmen to whom I had distributed my patronage, and related with fitting comments to me — the Honorable Reginald Finsborough — by tradesmen whom I had condescended to employ as Captain Sidney Fitzherbert de York. A similar satisfaction awaited me in regard to the Honorable Reginald when I was the Reverend Jeremiah Snuffle, a clergyman of highly evangelical principles, with a pair of black gaiters and plated spectacles; so that I can seriously recommend any person who is oppressed with unpaid letters, at once to look into the Court Guide or the Congregational Magazine, and select a good name. If he is afraid of having that filched from him by some of the myrmidons of the law — a process which, as Shakspere says, leaves him poor indeed, and not enriches them — I see nothing left for it but to follow my example one step further, and write a religious novel. It needs no intellect, no learning, no research; all that is wanted is a prodigious power of hypocrisy, and some strongly-colored descriptions, which you can borrow from the last glaring trial for divorce. If you prefer Socialism and theft, on the plea that your conscience won't allow you to descend so low as to compose a religious novel, Sir, I honor your magnanimity, and have nothing farther to say to you. My hints are addressed only to persons of a literary turn of mind, and by no means to gentlemen who keep a conscience.'

To any reader who desires to see how a large piece of bread may be covered by a small piece of butter, we commend the ' epistolary ' specimens which succeed, and which are to the life.

Our Contemporaries are beginning the year by brushing up their exteriors, and adorning the inner man with renewed interest and beauty. The ' Albion,' without a peer in its kind, assumes a new and handsome dress, and is otherwise greatly improved by an additional sheet of four pages, embracing foreign and domestic intelligence, notices of the drama, the arts, etc., leaving the original paper an entirely *literary* journal; and all this without any advance in price. Taking into consideration the choiceness of matériel, the beauty of execution, and the number and superior size and character of its engravings, (four of which are now in progress,) the ' Albion ' must be considered the best and cheapest weekly journal on this continent. Its excellent Editor has our warmest wishes for his continued success. · · · Our old acquaintance, the ' Mirror,' must not be forgotten; for in its replenished garb, and under the time-honored charge of ' the General,' it maintains its ancient reputation, and sustains itself against all sorts of dangerous ' weekly ' competition with a practiced self-reliance which is especially refreshing. May the General live a thousand years, and his goodly periphery be never the less! He may boast overmuch perhaps, on occasion; but then he has also that ' *hold-fast* ' which is better. · · · The ' Ladies' Companion,' under the competent care of its editor, Robert Hamilton, Esq., begins its new volume with a ' crack number,' containing an imposing array of contributions from well-known pens; among them, those of Longfellow, Willis, Park Benjamin, Simms, Fay, Mrs. Embury, Mrs. Sigourney, Mrs. Stephens, John Inman, etc. The Editor himself has furnished an interesting ' Tale of the Revolution ' in addition to the liberal performances in his own especial departments. An engraving of Madge Wildfire, from the ' Waverley Gallery,' a view of Baltimore, and a plate of the fashions, form the embellishments of the number, which is executed with its accustomed neatness. · · · Our young brother ' Arcturus,' (whose Editors give the *cheapest* suppers we were ever invited to a month after date,) has donned new garments, and appears justly felicitated thereat. Moreover, he is getting less monotonously didactic, and is otherwise improving. Success to him! By the way, we have ' a bone,' which out of courtesy for their kind remembrance of the Old Knick in their imaginary feast, we will pick with the Editors, with their permission. There is upward of considerable meat on it. And first, thus saith that pleasant journal, the *Boston Transcript*, under the ' nervous but inelegant ' head, ' Literary Fraud:' ' In the January number of ' *Arcturus* ' there is an article entitled ' The Old Maid in the Winding-Sheet: A Twice-Told Tale; by Nathaniel Hawthorne.' It is well called ' a twice-told tale,' for it is told, word for word, without a shadow of variation, in the July number of the *New-England Magazine* for 1835! The best of the joke is, that the conductors of ' Arcturus ' on the strength of this tale introduce Mr. Hawthorne to the public, in an elaborate article of three pages, as a contributor to their Magazine! It would not have cost them more if they had introduced the whole volume of his works to the acquaintance of their readers.' Now, gentlemen, ' how *could* you do so!' And how could you *keep* doing so, by copying from the Knickerbocker the poem of ' The Green Isle,' written some months since for these pages by Mr. Noble, and publishing it in the same issue as original? Highly improper! · · · We have great sympathy with and respect for the persevering spirit and energy of the proprietor of ' The Magnolia,' or Southern Monthly, published at Savannah, Georgia. After a prolonged struggle, the Magazine has been placed upon a permanent basis; and new attractions of a rare order have been secured for future numbers. The proprietor has been authorized by W. Gilmore Simms, Esq., and a distinguished literary gentleman of South Carolina, to announce to his subscribers that if they will use their exertions to extend the circulation of the work one thousand additional copies, these gentlemen can be secured as co-editors.   The offer, we may well believe, will be deemed sufficiently seductive by the friends of 'The Magnolia' at the South, who owe it to themselves to cherish so meritorious a publication.

GOSSIP WITH READERS AND CORRESPONDENTS. — A friend in the country, who seems aggrieved at a little anecdote in the November KNICKERBOCKER concerning an imaginative passenger in one of our packet ships, informs us that 'whoever related the story must have been profoundly ignorant of the pages of SWEDENBORG.' This we can very well believe. 'B. J. F.' does us no more than justice in assuming that we would not willingly cast ridicule upon a sect whose creed includes some of the most grateful and consoling views of heaven and a hereafter that it is possible to conceive.   Will our friend furnish us with a brief and comprehensive digest of the Swedenborgian theory? . . . '*A Welcome to the Infant Duke of Cornwall*' is very loyal but not very poetical; far less so indeed than the emotions which crowd upon the mind, in thinking of the vast possessions over which the royal prince will one day be called to preside. Salutes, for example, in honor of his birth will ere long have been fired : *in America*, on the shores of Hudson Bay, along the whole line of the Canadian lakes ; in New Brunswick, Nova Scotia, Newfoundland ; in the Bermudas, at a hundred points in the West Indies, in the forests of Guiana, and in the distant Falkland Islands, near Cape Horn ; *in Europe*, in the British Islands, from the Rock of Gibraltar, from the impregnable fortifications of Malta, and the Ionian Islands ; *in Africa*, on the Guinea coast, at St. Helena and Ascension, from the Cape to the Orange River, and at the Mauritius ; *in Asia*, from the fortress of Aden in Arabia, at Karrack, in the Persian Gulf, by the British army in Affghanistan, along the Himalaya mountains, the banks of the Indus and the Ganges, to the southern point of India, in the Island of Ceylon, beyond the Ganges in Assam and Arracan, at Prince of Wales Island and Singapore, and on the shores of China at Hong Kong and Chusan ; and in Australia, at the settlements formed on every side of the Australian continent and islands, and in the strait which separates the islands of the New Zealanders. Well might Mr. WEBSTER extol in glowing terms the extent of a dominion wherein were heard continually the 'martial airs of England !' . . . The '*Running Review of Barnaby Rudge*' is too copious in extracts and too crude in commentary for our purpose. One passage only we subjoin : ' I think that in the *final* disposition of his characters Mr. DICKENS is preëminently felicitous. There is no confusion, no infringement of the natural. The old lethargic inn-keeper WILLET retiring in his dotage and with his ruling passion strong upon him, scoring up vast imaginary sums to imaginary customers, and the lament of the elder WELLER at the death of good old MASTER HUMPHRY, are not only characteristic — they are perfect : ' And the sweet old creetur, Sir,' said the elder Mr. WELLER to me in the afternoon, ' has bolted. Him as had no wice, and was so free from temper that an infant might ha' drove him, has been took at last with that 'ere unawoidable fit of the staggers as we must all come to, and gone off his feed for ever! I see him,' said the old gentleman, with a moisture in his eye which could not be mistaken, ' I see him gettin', every journey, more and more groggy ; I says to Samivel, ' My boy ! the Gray 's a going at the knees ; ' and now my predilections is fatally werified ; and him as I could never do enough to serve or show my likin' for, is up the great uniwersal spout o' natur'.' . . . A clerical friend (who has our cordial thanks) has called our attention to the following beautiful passage from a recent discourse of an eloquent divine, ' as illuminating, he would fain hope, the vague lessons of nature to which the Editor alluded in one of his late conversations with his readers and correspondents:' ' I must confess that the teaching of nature is too general to satisfy the wants of my mind ; and that the revealings of my mind, again, are too doubtful and defective for the needed reliance. I am ignorant ; I am weak ; I am sinful ; I am struggling with many difficulties ; the conflict is hard — it seems too hard for me at times ; and nature around me moves on meanwhile in calm uniformity, as if it did not mind me, and as if its Author did not regard the dread warfare that is going on within me. The universe lies around me, like a bright sea of boundless fluctuations — studded with starry isles indeed, but swept by clouds of obscurity — and whither it is tending and where it is bearing me, I know not. I feel at times as if I were wrapped with an infinite envelopement of mystery ; and I ask, with almost heart-breaking desire, for some voice to come forth from the great realm of silence, and speak to me. I say : ' Oh ! that the great Being who made the universe, would for once touch, as no hand but his can touch, the springs of this all-encompassing, mysterious ORDER, and say to me, in the sublime pause — in the cleft of these dread mountain heights of the universe — say to me : ' I love thee ; I will care for thee ; I will save thee ; I will bear thee beyond the world-barrier, the rent vail of death and the sealed tomb, away, away ! — to blessed regions on high, there to live for ever !' It has COME ! — to my faith, that very word has come, in the mission of

CHRIST.' - - - We cannot admit the '*Defence of Friends*' against the harmless satire of the early strait-laced Quakers, contained in the story of 'The Burning of the Ships.' Our correspondent, who is evidently *not* a Friend, is ' begging the question ' altogether. No such ground as he indicates was ever taken. He might as well denounce HOOD for saying that a Quaker could n't have a fever, because there was ' nothing for it to hang on by ; no nervous irritability, no peccant humor ; nothing to forment with ; ' or with as good cause level his denunciations against the apothecary's apprentice, for declaring that even hydrophobia was powerless against a Broadbrim, he having known one who was bit in nine places, but who would n't have one of them cauterized or cut out, and yet never ran mad ! ' He walked it, and never gave tongue ; only bit one little baby, and then not quite through the skin ; shook his head at water, but lapped warm milk ; and finally went home, got into bed of his own accord to be smothered, and died like a lamb.' The Society of Friends has not a more fervent admirer than the Editor of this Magazine ; but it is not impossible that its individual members may sometimes conduct unseemly. The female Friend who was moved to enter stark naked into a church in Newbury, (Mass.,) where she formerly worshipped, and was highly extolled for her submission to the inward light that had revealed to her the duty of illustrating the spiritual nakedness of her neighbors by this indecent exhibition of her own person, was neither the first nor the last member of a proverbially irreproachable sect who has committed very foolish acts. The chaffering tradesman depicted by our correspondent is in a kindred category. · · · Is there any doubt in the mind of the reader that the following love-ditty proceeds from a countryman of woman-and-wine-loving TOM MOORE ?

> ' WHEN Julia in her garden roves,
>   Or simpers in her bower,
> Or culls sweet blossoms in the groves,
>   Oh would I were a flower !
>
> And when adown the lawn she trips,
>   Ere comes the vesper hour,
> Just when the rose-bud meets her lips,
>   Oh would I were a flower !
>
> And when within her bosom fair
>   She hides it from the shower ;
> Oh then dove-like I 'd nestle there,
>   If I were but a flower ! '   M'G.

If ' J. P.' will allow us to curtail the last two chapters of '*My Grand-mother's Mystery*,' his story shall appear. Curiosity is in the main well stimulated, but we tire for the rising of the curtain. The story is something akin to one which appeared in an English periodical, concerning a murderer who from the time he was first arrested for killing an old woman, resisted all inquiries as to what induced him to commit the horrid deed. ' He could n't tell,' he said ; ' it was a sudden impulse — a sort of whisper ; Satan put it into his head. He had no reason for doing it ; the why and the wherefore he did n't know himself.' Curiosity stood tip-toe on one long leg. Ladies brought tracts and cakes to him in prison, and begged him to make a clean breast of it. Why did he do it ? ' Lord knows,' said he, ' *I* do n't.' The jury after his trial brought him in guilty, but recommended him to mercy, ' provided he gave his reasons.' ' He said he had n't any ; he had killed the old-woman off-hand ; it was a sudden start — the same as a frisk ! He could n't account for it ; it was done in a dream, like.' At length the day of his execution arrived:

' The sheriffs and under-sheriffs, with their respective friends, the ordinary, and the extraordinary clergy, the reporters, and other official or officious persons, were assembled in the press-room. The convict's irons were knocked off. ' If you have any thing to say,' stammered the senior sheriff, ' now is the time ' ' To cleanse the bosom of the perilous stuff,' put in a celebrated tragedian. ' It is not yet too late,' began the ordinary. ' Come, let 's have it,' said a penny-a-liner. ' Now then,' muttered the jailer. But the convict shook his head, and repeated the old story. A phrenologist, who recollected that ' Murder will speak with a most miraculous organ,' now felt the devoted head, but was none the wiser. Nothing remained, therefore, but to beg for keep-sakes ; but as the turnkey and his wife, and the ladies of quality, and the peers, and the M. P., and the editor, and the exhorters of all denominations, had already received a lock of his hair a-piece, the last comers were obliged to put up with a few carroty clippings ; (and all the while, there thou wast, poor old Honesty ! toiling for a shilling a day, wet or shine, in the fields, and not one christian man or woman to ask thee for so much as one white hair of thy head !) the last comers, I say, had but a few carroty clippings, so closely the murderer had been cropped. And in this plight he was led forth to the scaffold, in the gaze of ten thousand sons and daughters of curiosity, in the street, at the windows, and on the house-tops. And now the last hope rested on Jack Ketch, who took his opportunity while he adjusted the rope. But after a whisper, even that functionary shook his head, and intimated to the company, in two brief syllables, that it was ' no go.' The criminal, like the ' Weary Knife-grinder,' had no tale to tell. So, in despair, the ordinary at last began to read the burial service ; when, lo ! just as the fatal bolt was about to be drawn, a desperate individual in a straw hat, a light-blue jacket, striped trousers, and Hessian boots, with an umbrella under his arm, dashed in before the clergyman, and in hurried accents, put the old question, ' Now or never ! why did you do it ? ' ' Why, then,' said the convict with an impatient motion of his cropped head, ' *I did it — TO GET MY HAIR OUT !* '

We have n't a notion of the drift of ' *Phocion.*' We thought, in trying to read his essay, that he must be some delegate from the ' inworld ' of Boredom. We would wager a ducat that if he were asked to explain what he intended to convey in the paragraph beginning ' And thus my life indwells with Nature,' he would be compelled to answer with RICHTER, ' When I *wrote* that passage, God knows that I knew the meaning of it. Possibly God knows now ; but I have forgotten ! ' · · · We have seldom laid before our readers a number of the KNICKERBOCKER which for variety and contrast of different excellences impressed *us* more favorably than the present. With Bavant, Mary Clavers, Sanderson, Harry Franco, John Quod, the 'Country Doctor,' and our additional rare recruits, it could scarcely be otherwise. *Apropos* of our 'Americans in Paris:' a Boston friend at our elbow says that his steam-boat captain, so 'grave by his piety,' reminds him of an old school-mate of his who not long since commanded one of our packet-ships. When a lad, he was a roystering, harum-scarum fellow, the bully of the 'North End,' and the terror of every boy who knew him. His friends could do nothing with him; and at last, as he grew older and more reckless, they determined to send him to sea. A seaman's berth was accordingly secured for him with Captain M——, a nephew of the noted Munoo, who then commanded an East-Indiaman. While on his way to the vessel, to make the acquaintance of his new master, our rollicking blade was informed by a graceless, quizzing comrade that Captain M—— was a very *religious* man, and that he must be careful not to offend his prejudices, as the least slip of the tongue might ruin his prospects. 'Never you mind,' was the reply; '*I* know how to humor him.' Accordingly, after having encountered and made himself known to the Captain, he began his assumed autobiography: 'I have been *through* all the town schools,' said he, (that was a fact!) 'and three years to a Sunday-school. I belong to the Tract Society, and am a member in full standing of Dr. S——'s church.' The Captain's face glowed like a furnace: 'A Sunday-school scholar!' exclaimed he, 'and a member of the church!! Why, what in h—ll do you expect to do aboard my ship, with your d—d Sunday-schools, and tracts, and church-goings!' Our hero was quite unprepared for such a violent explosion of piety; and though taken all aback, he soon rallied, and burning with rage and resentment, replied: '"What can I *do* aboard your ship?'—you d—d old fool!—what can I do? Why I can thresh you and your whole crew—*that's* what I can do! I can knock you all to the d—l in less than no time!' This soft answer operated like a charm in turning away the wrath of the Captain, who said, tapping him on the shoulder: 'Young man, you're just the chap I want—step aboard;' and he shipped him immediately. . . . The following forms the concluding portion of an explanatory article from the Editor of this Magazine, which appeared in a New-York daily journal, in answer to a defensive card from Mr. J. H. Ingraham, repelling the charge of plagiarism of the romance of 'Lafitte.' An unexpected delay in its first publication has prevented the timely appearance of the *entire* article in our pages: 'We require no incentive of any sort to render justice to a man who complains of an injury received through our pages; and in making the original announcement referred to, we expressly stated our willingness to open the Knickerbocker to any explanation which Mr. Ingraham might give of a report which, if false, he owed it to himself to deny and disprove. We were wholly ignorant of his address, and had not seen him, to our remembrance, for at least eighteen months. The same offer was tendered him in our interview at the Carlton-house, and we gave his *denial* of the charge, as made at our publication office, in our last number. And we now take the first opportunity which has been given us authoritatively to state, that the parties to whom our informant referred *acquit him* of the alleged act of plagiarism; that the charge resolves itself into simply this: that Mr. Ingraham made use of a 'cave scene' which appears in the novel, and for which he expressed his willingness to acknowledge his indebtedness in the preface to a second edition, but which tribute the originator himself declined. Our informant, *his* informants, and the alleged plagiarism, were alike entirely unknown to us, until revealed in the manner we have mentioned. Toward Mr. Ingraham personally we had and have no feeling of animosity. Our opinion of his works, it is true, has been freely and publicly expressed. What we could conscientiously commend we have commended in these pages, as in the instance of his entertaining 'South-West, by a Yankee;' and we have as conscientiously condemned the style and tendency of many of his romances. With the foregoing explanation of the matter in question—to the accuracy of which, according to the best of our knowledge and recollection, we are ready to make oath—we leave the subject with our readers.' . . . 'L. B. D.'s 'contingent promise' is not unlike the note-of-hand proposed by a modern financier of the Diddler family to his schneider, viz: 'Thirty days *after it's convenient*, I promise to pay,' etc. However, we shall be rejoiced to hear from our friend at *any* time. . . . '*Remembrances of the Dead*,' although soft and musical in expression, are false in philosophy. Sure we are, that the lines proceed from one who has never known that *one* sorrow which makes us feel the impotency of consolation. Of such inevitable memories it is that Byron speaks:

'And ever and anon of griefs subdued
There comes a token like a scorpion's sting—
Scarce seen, yet with fresh bitterness imbued.'

'Grenada and the Alhambra,' No. 2; 'My Grand-father's Port-Folio,' No. 3; an Essay on Ralph Waldo Emerson; 'The Past;' 'Song of the Winds;' 'Storming of Stoney-Point;' 'Neck-Nothing Hall, a Hunting Sketch;' and several other communications which we have not space to specify, are either filed for insertion, or awaiting consideration. . . . Several notices of periodicals, books, lectures, etc., are unavoidably omitted.

LITERARY RECORD.

THE AMERICAN REVIEWS. — The 'New-York Review' for the January quarter reached us at a late hour, so that we have only found occasion to glance through a few of its articles. The elaborate papers are upon the Life and Character of JOHN ADAMS; BRADFORD's 'American Antiquities;' 'Collections of the New-York Historical Society; PALMER on the Church of Christ; KENNEDY's Novels; PARK's Pantology; WILLIAM COST JOHNSON's speech on appropriating the Public Lands for purposes of Education; 'American Naval Battles in the War of 1812–13;' and a review of 'Monaldi,' by WASHINGTON ALLSTON. The shorter 'Critical Notices,' so far as we have examined them, may be deemed models of this style of reviewing. Brief, sententious, and to the point, they convey their aim and impress their influence at once, and with striking effect. LESTER's 'Glory and Shame of England' is here demolished with a few well-directed strokes of a trenchant blade; and 'My Progress in Error and Recovery to Truth,' a recent canting, common-place publication, shares a similar fate. A little passage in the author's experience is thus disposed of: 'One morning,' says he, 'I shut myself up in my room, *determined* not to go out of it again till the great point was settled, and I had declared either for God or against him.' 'The specific result,' says the reviewer, 'of the sinner thus *cornering God's grace* is not given; and what we more regret, no recognition of its impious folly.' High praise is awarded to Mr. KENNEDY as a national novelist, in a review of his works which forms the fifth article of the number. The reviewer, we observe, alludes to the fact mentioned in our December issue, that the present period is one altogether unpropitious to novel-writing. 'There are as many good critics of novels now as there were readers of them formerly. Publishers have grown cautious; the public taste has grown nice, and the public demand regulates the profits.' We are glad to announce that 'these be truths.' However unpalatable they may be to minor *producers* at home and abroad — with stores of melodramatic matériel, murders, seductions, robberies, and rapes, on hand — they will be greeted with satisfaction by many who have heretofore been *consumers.* The last 'North-American' has not been sent as heretofore to our address. We perceive, however, that the ambitious antagonist of Dr. ANTHON, who has already been put *hors du combat* some half-dozen times, as our readers can testify, has been making new arrangements to emerge once more from the 'diminutive end of the trumpet.' In an attack which he has seen fit to make upon that monument of learning and industry, the Classical Dictionary of LEMPRIERE, he has again 'written himself down,' but not the book he assails, nor its eminent editor. If he were to learn the opinion, which we lately perused, of one of the most distinguished men and scholars in New-England, touching this same work, our determined hypercritic might be brought perhaps to doubt the infallibility of his judgment, and to believe that after all, Dr. ANTHON might be a passable scholar, although he does n't go to school at Cambridge.

LIEBER ON PROPERTY AND LABOR. — We regret that we did not receive in season for a few extracts an excellent volume of an excellent series, HARPERS' Family Library, containing 'Essays on Property and Labor, as connected with Natural Law and the Constitution of Society; by FRANCIS LIEBER.' We agree cordially with Rev. Prof. POTTER of Union college, who in introducing the work to the public predicts that 'no person will rise from the perusal of these essays without a high respect for the author's powers, or without feeling that he has gained new light on a difficult and much-contested subject.' The discussion is enriched with many pertinent and striking illustrations derived from travellers and historians, and is pervaded by that *suggestive* spirit which belongs only to works of the higher class in philosophy, and which has a peculiar charm for the thoughtful reader. 'The author has taken a judicious mean between those who would hedge property about with needless safe-guards and those who would leave it without protection. He is the advocate of an enlightened freedom; a freedom tempered only by such restraints as are indispensable to its own preservation, and inseparable from the present lot of humanity. He has unfolded some of the purposes with which a beneficent Creator has assigned to man an earthly inheritance of labor and care. He has pointed out the wisdom of that beautiful provision by which GOD has connected the progress of our race with the humble labors of industry, and how far such labors are from degrading those who pursue them, or from diffusing through society a sordid or unworthy spirit. We have already spoken in terms of deserved praise of Mr. LIEBER's lucid exposition of the International Copy-right question; and we are glad to perceive a long and very thorough review of it in a late German law periodical, in which its merits are noted and highly commended. It is not too much to say, indeed, that Mr. LIEBER illumines every theme which he investigates; and we would cite the above-mentioned dissertations, together with the author's sound and judicious views on the subject of the Post Establishment of the United States in the seventeenth number of the 'New-York Review,' heretofore referred to in these pages, as among the many evidences which he has furnished of the justice of this encomium.

LIEBIG's ORGANIC CHEMISTRY OF AGRICULTURE AND PHYSIOLOGY, from the press of Mr. JOHN OWEN, Cambridge, (Mass.,) with an introduction and notes by Prof. WEBSTER, of Harvard University, has passed to a second edition. The interest excited in Great Britain on the appearance of this work, from one of the most eminent chemists in Europe, and the high encomiums bestowed upon it by individuals and learned bodies, together with the various notices which have been published by Prof. LINDLEY, Prof. DAUBENY, and others, all concurring in the opinion that the information it contains is of great amount, and that from its publication might be dated a new era in the art of agriculture, induced the American editor to suggest its republication in this country. The peculiar views of the eminent author have been put to the test of actual experiment in the neighborhood of Boston, and a variety of plants have been cultivated with satisfactory success upon the principles developed in the work. An introduction and explanatory notes render the text clearly intelligible, and an appendix contains many theoretical and practical matters, embracing the views of distinguished American chemists who have engaged in the investigation of the chemistry of agriculture. It is a very valuable work, and appears in a garb befitting its character.

BOSTON ALMANAC FOR 1842. — A very beautiful and comprehensive little Almanac, from the pen and the press of Mr. S. N. DICKINSON, Boston, has been sent us by the publishers, Messrs. THOMAS GROOM AND COMPANY, Stationers' Hall, State-street. It seems to us absolutely *wonderful* that so much interesting and valuable information could be contained, in an easily accessible form, in such a brief compass. In addition to the 'Almanac' proper, we have records of chronological cycles, eclipses, tables of tides; ruled blanks for every-day memoranda; general, state, and city governments — political, legal, and social; legal tenders of coin; events in Boston in 1841, and *general* events every where, for the same year, arranged under each month in which they occurred. In addition to all this, the volume contains a complete miniature Business Directory, with the city wards, their boundaries and places of meeting; public buildings; packets and their stations; stage-routes; societies and institutions, newspapers, etc., etc. Altogether, the handsome little thing is 'a curtailed abbreviation compressing all the particulars of a Multum in Parvo!'

AMERICAN CRIMINAL TRIALS. — We sincerely trust that the first volume of 'American Criminal Trials' by PELEG W. CHANDLER will prove the forerunner of a continuous series from the same hand. The style is exceedingly natural, and the impression left upon the reader seems little short of actual observation of the scenes and events described. The trials for sedition and heresy; for witchcraft, blasphemy, and treason; of the Quakers, and of the soldiers who were engaged in what is usually termed 'the Boston Massacre,' etc., which have rendered memorable the early history of Massachusetts, are here recorded; and the reader may be assured that he will not relinquish the work, after having once taken it up, without having made an agreeable and familiar acquaintance with its contents. It is an honor to the author, and externally to the care and taste of the publishers, Messrs. C. C. LITTLE AND JAMES BROWN, Boston.

PUBLICATIONS OF MESSRS. APPLETON AND COMPANY. — Among the later and smaller publications of this popular house, are the following: 'Which is the Wiser?' a beautiful story by MARY HOWITT, who could not write an indifferent one; 'Norway and the Norwegians, or Feats on the Fiord,' a tale by Miss MARTINEAU; and a delightful little volume by the good Bishop JEREMY TAYLOR, entitled 'The Golden Grove: a Choice Manual, containing what is to be believed, practiced and desired, or prayed for; the prayers being fitted to the several days of the week: to which is added, A Guide for the Penitent, or a Model drawn up for the help of Devout Souls wounded with Sin; also Festival Hymns, composed for the use of the Devout.' The two first-named are illustrated with beautiful engravings on steel.

THE 'CORRESPONDENCE OF MRS. ADAMS,' daughter of JOHN ADAMS, second president of the United States, edited by her daughter, and recently published by Messrs. WILEY AND PUTNAM, is a little volume which will commend itself to the attention of American readers; to whom all things which appertain to our early history and struggle for an independent existence among the nations of the earth we may hope will be deemed themes of interest through all time. The volume was suggested to the editor by the favorable reception given to the 'Journal and Correspondence of Mrs. Adams.' It is neatly printed, and embellished with a good engraving of TRUMBULL's Battle of Trenton.

THE NEW-HAMPSHIRE BOOK. — We admire the 'state pride' that prompts the collation and publication of such works as 'The New-Hampshire Book,' which we find on our table, through the courtesy of the publishers, Mr. DAVID MARSHALL, Nashua, (N. H.,) and Messrs. JAMES MUNROE AND COMPANY, Boston. We hope to see the spirit which has dictated the preparation of this and kindred works emulated by every State in the Union. The Granite State has contributed her share to the literature of the country, and her full quota of distinguished men, political and literary. We shall embrace an occasion, when we have more space and leisure, to do better justice to the volume before us; which we should add, reflects scarcely less credit *internally* upon New-Hampshire, than it does *externally* upon *the* DICKINSON of Boston, whose immense and multitudinous 'printing-house' is one of the lions of the American Athens, and who has won to himself the reputation of being the most tasteful and accomplished professor of the 'art preservative of all arts' to be found in the United States.

'SKETCHES OF THE COUNTRY.' — Our readers who have enjoyed the beautiful 'Sketches of the Country' which have appeared from time to time in the KNICKERBOCKER, will be glad to learn that they are soon to form, with many others, hitherto unpublished, a volume, to be entitled 'Sketches of New-England, or Memories of the Country.' We have had the pleasure to peruse four or five of the additional papers, in the proof-sheets of the publisher: and the reader will deem it sufficient praise when we say, that they not only sustain the high promise of the published sketches, but that some of them even exceed their predecessors in unpretending but attractive and natural incident, and in simple ease and grace of style. The volume will soon be issued by Mr. E. FRENCH, 149 Fulton-street.

MEMORIAL OF BAYARD. — Messrs. APPLETON AND COMPANY have recently issued, in a handsome volume, a 'Memorial of the Rev. LEWIS P. BAYARD, D. D., containing a memoir of his life, extracts from his journals and correspondence, notices of his tour through Europe and the Holy Land, selections from his sermons, and the Discourse preached on the occasion of his decease, by the Right Rev. Bishop ONDERDONK of this city. The editor, Rev. J. W. BROWN, A. M., has done good service to the church and to the christian public in collecting for enduring preservation a memorial of one 'whose years were spent in the faithful and zealous discharge of christian duty, no less in the private walks of social and domestic life than in the christian ministry, and in the various honorable and responsible posts which he occupied in the general concerns of the Church.'

HISTORY OF THE LIFE OF RICHARD CŒUR DE LION. — It needs but the announcement of a work upon so teeming and rich a theme as this, from the pen of Mr. JAMES, to insure its eager acceptance at the hands of the public. 'Mr. JAMES,' says the New-York Review, 'has framed his romances out of history: but he has not, as it might have been feared, reversed the operation, and filled his histories with romance; on the contrary, they are distinguished by their fidelity; and this his most recent we regard as the most valuable that has come from his pen.' The volume is from the press of the Messrs. LANGLEY, which is all that is necessary to say in reference to its outer appointments.

HARPERS' FAMILY LIBRARY maintains its high character unabated. Three of the recent issues contain the 'Epitome of the History of Philosophy,' adopted by the University of France for instruction in the Colleges and High Schools, and admirably translated by Prof. C. S. HENRY, of Princeton; and in one volume, the 'Lives of the Ancient Philosophers,' translated from the French of FENELON, with notes, and a life of the author, by Rev. JOHN CORMACK. Both these publications are works of eminent repute and standard value, and well worthy the entertaining and instructive series of which they form a part.

RIGHT OF SUFFRAGE. — Messrs. OTIS, BROADERS AND COMPANY, Boston, have issued in a handsome volume a 'Treatise on the Right of Suffrage,' in which (and we believe for the first time) this subject — so important to the American people, and to others who possess or would establish a representative government — is fully examined, and reduced to the true principles by which the exercise of the right ought to be regulated. The author, SAMUEL JONES, Esq., has supplied an important desideratum by this timely publication.

'HINTS TO MOTHERS.' — Messrs. WILEY AND PUTNAM have published a volume entitled 'Hints to Mothers, for the Management of Health during the period of Pregnancy, and in the Lying-in Room;' with an exposure of popular errors in connexion with those subjects. The author is THOMAS BULL, M. D., the distinguished physician-accoucheur of London. An American physician of eminence has given valuable additions, including an important table, called 'The Ladies' Perpetual Calendar.' The work is deemed one of the very best of its class, and it has already passed to a third edition.

THE KNICKERBOCKER.

Vol. XIX.   MARCH, 1842.   No. 3.

GRENADA AND THE ALHAMBRA.

BY REV. GEORGE B. CHEEVER.

THE entrance to the city from the luxuriant vega is by a broad and well-paved street, inclining upward from the border of the plain, and opening through the straggling suburbs upon a large square just outside the gates, in the midst of which was situated an immense amphitheatre for bull-fights. From this open square Battiste plunged at once into the intricacies of the city, winding toward its best inn, the *Fonda del Comercio*, to dispose of his passengers, but managing to pass his own *posada* in the way, to tell his old acquaintance there, who seemed highly delighted to see him, that he was going to take up his abode with them as usual. The Fonda del Comercio is situated quite in the heart of the best quarter of the city, near the Alameda, the Cathedral, and the Theatre, three important points for a Spaniard, and not far from the *Calle de Gomeler*, or the street by which there is open access from the city to the Alhambra. It was on the whole one of the best inns I have visited in Spain; nor were the charges extravagantly high, although the table spread for us was profusely supplied with several courses of Spanish dishes. The inn seemed quite full of company, among whom was no less a personage than the chief *matadore*, a bull-killer of considerable celebrity, who had arrived in Grenada on occasion of the first bull-fight for the season in that city. The barbarous and savage spectacle was advertised for the next Sabbath, and would have taken place on that day, had it not been for a few clouds in the atmosphere; the people not being satisfied with any but the clearest and finest weather for the enjoyment of this amusement. A great deal of card-playing as usual was going on in the inn; and every evening a large hall was filled with Spaniards spending their time in nothing but the idle game of dominoes, and sipping a cup of chocolate or a tumbler of *orgeat-almendra*, in couples at separate tables; but there was no appearance whatever of intemperance or noisy dissipation in any shape.

Our first business after getting settled in our rooms was to send for the noted guide, Matteo Ximenes, a garrulous, good-natured, persevering cicerone at the Alhambra, upon whom WASHINGTON IRVING has conferred a celebrity of which Matteo is very naturally a little vain. Beside his occupation as chief guide to the Alhambra, Matteo has a silk loom in one of its dilapidated buildings, where his family live, and where they weave silk ribands with ave-Marias and other Catholic inscriptions upon them, and thus help to support the household. The next morning we were awakened early by the ringing of all the bells in the city, with the reports of cannon and fire-arms, it being Good-Friday of the Holy Week, a day devoted to the celebration of our Lord's resurrection. It was ushered in with quite as much noise as used to attend the dawning of the Fourth of July in our own country, and was spent still more completely as a holiday. The people here, as elsewhere in Catholic countries, have the ceremony of hanging Judas Iscariot during the Holy Week. Being entirely ignorant of the custom, I was surprised, in wandering about the streets, at the spectacle of a black figure ingeniously stuffed and dressed in the shape of a man and hung by the neck from poles stuck out of the windows, or from cords stretched across the streets in different parts of the city. Some of the images they had contrived to render truly frightful, and so well resembling a human being that at first it was a startling sight. They hang the traitor Iscariot with great glee, and one might suppose with a holy indignation at the iniquity of his conduct; but it is the same thoughtless hypocrisy with which the Pharisees of old garnished the sepulchres of the prophets. What a moral lesson it conveys, to see a whole nation hanging the betrayer of our Lord in effigy, and crucifying the Lord himself in reality, even in the very nature of their religious rites and establishments! What thoughtless, melancholy ignorance of their own hearts, and of the falsehood and depravity of their own system! A whole people lulled and hurried to perdition amidst the mummery of a scheme that takes from the cross itself its power of salvation, and converts it into a sign of superstition and an emblem of the Man of Sin!

Our first visit was to the church of San Juan de Dios, near the inn, on one side of the broad street-esplanade that leads down to the Alameda. It was filled with images and decorations quite as tawdry as usual, but so darkened by the exclusion of the day-light, and crowded with silent kneeling worshippers, that its dim recesses, images and paintings, amidst the blaze of wax tapers, wore an air of great richness and solemnity. We could not but notice one of the pulpits, exquisitely carved from one solid block of green-veined marble from the neighboring Sierra Nevada. On the platform before the high altar were large images of the Virgin in deep mourning, and of the Saviour clad in an immense black robe and bearing his cross, with a countenance full of agony, and pale as death. I doubt not that the sight of these images on such occasions diffuses a sort of superstitious awe and sympathy over the assembly, which they could easily mistake for religious veneration and sorrow. Our guide seemed to exercise a sort of privileged boldness on this occasion, for he carried us right across the platform in front of the altar and in sight of the crowd, from one side of the church to the other, bowing and crossing himself however, before the images, with all the devotion of a good Catholic.

The service of the choir and the altar had not commenced, and we emerged from the crowd and the pageantry to visit the cathedral, in an opposite direction.   This is a very large pile altogether, composed of the cathedral itself, the *sagrario*, or parish church connected with it, and the chapel of Ferdinand and Isabella.   At the main entrance the outside of the pile presents a front of imposing grandeur, and the effect on first entering is also imposing, from the vastness of its dimensions, the innumerable columns, the high altar centrally insulated beneath a gorgeous lofty dome, the broad area around it, the beautiful marble pavement, the chapels, the pictures, and the statues.   But as you wander along from chapel to chapel and through the pillared aisles, you find the grand effect is lost in irregularity and confusion, and that it is quite impossible to gain any impression of unity or simplicity of design or proportion.   The great dome is crowded with statues and paintings, but the ornaments which make a show of splendor at a distance are found to be vulgar and theatrical, though there are some exceedingly fine paintings over several of the altars, and among them specimens of Espangolitto and Murillo.   The cathedral and the sagrario were crowded with worshippers passing from one to the other through the curtained passages, or rather with gazing spectators of the superstitious and idolatrous rites ; and in truth one could not but admire the perspective view of the priests in their most gorgeous robes ministering around the central altar, in presence of the assembled multitude.   Here, as in the first church we visited, the dark green marble from the Sierra Nevada is cut in large blocks and sculptured into pulpits of very great beauty. In one or two of the aisles our attention was drawn by an inscription warning all persons against walking merely for pleasure, or conversing with women in any of the chapels, upon pain of excommunication.   A very droll menace ; supremely ridiculous indeed, when compared with the known licentiousness of the Romish church in Spain.

We witnessed a procession around the cathedral, with a tawdry canopy and old worn-out priests shuffling along ; as complete a burlesque and caricature for a religious ceremony as can well be imagined.   We were also shown the identical sheet in which the body of our Lord was wrapped after the crucifixion !   It was pinned upon a curtain of red damask, and drawn before one of the chapels for the devotees to worship.   It had been stained or painted with a dim impression of a human body ; and our guide gravely assured us it was the same cloth in which the Saviour was buried, and that it had never been washed !   It was a revolting, painful scene, but not half so much so as the spectacle of a ghastly human figure, inclosed and shrouded in a glass case, and laid before one of the altars as a representation of *Corpus Christi*, or our Lord's dead body.   The people seemed to gaze upon it with all the awe that an actual corpse would have inspired in that situation.   In the sacristy, or vestment-room of the priests, we were shown likewise *the handkerchief of the Virgin Mary*, stretched in a triangular frame of metal, set with heavy ornaments, and covered with a steel netting, so that it might be kissed without injury by the worshippers.   The priest offered it to our lips, but we politely declined the honor, though we saw several devotees, and our guide Matteo among the number, kneel before it and kiss it with much apparent reverence.

In the royal chapel, which is connected with the cathedral, are contained the tombs of Ferdinand and Isabella. From this circumstance, and the curious splendor of its own decorations, it is an interesting spot; the burial-place of sovereigns who united the divided Spanish monarchy, and made it for a time signally illustrious, and one of whom was almost the only truly generous and noble-spirited personage that has filled the Spanish throne. The fortunes of Columbus, the discovery of a new world, the destruction of the Moorish monarchy, the expulsion of the Jews, the establishment of the tremendous tribunal of the Inquisition, and the full sweep of all the influences of Popery across the kingdom, just at the time when the light of the Reformation was beginning to irradiate and awaken the human mind in Northern Europe, make that period in the history of Spain a time of singular interest; as an epoch which unites the causes both of the nation's temporary greatness and its centuries of degradation and decay. The tomb of Ferdinand and Isabella and that of Philip and Juanna are certainly among the most splendid mausoleums in the world, composed of pure white marble, most exquisitely and elaborately wrought. They were constructed probably during the reign of the Emperor Charles V., by Italian artists. The two Catholic monarchs lie side by side, pillowed upon the pile of sculptured marble, wrought with various emblematic images; and opposite to them, upon a similar pile of equally admirable workmanship, repose the statues of Philip the First and his queen Juanna. While we were there, some French artists were engaged in the preparation of large casts of these mausoleums for the Museum at Paris. The sepulchre is beneath, reached by a flight of steps, and illuminated by torch-light; and the four bodies, with that of the young son of Philip, are inclosed in lead coffins, plain and clumsy, without any ornament.

'Earth's highest station ends in ' *Here he lies.*' '

The marble mausoleums receive the admiration once paid by kneeling multitudes to the dust and bones now hidden from the sight, and hermetically sealed, as an offence against the atmosphere!

Above the altar of the chapel there are some very curious figures carved in wood, supposed to be of the time of Ferdinand, representing on one side of the altar the surrendering of the keys of Grenada from its conquered Moorish king to the Catholic conqueror, and on the other exhibiting the baptism of the Moors by the priests; an inquisitorial, bigoted mummery, enforced upon them under pain of flames and death, and which must have been for that very reason unspeakably detestable. The Moorish women are represented with their faces almost entirely concealed, and their dress is supposed to be a faithful picture of that of the period they refer to: the faces of the priests on the other hand are drawn as ugly and revolting as they often appear in actual life upon the shoulders of the modern canons. Among other curiosities in this chapel we were shown the cloak of Isabella, gorgeous and stiff with gold, said to have been wrought by her own fair and gentle hands, and certainly an interesting specimen of her domestic industry.

From the cathedral we passed through several narrow streets into the *Viva Rambla,* an oblong square of four hundred feet by two hundred, surrounded by aged, lofty, dark-looking buildings, and supposed to be very little altered from what it was in the time of the Moors.   We entered the inclosure through an antique Moorish gate-way, which is said to be the same through which the daring warrior Pulgar impetuously rode from the Catholic camp, and affixed an insulting inscription upon the gate of the principal mosque in the heart of the city.   Irving's 'Conquest of Grenada' will bring this feat of romantic chivalry to your remembrance.   Every thing in this square and in the long narrow street which leads northward out of it is so oriental in its aspect ; so impressed with the genius of another world than that we are accustomed to; so illustrative of the abodes, shops and manners of the Moors ; that it seems as if that swarthy, turbanned, fiery race were still peopling the scene before you.   Every thing wears an air of the picturesque and romantic ; and in this neigborhood is to be seen a curious old building called the *Casa del Carbon,* so named for no apparent reason, it having been a grand royal post-house of the Moors, where they kept the fleetest horses ready at a moment's warning.   The entrance to this building is an antique Moorish gate-way, even at this day partially covered with Arabesque work, and containing above the arch a very long inscription in Arabic letters, taken doubtless from the Koran.   Matteo told us that the whole interior of the building was formerly covered with beautiful Arabesques in good preservation, but that they were destroyed by the governor of the city, in order to convert the building into cells for prisoners.

I was quite as much interested by one of the portals in the cathedral as by any thing else within its precincts; a Gothic gate of exceedingly beautiful architecture, and said to be of a date posterior to the conquest of Spain by the Moors.   If so, a part of the present cathedral must have been the site of an old Gothic church, of which some of the external pillars indeed seem to be still standing, for they are totally unlike any thing else in the pile.   There is a very similar portal at the entrance to the sagrario, or parish-church of the cathedral in Malaga, which is eminently beautiful.   It formed the principal entrance to a great Moorish mosque, which occupied the spot where the cathedral now rises, and possibly may have been part of a previous Gothic church converted by the Moors into their own temple.   Goths, Moors, Catholics — the very edifices mark the progress of these successive conquerors. The portal is arched with great lightness and symmetry, and the carving is exquisitely wrought out of a sort of free-stone, and preserved with wonderful perfection.

Before proceeding to the Alhambra, let us notice the Alameda of Grenada, and the history of the city.   The Alameda is one of the most beautiful, perhaps the most so, in the kingdom ; and its beauty will be still greater, when its improvements and enlargements, now in progress, shall have been completed.   The river Xeuil runs directly in the midst of it, embowered in trees, and crossed by an arching stone bridge, to which you ascend by steps from either side the stream to cross over and extend your walk on the other.   The broad gravelled walks of the Alameda are interspersed with gardens, and shaded by rows of trees; and at each end of the principal esplanade a fountain plays perpetually from an immense marble basin, supported on the head and shoulders of a number of grotesque gigantic forms, who spout the water from their mouths into the rim of the basin beneath. The entrance to Grenada along the banks of the Xeuil toward the Alameda is very beautiful. Here indeed, between the two long mountain ridges through which, in the middle of a lovely valley, the Xeuil winds its way, is one of the most romantic walks in the region. The waters of the Xeuil have been turned into two channels several feet above its bed, one on each side the valley, where they murmur along, overhung by cliffs and cottages, with a thick border of woods, toward the city and the opening of the great vega.

The city of Grenada was entirely built by the Moors in the tenth century, at which time the region belonged to the kings of Cordova. In 1235, under the Moorish king Alhamar, Grenada became the capital of a new kingdom of the same name, and the most celebrated of all places in the Moorish annals; the grand bulwark indeed, and the last, most favorite and beautiful retreat of that noble race in Spain. Ten thousand cavaliers from Syria and Irak, supposed to have been of the princeliest line in Arabia, came from their native deserts and settled amidst this southern paradise. When the kingdom thus formed and supported was conquered by the Catholic kings, it was seventy leagues long and thirty broad, containing thirty-two great towns and ninety-seven smaller ones, with upward of two thousand boroughs and villages, and three millions of inhabitants. Its annual revenue amounted to seven hundred thousand ducats. When the city was besieged and conquered by Ferdinand and Isabella it is said to have been nearly twelve miles in circumference, defended on its ramparts by ten hundred and thirty towers, including within its walls seventy thousand houses and four hundred thousand inhabitants. The fortress of the Albaycin as well as that of the Alhambra was capable of containing forty thousand men. The number that defended the ramparts during the siege was nearly a hundred thousand. The population of the city was greatly augmented toward the close of the Moorish dominion in Spain, by those who fled from other conquered places, and sought their last refuge in a city which they fondly hoped would prove as impregnable, as it was beloved and beautiful. The diminution of the population in Grenada is but a specimen of what has taken place in all Spain under the ruthless influences of civil and religious ignorance, bigotry, and despotism. At present the number of inhabitants in the city cannot be much more than seventy-five or eighty thousand. We heard them computed at about seventeen thousand *vecinos*, or families; which, allowing five persons to a family, would make eighty-five thousand.

It is difficult to conceive a more splendid, commanding, royal situation for a city than that which the Moors chose in this magnificent region. They selected two rising mountainous undulations, right at the northernmost end of the vast and fertile plain watered by the Xeuil and the Darro, and directly beneath the towering ridges of the Sierra Nevada. Each of these mountains were precipitous on one side, and susceptible of the strongest fortifications, and over one of them, with its southern base gradually sloping toward the plain, they threw the fortresses, castles and habitations of the common city, calling it the *Albaycin;* and over the other and the loftiest elevation they spread the palaces of the Alhambra, begirt with massive lines of towers and fortifications, and looking abroad over the city and the plain below, as a battlemented crown upon the forehead of the mountain. Between this city of the monarchs and the city of the people ran the waters of the Darro through its narrow winding vale, the western towers of the Alhambra rising directly on the borders of its steep precipitous glen, and looking up the romantic gorges through which it emerged from the bosom of what might be called the Spanish Alps. There, northward, the range of the Sierra Nevada pierces the clear blue sky, snow-mitred and pinnacled the year round, the Alhambra and the city appearing at a distance as if hanging at its dark-green base, while the eye roams from its declivities, south, east, and west, over a vast inland sea of vegetation, surrounded and framed in by a continuous picturesque amphitheatre of mountains. Studded with populous towns; humanized and domestic to a degree uncommon at that age; with a spirit of toleration and intelligent industry equally rare; busy and stirring with arts, trade, and manufactures; how beautiful must the scene have been under the flourishing dominion of the Moors in the full tide of their prosperity! And what a singular history is theirs! — romantic, even in its reality, to a degree of fiction.

THE PAST OF LIFE.

I LOVE the Past! Those buried hours
Whose shades still round the Present linger,
As Memory with faithful finger
    Points to the flowers
Upon their green graves flourishing,
    In the fresh bloom of spring!

I love the Past! Its teachings tell
The listening heart its own wild story:
Its youthful dreams of fame and glory,
    With love's bright spell
Inwoven and blended like the light
    Of distant stars at night.

I love the Past! Its records bear
Affection's earliest, fondest traces,
The lines of first familiar faces;
    The words of prayer
First gathered by my infant ear
    In tones forever dear.

I love the Past! Its memories cling
Around my heart, like hopes of heaven!
And bright as sun-light hues at even,
    Or seraph's wing,
Comes back the first-born hope to me
    Of immortality!

MOONLIGHT NIGHT AT SEA.

BY AN ENGLISHMAN.

I.

Oh the sweet calm, at dead of night,
  On boundless Ocean's moonlit waves,
When on its breast there beams the light
  Which glitters through its coral caves,
And softly blends the seas around,
That echo back the faintest sound!

II.

This is the hour that lures the soul
  From all the selfish cares of life;
Awakes the mind beyond control
  Of all its stirring scenes of strife;
And wafts unnumbered feelings back
To brighter spots on Memory's track.

III.

Thou art as calm, serene, and bright
  As when my early childhood's gaze
Delighted saw that flood of light,
  And grasped to catch those fleeting rays
That wavered on the deep-blue sea
Like threads of golden tracery.

IV.

But, tenants of the passing hour,
  We gleam along life's troubled tide;
Around us ever tempests lower,
  To whelm our bark in all its pride:
While that deep flood still wanders on
As ever, from its primal dawn!

V.

Yes! as I gaze on yon clear moon,
  I think of one who oft with me
Did pensive muse at midnight's-noon
  By that bright orb and silvery sea:
My mother! for 't is *thine* the smile
I see reflected there the while!

VI.

Perchance not mine alone the eye
  Which bends on thee its loving gaze;
My mother! dost thou from on high
  Watch with me now those heavenly rays?
Oh *is* it thus? May it not be
Thou too dost watch that moon and sea?

MY GRAND-FATHER'S PORT-FOLIO.

NUMBER THREE.

THE manuscript from which the following tale is extracted bears no date, and no internal nor external marks by which I can ascertain the year when the journey was undertaken, in the course of which my grand-father became the interested spectator of the scene which he describes. Indeed, I am unable to affirm that it is narrative of facts. All the information which I possess in relation to the matter may be laid before the reader in a very few words. One of my aunts, my grand-father's eldest daughter, became the wife of a gentleman who possessed a large tract of land in Ohio. Being an enterprising and brave man, and finding a sympathizing companion in his high-spirited partner, he resolved to strike into the wilderness, and lay the foundations of their future home amidst the grand forests of the West. Whether my grand-father ever hazarded the fatigues and perils of a journey to his daughter's residence is a circumstance upon which I cannot undertake to decide. Certain it is, that I find among his papers several short stories like the following, whose scene is laid in the West. These however are all of them destitute of those exact local descriptions, that continuity of narrative, and those data of time and place, which naturally attach to the records of an actual tour. Beside, I have ascertained that the good old man was somewhat addicted to romancing, and drew largely upon his imagination, to beguile the intervals between the more serious and wearisome engagements of his professional labor. If therefore it should seem to the reader that the subjoined tale has more the air of fiction than of fact, he is at liberty to use his own better judgment in deciding a question, the answer to which, whatever it may be, will not I hope be prejudicial to the interest of the simple story that I humbly trust will be found worthy of a place in the select company under whose auspices it is ushered into notice.

THE BACKWOODSMAN'S SACRIFICE.

I HAVE been jogging on my equestrian journey for three summer weeks; following out every path that has opened invitingly before me; suffering myself to be turned aside by the smallest thing; tracing a brook or ascending·a hill; penetrating a deep shade, chasing a squirrel; led on by the scented air to the quiet home of the wild flowers and the fern.   .   .   .   .

The journey of to-day has been more delightful and exhilarating than the wasted dyspeptic ever dared to hope to enjoy again. During twenty-five miles gone over, I have passed not so many human dwellings, and those all built of logs partially squared, and piled one upon another. A beautiful river has been in sight or hearing all day long; which now has expanded between the more gentle and yielding banks, broadly, as if it were an inland lake; while its waters seemed to have stayed their onward flow, as if there were a spirit in *them* too that sighed for rest, and they would have loved to linger in the domain of peace for ever; and anon has crowded up its forces into itself, and darted by, where the impending shores pressed more rudely against it, as if, like human tyranny, they would check its joyous and natural career.

The path which I have travelled since the morning has been pursued at random; one only star pointing out its direction, and that the sweet promise of seclusion. It has been winding about nearly the whole distance in the deep shade of a majestic forest, like which New England has none; whether in respect to the grandeur of its regal individuals or to the vastness of its grave and reverend community. The air has been bland and genial as ever fanned the broad palm-leaf in the sweetest garden of the earth; and yet as inspiriting as ever kissed the glowing cheek of Alpine nymph, while it has breathed into her heaving bosom a life of health, whose source she does not think to inquire into, any more than to pause in her mountain chase to ask herself if *she is happy*.

It has been one of those rare and precious days for whose boon all that lives insensibly gives thanks; when life itself is gratitude. One of those days when Nature seems to be surcharged with the Spirit of Love; so that even the most misanthropical and pertinaciously-wretched of hearts is imperceptibly wooed out of its self-erected charnel-house; and the slow pulse dances, and the dull eye lightens up, and the marble cheek glows red; and the patient in his confinement has the casement lifted and another pillow placed beneath his languid head; and mothers may be seen, the country through, carrying abroad their pale and sickly progeny to take their share of God's blessing, and bathe in the warm and limpid air; and sons and daughters propping up their aged sire or dame, as they totter out to bask their chilled frames in the sunshine once more, and freshly dream of life's morning glow, and look back over the long hill of life to the garden on the other side where the sun always shone; one of those days in fine when it seems to be the purpose of God to give to all his children, both the just and the unjust, a holiday; while heaven lends its choicest influences to earth, and smiles from end to end to see all creatures glad.

I have been more happy than I can tell. Let me never forget this day. Let its memory come over me in other desponding days and dark and dreary nights, when the whole head shall again be sick and the whole heart faint, and the sun and the moon and the stars shall not give to me their light; let it come as a token of the *ever-smile* that my own clouded breast cannot then see; let it come as a sign of the power of HIM in whom alone I live and move to give at any hour perfect bliss to my thirsting soul; let it come to me as a sweet harbinger of what perchance *to-morrow* may bring with it: let it come as an antepast of what eternity shall be, if I but trust and hope in the stormy hour, and follow on through shade and sun after the light of that countenance whose reflection I have to-day brightly seen, in order that I might know that it is *that only* for which my heart and my flesh do cry out, and that I might henceforth never let it go from before my longing eyes!

Early in the afternoon, after a primitive and sweet noon-feast, made up of a dainty bit from my saddle-bags and a quaff from a clear rivulet — the latter shared with infinite relish by my most companionable and temperate horse — I came suddenly upon a little knot of buildings, consisting of three houses with their complement of small and rudely-constructed sheds for domestic animals, all closely clustered together in the midst of a narrow and partial clearance.

'It is singular,' I thought, 'that I see and hear no signs of occupancy in this most pleasant and comfortable of forest abiding-places. Where are the silver-haired and trumpet-tongued cherubs that I should have looked for to be already surrounding and climbing upon the stranger's horse, as they poured forth, impelled no less by genuine western hospitality than by childish curiosity, from the 'multum in parvo' of a back-woodsman's abode?' And where are the hale and brown-visaged mistresses of these houses of logs?— queens of noble bearing, of warm and honest hearts, and of wide domain? And where are the huge dogs that even after long experience of their harmlessness to an open brow, I hardly dare to face, and before which it would ill become a bear to stand? Surely something extraordinary has happened to this little neighborhood, who have nothing to protect them but their courage, their honesty and their God. Pray Heaven that it be no ill!'

I spurred forward, sprang to the ground, cast the reins freely upon my horse's neck, and entered the open doors of one after another of the huts, until all had been completely examined and found to be silent and deserted. Nothing within them however indicated harm or a hurried remove: and feeling assured that those whom I sought could not be far off, I took the first foot-path that presented itself, and went on if perchance to find them.

Fortunately I selected the right avenue, and after a brisk walk of five or ten minutes came upon the assembled party. On looking down from a gentle acclivity, I saw standing all uncovered in an easy and graceful group around an old man (whose locks were long and white, but whose form was erect and powerful, and whose face showed no sign of age) it might be a score of emigrants, older and younger, male and female, in attitudes of the profoundest reverence, and as was easily manifest, engaged in prayer. Instantly my steps were staid. The influence of the scene took possession of my soul; and although I could learn no words of their petition, I let my heart go heavenward with theirs, in indefinite but not the less true and earnest supplication.

As soon as a little stir in the assemblage warned me that the spirits of my brethren had come back to earth again, I stepped carefully down, and unimpeded and almost unnoticed, took my stand among them. Immediately the whole mystery of the scene was revealed to me; for I heard the old man who had acted as priest to kindle the altar of their devotions, say, as he spread out his arms, and a smile like that which illuminated the face of Jesus when he blessed little children played upon his weather-worn countenance: '*Let the children be presented for baptism.*' He was an itinerant evangelist whom the SPIRIT led hither and thither among the wanderers of the wilderness, to publish sweet tidings of salvation; to break the bread of life; to pour out the cup of blessing, and place the seal of the Good Shepherd upon the foreheads of his scattered lambs, so that not one of them should be lost.

Three fathers in turn presented each their children to the holy man; and he dipped his finger into a natural basin of rock, into which the overflowing drop of a perennial spring, clear as innocence itself, trickled down, and sprinkled the symbolical water upon their heads; and looking up to heaven, as he raised his hand thitherward from off each up-turned and sunny brow, repeated the deeply significant and soul-moving words divinely appointed for the sacred rite: '*I baptize thee in the name of the Father, and of the Son, and of the Holy Ghost. Amen.*'

And now, two of the grateful sires, as soon as they had offered their children — who seemed to feel as if something mysterious and holy and yet most happy had been done unto them — led them back to the side of their mothers, who, silent and subdued, had waited apart at a little distance with thrilling interest for the issue of the sacred work.

One of the fathers with his three sons remained looking for the third *mother* to come up, who carefully unfolding the clean white drapery which enveloped the tenderest and fairest of her precious jewels, placed an infant of but a few days' age in the arms of the holy man; while he, with a feeling of reverence, as if he were dealing with an unfallen angel, just ruffled the water in the bowl of rock, and raised his hand, tremulous from the sincerity of his interest, to place the mystical signet upon a brow that reflected the purity of heaven.

Every eye was intently fastened on him, and every heart was altogether gone out to him. But his hand remained lifted on high; an ashy paleness spread over his cheek; and, pausing for one moment to command his evidently agonized emotions, while we all stood breathless in bitterest suspense, at length with a calmness and tenderness of tone that could not fail to still the most tempestuous grief, instead of the wonted baptismal words, he ejaculated, as he gave back the soulless body to the bosom of the awe-stricken mother: 'THE LORD GAVE, AND THE LORD HATH TAKEN AWAY; AND BLESSED BE HIS HOLY NAME!'

CONSCIENCE: A SONNET.

THY voiceless, loud rebuke the bravest shun,
CONSCIENCE! thou stern detector of each art
That would to Wrong a robe of right impart,
Woven of delicate distinctions; spun
Like webs that on the meadows meet the sun,
But with the dew that spangles them, depart.
Shechina in the temple of the heart!
Visible presence of the viewless One!
Thou art a native tenant in the breast
Of man, where'er yon blue etherial dome
Hangs o'er a hearth, curtains a human home,
Or veils a lonely hunter in his quest:
Where'er a portion of our race may rest —
Where'er we, universal brothers, roam.

SONG OF THE WINDS.

"BLOW WINDS, AND CRACK YOUR CHEEKS!—RAGE!'—SHAKSPERE.

Now the weary world is sleeping;
 Every human sound is still :
Faëry sentries now are keeping
 Watch on every shaded hill;
O'er the vales where ghosts are straying,
O'er the sports that sylphs are playing
 To the song of whip-poor-will.

This was made our festal night;
See ! the silver orb of light
Lifts from th' east her magic ring,
Signal for our gathering.

Then gather we ! gather we ! spirits of air !
But hushed be our tread, as we hither repair.
One venturing cricket is filling his song;
Tread noiseless above him, while gliding along.
Then gather we ! gather we ! haste from afar;
Our coursers are waiting, and ready our car.

Come, Boreas ! come from thy home at the pole,
Ere the cold Northern Bear his full night-circle roll;
And the strength of thy breath, and the speed of thy wing,
And thy trumpet made ready, all silently bring.
Then gather we ! gather we ! haste from afar;
Our coursers are waiting, and ready our car.

Come, Child of the South ! from thy dwelling of death
Where the desert-born Simoom is blown on thy breath !
Come sweeping o'er Ætna's red chimney of hell,
Borne on his black sulphur-cloud, fearful and fell.
But darkness and silence spread under thy wings,
As they sweep o'er the leaf where the night-cricket sings.
Then gather we ! gather we ! haste from afar ;
Our coursers are waiting, and ready our car.

Come, Breath of the East ! from thine ocean-lashed cave,
With thy storm-dripping pinions skim over the wave.
Roar across dark Asphaltus, and sprinkle the gloom
That floats on the billows o'er Sodoma's tomb ;
And gather the mists reeking up from the fen,
Where ghosts smell the blood of the night-murdered men.
But stealthily marshal thy heavy-winged train,
As they pass where the cricket is pouring his strain.
Then gather we, gather we ! haste from afar;
Our coursers are waiting, and ready our car.

Come, Zephyr ! soft blown from the hills of the West,
Where thy spirit is fed in the Isles of the Blest ;
Sigh over the fields and the gardens of bliss,
Till their odors are wooed by thy languishing kiss;
With each lingering whisper that waits on a dream,
Or lurks in the willow that bends o'er the stream ;
With the sigh of the lover that dreams of the hour

When his soul shall be blest in the moon-lighted bower;
With the breath of the love-kiss that lingers so sweet
Ere it breaks on the soul-speaking lips as they meet.
Come, Zephyr! so laden; but heed as ye pass,
And charm not the cricket that sings in the grass.
Then gather we, gather we! haste from afar;
Our coursers are waiting, and ready our car.

Come, wandering Breezes! wherever ye roam,
O'er the graves of the dead or the ocean's mad foam;
Come, fly from your caves by the surf-beaten shore,
From the deep-sounding gulfs where the cataracts roar;
Come hie o'er the mountains, come haste o'er the sea,
Where Dryad and Mermaid shout up to your glee.
Then gather we, gather we! haste from afar;
Our coursers are waiting, and ready our car.
But hist! as ye settle, be viewless and still
Till the song of the cricket is sung to its fill.

    .   .   .   .   .

Now all are here!
The sand has run:
Hark! chanticleer
Calls up the sun!
The final signal's near:
There — hark! the cricket's song is done;
Now hist once more! · · · The convent-bell strikes, one!

Shout! Now the earth is ours!
Shout, all ye wingéd powers!
Shout, till the convent-towers
Roar back the sound!
Shout, as we upward rise!
Shout, as our chariot flies!
Shout, as we seize the skies,
And sweep the vast profound!

All hail our festal night!
See Dian's orb, how bright!
And through her fields of light,
There wanders not a cloud.
We'll use awhile her ray,
As at our freaks we play;
And when we work a fray,
We'll wrap her in a shroud.

Our festal night, all hail!
Shout through the rocky vale!
Hark! hear that frightened wail!
A ghost is shrieking there!
We'll chase him to his den,
And scare him out again;
We'll drive him through the fen,
And twist his horrid hair!

Now roar we through the forest,
Where reigns the fearless oak:
He cares not for our coming,
But we'll lay him with a stroke.
Sweep! — roar!
'T is o'er!
He lies with all his leaves! the monarch's strength is broke!

The frightened birds are shaken from their nest;
　The black bear, trembling, glares from out his cave:
The roaring fury breaks the dead man's rest,
　And scares his ghost up from the unsafe grave.

　　　Now mount we to the sky,
　　　　And scour the upper air:
　　　We 'll carry war on high,
　　　　And work a wonder there!
　　　We 'll shake the very stars,
　　　And startle bloody Mars:
　　　　Blow fiercer! blow
　　　　　With all your might!
　　　　There! see they go!
Shooting down headlong through the sea of night!

　　　Boreas, take thou the reins:
　　　Guide the steeds to Siber's plains.
　　　Swiftly! swiftly! we must play
　　　Fearful tricks before the day.

Merrily, merrily ride we now!
And see, far below how the forests bow!
Where Caurus descending is making rare play;
See him wreck the black hovel that stands by the bay!
　Ha! those young sleeping wretches! there 's one, two, three!
All wrapped in one blanket he 's raised with his breath,
　And blown them far out o'er the sea!
Rush! rush! as we travel our Caurus shall play:
There 's a beggar asleep; clutch his basket away!
Now merrily, merrily drive to our goal;
See, Cynosure rises! we 're nearing the pole!

　　　There glows the Northern Fire,
　　　　Up through the stinging air!
　　　We 'll catch its freezing flames,
　　　　And wreathe them with our hair.

　　　Plunge to the hills of snow,
　　　　And lift the storm on high!
　　　And sweep the powdery blast
　　　　Through all the smothered sky.

　　　Rifle old Winter's treasures;
　　　　Let him grumble if he dares!
　　　We 'll beard him in his palace,
　　　　And flaunt his frosty hairs.

　　　What care we for his weapons?
　　　　Toss up his armory!
　　　We 'll spoil the grim old spoiler,
　　　　And mock him in our glee.

　　　Drive round his throne, good Boreas,
　　　　His sparkling throne of ice;
　　　We 'll dash his temple as we pass,
　　　　And spoil him in a trice.

Ha ha! we are strong, and our promise is done:
Our goal we have reached, and its circle have run;
And braved the old tyrant that wars with the sun!

Now to the left we 'll bear,
    To Norway's boisterous shore,
To play a frolic there,
    And hear the Maelstrom roar.

Now o'er Caucasus we fly,
But we 'll keep our path on high:
Nor disturb them as they flow —
Wolga's waters dark below.

Here we 're passing in a trice
Russia's sporting hills of ice:
Leave them in their silver light:
We will spare the Russ to-night.

Bend we now the Northern way,
Where the Lapland witches play;
Where grim Hecate's imps are bred,
On the milky moon-beams fed.'
See the fiendish, filthy brood,
Dabbled o'er with human blood !
Dancing hellish festival
Round a cloven, bleeding skull.
Leave their merriment alone —
We have frolics of our own:
We shall see a dreader scene
Ere the morning light, I ween !

Here rolls the Western wave,
    Insidious in its play;
But murderous waters rave
    To whelm their evening prey :
And the mermaiden sits on the rocky isle,
    And chants o'er the bright dancing waters her song :
Ah, little they deem that she 's weaving the while
    Her spell o'er the listeners, fatally strong !

Go, mermaiden ! haste to thy coral-built cave,
    And spread the pearl-couches far down in the deep;
For the crew of yon vessel now floats o'er the grave,
    Where the sun of the morning shall find them asleep.

Now stoop we to the shore,
    And lift the angry sea :
And bid the whirlpool roar
    As horrible as we !
Up to the skies the mountains rise,
    Their bright tops shattered into spray ;
Now down they stoop with fearful swoop,
    As 't were to sweep the earth away !

The sails are driven !
    The masts they fly ;
To splinters riven
    They shoot on high !

Now shall come the fearful wail !
Now the iron heart shall quail !
Caurus, draw the pitchy cloud,
And the trembling moon enshroud.

See the towering iceberg loom
Through the doubtful, horrid gloom !

Onward it comes! and on its brow
See the hell-brood gathering now!
See the spirits o'er it glide,
With their white hair streaming wide.
Hear their shout that 's raised on high,
With the sea-calves' 'larum cry.
Now on tip-toe see them stand,
Lifting each long white skinny hand;
Straining with their fiery eyes
To behold their fated prize.

Now for mercy shrieks the crew,
 But their shriek shall rise in vain;
Pierce them, Terror, through and through!
 Ha! they shriek again — again!
 High on the final wave
 Lift them above their grave!

Sweep o'er them the dark wing;
Eurus, their death-knell ring:
 Crash! — it is done!
Hark! hear that rending cry!
Blow! drown their agony:
 Grave, thou hast won!

Ha! ha! aloud, aloud
Shout, shout ye fiendish crowd!
And drop your flapping shroud:
 Leap on it, and descend.
Now shout we as they go
To watch their prey below:
One awful blast we 'll blow,
 And then our fray shall end.

Upward! upward! turn on high
Till the dread commotion die;
Till the billows be repressed,
Lulled by mermaid's song to rest.

We have had our festal night,
And the morning smells of light:
Day-dawn in the east afar
Melts the newly-risen star.
We must sever ere the day
Pales Diana's western ray.

Now our festival is done:
Eurus, fly and meet the sun.
Greet him with a sweetened breath —
Let it bear no tale of death.
Notus, to thy home repair,
Stealing through the misty air;
Skimming stilly o'er the deep,
Hushed at length to quiet sleep.
Zephyr, chase that whispering wave,
Straying o'er the recent grave.
Boreas, with noiseless speed,
Homeward turn our mettled steed.
Homeward, homeward, every breeze!
Homeward o'er the earth and seas!
Homeward, homeward! see, the morn
Lifts the sun — the day is born!

         E. A. S.

EDWARD ALFORD AND HIS PLAY-FELLOW.

BY THE AUTHOR OF 'WILSON CONWORTH.'

CHAPTER FIRST.

'IT was an high speech of SENECA, after the manner of the Stoics, that the good things which belong to prosperity are to be wished, but the good things that belong to adversity are to be admired.'   BACON.

WE must carry back the reader to the time when the child whose history we are about to relate slept upon the arms of its nurse; when the sun was shut out from the window, and the darkened room and closed shutter showed that weakness and pain were the purchase of this new being. The child was a boy; like his father, he seemed his very fac-simile. His fine hair lay upon his head with the outline of his father's head, and he looked prematurely old, from his resemblance to one already in years. The mother who bore him lay languid upon her couch, happy that she had given birth to a man. The luxuries of wealth were about her; the rich bed-stead, the carved furniture, all the elegant conveniences that art could supply, were there. But all these, and the down and linen that wrapped her limbs, could not allay the pain in her joints. The soft tread of domestics could not bring softness and repose to her racked frame. She was passing through the trial all mothers feel and must feel in gaining the great privilege of giving birth to a human being. She seemed insensible to all attempts to soothe her pain; and only when the child was brought to her and suffered to nestle in her bosom did an expression of ease pass over her face. Then she did smile faintly, but in such a sort as if the frame was too weak to express the deep joy of her heart. But she was happy; all her own pangs were forgotten in the warm gushings of maternal love. Bountiful Nature! how hast thou supplied in our moral constitution a medicine and solace for that which is beyond the reach of surgical skill, or any human contrivance! Thou calmest the mother's anguish by giving her a feeling which swallows up all physical suffering, and spreads through her frame a thankful joy!

At the same hour that this event was going on in the sick chamber, a poor foreigner just landed on our shores, and travelling into the suburbs in search of food and shelter, was taken ill near the gate of the house with the pains of child-birth. The husband who accompanied her asked leave to be permitted to lodge his wife in the barn; a favor at first refused by the English coachman, who said he was afraid his horses would take some disease from such ragged customers; but an American servant of the family representing the case to his master, the woman was comfortably lodged in an out-house that served the family with extra room in case of much company. The village apothecary and surgeon were sent to her, and her delivery was as comfortable as any lady's in the land could be. The bed she lay upon was coarse in its apparel, but clean and wholesome. The furniture of the room was simple and only what was necessary.   The darkness was as complete in the apartment she occupied as it could be in the chamber of the lady we have been speaking of.   The air was as pure in the one as in the other, only perhaps the humble room had the advantage in this respect.   But she had also the same stillness about her, and more than all, the same kind Nature presided at her bedside, filled her heart with the yearnings of maternal love, and made *her* to forget the pains and languishment of labor.   Beside, the woman·had been used to toil, and her sturdy frame more easily underwent the trial than that of her whose life had been passed in ease and luxury.

Her child too was a son, and it made the heart of the father glad that it was so; for, thought he, the lad will be able to help me on the farm, and can take care of himself, and will not need the looking after that girls require.   He will be beset with temptations to be sure, but not of the kind that vex the days and nights of poor anxious parents for their daughters, sent out in the world to earn their bread, with the strong passions of our nature at work in their hearts, and but little aid of education and pride of station to counteract them.   Poor parents may not talk much about this fear, but it is one that lies heavily on their hearts, when in the intervals of labor they think of the prospects of the offspring about them.

But on the score of profit, the birth of a son is considered by the farmer twice as fortunate as that of a daughter.   The rich man congratulates himself upon his good fortune when a son is born to him, because he can take his name and support the title and dignity of his family ; the poor man arrives at the same result by thinking of the dignity of labor and the title to land.   ' This son of mine,' says he, ' can work ; he can earn his bread; he will save me the hire of a hand ; and if I should die, can carry on my farm and support his mother and the children.'   There was much meaning conveyed in the remark of a poor man who, on being told that a neighbor's wife had brought forth a daughter, said, ' What ! *only* a gal ? '

But it is time that we introduce more particularly to our readers the persons destined to figure in this history.   Mr. CHARLES ALFORD was the fortunate owner of the country-seat where his beautiful wife had just given birth to her first child.   He had inherited a large fortune ; nature had bestowed upon him a fine constitution and amiable disposition ; the last almost a necessary consequence of the first.   He had received a ' good education,' as the phrase goes; had been at college ; had travelled ; seen the old world, and returned to close the eyes of his father, and assume his wealth.   He soon after married a pretty girl moving in the polished society of Boston with great éclat, and had about a year previous to the event which commences our story purchased this country-seat about twelve miles from the city.

Mrs. AMELIA ALFORD was the daughter of a merchant in high standing.   She had been educated at one of the fashionable schools, and subsequently in the most fashionable society of the most polished city in the Union.   It would seem, and the world said, that two people never came together over whom fortune had showered so many favors. They had wealth, health, polished manners, fine tastes, mutual love for the fine arts and literature, and a fashionable regard for the Sabbath and the ordinances of religion. Not a stain marked either character that any human eye could see; and their greatest misfortune seemed to be that they had nothing more to hope for. The birth of little Edward crowned a cup already overflowing with happiness; and the happy father, as he contemplated his lot, was fairly forced by his satisfaction and delight to utter a prayer of thanks to his Maker for so great blessings. It was sincere and heart-felt, and the better because he did not feel at the time that he was doing any thing very good in the sight of God, but on the contrary felt more keenly than ever before the neglect and indifference he had manifested in his heart, if not in his manner, to so kind and beneficent a Being.

Poor John Towley and his wife Jane, in the out-house, had also their satisfactions and thankful prayers. They agreed to call their little son Thomas; partly because it was the name of his grand-father, and partly because the name was in the Bible; for the poor and uneducated have a great respect for Scripture names and words, as well they may.

John was an English gardener out of employment, and sought a home in America for his family, consisting of several children, whom he had left behind him in England in such places as he could procure for them. Putting one with a brother, another with his aged father, one at service, and leaving one to the care of the parish, he and his wife had determined to emigrate. Before he had sailed, nearly all his means were exhausted; and with barely enough to pay their passage-money, they had landed on this hospitable shore.

When Mrs. Alford learned that a child had been born so near her at the time of her own delivery, she felt a natural sympathy with the mother, and longed to see her and comfort her. She gave directions that she should want nothing; sent her food from her own room, and did so many acts of kindness for her, that Jane began to think that there was some truth in all she had heard of the easy way of living in America. The child must be brought to her; and little Tommy in an extempore dress was presented in her chamber. A stout, bright-eyed little fellow he was; and looked like a young giant beside the delicate babe that lay wrapped in lace and flannel in some newly-fashioned cradle. Tommy when only four weeks old crowed outright, and came by his noisy delight near to frightening little Edward into a fit.

The mother being established in the kind sympathies of Mrs. Alford, for the more favors we do a fellow-creature the more we are disposed to do, she could by no means think of permitting her to leave the room she occupied. Jane by this time was as well as ever; she was able to assist the servants in many of their labors; and the humility and gentleness of the foreign woman began to make friends for her even among the selfish and hard-hearted domestics of the family. It was in due time found out that she was an excellent washer and mangler; could clean house, cook, work in the field, if necessary; in short, make herself generally useful; the latter property being invaluable in an American servant. John too had established his reputation as a good gardener; and Mr. Alford, at the solicitation of his wife, agreed to retain the pair Heaven had dropped at his gate, as servants in the establishment. They were to occupy the small house of the gardener, which was vacant, and receive all they could show themselves capable of earning.

It was a happy day for John and Jane when this arrangement was closed, and their sore hearts began to heal in the prospect of soon being able to send for their children. Little Tommy too crowed louder than ever, and seemed to partake of the general joy.

It was early spring-time, and both the children grew apace. Mrs. Alford by this time could sit up in her easy chair, though no breath of heaven disunited with coal-smoke and the dust of sweeping was suffered to enter her lungs. All the air she breathed must first be warmed by artificial means; and so by extra care and attention she was kept in a languid and weak condition for two or three months. It certainly would have been very vulgar if she could have recovered as soon as poor Jane did. A sense of propriety kept her still in her room, when she longed in her heart to accompany little Edward in his rides with the nurse. From her window she could see Jane at work at the wash-tub, with the sleeves turned up from off her brawny arms, her child rolling on the grass and snatching at the flowers, taking the deepest delight in the green colors about him, and his ear evidently pleased with the songs of the birds, as in their flight they wheeled close to him. The poultry began to acknowledge little Tommy as a playmate, and the large watch-dog would lie down before him and gaze curiously in his face. It is not strange that Mrs. Alford felt a feeling of inferiority to this poor woman, as she watched these movements. Nature and truth asserted themselves in her heart; and she would question for a moment the customs and habits which penned her up in a gaudy chamber, without the least disease upon her, while this woman of charity was enjoying the pure air and the bright sun, with liberty to go whither she pleased and do whatever she liked.

We talk of the confinements of labor; the daily toil and dull routine of the same pursuits; but there is no thraldom so hard as that of fashion. The king is the greatest slave on earth. He can only wear certain garments, and must appear at stated intervals in a certain manner. He must walk just so, and not otherwise; ride at a prescribed pace, and keep up an accustomed dignity. The queen cannot surrender herself to her feelings as the village maiden can; it would be unseemly for her to undress herself or put on her own clothes. She can have no solitude, no nature, no repose. Both king and queen move in one eternal round of state, to which nothing is so near alike as a horse in a cider-mill. As we descend from this rank, the sphere of liberty is enlarged: the wealthy commoner enjoys more than the noble; the poor laborer more than the rich nabob; until we come to those who enjoy the largest liberty of all; those who draw their support from the bosom of mother Nature; who regulate their hours by the clock-work of the heavens; rising with the sun; reposing when he seems to stand still, as he does at noon; going to sleep when he goes out of sight; earning rest by labor, hunger by abstinence, and health and happiness by all.

We do not propose to go into the detail of the different management of the two children. It can readily be imagined how tenderly the child of wealth was nurtured; what quantities of physic he swallowed; how often the city physician was summoned post-haste upon the slightest token of ailment, and the long consultations held over his infant complaints by all the female members of the family. It is enough to say that he barely escaped with his life; having achieved before he was three years of age the establishment of the reputation of more than one physician; the new painting and glazing of the shop of the apothecary, beside putting into fashion the newly-invented cradle which rocked his infant slumbers. But he saw his third birth-day, a feeble under-sized boy, but yet his mother's darling and his father's pride.

Little Tom, for by this time he had become too much of a man to be called Tommy, weighed twice as much as he. With a fine broad chest, which he had expanded in gambols with the dog, in rolling on the grass, in reaching and climbing, running and shouting, he bade fair to be able to earn his bread and fight his way through the world, if the passage was not granted him. He had had all the advantage of simple habits, with the additional one of cleanliness. Being often invited to the nursery of the Hall, Mrs. Alford would not allow of his admission unless he was neatly dressed and washed; and this no doubt was an unusual privilege he enjoyed. If poor parents only knew how much disease and expense they would save themselves by the simple application of cold water to the limbs of their children, it would seem they would be willing to use this cheap prevention. But unluckily for these little urchins of poverty, the hands and face are generally considered the only washable parts of the body after a child gets able to walk. The accidents to which tended children are liable insures corporeal washing until this period, and we do not question but these very accidents are intended by kind mother Nature, who always takes better care of us than we take of ourselves, as hints to this very habit. Cats and dogs lick and wash their young. Older animals exchange the compliment of scratching each other. Even the pigs take care of their skin, as many a well-worn post in the stye will witness; but it is only for man endowed with reason, hands, and bathing-houses, to neglect this natural law of health — cleanliness. We brush our clothes, our hats, and boots; we encase our necks and bosoms in white linen, and imagine we are clean.

Tom, for we must drop the *little* also, gained every thing in health from this order of Mrs. Alford; and this, with the out-o'-door exercise he took, gave a brightness to his eye and complexion which fairly outshone the delicate beauty of Edward, who was destined to live, though with a frail hold upon life.

The children soon came to love one another. They as yet knew not but they had equal privileges in the world. They had their little quarrels and contentions about the possession of play-things and bits of cake, but oftener they were to be seen together with a spirit of mutual love and pleasure in each other's society. Tom became the supporter and assistant of his play-fellow; and thus early began to learn the superior satisfaction of giving to receiving. The applause and caresses he received from Mrs. Alford upon these occasions by and by caused him to show a generous yielding of his own wishes and desires to his weaker companion; and Edward began to look to him for that protection and guidance, as to where to go and what to do, which while it protected him was invaluable to Tom in giving him force and self-reliance. The fact that he had another to look after beside himself made him thoughtful and considerate; and in these childish sports and pastimes he was insensibly forming the most useful habits of mind.

.Though Tom was clad in coarse yet clean garments while his play-fellow was robed in the most expensive and elegant fabrics, the children not yet seemed aware that there was any difference in their dress. Too happy were they in their plays in the newly-mown fields, among the flowers of the garden, or under the broad shade of the spreading elms, to be thinking of such trifles. While all the servants and villagers looked at Edward with admiring eyes, as the heir of wealth and the son of a gentleman; while Tom was only a fine healthy boy, fitted for work; Edward himself looked up to Tom as his superior, because he really *was* so; and his native good sense was stronger than all the lessons he received from his nurse, and the false judgments of those about him, in producing this feeling.

Time wore on in this manner until the children were six years of age. By this time Edward had learned to read in a famous infant school in the city. He could sing little hymns and repeat many verses, while his play-fellow had not yet learned his letters. Unfortunately, or fortunately for him, as the sequel will show, neither John Towley nor Jane had been trained in reading and writing. But the boy knew things if not words. He knew all the flowers in the garden, their habits and culture. He could weed out a bed of onions and transplant roots equal to his father. If Edward knew that horse, *equus, ippos, cheval,* all stood for the name of that domestic animal, Tom knew more than he about the creature, and could ride him to boot, while he called him and knew him only as an ''os.' If Edward had learned to tell the time of day by the little watch he carried in his pocket, Tom could tell it by looking at the sun, or by the cravings of his stomach for dinner or supper. The one knew the names of many things without knowing any thing more about them; while the other knew the nature and uses of many things without knowing their names. Edward had the most *information*, but Tom had the most *knowledge.*

Although John Towley could not teach his son to read, he could and did teach him always to speak the truth. He could and did teach him the elements of religion; that he had a Father in heaven; that this Father saw all he did, and knew even his thoughts; that he was pleased when he did right and spoke the truth, and offended when he did wrong and spoke a lie; that he was to live for ever in a place where goodness would be the only distinction; that in the sight of this Heavenly Father he was as precious as if he wore fine clothes and could repeat ever so many verses. Tom had never thought at all about his clothes before he heard this; and the next time he met Edward he did compare their garments, and concluded that Edward's were nicer than his. This thought did not get out of his mind for weeks, if it ever did.

Edward likewise had been taught religion. He had been to the Sunday-school, and could say the whole catechism. If asked, 'Who died to save sinners?' he gave the correct answer. He would say that he was an 'utterly depraved creature,' in answer to a certain question; and, in short, could go without stumbling through the whole body of divinity. But his mind was so crowded with terms, and he had been taught so many words and phrases, that he had no time to think of any thing else, and was glad to escape from teachers who looked so sad and solemn, and whose voices had that sepulchral sound he had heard his nurse say was heard about grave-yards o' nights.

The two youngsters were one day on the banks of the pond near Mr. Alford's house in which the white lily grew, and it was just fit to be plucked. They had been told never to go into the water, and it was only by special privilege that they were suffered to go near it.

'Oh, get me a lily, Tom! What would I give for a lily! How white and pretty they look!' exclaimed Edward.

'No,' said Tom; 'mother said I must not go into the water; and your mother too told *you* not to.'

'But nobody will see you,' says Edward. 'You have no shoes and stockings on; you can strip up your trousers, and then we can have some lilies! Oh, *do* go, Tom! — that's a good fellow!'

Tom looked at his play-mate with surprise, and then said: 'God will see me!'

'Oh no he wo'n't!' said his companion.

But Tom would not go. This conversation may give a fair view of the religious education of the two children.

Having recorded the chief influences that marked their infancy, we propose in a succeeding chapter to show the effect of opposite plans of education; the one the study of contrivance, the other the work of necessity.

SONNET.

ON A MEDALLION REPRESENTING TITYOS CHAINED IN TARTARUS.

BY MRS. MARY E. DEWITT.

O! wondrous marvel of the sculptor's art!
  What cunning hand hath culled thee from the mine,
  And carved thee into life, with skill divine?
How claims in thee Humanity a part!
Seems from the gem the form enchained to start,
  While thus, with fiery eye and outspread wings,
  The ruthless vulture to its bosom clings,
With whetted beak deep in his victim's heart.
O, thou embodied meaning, master wrought!
  So taught the Sage, how, sunk in crime and sin,
  The Soul, a prey to Conscience, writhes within
Its fleshly bonds enslaved; while ever Thought,
The vulture fierce, with beak remorseless, tears
At life — the hell whose chain the soul in torture wears!

F L O W E R S.

THE SICK POETESS' REQUEST TO HER LOVER.

Ah! go love, and bring me the flowers that bloom bright
   In the depths of the glen, near our favorite hill;
I dreamed of their freshness and fragrance last night,
   As they hang on the edge of the glittering rill.

Bring me the blossoms that fall from the lily
   Which grows 'neath the shade of the low-bending yew;
I love the pure grace of that child of the valley —
   And forget not a bunch of wild violets too.

Wild violets! they were the flowers thou didst wear, love,
   Long, long near that faithful and fond heart of thine,
When I, on beholding their beauty was o'er, love,
   Had flung them all withered and scentless from mine!

Oh, bring them! oh, bring them! I long for their perfume!
   Bring them now, with the dew on their blossoms like rain!
And closing my eyes on my sick chamber's cold gloom,
   I 'll wander with *thee* in the green glades again!

Killoley House, Enniscorthy, Ireland.   ALICIA JANE SPARROW.

STRAY LEAVES

FROM THE PORT-FOLIO OF A GEORGIA LAWYER.

NUMBER TWO.

ONE of the striking peculiarities of our people is the disposition to
talk tall; that is, to use the largest and the longest and the most difficult words to express the simplest ideas. It was this same error which
made Sir James Mackintosh and Sir Edward L. Bulwer fail in their
legislative career. They were both (especially the first) of eminent
literary attainments, highly 'talented,' and good judges of human
nature; and it was but fair to presume that thus gifted, they would have
distinguished themselves greatly in parliament; but they spoiled every
thing by coming there steeped in dictionary, and 'talking tall;' or to
express the idea in the language of an English writer, 'they spoke over
the heads of other people.'

This peculiarity is indigenous in Georgia, but it grows elsewhere also.
When General Lafayette came to Savannah in 1825, he was feasted, and
paraded, and invited about, until the excess of hospitality made him sick.
His son, George Washington Lafayette, seeing his father's condition,
and dreading that he might be made seriously ill, exclaimed, wringing
his hands Frenchman-like, in an agony of grief: 'They will *assassinate*
him by kindness!'

This mode of expression developes itself on every occasion; at the bar and on the bench, at home or abroad, drunk or sober, our people 'talk tall.' Ask a man for instance in one of our frontier or upper counties what kind of ague he had had, and he will tell you that it was 'exorbitantly chillyish.' Demand of him what kind of fever followed on, and he will answer that 'it was not *extravagant*, but it rather *ascended* into bilious.'

Another species of this peculiarity is to twist large words out of their original meaning, and give them a signification which no dictionary or usage would sanction. They come to the knowledge of the words by hook and by crook, and they are determined to use them in the same way. An instance of this kind occurred in the county of ——, a short time since. In a criminal case which had created considerable excitement, a large number of jurors had been summoned in the afternoon, and it being too late to proceed with the case that day, they were adjourned over until the morning, with strict injunctions from the Judge that they should report themselves then and there duly sober. The morning came, and so did the jurors. They had remembered one part of the court's command, but they had forgotten the other, and some of them were in a very 'spirited condition.'

'Call the first juror,' said the Judge.

'William Jones!' bawled the officer.

'He-e-e-re!' answered 'Bill,' with a loud shout, and a prolongation of the word for about a minute. As soon as he could be heard, the Judge kindling with indignation, thus addressed the delinquent:

'How dare you come into court, Sir, in this condition? Did I not tell you not to appear here drunk? Stand up, Sir!'

Jones made a desperate effort and stood upright, steadying himself upon the shoulders of his adjacent fellows. 'May it please your Honor,' at last stammered he, 'I am not drunk; I am only *slightly interrogated.*'

That word has formed ever since a part of the vocabulary of the county; and no one there dreams now of applying any other term to a man who is greatly intoxicated than that he is 'slightly interrogated.' By the by, I don't know that Jones was much out of the way in his answer, for as a juror he certainly was in a very question-able attitude.

This propensity is displayed in another manner. If a man is a tailor, for example, he will use similes and tropes and words relating to his trade, when he is speaking of quite a different subject. I will give an instance of this, which will enable me also to relate a reminiscence of the circuit. A few years ago I attended the Superior Court for the county of ——. The court adjourned late in the night, and the Judge and Bar being very weary, retired to their beds immediately thereafter. We were all in the same room, and immediately adjoining to us was the bar-room, and the chinks or vacant spaces in the partition enabled us to see and hear all that was going on. Shortly after we had retired, about forty men, 'pretty well corned, and up to every thing,' entered the liquor-room. No sooner had they arrived there than they commenced boasting. 'I'm the step-father of the Earth!' said one. 'I'm the yellow blossom of the forest!' exclaimed another, and requested his fellow citizens then and there being 'to nip the bud, if they dared.'

'I'm kin to a rattle-snake on the mother's side!' shouted the Earth's ancestor. This seemed to be a '*socdoliger;*' (which translated into Latin, means a *ne plus ultra;*) for the 'yellow blossom' stopped to consider what answer he could possibly make to this high claim of ancestry. A happy thought struck him.

'Will you drink or fight?' roared he, in a voice of thunder.

A dead silence ensued, or at least a subdued murmur, ''twixt which and silence there was nothing.' Perhaps a more embarrassing question could not have been propounded. The rattle-snake's son was exceedingly thirsty; the sands of Arabia were not more so; and liquor was the idol of his heart. He loved it dearly, but he loved fighting also; and here was a glorious chance to 'lick' an adversary he had long longed to get at. *Curia vult advisare.* He was deliberating between these equally pleasant alternatives, when it occurred to him that it was possible to accomplish both.

'*Both!*' responded he, 'both. I'll drink first — I'll fight afterward.'

A loud shout of approbation rose from the crowd. The liquor was called for — a pint of buck-eye whiskey — and impartially divided into two tumblers. The adversaries each took one, and grasping each other with their left hands, and touching the glasses together in token of amity, drained their respective goblets to the last drop, and then smashed them over the heads of each other, and at it they went. A clamor ensued so terrific that the English language has no word that would be sufficiently expressive of it. All sorts of encouragement were offered by the friends of each combatant, and an amateur who had no particular predilection for either, jumped upon the counter, and commenced singing a poetic description of all the naval battles of America, from the time of Columbus to the present day, (which somebody has had the barbarity to put into miserable verse,) keeping time with his heels on the counter. Just as he had got to the one hundred and ninety-ninth verse, and was in the midst of what he called 'the Wasp and Hornet arrangement,' his melody was stopped by a shrill cry from the 'yellow blossom of the forest,' who began to fall into the sere and yellow leaf, and gave manifest symptoms of being whipped.

'He bites!' screamed he.

'I get my livelihood by biting,' said the other, relaxing his hold for a moment, and then taking a fresh start.

''Nuff! 'nuff! take him off!'

Up rose the rattle-snake, amidst loud cheerings. His first impulse was to crow like a cock; then he changed his genus very suddenly, and declared that he was a 'sea-horse of the mountain,' and that he had sprung from the Potomac of the earth : then he was a bear with a sore head; a lion with a mangy tail; a flying whale; in short, he announced himself to be every possible and every impossible bird, beast, and fish, that the land or the sea has ever produced.

His wit having exhausted itself, some fresh excitement or novelty was requisite. 'Let's have *Bingo!*' suggested a by-stander. 'Huzza for Bingo!' echoed the crowd. Well, thought I, I do n't know who and what Bingo is, but I do know that when things reach their worst condition, any change must be for the better; and as any change from this terrible riot must be for the better, I say too, 'Huzza for Bingo!' Alas! as the sequel proved, I deceived myself greatly.

A gallon of whiskey with spice in it, and a gallon of Malaga wine were placed on a large table, around which about forty men seated themselves, having first elected a president *vivâ voce.* The president elect commenced the game by singing at the top of his voice:

> 'A farmer's dog sat on the barn-door,
> And Bingo was his name, O!'

And then they all shouted in chorus:

> 'And Bingo was his name, O!'

'B,' said the president, 'I' said the next, 'N' the third, 'G' the fourth, 'O' the fifth; and then the chorus, taking up the letter 'O,' again shouted:

> 'And Bingo was his name, O!'

If either missed a letter, or said 'n' for example, when he should have said 'i,' his penalty was to take a drink, and the company as a privilege drank with him; and with such slight interruptions as the time for drinking would occupy, this continued for about six hours.

At last the patience of the Judge (who was quite a young man, and who is not more than a squirrel's jump from me while I write) became exhausted, and he called for the landlord. Our host, who was a tailor by trade, and who was also one of the Bingo fraternity, made his appearance with a candle in his hand and a very affectionate and drunken leer upon his countenance.

'Go, Sir,' said the Judge, 'into the next room, and tell those drunken lunatics that if they don't stop their beastly noise I'll commit every one of them to jail in the morning for contempt of court.'

'Oh, Judge!' answered our host, holding up his unoccupied hand in token of his amazement: 'oh! Judge, you'll give me the *double-breasted horrors!* Why, Judge, work is *scace* and people's pertikler; and if I was to preliminary your orders to that crowd of gentlemen, why Judge, I'd pick up a lashing in a leetle less than no time;' and off he staggered. Bingo was forthwith resumed, until gradually the chorus became more confused and indistinct. Chaos had come again. The actions of the virtuous gentlemen there assembled ceased to be above-board, and were carried on under the table. Some were snoring, others hiccuping, others cascading. Bingo had ceased to be, except when some sleeper, feeling some painful sensation from his attitude, etc., would exclaim, 'Ou!' which would wake up his immediate neighbor, who, the ruling passion strong in death, would exclaim, 'And Bingo was ——,' and then relapse into such silence as a drunken man usually falls into.

———

YEARS have passed away since that awful night. Joys have blessed me; afflictions pained me; but all the vicissitudes of life have failed to drive out of my memory that terrible game and tune of Bingo. It haunts me like a dun in the day, like a ghost in the night. If I hear any one say, 'Oh!' the sequel immediately occurs to me : 'And Bingo was his name, O!' I am not much of an anatomist, but I am satisfied that when a post-mortem examination is had upon me, the whole matter of Bingo will be found incorporated with my pia-mater, or dura-mater, or some other portion of my brain. I can't tell the process or the manner by which and in which it has become a part and parcel thereof; but this much I know, that if my operator is a skilful surgeon he will find there developed in characters that *he* can read, the distinct statement, that there was a farmer who had a dog whose peculiar habit and custom was to sit upon the barn-door, and that he answered to the classical and melodious name of 'Bingo.'

In a very heavy equity cause which was tried some years ago in our circuit, one of the jurors, who had been inundated with cases from 'Vesey Junior,' expressed a wish 'that Vesey Junior had died *before* he (Vesey, Jr.) had been born.' I have something of the same feeling toward 'Bingo.' Have not you also, reader?

THE LAY OF THE HAWK.

BY I. M'LELLAN, JR.

I.

O'ER the wild mountain,
 O'er the rough stream,
Where the white fountain
 Reflects the sun-beam;
O'er the pine forest
 All lonely and dim,
And where the Fall pourest
 Amidst deserts grim;
There swiftly my strong wings
 Urge onward their flight,
And shrilly my cry rings,
 Creating affright!

II.

I soar o'er the village,
 I swoop o'er the farm,
And living by pillage,
 Am fearless of harm.
Over cities I soar,
 High above each dark roof,
Hearing well its uproar,
 Though myself far aloof.
I scorn the pale race
 Of mankind as I go,
As they creep at snails' pace,
 Like insects below!

III.

There poised on my pinion
 In wide circles I roam,
The skies my dominion,
 The bright clouds my home!
I sweep o'er the valley,
 I gaze on the plain,
On the city's dark alley,
 On the king's wide domain :
I view all the glory
 That earth has to boast —
Each mountain-head hoary,
 Each sun-brightened coast!

IV.

Wide, wide o'er the ocean
 I stretch my long flight,
When the waves in commotion
 Are angry and white.
I poise on the mast
 Of the voyaging ship,
And borne on the blast,
 The proud fleet outstrip.
I am near when it lies
 With rent spars and torn sail,
And I hear the wild cries
 Of the lost in the gale!

STORMING OF STONY-POINT.

A REMINISCENCE OF THE REVOLUTION.

It has always appeared to me a sad misfortune that so little pains have been taken to chronicle events connected with our revolutionary struggle. I cannot account for it otherwise than by supposing that individual acts of heroism have been merged in the wonder and astonishment of the world that a country with a population of three millions, and even that divided against itself, should have kept Old England at bay for seven years, and finally constrain her to let the darling object of her ambition assume an independent attitude among the great powers of the earth. This undoubtedly *is* one cause; but a more prominent one perhaps may be found in the fact that years of unmitigated toil were necessary to recover from the state of desolation in which the country found itself after the conflict was over. Men in those days literally earned their bread by the sweat of their brows; and the learned and the unlearned toiled side by side in retrieving their fortunes from the poverty incident to a civil war.

The writer of this sketch was brought up by grand-parents who had suffered severely in the revolutionary struggle, not only by the loss of property but by deaths of near connections. My grand-father was an Englishman by birth, who came to this country in early life, strongly imbued with the old cavalier spirit of the times; and with his dashing exterior and consequential air, connected himself in marriage with Miss GRACE STERLING, upon whose family he had impressed the idea that he had conferred a great honor by the union.

He had many good traits of character, however; and behind all his blustering there was an unusual degree of honesty, and a bravery that would not have discredited the best cavalier of the olden time; and although he became thoroughly American in his feelings, yet for the sake of argument he was continually drawing comparisons between his own and the country of his adoption not very flattering to the latter; and when hard pressed as to why he remained here, he would end the discussion by applying the old salvo, 'that it was better to reign in h——l than serve in heaven.' This blaspheming was a poser to the parishioners; and in the absence of reply, a little vanity on his part easily construed silence into victory.

Upon the breaking out of the revolution he obtained a lieutenancy in a company of grenadiers attached to the 'Continental Line,' as they were termed in those days. A brother was killed by the British and Indians at the battle of Wyoming; another lost his life on the field of Brandywine; and a third was maimed for life at the surprise at Paoli. With such an impulse to vengeance, Lieutenant B —— girded around him his Damascus blade, and entered into the conflict heart and soul; and although he was at the principal great battles of the revolution, and on each occasion signally distinguished himself, yet he was sure immediately after to commit some act of aggression and outrage upon his superior officers that cancelled all claims upon the appointing power. And it was rather fear in the officers appointed to try him than inclination that he was not dismissed the service; for on the very day of the Battle of Monmouth he struck his brother-in-law, Captain De F——, for interfering with one of his men while he was quenching his thirst at a brook in the heat of the engagement. Captain De F——'s intentions were good, for the day of that battle was one of the hottest of any we have on record; and as the men were in the last state of exhaustion, many on that memorable day never arose from the stream at which they slaked their thirst. Lieutenant B—— was immediately ordered under arrest; but as he supposed he could better fight out his excuse than by retiring into the rear, he charged with his company a small body of infantry that lingered about the bridge at the foot of the hill where WASHINGTON was stationed. The onset was so unexpected that they broke and fled at once. This was done directly under the eye of the Commander-in-chief. The discomfiture of the English at this point was so unexpected, by so inferior a force, that although it was done without orders, and against all rules of fighting, yet success insured forgiveness of all past offences. This offence was but one of half a dozen others equally flagrant.

But I intended merely to repeat, as nearly as an interval of twenty years will permit, one of the oft-told tales of the old gentleman over his glass of whiskey-punch of a cold winter's night. Old men find so few to commune with, and are such strangers on the earth, that they prefer intercourse with the dead rather than the living; and they never are young again, save when recounting over events long gone by, with those who, like the events themselves, are passed away for ever.

It was on one of these occasions that my grand-father, holding me on his knee, and my grand-mother, the once beautiful Grace Sterling, were seated around a blazing beach-wood fire; when the old gentleman began 'to fight his battles o'er again.' His subject was the storming of Stony-Point, his favorite battle. Why, I know not; for an incident occurred there which was painful in the last degree to my grand-mother. Eliza G—— was her intimate friend. She was but seventeen when she accompanied her sister and her sister's husband, Captain Burgoyne, a British officer, to the fortress of Stony-Point, where his regiment was stationed. I have often heard my grand-mother speak of her as a lady of surprising loveliness; with slight sylph-like figure; and in whose large dark and lustrous eyes benevolence and kindness were reflected. 'We arrived,' said the old gentleman, 'at eleven o'clock at night within a mile and an half of the fort, on the 15th of July, 1779; and a d——l of a night we had of it! I never knew it darker. 'Mad Anthony' formed us in hollow square, gave his orders, and selected the storming party. He made us take our flints from the locks, for two purposes; the one to avoid an accidental discharge and thus discover our position, and the other that the bayonet could be best relied on in the night. Our clothes,' continued he, 'were torn into shreds by the under-brush, and our limbs dreadfully lacerated. The watch-word was 'Remember Paoli!' It was one that we should not be likely to forget; for we had been completely surprised there, and scores were bayoneted while asleep in their tents; and *there* (showing a scar through his hand) that was done while asleep, and it saved my heart from the steel that was aimed at it. My whole company had been surprised; and out of ninety rank-and-file, twenty-eight were killed or wounded. But my brave fellows that escaped actually carried off forty prisoners! They not only fought their way out, but charged back again, and aided the retreat of the rest. Wayne knew my men's fancy for the bayonet. Yes,' continued the old gentleman, his eye gleaming with energy, 'there was not a man under six feet in his stockings. They had never been beaten. I was a little surprised when Sergeant Reinford came to me and said that private Summers wished the liberty of speaking to me. I of course granted the request; when Summers advanced from the ranks, touched his hat, and said: 'Sir, it is the request of the men that you will lead us into the fort as soon as we approach it, without signal from the commander. We can take the fort *alone*, Sir!' I made no reply; but of course I dared not break orders. Ah! poor Summers! he died nobly in the fort, and so did one half of my company.' Here the old gentleman's nerves gave way, and he cried like a child. 'Yes,' said he, in a suppressed voice, 'they died in saving me my company. Wayne sent for me, and said in a stern manner: 'Lieutenant B——, I shall depend upon you in the escalade at the south of the fort. You will be supported by Major ——, and Colonel —— will look after the upper side. They have their orders. The signal will be a rocket thrown as nearly over the fort as possible, precisely at twelve. You will get close under the walls and lie still until you see the signal.'

'We were led by a guide, and by good luck crossed the moat which surrounded the fort. The water was up to our waists, and we carried our muskets over our heads to keep them dry. We got to our assigned posts undiscovered. I can attribute our good luck to nothing but the noise of the whip-poor-wills. The hills appeared to be alive with them. Our men in the darkness were pitching and diving about from precipice to precipice, like drunken men. At times they would wound themselves with thorns, and curse old Wayne, and inquire of each other why he did not fight in the day-time, and not go thieving about like an old burglar in the night. However, we arrived under the walls undiscovered by the English. It now wanted a quarter to twelve. There was only one thing to trouble me. I knew Eliza G—— was in the fort, and I knew the storming would scare her to death, even if she should otherwise escape. We lay close to the ground, hardly daring to breathe.

'The sentinels on the walls of the fort were at this moment relieved, and others left in their places; and as the guard passed just over our heads, they little anticipated that in five minutes more the mortal struggle would commence; that the gay, the gallant, the high-born would bite the dust in the agonies of death; that the blood of the same race (we had no French there) would stand in pools upon the earth. At length came the signal. It curved high in air like a flying dragon. 'Three cheers, boys! Remember Paoli! Into the fort, you dogs!' No sooner said than done. Some went through the portholes and some got in upon the shoulders of others. The confusion within was astounding. The camp-women instead of cursing us for rebels were crying, 'Good Americans! save us! Mercy! mercy!' As the world calls these creatures women, there was an end of the argument. We saved them, although we knew that these same wretches at Paoli after the battle stabbed many wounded officers in order to plunder them of their clothes, which they stripped from their bodies while they were yet gasping for breath.

'The British made a stand in considerable numbers, while their artillery did great execution without the fort. ' Our forlorn hope were principally slain. For fifteen minutes my brave grenadiers sustained themselves against the whole force within. The storming party sent on the north side now came pouring in : we were about three hundred strong inside. We now gave three cheers, and at it we went with the cold steel. 'We surrender! we surrender!' was now heard on every side; and as the besieged were entitled to quarter, inasmuch as they had not been requested to surrender, the battle ceased, although the men were quite willing to retaliate for the loss sustained at Paoli. The shipping that lay under the point slipped their cables and drifted down the stream. The dawn of day,' continued the old gentleman, 'presented a dreadful scene. The moans of the dying were most piteous; the young wife wailing over her dead husband, and the young child clinging to its mother for protection.'

The old gentleman now arose from his seat, and unlocked a huge oak chest. He drew from it a letter, yellow with time, which bore date a few days after the battle. It was addressed to my grand-father, who had been despatched to head-quarters early in the morning after the engagement, with intelligence of the success of the expedition. 'Boy,' said he, 'read; my glasses are getting too young for me.' I commenced :

'DEAR B ——: Among the slain, poor Eliza G—— is found! Do not tell Grace; it will kill her. You know how much they were attached. The scene to me you must well know is indescribably painful. The last time I saw her at your house in Fairfield I half lost my heart; and had I not known her *penchant* for D——, I might possibly have despaired, and surrendered at discretion to that palpitating rebel. I was directed to see to the burying of the dead, and have just performed that sad office for poor Eliza. She was slain by a shot from the English, as they were firing upon us. When I found her she was lying upon a couch, where she had sought repose. Poor girl! — she little dreamed that her snowy night-dress was destined to be her winding-sheet! · · · If she was beautiful in life, she was even more lovely in death. In the contemplation of her beautiful features, well might one exclaim : 'O Death! where is thy victory! O Grave! where is thy sting!' I pity from my soul poor D——, even though he *is* a tory. By the by, I look like a tory myself. My coat was so completely torn to pieces by the bushes, that I have borrowed a red one from Burgoyne.

Strange juxtaposition!   He and I old class-mates, and he my prisoner!
We are together half our time.   He appears to be quite heart-broken.'

———

I now looked up, and perceived both my grand-parents nodding a
sleepy assent to all I read; the old gentleman occasionally in broken
accents exclaiming: 'Poor Summers! you died to save my life!' and
my grand-mother, in dozing sympathy, muttering: 'I *told* Eliza to
keep away from the forces.'   The apathy of the old is a sad memento
to the young and exuberant heart.   I have heard the old gentleman so
often describe sometimes one portion of this engagement and sometimes another, that the interest it had created induced me, while
attending one of the circuits last winter, to visit the Point.   Accordingly my friend and myself crossed upon the ice from the east to the
west side of the Hudson; and although the wind swept with the force
of a hurricane down the river, we gained the Point in about half an
hour.   Its lines of defence are still visible.   After taking a survey of
the scene, once so sanguinary, we hurried to the place where the dead
were buried.   Here and there a flat stone is to be seen, denoting the place
where some distinguished officer lies.   We found also a piece of board
with the letters 'E. G.' as nearly as could be deciphered; for time
with it, like the individual commemorated, had done its work.   The
'desolate and dying year' was in unison with the place.   The snow
was a foot deep; the winds whistled solemnly from the hills.   'What
mock solemnity,' thought I, ' is the pageantry of funeral rites compared
with a scene like this!'   The funeral dirge swelled on each blast that
withered life itself, and spirits of the air whispered, ' Be ye also ready!'
   It was nearly night, and we hastened to our lodgings, hungry and
fatigued.   I was haunted after retiring with remembrances of ' poor
Eliza.'   I shall hope at some future time, Mr. EDITOR, to prepare for
your pages some account of the fate of poor D ——.   It is sufficient
now to state that he was taken in the American camp, and was tried
and hanged as a spy.   Sufficient evidence however has since appeared,
to convince his friends that his mind had lost its balance.   Several of
his letters to them give every indication of the fact.   His chivalrous spirit was so opposed to any thing that might savor of duplicity,
that they would never admit for a moment that he could, while in
his right mind, be capable of acting the part of a spy; although the
necessity of the case and the usage of nations has sanctioned the practice as compatible with the character of a gentleman.   My own notion
is, that no man, with proper respect for himself, could ever be induced
to play the hypocrite, even though it were to gain him the applause of
a sovereign.   B.

— — — — — — — — —

EPIGRAM ON A SUICIDE.

I WOULD not joke with theme so grave,
   Or any ill-timed wit display;
But if you never was a knave,
   You 're now a *cut-throat*, any way!

FORGETFULNESS.

AN EARLY POEM BY THE LATE WILLIS GAYLORD CLARK.

I.

Oh ! think not of that vanished dream, thou lovely one and young,
Forget the warm impassioned vow on Love's beguiling tongue ;
For time hath not one balm to heal a wounded breast like thine,
Whose purest faith was offered up on a delusive shrine ;
And though thy sweet voice triumphed, when the soul's confession fell
From lips that sealed it with a kiss, whose rapture none may tell,
Yet it died when from thy burning cheek the heart's tumultuous blood
Rolled back in silence to its cell, a swift and heavy flood !

II.

Why is it that at such an hour, the purple currents rise,
To bathe in varying hues the face, and light the swimming eyes ?
Where thoughts of tenderness untold are palpably revealed,
As each fond glance of transport given, by plighted vow is sealed :
It is that by that thrilling spell the heart in fellowship
Sends up its flood, to paint the cheek, and warm the faltering lip ;
That melting in continual flow, the inconstant tide may be
A pure libation of the soul, victorious LOVE, to thee !

III.

Yet school thy heart a veil to fling o'er the lamented past,
Where all was bright and beautiful — too beautiful to last ;
And let the waves of Lethe roll above thy perished spring,
When Time, with laughter on his brow, shook diamonds from his wing ;
And let the smile, the vow, the tear, be each beneath the pall
That from Oblivion's dusky plume shall like a curtain fall !
What recks it that life's faded hours passed like a summer stream ?
Alas ! where *now* have fled away their glory and their gleam !

IV.

Oh ! if within thy heart of hearts the memory should live
Of dreams so passionate and deep, and yet so fugitive,
It will but wake a quenchless thirst for moments vanished now —
It will bring ashes to thy lip and fever to thy brow !
And clouds from the lone spirit's cell in sable throngs will come,
To clothe each image of the brain in drapery of gloom ;
Till, faint and sick, the autumnal hue upon thy cheek shall lie,
And futile longings fill with tears thy dim and pensive eye !

V.

Then think of Love's departed hours, in dallying rapture spent,
As glimmerings of a melting wave, with sunset colors blent ;
Bright, but so changeful as to fade upon the gazer's eye,
While yet it drinks the glory of the occidental sky !
Love comes upon a rosy plume, and borne in light along,
He pours his radiance on the brow, and wakes the soul to song :
But the golden bowl is broken soon, and when the heart is bowed
The wrecks of his dominion are the shadow and the cloud !

TORQUATO TASSO.

'THUS ill-fated TASSO, whom you praise,
  Romans! amid his wrongs, could yet console
  The beautiful, the chivalric, the brave,
  Dreaming the deeds, feeling the love he sung.'

IT was a festal night at the ducal palace. The princess LUCRETIA, after a few years of wedded misery, had returned to her brother's house to claim his and her mother's protection; and all Ferrara were summoned to give welcome to their beloved lady.

A gay and brilliant scene it was — that lofty palace blazing with lights, which were flashed back and magnified by the sparkling jewels that glittered in the dark hair and on the white arms and slender waists of the fair Ferrarese. Lordly nobles, stately dames, the high in rank and the gifted in genius, were gathered there; for all such did Alphonso love. But none knew his neighbor. The mask concealed all faces; and it was only by the voice or air that friend recognized friend. Yet this was no restraint upon the gayety of the scene. In the large hall of the palace, inspiring music sent forth its call, and young men and maidens obeyed its summons. Others formed themselves into groups, and the merry jest, the sharp hit and keen reply passed with more freedom than if the speakers had been face to face.

The company had been received by one of the officers of the household, and the Duke and his fair sisters did not make their appearance during the early part of the evening. The guests had begun to speculate upon the cause, when a peal of martial music announced their approach. The large doors at the end of the saloon were thrown open, and the Duke, with Lucretia leaning on his arm, attended by her sister and many of the ladies of the court, entered. Silence for a moment prevailed, then a spontaneous burst of welcome was uttered, and the guests were pressing forward to greet their much-loved lady, when one in the garb of a troubadour, with a low hat and drooping feather concealing his face, a small lute resting on his arm, stepped before the rest, knelt with lowly reverence at the feet of the Duchess, and poured forth in the name of all Ferrara a heart-felt welcome. It was only a sonnet's length, but each word was forcibly expressive; and as he finished, a murmur of applause rang through the room.

With moistened eye and swelling heart, Lucretia bent on him her sad sweet glance: 'Thank you, Sir Troubadour,' she said, 'for your greeting. I receive it as the expression of the feeling of my beloved Ferrara, which is rendered dearer to me than ever, by my long absence and many sorrows; and for you, willingly would I bind you to become my minstrel; to relinquish the wanderer's garb, to dwell with us in our courtly circle; to greet the .coming and bless the departing with your magic lays. Say, is there any way in which we can chain you to our service?'

As she spake, she unclasped from her throat a delicate chain, to which was attached a Maltese cross of great value, and threw it over the neck of the minstrel, who still knelt with bended head before her.

'Lady, it needs not golden fetters to bind where the heart is already a slave. I live but to do thy bidding and that of thy noble sister, and am but too happy if my feeble lay has given you pleasure.'

Leonora, who had watched the scene with much interest, on hearing the allusion to herself came forward, and drawing from her finger a ruby ring with her own signet upon it, gave it to the seeming troubadour, saying:

'Accept this token, not as a reward but as a remembrance of this pleasant hour.'

The troubadour pressed the ring to his lips, and bending low, rose and mingled with the crowd.

'It is Tasso!—it is Tasso!' echoed a hundred voices. 'Thanks to Tasso for so nobly expressing the welcome of Ferrara!' They all crowded round the Princess, whose feelings almost overwhelmed her at these proofs of the love of her people.

Having divested himself of his troubadour dress, Tasso returned to the company, and was graciously received by the Duke and Princesses; and no allusion was made by them to his appearance before, although the chain of Lucretia still glittered on his neck. The dance and the song went on; the masks were retained till supper was announced, when each one removed the velvet covering which had concealed his or her face, and gathered round a table heaped with all the luxuries of the time.

Tasso, the favored poet, was placed next to the fair Leonora; and his expressive intellectual face spoke deeply of his happiness. She too was not indifferent. Her playful fancy, her highly cultivated intellect, were all called into play; and no one who listened to her could have wondered at the poet's fascination. But little recked that gay circle who looked with admiring and envying eyes at the distinction shown the poet, that this night, so fraught with pleasure, was but the herald of a morn of darkness; that the light which now illuminated all Italy, and to whom every one turned as the mid-day effulgence of a glorious sunrise would so soon go down in whirlwind and storm! Why did not some kind voice whisper the child of destiny to beware how he drank of the Circean cup which was hurrying him on to destruction!

- - - -

> 'Before you is Sorrento; dwelling there
> Was Tasso's sister, when the pilgrim came
> Asking asylum 'gainst the prince unjust,
> From former friends. Long grief had almost quenched
> Reason's clear light, but *genius* still was left.'

It was just at twilight on the 25th July, 1577, that a man with bent form and whitened hair stood at the portal of one of the noblest houses in Sorrento. With trembling voice he asked of the menials who waited in the hall, if their lady was at home, and whether he could have audience with her. With a sneering look at his humble dress, the servants coldly answered that their lady was not wont to give audience to such as himself; but if he had *business* with her he could be attended to by the steward of her household.'

'No,' replied the old man, taking from his bosom a letter; 'I have promised to give this letter into her own hand, and I must receive the answer from herself, which I am to convey to her brother in his prison-home.'

Well did the servants of that lofty mansion know that, however humble the messenger, one who bore tidings to their lady from her idolized brother would be welcome; and with added courtesy they asked the old man to be seated, while they went to see when it was her pleasure to receive him.

They soon returned to conduct him to the apartment, where, surrounded by every luxury which the taste and refinement of the sixteenth century could devise, was seated a lovely woman just past the prime of life. The traces of sorrow were upon her pale cheek, which not even the sunset glow that came through the rose-tinted curtains could color. A small marble table, covered with richly-illuminated books, was by her side. The old man entered with trembling steps, and advancing to the couch where the lady was reclining, and dropping on one knee, gave her the letter. With a soft low voice she bade him rise, and after she had read her brother's epistle she would question him farther.

The man withdrew into a shaded recess opposite the lady, and watched her intently while with eager haste she read the scroll. As she perused it her tears fell thick and fast upon the page, and she was almost suffocated with her emotion. The old man caught the infection of her sadness, and brushed away the tears which blinded his heavy eyes. When she had finished reading the letter, she almost reverently kissed it, and placed it in her bosom. Looking up, she caught the eye of the messenger gazing earnestly upon her. In her excitement, she had forgotten his presence; and she involuntarily uttered a slight scream when she met his piercing gaze; but recollecting herself, and the many questions about her brother which she wished to ask, she called him to her side. He sprang forward, and seizing her hand pressed it to his lips.

'Oh my sister! my sister!' he exclaimed, 'my beloved Cornelia! — am I indeed so changed that you, the child of the same mother, the companion of my childish sports, and the sympathizer of my maturer years, know me not!'

The bewildered and terrified lady looked with fascinated eye upon the stranger. Could it be? Was it indeed *possible?* The voice was the same that had soothed her infantile griefs, and aided in her studies; but not one trace could she find in the stooping and worn figure before her, of the noble form and lineaments of him whose wandering mind and prisoned body she had mourned for many a long year, with more than the grief of the mourner who has laid the loved and lost in the cold earth; for to such Time brings the healing balm, and fans with his cooling wings the fever of bereaved affliction; but to her each day had brought the bitter recollection that he, the gifted and the loving, was condemned, not only through his own imprudence but from the envy of those above him in rank, to a life of solitary confinement, where his lofty mind, deprived of the companionship of those who could sympathize with his joys and sorrows, could only feed upon itself.   Overwhelmed with emotion, Cornelia threw herself into his arms and sobbed her welcome.   A strange sight, and one deemed worthy of the painter's pencil.*   The beautiful and richly-dressed lady, every article upon and around her speaking of rank and wealth, just recognizing in the travelstained wanderer her *brother*, the son of genius!   It was long before they were either of them sufficiently composed to speak ; and before Cornelia expressed her own deep feelings of anxiety, or listened to the sad detail of her brother's sufferings, she constrained him to refresh himself by the bath and the rest he so much needed.

Thus did TORQUATO TASSO appear among his friends after the imprisonment which the pride of Alphonso Duke of Ferrara had condemned him to endure for the crime of loving his sister.   Flattered and caressed as he had been by all Italy, the favored of princes, and encouraged as he was by the lady Leonora, who, won by the poet's fame and gratified by the homage he rendered her, received his attentions with complacency ; what wonder then that he forgot the distance between himself and his patron's sister, and dared to hope for an alliance with her?   The rash act, that of publicly saluting the princess before a crowded assembly, which was the immediate cause of his confinement, can only be excused by the incipient madness which fevered his brain and clouded his sense of propriety.   But the cruel rigor of Alphonso in his long imprisonment for so slight an offence, which should rather have been tried by the Court of Love, and punished by frowns and simple banishment from his lady's presence, will never be forgotten or forgiven ; and wherever the ' Jerusalem ' with its spiritstirring scenes and tender pictures is read and loved, Alphonso's name will be banned as the tyrant who would have crushed a genius so formed to delight the world.

Tasso from his birth seemed marked out for misfortune's child.   His father, BERNARDO TASSO, a poet of some reputation, but better known as the parent of the illustrious Torquato, was secretary to San Severino, Prince of Salerno, and he shared his honor and disgrace.   The prince having made a complaint to Charles Fifth against the viceroy of Naples, who had striven to introduce the inquisition into the kingdom, he was condemned to death, and the cruel sentence pronounced not only against him, but his secretary and his son, the future poet, not then nine years old.   With great difficulty they escaped by night from the fatal punishment, and withdrew to Rome, where the young poet composed verses, and compared his escape to the adventures of Asconius and Æneas flying from Troy.

The Jesuits had just established one of their celebrated colleges at Rome, and the young Torquato was placed under their care; and so rapid was the developement of his mind that the most wonderful stories are told of his progress.   His father was exceedingly anxious that he

---

*, A painting representing this scene is, or was a short time since, in the gallery of the Louvre.

should study civil law, not realizing what drudgery it would be to the poetic mind of his son to give up the dreamy luxury of belles-lettres for the dry commentaries on Justinian.   He therefore sent him to Padua, where, instead of attending to his studies,

> ' He waved his magic wand,
> Peopling the groves from Araby, and lo !
> Fair forms appeared, murmuring melodious verse.'

He composed many beautiful pastorals and odes, which pleased his friends so much that they urged him to commence a larger work. Thus encouraged, he began his ' Rinaldo,' although with much fear lest his father should discover it, and forbid a design which must necessarily withdraw his mind from his more important duties.   But he had the satisfaction of learning, when it did come to Bernardo's ears, that he should be left to finish his poem undisturbed, and also that he should be permitted, if he desired, to change his present duties for the more agreeable studies of philosophy.

When he had completed his poem, Torquato sent it with a trembling heart to undergo the ordeal of his father's judgment.   He feared his critical taste, which was admirable ; and he knew that a parent's feelings would not bias his opinion.   It would perhaps be impossible fully to estimate the happiness of Bernardo, when he had perused the work, and found it so far superior, that it became in his eyes the forerunner of his son's future fame.   He readily yielded his consent to its being published ; and in April, 1562, when its author was but eighteen, it appeared under the auspices of Cardinal D'Este, to whom it was dedicated.

Great was the fame gained for the youthful author.   It attracted the attention of men of letters, and all united in its praise.   The enthusiastic admiration with which it was received must have added not a little stimulus to Tasso's love of poetry, and encouraged him to cultivate the talent which gave so fair a promise.   Later ages have judged more calmly of ' Rinaldo ; ' and though none of his works were more popular during his life-time, it has now passed away.   Even before his death, Torquato was unwilling to recognize it among his works.   Menagio, in his preface to the ' Aminta,' remarks that the ' Rinaldo ' was the ' work of a youth, but of a youthful Tasso.'   Verily, ' the child is father of the man.'

But though engaged in his own composition, Tasso did not neglect the general cultivation of his mind.   He held literature in the highest veneration, and attended most studiously all the lectures of the professors on the profoundest branches of education.   Soon after the publication of his ' Rinaldo,' he received the gratifying compliment of being invited by the Bishop of Narni to enter the University of Bologna which had just been reëstablished by Pope Pius Fourth and the good Bishop Donati Cesi, who sought for young men of the most promising talents to become leaders in his new school.   The time passed here by Tasso was well improved ; and he was just prepared to take his degree in theology and philosophy, when certain ill treatment which he received in consequence of being supposed the author of some idle pasquinades upon the college, so offended him, that he took an abrupt leave of Bologna, forgetting in his fiery impatience the debt of gratitude he owed the bishop.

He now reverted to the idea of the epic poem, the plan of which he had sketched while at Bologna, and to which he had directed all his studies. He had collected from the works of the most celebrated writers all that could aid him in his project; and he once more entered his name as a student at Padua, and devoted himself unremittingly to his classical pursuits. At the end of his first term, Torquato visited his father at Mantua. The happiness of the old man, then seventy years old, at this meeting, was only equalled by that of the son; and the joyous hope which the parent expressed at the prospect of his glorious future made a deep impression on Tasso's heart. 'He said to me,' observed our poet, 'that his love for me had made him forget that which he had for his poem; that no glory in the world, no perpetuity of fame could ever be so dear to him as my life; and nothing more delightful than my reputation.' What a beautiful picture of a poet-father and a poet-son! — the former forgetting his own literary offspring and poetical aspirations in the dazzling brilliancy of his son's morning light. Bernardo Tasso was no mean poet; and had not Torquato so far eclipsed him, he would have taken a high rank among the bards of Italy.

Anxious that Torquato should have some certain support, which would allow him to pursue his literary tastes untrammelled by the fear of want, Bernardo made every exertion to procure him some situation, and finally succeeded in securing for him an appointment about the person of Cardinal D'Este. Many of Torquato's friends advised him not to accept it, but to keep his genius unfettered by the bondage of a courtier's life. Its wings they contended must be clipped when it could fly only in humble obedience to a patron's command. And happy it would have been for him had he followed their advice; but he had not yet learned how much better it is to depend upon one's own resources than the caprices of the great.

Soon after his appointment he accompanied the Cardinal to Rome; and it was on his return from this journey that he first met the princess Lucretia and her sister Leonora, whose influence over his fate was so remarkable. These ladies, who had been educated by their mother Renata, daughter of Louis Twelfth, king of France, a woman endowed with the highest accomplishments of her sex, were gifted and lovely beyond any of their countrywomen. To exquisite personal beauty they added brilliant and cultivated minds, and a high appreciation of all intellectual acquirements. When Tasso first saw them, Lucretia was thirty-one and Leonora thirty years of age; but the elegance of their persons and their amiable dispositions had preserved the gracefulness of youth undiminished. The fame of the 'Rinaldo' had prepared them to admire Tasso; and his pleasing manners soon rendered him a favorite. They introduced him to the notice of the Duke Alphonso, their brother, and to the most distinguished persons of the court.

Here Tasso remained in the midst of the courtly circle, playing the

part of the laureat; writing sonnets for all court occasions, epithal-
miums for wedding festivities, dirges for the noble dead, and in his
leisure hours laboring upon his grand poem, till 1570, when he received
a summons from the Cardinal D'Este to accompany him to France,
whither he was called to attend to his diocese, which had suffered from
the rapid increase of the Huguenots. Before his departure he made
arrangements like a careful merchant for the disposal of his literary
property in case of his death. ' Since life is frail,' says this testament,
' if it should please God to take me while on my journey to France, I
pray Signior Ercole Rindonelli to take charge of my property. And
first, as regards my compositions, I would have him collect my amatory
sonnets and madrigals, and give them to the world. For the rest,
whether amatory or not, which I have written in the service of my
friends, I desire they may remain buried with myself, except that only
which begins,

' Or che l'aura mia dolce altrove spira.'

The oration I made at Ferrara at the opening of the academy I should
be glad to have published; and also four books on heroic poetry; the
last six cantos of Godfrey, and of the first two, such stanzas as may
seem least faulty, if they be all previously corrected by Signior Scipio
Gonzaga, Signior Venieri, and Guarini, who from the friendship and
connection I have with them, will not I am persuaded refuse to take
the trouble : let them know moreover I would have them cut out and
repress any thing without saving which may appear superfluous or
indifferent. But in making additions and alterations let them be more
particular, as the work cannot be other than imperfect. If any other
of my compositions should be deemed worthy of publication, they are
at liberty to dispose of them as they please. As for my robes, they are
in pledge to Aaron for twenty-five lire, and seven pieces of tapestry
which are in pledge for thirteen scudi to Signior Asconorio. As for
the rest in this house, I wish it to be sold, and the money appropriated
to placing the subjoined epitaph on the tomb of my father, whose body
is buried in St. Paul. And if any impediment should occur in effecting
these objects, let Signior Ercole apply to the most excellent Madame
Leonora, who I think will on my account be liberal to him.'

This singular document proves the low state of Tasso's finances,
since his very garments were pledged; and it bears a touching proof of
his devoted love to his father, and his wish to perpetuate it by erecting
a suitable monument to his memory. But it was not to be the poet's
fate to require the aid of executors so soon. He had but barely tasted
the troubled cup of life, and he was to live to drain its very dregs,
made doubly bitter by cruel neglect and misunderstanding.

At the French court Tasso met with the most gratifying reception.
Charles Ninth was a warm patron of literature and the fine arts, and he
heaped many testimonials of regard upon the poet. Perhaps the most
gratifying one to Tasso's feelings was the life of a poet who had seriously offended his Majesty, and was condemned to death. Friends
interceded for him; his wife and children supplicated with tearful eyes,
on bended knee; but Charles was inexorable, till Tasso, who had

become interested in the hopeless fate of the poet, begged his life as a personal favor to himself; and the monarch granted to the request of genius what he had refused to natural affection.

But Tasso did not long enjoy his residence at the French court. His poverty subjected him to much insolence from the pampered menials of the Cardinal, and his sensitive pride took alarm at some fancied coldness of his patron, which he attributed to the evil influence of the enemies which the favor he enjoyed with the monarch had raised up against him. He shrunk from the idea of being a neglected dependant, and asked and obtained permission to return to Italy; and he was soon once more in Ferrara, basking in the light of Leonora's presence.

He made application to be once more received into Alphonso's service, and the request was not only granted, but the conditions on which he entered it made so very advantageous, that he was enabled once more to resume his studies and literary pursuits. His gratitude to the Duke for this indulgence was expressed with the greatest fervor, not only when speaking of him, but in his poems. In the commencement of the ' Jerusalem' he thus addresses him:

> ' August ALPHONSO! whose benignant hand
> Welcomed a wandering stranger to thy land,
> And guided safe, mid rocks and billows tost,
> My sinking bark; to thee, much-honored host,
> The grateful off'rings of my Muse belong;
> Nor thou disdain the dedicated song:
> Thy name perchance my future theme may be,
> And the great deeds I tell be told of thee.'

' He drew me,' said the poet to his friend Gonzaga, speaking on this subject, ' from the darkness of my base condition to the light and reputation of the court. He relieved me from distress and placed me in a comfortable position. He gave value to my writings by hearing them often and willingly, and by honoring me with every kind of favor. He deemed me worthy of a seat at his table and intimate conversations, nor was I ever denied by him any favor I asked.'

It was now that he felt himself in a condition to continue his ' Jerusalem Delivered' with the steadiness it required; and he pursued it with unabated ardor until interrupted by a serious illness, which left him in an exceedingly weak and nervous state. Before he had regained his usual health, the Duchess Barbara died, and he was obliged to tax his powers for the condolence of the Duke, who was deeply grieved by the death of his amiable consort. At this time, and for his patron's amusement, he composed the ' Arminta,' a beautiful pastoral.

Before he could resume his pursuit with any ardor, he was attacked by a quartern-ague that prevented him from writing through the winter. We may imagine with what delight Tasso welcomed the return of spring, which he trusted was to relieve his frame from illness, and open to him his usual sources of enjoyment. In the month of April he writes thus to his friend Albano at Rome:

' After a distressing ague, I am by the mercy of God restored to health, and have at last, after much labor, completed the poem of ' Goffredo.' And this liberty from sickness which I now enjoy, and which I shall also soon enjoy from my poetical occupations, is for nothing else more gratifying than that it will permit me to attend to your commands. If I am able to send my poem to press this September, I shall then spend some months at Rome, which I should not have thought it right to do had I not fulfilled my obligations to my patron the Duke, which I shall partly seem to have done by the dedication of my poem.'

The assistance and inspection of Tasso's critical friends in his poem proved a source of great annoyance to him, for they disagreed among themselves in all points, and made many objections to the design though not to the execution of the work. But he combatted them in a vigorous and curious manner; and his fine scholarship was shown in his replies. But there were other trials that Tasso had to contend with, which affected him more deeply. The Duke's favor had made him many enemies in the court, who contrived by a thousand ways to render his residence there disagreeable; and although his patron was uniformly kind, he felt himself very unhappy, and determined as soon as his poem was published, to retire to Rome and live as independently as his limited means would allow. His weakened health and shattered nerves rendered him peculiarly sensitive to any annoyance, and he became almost insane by discovering that during a short absence his desk had been opened, and copies taken of many cantos of the 'Jerusalem.' Indignant at the baseness of the theft, he applied to Alphonso for redress. But as it was impossible to point out the criminal, nothing could be done; yet Tasso suspecting a person of the name of Madalo, and meeting him one day as he was crossing the court of the palace, he gave him a severe rebuke for his perfidy; to which Madalo replied in such insulting language that the poet struck him on the face with the scabbard of his sword. At this the weak courtier fled with precipitation, but soon returned with his brothers, and following Tasso, endeavored to wound him in his back; but not succeeding, the whole party retreated, and made the best of their way to Tuscany.

Manso, Tasso's biographer and most devoted friend, asserts that from this time his mind became disturbed, and he gave the first symptoms of approaching insanity. The Duke seeing his perturbed state, soothed him by all the means in his power, and sent him to Belrignordo, a most delightful estate belonging to the Duchess D'Urbino, trusting that its quiet and retirement, the perfect enjoyment of nature, and the influence of Lucretia, who resided there altogether, would have a happy effect in restoring the equilibrium of his mind. He was just beginning to show the healthful influence of the place, when he received the news that the parts of his poem which had been pirated were being printed in various parts of Italy. Anxious as he had been that it should appear in the most correct form possible, and looking forward to it as the reward of all his labors, he was greatly distressed, and implored Alphonso to interfere and prevent the circulation of any edition which might appear in this way. Alphonso accordingly wrote to the princes of Italy requesting them to stop the publication, and his example was followed by the Pope, who exerted his authority in the same manner.

While these powerful friends were interested in his behalf, the Count Torsoni persuaded him to visit Modena, where he hoped by the change of air and gay society to relieve him from the melancholy which was rapidly taking possession of his spirit. But neither the society of the gifted and intellectual, the charm of wit, nor the delights of music, could cheer his perturbed mind, or restore the buoyancy of his spirits. Wearied with the effort of appearing gay to gratify his friend, he returned, oppressed as with an incubus, to Ferrara. Perhaps no portion of Tasso's life presents a more melancholy picture than the present. About ushering into the world a poem as yet unequalled, which was to make for him a name which should echo wherever Jerusalem was known, he becomes the victim of the most dire malady to which our frail natures are subject. Slowly and silently it creeps along, dimming the brightness of the intellect, and crushing with its stealthy steps the heart's happiness. His bewildered eyes are seeking for the unknown enemies, the phantasmagoria which his imagination has conjured up. Haunted by fear, oppressed with illness, he soon became exhausted by the wearing conflict; the struggles of insanity with beclouded reason. Tasso's biographers differ in the causes which led to his derangement; some attributing it to the high mental excitement produced by his close attention to his studies, and the feverish action of his poetical temperament; others to his attachment to the Princess Leonora, and can view alone in this an excuse for Alphonso's cruel rigor.

The limits of this sketch will not allow us to follow through all its sad changes the commencement of his malady; his flight from Ferrara, and the places of obscure refuge which he sought in the hope of escaping his haunting fears; his dread of the fearful inquisition, and his sufferings from actual poverty. He was at one time so reduced as to be obliged to sell the ruby ring given him on the festal night by Leonora, when light and happiness encircled him, and which he had always worn as a talisman of affection. A beautiful golden collar too, the gift of Lucretia, he sold to procure food. But these afforded him only temporary relief; and at last, wearied out with suffering, he once more sought refuge at the court of Ferrara. But here, alas! all was changed; not only by his distempered fancy, but the coldness of the Duke, who looking upon him as a mad-man, would not even grant him an audience. Annoyed and irritated 'to the top of his bent,' the unfortunate poet vented his spleen in severe sarcasms upon the whole ducal court, which coming to Alphonso's ears, alienated him still more; but at last through the intercession of Leonora he was once more admitted to the palace, and though coldly received, was tolerated by the Duke.

It was at this time he committed the imprudence which was visited upon his head by so many years of intense suffering, and which his disordered intellect, that extinguished the sense of propriety, can alone excuse. Entering the palace uncalled for, on the night of one of the ducal balls, following a momentary impulse, he advanced to the Princess Leonora, who was surrounded by foreign ambassadors and men of distinction, and in the face of the assembled company, saluted her! The Duke, irritated beyond measure, and perhaps gladly availing himself of the excuse, had him immediately arrested and sent to the hospital of St. Anne's, an institution for lunatics. In whatever light we look upon this procedure of the Duke's, it must be considered unjustifiable. The poet had, it is true, no claims upon him but those of genius; but this should have rendered him sacred; and Alphonso sinned not only against his own nature, but the feelings of a whole world, in immuring Tasso in a dungeon. Though weak and flickering, the fire of genius was still in his heart, and should have been cherished and guarded from outward harm, so as to have kept if possible the divine spark from being extinguished.

No one can read without a shudder Tasso's own description of his melancholy situation: with enough of the light of reason to feel acutely the horrors which surrounded him; the shrieks and groans of the maddened inmates continually in his ears; those organs formed only to receive harmonious sounds, and so sensitive, that he shrunk from any discord as from the surgeon's probe. The constant dread of becoming like those whose howlings disturbed his midnight rest, produced in the end the very effect he dreaded. Writing to his friend Manso, he says: 'My mind becomes slow of thought, my fancy indolent in imagining, my senses negligent in ministering to them images of things: my hand refuses to write, and my pen even to execute its office. I seem indeed to be frozen, and am oppressed by stupor and giddiness in all I do. Nor shall I ever be able, without some demonstration of courteous kindness, to revive in myself that vivacity and spirits not less generous in prose than verse.' What a sad picture do these few lines present of their impulsive writer; his warm emotions, his kindling thoughts, his high aspirations, chilled by the wintry frost of unkindness, into stalactites, which no after sunshine or warmth could dissolve! The kindness of friends, the soothings of affection, the flatteries of admirers, were what the sensitive nature of Tasso required. Coldness from those he loved broke the strings of his lute; and when once rudely snapped, it was impossible for any skill to restore the harmony of the instrument.

His friends were ceaseless in their endeavors to mitigate the resentment of Alphonso. Not only those who personally knew him, but crowned heads and the princes of the land, who knew him only as Tasso the poet, used every endeavor to obtain his freedom; and gleams of hope would come upon his blighted spirit as one after another wrote to promise him their influence. When thus stimulated, he would attend to his literary pursuits. 'Gerusalemme Liberata' or 'Goffredo,' as it was entitled, appeared in Venice in 1580; and shortly after he wrote the dialogue 'Il Padre di Famiglia.' He also revised the minor poems he had composed during the last two years, and having collected them in a volume, sent them to the Princesses Lucretia and Leonora, with a letter expressive of his devotion to them. But this proof of his continued affection came too late for Leonora. She was on her death-bed, and too near her end to be cheered even by the genius of Tasso. The token of affection could not recall her from the spirit-land to which she was fast hastening.

The news of her illness and death affected Tasso deeply, but it did not, as might have been expected, inspire his Muse; while all the host of Italian poetasters poured forth their elegies and lamentations, and one dirge resounded through the country. The master-spirit of them all hung his harp upon the willow, and touched not its strings till her name had passed away from the lips of her people, though her memory was enshrined in their loving hearts. Many reasons were assigned for this singular silence on the part of Leonora's devoted lover. Perhaps he felt too deeply, to trust himself to speak of her, or perhaps he was not gifted in that style of elegiac composition.

Time passed on, though with slow and solemn footsteps, to the poor prisoner at St. Anne's; but the year 1584 brought new hopes to his heart, and some relaxation from the severe discipline to which he had been subject. He was allowed to attend church and to visit some of his friends. These indulgences tranquillized his mind; and he once again began to compose with freedom. All the cities of Italy interested themselves in his fate. Bergamo sent a delegation to Alphonso with bountiful gifts, imploring his freedom. The Duke accepted the gifts, and gave in return fair promises, which he had no intention of fulfilling; and as he saw that advantage was taken of his late leniency to press the suit in Tasso's favor, by all the neighboring princes, he once more increased the severity of his confinement, and forbade the indulgences he had heretofore granted.

The oppression renewed, Tasso's mind became more and more disordered. He yielded himself to the fancy that he was haunted by an evil spirit, whose sole delight and occupation was to annoy him, thwart his plans, and watch him day and night. He writes an account to his friend Cataneo of this affliction : 'I have received two letters from you, but one vanished as soon as I had read it, and I believe the goblin has stolen it, as it is the one in which he is spoken of; and this is another of the wonders I have seen in this hospital. I am sure they are the work of some magician, as I could prove from my arguments, particularly from the circumstance of a loaf of bread having been taken from me while my eyes were wide open, and a plate of fruit vanishing in the same manner when the amiable young Polocco came to visit me. I have also been served thus with other viands, when no one has entered the prison, and with letters and books which were locked up in cases, which I have found strewed about the floor in the morning. Beside the miracles of the goblin, I suffer by my natural terrors. I see flames in the air, and sometimes my eyes have sparkled to such a degree, I feared I should lose my sight; and sparks have visibly flown from me. I have also seen amid the spars of the bed the shadows of rats which could not naturally be there. I have heard fearful noises, have felt a whistling in my ears, a jingling of bells, and tolling of clocks for an hour together. But amid so many terrors, I have had appear to me a glorious vision of the Virgin with her Son in her arms, in a circle of colors and vapors; wherefore I will not despair of her grace.'

How sad it is to trace in this letter to his friend the disorder of his imagination! The soaring flight, the brilliant coloring are there, but broken and disjointed, and yet like the bits of colored glass in the child's toy, the kaleidescope, forming from its very chaos beautiful and distinct images. Soon after writing this letter he was attacked with a violent fever which brought him to the verge of the grave; and he attributed his recovery solely to the interposition of the Virgin, who frequently appeared to him. When he was sufficiently recovered to bear the joyful news, he was told that Alphonso had consented to his liberation. Poor Tasso could not sleep the whole night after hearing it, so anxious was he to escape the gloomy prison which had been even worse than the weary pilgrim's Slough of Despond, since no efforts of his own could effect his release.

None but a Silvio Pellico or Maroncelli can know fully how to sympathize with the liberated prisoner's feelings. When the day arrived which was to restore him again to freedom, his heart was too full for expression; and it is almost a wonder that the powerful excitement did not quite overturn his newly-acquired balance of mind: but his happiness was subdued by the remembrance of his sorrows and sufferings, and he turned from his prison door, a chastened man. His first visit was to his sister at Sorrento, and her welcome was as warm as when he sought her home in the first years of his derangement, when in the disguise of an old man he hid himself from Alphonso's resentment. After remaining with her a month or two, he took up his residence with the Duke of Mantua, and being quietly established there, resumed his literary pursuits. He wrote his 'Lettera Politica' and his tragedy of 'Torrismondo;' but the demon of unrest again took possession of him, and he insisted upon leaving Mantua for Rome, where he thought he should enjoy more freedom.

It was on this journey to Rome that Tasso received that tribute of respect from the brigand captain, Marco di Sciarri, which has been so beautifully commemorated by the English bard of Italy:

> ' On the watch he lies
> Levelling his carbine at the passenger,
> And when his work is done, he dare not sleep.
> Time was, the trade was nobler, if not honest;
> When they that robbed, were men of better faith,
> Than kings or pontiffs; when such reverence
> The poet drew among the woods and wilds,
> A voice was heard that never bade to spare,
> Crying aloud, ' Hence to the distant hills;
> Tasso approaches; he whose song beguiles
> The day of half its hours, whose sorcery
> Dazzles the sense, turning our forest glades
> To lists that blaze with gorgeous armory,
> Our mountain caves to regal palaces:
> Hence! nor descend till he and his are gone.
> Let him fear nothing.''

This fact has been recorded by Manso, who was with Tasso at the time. Marco de Sciarri, at whose name all Italy trembled, withdrew his troops from the neighborhood of Mola Di Jaëta, that Tasso might pass without molestation; a like tribute to that paid a few short years before to Ariosto, and which shows how much more willingly even common minds yield to the empire of genius than to that of rank or wealth.

Happiness seemed now once more to hover over the poet, and to promise a bright and peaceful close to his fitful career. Apartments were prepared for him at the Vatican, and he proceeded to the completion of a new epic, 'Gerusalemme Conquista,' as it was termed, for which he said ' he felt so much affection that he was alienated from the ' Liberata ' as a father from a rebellious child of whom he suspects the legitimacy, but that the ' Conquista ' was born of his mind as Minerva from the head of Jove, and to this he would intrust his reputation.' This delusion adds one more proof to the many that the best authors are not the best judges of their own writings. Even Milton thought his ' Paradise Regained' better than his ' Paradise Lost !'

In 1594, finding his constitution much shattered, he went to Naples, hoping the fineness of the climate would renovate him; and here he experienced the greatest devotion and kindness from his friends. Manso provided every thing for his comfort, and watched over him with the tenderness of a brother. He might have received great benefit from the quiet life he led; but unfortunately one more honor was proffered to him, the anxiety to receive which cost him his life.

The Pope Clement Eighth, in a full conclave of cardinals, determined to give him a public triumph; and as a recompense for his past sufferings, to confer upon him the poet's crown. This honor had not been conferred upon any one since the gentle bard of Vaucluse bent his knee to receive it from the assembled world; and Tasso was gratified that the same homage should be rendered him. The distinction was proffered too in the most flattering manner. ' It is my wish,' said the sovereign pontiff, ' that the crown which has hitherto been an honor to those upon whom it has been conferred, should now be honored by your acceptance.' Accordingly Tasso left Naples, accompanied by Manso and a deputation from the Pope, and at a short distance from Rome was received with all due honors. The most magnificent preparations had been made in the capitol for the ceremony. But vain are the expectations of man ! A higher than pope or cardinal determines to whom honor shall be given. At the moment when Tasso's name was resounding through Rome, and the laurel crown was waiting for him, he heard a voice bidding him exchange the garments of an earthly coronation for the robes of immortality, which were awaiting him in another world; and obedient to the call, his wearied and exhausted frame yielded up its pure spirit on the very day destined for his crowning honor, and the preparations for his triumph ended in a funeral procession.

His remains were interred in the monastery of St. Ormphrius, and a marble slab was placed over him by Manso, who wished to erect a fitting monument to his friend; but Cardinal Cynthio prevented him, observing that he himself intended to build a worthy mausoleum over the poet. He therefore only yielded Manso permission to place the name and date of his death upon this simple slab, and to this, which would have been all he himself desired, were confined the monumental honors of the immortal Tasso. For Cynthio, occupied with the cares and pleasures of the world, forgot the dead in the living; and it was not till a century after, that Cardinal Bevilacque placed his remains in a prouder receptacle, and attached a more sounding but not so noble an epitaph as the ' *Hic Jacet Torquatus Tasso* ' of his friend.

Most of Tasso's celebrity has been derived from his magnificent epic of ' Jerusalem Delivered ; ' a work abounding with the most thrilling events of the crusades, blending with the most pleasing descriptions of tender scenes, combined with a majestic flow of language which captivate and overpower the reader. It is most singular that Tasso's dying request to Cardinal Cynthio was, that he would collect all the copies of his ' Jerusalem Delivered,' wheresoever they might be found, and commit them to the flames, that no trace of it might be left. The Cardinal gave an equivocal answer, which satisfied the dying man; but it is needless to say he never intended to fulfil so extraordinary a request. This work is well known to the English reader by its many fine translations. His 'Jerusalem Conquered,' 'Arminta,' and 'Rinaldo' would alone have gained Tasso no ignoble fame; but they were extinguished in the blaze of his more brilliant epic.

The sad tale of his life has thrown a deep interest around Tasso; and we linger about it with melancholy emotions, longing to pour some sunshine through the dark cloud which rested over him. This was not to be, in the present world; but as his life was pure and blameless, and he was resigned to the will of his Heavenly Father, we may trust that he is now where all is brightness and peace, and where the mind so dimmed and disturbed in this life finds eternal brightness and repose!

THE HAUNTED HOUSE.

FAR down a hollow dark and drear, between two lonely hills,
Where the hazel grows and briar, and never-failing rills
O'er the pebbles clad with moss in ceaseless murmur flow,
Stands a lone deserted house, built many a year ago.
The night-wind makes a solemn wail the broken chimney o'er,
The shingles rattle on the roof, and creaks the swinging door;
The garden-fence is all decayed, the garden full of weeds,
And on the barren heath and hill the flock no longer feeds:
The school-boy goes not near the spot, but passeth far around;
And the ploughman coming late at eve unto this wizard ground
Looketh never toward the haunted-house lest he a ghost may spy,
But with fearful step and stolen glance, he passeth quickly by.

A hated man lived in this house 't is said, in olden time,
Who hung himself upon a beam, remorseful of some crime:
And beldames oft have seen a sprite who slowly twists a cord,
And waves them with his hand away, yet speaketh ne'er a word.
One stormy night amid these hills a soldier lost his way,
Who coming wounded from the wars, had travelled many a day.
His fearful cry for help was heard far o'er the waste of snow:
A strange man came unto his aid, and told him where to go;
To rest within this lonely house until the break of day,
Yet stabbed him sleeping on the hearth, then plucked the knife away:
The bleeding soldier started up, but fell upon his side,
He rolled his dim eyes toward the light — stretched out his feet, and died!
And thinking of his crime, 't is said, the murderer lost his mind:
He saw the soldier in the dark — he heard him in the wind;
Oft from his seat he started up, and cried with strange surprise,
'His dying hand is quivering! See there! how glare his eyes!'

And whence he came or where he fled, no mortal tongue can tell,
Nor since his time within his house hath man been known to dwell.
For many a day a cock was heard around the scene of blood,
Sending his loud and clear 'too-who' through all the lonely wood.
A cat would sometimes mew at eve upon the chimney-stone —
But very still the glen is now, for even these are gone.
The night-wind wails with wilder blast adown that hollow drear,
The forest wears a sickly hue through all the changing year;
Along the winding rocks the stream goes faster on its way,
And what yet makes the wood more drear, the owl hoots there by day!

LIFE IN HAYTI.

NEW-ENGLAND boy as I was, to whom snow-banks were as familiar as green fields, the hot weather of Hayti in mid-winter began after a time to be very tiresome. December gone, January passing away, and nothing but a succession of bright suns, unclouded skies, and hot days! Nature rebelled against such unnatural weather, as much as the natives would have done against an atmosphere at zero.

At length there were tokens of some relief from the incessant brightness of the day-god. Clouds began to roll over from the northward; the sea assumed a darker hue, and sent forth low moans, like a chafed beast of prey. There was no wind, but the clouds grew larger and darker, and now and then a wave combed over, 'feather-white,' to seaward, like a tiger showing his teeth; and occasionally a 'roller' came in upon the beach with a voice of thunder. Then comes a puff of air from the north; another and another follows at short intervals from the same dreaded quarter, which increase in violence until the 'norther' is fairly declared. And now, sailors! look to your ground-tackle! Make all snug, and prepare for a gale!

The sky is now completely overcast with the murky rack; and the sun for a rarity is hidden from the view, though still making faint attempts to break through the unusual barrier. The waves roll higher and higher, and break terrifically upon the shore. The coasting craft are hauling round as far as possible behind the point, and boats in the harbor are plying back and forth, bearing extra cables and anchors, and the loud sea-song of the black sailors is borne on the gale. As the storm increases, the rock-bound shores resound with the noise of the billows, which come crashing in as if they would tear terra-firma from its foundations. I now began to feel more at home. To be sure it was not equal to a winter storm in father-land, with its driving snow; but it was a respectable imitation, even though the mercury did not fall below sixty degrees of Farenheit. I observed that as soon as night came on the houses were all closed; and on inquiring the reason, was told that it was on account of the coldness of the weather; a fall of twenty degrees from the usual temperature of eighty being too much for Creole constitutions.

In order more thoroughly to enjoy the storm, I went down in the evening to the quay or wharf, where I could feel the blast and see and hear old Ocean. The streets were deserted, and the soldiers on sentry duty were cowering in the guard-house. Getting to the farthest end, with the waves crumbling among the piles beneath my feet, I clung to a post and watched the swift-flying clouds, as one after another they blotted out the moon, amid 'the noise of many waters.' And there, like a lonely exile, I stood an hour, and thought of home and friends, and the school-mates from whom I had so recently parted. Many a young form passed in review before me, and I longed to clasp their hands once more, and enter again with them into the sports and cares of boyhood. Gathered as we had been at ———, from all parts of the Union, it was natural that we should be scattered again like leaves of the forest; but I felt in that solitary hour as if no one of us had been wafted farther from his parent-tree than myself. The rain fell while I was thus 'chewing the cud of sweet and bitter fancies,' and when I returned to the house I was drenched to the skin.

My entrance was greeted with upraised hands and eyes, and a volley of exclamations from the servants, which proved to be a mixture of scolding and lamentations for the poor '*petit blanc,*' who would most assuredly have a fever the next day. The fever! This was a part of the performances which I had no relish for; so following their eager advice, I tore off my wet clothes and went to bed. The next morning I awoke with a severe attack from the dreaded enemy, which however was speedily mastered by a clever Frenchman who in France had kept a '*boutique d'apotecaire,*' but in Hayti was a regular M. D. So much had he gained by going 'to the colonies,' or rather away from home; for 'a prophet is never honored,' etc.

As the troops of children passed our doors on their way to and from school, it was amusing to witness the variety of complexions they exhibited. Positively no two of them were of the same color. Every nation on the face of the earth might find its representative in complexion, be they white Saxons, black Africans, or yellow Chinese; dark Moor, red Indian, or swarthy Spaniard; or any of the intermediate lights and shades of the human face divine. All I say would find in this (and nearly every other West-India town) their counterparts in color. The principal boys' school was on the Lancasterian plan. The master is an intelligent native, who fled his country in revolutionary times; and in his search after a quiet life found himself (of all situations to gratify such a taste!) a soldier in Soult's army in Spain. He had found his way home at last, bringing light pockets and a ball in a limb; and his experiences had given him a fund of anecdote, a reverence for 'L'Empereur,' and a limp in his gait. And how many of the sons of France had found *their* ways home after the weary wars of Napoleon, in the same plight with this unfortunate Dominie! And yet they all sang:

'It was a glorious victory!'

I am inclined to believe that the worthy pedagogue was in the habit of 'fighting his battles o'er again' to his boys, thereby inspiring them with a military spirit. Certain it is, that a majority of the urchins were usually arrayed in a miniature soldier's coat, having a standing collar, army buttons, and trimmed with light-blue or scarlet cloth; the same being in close imitation of the garments worn by their captain or lieutenant sires. It cannot however be the spirit-stirring tales of Maitre Cleverin which have clothed his youngsters in warlike vestments, for the chivalrous fashion prevails in other parts of the island. The same spirit is inculcated by the Commandant, who puts his little boys into the regiment, and makes them exercise with the troops in line.

The difference in the habits of the hardy sons of the north and the languid people of the south displays itself in early life. Here were no athletic games to wile the out-of-school hours away. The youngsters would as soon have thought of jumping over a house as over each other's heads at a game of leap-frog; and they would have shrunk away from a well-contested game of foot-ball, such as come off in the grounds of our northern seminaries, where 'Greek meets Greek' with a 'tug of war' scarcely equalled since the days of the tournaments. At school however many of these boys are far from being dull scholars, but make good proficiency in the simple branches of education which they are taught. Specimens of their chirography for example can be produced, as symmetrical and elegant as copper-plate. The mention of this art brings to mind an article of stationery of fine quality, which is found here. The sea-beach is a black sand, as coarse as common gray sea-sand; but there is one spot of ten or twelve yards square which is of fine grain and of the brightest purple, with all the hues and tints of a rich velvet. This we prepared by washing in fresh water, and sent it by sacks-full to our friends. This is the only spot where I have ever seen the black sand of stationers; and it appeared very singular that it should never be mixed with the coarser sands lying on all sides; although it is covered by the sea at high tide.

The remark is often heard, that in all parts of the earth are to be found Scotchmen; and moreover, that a 'cannie Scot' will thrive in any land and in any clime. Among the handful of whites residing here, there was one who was born not exactly in the 'land o' cakes,' but a little to the northward, in the Ultima Thule itself, and in no less renowned a spot than the island of jolly Magnus Troil, and in sight, as he assured me, of his house. With the fair Minna and Brenda still fresh in memory, and the roar of 'Sunburgh Head' still ringing in my ears, my wonder may be conceived on finding one day that I had been discussing the merits of 'the Pirate' with a veritable compatriot of Triptolemus Yellowly and of Norna of the Fitful Head!

The story of my new and agreeable friend was singular enough. When he left his home to seek his fortune he bent his steps, like all Englishmen, first to London; thence to the United States with a British consul; and from there to St. Domingo, where he had been an eye-witness of many of the atrocities of Dessalines and others, although he had always felt safe as a British subject, while transacting, as he did at one time, a large business. He was a well-read man, and of no little value to our small circle; although, like a true John Bull, full of eulogies on British power and influence, and full of sarcasm for every thing French, from Charles the Tenth to a poodle-dog; and I never could see that either their elevation or abasement of kings ever tended to exalt the people in his estimation. One being as curious to hear something of New-England as the other was to learn more of the Orkneys, we exchanged information as far as our respective abilities would allow; and at the same time were refreshed by an opportunity of using our mother tongue instead of the Creole jargon which was jabbered from morning till night on every hand. He had left his northern home long before Walter Scott visited it, otherwise he would have had an opportunity of 'ciceroning' the Baronet about the Island, and of pointing out those localities afterward depicted so vividly in the pages of 'The Pirate.' Such an occupation would have been to my friend an inexhaustible source of pleasant fancies ever after; and perhaps he would have gone with Scott to Edinburgh, and so have altered entirely his fortunes, and probably not for the worse. But it was not so to be; and Mr. S —— has lived thirty years in this distant corner of the south, and for most of the time the only British subject within as many leagues.

Another of our little circle of 'blancs' was a Spaniard, born in Cadiz. He too had emigrated from the old world to the new, in his youth, in search of an honorable independence. His first place of residence was in the city of Caraccas, where he acquired property and lived happily, until the fearful night of the great earthquake which overthrew that capital. He was roused from his slumbers by the rocking of the house, which was of stone; and in a few moments it was hurled to the ground. He escaped miraculously, and left the hapless city an impoverished man. In his wanderings he visited Hayti and settled in this community, and was again at the head of a prosperous business, when a relentless fever took him from among us; not however until he had seen another of the elements bursting from its natural bounds, and spreading still greater desolation in its path than was caused by the earthquake of Caraccas. Signor Champana was this time however more fortunate; for the roof only of his house was lifted off and deposited in the road by the hurricane of 1831; whereas the earthquake had razed his mansion to its foundations. This gentleman enjoyed thus the unenviable distinction of having had one house shaken to pieces and another blown away by the unruly elements.

There was in command of a regular trader between our port and Philadelphia a worthy 'ancient mariner' who had been there fifty years before, in the capacity of cabin boy. His account of the state of things at that time was almost incredible; yet it tallied well with the stories of the old people; and we had no other way of getting at any thing like statistics, all public records having been destroyed. He assured us that the harbor now so deserted was then filled with large French vessels, and that the quays and stores were loaded with sugar, coffee, rum, and indigo, the produce of the plantations in the district. What a wonderful change has come over this fair island! Not a pound of indigo has been manufactured for a quarter of a century, although the frequent occurrence of the shrub growing wild shows it to have been once abundant. In place of the huge hogsheads of sugar which filled ship after ship, and supplied half Europe, the whole produce of the island is now a few hundred barrels, not one of which is exported. In fact, white sugar is frequently imported into this island from the United States. The quantity of rum produced is also very small compared with former times, none being exported, although great quantities are unfortunately distilled for 'home consumption.' And lastly, in place of the three or four millions of coffee, which this custom-house now exports, there were then exported forty millions of pounds! — equal to nearly the whole crop of the island at the present time. In *those* days it was not uncommon for a planter to raise one hundred thousand pounds. In *these* days he is a fortunate proprietor who can deliver six thousand, of which one half goes to the cultivators.

The agricultural habits of this people are in a state of transition, and not exactly of stagnation; as might be inferred from the enormous deficits in all their crops. Each year the tillers of the soil grow more averse to living upon land which they do not own, as the tenure of occupancy compels them to divide the produce with the owner. The facilities for purchasing land have vastly increased. The average price for many years has been about twelve dollars Haytien (two of which make one Spanish) per acre. In 1826, the grower received for his coffee six dollars and a half per hundred pounds. With a depreciating currency, the price has constantly increased until 1840, when the price was nineteen dollars. But as the price of land did not increase in value as well as its products, (a bad sign in any country,) we see the cultivator now able to purchase thrice as many acres with his bag of coffee as he could fifteen years ago. With such facilities and advantages staring them in the face, the negroes must be inconceivably degraded and stupid not to profit by them, and thus become not only the tillers but the owners of the soil. Indeed so valueless have the estates become to the colored proprietors living in the towns, that they readily give credit to the purchaser.

In tropical climates the land-holders are usually the richest portion of the community. Why then, it may be asked, do the colored people, the mixed bloods, (who are more intelligent and better educated than the blacks,) thus willingly part with their territorial possessions? Have they trades or professions which are more lucrative than that of the agriculturalist? The answers to these questions involve facts in regard to the race whose characteristics we are describing which will perhaps be novel to many of our readers. In the first place, there is in this state of Hayti, this black republic, whose motto is 'Liberté, Egalité,' a great amount of ARISTOCRACY. There is an aristocracy of money, of place, of military renown, of education, of family, and strongest and most conspicuous of all, of color. The first is to be found in the richer merchants and shop-keepers, male and female, of whom there are some in every town, who exert a great influence over their fellow citizens. The aristocracy of place includes not only all those on the civil list, but all the officers of the army; not only judges and 'commissaries,' secretaries of departments, treasurers, collectors, *et hoc genus omne*, but also generals and commandants, colonels and captains, innumerable; all of whom attach sufficient importance to their several situations, and are presumed to be friendly to the government.

Quite a number of young men are sent to Europe (usually to France) for an education; some of these return accomplished and refined by their sojourn in good seminaries: others bring back to their native soil all the fopperies and vices of Paris. There are probably not far from a hundred Haytien students in France at all times. These may be called the *learned élite*, and they adopt either the medical or legal profession, the priesthood not being popular with them. The pride of *family* forms still farther material for the formation of 'caste.' The casual observer sees nothing of this, but an intimate acquaintance proves to him that there are as strongly marked lines in this respect as in any other; and there is sometimes found a 'clannishness' worthy of the banks of Loch Lomond. The pride of color needs no explanation. Nearly all the families of mankind look upon the white race as the most highly endowed. In a country therefore where one portion of the population is allied to this superior race while another portion is not, it follows that there must exist a *natural* aristocracy, and such I conceive to be emphatically the case in Hayti.

It must not be supposed however that upon these different foundations, more or less substantial for creating differences of rank, there is allowed to be raised any proud superstructure which shall tower over the heads of the people. Though all these feelings exist, yet any attempt to show them or to follow out the views of their possessors, would be instantly crushed by the mass. Where a conscious feeling of superiority exists, great care is taken that it does not break the bounds prescribed by the constitution, comprised in those magical words, ' *Liberté, Egalité.*'

A great source of recreation as well as of health we found in the beautiful river which winds through the hills back of the town. Its pellucid current flows briskly along over a bed of pebbles, and the banks at our favorite bathing places were of clean ' shingle,' shaded by clusters of the graceful bamboo. The path lay through a plain which once formed the rich sugar estate ' Benquier ; ' but in place of the canes there was now a dense forest of guava-trees, from which we plucked the fruit as we rode along. This tree and the logwood have sprung up spontaneously on the deserted lands, and where unchecked have formed impenetrable thickets. We resorted frequently to the banks of the river in the cool of the afternoon, and lingered till dark, watching the ' crabier,' a small snow-white crane, stalking ' silent and thoughtful by the solemn shore,' or listening to the murmuring stream and the soft breezes playing through the trees ; and as we looked beyond the scenes before us to the gentle outlines of the undulating hills, and heard the merry notes of the oriole from the groves on every hand, we could not help confessing that life in such a land might be as sweet as it is possible to be on earth. There was nothing to operate as a drawback upon these smiles of Nature. Those terrors of tropical rivers, the alligators, are unknown. The huge serpents and ferocious beasts which render the solitudes of our southern continent so hazardous, are banished from this terrestrial paradise. Instead of the venomous reptiles so common to these latitudes, we saw on every side little chameleons or lizards running nimbly and harmlessly along the ground, or over the trunks and limbs of the trees.

Now and then the noisy laugh of some neighboring rustic or of merry wayfarers would pierce the air ; and if they came in sight, a distrustful scowl, or saucy joke, or civil greeting would meet us, according as the feelings of the individual were favorable or otherwise toward the ' blancs.' If we wandered farther up toward the ' passe,' or ford, we amused ourselves with watching the people crossing the river ' *à la nage.*' They dodged the ferry-boat below, and took to the water like ducks, men, women and children, and waded, swam, and scrambled across, as the river happened to be high or low. If they chanced to have a horse or a donkey in charge, they transferred the huge bundles of grass or bananas from their own heads to the already loaded backs of their animals, and so ' plunged in and buffeted it with lusty sinews.'

There is one rural occupation, which we of the north are wont to consider the most delightful of all, which is unknown in the tropics. I mean that of the hay-maker. The graceful sweep of the mower's sythe, the busy rakers, and the fragrant hay-stacks are never seen. The coarse guinea-grass grows at all seasons, and is the common provender for animals from the beginning to the end of the year, being cut daily to furnish the daily supply.   Horses after eating it for some time will not touch the best hay.   But the loss of the cheerful song of the hay-maker is not the only thing missed in the rural life of the tropics.   In a country where 'the quarters' succeed each other in monotonous similitude, with nothing to mark the ingress of the one or the egress of the other, we lose the greatest charm of life — the change of the seasons.   How delightful is Spring, with its soft mornings, and buds and blossoms, when Earth has shaken off the icy hand of Winter! How pleasant is Summer, with its bright days and flowers, and rural scenes and refreshing showers! — contrasting all, as we constantly do, with the sternness of a more inclement season.   How delicious are the golden days of Autumn, each one of which we would cleave to for ever ; when the fields are heavy with the golden harvest, and the gardens hang with ruddy fruits, and the sun, shorn of his fiery beams, is succeeded at night by the harvest moon!   And when old Winter comes round again, has he not his thousand delights?   The bright fire-side, with pleasant friends or pleasant books ; the merry sleigh-bells, the gay reünions, the intellectual feasts?   Is it not the season when, spite of the freezing air without, the flow of soul gushes most sparkling within? Its chilling breath may blight all nature without, yet it is powerless upon the heart and soul of man.   Does it not rather rouse and stimulate his energies to prepare for its coming?   It is an affecting type of that other winter which will follow it ; that long cold freezing winter, 'in which no man can work!'   St. Croix.

'WHAT IS OUR LIFE?'

We are born, we laugh, we weep;
  We love, we droop, we die!
Ah! wherefore do we laugh or weep?
  Why do we live or die?
Who knows that secret deep?
  Alas! not I!

Why doth the violet spring
  Unseen by human eye?
Why do the radiant seasons bring
  Sweet thoughts, that quickly fly?
Why do our fond hearts cling
  To things that die?

We toil, through pain and wrong ;
  We fight — and fly ;
We live, we lose — and then ere long
  Stone-dead we lie!
O Life! is *all* thy song
  'Endure and — die!'

THE QUOD CORRESPONDENCE.

The Attorney.

CHAPTER XVI.

ON the following morning an elderly man was seen walking briskly toward the lower part of the city. He was a hale hearty old fellow, not too fat, nor thin; with a merry joyous eye, and a good-natured cheery face that had a smile in every wrinkle. He was dressed in a plain suit of black, and under his arm he carried a cane which he sometimes transferred to his hand, for the purpose of aiding him in walking. He must have been past sixty, for his hair was silvery white; yet his cheek was rosy, and his step firm and elastic, like one in a green old age; who in spite of time and trouble kept a young heart in his bosom; and as he walked briskly along, looking now at the blue sky, now at the houses, now at the throng who toiled through the street, and now pausing at a shop-window to examine some trifle that caught his fancy, or nodding with a frank good-humored smile to a passing acquaintance, there was so much buoyancy and sunshine in him that it made one young to look at him. It was just the day too to meet such a man; a soft warm morning in the midst of winter. Ice and snow were melted, and the genial hours of spring seemed stealing back at a time when all nature was bleak and desolate.

The old gentleman had a companion, who as he walked gaily along, pausing or increasing his pace as suited his humor, adapted his gait to his; stopping when he stopped, going on when he did, and listening quietly, yet with deep interest to the remarks which dropped from him. This person was a young man of three or four and twenty; tall, thin, with a quick bright eye, black hair, and rather pale. There was a strong contrast between him and the old man. There was more of earnestness, perhaps of sadness in him, and he bore the look of one who had buffeted his way through the world, and even in the outset of life had become a stern and determined man. The expression of his face was prepossessing; for even amid its seriousness, frankness was stamped on every feature; and when he laughed, which he frequently did, as they went along, there was something gushing, heart-felt and child-like in its tone, which showed that trouble and not nature had wrinkled his brow and saddened his spirit.

They were apparently conversing on a subject which interested them both deeply, although that interest displayed itself differently in each.

'Keep cool, my boy, keep cool!' said the old man, looking merrily out of his blue eye, and placing his cane under his arm and his hands under his coat-tails; 'keep cool, we'll match him yet; but we must fight him with his own weapons. Above all things, do n't get excited.'

'I am not in the least excited,' replied the other gravely. 'Indeed, Doctor, of the two I think you are the most so,' said he, smiling. Then after a pause, he asked : 'Do you think her father ever made such a will ? It seems scarcely possible.'

'I do n't intend to think about it,' replied the old man. 'It 's strange ; but strange things happen every day. It *is* strange — very strange. If it was n't for the sin of swearing, I should say it was d — d strange, if that 's any comfort to you.'

'Well,' said his companion, laughing, 'if you wo'n't commit yourself on that point, of course you will not undertake to think whether the law will uphold such a will or not.'

'Of course I wo'n't ; for that 's just what we are going to a lawyer to inquire about,' replied Doctor Thurston, for he it was. 'After we 've seen him, I 'll think boldly, and not till then. Here 's the place.' As he spoke, he pointed to a brick building, two stories in height, be-labelled from top to bottom with small tin signs, indicating in gilt letters that the crop of attorneys was numerous and flourishing. Among these was one sign, discolored and gray, and almost illegible from age. On it were simply the words 'D. FISK.'

'That 's the man,' said the Doctor, pointing to the sign. He 'll ferret his way to the very bottom of this matter, depend on it. I know him well.'

Having thus expressed his faith in the abilities of the professional gentleman whose territories he was preparing to invade, he opened a small glass door at the bottom of a narrow stair-way, and ascending, found himself in Mr. Fisk's outer office.

Law certainly engenders dust and decay ; for every thing was covered with the first, and seemed in a very advanced stage of the last. There were three tables in the office ; broken, and covered with ragged baize ; six or seven chairs, some lame of a leg, and one or two deficient in an arm, or weak in the back. Loose papers were lying on the tables, and empty ink-bottles and old hearth-brushes under them, half buried in dirt, cobwebs, and shreds of paper, apparently the accumulated sweepings of years ; and indicating, either that Mr. Fisk was too much immersed in the duties of his profession to care about the cleanliness of his office, or else that dust, cobwebs, and empty bottles, and broken chairs and tables, were essential to the proper management of an extensive law practice.

At one of the windows a young gentleman, belonging to the class of individuals usually denominated 'students at law,' was intently occupied in the abstruse employment of blowing with his breath on the glass, and cutting the initials of his name thereon with his fore-finger. Another young man, with light hair and spectacles, clad in a coat sufficiently exploded under the arms and ragged at the elbows to belong to that class of habiliments technically called 'office-coats,' was slumbering sweetly over a lucid work on Law Practice ; while behind him at the fire a third student, a promising young gentleman, out at the elbows, and with no buttons on the back of his coat, was engaged in the rather matter-of-fact employment of roasting chestnuts on a broken shovel, with a large hole in its bottom, carefully keeping the nuts in their place with the feather end of a quill.

In front of the fire, with his back to it, his hands in his breeches pockets, a pen in his mouth, and one behind his ear, indicating that it required the active exercise of several pens at the same time to keep up with the heavy business of the office, stood Mr. Cutbill, a gentleman with thin whiskers and a Roman nose. He was the head-clerk; worked hard, talked equally hard when he got an opportunity, and stood in wholesome awe of Mr. Fisk.

'Ah! Doctor!' exclaimed he, advancing and offering his hand as soon as he saw who they were; 'glad to see you; *very* glad to see you. In law again? It does one good to get a Doctor in a lawyer's hands; indeed it does. You bleed us, and we bleed you! Ha! ha! But I suppose you 'll pay off the score when you get us on our backs.'

Doctor Thurston laughed, and said that he might trust him for that.

'No doubt, no doubt. Sit down, Sir; sit down both of you,' said he, bowing and smirking.

'Can I see Mr. Fisk?' inquired Doctor Thurston, without taking a seat.

'He 's engaged just now,' replied the clerk; 'quite busy.'

'Will he be so long?'

Mr. Cutbill pursed up his mouth, looked at the ceiling with his left eye, as if he were going through some abstruse mathematical calculation, by which he would be enabled to give the precise time in minutes and seconds; after which he said he thought not, and drew the skirts of his coat open behind.

'Take a chair,' said he, pointing to an article of that description with no bottom to it. 'Oh! ah! I beg pardon; do n't take *that*; we keep that for the long-winded fellows who tell the same story over every time they come here. It 's uncomfortable, and they do n't sit long.'

Here Mr. Cutbill laughed in a subdued manner, and said: 'We wo'n't give *you* that chair, Sir;' and he pushed two others toward them.

'Fisk has his hands full, eh?' inquired the Doctor, as he and his friend seated themselves.

'Run down, Sir, run down,' replied Mr. Cutbill, straightening himself up, and throwing his chest forward by way of exercise. 'Clients, clients, from morning till night. In a confidential way, Sir: he has the best run of clients in the city; all first-raters. I think,' continued he, relapsing into a deep calculation, 'that I may say Mr. Fisk has not a single bad client; none of those who sneak into an office as if they had no business there. None of those who open a door on a crack, and peep in, while they ask advice; none of those who knock: now take my advice,' said he, growing animated; 'never open a door to a knock. We never do it — do we, Torker?'

'Devil a bit; catch *us* at it!' replied the person thus addressed. After which he breathed violently on the window-pane, and with the fore-finger of his right hand cut a capital T with eminent success.

'If you do,' continued Mr. Cutbill, 'ten to one, you 'll stumble on a dun, or a perambulating female, begging for a donation to some unheard-of charitable society, of which she is both member and object, or a small gentleman in a white cravat, anxious to found a church on the top of an iceberg, where he is to preach to the Esquimaux on the sin of luxury and high living. Confound it! Mr. Juniper,' exclaimed he, breaking off an enumeration which promised to be a long one, and addressing the young gentlemen engaged at the fire : 'you 'll have Fisk on us if you do n't keep those chestnuts quiet.' This abrupt remark was elicited by a succession of sudden reports, emanating from the culinary department, like a volley of small artillery.

'Can't help it,' replied Mr. Juniper, composedly continuing his occupation ; 'a man must eat when he 's hungry. I wanted a knife to nib their noses, but I had n't one ; so I 'm blow'd if they may n't bu'st just as much as they please. You 're always grumbling, but bloody ready to eat 'em.'

Mr. Cutbill turned very red, and assumed an air of extreme dignity, for the purpose of overcoming any ill impression which this remark might have made on the clients. At the same time he told Mr. Juniper that he had always, up to that time, thought him a gentleman. In reply to which, Mr. Juniper informed him that he was a 'poor squirt,' and if he again let his coat-tail fall in his shovel, as he was doing at that particular moment, he would set it on fire.

Farther conversation of the same pleasant character might have followed, but just then there was a stir in the inner office.

'By Jove! there he is!' exclaimed Mr. Cutbill. 'Go in, Doctor, and you, Sir,' said he, bowing to his companion. 'Quick!—do n't wait for him to come here, or there 'll be the deuce to pay. That Juniper,' he added, sinking his voice, 'do n't care a straw how much of a row he kicks up, because I 'm head-clerk, and take all the blame. Mum!' said he, placing his finger significantly on his lips, and favoring the doctor with an infinite series of sudden, sharp winks. At the same time he seized a law book, and plunged over head and ears in an intense perusal of its contents. The door of the inner room opened, and a voice said, 'Good morning.' Then a man passed through, nodded slightly to Mr. Cutbill, who bowed deferentially, and went out.

Without waiting for any farther suggestion, the doctor and his companion ushered themselves into the presence of Mr. Fisk.

He was a small man, thin and wrinkled, with a large prominent and bright eye. His hair was matted and twisted in every direction, from a habit of running his fingers through it, when in deep thought ; but other than this, there was nothing peculiar about him, except an immoderately large shirt collar, which stuck up under his ears, apparently supporting his head on his shoulders. The table in front of of him was covered with bundles of papers tied with red tape, either waiting their turn to be perused, or laid aside after having been read ; and a great many loose ones were strewed around in the utmost disorder. All the chairs in his immediate vicinity were covered with open law-books with the faces down, and some were even lying on the floor. Before him was a paper on which he had been writing. When they entered, being deeply engaged in investigating the various means by which an insurance company might receive a premium of insurance, and in case of fire not pay their policy, he did not look up until Doctor Thurston spoke.

'Ah! Doctor! I'm glad to see you. Sit down,' said he, pointing to a chair.

'This is Mr. Francis Wharton, of whom I spoke to you,' said the other, by way of introducing his companion; 'an intimate friend of Miss Crawford.'

The lawyer looked significantly at the person thus presented to his notice, and shaking hands with him, again requested them to be seated. At the same time he took a chair opposite, and without speaking, looked at them, as if to know the object of their visit.

'I came here on the same business about which Doctor Thurston has already spoken to you,' said Wharton, in reply to the look which seemed more particularly directed to him.

Mr. Fisk merely bowed.

'I am not aware whether the particulars were fully detailed then.'

'It would be well to mention them again,' said Mr. Fisk, quietly. As he said this, he pursed his mouth up into a point, and folding his hands on the top of his head, leaned back in his chair, with his eyes fixed on the wall. He did not speak nor move until Wharton had given the whole history of the claim set up by Bolton, and of his two interviews with Miss Crawford. He mentioned that until that will was produced, nothing had ever transpired to make them suppose her other than her father had always represented her to be, his legitimate child. When he had got through, Mr. Fisk sat up in his chair.

'And you wish me to resist the probate of that will?' said he, as composedly as if resisting the probate of wills was an every-day matter with him.

'Most certainly!' interrupted Doctor Thurston, who had held in as long as his nature would permit; 'most certainly we do!' repeated he warmly, and thumping his cane on the floor.

'On what grounds?' inquired the other, nibbing a pen, and laying it on the table, in readiness to continue his writing as soon as they should be gone.

'On the ground that it is a forgery.'

Mr. Fisk gave a slight and unsatisfactory cough, and then said: 'What proof have you?'

Doctor Thurston started up, and walked rapidly up and down the room. 'Proof, proof,' exclaimed he; 'the will itself proves it. On the very face of it, it is a foul, glaring lie. Does n't it set forth this girl, my own little Ellen Crawford, as illegitimate! What could be more false than that?'

'Perhaps she is,' said Mr. Fisk, with a quiet smile; and not a little amused at the fiery old man, who paced up and down the room like a lion at bay.

'My God! Helen Crawford illegitimate! Haven't I known her since she was no higher than my knee?—very shortly before her mother's death? Did n't her mother on her death-bed call me to her, and put that little child in my arms and bless it, and beg me to love and watch over it as if it were my own?—and have n't I done so? Crusty and crabbed an old fellow as I am, has n't there always been a warm spot in my heart for her? God bless her! and do n't I love that dear little girl more than all the world beside? Would n't I protect her with my heart's blood? I 'd like to see the man who 'd wrong her while this old arm can strike a blow!' said he, clutching his cane, and shaking it fiercely, as if at that moment he would have derived intense satisfaction from breaking the head of somebody. 'I 'll tell you what it is, Mr. Fisk,' said he, striding up to the table, and striking his hand vehemently on a pile of law papers, and thereby raising a cloud of dust; 'if she 's illegitimate, so am I;' and he again struck his fist down, as if he had driven a nail home and was clenching it.

'Did you see her mother married?' inquired Mr. Fisk; 'did you ever know any one who did? — or did you ever see her marriage certificate?'

'No.'

'Did you ever see the clergyman who performed the ceremony?'

'How could I? He died very shortly after it; before I knew the family.'

'Did you know his name? — and did you ever see the church-record containing the memorandum of their marriage?'

'No.'

'Do you know in what church it was performed, or in what city?'

'No.'

'Then you know nothing about it,' replied Mr. Fisk, 'nor whether it is true or not. Her father in his will says she is a natural child; and he certainly ought to know something about it.'

'What 's to be done then?' demanded the doctor, impatiently.

'I 'll tell you. In the first place, although the character of this Bolton is bad enough to justify suspicion of the worst kind, still nothing can be done without *proof;* and it would be worse than useless to advance so sweeping a charge as that of forgery, unless we have strong testimony to support it. You must ascertain if possible whether Mr. Crawford was really married to his daughter's mother; also when and where; the name of the clergyman, and of those present at the ceremony; and whether any of them are still living; if a marriage certificate was made out, who saw it, and what has become of it. Any thing that will tend to substantiate Miss Crawford's legitimacy will be useful of course only to cast suspicion on the will. You might also learn whether Mr. Crawford at any time made a previous will, and how he disposed of his property in it; and how he there mentions his daughter. When you are able to give me more definite information on these points, I shall be able to advise you more effectually. Your opponent is a vigilant fellow, and one who manages his cards adroitly; and I will frankly tell you that I fear you will find the proof of these matters not so clear as you imagine; for you may be sure that Bolton sifted this thing thoroughly, and knew the strength of your testimony to a hair, before he committed himself so boldly as he has done. He is shrewd, sagacious, and unprincipled, and would stick at nothing to accomplish his ends.'

'Depend on it he never offered to marry Miss Crawford without some ulterior object. He was afraid of her. I'd stake my life on it!' exclaimed the doctor, earnestly.

'It looks suspicious indeed,' replied the lawyer, drumming with his fingers on the table. 'Who did you say were the witnesses?'

'Two fellows I never heard of, nor ever heard him speak of. I forget their names.'

'He has not yet applied for letters testamentary, I suppose?' asked the lawyer.

'I don't know,' replied Doctor Thurston, 'but I think not. He told Miss Crawford he intended to. She has not heard from him since.'

'She being illegitimate, it would not be necessary to cite her.'

He drummed on the table for some time, and then said, rising to give them a hint that they had occupied enough of his time, 'I'll attend to it; and you must n't fail to communicate any thing you may learn. Good morning.'

He bowed as he spoke, and neither the doctor nor his companion having any thing more to communicate, they took their leave.

———

CHAPTER XVII.

'Now then to my work!' muttered the Attorney, a few days after his interview with Miss Crawford; 'there's nothing left but law, and all depends on skill and management.'

Now that he had abandoned all hope of compromise, and was determined to advance, and support his claim at all hazards, and to abide the event, whatever it might be, he was a different man; cold, calm, and calculating. He measured every difficulty, fortified every weak part of his cause, and shutting his eyes to those things which he knew might happen, to blast him, but which he could not prevent, he waited patiently for the result. He lost no time in presenting the will for probate; and to avoid all appearance of apprehension, he caused a citation to be served on Miss Crawford, apprizing her of the time when the will would be proved, and summoning her to attend. These steps taken, nothing more could be done for fifteen days, as the law required the lapse of that space of time between the serving of the citation and the proving of the will; and fifteen days of intense anxiety they were to Bolton.

In the mean while, neither the friends nor the counsel of Miss Crawford had been idle, although they kept their operations profoundly quiet. On questioning her, they learned that her father had frequently spoken of his marriage with her mother, and had mentioned that she was poor, and an orphan at the time, and that from opposition on the part of his parents, the ceremony had been performed in secret, and with none present except the clergyman and two witnesses. She had never heard the names either of the clergyman or of those who were present, nor had she seen her mother's marriage certificate. She knew that she had once possessed one, but she believed it to be lost. In the course of their investigations, however, they stumbled upon a will made by

Mr. Crawford, several years previous to his death, in which he mentioned Helen Crawford as his only child by his wife Catherine, and left her sole heir to all his property. On this document, however, there was a memorandum, stating that it had been revoked by a will of a later date, which they were unable to find.

These facts having been communicated to Mr. Fisk, fairly awakened his suspicions, and he knuckled down to his work in good earnest. He set on foot inquiries respecting the character of Wilkins and Higgs, by which he discovered that they were men of the worst possible reputation; familiar with crime, and the intimates of those who followed it as a regular means of livelihood; and as he proceeded in his investigations, many other little matters leaked out respecting the habits of those two gentlemen, which in all probability they would have preferred should remain in obscurity, or known only to themselves. By his ingenuity also, a friendly communication was opened with persons frequenting the same haunts with the two confederates, and several of them were paid to keep an eye on their motions and conversation, and report what they dropped to the watchful lawyer. But little however was gained in this way; for Wilkins was too sullen and moody, and Higgs too much on his guard, to let any thing escape that might implicate them. They however were several times traced to the lawyer's office, and had once or twice been observed in earnest and excited conversation with him in the street.

The visits of Wilkins to the widow had likewise been observed, and as they were frequent, Mr. Fisk naturally supposed that his intimacy in the family must be great; and with no other object than that of leaving nothing untried, he determined to spring a mine in that quarter. Matters were in this state, when about nine o'clock one cold frosty morning, a stout man with a pimpled face verging into purple toward the end of his nose, opened the door of a small tavern in the neighborhood of Centre-street, and stepped into the open air. He looked up and down the street, then at the sky; stamped his thick cane shod with iron heavily on the pavement, and cleared his throat; after which he deliberately placed his cane under his arm, and buttoned his coat up to his chin. This done, he turned slowly round, and looked in the door.

'Come along you cuss, will yer? P'raps you're waiting for a perswader. If y' are, ye'll get it, blast yer!' And he shook his heavy stick insinuatingly at the object of his remarks.

Thus encouraged, a large white bull-dog walked to the door with a step as deliberate as that of his master, stared up and down the street, then at the sky, the same as the gentleman who preceded him had done; after which he seated himself on end, and looked pleasantly up in the face of Mr. Rawley, as if he had nothing to do with a volley of epithets which that gentleman was just then showering upon him, and as if he wished him not to hurry himself in the least.

Mr. Rawley having unbottled his anger, pulled the door of his house to, put his stick under his arm, and thrusting his hands in his breeches pockets, walked briskly down the street, followed by Wommut, who kept so close to his heels that it seemed a matter of some singularity that his nose escaped collision with them.

Mr. Rawley walked on for some distance, when suddenly he stopped and uncorked again: 'Come along, you cuss!— you in-*fer*-nal cuss! Must I be a bustin' my lungs all day a callin' arter you?'

These remarks were addressed to Wommut, who was again delinquent, and who had paused at the corner to watch the progress of a fight which was going on between two small dogs, with the eye of a connoisseur, who seemed desirous of dropping a hint or two to them on the subject.

'Come, I say!" shouted Mr. Rawley, brandishing his cudgel.

Wommut approached in an oblique direction, which brought him a little nearer his master, and a great deal nearer the combatants, and then paused and looking over his shoulder at his master, winked his eyes slowly, and made a painful effort at swallowing, which showed that his feelings were deeply interested.

'Come here, will yer?' bawled out Mr. Rawley.

Wommut deliberated a moment, then pitched headlong into the fight, and shook both dogs violently, by which piece of exercise, being apparently much relieved, he went to within twenty feet of his master, and placidly seated himself, waiting for him to go on.

'Have n't I brung you up in in the best of 'ciety, yer brute yer? and is this the way you 're going for to disgrace me, by stickin' your ugly muzzle into every wulgar rumpus atwixt all low-lived mongrels you meet, and you a reg'lar thoroughbred bull? Do it agin, that 's all; do it agin!'

And Mr. Rawley shook his stick ferociously at the dog, who kept at a respectful distance, until his master had become somewhat mollified, after which he gradually narrowed the space between them, until he followed as before, with his nose almost touching his heel.

It was a fine cold morning. The air was quiet; the sun shone cheerily, and every thing looked gay and bright. Even the old houses in that ruinous part of the city had a fresh appearance. Mr. Rawley walked sturdily on, thumping his cane on the stones until they rang, and clearing his throat manfully. He struck into Chatham-street, and along that thoroughfare he directed his course, jostling his way among the crowd, and giving way for nobody. Through Chatham-street, along the Park, and down Broadway he kept on, and close at his heels followed Wommut, until they came near Wall-street, a few blocks above which Mr. Rawley turned off into Nassau. It was early in the day, and that narrow street was thronged with people, among whom he drifted on, until he came to the small two-story building, on the outside of which Mr. Fisk kept his sign, and in the inside of which he kept his office.

He ascended the outer steps, and pulled open the door at the foot of the inner staircase.

'Go up!' said he, holding open the door, and looking over his shoulder at the dog.

In obedience to his hint, and aided by the application of Mr. Rawley's foot, which accompanied it, Wommut preceded his master, until he reached the top of the stairs, where he gave a short asthmatic cough, and seated himself.

'Is this 'ere where Mr. Fisk keeps?' inquired Mr. Rawley, after he had attained the same eminence with the dog, and looking very hard at Mr. Cutbill, who was looking equally hard at Wommut.

'This is his office,' replied the head-clerk, continuing his earnest gaze at the dog.

Mr. Rawley, on receiving the answer, took off his hat and placed it on the floor, laid his stick beside it, pulled off his gloves and threw them in his hat, unbuttoned his coat and shook it gently, after which he drew from his pocket a dirty spectacle case, and an equally dirty pocket-book of a large size. Laying the last on his knee, he opened the first, and fixing a pair of iron spectacles carefully on his nose, he proceeded to unstrap the pocket-book, from which he took a letter, and without saying a word reached it to Mr. Cutbill. Having successfully accomplished this feat, with equal deliberation he replaced the pocket-book, and spectacles, buttoned his breeches pocket, pulled down his waist-coat, and stared Mr. Cutbill full in the face.

That gentleman read the letter through, and then said:

'Oh, Sir, you're Mr. Rawley?'

'Yes, Sir, I am that individooal.' And Mr. Rawley looked as if asking, 'And now that you know it, what you going to do about it?'

'I'm delighted to see you; and so will Mr. Fisk be,' said Mr. Cutbill, advancing, and rubbing his hands. 'We were quite anxious to see you, indeed we were. A fine dog that, Sir, a *very* fine dog!'

'He *is* a fine dog,' replied Mr. Rawley, with some emphasis; 'a remarkably fine one.'

'Upon my soul, I think I never saw a finer. A pointer, I think?'

'No Sir; a bull — a regular bull; a real out-and-outer.'

'Fine fellow! — fine fellow! Poor pup — pup — pup!' said Mr. Cutbill, looking insinuatingly at Wommut, and patting his own knee, by way of hinting to him that his intentions were friendly. 'Is he vicious? I hope he ai'n't.'

'He wicious! Let me catch him a-being wicious — that's all! He never killed nobody. He used a young nigger rather rough last fall, and bit a hole in the bowels of a small Irish infant; but it was all in play. He's the best naturedest dog in the world, if you let him alone.'

'Oh! we wo'n't disturb him then,' said Mr. Cutbill, increasing the distance between himself and the amiable animal; 'we wo'n't notice him; but he's a prodigiously fine dog. I think Mr. Fisk is at leisure to see you; and you had better go in and take him with you. I'm sure Mr. Fisk will admire him; he's such a noble specimen — so like a lion. If he do n't like my looking at him, I wo'n't. He looks as if he did n't.'

'It ai'nt you that's a 'citing him,' replied Mr. Rawley. 'It's that chap there,' said he, pointing to Mr. Juniper, who was saluting the dog with sundry pellets of chewed paper, ejected through a tube; while Wommut, laboring under the delusion that his nose was beset by divers flies of a species hitherto unknown, kept snapping in every direction. 'Let me tell you this, my chicken,' continued Mr. Rawley, 'if you've cut your wisdom grinders, you'll let that animal alone; for when his dander's fairly riz he's h — ll for assault and battery. A gen'leman worried that same dog one fine day, and the next year that same gen'leman wore a wooden leg. I only mention the fact; that's all.'

'Mr. Juniper, for God's sake do n't disturb the animal!' exclaimed Mr. Cutbill, earnestly; 'of all abominable things, cruelty to dumb beasts is the worst. Poor fellow! poor fellow! I hope he do n't make mistakes when he's excited, and bite the wrong person?'

'Not often; but he does sometimes, 'specially when he's aggravated about the nose.'

'Indeed! ah! I think you had better step in the next room; Mr. Fisk will see you at once. He's very anxious to. Walk in sir; *do* walk in. Take the dog with you; a splendid animal! — beautiful! — a perfect study!' And Mr. Cutbill fairly bowed Mr. Rawley and his companion into the back office and shut the door.

Mr. Rawley remained for some time shut up with Mr. Fisk, and when he came out both he and Wommut wore an air of profound mystery. He looked at Mr. Cutbill, and then strode down the steps without saying a word. Wommut had already descended two steps, in pursuance of his example, when he detected Mr. Juniper in the act of throwing the cover of a book at his head; and turning short round, was ascending for the purpose of taking a gentlemanly notice of the aggression, when he was arrested by the voice of Mr. Rawley. He paused on the top step, looked Mr. Juniper full in the face, raised his upper lip, and favored him with a sarcastic smile which displayed all his teeth, and then quietly descended the steps, and made his egress from the door, being somewhat aided therein, as in his ascent, by a kick from his master.

That gentleman now directed his course to the upper part of the city. He did not stop at his own tavern, but dodged in and out of various places in obscure parts of the town. He had undertoned gossipings in corners with several suspicious fellows, apparently obtaining but little satisfaction to his inquiries. He then went to Wilkins' house and had a long and mysterious conversation with the red-headed lodger on the second floor, who treated him with singular deference. Thence he directed his steps to a small house in the Bowery; and very shortly after might have been seen holding by the button no less a person than Aaron, the drab-colored body-guard of Mrs. Dow. Their colloquy must have been most satisfactory, for he chuckled and laughed to himself as he left him, and snapped his fingers, and swore lustily at the dog, which last demonstration of pleasure he did not intermit until he reached his own house.

What the nature of the conversation was, has not transpired; but during the whole of the evening succeeding it Aaron was observed to wear an air of profound and uneasy gravity. He shook his head ominously in the kitchen, and threw out so many cloudy hints that a certain gentleman who should be nameless, but whom they all knew, and particularly Mrs. Dow, and who came in and out of a certain house as if it were his own, and spoke to a certain respectable man-servant as if he were a dog, would 'get his bitters soon,' that the red-haired cook with prominent teeth, to use her own expression, 'was ready to bu'st with cur'osity.'

A dozen times in the course of the evening Aaron thrust his head in the little parlor, (where Mrs. Dow was dozing over a large Bible and a small prayer-book, with a small stove under her feet,) to see what the hour was. Eight o'clock came, then nine; a quarter after, then half after, and at last ten. As the clock struck, Mrs. Dow lighted an under-sized lamp, with a particularly large extinguisher attached to it by a brass chain, and examined all the windows, doors, and latches, to see that they were properly secured. Having satisfied herself in this particular, and having thrust a long sharp-pointed stick violently under every chair, sofa, and side-board, and into every dark closet in the lower part of the house, and having closely scrutinized every drawer of sufficient magnitude to contain any thing larger than a rat in the last stage of decline, she felt morally certain that there were no hidden interlopers in the house; and accordingly took herself off to bed, first giving Aaron a particular charge not to set the house on fire, in any accidental manner whatever.

No sooner did Aaron hear the door of her room double locked, and the bolt drawn, than he clapped his broad-brimmed hat on his head and sallied out; and being somewhat flurried at the stealthy nature of this proceeding, he ran with all his might, two blocks in a direction contrary to what he wished to take before he stopped to think. He then paused, buttoned his coat up to his chin, fixed his hat firmly on his head, and changed his course.

The crowd had begun to thin off from the more public streets; and the narrow ones were comparatively quiet and deserted. It was a long time since Aaron had ventured out at such an unseemly hour, and his courage being of the passive rather than the active kind, he began to feel far from comfortable at the loneliness about him. He kept a wary eye on all the dark corners, and gave a wide berth to every alley; which he felt certain was a lurking place for tall black-bearded ruffians armed with ropes, ready to sally out and strangle him on the spot, pack him up in an empty pork barrel, and sell him to an eminent physician, who would ask no questions, but would quietly boil him down, and make a skeleton of him before that time to-morrow night. At length he came to a street more dimly lighted than the others, and at the corner of this he stopped. It was so dark that he could not see a hundred yards; but within that space there was no one stirring.

'Here's a go!' muttered he, looking suspiciously about; 'a wery lonesome street! How a man might be invited to die here, wiolent! It smells of murder and arson, and sich. No matter,' said he, clearing his throat very loud, and straightening himself up: 'I'm under diwine pertection here as well as in my bed; though it *does* strike me that diwine pertection in my bed is a securer kind of pertection than diwine pertection just in this neighborhood.'

He continued standing still for full ten minutes, as if in expectation of the arrival of some person. But the only one who did make his appearance being a single man of a very cut-throat expression, who loitered slowly past him, his resolution was fast evaporating.

'If he is n't here in five minutes more,' he muttered, 'I'm off.'

To employ his thoughts during that interval, he very devoutly struck into a hymn, which considering all circumstances, he was delivering with a great fervor, when a gruff voice exclaimed in his ear :

'What yer raisin' such a row about? If there *is* a land of pure delight, where saints infernal dwell, as you 're tellin' all this 'ere neighborhood, *this* ain't it.'

'Is it you, Mr. Rawley?' inquired Aaron, a little tremulously.

'To be sure it is; and you — you 're the rummest man of your years I ever *did* see. Here 's this 'ere animal,' said he, pointing to his dog, 'has been a wantin' to walk into your mutton ever since we turned the corner. He hates melancholy tunes, and supposed you wanted to pick a quarrel with him.'

'It is a lonely spot, and a savage,' replied Aaron gravely.

'Pshaw! come along! There ain't much danger when you 've got *him* with you;' and Mr. Rawley nodded his head toward Wommut as he spoke.

Without farther remark, he turned on his heel, and walked rapidly on, (followed by his dog and Aaron, who took especial care to keep under the wing of so valiant a protector,) until he had crossed Broadway, and found himself in front of a large house in the neighborhood of Hudson-Square. Here he stopped.

'You wait here till I call you,' said he. He ascended the steps, rang the door-bell violently, and in a few moments was ushered into a richly-furnished room. At a table sat Mr. Fisk engaged in writing. A number of papers were unfolded in front of him ; and one or two law-books were lying open, as if he had just been referring to them.

He looked up as Mr. Rawley entered, but did not speak or rise.

Mr. Rawley deliberately walked to the table, laid his cane on it, and wiping his forehead with a cotton handkerchief which he drew from his hat, said :

'I 've brung the indiwidooal.'

'Who?' demanded Mr. Fisk.

'Him — the widder's man — the one we was arter."

'Where is he?'

'In the street. You need 'nt call him till you want him.'

'I want him now ; beside, he might get tired and go off.'

There was something so ludicrous in the idea of Aaron's going off, that Mr. Rawley shut his eyes, and compressing his lips, indulged himself in a fit of violent internal laughter, which threatened to shake him to pieces, and caused his stomach to quiver and undulate like a large jelly.

When he had partly recovered, he said :

'Bless your soul! *He* go! He can 't! When I came in, I tipped Wommut a wink ; that was enough. *Let* him go off arter that, that 's all. If he does, he 'll leave a pound of man's flesh in the keeping of that there waluable animal.' And here Mr. Rawley was attacked by another violent fit of merriment. 'There ain't a constable,' he continued 'nor deputy-sheriff like him for hanging on. A bone won't buy him off. He settles all the quarrels between me and my customers, and seems to take a pride in it.'

Mr. Fisk then told him that as it was growing late, and it would be better to introduce Aaron at once. Whereupon Mr. Rawley vanished, and in a few minutes returned, followed by the man-servant and Wommut. The latter walked stiffly across the room, and seated himself on the rug directly in front of the fire, while Aaron paused at the door. Mr. Fisk told him to come in, and to take a chair, which he did; and having perched himself in a very uncomfortable position on the extreme edge of it, attempted to look about him with an air of total unconcern, in which he signally failed. Mr. Rawley in the mean time betook himself to a long arm-chair, planted the end of his cane firmly on the floor, and clasping both hands over the head of it, rested his chin on them, and rolled his eyes from Aaron to the lawyer with a look of keen and cunning interest.

Mr. Fisk, after a few casual remarks, during which Aaron so far recovered his composure as to seat himself comfortably, asked if he was acquainted with one George Wilkins.

'Of course I am,' replied Aaron, confidently: 'have n't I let him in at the widder's twice a week reg'lar, except the two months he was away at the South?'

Mr. Fisk made a memorandum on a piece of paper in front of him. 'Now Aaron,' said he, 'I want you to answer, as accurately as if you were under oath, all that I shall ask. You know my object, I suppose?'

'This gen'leman,' said Aaron, pointing toward Mr. Rawley, 'says you're to prevent that Wilkins from marrying Mrs. Dow, the widder. I want the same thing too.'

Mr. Fisk looked at Mr. Rawley, who was going through a series of the most extraordinary contortions of countenance, for the purpose of giving him a hint to confirm the story which he had fabricated, to enlist Aaron in their interest. Then without paying the slightest attention to the extraordinary performance, he said:

'Such was *not* our purpose; although, if we succeed, Wilkins will have something else to do than to persecute your mistress with his attentions; and may find his motions somewhat less at his own command than they have hitherto been.'

Aaron looked earnestly at him, and then uttered with an interrogatory jerk of the head the single word 'Penitentiary?'

Mr. Fisk nodded.

'Go on, Sir — go on!' exclaimed the other, rubbing his hands violently, and giving several other peculiar indications of intense satisfaction. 'I 'm ready.'

'Well then,' said the lawyer, 'to save time, confine your answers strictly to the questions I shall ask. You mentioned that you knew this Wilkins?'

'I do,' replied Aaron laconically.

'What kind of a man is he!'

'Tall man, black hair and whiskers; owdacious and rascally; bad cut to his eye.'

'Wounded in the eye?' inquired Mr. Fisk.

Aaron stared at him, as if he did not understand.

'You said he was cut in the eye,' repeated the lawyer.

'I did n't,' replied Aaron, energetically. 'I said the cut of his eye was bad.'

Here Mr. Rawley laughed so prodigiously, that he was attacked with a violent fit of coughing; whereupon Wommut rose, and walked leisurely around the table, to see if any thing was required in his line. Finding that there was not, he returned to the rug, where he remained the rest of the evening, winking and blinking, with his nose so close to the fire that he could not keep his eyes open.

When Mr. Rawley became somewhat composed, Mr. Fisk went on with his inquiries.

'When did Wilkins go to the South?'

'In the end of July last.'

'Ah! that's important.   You 're sure of that?' said the lawyer, with some animation.

'I 'll swear to it,' replied Aaron, resolutely.

'When did he come back?'

'In the middle of September.   I can tell the very day when I get home.   I made a note of it.'

Mr. Fisk rubbed his hands with an appearance of still greater animation.

'Are you sure he did not return before that?'

'I am,' replied Aaron; 'but he wrote reg'lar.   His letters was n't post-paid nuther.'

'How do you know he wrote them?'

Aaron, acting upon the well-known principle of law that no one is obliged to criminate himself, remained silent.   Mr. Fisk saw the dilemma, and inquired what they contained.

'Love, of the sweetest mixtur'.'

'Could you get one of them?'

'It can't be did,' replied the other, with the decided manner of one who felt confident of what he asserted; 'it's totally onpossible.   They 're under lock and key, in the red box with her best teeth, and she keeps the key herself.   Them letters was of the urgentest kind,' said he, with increasing animation; 'they was alarming in their natur'; and what 's to be did, must be did soon; for it 's not onpossible that the widder might elope with him if it 's put off.   She 's getting dreadful desp'rate.'

'No fear of that!' replied Mr. Fisk.   'If *she* is ready Wilkins is not.   He 's married already, and will not risk taking a second wife untill he gets rid of the first.'

The man-servant rose erect, his hair bristling nearly as straight up as himself, as he exclaimed:

'Married!   Got a wife!'

The lawyer nodded.

Aaron gave a rapid flourish of the right leg, intended for a caper, snapped his fingers, uttered a loud laugh which terminated in a whistle, and then suddenly recollecting where he was, stopped short, and looked earnestly at the opposite wall, as if he had just made some important discovery in that quarter.

Mr. Fisk waited until this violent effervescence had in a measure subsided, and then said: 'I wish you to remember that this conversation is strictly confidential; and that whatever you may learn from either Mr. Rawley or myself respecting Wilkins or his associates is not to be communicated to any one, and least of all to Mrs. Dow.   It is not our intention that he shall escape us, or be enabled to carry out his designs against your mistress or any other person ; but in order to insure success, we must be secret ; for if our plans are discovered before they are ripe, they will be frustrated.'

Aaron promised the required secrecy ; and a long conversation then followed between him and the lawyer, in which the latter learned much respecting the habits and character of Wilkins ; though but little as to that of his companion Higgs, of whom Aaron had never even heard. Enough however had been elicited to satisfy Mr. Fisk that he had obtained a clue which would enable Miss Crawford to contend success-fully against the will, and to throw upon it a suspicion of forgery, which he imagined it impossible that they could remove.

After making several notes and memoranda, he threw down his pen with the air of a man satisfied with his work, and told Aaron that he considered his information of much importance, and appointed a time at which to see him again.   He then thanked him for the trouble he had taken ; and said that he would not detain him any longer.   Aaron understood this as a hint to go about his business ; so he took up his hat, and being again assured that his mistress should come to no harm, and once more enjoined to secrecy, he departed, after lingering for a moment, in the hope that Mr. Rawley would offer to accompany him. That gentleman however made no motion of the kind ; so he set out alone.   His way was through streets dimly lighted, traversing a part of the city notorious for crime and midnight violence.   Stealing along like a thief, now muttering a prayer, now an exclamation of terror, and now startled at the sound of his own footsteps as they echoed on the stone pavement, he at last reached the door of his home.   Cautiously unlocking it, and closing it noiselessly, he stole up stairs and crept into bed, where his heavy breathing soon indicated that for the present he was at rest.

A H ,   C O M E   T O   M E .

In deep and utter loneliness,
In the very earnest wretchedness
Of sorrow and heart-weariness,
I call on thee : Ah! come to me, Mary.

The hours that once flew swiftly by,
Too swift indeed when thou wast nigh,
Now labor onward heavily :
How heavily ! Ah! come to me, Mary.

Come, let me yield me to thy spell,
For oh! I love — how truly well
These quivering lips, these hot tears tell,
Couldst thou but see : Ah! come to me, Mary.

Come with thy smile of other days,
Come with thy gentle, winning ways,
Come with thy gloom-dispelling rays!
I yearn for thee : Ah! come to me, Mary.

LITERARY NOTICES.

GOD THE GUARDIAN OF THE POOR, AND THE BANK OF FAITH : or a Display of the Providences of GOD which have at sundry times attended the Author. In one volume. 8vo. pp. 350. Lowell, (Mass.) P. D. AND T. S. EDMANDS. Boston: SAXTON AND PIERCE.

'WILLIAM HUNTINGTON, S. S., Minister of the Gospel at Providence Chapel, Little Titchfield-street and at Monkwell-street Meeting,' London, and the author of the volume whose title is given above, is one of that class of groaning and garrulous gentlemen of whom SIDNEY SMITH wrote ; one of those didactic artisans who through indolence and impudence come at last to be denominated 'gospel preachers and vital clergymen,' and who go itinerating about, practically to set forth how narrow is the interval between a church and a lunatic asylum. Having tried the business of coal-heaving, with other intellectual avocations, including cobbling, our Jack-at-all-trades being at conventicle, is seized with 'a call' as he conceives thenceforth to 'dispense the word.' We accordingly soon find him assiduously engaged in his new avocation ; itinerating, preaching, and begging ; in short a clerical JEREMY DIDDLER, infinitely more accomplished in his art than his great prototype ; fancying, moreover, that the ALMIGHTY has an *especial* eye upon his temporal wants ; looking after his wardrobe, and securing him little conveniences of various sorts, which he had previously intimated he would be very glad to obtain. At one time we find him 'greatly in need of a parsonic livery ;' and having prayed for a new suit of clothes, he tells us :

"A few days after this I was desired to call at a gentleman's house near London. Indeed it had been impressed on my mind for six weeks before, that God would use that gentleman as an instrument to furnish me with my next suit. And so it fell out : for, when I called on him, upon leaving his house he went a little way with me ; and while we were on the road he said, 'I think you want a suit of clothes.' I answered, 'Yes, Sir, I do ; and I know a poor man that would be very glad of this which I have on, if my Master would furnish me with another.' When we parted he desired me to call on him the next morning, which I accordingly did ; when he sent a tailor into the room, and generously told me to be measured for what clothes I chose, and a great-coat also. When I got the new, I furnished the poor man with my old suit. This was the fourth suit of apparel that my Master gave me in this providential manner, in answer to the prayer of faith. Thus God, who kept Israel's clothes from waxing old, though in constant use for forty years, gave me a new suit every year."

We next find our reverend coal-heaver complaining that travelling on foot from pillar to post, preaching twenty or thirty 'sermons' a week, is no joke; and he adds, reasonably enough :

"Finding myself wholly unable to perform all his labor, I went to prayer, and besought God to give me more strength, less work, and a horse. I used my *prayers* as gunners use their *swivels* ; turning them every way as the various cases required. I then hired a horse to ride to town ; and, when I came there, went to put him up at Mr. Jackson's livery-stables, near the chapel, in Margaret street ; but the ostler told me they had not room to take him in. I asked if his master was in the yard. He said, yes. I desired to see him ; and he told me he could not take the horse in. I was then going out of the yard, when he stepped after me, and asked if I was the person that preached at Margaret-street chapel. I told him I was. He burst into tears, saying he would send one of his own horses out and take mine in ; and informed me of his coming one night to hear me out of curiosity, because he had been informed that I had been a coal-heaver. He said that some of my friends had been gathering money to buy me a horse, and that he gave something toward him. Directly after I found the horse was bought and paid for ; and one person gave me a guinea to buy a bridle, another gave me two whips, a third gave me some things necessary for the stable, another trusted me for a saddle ; and here was a full answer to my prayer. So I mounted my horse and rode home ; and he turned out as good an animal as ever was rode. I believe this horse was the gift of God, because he tells me in his word that all the beasts of the forest are his, and so are the cattle on a thousand hills. I have often thought that, if my horse could have spoken, he would have had more to say than Balaam's ass ; as he might have said : 'I am an answer to my master's prayers ; I live by my master's faith, travel with mysteries, and suffer persecution, but I do not know for what :' for many a stone has been thrown at him.''

Our clerical cobbler need not have gone so far back to find an ass that had more to say than Balaam's, and much less to the purpose. Meeting with such invariable success — not a little enhanced, we may suppose, by emulous auditors of his 'experiences' in this kind — it is not to be wondered at that our mendicant divine continues his exertions :

" Having now had my horse for some time, and riding a great deal every week, I soon wore my breeches out, as they were not fit to ride in. I hope the reader will excuse my mentioning the word *breeches*, which I should have avoided, had not this passage of scripture obtruded into my mind, just as I had resolved in my own thoughts not to mention this kind providence of God : 'And thou shalt make them linen breeches to cover their nakedness ; from the loins even unto the thighs shall they reach. And they shall be upon Aaron and upon his sons when they come into the tabernacle of the congregation, or when they come near unto the altar to minister in the holy place ; that they bear not iniquity and die. It shall be a statute forever unto him and his seed after him.' · · · 'When I came to London I called on Mr. Croucher, a shoe-maker in Shepherd's Market, who told me a parcel was left there for me, but what it was he knew not. I opened it, and behold there was a pair of *leather breeches* with a note in them ! — the substance of which was, to the best of my remembrance, as follows :

" 'Sir : I have sent you a pair of breeches, and hope they will fit. I beg your acceptance of them ; and, if they want any alteration, leave in a note what the alteration is, and I will call in a few days and alter them. ⸱. s.'

" I tried them on, and they fitted as well as if I had been measured for them ; at which I was amazed, having never been measured by any leather-breeches maker in London. I wrote an answer to the note to this effect :

" 'Sir : I received your present, and thank you for it. I was going to order a pair of leather breeches to be made, because I did not know till now that my Master had bespoke them of you. They fit very well, which fully convinces me, that the same God who moved thy heart to give, guided thy hand to cut ; because he perfectly knows my size, having clothed me in a miraculous manner for near five years. When you are in trouble, Sir, I hope you will tell my Master of this, and what you have done for me, and he will repay you with honor.' ''

MAWWORM, in the play of the 'Hypocrite,' and the REV. MR. STIGGINS, one of DICKENS' striking creations, have been thought to be caricatures ; but the 'experiences' of such prelates as Mr. HUNTINGTON would seem to establish the identity of their class beyond all gainsaying. But let us present one more 'remarkable providence :'

" Another year having rolled over my head, I began to look about for my livery ; for I always took care to let my most propitious Master know when my year was out. And indeed I wanted it had enough, for riding on horseback soiled my clothes much more than walking did. · · · At length I was informed by Mr. Byrchmore that a gentleman in Wells-street wanted to see me. Accordingly I went ; and was admitted into the parlor to the gentleman and his spouse. He wept, and begged I would not be angry at what he was going to relate ; which was, that he had for some time desired to make me a present of a suit of clothes, but was afraid that I should be offended at his offer, and refuse it. 'Ah !' says Envy, 'there need be no fear of that, for Methodist parsons are all for what they can get.' It is true ; for we are commanded to 'covet earnestly the best things ;' and so we do, and expect a double reward of the Lord — one in this world, the other in the next. And this is no more than our Master has promised to give us ; for we are to 'receive an hundred fold in this world, and in the world to come, life everlasting.' I told the good man that I had been for some time expecting a suit of clothes, but knew not how to procure them. They both wept for joy upon my accepting them, and I wept for joy that they gave them so freely. As they had been fearful that I should be offended at their offer, and not receive them ; so I had been much exercised in my mind, lest my Master would not give them to me, as he usually had done. However, our minds were now eased of our fears, on both sides, and I was clothed ; and it was the best suit that I ever had. This is the fifth livery that my trembling hand of faith put on my back, and every one came from a different quarter.''

'It pleased God,' says Mr. Huntington, 'to keep me depending on his providence from hand to mouth, throughout the whole course of my pilgrimage.' At one time we find him complaining of the great difficulty of 'carrying on preaching a dozen times a week, and the business of cobbling at the same time;' and he therefore disposes of his 'kit of tools and a little leather, and throws himself entirely on the propitious arm of Providence;' not without evident internal grumbling at the small temporal reward he had hitherto received for exercising his clerical functions. He lacks the candor of the Indian missionary at Catawba, who received ten dollars a month for preaching to his red brethren at two 'stations,' and who, in answer to the remark of a profane layman that 'that was d—d poor pay,' said: 'Yes; but d—d poor *preach* too!' It is certain that Mr. Huntington's manner was not of the most polished description. He himself tells us: 'Being a native of the Wild of Kent, which is none of the most polite parts of the world, I retained a good deal of my provincial dialect; and many of my expressions, to the ears of a grammarian, sounded very harsh and uncouth. This circumstance caused many unsanctified critics to laugh and cavil at me. But, when God permitted me to drop promiscuously into company with any of those who were so very learned, and they began to pour contempt on some of my expressions, I generally found them very deficient in the work of the Spirit on their own souls.' It is to be feared also that his habits were slightly lax, especially in the matter of temperance. The beer he tells us which he drank for some years together, 'brought him at one time so low that he was compelled to gird his stomach with a handkerchief as tight as he could bear it, in order to gather strength to enable him to deliver three discourses a day!' At length he 'got so weak and low, that a pint of good beer rendered him incapable of walking steady,' and he could no longer gird up his loins and address himself to his great task. Howbeit, leaving off beer, he finally recovers; and soon after appears as an amateur gardener; adding to his professional gains by secular labors and 'home vegetables.' His new recreation had probably been suggested by looking over the religious advertisements of his sect, mentioned by the Edinburgh reviewer: 'Wanted, a man to take charge of a carriage, and a pair of horses of a religious turn of mind;' 'Wanted, a pious gardener, to take charge of a charity garden; pleasant employment, and small wages,' etc. *Apropos* of this. Here is an example of the manner in which our author 'improves' all subjects:

"While I was walking about by myself among the flowers, a well-dressed motherly-looking woman stepped up to me, and supposing me to be a gardener, (for my appearance was more like a slave than a prelate,) she thus addressed me in a free and jocose manner: 'Now, Mr. Gardener, if you please, I want a root to put in my pot; and it must be a root that will last.' I looked up very seriously at the lady, and replied: 'Well, I believe I can tell you where you may get such a root.' At this answer she smilingly asked, 'Where?' I answered, 'In the book of Job; for he says 'The root of the matter is found in me.' Job xix, 28. And if you can get that root into your pot, both the root and the pot will last for ever.' She then asked, 'And pray have you got that root in you?' I answered her, 'I verily believe I have.' Upon which she replied, 'It is well with you, and it is very true what you have said.' "

The volume before us is from the *seventh* London edition; and our readers will perhaps find in this fact an excuse for devoting thus much of our space to its discussion. The ignorance, impudence, vain-gloriousness, and hypocrisy of the author, we would fain hope, will find fewer admirers in this country. Such books and such divines bring religion into contempt; and that which might have its perfect work if rightly dispensed, becomes a mockery and a by-word. The volume was written 'to get a little money,' 'God's hand having been quite shut up for some time,' and the author suffering at the same period, as he informs us, with his usual infirmity, 'gout in the pocket.' He 'wrote the work off hand,' and doubted not the Almighty would cause it to turn out a very fair speculation! What wretched profanity and self-delusion!

SKETCHES OF NEW-ENGLAND, OR MEMORIES OF THE COUNTRY. BY JOHN CARVER, Esquire, Justice of the Peace and Quorum. In one volume. pp. 286. New-York: E. FRENCH, Fulton-street.

WE have already announced the volume before us, and informed our readers that several of its divisions had heretofore appeared in the KNICKERBOCKER, under the general title of ' *Sketches of the Country.*' These pictures of New-England are dedicated to ' Yankee absentees, than whom none better know that ' Home is home, though never so homely.' The author is evidently devotedly attached to Yankee-land. He was born, he tells us, on the banks of one of her beautiful rivers, and was nurtured among her mountains. He boasts his descent ' direct from one of those stern old Puritans who chartered the Mayflower, and much of his childhood was spent on the very homestead where the good man pitched his tent and cleared his land. Like many of her sons indeed, he has in riper years wandered over sundry parts of the world, and has seen and known much of its excellence and beauty; but he has always returned to the ' rude and rocky shore' of New-England, with new love for her homes and her institutions — new respect for her hardy sons. He is willing to confess that all his predilections are for New-England; that although ' Abana and Pharpar, rivers of Damascus, are better than all' her streams, he loves them not as well; that he would live upon her barren soil, and die there among his kindred.' The writer assures his readers that his description of manners is of what he has *seen*, and his delineations of character are of those who have been his neighbors and acquaintances. Hence we can well believe with him, that ' there are many whose memories will bear testimony to the faithfulness with which he has endeavored to transfer to paper an outline of the beautiful scenery which is spread all over the hill-sides and river banks, and rich cultivated meadows of New-England; and not a few will follow him through her homesteads and into her cottages with the awakened feelings of a glad and hardy boyhood.'

The readers of the KNICKERBOCKER being familiar with the characteristics of our author's style, we proceed without comment to one or two extracts from ' The Village,' a sketch as we infer of the writer's native place. The whole reminds us of an admirable article written for these pages by Miss SEDGWICK, entitled ' *Our Burial-Place.*' Each is a reminiscence of departed friends:

" I must not forget good Deacon B——, the spiritual father of our Israel! He was the conservator of the church, the keeper of the flock, the shepherd of the little ones, the right-hand man of the pastor. Good old Deacon B——! Light lie the earth upon his ashes! Methinks I see him now, his gray head raised above the people at the evening conference, his trembling hands folded before him, pleading earnestly with his God for spiritual blessings to descend on the Zion he so dearly loved. He lived for Christ, and died as he had lived. On the day of his death, as he sat calm, unmoved, cheerful, smoking his pipe, and dwelling on the goodness of his Saviour, his constant theme, his daughter said, ' What message shall I give to the children, father, when I see them?'

" ' Tell them,' said the good old saint, ' in the words of my blessed Master, that having loved my own that are in the world, I have loved them unto the end.' And so, full of days, peaceful, trusting, he went to his grave, as a shock of corn fully ripe cometh in, in its season."

From a very graphic sketch of the village doctor we segregate the annexed pleasant anecdote:

" Dr. Biddle was no contemptible humorist; and his jokes, poor man! are still remembered by his townsmen, and repeated far oftener than his wonderful cures. At a social supper one evening, when all the family were present, and merriment and good humor had prevailed, Dr. Biddle, who was somewhat of a proser over his cups, had wearied the company with a long story of a child, and patient of his, having been gazetted as dead in the county newspaper, two days before its decease took place. ' What did they mean? How in Heaven's name could they know, two days beforehand, that the child would die?' ' Well enough,' says Dr. Biddle. ' How so?' replied the other; ' from the nature of the disease?' ' No, no!' dryly responded Biddle; ' but from the nature of the *physician!*'"

The following incident in the life of the good old minister of P —— is not rare in the history of many of the patriotic divines of his day:

"His early interest in behalf of the struggling colonies for their independence, and his own active exertions in the good cause, will not be soon forgotten. He marched with the recruits, who hastily enlisted when Burgoyne was on his rapid march from the Canadas, encouraged them by his eloquence and example, cheerfully endured their fatigues and hardships as a common soldier, and took an active part in that engagement which brought such glory to the American arms. It is related of him, that on arriving in sight of the British army, with his characteristic enthusiasm and fearlessness of danger, he mounted a stump and called out with his stentorian voice, ' In the name of God and the Continental Congress, I command you to lay down your arms.' A hundred balls came whistling at once through the air around the veteran, who, waving his hand with undaunted defiance, quietly dismounted from his dangerous position, and fell back into the lines."

In the sketch of the village of P —— we have this picture of a ' brave old elm' which stands in its centre-park:

"Beneath it the boys play their games of cricket and bass, and have played them an hundred years ; the swain whispers there his soft tale to the ruddy cheeked lass he loves ; the school-girls circle round it, in their soft-toned merriment ; Fourth-of-July brings to it crowds of mimic, noise-loving heroes, whose shots, and bruises, and unceasing crackings, the Old Tree, dressed in gay pennons and waving flags, receives upon his rough sides, like a hearty, hale veteran, as he is. The grave go there to meditate, and the gay to dance ; and strangers stand and admire the broad base and erect trunk of the unmatched elm."

The sketches which have already appeared in our pages, not less than these extracts, will doubtless attract attention to the excellent and various volume which we have pleasure in commending to general acceptance.

The Life of the Countess Emily Plater. Translated by J. K. Salomonski, a Polish Exile. In one volume. pp. 286. New-York: John F. Trow.

This interesting volume records one of the most prominent among the many instances of devotedness and patriotism to which the late Polish revolution gave birth. The name of Emily Plater, says our author, ' excites a thrilling emotion in every heart which is not insensible to feelings of honor and patriotism.' She was a young and lovely lady, of high birth, who served as a soldier in the national struggle, and died while yet in her prime, in the service of her unhappy country. The author, who was connected with the brave and beautiful countess by old family ties ; was proprietor of an estate in the neighborhood of her own, and her companion in arms on the plains of Lithuania ; has followed his heroine through her whole career. Having been made the confidant of her thoughts as well as a sharer in her dangers, the writer may well claim that her whole life is known to him. ' When proscribed,' says he, ' and, cast on the Prussian soil, I was compelled to seek an asylum in France, I lost sight of Emily Plater. Then, overcome by her continued fatigues, she was approaching her end. At the early age of twenty-six, she paid the forfeit to which the dreams of her ardent and almost supernatural enthusiasm had exposed her. But the particulars of her death have reached me. I have received letters dated from her sick chamber, and have personally questioned those who closed her eyes.' The reader will perceive that our author was in the outset in possession of all the materials necessary for a full biographical sketch of his noble heroine ; and they will find, on perusing his work, that he has made a good use of them. We are continually reminded, in perusing the spirit-stirring appeals and gallant deeds of the noble girl, of her great female prototype, Joan of Arc ; and if our readers desire to enjoy a kindred picture of single-minded, devoted heroism, let them peruse the records contained in the latter half of this beautiful volume. Then let them turn to the mild, sweet face in the beginning, and ask whether with *such* hearts Poland should not have been free.

EDITOR'S TABLE.

AN ARTISTICAL LETTER. — Dropping in the other evening upon an old and favorite correspondent, partly for the purpose of pleasant gossip, and partly to 'flesh our maiden spoon' in a tureen of authentic and savory *chowder*, we found him engaged in perusing a long epistle which he had just written he said to an artist-friend of his, and which he added he would read to us, if haply it might prove to our edification. It *was* edifying; insomuch that we begged permission to rob his correspondent of its perusal until he should encounter it in these pages 'in all the dignity of type.' Looking fondly at his new portrait, which has an *interior* look, as if the living, thinking original had himself stepped into the frame, he 'with unwilling willingness gave a faint consent' to our request; and the following is the result.

LETTER TO W. PAGE, ARTIST.

'SIR: According to your wish, I will recount to you the opinions of my household on your picture. But I must confess that I could not at first understand why you were anxious to know the judgments of those who (as I thought) were the most unfit persons in the world to give an intelligent opinion as to the merits of a portrait. Subsequent observation however has convinced me that a man's 'wife and weans' are the most competent judges in such a matter; upon the same principle that the birds which pecked at the painted cherries, and the bees that would not alight on muslin flowers were the most exquisite critics of their day, although they were as ignorant of the rules of art as birds and bees are now.

'It was Christmas eve, and I had promised Mrs. F. a present; but as I wanted to enjoy her surprise, I would not tell her what it was to be; consequently when I reached home I found her in quite a feverish condition; but I pretended not to notice it, and told John, in a careless and unconcerned manner, to take *the box* into the back parlor and bring me the key of the door. The Christmas-tree for the children was in the back parlor; and you may be sure that my wife's face was not the only one that looked a little flushed when we sat down to tea. Every thing went wrong at the table, and nobody was suited. One had too much milk, and another too little; C. complained that his tea was too strong, while his sister got nothing but water. It was very evident that the presiding officer was disconcerted; and I began to grow apprehensive that I had carried the joke a trifle too far; but I preserved the most perfect self-possession, and regarded the anxious looks of my wife and children with the air of a juryman about to pronounce judgment upon a trembling culprit.

'When at last the ceremony of tea-drinking was over, I proceeded leisurely to the back parlor, previously requesting Mrs F., when she heard a rap on the floor, to come in with all the children and the servants. While John and myself were engaged in hanging the picture, we heard a good many feet creeping stealthily past the door, and once I thought I could hear some body breathing at the key-hole; but as my wife solemnly averred that she did not move from the tea-room until I gave the signal agreed upon, I must acquit her of any undue curiosity, although I am not sure that she did not commission her sister to try to get a peep at the 'present.' When the picture was properly hung, and the candles on the Christmas-tree all lighted, John threw open the folding-doors, and in rushed the children with a joyous shout, the cook and chamber-maid, my wife's mother and sister, and last of all, my wife. It was a great exercise of virtue in her to bring up the rear; and knowing what it had cost her, I could not but reproach myself for having tried her so severely. The Christmas-tree with its bright lights and trinkets attracted the first looks; but the portrait soon caught their attention; and then such a clapping of hands followed as sometimes welcomes a favorite orator at a public meeting. They all declared with one voice that it was 'first-rate.' My wife said at first that it was worth a thousand dollars; but after looking at it a short time longer, she declared that ten thousand dollars would not tempt her to part with it. This was a high compliment to both you and me; and I do not know but that it might have been carried to a much greater extent, had I not in the excitement of the moment clasped her to my breast and kissed off a tear that I saw trickling down her cheek. This slight diverticle caused something of a sensation among the children.

'Order however was soon restored, and they all began to deliver their opinions. Wife's mother declared with an earnestness that left no doubt of her sincerity, that it was 'the completest pictur' she had seen since she first breathed the breath of life,' a period of time supposed to include about seventy years, although nothing certain is known on the subject, she having with the ingenuousness of a young girl of thirty torn the leaf out of the family Bible in which the date of her birth was recorded. Little Mary, my pet of all the little ones, merely said 'Oh that's papa!' and then looking at me, she added: 'And here's my papa!' It was clearly a puzzle to her how I could be in two places at once. But she was not philosopher enough to doubt the evidence of her eyes. She saw an impossible fact, and was willing to believe it, although she knew it could not be true. The cook gave a decided opinion at the first glance: 'Well now, I declare if that aint the Governor himself! Sure an' it is! Upon my sowl, Mr. F., he has done you to a turn! Only look at the mouth! It is all ready to eat something. Upon my conscience, Mr. F., I don't believe the Lord-leftenant of Ireland was ever served up better nor that. Indeed I do n't.' This was extravagant praise, considering whence it came; for Mrs. Dougherty is fully alive to the sentiment that 'fine words butter no parsneps,' and she has never been famous for using them too lavishly. Ellen, the chamber-maid, being asked how she liked the picture, replied that 'it was no picture at all; it was life.' This was a very satisfactory reply, and it convinced me that Ellen was not always a chamber-maid; an opinion that I have long held. I cannot say that she has seen better days, for she seems entirely happy; as well she may, having a quiet home, light work, and good wages.

'The boys, rogues that they are, said a good many things to each other in an under tone, that caused no small merriment among themselves; but each one declared in turn that some particular feature was the best; so that the eyes and mouth and nose each found an advocate, which satisfied me that neither was exaggerated. My wife's sister, who has recently returned from Boston with a slight tinge of transcendentalism, was the last to give an opinion. She thought that the finest part of the picture was the soul. This caused every one to look with a closer scrutiny than before. Unlike other portraits that she had seen, the spirituality of the subject was more apparent than the paint; she did not know why or how it was, but there was a quality of life about it that seemed to sympathize with her. She knew that it was an illusion, and she was trying to detect the art by which it was produced, but she could not. She could now realize something of the enthusiasm of those who had seen and knew how to appreciate the great works of the great masters. – Here was the grand effect of art that she had often sighed for but had never seen before. It was like reading a fine poem, or as she expressed it, a *true* poem, when the spirit of the poet infuses itself into the reader without a consciousness on his part whether it be conveyed in blank verse or rhyme. And what surprised her more than all was, that the longer she looked the more perfect the illusion grew; and instead of detecting the art which produced it she lost sight of it altogether; and at last she begged me to speak, that she might know which was the picture. She would not trust herself alone in the room with it, lest she might be tempted to scratch it, to convince herself that there was not life beneath the surface. As I have had some astounding experience in regard to female curiosity, I have determined to carry the key of the back parlor in my pocket until my wife's sister goes home.

'Many more remarks were made, but they were all of the same tenor; and as you will be able to gather from what I have recorded, the general suffrage, and so judge of your own work by the opinions of others, I will relate no more of what was said, but 'conclude with a few general remarks,' as sermonizers have it, relating to the subject, which I let fall myself. Ellen the chamber-maid and Mrs. Dougherty our culinary professor having withdrawn to the kitchen, I requested my wife and the children to be seated, and having wiped my glasses and adjusted them with that degree of solemn precision which usually indicates a set speech in those who wear such dignified adjuncts, I delivered the following remarks to a very attentive auditory. Whether they listened or not I do not know; but as they knew what the consequences of seeming inattention would be, they *appeared* to take especial note of what I said.

' 'It is very common for thoughtless people to say that they are no judges of paintings; and even you, Fidelia, (turning to my wife's sister,) have often said the same thing; and yet your remarks this evening prove you to be a very competent judge; and even our darling little Mary, who never saw a picture before, is a very good judge; and I am very much mistaken if Mr. Page be not more flattered by her decision than he would be by that of any grown-up connoisseurs.' At this my little pet opened her bright blue eyes and laughed, as much as to say, 'That is *so* funny!' And then I was forced to suspend my observations while each one of the audience gave little Mary a kiss; after which, to avoid farther interruptions of the kind, I did violence to my feelings, and ordered her to be taken down to the nursery, and then resumed my remarks.

' 'The best judgment on a picture is by no means that which is expressed in artistical terms. Painting being above all others an imitative art, the merits of a picture must be felt; and nature being the only standard by which it can be tried, the conventional terms of art are too positive to convey an idea of the relative quality of a work, the merit of which must depend altogether upon its resemblance to an original. You may say that a picture has great breadth, or warmth, or truth; but if it be not as broad, and as warm, and as true as truth, how can you express the degree of truth it may possess? The only merit that a painting can have is its truthfulness; and to judge of this, no artificial schooling is required; but to learn to distinguish the works of one painter from another, which is rather done by studying their defects than their merits, requires a peculiar organization and opportunities for observation which but few enjoy. And it is this talent which gives a man the distinction of being a judge of paintings, rather than the ability, which most men possess, to judge of the excellence of a picture *per se.*

 ' 'This picture is probably the only good painting that either of you has ever seen; and yet you cannot be fully conscious of its merits, unless you compare it with one of an inferior order. It may appear paradoxical to you, but it is nevertheless true, that its great excellence is the cause of its not striking you as an extraordinary production. It is simply a true copy from nature; and while you see the original before you, it cannot strike you as a wonderful thing, unless you know something of the difficulty of producing it. I have seen, as you know, many of the famous pictures in Europe, and all that are worth seeing in our own country; but I am constrained to aver that I have never seen but one finer portrait, and that was painted by the same artist who painted this. You think this extravagant praise, and so it is. All praise is extravagant that exceeds the general opinion; but there must be a beginning in pronouncing right judgment; and why should I hesitate to declare what I feel to be true, lest it should conflict with the prejudices of those who watch the wind of public favor before they shape their opinions? The great names in art whom all men now praise once stood in need of the commendations of their neighbors. Even the picture that I have just alluded to was last year pronounced ' unfit for exhibition ' by a newspaper critic who made use of terms of art as freely as though he had been cradled upon an easel; and yet an artist fresh from Florence pronounced the same picture equal to a TITIAN. And so it is.

 ' 'The merit of this picture is very great. It has all the excellences of the art. The drawing is faultless; the position is free without carelessness; and while the most perfect truthfulness is preserved, it is neither common-place nor familiar; but a certain air of historic dignity is imparted to the subject, without in the least destroying its vraisemblance. It possesses that rare quality which modern painters have imagined, from their own inability to impart it, belonged to the subjects of VAN DYKE rather than to his skill; but if they had reflected that the contemporaries of VAN DYKE failed where they have failed, they would perhaps have attributed the effect to the right cause. Here are none of the aids of a novel or picturesque costume; and it is doubtful whether a ruff and a velvet doublet would add any thing to the picturesque effect of the painting. The face is by no means handsome, and the skin is bilious; perhaps a painter could not have a worse subject; and yet how real and life-like is the flesh; how sweetly the double-lights are managed; and how clear and transparent are the shadows! They are entirely free from that smuttiness so common in the works of the great mass of modern painters. Observe how clean the linen is, and yet there is nothing in its appearance that reminds you of white paint. See how the light glistens in the hair; you feel that a breath of wind would rustle it. It is a near approach, if not equal, in this regard to some of PAUL POTTER'S pictures. The hand is a real living hand, composed of bones and muscles.

It does not remind you of a bunch of parsneps, as most hands do that you see in portraits; but you feel an inclination to extend your own toward it to grasp it.   But the picture possesses a merit above and beyond all these things.   As Fidelia said, it has a *soul.*   It is not a mere frontispiece, a mask with shoulders, but it has a basiliar region as well as a frontal; and there is a sentient spirit beneath the surface, which you can feel although you cannot see it; and there is a warm fleshly heart and blood and bones beneath that brown vest.   This is the highest reach of art.   The mind sees more than the eye.

'' All the great painters have a manner of their own, but scarcely any two of Mr. PAGE's pictures are alike.   His only peculiarity is his excellence.   His fertility of expression is wonderful.   Some have said that he experiments too much; but his experimenting is not like SIR JOSHUA's, for he is as certain of his effect as the house-painter that paints your Venetian blinds   In truth, he rather plays with his pigments than experiments with them.   You are apprehensive when he takes up his brush, from his seeming indifference, that he will spoil the effect he has already produced, and you discover that he has bettered it, although you thought it impossible.   He has neither strong lights nor deep shadows, and yet his subjects come out of their canvass as if by some magical influence.   You see one of his old men, and you think that old men are his forte; but you turn to his women and children, and you think that he is most at home in the drawing-room and the nursery.   The secret of his success is, he copies Nature without exaggerating her, and he has the discrimination to copy only her most pleasing points.   Perhaps it might be infringing on his rights to detail his method of handling; but if you would know his secrets go and sit to him.

'' Mr. PAGE has had but scanty encouragement from the press, although his merits are fully appreciated by the discerning few who are acquainted with him and his pictures.   Perhaps the critics are afraid of spoiling him by too much praise; I have seen such ideas in print; but what a poor creature a man must be who can be injured by praise!   No true genius ever was.   Could praise have spoilt SHAKSPERE or HOGARTH?   Surely, if excessive laudation could hurt a noble spirit, or render nerveless the soaring wings of genius, the world's favorite, the pet of two hemispheres, the inimitable DICKENS, would have been a ruined man in the first year of his literary advent; for like the young scions of royalty, the first words that greeted him were those of adulation and praise.   But the sun's rays never melted but one pair of wings, and those were waxen.

'' Mr. PAGE has never seen a really fine picture, except those that he has painted himself; for he has too much patriotism to leave his own country, and too much good sense to imagine that excellence can be attained in the arts by studying in any other school than that of Nature.   From these considerations alone he has resisted all the allurements held out to him to visit Italy, (an artist can well understand how potent these can be,) and this should insure him the very highest regards of his countrymen, even though his merit were not half what it really is.   He is at present engaged on a large historical picture, which when finished will cause a sensation in the world, and give a character to American art that it has never yet attained; although we can number among our painters such names as STUART, ALLSTON, and TRUMBULL.'

'' Of course,' said my wife, ' Mr. PAGE is overrun with sitters.'

'' That is a very natural supposition, my dear,' I replied; ' for I know of no better investment, in a pecuniary view, than to lay out the money that it would cost in buying one of his pictures; nor a dearer legacy that a parent could bequeath to his children than one of his portraits. What would I not give for such a portrait of my poor mother as he could have painted!'

'Or of our little Emma, who is now in heaven,' said my wife.

'This last remark gave such a serious turn to our thoughts, that to restore cheerfulness once more, I dropped the subject of pictures, and turned round to the Christmas-tree to distribute the little gifts with which its branches were loaded. But alas! The Christmas-tree was not there. My wife! where was she? The boys were gone. Even the boys and wife's mother, like Fidelia and the rest, had never been. They were phantoms to whom I had been talking. The very fire which had glowed so brightly was not! It had gone out with the things that haunt us and depart, perchance to haunt us again The portrait alone was left. The clock ticked sharply in the dead silence of midnight; it was the only voice that responded to mine; and I was left, as I fear this may find you, dear P., literally without a sitter. H. F.'

'LITTLE-PEDLINGTONIANA.' — There turned up recently among our miscellaneous collection of original manuscripts, a mislaid sheet of a review of POOLE's 'Notes of a Residence in Little Pedlington,' published in a series some eight or ten years since in a London Magazine. To some of the earlier chapters we adverted at the time in these pages. Little Pedlington, it will therefore be remembered, is one of those petty villages, isolated from the great metropolis, but in the opinion of its little-great inhabitants altogether superior in point of interest to the great Babylon itself. It has its petty authors, bankers, clergymen, editors, actors, painters, etc.; its architectural wonders, and its natural curiosities. The writer arrives in the night, and takes his first breakfast in his apartment at one of the two inns of the village. His etching of this meal is *Cruikshankian* to a degree: 'Poured out from a huge japanned-tin vessel, standing eighteen inches high, a nankeen-colored liquid. Rose for the purpose of looking into the unfathomable machine. Full to the brim! Made according to the latest approved recipe: 'To half an ounce of coffee add a quart and a half of water.' The remainder of his breakfast is only surpassed by his dinner: 'Returned at four to 'as nice a little dinner as I could wish to sit down to ' — such as I was promised by mine host. Thermometer at eighty-four: huge hot round of beef, which filled the room with steam; hot suet dumplings, and hard, hot carrots; and scalding hot potatoes, *in their skins.* 'Nice little dinner' indeed — for the season! Finished dinner, and ordered some wine. Wine fiery as brandy, and warm. Complained of it. SCOREWELL undertook to 'try again.' While he was away, fancied I heard a pump-handle at work. Returned; wine by no means so strong, and much cooler.'

The next day the writer sallies out, under the guidance of FELIX HOPPY, M. C., (Master of Ceremonies,) to look at the Little-Pedlington lions. The town-pump, after the model of a native architect, and from the best point of view, so impresses him, that he is compelled at once to admit that there is 'nothing like *that* in London.' 'Do you see that lady in a green veil?' eagerly asks his 'guide.' Yes. 'You are familiar with *her* in London, of course?' He had never heard of the lady. 'Why that, Sir, is 'ENAJ SBBURCS,' who writes the sweetest poetry for the Little-Pedlington 'Weekly Observer!' Yes, Sir, that is JANE SCRUBBS, whose reversed name has created such a sensation throughout England! Never heard of *her*, Sir! Impossible!' It was a matter of great marvel to Mr. Hoppy also why his 'Guide' and Rummins's 'Antiquities of Little-Pedlington' had not been noticed in the 'Quarterly' or the 'Edinburgh.' 'Quite superior to all such pettiness at Little-Pedlington. The Pedlington 'Weekly Observer' *had* spoken of Rogers and Moore, Campbell and Coleridge, and such writers — ay, and with great kindness too, notwithstanding.' · · · We have already given, we believe, the visit to Hawkins, the banker, and to '*the Zoo*,' as Mr. Hoppy terms a collection of two monkeys and a few stuffed birds. As the writer and his guide are on their way to 'Hygeia Lodge,' a Pedlingtonian hurries past, who is thus introduced to the stranger : 'That man, Sir, ought to be the happiest fellow in Little-Pedlington, for he 's making a fortune. It is Diggs the undertaker ; just married Dr. Drench's eldest daughter; great connexion for *him*, Sir!' At 'Hygeia Lodge' the visiter 'saw a man busy planting shrubs and trees about a deep hole.' On inquiry, was informed that Doctors Drench and Drainem had had the good fortune to discover there a mineral spring of the nastiest water that mortal man ever put to his lips. The Little-Pedlingtonian wondered what was to become of Cheltenham and the like watering-places. 'However, poor devils! that 's *their* affair.' Fancied I smelt something like the detestable odor of a tan-yard. Peeped through the window of a small shed, the door of which was fastened by a strong padlock. Saw a box of sulphur, a couple of bags of iron-filings, a pile of stale red herrings, some raw hides cut into strips, and a quantity of bark, such as the tanners use. Wondered what *that* was for !'

'The Little-Pedlington 'Weekly Observer' and its 'intensely gifted editor, Simcox Rummins, Jr.' undoubtedly suggested to Mr. Dickens the 'Eatonswill Gazette' and its querulous contemporary. The manner in which Mr. Rummins lays down the law to the Emperor of Russia is 'a caution ' to that monarch : 'Once more we call the attention of His Imperial Majesty to what we have so often said, and what we have now repeated — shall we add, for the *last time ?* He may continue to *not* notice us in any of his decrees or manifestoes, and thus *affect* to be indifferent concerning what we say to him ; but we have it on the best authority, that our warning voice, wafted on the wings of the viewless wind, pierces the perfumed precincts of the palace of Petersburgh, and carries conviction like the roaring of the rushing cataract into his mind. But if the 'Little-Pedlington Observer' does sometimes address the Autocrat in terms of more than usual severity, let him remember that we do so more in friendship than in anger; that we regret the necessity we are under of giving him pain, but that like skilful surgeons we must probe in order to cure !' The following, from the same journal, is an admirable specimen of editorial non-committalism. The theme is the new drop-scene of the Little-Pedlington Theatre, by the unrivalled Daubson · 'The subject is a view of the New Pump in Market-square, as seen from South-street ; though it seems to us the painter would have done better had he represented it as seen from North-street ; not but that we think South-street a very favorable point for viewing it ; and no man has greater taste in these matters than Daubson, when he chooses to exercise it.'

Apropos of Daubson: The metropolitan visiter is taken to see the 'all-but breathing Grenadier,' the *chef-d'œuvre* of this great master. As he approached it he involuntarily took off his hat. The picture, he tells us, did not put him *much* in mind of Titian or Vandyke — *not at all of* Rembrandt.' 'Daubson is no servile imitator — in fact no imitator at all. Perhaps a military critic might object that the fixed bayonet is *rather* longer than the musket itself.　Be this as it may, owing to that contrivance it appears a most formidable weapon.　In order that the whole arms and accoutrements may be seen by the spectator, the painter with considerable address has represented the cartridge-box and the scabbard of the bayonet *in front*.　Scabbard about one-third the length of the bayonet.　Judicious.　Nothing formidable in the appearance of a long scabbard, whatever may be thought of a long bayonet.　Legs considerably thicker than the thighs : grand idea of stability, and characteristic of a ' Grenadier Standing Sentry.'　Having drank in the matchless beauty of the picture, it is not perhaps surprising that the stranger should be anxious to look upon its distinguished creator.　He was therefore presently ushered by the officious ' M. C ' into the presence of the great artist, whom he found cutting paper profiles with a machine that conducted a long wire, with a knife at the end of it, over the face of the sitter, who was fastened bolt upright in a high-backed chair.　A verdict is pronounced upon his ' Grenadier,' in the true pseudo-connoisseur style : ' Mr. DAURSON, I assure you, that for design, composition, drawing, and color; for middle-distance, fore-ground, back-ground, *chiar-'oscuro*, tone, foreshortening, light and shade ; for breadth, depth, harmony, perspective, pencilling, and finish, I 've seen nothing in Little-Pedlington that would endure a moment's comparison with it.　How is it, Sir,' said I, in conclusion, ' that so eminent an artist as yourself is not a member of the Royal Academy ? '　' D — n the Royal Academy ! ' exclaimed he, his yellow face turning blue ; ' d — n the Royal Academy ! They shall never see *me* among such a set !　No, Mister, I 've thrown down the gauntlet and defied them.　When they refused to exhibit my ' Grenadier,' I made up my mind never to send them another work of mine ; never to countenance them in any way ; and I 've kept my resolution.　It 's only last year that *a friend of mine, without my knowledge,* sent them one of my pictures, and they rejected *that !* They knew well enough whose it was.　But I considered that as the greatest compliment ever paid me ; it showed they were afraid of the competition.　D — n 'em ! they did n't *dare* to exhibit it !　If they did but know how much I despise 'em ! Mister, that den must be broken up.　There will be no high art in England while *that* exists ! '　We commend this ' Diary ' to the manager of the ' Olympic ' Theatre.　In his hands it would be found full of comic capabilities.

' TWICE-TOLD TALES.' — Messrs. JAMES MUNROE AND COMPANY, Boston, have recently issued, in two very neat and compact volumes, the ' Twice-Told Tales,' to the number of thirty-six, of NATHANIEL HAWTHORNE.　Many of these papers appeared originally in the KNICKERBOCKER ; and so great was the admiration which they excited, that our readers will require no additional recommendation to seek out and peruse the volumes before us.　We scarcely know Mr. HAWTHORNE's superior as a quiet yet acute observer and most faithful limner of Nature.　His mind reflects her images like the plates of the Daguerreotype, while his fine imagination *colors* the picture with the most life-like hues.　In many respects Mr. HAWTHORNE reminds us of LAMB.　' ELIA ' might have written, for example, the ' Rill from the Town Pump,' in which that peerless essayist's graphic limning and felicitous meditations are alike embodied ; and there are other portions of the volumes which are imbued with that combined simplicity, naturalness, and grace, which are scarcely less the characteristics of LAMB than of HAWTHORNE.　These ' Tales,' though they were *thrice* told, would scarcely fail to meet with a wide and general perusal.

'BURNS' ANNIVERSARY.' — We know not when we have enjoyed a social and festive scene with more *gout* than the BURNS' Anniversary, recently celebrated by his countrymen and several American guests at the Waverley House. We lack space to publish, what we should be but too happy to present, many of the brief and sententious speeches and toasts given on the occasion. Dr. CUMMING presided with dignity and ability, and was supported on the right by Mr. WILLIAM CULLEN BRYANT, L. GAYLORD CLARK, and JAMES LAWSON, and on the left by Dr. CALDWELL, A. WATSON, Esq., and Dr. ELLIOTT. Mr. JAMES LINEN acquitted himself ably of the office of Vice-President. Dr. CUMMING arose, amidst prolonged applause, and after a few terse and feeling remarks upon the life and character of BURNS, preparatory to a toast to his revered memory, he favored his auditory with a poem on 'The Land of BURNS,' in which, as in CHARLES SWAIN's invocation to the characters of SCOTT, 'the Bard of Ayr and the scenes he loved passed by like BANQUO's train.' The following will afford the reader an idea of the spirit and variety of this performance :

BEHOLD! his noble form erect,
   As wrought by FLAXMAN's hand,
And near in varied form appear
   His soul-created band.

Around we mark the classic scenes
   Which fired his passions strong,
The woods, the streams, and meadows green,
   Immortal in his song.

There Carrick, Kyle, and Cunningham,
   Dumfries, and Ayr, are seen ;
The Tay, Clyde, Ettrick, Doon, and Tweed,
   And ilka hill between :

These shine in many a lofty lay,
   Are lisped by many a tongue ;
And while a Scot has soul, they 'll be
   The burden of his song.

There stands the auld clay-biggin' where
   The peasant-bard was born,
And where from hoary age he learned
   That man was made to mourn.

And there the ancient brig o' Ayr,
   Close by the gude auld toun,
Where Freedom's champion, WALLACE hight,
   Slew many a Southern lonn.

And there auld Alloway's haunted wa's,
   Where martyred worthies sleep,
Where brownies, bogles, elfs, and imps
   Their midnight revels keep.

And yonder, skelpin ower the brig,
   Bauld Tam O'Shanter's mare,
And Cutty Sark, the jade, exults
   To see her hurdies bare.

And there 's the spot, near Mossgiel farm,
   Where he the daisy mourned,
And where the ploughman's humble lot
   The ploughman-bard adorned.

There too was caught th' inspiring theme
   Which lit the poet's soul,
And gave to Fame the brightest name
   That ere illumed her scroll.

'T was Love that woke the poet's lyre,
   To sing his NANNIE's praise,
And mourn his Highland MARY's loss
   By wild Montgomery's braes.

And there the jolly beggars sang,
   Frae mornin' until e'en,
And there the Cotter's social hearth
   Displayed its hallowed scene.

And now, in fair Edina's halls
   He feels the glow of pride,
When DUGALD STEWART and GLENCAIRN
   Are seated by his side.

And now, his lowly home he seeks,
   With Fame's green laurel crowned,
And see! his aged mother hears
   His well-known footsteps sound.

'Oh! ROBERT!' is her simple cry,
   Her heart 's too full to speak ;
A world of joy is in her eye,
   Tears trickle down her cheek.

And there he meets his lovely JEAN,
   The lass he lo'ed the best,
Who shared his joys, who dried his tears,
   And soothed him when distressed.

Now, Ellisland appears in view
   On Nith's alluvial plain ;
The sun has left Dalswinton's towers,
   Darkness and silence reign :

And there, stretched on a mass of straw,
   While deep groans rend his breast,
He sees, in that bright glittering star
   His MARY's blissful rest.

The poet followed the Bard to his mausoleum at Dumfries, that 'Mecca of the mind,' and animadverted with just satire upon Scotland, who could permit her gifted son to live and die neglected, and then honor him with — an urn ! The conclusion, invoking the reverence of the Present for the glorious bards of the Past, was not less striking and felicitous than the extracts which we have given above. A characteristic letter from Mr. HALLECK, who was unable to be present, was received and read with much applause. American poets were not forgotten in the honors, which called up Mr. BRYANT, the king of them all, who gave in response, after a few spirited remarks, a toast to 'The authors of the Anonymous Ballads of Scotland.' The party separated at an early hour; and nothing occurred from first to last to mar the festivities of the occasion.

FOREIGN REVIEWS AND MAGAZINES FOR JANUARY. — Through the prompt attention of Messrs. WILEY AND PUTNAM, of London and New-York, we had early on our table all the January Reviews and Magazines from the other side of the great water. A running commentary upon some of them, accompanied by a few brief extracts, may not be unacceptable to our readers. We are especially struck with the altered tone and manner of the London *Quarterly Review.* After abusing our country, its institutions, literature, and people, for the last ten years, it seems at length to have become ashamed of its course in this regard, and resolved to do us at least unavoidable justice. Four of the best papers in the number are upon American works: STEPHENS' Travels in Central America, ROBERTSON's work on Palestine and the Holy Land, IRVING's Memoir of LUCRETIA DAVIDSON, and the 'Correspondence,' etc., of JOHN ADAMS. The 'Incidents of Travel' are warmly commended for their variety and sustained interest, their lively spirit and gay, healthy-minded tone, and the language is pronounced to be correct, clear, and concise, 'with but one or two American peculiarities.' The reviewer of ROBERTSON's work honestly 'confesses to a little national jealousy.' 'We are not altogether pleased,' says he, 'that for the best and most copious work on the geography and antiquities of the Holy Land, although written in English, we should be indebted to an American divine;' and he proceeds at great length to award it the highest praise. In opening the notice of ADAMS' Letters, the reviewer has this characteristic paragraph:

'AMERICA is, we believe, in personal feeling the most aristocratic country on the face of the earth. Each man's rude assertion of equality is no better than a disguised assumption of superiority; and whenever the pressure of condensated society shall force the more consistent particles to the surface, there will emerge *some* form of aristocracy, probably as decided and distinctive as any thing which we have in Europe; and perhaps some ADAMS may shine in future Red books, as Duke of Massachusetts, Earl de Quincy, Viscount Braintree, and Baron Adam of the Garden of Eden! Let it not be supposed that we either ridicule or deprecate such a result. It is the natural course of human events; and few ennobled families could have a more respectable stock or a deeper root of public services than the descendants of JOHN ADAMS; but we cannot help smiling at the inconsistency which fosters such natural and laudable feelings under a sour parade of republican simplicity.'

We reciprocate, in common we are sure with every right-minded American, the annexed timely and honorable concessions:

'IT is impossible that any other two independent nations can have such a community of interests as England and America. In truth, we know of no material and substantial interest in which they are opposed — nay, in which they are separated: their origin, their laws, and their language are the same; their business, their prosperity are identified. New-York is but a suburb of Liverpool, or if you will, Liverpool of New-York. The failure of the Pennsylvania United States' Bank ruined more fortunes in England than in America; the manufacturers of Manchester share more wealth with Carolina than with Middlesex. We are not merely brothers and cousins; the ties of consanguinity we know are not always the bond of friendship; but we are partners, joint tenants as it were, of the commerce of the world; and we have had, as we have just hinted, melancholy experience that distress on either shore of the Atlantic must be almost equally felt on the other. 'And why should we quarrel? What are the grounds or objects of any difference between us? We know of but two, or at most three, points of difference on which the most captious on either side of the Atlantic have raised even a question. And what are they? Matters which, we firmly believe, two intelligent and honest negotiators might settle in a fortnight, and which owe their chief interest to their being made the pretexts of those who wish, for private or personal objects, to blow up a conflagration. · · · We conclude with repeating the expression of our anxious but respectful hope — we might say our conviction — that taking them altogether, the points of difference existing between England and America are so inconsiderable, compared with the vast importance of the common interests which should unite them, that the wise and honest statesmen who now principally influence the foreign relations of the two countries will be enabled to bring all those differences to an early, honorable, and final close, and to give to that community of interests such additional cordiality and confidence as may make our two countries in feeling — what as compared with the rest of mankind we really are — independent but friendly branches of one great family."

The *Westminster Review* has three or four very able papers, and among them one by CARLYLE, which partakes of that writer's fire, originality, and singularity. It is a review of an Edinburgh work upon the Life and Character of ' Baillie of Kilwinning,' a prominent actor in the days of CROMWELL and the Rump Parliament. How vivid, how sententious is the following passage:

'SESSION sixteenth vanishes thus, in a flash of fire! Yes; and the ' harsh untunable voice ' of Mr. O. CROMWELL, member for Cambridge, was in that shout of ' Withdraw!' and Mr. CROMWELL dashed on his rusty beaver withal, and strode out so — in those wide nostrils of his a kind of snort. And one Mr. MILTON sat in his house, by St. Bride's church, teaching grammar, writing Areopagitica; and had dined that day, not perhaps without criticism of the cookery. And it was all a living colored time, not a gray vacant one; and bad length, breadth, and thickness, even as our own has! But now, also, is not that a miraculous spy-glass, that perceptive faculty, soul, intelligence, or whatsoever we call it, of the Reverend Mr. Robert Baillie of Kilwinning? We will *see* by it things stranger than most preternaturalisms and mere common-place ' apparitions ' could be. ' Our fathers where are they?' Why, there; there are our far-off fathers, face to face, alive; and yet not alive; uh, no! they are visible, but unattainable — sunk in the never-returning past! Thrice endearing, we cannot *embrace* them; *ter manus effugit imago.* The centuries are transparent, then; yes, more or less; but they are impermeable, impenetrable, no adamant so hard. It is strange. *To be, To have been*; of all verbs the wonderfullest is that same. ' Time-element,' the ' crystal prism!' Of a truth, to us, sons of Time, it is the miracle of miracles.

'Such is the drama of life, seen in Baillie of Kilwinning; a thing of multifarious tragic and epic meanings, then as now. A many-voiced tragedy and epos, yet with broad-based comic and grotesque accompaniment; done by actors not in buskins; ever replete with elements of guilt and remorse, of pity, instruction, and fear! It is now two hundred years and odd months since these Common's members shouting, ' Withdraw! withdraw!' took away the life of THOMAS WENTWORTH Earl of Strafford, and introduced, driven by necessity *they* little knew whither, ' horrid rebellions,' as the phrase went, and suicidal wars, into the bowels of this country. On our horizon too there loom now inevitabilities no less stern; one knows not whether not very near at hand.'

In the *Church Quarterly* is to be found much good reading. We noted especially the following remarks upon the art of writing a good familiar letter: ' To impart pleasure, it should recall to our minds the writer. We wish to be reminded of our friend not only by his seal, his hand-writing, by knowing his occupations and his whereabouts, but by touches which are *like him ;* by seeing that he looks at things in his old point of view; grave, humorous, fanciful, shrewd — even, we may say, if it be only a little, wrong-headed. We like to remark *his* expressions; we like to be reminded of the tone in which he would have *said* what he now *writes.* Over and above the happiness of thought and expression, the life and depth, the terseness and clearness, which are the merits of familiar correspondence, in common with any other kind of composition, it appeals to a common fund of recollections, and has for its principal the reviving and increasing these.' In a review of a volume of German Hymns, there is one quoted, *Kindliches Gemuethe,* or ' Child-like Temper,' from which we take the subjoined simple yet graceful stanzas:

' His mother's arms his chief enjoyment,
To be there is his loved employment;
Early and late to see her face,
And tenderly her neck embrace.

' O Innocence! sweet child's existence!
This have I learnt through GOD's assistance:
He who possesses thee is wise,
And valued in the ALMIGHTY's eyes.

' O Childhood! well beloved of Heaven!
Whose mind by CHRIST alone is given,
How long my heart to feel like thee;
O JESU! form Thyself in me!'

The following, from an extended hymn, '*Ewigkeit*,' or Eternity, is forcible and felicitous :

> 'Eternity! eternity!
> How long art thou, Eternity!
> A ring whose orbit still extends,
> And ne'er beginning, never ends ;
> *Always* thy centre, Ring immense !
> And *Never* thy circumference:
> Mark well, O Man ! Eternity !'

The magazines strike us as being rather under their average quality. BLACKWOOD has an article upon the copy-right question, to which we had hoped to be able more particularly to advert. This assumption of the writer may be taken as a 'veritable verity,' as many of our own correspondents can bear honorable witness : 'The days are gone past when JOHNSON wrote his sonorous periods in a garret in Fleet-street. The vast increase of readers, particularly in the middle and lower ranks, has opened sources of literary profit, and avenues to literary distinction, unknown in any former age. A successful article in a magazine brings a man into notice in the literary world just as effectually as a triumphant début makes the fortune of an actress or singer.'

ENGLISH ETYMOLOGY. — We are indebted for the following to the correspondent who furnished for our October issue the valuable essay upon English synonyms :

SINGLE English words, when examined historically, often exhibit in their form marks or impressions of very different ages and nations. The historical formation of a word is often, on this account, highly interesting to the philosophic and curious mind.

I propose to take the common English adverbs, *dogmatically, dramatically, grammatically, phlegmatically, pragmatically*, and *schismatically*, and to investigate them etymologically.

I. These adverbs are formed from the adjectives *dogmatical, dramatical, grammatical, phlegmatical, pragmatical*, and *schismatical*, by means of the Teutonic suffix *ly ;* (Goth. *leiks*, Old Germ. *lih*, Germ. *lich*, Anglo-Sax. *lic*, Dutch *lyk*, Dan. *lig, lige*, Swed. *liger*, Icel. *ligt*, connected with Goth. *galeiks*, Old Germ. *kalih, gelich*, Germ. *gleich*, Anglo-Sax. *gelic, lic*, Dutch *gelyk*, Swed. *lik*, Dan. *lig, lige*, Eng. *like ;*) constituting adverbs of adjectives.

As a Teutonic suffix is here annexed to a Latin word, it must have taken place since the confluence of the two streams, (the Teutonic and the Latin,) which constitute the English language. These adverbs, then, have been formed in English times on English soil, and belong to no other language.

II. These adjectives, *dogmatical, dramatical*, etc., are formed from *dogmatic, dramatic, grammatic, phlegmatic, pragmatic*, and *schismatic*, by means of the modern Latin suffix *al ;* (Ital. *ale*, Provenç. Span. Port. Fr. *al*,) which has been appended to them without any apparent significancy.

As this pleonastic use of the suffix *al* does not belong to classic Latin, (*grammaticalis* being first found in Sidonius, a writer of the fifth century,) these adjectives, *dogmatical, dramatical*, etc., have been formed in the middle ages and on modern Latin soil.

III. These adjectives, *dogmatic, dramatic*, etc., are formed from *dogma*, Gr. δόγμα, (gen. δόγματος ;) *drama*, Gr. δρᾶμα, (gen. δράματος ;) Gr. γράμμα, (gen. γράμματος ;) *phlegm*, Gr. φλέγμα, (gen. φλέγματος ;) Gr. πράγμα, (gen. πράγματος ; and *schism*, Gr. σχίσμα, (gen. σχίσματος ;) by means of the Græco-Latin suffix *ic*, (Gr. ικος, Lat. *icus*,) signifying *related*, or *belonging to*, and forming adjectives from nouns.

As a Græco-Latin suffix is here attached to words originally Greek, but derived to us from the Latin language, these adjectives, *dogmatic, dramatic*, etc., must have existed in Græco-Latin times and on Græco-Latin soil.

IV. These Greek nouns, δόγμα, δρᾶμα, γράμμα, φλέγμα, πρᾶγμα, and σχίσμα, are derived from the Greek roots,

δοκ,	δρα,	γραφ,	φλεγ,	πραγ,	σχιδ,
THINKING;	ACTING;	WRITING;	BURNING;	DOING;	DIVIDING,

by means of the Greek suffix μαr, denoting passive concretes.

This process must have been in Grecian times and on Grecian soil.

These words, then, *dogmatically, dramatically*, etc., bear the impress, not of one moment only, but of ages.

GOSSIP WITH READERS AND CORRESPONDENTS. — WE agree entirely with ' J. E.' in the animadversions which he makes upon the theory of the ' Learned Blacksmith ' in relation to the general equality of intellectual capacity or talent. Mr. BURRITT, for whom we have the highest respect, is himself a practical illustration of the false premises upon which the lecture to which our correspondent refers was based. ' It strikes me,' he writes, ' that the great error in the process of education at the present day is the appointment of an uniform measure of cultivation to all, and the endeavor to bring every individual to that measure, as if there was but one standard of human intellect, and all men were capable of attaining to the same perfection ; whereas if regard were paid to the strength and peculiar combination of the several faculties of each learner, and these faculties educated to the highest perfection of which they are susceptible, the result would be the production of an infinitely greater number of original minds, and a higher degree of general capacity. It was not chance and a combination of fortuitous circumstances, that made NAPOLEON ; for we see his mighty genius for war bursting forth in startling scintillations while yet a stripling school-boy at Brienne. It was not study that produced a BYRON, who at the early age of twenty-two years amazed and delighted both hemispheres with his ' Childe Harold ; ' thenceforth hoping, and not vainly, to ' be remembered in his line with his land's language.' It was not study that gave to the world a SHAKSPERE, who ' lisped in numbers,' and dissected each maze and intricacy of character with a skill that has never been equalled ; who looked through the infinitely diversified human heart, as though it were to him a transparent record. Modern sculpture, with the same models for imitation, and equal ambition and application brought to its pursuit, has never attained the perfection of art which is manifest in the productions of a PHIDIAS or PRAXITELES. Modern painters may seek in vain to vie with the undying productions of a TITIAN, a RAPHAEL, a DA VINCI ; and ELIHU BURRITT, with all the indefatigable perseverance and industry which distinguish him, would have labored in vain for his present position, were he not imbued with a higher order of intellect than is vouchsafed to the majority of mankind. It is to superiority of mental *capacity*, rather than to *contingency*, that the bright names which illuminate the pages of history owe their proud eminence.' · · · The ' Parallel between NAPOLEON and WELLINGTON ' finds some objectors we perceive among the fervent admirers of the former. In this class is our correspondent ' *Austerlitz*,' who writes like a Frenchman, as doubtless he is. A favorite contributor sends us the following lines by the Hon. RICHARD HENRY WILDE. They are ' twilight reflections' which rose in the writer's mind at Saint Helena :

> ' Faint and sad was the moon-beam's smile,
> Sullen the moan of the dying wave,
> Hoarse the wind in Saint Helen's isle,
> As I stood by the side of NAPOLEON'S GRAVE !'

The fine poetical spirit of the stanzas gives additional force to the biting irony with which they are imbued :

AND is it here that the Hero lies,
Whose name has shaken the earth with dread?
And is this all that the earth supplies?
A stone his pillow — the turf his bed !

Is such the moral of human life?
Are these the limits of glory's reign?
Have oceans of blood and an age of strife,
A thousand battles, been all in vain?

Is nothing left of his victories now
But legions broken, a sword in rust?
A crown that cumbers a dotard's brow —
A name and a requiem? — dust to dust !

Of all the chieftains whose thrones he reared,
Were there none whom kindness or faith could bind?
Of all the monarchs whose crowns he spared,
Had none one spark of his Roman mind?

Did Prussia cast no repentant glance?
Did Austria shed no remorseful tear,
When England's faith, and thine honor, France,
And thy friendship, Russia, were blasted here?

No ! Holy leagues, like the heathen heaven,
Vassal-like shrunk from the giant's shock,
And glorious TITAN, the unforgiven,
Was doomed to his vulture and chains and rock !

And who were the gods that decreed thy doom?
A German Cæsar, a Prussian Sage,
The Dandy Prince of a counting-room,
And a Russian Greek of the middle age !

Men call thee Despot, and call thee true ;
But the laurel was earned that bound thy brow ;
And of all who wore it, alas ! how few
Were as free from treason and guilt as thou !

Shame to thee, Gaul ! and thy faithless horde !
Where was the oath which thy soldiers swore?
Fraud still lurks in the Gown — but alas ! the Sword
Was never so false to its trust before.

Where was thy veteran's boast that day,
' The Old Guard dies, but it never yields ! '
Oh ! for one heart like the brave DESAIX,
One phalanx like those of thine early fields !

But no ! ah, no ! it was FREEDOM'S charm
Gave *them* the courage of more than men ;
You broke the magic that nerved each arm,
Though you were invincible only then !

Yet Saint Jean was a deep, not a deadly blow —
One struggle, and FRANCE all her faults repairs :
But the mild PAYETTE and the stern CARNOT
Are dupes, and ruin thy fate and theirs.

We are quite obliged to ' *Wilton*,' but the attempt was vain. We detected his plagiarism at the first glance. Moreover, we *think* we have detected the impostor. Speaking of plagiarisms, leads us to say, that we have seen recently in the ' Mirror ' as from ' a late British work ' a story of Sir ROBERT BARCLAY, who lost an arm in the battle of Lake Erie, and an anecdote of LAMB's being ' all full inside ' on one occasion. Both these were derived from Mr. WASHINGTON IRVING, and first published in this department of the KNICKERBOCKER. Going to England and coming back *stamped*, however, we presume to be ' warrant good enough ' for their present re-circulation in the journals. Our friend WHITE of the ' Southern Literary Messenger,' we may say here, has again been imposed on by a plagiarist. The lines entitled ' *Too Soon*,' in a late issue, are stolen bodily from an English magazine, in which they appeared several years ago. · · · A friendly correspondent in a sister city, after some comments upon the sketches from ' *My Grand-father's Port-Folio*,' which he warmly commends for their simplicity and truthfulness, gives the following passage from the unwritten history of ' Deacon T.' one of our good ' Grand-father's ' trio : ' I knew Deacon T. well. He was the guardian of my early years, and I resided with him for a considerable period. There is some mistake I think concerning his charity. ' My Grand-father ' must have confounded the act of some other individual with those of Deacon T. He was never known to give money in charity but once, and that was a bad fourpence-ha'penny which had come back to him some twenty times in the way of trade, and which he at last gave away in a fit of desperation. He always said, when applied to for charity ; ' Go to Hannah ; (his wife ;) she always attends to such things.' *She* was a woman in whose economy and discretion in matters of benevolence he could place the most implicit confidence — and he knew it. On one special occasion, a birth-day I believe, the good lady made up a batch of extra-nice custard pies ; so nice in fact, that after they were done, she had n't the courage to eat them ; but hoarded them up until they became sour and mouldy, and then endeavored to force them down the throats of her family. But they ' would n't go down.' She then mixed them all over again into a pudding, hoping to disguise the taste by the addition of pearlash and other culinary arts. This was a failure. The parlor-folk quietly declined being helped to it, and the kitchen-girls turned up their noses over it. But the old lady's ingenuity was not exhausted. She had a sick neighbor, a poor woman who had been languishing for months in a consumption, and with characteristic benevolence she determined to administer the rejected pudding to her. It was accordingly again dressed over and served up in the shape of cup-custards, and carried to the sick woman by the old lady herself. But she was too ill to eat them ; and the next day and the next passed away, and they still remained untouched. At last the nurse, who had looked at the nice little things with a longing eye, ventured to taste one. She thought it was sour ; she tasted again, and was *sure* of it. The whole was then consigned to the pig-stye ; and its occupant, ' who came in immediately after,' thrust his snout into the trough, and then upset it ; and thus the custards were lost beyond redemption. But the Deaconess enjoyed the credit of the good deed ; and months after, I heard the poor sick woman lamenting the loss of her custards : ' If she could only have eaten them when they were first brought !'' Apropos of the old gentleman's ' Port-Folio.' If our readers can peruse ' The Backwoodsman's Sacrifice ' in the present number, without finding the ' fruitful river i' the eye ' swelling its channels, they have few emotions in common with us. · · · A friend who recently removed from this city to the West, writing from Illinois, gives us a pleasant picture of one of the *Manitou Islands* in Lake Michigan. ' On our passage out,' he writes, ' we had rather a tough time on the lakes ; but even this afforded us pleasure, as we were compelled to ' lay by ' at one of the Manitou Islands in Lake Michigan. This gave me an opportunity to explore the Island, which I gladly improved. Connected with it is a great deal of Indian lore, which you know is getting to be *literary*, as it has been *romantic*, for many years. There is a beautiful secluded lake in the centre of the island by which the Indians supposed the spirits of the departed made their entry into the happy hunting-grounds of the blest. Its romantic situation, lone and silent ; the beautiful transparency of the water ; and the fine pebbly beach, impress the visiter with agreeable thoughts, linked with the Indian traditions. There is only one or two houses on the island, and those are inhabited only in the summer season by wood-cutters, who ' receive calls ' from the steamers between Buffalo and Chicago, for wood ; the island being covered with the largest beach and fir trees. The lake I have mentioned lies about two miles in the interior. There is no harbor, which vessels can make in a gale from the coast, between Mackinac and Chicago, except this in the Manitou Islands. Our own vessel put back one hundred and twenty-five miles in a storm, to reach it. We lay there twenty-four hours ; and it was the pleasantest part of our whole trip. I hunted, fished, and rambled through the woods the whole day, losing my way once or twice, by the way of varying the amusement.' · · · ' P's.' defence of his Lines, ' *Remembrances of the Dead*,' noticed in our last ' Gossip,' is received, and in the spirit in which it was written. We cannot argue the point with our correspondent. GOD grant that he may never know by experience how vain is his ' consolatory philosophy !' It is true indeed that ' scenes, events, and things pass away,' but as always nor often do 'their sad associations die also.' In the words of one who had *himself* mourned the loved and lost:

'These things may pass away,
But past things are not dead ;
In the heart's treasury
Deep, hidden deep, they lie
        Unwithered.

And there the soul retires
From the dull things that are,
To mingle oft and long
With the time-hallowed throng
    Of those that were.

Then into life start out
The scenes long vanished ;
Then we behold again
The forms that long have lain
        Among the dead.

We feel their grasp of love,
We meet their beaming eye,
We hear their voice — ah, no !
'Twas our own murmuring low,
        Unconsciously.'

The desolate awakening from dread memories like these would prove a painful but irresistible argument to our friend. . . . 'P. Q. D.' (Lancaster, Pa.,) is illustrating an old 'bull' in his '*First Night in a City Tavern.*' Does he not remember the Vauxhall Garden waiter's alarm-call to one of his fellow-servants : 'Look out, Bill ! There 's a Brandy-and-water gettin' over the fence, and a Cup-o'-coffee and a Muffin slinkin' out o' the back gate ! Stop 'em !' SAM WELLER adopted this figurative language with his boots, shoes, and pumps ; and it is quite common in the mouths of musicians. We remember hearing the daughter of an actor threaten (in revenge against an obstinate father who had prevented her marrying the 'first fiddle') to run away with the bassoon !' . . . We have great pleasure always in welcoming such gossipping reminiscences of the darker days in our history as are contained in the '*Conversations of my Aunt,*' for which we are indebted to an obliging and congenial friend : 'When the British,' said my Aunt, 'had possession of New-York, they treated the American prisoners very badly, and many charitable people furnished them with food and other necessaries. Several families, I remember, made soup for them. Among those who did the most for them were some of the Quakers. The Friends of Long-Island sent down whole quarters of meat and great quantities of vegetables to OLIVER HULL, a Quaker, who lived on the south-west corner of Beekman and William-streets. Mrs. Hull used to have it made into soup, almost every day, and GARNER BAKER, a poor boy they took to bring up, carried it in two pails with a hoop to the prisoners at the Sugar-House in Liberty-street, and other prisons. Mrs. Hull found out that the nurse, who was a cruel ugly creature, treated the sick very badly, and sometimes threw away the soup and tea which was sent to the prisoners. She complained of her conduct to the attending physician, and had her turned away. I recollect my mother sending tea, sweetened and poured in bottles, to the sick prisoners, by young BAKER. We were going to meeting one day, (when the meeting-house was in Liberty-street, where THORBURN's seed-store afterwards was) and as we passed the old Sugar-House, a prisoner called out to us from a window : 'Do n't be discouraged, dear ladies ! The rebels are not discouraged ; they 'll never give up !' ROBERT MURRAY did a great deal for the prisoners ; and his son JOHN, JR., who lived afterward in Franklin-Square, was a very smart young man, and very active in their behalf. Another Friend did so much for the prisoners, and said so much about their cruel treatment, that he had to leave town to avoid the jealousy of the British. Old Friend DELAPLAINE broke up keeping shop, and went to Shrewsbury, because he would not take continental money. He said it was made for the purpose of war, and he could not conscientiously take it. But my father had confidence in it, and laid it up. He was a very strong Whig. Father sent me and my sisters out of town to stay a few months with uncle TEDDEMAN at Purchase. While we were there the battle of White Plains took place, and we heard the guns. A Scotch servant-girl who lived at uncle TEDDEMAN's had a brother in the battle, and she cried very hard, fearing he might be killed. A British officer was billeted for awhile at our house. He was a very civil man, and read his Bible. He was sick, and mother used to ask him to come and take tea with us. After he went away, another officer with his wife and daughter staid there. They behaved very well until the officer went away, and then his wife and daughter would often quarrel. The mother sometimes chased her daughter down stairs with the broom-stick. I was very much afraid of them. The daughter was not, I guess, very good. There was a very handsome Hessian officer whom she used to admire. He was called the 'Hessian beau.' Another revolutionary sketch, 'The Storming of Stony-Point,' from the hand of an eye-witness and an actor in the scene, will have attracted attention in preceding pages. . . . '*The Sham Duel*' has several good points, but it is too broad a caricature. Our correspondent's BOB ACRES had as narrow an escape as Sir ROGER DE COVERLY, whose blood would inevitably have been shed in defence of his country, only that he was sent out of the field upon a private message the day before the battle. The brave German SCHMELZEL tells us that he was always accustomed several hours before a battle to withdraw so many miles to the rear, that the men, so soon as they were beaten, would be sure to find him. 'A good retreat,' says he, 'is reckoned the master-piece in the art of war ; and at no time can a retreat be executed with such order, force, and security, as just before the battle, when you are not yet beaten.' · · · · '*Science and Invention*' shall appear so soon as we can find space for it ; *not* omitting the speculative passage, which is left at our discretion. The predictions of the writer are as likely to be fulfilled as those of ROGER BACON, who in the thirteenth century anticipated the invention of the steam-boat, locomotive engines, the diving-bell, suspension-bridge, and the science of projectiles. 'Men,' said he, 'may yet construct for the wants of navigation such machines that the greatest vessels, directed by a single man, shall cut through the rivers and seas with more rapidity than if they were propelled by rowers : chariots may be constructed, which without horses shall run with immeasurable speed. Men may conceive machines which could bear the diver, without danger, to the depth of the waters. Men could invent a multitude of other engines and useful instruments, such as bridges that shall span the broadest rivers without any intermediate support. Art has its thunders more terrible than those of heaven. A small quantity of matter produces a horrible explosion, accompanied by a bright light ; and this may be repeated so as to destroy a city or entire battalions.' 'Where steam is now,' says a late London Quarterly, 'electricity may come to be ; for all this hissing and panting drudgery a silent flash. A hundred years hence ARKWRIGHT's best jenny will we doubt not be considered as an antiquarian curiosity, much on a par with the hand-loom of the Hindoo.' · · · · There is a good degree of tragedy in the '*Adventures in the Country.*' The hero could not say with the verdant country youth who bought a horrid old 'screw' at Tattersall's , in 'Tom-and-Jerry,' 'I think I know what an '*orse* is — I 'm not a *hass ;*' for he buys a Bucephalus of a Buckeye, and while travelling a short distance in a wagon, over an intolerably muddy Ohio road, with his wife by his side, he is inexpressibly annoyed by two wags who walk along by the side of the road, and every now and then call out 'Whoa !' The horse stops, nothing loath. A shower of blows are rained upon the poor beast's back, and he starts again ; but the reiterated 'Whoa !' brings him up once more with a round turn ; and thus the unhappy pair journey for five miles ! The imploring looks of the lady and the remonstrances of the husband were alike powerless in quelling the spirit of fun in the breasts of their tormentors. · · · · '*The Mist-Cloud*' describes what we have often seen on Long-Island Sound, but the poem possesses more correctness than poetry. Beside, MILTON has anticipated half of its pictures in these brief but matter-full lines :

> 'Ye mists and exhalations that now rise
> From hill or steaming lake, dusky or gray,
> Till the sun paint your fleecy skirts with gold,
> In honor to the world's great Author, rise !
> Whether to deck with clouds the uncolored sky,
> Or wet the thirsty earth with falling showers,
> Rising or falling, still advance His praise !'

'*Mr. Dunn, a Sketch,*' is not *well* done. 'M.' will find a plan better likely to succeed, by studying the work of '*CHAWLS YELLOWPLUSH, Esquire.*' His master thought himself while in Paris quite beyond the reach of his London creditors ; 'as sure as any mortial man can be in this sublinary spear, where no think is sutln excep uneuttnty. It is a maxim in Franse,' continues Mr. YELLOWPLUSH, 'that after dark no man is lible for his dets ; and in any of the Roil gardings — the Twillaries, the Penny Roil, or the Lucksimburg, for egsample, a man may wander from sunrise to evening, and hear nothink of the ojus duns. They an't admitted into those places of public enjyment and rondyvoo any more than dogs ; the centuries at the garding-gait having orders to shuit all such.' But although ALGERNON DEUCEACE, Esquire was a 'leader of the *ho-tong*' and very sly, he fell a victim to *his* 'Mr. DUN,' and in a far more romantic way than the personage described by our contributor. · · · · We agree entirely with '*A Washingtonian,*' and trust he has seen nothing to militate against his views in these pages. The eminent examples cited are remarkable, certainly ; and let us hope they will stand firm ; but alas ! it was SWIFT (precept *vs.* practice !) who, speaking of BOLINGBROKE's poor health, said : 'Tell me, is not temperance a necessary virtue for great men, since it is the parent of ease and liberty, so necessary for the use and improvement of the mind, and which philosophy allows to be the greatest felicities of life ?' · · · · '*A Chapter on Faces*' has some admirable hits at the expressionless, pursed-up mouths and straight noses which garnish the faces of the 'fashion'-able females represented in our lady-periodicals. But the article goes into other matters, and evinces we think personal pique toward one of our contemporaries. Speaking of 'fashions for the month,' here is a part of the report for January, for a certain section of London. A similar style prevails in some circles in this city : 'Coats are very much worn, particularly at the elbows, and are trimmed with a shining substance, which gives them a very glossy appearance. A rim of white runs down the seams, and the covering of the buttons is slightly opened, so as to show the wooden material under it. Hats are now slightly indented at the top, and we have seen several in which part of the brim is sloped off, without any particular regard to the quantity abstracted.' · · · · '*Israfel, an Elegy on the Death of Willis Gaylord*

Clark,' by ' T. H. C., M. D.,' is fervent in spirit, but the writer is in error in an important fact. The cherished companion of the dear Departed mourns *not* ' for him who lies low with the dead,' for she was among the ransomed in heaven long before his own body was ' married to that dust it so much loved.' *He* it was who lamented for many a weary month, with the affectionate and sorrowing MAL-COLM:

' Is ours fair WOMAN's angel smile,	' Beyond the hills, beyond the sea,
All bright and beautiful as day ?	Oh ! for the pinions of a dove !
So of her cheek and eye the while	Oh ! for the morning's wings, to flee
Time steals the rose and dims the ray !	Away, and be with them we love !
She wanders in the Spirit Land,	When all is fled that 's bright and fair,
And we, with speechless grief oppressed,	And life is but a wintry waste,
As o'er the faded form we stand,	This, *this* is then our only prayer,
Would gladly share her place of rest !	To flee away and be at rest ! '

' *The Death of Schiller,*' and the ' *Lines* ' upon reading a poem of MOTHERWELL's, do not lack feeling nor merit; but the versification is far from melodious, and the *labor* is too apparent. The same remarks apply to the ' *Pilgrims of Life.*' It requires something beside *form* and *measure* to approach the model which the writer evidently had in his mind. · · · ' Noor-Mahal, or the Light of the Harem ; ' ' Grenada and the Alhambra,' Number Three ; ' My Grand-father's Port-Folio,' Number Five ; ' Edward Alford and his Play-fellow,' Number Two ; ' An Adventure on the Blue Ridge ; ' ' Life in Philadelphia in 1841 ; ' ' Letters from Rome,' by GEORGE WASHINGTON GREENE, Esq., ' Exeter, a New-England Sketch ; ' ' My Native Land ; ' ' The Old Year and the New ; ' ' Song over the Cradle of two Infant Sisters sleeping,' from the Spanish ; ' Life's Seasons ; ' To ' Miller's Bridge ; ' with several other articles, are either filed for insertion, or awaiting examination. · · · *Errata.* — In the first line of the last stanza of ' *England's Merrier Day,*' on page 163 of our February issue, play-*mates* should read play-*wrights* — an important distinction doubtless with good ' QUEEN BESS.' ☞ ' Several books, pamphlets, periodicals, etc., have escaped notice in the present issue. February is a short month ; and owing to our increased circulation, it is found necessary, for an early publication to have all our matter in the hands of the printers by the twelfth of each month.

CLASSICAL AND COMMERCIAL SCHOOL. — We are glad to perceive that Mr. JOHN W. S. HOWS is again among his numerous friends in town, and that he intends soon to open a Classical and Commercial Day School at 136 Mercer-street, near the Panorama, where he will carry out the same system of sound practical education to which he has devoted himself during the six years he presided over the ' Woodlawn Institute,' and which he believes may be improved upon by a residence in the city, from the facilities afforded in procuring the aid of the best assistants. By this arrangement, Mr. HOWS will be able to appropriate a portion of time to the instruction of adult classes in Elocution ; and the study and experience he brings to this important branch of every American's education, cannot fail to obtain for him the confidence of the public. Previously to opening his classes, Mr. HOWS will give a course of four lectures, with a free introductory, intended to illustrate the different styles of elocution, with scriptural, forensic, poetical, and dramatic illustrations.

CHARLES DICKENS, ESQUIRE. — At a time when the public press and society at large are replete with the hearty welcome given to this distinguished writer and excellent man, it will not be expected of us to indulge in enlarged comments upon his career thus far in this country. Suffice it to say, that wherever he has journeyed, his has been a triumphal progress ; too much so indeed, we fear, for his personal comfort, not to say health. Boston yielded him ample and most tasteful honors ; Hartford followed Boston ; and New-York has excelled herself in the brilliancy of his reception. Such ever be the reward of high and varied genius !

LITERARY   RECORD.

DR. MOTT'S TRAVELS. — The BROTHERS HARPER have just published the 'Travels in Europe and the East' of the eminent physician and surgeon, VALENTINE MOTT, M. D. The volume is printed upon a large clear type and beautiful paper, and embraces observations made between 1834 and 1841, and during a tour through Great-Britain, Ireland, France, Belgium, Holland, Prussia, Saxony, Bohemia, Austria, Bavaria, Switzerland, Lombardy, Tuscany, the Papal States, the Neapolitan Dominions, Malta, the Islands of the Archipelago, Greece, Egypt, Asia-Minor, Turkey, Moldavia, Wallachia, and Hungary. So wide a sweep of observation, to a mind like that of our author, cannot fail to have been productive of ample matériel for American readers. We shall refer again to the work, and to another which accompanied it — the popular 'Parlor Melodies.'

'KABAOSA, OR THE WARRIORS OF THE WEST.' — We have been in no small degree entertained and instructed by a tale of the last war, now publishing in parts, under the above title. It is from the pen, as we learn, of a lady of this city ; and her readers will readily perceive that she is either personally conversant with the scenes she depicts, or that she has made her theme the subject of close scrutiny. The style is spirited and natural, and the incidents stirring and picturesque without being improbable. We await the conclusion of the work with some impatience. It is *American*, and embodies moreover a very fruitful era of border romance and desultory Indian warfare. D. ADEE, New-York, and SAXTON AND PEIRCE, Boston, are the publishers.

JACOB'S GREEK READER. — Mr. WILLIAM E. DEAN, No. 2 Ann-street, has just published, on a clear and beautiful type, and in a volume of convenient size, 'A Translation of JACOB's Greek Reader, (adapted to all the editions printed in America,) for the use of schools, academies, colleges, and private learners ; with copious notes, critical and explanatory ; illustrated with numerous parallel passages and apposite quotations from the Greek, Latin, French, English, Spanish, and Italian languages : and a complete Parsing Index ; elucidated by references to the most popular Greek grammars extant. By PATRICK S. CASSERLY, author of 'A New Literal Translation of Longinus,' etc. The volume is dedicated, in an affectionate epistle, to the author's children

---

MR. BELLOWS' 'LECTURE UPON LECTURES,' delivered recently at the Clinton Hall, was one of the best of the numerous class of which it treated. With a determination to show the *accessibility* of much knowledge that is too often clouded under scientific nomenclatures or conventional terms, and to expose the humbuggery of those who would hedge learning about with forms and ceremonies, we cannot but think that Mr. BELLOWS will find his proposed course so popular, that a repetition will be called for in our sister cities.

'TECUMSEH.' — This admirable narrative poem by a young American is we learn passing through the press. Should it appear in season, we shall review it in our next number ; and we have little fear that our readers will not agree with us, that it is a production of rare merit, and one which will reflect honor alike upon the author and upon our literature.

THE KNICKERBOCKER.

VOL. XIX.   APRIL, 1842.   No. 4.

LETTERS FROM ROME.

BY GEORGE WASHINGTON GREENE.

LETTER THIRD.

You are tired you tell me of lingering so long upon the threshold. You would enter at once into this time-hallowed sanctuary, and give yourself up, mind and soul, to the contemplation of its wonders. I can readily believe you. It would seem as if nothing could be more tantalizing than these long introductions which arrest you just as your feelings are beginning to warm, and chill your enthusiasm before they allow it to approach its legitimate object. And yet there is one thing more painful than even this delay : a doubt in the authenticity of what you behold ; a distrust of the science that guides you. The moon may shine ever so sweetly upon arch and column, and the soft air bring none but the low and spirit-like sounds that harmonize with the scene. For the picturesque there is more than enough in the rudest and least-defined fragments of Roman grandeur. But it is not the picturesque alone that you seek in Rome. There are feelings that lie deeper than the transient glow of admiration ; sympathies which, although they may be awakened by the imagination, can only be kept active by an unwavering and deep-rooted conviction. Is there certainty enough in our knowledge of Rome to justify these sympathies ? Is it to reason or to credulity that we yield up our conviction ? We speak of palace and temple as of familiar things, and assign to each its limits and its date. But how can we trace in ill-assorted fragments the beauty of their primitive form, or fix the epoch of ruins that have no inscription ? These are questions that have again and again been addressed to me upon the spot ; nor is it unnatural to suppose that they must often suggest themselves to those who may read my descriptions at a distance. It is to a brief exposition therefore of the sources of our knowledge of Roman topography that I shall confine myself in the present letter.

Rome was divided by Augustus into fourteen regions or wards, each of which derived its name from some remarkable edifice comprised within its limits, or from some well-defined peculiarity in its situation. This division was preserved without material change till the middle of the sixth century; and various catalogues or registers were undoubtedly compiled, both of the limits of each ward and the chief edifices which it contained. Of these, three, originally prepared for the use of the Prefect of the city, have been preserved to modern times, and are commonly known as the *Regionarii*. The first bears the name of Publius Victor, the second of Sextus Rufus, and the third is usually designated by the title of the larger work of which it forms a part, and which is cited by historians as the 'Notitia Utriusque Imperii.' They were all composed during the fourth or fifth century. The third is attributed with much probability to the reign of the second Theodosius. It is not description that you are to look for in these catalogues. They contain a simple enumeration of the principal edifices of each ward, a list of the streets and chapels, of the palaces and blocks, the magazines, ovens, private baths and flowing fountains, together with the number and title of the subaltern magistrates and their assistants. Panvinio I believe was the first who thought of using the works of the Regionarii for the elucidation of the topography of Rome upon a plan sufficiently comprehensive; but his early death in the midst of far more important avocations prevented him from accomplishing the design which he had so ably sketched out. This loss was supplied by the copious erudition and untiring perseverance of Nardini; and these catalogues have continued to form the basis of every subsequent research.

A fourth monument, which, though but a partial catalogue, deserves to be classed with the lists of Rufus and Victor, is an inscription which originally adorned the base of a statue of Hadrian, and may still be seen in the palace of the Conservatori. This statue was erected by the vicomagistri of the wards; and fortunately for posterity they caused their own names and those of the streets of five of the wards to be engraved upon its pedestal.

Very different was the aim of the next writer, who in the dearth of more valuable materials has acquired an importance and a celebrity to which he probably never aspired. His name not having reached us, his work is known by that of the celebrated antiquarian by whom his labors were first brought to the light, and is cited as the 'Anonimo of Mabillon.' It is generally agreed that he must have written about the year 800. His work is a meagre itinerary for the guide of devout pilgrims, whose attention however he has fortunately directed to the most important remains of antiquity which lie in their way from one to another of the sanctuaries of the Holy City. Martino Polono, who visited Rome in the thirteenth century, is the next writer whose labors have served to lighten the researches of the local antiquarian; and with him may be classed the Mirabilia Romæ, from which, meagre as they are, some precious notices have been extracted for a more accurate knowledge of the state of the city and its monuments during the middle ages.

Although none of the classic writers have left a description of Rome in the days of her glory, yet there are innumerable passages scattered throughout their writings which have a direct bearing upon this subject.

The description of Strabo, though very general and confined solely to the most striking features, contains important facts for a correct estimate of the embellishments of Augustus. The poets too have introduced names of places and fragments of description which serve, with judicious criticism, to supply the want of minuter information. And what shall I say of the orators and historians? Open almost any page of Cicero or Tacitus or Livy, and you will find yourself transported into the midst of Rome. All of these scattered rays have been carefully united, and their light brought to bear with full force upon every branch of Roman topography. How little did Cicero dream, of the importance which after times would attach to his casual mention of the senate-house or therostrum! Or what would Virgil have said, could he have foreseen that many who are insensible to the poetic beauty of his verses would have held them above all price for their frequent reference to places and names!

But the most precious monument of all antiquity, and which, had our good fortune preserved it to us entire, would have amply supplied the place of description, is the plan of Rome which was engraven upon marble during the reigns of Septimin Severus and Caracalla, and discovered in the fifteenth century behind the church of the S. S. Cosma e Damiano. This inestimable monument is supposed to have been designed for the pavement of the temple of Romulus, near which it was found; and this conjecture, though unsupported by direct evidence, is so probable in itself that no archaiologist has, as far as I am aware, ever thought of calling it in question. It was drawn upon a scale of the two hundred and fiftieth of the actual size of the city, and contained an exact plan of every street and square, and every edifice both public and private. Unfortunately it was first discovered in an age unable to appreciate its importance, and suffered to remain for many years inlaid upon the walls of the building near which it had been excavated. From thence it was removed by order of Paul III. to the Farnesian gardens, until finally the providential care of Benedict XIV., to whom we are indebted for the preservation of so many of the mutilated monuments of antiquity, caused it to be placed in the conspicuous and sure station which it now occupies as a part of the Capitoline Museum. In each of these removals some new injury was inflicted upon the fragments so accidentally preserved, and the difficulty of arranging and explaining them increased. Nothing however can damp the ardor of a genuine antiquary; and these remains, mutilated as they are, justly continue to hold the first place in the class of unwritten documents.

The numerous inscriptions which may be found in every museum and church, and I had almost said in every edifice of Rome, and which have been collected and arranged with so much assiduity and with such rare erudition by Grutorius and Muratori and other distinguished scholars, afford also important data, which have been applied with great success to the solution of some very difficult questions. Were I not afraid of exhausting your patience, I would cite some examples at length. One at least you must bear with; it is such a beautiful instance of ingenious research, and withal so convincing. In the garden of the convent of Palazzola, which stands upon the site of the ancient city of Alba Longa, there is a tomb hewed out in the rock, and adorned with the consular fasces united to the insignia of the pontificate. No inscription gives the name of the personage to whose honor it was dedicated, or the date of its erection. How can we venture to supply this silence? The style of the monument is of the second Punic war. It is the only instance too in which the consular fasces and distinctive emblems of the pontificate have been found united. Now by referring to the Fasti Consulari you find that these two dignities were united in the person of a consul who held his office in the year 578 from the building of the city. His name was C. Cornelius, and he died during the year of his consulate. Thus far the evidence, though probable, would seem not to be wholly conclusive. But from the 'Fasti' we are naturally led to the historians; and Livy, speaking of the same individual, relates that his death was the consequence of a stroke of apoplexy which seized him while on his way home from celebrating the *Feriæ Latinæ* upon the Alban Mount. Is conjecture pushed too far when, knowing as we do that his way from the mount led him within a few paces of the spot occupied by this monument, we say that it was to his memory that it was erected?

The science of medals, which has thrown so much light upon obscure questions of chronology, has also been applied with the greatest success to the study of ancient buildings. Upon the erection of a new building a medal was frequently struck in honor of its founder, or as a record of his magnificence. Upon this a portico or a colonnade, or sometimes an outline of the whole edifice, carefully preserved the order of the architecture and the embellishments united with it. The beauty of the execution often vied with the splendor of the monument it was designed to illustrate, and it is to these fragile records that we are in a great measure indebted for the materials of those exquisite illustrations which have added so much to the pleasure and facility of topographical research.

I have reserved for the last place the most important of all the standards of archaiological criticism; I mean the style of different works as indicative of their date. In sculpture this test is familiar to every reader. In architecture it supplies a guide equally trusty. The use of different materials, the mode of employing them, and the degree of taste with which ornaments are chosen and introduced, form so many positive tests, which judicious criticism can apply with scarce the chance of a mistake.

Of the period of the kings we have five monuments of unquestionable authenticity. The same style of construction is rigorously preserved throughout them all. The material is *tufa* from the quarries of the city, mixed in one instance with *peperino, gabian stone* and *travertine.* The stone is cut in oblong cubical masses, which are laid with so little regard to the position of the joinings that they frequently fall in a line one upon the other. The inner mass is composed of scales of flint. This style continued in use during the first years of the republic.

From the year of Rome 245 to 365, we have no monument of certain date. But from this last date and beginning with the walls of Camillus behind the palace of the Conservatori at the Capitol, of which Livy speaks as a work *vel in hac magnificentia urbis conspiciendum,* we find fifteen different structures in unequal grades of preservation, which bring us down to within about forty years of the commencement of our era. In all of these structures, till the building of the Theatre of Pompey in the year 701, the same materials are employed that I have enumerated as being in use during the rule of the kings. The stones too are cut in large cubes, but in the manner of laying them you perceive a decided progress toward a purer and more cultivated taste. The joinings are regular throughout, and arranged in a checkered line, like the squares of a chess-board. In this too there is another step, of which a beautiful instance may be seen in the Tabularum, where the layers are placed in alternate strata of breadth and length.

In the Theatre of Pompey we find the first example of the introduction of the *opus reticulatum*, which began about that time to take the place of the *opus incertum* or *antiquum*. These terms are applicable only to the intermediary walls, and which were designed to receive a covering of stucco or of marble. The *opus incertum* is composed of small conical polygons, arranged without any regard to the symmetry of their lines. The examples of this style must be chiefly sought in the environs of the city, the only specimens within the walls being some ruins on the Palatine and at the Navalia. The *opus reticulatum* derives its name from the net-like appearance produced by arranging the stones which compose the fabric in such a manner as to form a diagonal of the lines of their joinings. In the Theatre of Pompey the want of that perfect symmetry to which this style was soon after carried, would seem to show that its introduction was as yet recent. It seems in fact a specimen of the transition from the *opus incertum* to the *opus reticulatum* in its more perfect state. The materials of both of these are the stones of the quarries nearest to the edifice. Brick was first used in the tomb of Cecilia Metella; or at least this is the earliest example that we know of a certain date. It attained to the highest point of perfection during the reign of Trajan. To those who have never seen the brick-work of the Romans it is impossible to convey any idea of the extent of that perfection. The indications of an approaching decline are perceptible in the edifices of his successor, notwithstanding his personal claims to architectural genius. The progress of decay is marked with a precision that is almost painful. Scarce an emperor but has left us some token of the corruption that was rapidly invading every branch of the arts. Large strata of cement are found intermingled with strata of brick, and no longer in proportion with the end for which cement is used. In the circus of Romulus, layers of brick are alternated with layers of stone; and even under Hadrian we find parallelipipides of stone occasionally used in the place of brick, as if the latter were already becoming scarce. In the ninth century this style came again into vogue with the name of Saracenesque, and before the close of the middle ages was carried to a pitch of perfection which readily deceives the unpracticed eye.

Similar observations might be made with regard to the successive introduction of the orders of architecture. The Doric and Ionic were the first in use; the Corinthian came next; and in each the proportions of their Grecian models were for some time rigorously observed. Then came a desire for innovation under the name of improvement.

The Doric column was elevated upon a base; the Corinthian capital was prolonged; the volutes of the Ionic became angular; and at last, as if their own exquisite simplicity fell short of the full perfection of beauty, the two orders were blended in the Composite.

With data like these, it is easy to see how a standard may be formed for ascertaining the date of monuments that have no inscription, by comparing them with those that have. The rigid application of the rules thus deduced has given to the science of archaiology a degree of certainty to which it could never have attained by any other means. Mistakes are still made. Many questions are still acrimoniously agitated. Passages of the classics are misapplied, and the characteristic style of one period may sometimes seem to run into that of another. But with all this, there is certainty; conviction in the writer; conviction too that gains upon you as you read, and chases the coldness of doubt away. It is Rome; the Rome of a thousand triumphs, and a thousand associations for every mind and every age.

———

LETTER FOURTH.

It is with a singular feeling that you walk the streets of modern Rome. The pavement of the original city is every where buried beneath the actual level; and though its average depth does not exceed fifteen feet, yet there are parts in which it extends to over three times that number. Columns and porticoes rise midway from the bosom of the earth, and you can almost lay your hand on the richly-carved frieze that once was visited only by the birds of the air. Nothing is more frequent than to meet the remains of an ancient edifice in digging for the foundations of a modern building; and many of the most precious inscriptions and choicest works of art have been drawn forth from heaps of ruin at great depth below the surface of the soil. When you think of the treasures that still lie hidden beneath this surface; of the wrecks of temples and palaces; the intermingled spoils of the barbarian, of fire and of flood, of which the soil itself is composed; you feel as if walking in some vast cemetery, where every footstep falls upon what once was a living being. The streets of Pompeii itself are scarcely more melancholy.

In seeking for the causes of this great change, you feel at once as if no single agent could have produced it, and that even the concurrent action of many would have been inadequate except in spots long and thickly inhabited. Whatever system we adopt with regard to the foundation of Rome, its origin must be carried back full twenty-six hundred years. During the whole of this long period the soil has been subject to all the caprices of man, and filled up or removed to suit his whims or his necessities. The mere circumstance of so many millions of human beings having successively dwelt within this comparatively limited circle would alone account for many and great changes. But to this must be added the peculiar features in the history of Rome; its gradual rise from the humblest original; its revolutions of kingdom, republic and empire; the infinite gradations of taste and caprice by which the structures of one age gave place to those of another; a palace to a bath and a portico to a temple; fires, inundations, and the insensible but unerring action of the atmosphere.

And in the first place it should be observed that the Romans, in erecting a new building upon ground previously occupied, seldom if ever carried beyond the walls the rubbish formed by the demolition of the original edifice. If no other convenient place of deposite could be found, it was carefully levelled and worked into the foundations of the new structure. This usage is still followed; and in the excavations made for ascertaining the position of the original soil, the difficulty of finding a proper place for the earth that is removed contributes not a little to retard the progress of these interesting researches.

If now you consider how many works of the early kings must have been found inadequate to the wants or not in proportion to the progressive taste of their successors, you will readily conceive what changes must have taken place even within the first two hundred and fifty years from the building of the city. During the republic, it was no longer the caprice of an individual, but the will of a whole people that called for change. Circuses were to be built; theatres erected. Distinction could only be purchased by bowing to the popular will; and this commanded costly shows, and edifices equally costly for the exhibition of them. Their gods too were no longer the gods of a single city but of a mighty nation; and every art was called into requisition to furnish forth habitations worthy of their power. Still more numerous were the changes under the empire. The well-known vaunt of Augustus shows how large a part the first emperor bore in these revolutions; and the time had not yet come when one man, though emperor of Rome, could venture to depopulate whole wards in order to make room for a single palace. The base of the column of Phocas is twenty-seven feet below the modern level of the Forum; and yet the soil by which that base is supported is composed of the ruins of earlier fabrics.

The repairs of the streets and pavements was another cause no less sure in its results, and equally constant in its action. The gate of St. Lorenzo, although of the time of Honorius, is nearly upon a level with the actual surface. But the monument just within it, a work of the republic, is buried so deeply that a loaded cart can hardly pass under its arch. A few paces beyond this gate, in digging for the foundations of a chapel, three successive pavements were discovered rising in layers one above the other. If we suppose these repairs to have been made no oftener than once in a century, yet each new layer being formed upon the ruins of the old, a much shorter duration than that of Rome would have been sufficient to change the whole surface.

Rome was more than once exposed to the outrages of a victorious enemy. The first sack by the Gauls under the guidance of Brennus left all but the Capitol and the walls a shapeless mass of ruins. It seemed as if it was never again to be made habitable. The populace shrunk from the task of restoration, and but for the firmness of their Dictator would have sought a home in their newly-conquered Veii. But the eloquence of Camillus was triumphant. The city arose from its ruins more closely built, and in a few years was more beautiful and more populous than ever.

In the year 409 of the christian era, a period before which it had already reached the highest point of wealth and splendor to which it ever attained, a hostile army once more appeared before its walls. During the night the hand of a traitor threw open the Salarian gate, and in a few hours the magnificent fabrics of the Pincian and a portion of the Quirinal were a prey to the flames. It is impossible to estimate the amount of destruction. The narrations of contemporaries differ in their details; but nearly all agree in representing it as having embraced the greater part of one of the most ornamented quarters of the city.

During the sack of Genseric in 455, the prayers of a venerable pontiff preserved the city from the flames; but the barbarian army passed fourteen days within the walls in the unrestrained exercise of their wanton caprice, and seeking in every direction for whatever bore the marks of silver or of gold. Equally destructive was the sack of Ricimer in 472. In 546 a part of the walls was thrown down by Totila, and the inhabitants driven to the adjacent villages. The hasty restoration of Belisarius contributed still farther to the accumulation of ruins upon the ancient level. But the most terrible of all for its fury, and the most fatal in its results, was the sack of Robert Guiscard in 1084. It was in the name of a pope that the invader came; and though it is impossible to reconcile the contradictions of the contemporary chroniclers, yet the report most favorable to the barbarian and to his employer presents a picture revolting to every feeling of humanity.

The ruins accumulated during each of these sacks were either left to moulder upon the spot where they had fallen, or were levelled and interwoven with the foundations of the new edifices. Livy bears testimony to the haste with which the work of rebuilding was carried on after the sack of the Gauls; and there is hardly an excavation but brings to light some new proof of the destruction by fire and by the sword. As we advance in the middle ages, the very want of an adequate population contributed to hasten the progress of decay; and since the sack of Guiscard a large portion of the ancient circuit has been left without inhabitants; the ruins that encumbered its ways mingling by the silent process of decomposition with the earth on which they had fallen.

Similar in their results were the great fires of which so many are recorded in the native historians. The great fire which under Nero destroyed ten out of the fourteen wards of the city, and called down so cruel a persecution upon the christians, is I believe the only exception. The ruins occasioned by this conflagration were conveyed down the Tiber and used in filling up the pools at Ostia. But on every other occasion the new buildings were raised upon the foundation and amidst the remains of the old.

To these causes, attributable to the caprice, the cruelty, and the negligence of man, two must be added over which even in the height of his power he has but partial control. In a city situated like Rome, every violent rain must detach some particles from the hills and add something to the level of the valleys. The water, wherever it falls, must find an outlet; and none but an eye-witness can realize the fury with which it pours down upon the plain.

Sixty-six distinct inundations of the Tiber are cited as sufficiently remarkable in their results to be deserving of record. The extent and duration of each has been different; nor have they been uniformly fatal in their consequences. We may even venture to call in question passages in which they are represented as menacing the entire city with overthrow. But in whatever form they have come, some degree of injury has invariably attended them. On some occasions whole buildings have been thrown down by the violence of the shock. On others the waters have slowly undermined their foundations, and the work of destruction has been accomplished by imperceptible steps. Even when attended with no visible consequences, the deposites of the waters, and their stagnation for days and weeks on spots already covered with ruins, would bring gradual accessions to the soil, and sooner or later raise it above its natural level.

But although this process of accumulation commenced in ancient times, a considerable part of it must be attributed to the building of the modern city. Whenever you dig for the ancient level in parts hitherto unopened, you find at the bottom either a hardened fluvial deposite, relics of the flames, or remains of decayed edifices. Over these rises a mass of artificial matter of every description. In these few lines you have the history of this revolution. The uninhabited quarters of the ancient city have been used as a vast reservoir for the litter and rubbish of the modern. It was inconvenient or too expensive to carry it to a distance, and hence the Forum or any other spot not too remote was made its receptacle. The deposites around the column of Phocas are nearly all of the middle ages or our own. Those of the twelfth, thirteenth and fourteenth centuries rise but four feet above the original pavements; those of the last century seventeen; while those of our own complete the enormous distance of twenty-seven feet of wilful interment of the precious remains of antiquity.

Via del Quirinale, No. 49,
  June 30, 1841.

SONNET.

We gathered round thy harp, as at thy will
Its chords poured forth their music; which doth still
Sound through the inner temple of the soul.
It was a wild but noble melody,
And when the last clear note had ceased to roll,
And thy sweet voice was silent, then they vied
In praises of the hand that could so well
Enchain the human heart by music's spell.
I could not speak; for every note that fell,
Came as a holy thing upon my ear,
And bowed my heart in prayer — that each swift day
Might bear thy gifted spirit yet more near
Where thou shalt strike thy golden harp, above,
And angels bend to hear thee sing redeeming love !

TO 'MILLER'S BRIDGE.'

I.

FRIEND of my early days ! — o'er thee
　Full oft my feet have passed,
Since first amid the forest's gloom
　Thy logs their shadows cast
Upon the waves, which to and fro,
Tilted among the reeds below.

II.

Massy and old and worn thou art,
　And mid thy arches gray
The painted wood-birds swiftly dart
　Through all the golden day ;
And 'neath thy beams where spiders cling,
Mid moss and grass the lichens spring.

III.

Merrily over thee the wain,
　Year out year in, hath passed,
When fields were ripe with golden grain,
　And when the snows fell fast :
And country dames with mien austere,
And meek-eyed girls, have lingered here.

IV.

Nor idly, for the woods around
　With sweetest echoes ring,
And birds up-springing from the ground
　Perch on the trees and sing ;
And lowing herds at sunset's glow
In file across thy timbers go.

V.

And countrymen with broad-brimmed hats
　Here oft at hot mid-noon
Gossip, and watch the large gray rats
　Amid the flowers of June ;
While the still currents, dark and slow,
All bright with bubbles move below.

VI.

No stifling city-smoke comes nigh
　To mar a scene so fair,
But bright as silver is the sky,
　And sweet the river air ;
And pleasantly the glad waves shed
Their light upon the beams o'er head.

VII.

But now, old friend ! thou art waxed old,
　And under thee no more
Are childhood's blissful legends told,
　For my best days are o'er ;
And they are in the tomb who played
With me beneath thy grateful shade !

　　　　　　　　　　　　　　　　H. W. R.

EDWARD ALFORD AND HIS PLAY-FELLOW.

BY THE AUTHOR OF 'WILSON CONWORTH.'

CHAPTER SECOND.

——— 'The schools became a scene
Of solemn farce, where Ignorance on stilts,
His cap well lined with logic not his own,
With parrot tongue performed the scholar's part,
Proceeding soon a graduated dunce.'

COWPER.

THE village of Braintree, in which Mr. Charles Alford's house was situated, was like most other places in the neighborhood of cities. It had its gentry, persons of some property, who resided one half of the year in the country and spent the winter in the city, and who had no more to do with their country neighbors than was absolutely necessary. Their visiters were mostly from the city, together with the few families situated for the time in their country-seats, like themselves. We Americans may as well confess it; we do practically acknowledge distinctions in society. There are high and low here as well as in England. We have family pride, mostly based on wealth. Intelligent foreigners seem to understand our condition better than we do ourselves; as they who learn our language grammatically, speak and write it more purely than we who learn it by ear. And they say: 'You are a great republic. We love your country, not because you *are* so different from the countries of Europe, but because *you have it in your power to be.*'

Braintree also had its plain honest farmers, who did not seem to care a straw whether they were noticed or not, so that they were well paid for their produce and garden sauce. The farmer, living by himself more than any other worker, sees not the ostentations and assumptions of wealth. The carriages in the high-way never run over his heavy ox-team. On Sunday, when the fine folk come to church in their showy dresses, he is rather amused at the novelty of the glitter than envious of it. He himself is neatly dressed; and he does not dream of any treasure that can compare with his four stout sons and half-dozen rosy-cheeked daughters.

Here too was the usual number of thin, care-worn mechanics; men who were diseased in body and consequently in mind by confinement in hot work-shops. Here is the material for revolution. The mechanic feels more keenly than another the inequalities of fortune. He is by his occupation brought closely in contact with the wealth he covets. He is admitted to the rich chamber, the costly apartments of luxury, in the way of business. He sees what he cannot enjoy. He is treated with indifferent civility. He is constantly measuring himself by a false standard; and this together with his bilious stomach makes him uneasy, envious, and dangerous. The revolutions founded in religious principle, like that of Switzerland and America, originated with the farmers; while revolts and conspiracies are common among the artisans of Paris.

Nor was this village peculiar in having three or four doctors, each attempting to ride the others down; two or three ministers and as many churches, the members of which cordially hated each other; but only on the Sabbath, being united perhaps by political or business bands during the week. It had also its lines of opposition stages, opposition lawyers and apothecaries, and a set of advocates for each side of every question under the sun. Animal magnetism and phrénology were now in their glory, in that halo of obscurity which commands the greatest reverence from the people; and party religion and party politics, scandal, back-biting and meddling had also their share in the mess of things.

The sun had just gone down, and every thing denoted that the labors of the day were over. The merchant was sitting in front of his store quietly smoking his cigar, surrounded by a squad of idlers to be found in every country village, who are not willing to do any thing, though having enough to do; and who fret life away in useless repinings about dyspepsy and the weather. Some were leaning against the door of the store, in vain trying by change of posture for an easy position; others, with hands in side-pockets, manfully kicking little stones and chips about, in the intervals of conversation, thereby venting their spleen and impatience; others were standing bolt upright, as if in despair, to wrestle thus with the fiend ennui; while a few were walking to and fro as if half determined to go to some place, if any place could be thought of to which they might go, not wishing to stay where they were, because your idler is always restless and uneasy; the most unhappy devil in America of any country in the world. He has not the philosophy of the Frenchman; he wants the phlegm of the Dutchman, the pride of the Englishman. He is surrounded by practical rebukes upon his delinquences, and lives under the fear of public sentiment; for the world about him is busy and industrious. He is always thinking of himself and his faults, and often seeks occupation and oblivion by meddling in the affairs of others. He prys into secrets, and is more mischievous than an idiot, without being more useful.

Here straggled along the day-laborer, with his implements on his shoulder; and there might be seen boys riding weary horses bare-back to water, upon the full run. Pretty girls, whose delicate limbs and genteel attire showed them to belong to the better classes, were strolling along the streets in clans of three or four, perhaps in pursuit of diffident admirers among the young clerks and students of medicine and law; for females control society in the village as completely as in the city; and however men may boast of their superiority, they do stand in awe of the women. Hardly ever does an engagement take place, but the first fire comes from what is called the weaker sex, though the victim of the manœuvre is led to suppose that he is the prime mover of the matter.

Many wistful glances passed from the group of idlers as these beauties tripped along; and as many, meant to be meaning, were cast from the depths of bonnets toward them; yet no one dared to join them in their walk. If any one had done so, straightway there would have been a report that such a gentleman was very much pleased with such a lady, and the parties would have become the town talk; a kind of notoriety which, however pleasing to the fashionable belle, is viewed by country lads and lasses as the worst of evils.   And from this condition between the sexes we can trace the secret method the lover takes to win his mistress, which shuts him or her out from the advice of parent or guardian in an affair of such immense consequence, and is a cause of regret for a life-time.

A band of urchins had as usual chosen the most public part of the most frequented street for their evening sport; which went on happily for a while, as far as they were concerned, though to the great annoyance of passers-by and the old ladies who love to take their snuff in quiet after tea.   But ere long the strong began to oppress the weak, and a loud call was made for a ring, and every encouragement given to widen the breach for the sake of a fight.

One of the combatants was a short thick-set boy, about twelve years of age.   His dark curly hair seemed to curl tighter to his head, and his black eyes glowed brighter as he confronted his opponent, a large clumsy, vulgar-looking boy, who relied much upon his physical strength.

'What if my father *is* a gardener, and we work for a living?' said the smaller boy; 'does your father do any thing better; lending money and getting people's farms away from them?   I know I go to the town-school while you go to Mr. Magnum's, where you ought to learn better than to lie and bully little fellers out of their rights.   I say the ball did not hit me, and our side is not out.   There's Ned Alford, and he will say it did not; and he is on your own side.   We wo'n't give it up; and if you want to fight, come on, that's all!   I'll fight till I die before I'll give it up;' and he tossed down his jacket, and shook his fist at Bill Spooner.   Nothing staggers men or boys so much as a sense of injustice.   The bold assertion of truth has won more victories than were ever achieved by the sword.

Ned Alford did interfere in behalf of our friend Tom Towley, for the bold fighter was he; and told Bill Spooner that if he did 'nt look out he would get his father's coachman to give him a flogging.   Bill was fairly frightened before by the courage of Tom, over whom he anticipated an easy conquest; but the support of Edward in behalf of his play-fellow gave a new importance to Tom in the eyes of all the boys; for Edward's father was thought the richest man in the village, and the boys took rank and influence according to the respective property of their parents.   'Oh! well, Tom,' said Spooner, 'I was only in fun; then your side is not out.   I wanted to see if you had any pluck. You ought to come to our school.   ·Mr. Magnum's is the place for such a fighter.'   'I do n't want to go to your school, Bill Spooner,' said Tom; 'Mr. Wickliff keeps as good a school as Mr. Magnum any day. We do n't learn Latin and Greek at our school, but I am most through the Rule of Three; but we do n't lie and bully little fellers as you do;' and saying this, Tom gathered up his jacket and hat, and was walking off with a noble sense of being able to take care of himself.

The boys belonging to the town school collected around Tom, leaving the pupils of Mr. Magnum by themselves.   The victory Tom had just gained, in carrying his point, gave them courage to speak their feelings; and many a taunt, hitherto repressed, was thrown at the *ruffle-shirters*, as the town boys called them, together with other epithets too coarse to be recorded on paper. A general fight would have been the consequence had not some of the citizens interfered and dispersed the belligerent parties; but notwithstanding that blows were avoided, a rancorous hatred was established between the two schools by this slight circumstance, which interrupted all future harmony.

Perhaps in our whole country we have no influence more at war with the true spirit of republican institutions than the fashion of private schools. Children who enjoy the advantage, if advantage it be, of private education in a select school, soon begin to look upon themselves as beings of a higher order than those educated at the public school. Their parents also can generally afford to dress them better than their neighbors' children; and in numberless ways the distinction is fostered. It is thrown at the poor boy as a disgrace, that he is the child of charity and goes to the public school. He cannot be supposed capable of reasoning soundly upon the subject. He feels deeply a sense of inferiority; takes but little pains with the neatness of his dress, the propriety of his manners, and the choice of his expressions. He attempts to become distinguished often for a bold coarseness; and since fortune has denied him (this is a conclusion of his own) the chance of being a gentleman and scholar, he is determined to make the most of his lower faculties, and reap what enjoyment he can.

But really he need make but little effort to become coarse and vulgar and illiterate; for who does not know that our system of public education is a mere form without substance? This is not the case it is true in some favored places where the public school is the pet of the people, and is crowding out of existence all private establishments, those hot-beds of aristocracy and pride. We suppose it is pretty well understood that most of the public schools in the country towns are taught by young men who resort to the business to perfect their own knowledge of reading, writing and arithmetic, as a stepping-stone to something better, at about the same wages the farmer gives to his hired man for shovelling manure — ten and twelve dollars per month. There, in a room eight feet high and twenty-five feet square are collected from fifty to one hundred boys and girls of all ages and sizes and conditions. This room is warmed by a box-stove, and the temperature ranges from twenty to ninety degrees. The children are thawed and frozen so often that it is no wonder many of them become *soft*. The teacher, knowing little if any thing of ventilation and the laws of health, mistakes the drowsiness and stupidity of the little children who sit on the lower benches, where the air has the least vitality, for idleness and stubbornness, and perhaps flogs them severely. Their little hearts are almost broken by this injustice. They feel it is injustice, but they cannot tell how. Repeated instances of oppression and despair of any redress (for if they complain at home they often get another flogging) induces insensibility. A warfare is already begun between the teacher and his pupils. 'Stratagem is authorized in war,' reasons the boy; 'we will cheat you if we can, Mr. Schoolmaster.' All idea of improvement is forgotten or lost in this new excitement and struggle with the master; and the winter school, which all the Fourth-of-July orators say is the foundation of the liberties of our country, ends with having sown in the hearts and minds of these young-sters seven devils, where before were only two or three.

At the same time, there is going in this and every village of any size, a select school, to which the wealthier sort of people send their children. This school may and may not be better than the public school. It probably enjoys better air and better manners. The teacher has A. B. attached to his name; but he too probably has no permanent interest in education. He has no idea of making it a life business. He has per-haps just been graduated from college, and needs a little money to help him along in a profession. But what is to be done? the reader asks. If we could have our way, there should be no private schools; or if there were any, they should be private schools at their peril. The rich and refined should give their money and patronage to the public school. If their children have good manners and refined habits, these would be caught by the poorer and less favored classes. Such a course would enable the town committees to engage well-educated and competent teachers; men and women acquainted with the *art of teaching*. No longer would the unmeaning and anti-republican feeling be encouraged among the young. All minds would have an equal chance. The intel-ligent poor boy would have the opportunity of measuring himself with the son of the wealthy, and discovering that his garb and diet were no obstacles to elevation of mind and superiority in the higher attainments of his nature. And if the teacher were to do his duty and govern his school with impartiality, making scholarship and good deportment the test of his favor and commendation, and not wealth and attire, the young would learn to put a right estimate upon the accidents of fortune; and the zeal now evinced in the acquisition of wealth, and the love of show and equipage, would give place to a thirst for the acquisition of knowledge and a love of moral excellence.

There is no way in which a system of public instruction can be car-ried out upon any other principle. Our public schools as they are now conducted may keep boys out of mischief, and drill them in certain habits of order; may teach them to read and write and keep accounts; fit them to be the shop-boys of dry goods merchants; but is this what we are aiming at when we talk of the education of the laboring classes, the elevation of our political character?

Let there be a hall large enough to contain five hundred pupils; let it be an imposing building and not a barn; let it be such a place that the pupil, as he enters it, shall feel he is at the threshold of a temple and not a prison: the mind impressed with reverence will need no govern-ment, but will be a law unto itself. Here in such a place shall such a teacher as we would have (and the lower the grade of mind he addresses, the higher must be his power and faith) tell these five hundred pupils some elementary knowledge. Let it be a whole, and let him give the subject that grace and command which all elementary knowledge has, far higher in degree than we generally imagine, and they will learn, and have something in their minds which has become a part of themselves, while from books they may have lists of words, ready on the tongue, and fixed in the memory, with little or no knowledge of the subjects to which they belong.

Mr. Alford designed to send Edward to college, and at Mr. Magnum's school he studied nothing but Latin and Greek, and enough mathematics to enable him to enter at Cambridge. The object was not to train his mind and character, but to get him into college. 'So he is well off my hands,' thought Mr. Magnum; 'enters college with credit, and takes a high rank; my task is done.' He did not consider that the course of the boy at college would depend much upon the habits he had acquired at school. It did not occur to him that the superficial school-boy makes the superficial collegian and the superficial man; that the teacher holds in his hands almost the destiny of the youth committed to his charge. He did not consider these things, considerations which give quite a new coloring to the employment of school-keeping, and should cause us to doubt if any are competent to such labors, rather than intrust our children to any person who chooses to assume the care of such responsibilities.

Mr. and Mrs. Alford, like all fond parents, thought it a matter of course that their son would do well. They paid large bills for his education; bought him all necessary books; and so many not necessary, that he got quite a disgust at the very sight of a book. He had had from infancy all the expensive annuals for children, picture books, dissected maps to teach him geography, and all the helps Peter Parley's ingenuity could furnish, to make him a philosopher and historian, before he was suffered to go a mile from home by himself. The boy's mind lived through this hot-bed process wonderfully sound. The worst consequence was that he hated all patient study, and never had learned to apply his mind to any subject which did not yield immediate gratification. He played with the rules of arithmetic as with so many puzzles, as they are; but algebra seemed an insurmountable difficulty. When he came to deal with principles he was quite at fault. But algebra he must have, for it was required for admittance to college; and so the rules were committed to memory, the questions were solved mechanically; and by a great mystery to himself he could pass a very respectable examination, considering he knew nothing about the science. All this time he carried a heavy heart to school; he became pale, languid and spiritless, for which cause his affectionate mother fed him with dainties and sweetmeats, which only made the matter worse. The hope of being a collegian and wearing a long-tailed coat and high cravat was the only bright spot in his dog's life.

But what was Tom doing in the mean time? In the summer he worked with his father. In the intervals of labor how sweet was to him the perusal of the book he had taken from the village library! How eagerly he devoured every word from title-page to end! The prospect of the winter school cheered his summer toil. As his body grew with healthful exercise, and his corporeal power increased, new mental wants were aroused, which asked for culture. Not a day nor minute was lost of the precious privilege.

Mr. Wickliff could teach him but little, but he taught him that little well. The large number collected in the town school-house gave but a small share of time to him. Tom was left to work out his own sums; forced to depend upon himself; and his healthy frame enabled him to bear the bad atmosphere with impunity. Being of a kind and obliging disposition, and a general favorite with all the boys, and girls too, many a question and slate was brought to him for assistance, in giving which he improved his stock of knowledge, and the goodness of his heart to boot. The teacher always learns more than his pupil; and no elementary knowledge can be unveiled without some valuable suggestions to the mind which contemplates it. Tom in fact was a kind of under teacher; both teacher and pupil in the school; and if the truth might be told, he more than once helped Edward along with a difficult sum. All these circumstances gave him a consciousness of strength and a self-reliance more valuable than all the mathematical knowledge in the world.

Tom also wrote a good hand. He was taught to write in parallel lines. No time was given to flourishing in the public school. The copy for the whole school was written on the black-board large enough for all to see it. Famous writing-masters who teach a beautiful hand in twelve lessons found no encouragement from Mr. Wickliff. He used to say, ' Parallel writing is the whole secret; uniformity is the trick of beauty. If you write one letter at an angle of forty-five degrees, write them all so. If you write one letter perpendicularly, do the same with all, and your page will look neat and be legible. Be as simple as you can with your capital letters, and do not make the looped letters too long and high. Be not too anxious about a fine stroke from your pen. In life and business you will often be obliged to write with a stump of a quill.' No writing-master ever gave better advice. Beside, he did not require all his pupils to write in a certain way, but he endeavored to help each one in the manner to which by habit or physical constitution he was inclined. Some wrote a very sloping hand, others an upright hand; but he required all to write their letters parallel with one another.

In Mr. Magnum's school, on the contrary, a writing-master from the city came twice a week to give lessons. In the first place he brought with him spread eagles, men on horseback, beast, bird and fish, all cut on paper by a flourish of his pen. These were submitted to the curious eyes of the boys. This display was followed by an address to the pupils, in which he attempted to show that a good hand-writing is the highest attainment of the mind; that it involves the mechanical powers, chemistry, and is quite nearly related to painting, claiming thereby affinity with music and poetry; in short, a fine art. The master was elegantly dressed; wore a diamond ring upon his little finger, and quite captivated the boys with his perfumery and smiles. They were all made to sit in a certain manner; to write at a certain angle; little and large, long-fingered and short-fingered boys, all must observe the same manner of holding the pen. Every letter that admitted of a flourish got it. Writing became the order of the day. The walls of the school-room bore marks of their improvement; the fly-leaves of their books were besmeared with spread eagles and incomprehensible figures; and the moment the lesson was ended they recovered their original position, only to write worse than ever before. The afternoon spent with the writing-master was devoted by Mr. Magnum to taking a ride with his lady, and was hailed by the boys as a season of fun and mischief.

Let it in justice be said that writing-masters may benefit adults who will adhere to their rules for a length of time until the habit is formed; but parents will find all attempts to teach little boys and misses to write well in a few lessons worse than futile. Every person has a style of writing adapted to his physical organization; and this it is which gives that character to the writing, by which many undertake to decide upon the disposition of the writer; enables witnesses in courts of justice to swear to signatures with as much assurance as they would to the faces and personality of individuals. Now the patent writing-master oversets all this; he engrafts upon his pupil his own hand and style instead of correcting and improving, by judicious rules, that which he finds to belong to the person by nature. His purpose is answered. He gets his tuition-money, but he leaves the learner often worse off than he found him. He breaks up his old hand-writing without giving him any other he can adopt. The pupil in the hurry of business flounces about between the old and the new, so that his writing has no distinctive character. He writes his name in one manner to-day, in another to-morrow. No witness may dare to swear to a signature *now*, for the writing-masters teach all to write the same angular or anti-angular hand, as the case may be.

Tom Towley in the district school had this advantage; he was instructed in the general principles of writing, and then let alone. And so in other respects he was not educated to death. Every path and movement was not so circumscribed and hedged with rules and precepts that nature had no chance. He did not become a machine, like the pupils of Mr. Magnum, who knew every thing by heart in the books. Tom could in time solve almost any question in common arithmetic, but he could not repeat a rule from beginning to end. He could tell in his own language how questions of certain kinds were worked out; and this *was* the rule in fact; and yet he thought himself very deficient in comparison to Edward, who could repeat all the rules in the book, but with difficulty worked out the questions belonging to them.

The mind will no more acquire strength by having every thing done for it than will the body. It must be left to do its own work. It must work out its own salvation from the death of ignorance. Too much may be done by the teacher as well as too little. Would the child that should be carried about in the arms until ten years of age have any strength of limb? Does the boy not gain this by exercise of exertion? Must he not work for it himself? Can you fasten it upon him by any artificial means? Not so. Nor will the mind have strength and sinew except by vigorous action of itself, unaided and unsupported but by its own energies, latent in it, which necessity must and will summon forth.

Before Edward and his class-mates left Mr. Magnum's school for examination to enter college, there must needs be a great exhibition. The trustees of the school, whose names were paraded in the news-papers as such, but who never came near it except upon great occasions, were present. This august body consisted of the ministers, the judges, and the rich men of the town. The two former classes are always supposed to know more about education than other people, and the latter were added for their influence. It was an amusing spectacle to see the attempts of grave and sensible men to appear to understand the Latin and Greek, the algebra and philosophy paraded before them. They looked pleased, nodded at one another, smiled upon the crowd of pupils, and sat uneasily, as if some knowing fellow should discover their ignorance. They did sit out an examination of several hours with praiseworthy patience; but as to deriving any pleasure, it was out of the question. They learned one important truth — their own ignorance, and were made to feel it.

The boys enjoyed the show very much. They had been drilled in the answers to certain questions for weeks, and knew their parts well. But accidents will happen sometimes; and we have to relate one which we hope may often occur, and expose the imposition of show schools.

A little class was called out to be examined in history. Proudly the little fellows took their places in their snow-white collars and shining buttons and well-combed hair. The third boy in the class was unfortunately absent on account of sickness. Mr. Magnum did not observe his absence, and the boys were too full of the occasion and themselves to think of any thing but their splendid appearance.

Mr. Magnum. 'Charles, who discovered America?'

First Boy. 'Christopher Columbus, Sir, a native of Genoa.'

Mr. M. 'Very well. Next; under whose patronage?'

Second Boy. 'Ferdinand and Isabella of Spain.'

Mr. M. 'Correct. Next; from whom did the western continent take its name?'

Third Boy. 'Sebastian Cabot, Sir,' answered the little fellow. That was the answer to his question; but the sickness of number three had placed him one step out of his place. He heard not the nature of the question; he was only thinking of his answer. And so it went; every reply through the class was just one step ahead of the question. A few of the audience perceived the mistake; and Mr. Magnum, if he noticed it, wisely said nothing. The boys proudly marched to their seats, and the mothers smiled, and some shed tears of congratulation and joy at such wonderful precocity.

The examination being ended, Mr. Shakehands, the popular preacher, rose to make a speech. But before we give his words, he deserves a more particular notice.

Mr. Shakehands was a clergyman by profession. His father had been a distinguished politician, and he inherited the faculty of spouting. He was a proud, vain, superficial man, with a good deal of lumber in his brain, such as dates, names, and remarkable events in the town, but without a particle of common sense, or any power of generalizing and connecting his knowledge so as to deduce from it a single important principle. He was fond of authority and command, and would have made a first-rate boatswain aboard a man-of-war. He had some humor, and told a few good stories when he forgot his dignity and fell into his natural character. But being called upon constantly to enact a part in life, placed in a calling for which he was entirely unfitted by nature and disposition, he lived in a constant struggle; unhappy himself, and making every body uncomfortable about him. He never preached good sermons, and kept his place only by visiting the women of his congregation, shaking hands with the family, and praising the children. The men hated him; but being afraid of their wives, who adored him, they were averse to saying so. He had in great perfection the art of flattery; and here was an opportunity not to be lost of soaping the public by proxy, by laying it on the boys. He began:

'This is a great occasion, and *opens up* to us high hopes for the future. In this high day of glory for our village, which is second to none in New-England, and I may say without flattery, the world; endowed so richly with superior advantages of intellectual cultivation, together with the collateral aids of religion and virtue; boasting so many fair scions of fair races — ahem — what auspicious hours are these! Here the fond mothers can, like the mother of the Gracchii, point to their jewels in these precocious instances of educational illumination. Where are fairer mothers? where more hopeful descendants! Too much credit cannot be given to the learned and accomplished teacher of such a race of juvenile aspirants for renown. He is, I am proud to say, only second to the sacred office of religion, in this our flourishing department of our county, called by the sweet and euphonious name of Braintree. *Tree* did I say? Nay it is a broad *tree*, that will overspread the land with intelligence, emanating from this glorious and stupendous institution, under the supervision, tutelage and care of my much esteemed and learned friend, Mr. Magnum, A.B., who ought to be D. D., if such titles were ever given to school-masters.'

'I wish you were d——d!' whispered a lawyer to his neighbor, 'with your infernal blather!'

Mr. Shakehands did not hear. On he went in the full tide of his wordy nonsense; calling every pupil by name, and saying the most extravagant things of each one.

The audience dispersed highly delighted. The trustees adjourned to the hotel to eat a dinner at the expense of the fund, and to forget as soon as possible their own insignificance as scholars, in talking loudly upon subjects they did understand.

Edward Alford was admitted to college. Tom Towley went to learn the trade of a blacksmith, in the town of Cambridge, near to the college where Edward was to take another step in his education. But let not the reader suppose that Tom had not also entered upon another step in his education in the work-shop of the black-smith. But we must defer for another chapter the description of their new condition.

EPIGRAM ON A LAZY FELLOW.

If ' keeping Sabbaths' saves the soul,
   This man's must go to heaven;
Not satisfied with one a week,
   He hallows all the seven.

SONG

OVER THE CRADLE OF TWO INFANT SISTERS, SLEEPING.

FROM THE SPANISH.

SWEET be their rest! no ghastly things
  To scare their dreams assemble here,
But safe beneath good angels' wings
  May each repose from year to year.

Cheerful, like some long summer day,
  May all their waking moments flow,
Happier, as run life's sands away,
  Unstained by sin, untouched by wo.

As now they sleep, serene and pure,
  Their little arms entwined in love,
So may they live, obey, endure,
  And shine with yon bright host above!

Boston.   JAMES T. FIELDS.

LIFE IN HAYTI.

NUMBER FIVE.

THE entire absence of every thing like architectural remains would seem to be conclusive proof that the aboriginal inhabitants of this island were as distinct from their neighbors in Mexico in their origin, as their mild manners show them to have been from their contemporaries within the limits of our own country, or even from the savage Caribs who occupied Porto Rico and the other islands to the eastward. While so utterly different from the above-named tribes, there was such a homogeneousness between the Haytien and the Cuba and Bahama Indians, that we may easily believe them to have sprung from the same stock. And yet it is hardly credible that the Mexican, the North-American and the Haytien Indians were derived from three different families of man. It would be a bold proposition to assert that three different parties of adventurers or exiles landed upon the shores of the new world, from whom have sprung all the nations which inhabited it at the arrival of Columbus.

But if the aboriginal tribes had a common ancestry in the new world, how many ages must have elapsed before they could have become so completely changed in their natures and habits from each other! How long must it have taken the Haytiens to forget the art of building, for instance! How came the spirit of revenge and its attending evil spirits to be so completely quelled in the breasts of these mild people, while they raged so fiercely among the North-Americans?

The Europeans gave them all, from one end of the continent to the other, the unmeaning title of Indians, and 'by this sign' destroyed them. But they too were perchance Europeans; perhaps allied to the hardy Northmen who afterward poured upon the shores of France and England. Perhaps they were Phœnicians or Carthaginians, who had passed out by the Pillars of Hercules in search of new sources of trade. The love of sea adventure we know was rife among the ancients. Witness the wanderings of Ulysses, of Æneas and of the Argonauts. But leave we this deep sea of speculation to wiser heads; and ' *revenons à nos moutons.*'

Certain it is that the sun did not shine upon a more peaceful territory than was our island when first visited by Columbus. The great voyager was shipwrecked a few days after approaching the land, not far east of Cape François. ' The existence of these islanders,' says Mr. Irving, ' seemed to the Spaniards 'like a pleasant dream. They disquieted themselves about nothing. A few fields cultivated almost without labor furnished the roots and vegetables which formed a great part of their diet. Their rivers and coasts abounded with fish; their trees were laden with fruits of golden or blushing hue, and heightened by a tropical sun to a delicious flavor and fragrance. Softened by the indulgence of nature, a great part of their day was passed in indolent repose in this luxury of sensation inspired by a serene sky and a voluptuous climate; and in the evenings they danced in their fragrant groves to their national songs, or the rude sound of their sylvan drums.'

Contrast now, good reader, these happy valleys, this new-world paradise, with European life at that very epoch. Europe, destined soon to be the mother of new nations in this newly-discovered hemisphere, was then in a perfect whirl of war. The Spanish sovereigns were engaged in a fierce struggle with the Saracens of Grenada; Burgundy was ruled by Charles the Bold; France was distracted by civil wars which united many great fiefs to the crown; England was equally convulsed by the feuds of the rival houses of York and Lancaster; and if these domestic strifes ever were suspended on either side of the channel, it was done that the two nations might make war upon each other; Ireland was a fertile field for revolts and insurrections; the border wars with Scotland were unceasing. Such was the convulsed state of christendom when Columbus spread before its wondering eyes a new and boundless world, to which valor or avarice or ambition or persecution might equally bend their haughty way.

I know not how it was, but as I contemplated the beautiful landscapes every where spread out in this delightful island, my thoughts reverted much oftener to the original mysterious dwellers upon the soil, (placed there we know not when nor how,) than to any of the races who have since held it. They went back to those simple children of nature who had roamed so peacefully over these hills and valleys time out of mind, until at length the charm was broken by intruders, coming as they devoutly believed from the skies. A few short years found them, all unused as they were to effort, performing tasks far beyond their strength for inhuman task-masters; and thus they perished from sheer fatigue, as by a pestilence. The places that knew them, in an incredibly short space of time knew them no more; and then their weak and unprofitable labor found a valuable substitute in the brawny strength of the sons of Africa, whom the 'auri sacra fames' soon poured into the island by ship-loads.   But to return.

A very important part of the life of a people is doubtless their eating and drinking.   Some account therefore of this department among the Haytiens may not come amiss.   I have heard of a dog who saw water delineated so naturally in a picture that he ran to it to quench his thirst; and I can aver that the feastings of Scott always made me feel hungry.   Whether the appetites of my readers will be excited by the delicacies we are about to set before them, I cannot say; but the writer feels homesick at the very retrospect.   No Haytien, and indeed no West-Indian feels as if he has begun the day until he has swallowed a cup of chocolate or coffee.   The former is the favorite beverage with the Spaniards, the latter in Hayti; not served up however in a huge coffee-cup with piles of hot toast and ham, where the weak beverage plays a secondary part.   The abstemious creole leaves his apartment as soon as or even before the sun appears above the horizon.   With a capacious and showy robe-de-chambre encircling his limbs, and a bright-colored 'mouchoir' playing the part of a turban, he proceeds straight to the 'bonne,' who knowing the early habits of the inmates has risen still earlier, and already wields the little cafétiere, containing the boiling beverage.

Each member of the family receives in turn his or her portion, which flows from the biggin as strong as possible and as black as night, and holding all the delicate aroma of the berry.   Qualified with a little syrup (the form in which sugar is used) it is quite a different article from that which is made on a more 'extensive' scale for our northern breakfasts.   The coffee is burnt and ground as near as possible to the time of using it.   It is then put in a bag or pocket tapering to a point; upon this the boiling water is poured, and is ready to be drank as fast as it filters through.   Some persons are so particular as to separate the broken kernels from the others before burning, and burn them separately, so that all may be roasted alike.   (Do not burn your coffee *black*; how can you expect to make coffee out of *charcoal?*)   Particular persons also provide a year's supply in advance, so that they may always use that which is a year old.   This foresight however is not often practiced by the improvident people of whom we write.   The early American breakfast is unknown; the first repast, though called the 'dejeuner,' not being prepared before eleven or twelve o'clock.   This meal is composed of meat or 'salaisons' and vegetables; the only other meal, 'diner' is usually served up soon after dark, and is very similar to the other. With both these meals all who can afford the indulgence drink French claret.   The food of the poorer classes is confined almost entirely to salt provisions and plantains, which latter are the staff of life in all tropical countries.   The kitchen is a shed detached from the house, containing a fire-place either of earth or brick, where every thing is cooked in iron pots of various sizes, or upon the gridiron.   Thus, to prepare the food for a decent meal, the cook has to preside over a dozen different pots and kettles, each with its separate fire.   The meat is consumed on the day it is killed; and it is more ludicrous than agreeable to see the labor and culinary skill exerted to prepare it for the palate.

A 'biftek' for instance is first pounded tremendously; then it is rubbed well with sour orange; and then ninety-nine times in a hundred done to death. When the beef was good, which was not uncommon, and when done rarely, (which *was* uncommon,) this dressing produced a very nice beef-steak. Turtle of the hawk's-bill species (which furnishes the shell) is often to be had. It is cooked usually as a ragout; a soup made of it being an unknown mystery to a people who make soups of every thing else. This is not the same turtle which furnishes the calipash and calipee to the London and New-York aldermen, which are taken among the shallows and keys of the Bahamas. The mode of capturing the hawk's-bill on the coast of Hayti shows him to be as simple in his nature as he is valuable as a prize. Wooden buoys are made as like the animal as may be, to which are attached a number of strong lines furnished with loops; these are anchored at some distance from the shore, and the silly animal descrying, as he fancies, a playmate, frolics round it until he becomes entangled in the meshes, and thus remains a captive until the fisherman visits his snares at sunrise, when he is borne triumphantly to the shore. The flesh is sold at about the price of beef, and the shell for nine or ten dollars the pound.

Fish are abundant, and are taken in various ways. Early in the morning, while the sea is smoothed by the land-breeze, the fishermen go out a mile or two and fish with hooks; those which they take, weighing from half a pound to five or six pounds each. This is a small size for sea-fish; the cod, haddock, halibut and sturgeon of northern latitudes being unknown. Those which are most common were of two kinds, red and blue; the former, including captains and sea-mullets, are exceedingly delicate, and gratify the most epicurean palate. Another excellent dish is prepared from the 'piscet.' These are fish an inch in length, which are taken in the river at certain seasons of the year, and are sold at the rate of a shilling the quart. The negroes provide themselves with a small tub, which they float upon the water by their side, and then plunging, scoop them up with both hands. They are common to only one or two rivers of the island; but while they last, (some two or three weeks,) the whole population near their favorite rivers live on them, and they must be allowed a place as a most dainty and delicate item in our bill of fare. There is a small fish called the sardine, identical perhaps (certainly in size and appearance, being of a silvery white, and some five or six inches in length) with the fish of the same name, of which vast quantities are taken on the coast of France, and are put up in oil by the French, and sent to all parts of the world. These are taken in a very skilful manner with a casting-net, which in shape is a perfect cone, about twelve feet in height, and when spread, the base or mouth covers a circle of about the same diameter. The fisher wades along in the water, sometimes immersed to the arm-pits, and giving his net a dexterous toss, it expands and then drops lightly on the water at four or five yards distance, and the bullets with which the mouth is loaded carry it instantly to the bottom. He then draws it in gently by a cord attached to the top or small end, and the bullets keeping the mouth down, and gradually closing together, form a sack from which there is no escape, and he thus captures all the fish which happen to be within the circle.   Much skill and practice are required to cast the net properly.

Still another and the most effectual mode of warfare against the piscatory tribes is that of the seine.   This immense net is at least a hundred feet long and twelve or fifteen in width.   It is packed carefully in a canoe, ready for giving out, and this canoe is stationed near the shore. Another is in front having half a dozen lusty rowers, and in the stern is fastened the drawing-rope of the seine.   At the word of command, they start off at full speed, drawing the seine out of the other boat; and after describing a semi-circle pull with main force for the shore, paying out rope after the seine is exhausted.   The other boat also lands, and the crowd of spectators laying hold of the ropes, the seine is dragged slowly to shore by the strength of fifty men.   It is interesting to witness this operation; the fish, as they find the meshy wall narrowing round them, leap into the air by scores, and as a big fellow falls on the outer side and escapes, the multitude cheer and the fishermen curse the lucky spring.   And as the net gets into shallow water, what a hubbub!   Such a splashing among the poor victims, and such shouts from the by-standers if there is a good haul!   But no hand touches until they are all drawn safely up high and dry upon the sands; for beside being against rule, a meddlesome fellow might chance to get hold of a sea-porcupine.   As soon as the game is fairly bagged, the horn is sounded, and the populace flock to the beach, and find the fishermen busily engaged in stringing their captives in one or two or three shilling bunches, which are soon disposed of, not without a vast amount of haggling about their money's worth.   There are sometimes more than a dozen varieties taken in a sweep.   The most singular and beautiful is one of the size of a dollar, as round, and of the same silvery whiteness; and moreover as transparent as glass, even the vessels being visible.   I placed one on a book, and *read through it* with the same facility as if it had been a piece of plate glass.   The edges of this beautiful little creature were not thicker than paper, and the thickest part, in the centre, not more than a sixteenth of an inch.

Next in our list comes the land-crab, which the natives esteem as an article of food, but which foreigners do not fancy.   It is frequently poisonous, (supposed from feeding on the leaves of the mancheneel tree,) though not fatally so.   In some work on natural history it is stated that this crab is peculiar to the island of Jamaica and the western part of Hayti.   In the latter they are quite common.   They are of a yellowish brown color, having long and powerful claws; and being withal very pugnacious, they are dangerous to handle.   They burrow in the soil; and after a heavy rain, piles of earth which they have removed with their claws are found at the mouths of their little dens.   The negroes bring them in, tied up like a bunch of onions, with strong withes passed tightly round every inch of their bodies and claws.

Another denizen of these forests, and more renowned in history, is the soldier-crab.   Being once on a voyage to Port au Prince in a country sloop, we were becalmed near the delightful shores of Leogane, some thirty miles from the above-named city. The captain thought it would be a good opportunity to 'wood up' without expense; so lowering his boat, he got into it, followed by two of the crew with their axes, and myself, and we pulled ashore. Leaving them busily engaged, I strayed away into a fine open piece of woods, and found myself treading among what appeared at first sight an army of pebble-stones endowed with the faculty of locomotion. A closer inspection showed them to be dingy rough looking shells which were thus cutting fantastic capers 'before high heaven.' Some were moving slowly and laboriously along; others were scrambling off at the top of their speed, as if the sheriff were after them, now and then coming to a rough place where they would roll over and over; while others hearing a noise drew in and remained motionless. I had stumbled upon a great rendezvous of the soldier-crabs. Here they resort once or twice a year to take a salt-water bath, deposit their eggs, and exchange the shelly covering which has served them as house and clothing for the past year, for another of more ample dimensions. Each crab forsakes his old house and then hunts about in search of another. Sometimes he has to try on a great many before he can find one to fit. Sometimes two competitors for the same shell engage in battle, when a third steps in and appropriates it to himself; and here possession is the *whole* of the law, for it is not in the power of a legion of soldiers to oust him.

After spending a few days at their watering-place, when they have provided themselves with new houses and suits of clothes, they march deliberately back to the hills and woods of the interior, where they remain until the time of the periodical visit comes round, when they again come rolling, crawling or tumbling back to the rendezvous. The shells which they inhabit are of all sizes and shapes of univalves, some not much bigger than a pea, while others are of three or four inches diameter.

The soldier-crab is not an article of food in the West Indies, and is introduced in this place *en passant.* But mention should be made of excellent shrimps, as also of the crab-fish and a small oyster, which latter is well enough for persons who have never eaten them in the United States.

Another welcome visiter to the bon-vivant is a wild pigeon of large size, the 'ramier,' of a grayish purple plumage, which makes its appearance at certain seasons. They are in fine condition and flavor, having a slightly bitter taste, like some of our game, which only tends to stimulate the appetite. This taste is probably acquired from certain berries on which the birds feed. They are doubtless the same mentioned by Columbus as 'stock-doves of uncommon size and beauty, whose crops we found filled with sweet spices.'

Of poultry, they raise the common fowl in abundance. Geese are *rara aves*, but turkies, Guinea-hens and ducks thrive. The Muscovy duck however is apparently more at home than the common species. There is a supply of beef, mutton and pork; but as the climate will not admit of the meat's improving by age, the only alternative is to impart tenderness to it by a terrible pounding, as before observed. But the great charm of West-India living is the unceasing supply of fresh and delicate vegetables. And this is the more important, as man does not require so much animal food in hot climates as in more temperate latitudes.

Foremost among these is the banana, or plantain; an invaluable gift to man as a substantial, pleasant and easily cultivated food. Next is the yam, whose crop is more sure even than the plantain. This root, when prepared for the table, is as white as snow, and sometimes grows to the weight of twelve or fifteen pounds. The best variety is the 'couche-couche,' which seems to be peculiar to the district of which we are writing more particularly. It is smaller than the others, and more sweet and melting. It is eagerly sought after by the people in the other quarters of the island.

Sweet potatoes, white and yellow, are in common use. The former are best, being more mealy and delicate than the other. Both varieties are more extensively cultivated in other parts of the island, in the vicinity of Port au Prince and Gonaives and Cape François, than in this district. Then comes a host of minor vegetables. The palm among these I give to the 'poix rouge' (similar in appearance to the common red bean of the States.) This delicious bean may be had at all seasons; and though one have it on his table nearly every day in the year he will never be satiated with its delicate flavor. Then there are the 'poix source,' identical perhaps with that which is called at the north the case-knife bean; the 'poix Congo,' from the name probably of African origin, which is round, of the size of the marrow-fat, of a brown color, and a very good variety; the 'poix inconnu' is smaller and less palatable than the last. The list of 'poix' may be closed with that 'of France,' which was doubtless introduced from that country. It is small, delicate, and similar in taste and color to our green pea.

The purple 'melongene,' or egg-plant, grows to a large size. It is a superb looking vegetable, and is usually fried in slices, or mashed. It has a delicate flavor, and its appearance receives a hearty welcome from lovers of good things. The 'concombre,' fluted and pear-shaped, is a cheap and wholesome vegetable. It is boiled or stewed. The 'petit concombre,' or Jerusalem cucumber, is of the size of a large plum, and covered with soft spires; cooked like the last, to which it is similar in color and taste, being green and sweet. The name of the last would lead us to suppose that it is the same mentioned in holy writ. Says Isaiah: 'The daughter of Zion is left as a cottage in a vineyard, as a lodge in a garden of cucumbers.' And the Israelites say to Moses: 'We remember the fish we did eat in Egypt freely — the cucumbers and the melons.' In Hindostan, Palestine and Egypt the cucumber is still an important article of food, and has been from the earliest ages; and it is much more probable that it is one of the wholesome varieties just mentioned, than the useless vegetable which is cultivated in more northern climes, but which is doubtless before the mind of many who read the accounts in Burckhardt, Heber, or the Bible. The artichoke does not grow in the south part of the island, but is always to be found at the tables of Port au Prince. It is in shape a cone some three inches long and as many across the base.

The leaves, or scales, grow like those on the cone of the pine, while the centre is composed of downy threads, or filaments, which must be carefully removed, leaving at the base a fleshy substance resembling a slice of turnip, three quarters of an inch thick. This last, with the roots of the leaves, form the edible part, and are eaten with a sauce made of oil, vinegar and mustard. This vegetable is much prized; and though it is said to thrive in a northern climate, particularly where a sea-weed dressing may be applied to the soil, yet it is I believe unknown in the United States.

At the risk of satiating the reader I shall enumerate a few more articles in the culinary department, always recommending to him the good old maxim ' to leave the table with an appetite.'

The tomato which is cultivated in Hayti is as round, as red and as large as the largest cherry. It is used as a condiment with both fish and flesh, and is very ' appétissant ' and very wholesome. It seems particularly well adapted as an accompaniment to that familiar dish which no true-hearted Yankee ever forgets ' where'er he roams, whatever lands he sees '— I mean salt-fish; (which article, by the way, the Creole cooks understand ' getting up ' much better than do the housewives whose homes are nearer to the Grand Bank.)

But this little tomato has another property which I predict will excite for it one day a warm interest, particularly among the ladies. It makes the most delicious *preserve* for pastry, etc., which can be imagined. In a tub containing a young tree, which the writer brought home, there sprang up soon after it was landed (in April) a tomato plant; and though left in a shady, exposed situation, it grew vigorously, and in September was loaded with fruit which turned red, but did not become fully ripe. If a warm sunny spot had been selected, it would have come to perfection. This was many miles north of New-York; so that there is every inducement to introduce it there or farther south.

The ' truffle ' is a species of mushroom growing under ground. It is rarely found, and all that we saw came from a friend residing a hundred miles off. It is esteemed as giving a delicate flavor to many dishes. The ' jonjon ' is another of this family, which is found after a rain, and is cooked with rice. When served up, the dish has the appearance of being a mixture of dry tea and rice, in equal parts. The squash grows tolerably well. The young children are often seen gnawing a boiled fragment with great apparent zest.

Nor must we omit from our catalogue the ' choux palmiste,' which is the apex of the cabbage-palm, and is composed of the undeveloped and immature substance which would shoot forth into leaves or branches. This decapitation destroys of course the trees, which, though unvarying from each other in appearance, are perhaps the most symmetrical in the world. The part cut off is about two feet in length and four or five inches in diameter. It consists of concentric layers which separate readily, after boiling, when it is very delicate, though rather insipid. The tree forms the principal figure in the national coat-of-arms, as it is a beautiful feature in the landscapes of the island. Every town and village has one in the centre of its ' square,' where it is called ' L'Arbre de la Liberté,' round which is collected weekly all the pomp and circumstance of military parades. But though thus consecrated as the sacred emblem of liberty, the inhabitants destroy the tree annually by thousands, though the only benefit derived from its destruction be the 'choux,' which is worth one or two shillings in the market. As the ship passes along the picturesque shores of St. Marc, large groves are descried near the water side, composed of this species of palm, interspersed with tall cocoa-nut trees which tower high above the heads of the others.

The 'avocado,' vegetable marrow, or alligator pear, is by many esteemed the greatest luxury in the vegetable world. It is the fruit of a tree whose foliage is of the deepest green, the fruit itself being a pale green or straw color. It is of the family of gourds, and was brought from Persia. Some of them are pear-shaped, others of an oval form; in size, six or eight inches in length and three to four in diameter. In the centre is a heavy roundish kernel of the size of an egg; the rest of the fruit being the edible substance which is cut off in slices like those of a melon. It separates readily from the stone and rind; and when laid in a dish, the slices are a perfect imitation of good hard, golden butter. As the name implies, it is of an unctuous nature, and of a nutty sweetness, resembling perhaps a fresh olive. With the application of a little pepper and salt, it is eaten raw, and seems to come in place with either fish or flesh. We were very fond of it in the morning with bread and a cup of coffee.

And now, though very far from having exhausted the subject, we shall turn for a season from the luxuries which dame Nature has dispensed so generously upon this favored isle. If our discourse has been wearisome, the apology must be found in the subject-matter, which is attractive to those at least who can indulge in retrospective thoughts founded upon a practical knowledge of the matters touched upon. And in these arctic regions, where the only green thing seen from November till April is now and then a melancholy looking cabbage, I am ready sometimes to exclaim with the Israelites: 'We remember the fish we did eat in Egypt freely; the cucumbers and the melons!'

St. Croix.

FRAGMENT FROM A MANUSCRIPT POEM.

There is in all Earth's countless things
An innate power to touch the hidden springs
Of human sympathies, and without words
To rouse to lofty purposes their thousand chords.
Hills, with their proud old forests; lakes,
Wild mountains, torrent-streams, whose dashing makes
Eternal melody with the free wind;
Clouds on whose bosom the storm-spirits find
A home, and hold their revels; it may be
Old Ocean's all immeasurable majesty;
These are man's earliest, his ennobling page,
And they who ponder most, are ever far most sage.

NATURE'S   TEACHINGS.

I.

GREAT Nature loves the silent tongue,
  The watchful eye, the musing mind;
For only these her songs are sung,
  From hill to vale along the wind;
Their burden still : ' Ask what ye may,
And I will answer yea or nay.'

II

To these she tells her secret laws
  In open field or tangled wood,
Where all is murmuring of its cause,
  From quiet rill to roaring flood;
Whispering where hidden waters sleep,
Or thundering of the mighty deep.

III.

Nor only of to-day they hear ;
  The wondrous tale she tells of earth
Clear rings upon th' unsealed ear
  The ancient story of its birth :
Grander than orphic hymn of old,
That music sung — that story told.

IV.

Nor rock nor shell nor leaf-marked stone
  To listless souls have aught to tell ;
But to the faithful eye alone
  Reveal how ancient forests fell ;
How waters from their beds were driven,
Fulfilling each dread 'hest of heaven.

V.

Lo ! Time rolls back, and chaos gray
  Stands darkling to the patient eye,
That sees the long primeval day,
  Its moving things, its misty sky,
Sudden to wreck and ruin hurled,
A perished and imperfect world !

VI.

When Mammoth and when Mastodon
  Majestic strode the leafy plain,
While every leaf they looked upon
  Was theirs, from mountain to the main ;
Unmatched their strength by human guile,
Undimmed for them the sunlight's smile.

VII.

See too the steady earnest eye
  Gaze on the far-off planet world,
And triumph o'er its mystery !
  To Thought's strong eye the scroll unfurled
That hidden lies to earth's dim light,
  While gleaming on the inward sight.

VIII.

But dream not thou may'st look and see,
  Or sudden tear the veil away;
Full oft must thy communing be
  Ere thou shall hear or ' yea or nay; '
From morning tide to even-song
Must be thy watching, calm and long!

IX.

Then bring with thee, to nature dear,
  The loving heart and quiet soul;
None other hath the vision clear;
  On other ear shall never roll
The oracle and song divine
She singeth to her God and thine.

MY GRAND-FATHER'S PORT-FOLIO.

NUMBER FOUR.

FLORA B.

AT the period of my settlement at P., thirty years ago, there was one family in the parish more interesting to me than all the rest, and then in the enjoyment of every thing that one could desire to make life happy. Their house was situated on the outskirts of the town, in a charming valley, to which its inhabitants had given the name of ' Flora's Retreat;' not only on account of its verdure and quietness, but also in honor of their eldest daughter, who seemed fitted to be the presiding goddess of the fairest spot on earth. Not a week elapsed for several years without a visit from me to the home of Judge B——, whose valuable library no less than the delightful society and the rural beauties of his residence constituted a charm too potent to be resisted. Under his roof I always found a warm but ostentatious welcome. A large arm-chair and a desk in the library were appropriated to my especial use. Indeed, without any formal stipulation I gradually became the tutor of his children; esteeming myself amply remunerated for the labor by the privilege of having access to books which it would have been beyond my ability to purchase; by the friendship of such excellent persons; by the opportunity of meeting with the distinguished strangers who in great numbers enjoyed the hospitality for which the proprietor of the ' Retreat' was proverbial; and by the liberal supply of the rich and beautiful productions of the garden and the farm.

FLORA B., then in her fourteenth year, was the loveliest being I have ever known. Beautiful and graceful as the fairest flower that she nourished; lively as the gayest bird that nestled in the valley; loving and innocent as an angel, and withal full of intelligence; it was a never-cloying pleasure to be in her company; to watch her airy motions; to listen to her sweet voice; and especially to instruct and train a nature so luxuriant and so pliable.   Her brothers, one older and one younger than herself, though far less interesting — the youngest indeed decidedly dull and partially deformed, but good-natured and gentle — were not without their attractions to one who knew them so well as myself, and who for their parents' and sister's sake was predisposed to regard them with favor.

With this little circle closely drawn around me, I have spent many a happy hour in my arm-chair, endeavoring to instil into their young minds the discipline of knowledge and virtue.

But the felicity of this lovely family was too beautiful a vision long to endure; and within a few years after it first excited my admiration, it began to dissolve.   Judge B., while on a visit to New-York to look after the investment of a large portion of his property, was thrown from a carriage; sustaining an injury which terminated his life before the news of the accident reached his home.   His body was conveyed to P. and interred in a quiet corner of the garden that had been the scene of many of his happiest hours.   His wife, who was previously in delicate health, never recovered from the shock which his death occasioned; but directly retired to her chamber, and never left it again till about four months after the burial of her husband; when the verdant turf was uncovered for her lifeless remains to be laid to rest by his side.

I can never lose the remembrance of the melancholy day of this second funeral.   It seemed to me, when I followed to the grave with Flora almost borne in my arms, as if the zest of my own existence had been forever taken away.   When we returned to the mournful parlor, Flora's grief came over her like a flood.   She leaned her head upon my shoulder and sobbed as if her heart were breaking.   I tried to console her; but when in the most plaintive tone she murmured in my ear, 'I am an orphan now!' I could only press her to my heart; vainly attempting to ejaculate a prayer that God would show himself her father. My feelings were too sorrowful for utterance, and only my spirit interceded for her.

The guardianship of the children devolved upon me.   The 'Retreat' was sold, and the orphans were removed to the parsonage.   The eldest boy had always manifested a passion for the sea too strong to be discouraged; and after every effort had been vainly made to direct his thoughts into some other channel, I was reluctantly forced to consent to his engagement as clerk to the supercargo of a vessel bound on a distant voyage.   He sailed — and we never heard from him again.

Flora's favorite employment was to minister to her youngest brother. It seemed as if all the affections which had aforetime been divided among the several members of her family were now concentrated upon him.   She could not endure to be separated from him even for an hour. She read to him, instructed him, and walked by his side almost daily to the graves at the 'Retreat,' which had been reserved when the estate was sold, and neatly enclosed, together with a few trees and flower-beds, as a spot consecrated to filial love.

But Flora's cup was not yet full.   Her brother, whose intellect had always been feeble, was attacked with a fever that left him a complete idiot.   During his long sickness she never left his bed; and when at length he recovered, and the awful reality became too apparent to allow her sisterly affection to cherish a ray of hope that his reason would ever return, her own strength and heart failed her, and the same fever brought her near to the gates of death.   While her illness continued, there was not a heart in the whole town of P. that was not melting with pity and tenderness.   Old and young seemed to vie with each other in their attentions and expressions of sympathy.   Every one who possessed a garden, gathered its sweetest ornaments for her chamber; and those who had none, brought their fragrant offerings from every woody hill and every cool brook-side far and near.   Her youth and her serenity, though for many days her life was despaired of, gradually prevailed over the angel of sickness, and our good Doctor H. pronounced her convalescent.   Her beauty and every moral and intellectual grace soon came back to her; but her childish vivacity never returned.   She sat at my fire-side, fairest of the daughters of Eve; but with ever a soft shade of melancholy upon her countenance, which told of a lost paradise.   But she never obtruded her sorrows upon the notice or sympathy of her friends; nor refused to add her own gentle smile to the radiance of our domestic joys.   She did not retreat from the influence of the happy circle; but I observed that her preference was always for the society of the sorrowful; and that into every home of affliction she would early seek an entrance, and make herself a constant visitant.   And her visits were always welcome; for her own example sweetly chided inordinate grief; and she carried with her that silent but most availing of all consoling influences which accompanies the presence of one of whom our own hearts tell us that she has been acquainted with deeper griefs.

Though I often spoke to her concerning the past — for it was a theme dear to us both — yet I never ventured to obtrude upon her my poor consolations.   For once, soon after her recovery, when I had unexpectedly met her in a twilight stroll, and found her giving vent in secret to the fullness of her sorrow, upon my attempting to speak to her those comforting words which are always uppermost in our mouths on such an occasion, by a beseeching gesture she constrained me to silence; and in an hour afterward, on going into my study, I found upon my table, in a hand-writing which I could not mistake, the following verses:

Go and hush the raging brine
    To a perfect calm;
Then for this deep grief of mine
    Thou mayest find a balm.

Stay the chariot of the night
    In its solemn track;
Thou mayest bring the morning light
    To my bosom back.

Charm yon placid orb of eve
    From its azure dome;
Then bid this barbèd sorrow leave
    Its perpetual home.

Cease at length the fruitless care
  To remove a wo
Far too large for love to share —
  Far too deep to know!

But *one* Comforter is dear
  To a spirit riven:
Thy sweet whisperings I hear,
  Blessed Dove of Heaven!

The impassioned tone of the poetry, which was evidently a spontaneous outpouring of strong emotion, revealed to me the depth of her sorrow; and the pious resignation expressed in the last stanza declared, what indeed I had known before, that she had sought and found a spring of consolation compared with which the sympathy of human hearts is a shallow and unsatisfying fountain.

Her brother had an apartment to himself, in which he remained excluded from the view of all, save the members of my own family. There he sat, pale and emaciated, in a long and loose gown of white flannel; strapped to his chair or to his bed, to protect him from harm; making the most plaintive sounds; playing with a small silver rod, and displaying no sign of intelligence or interest, except in regard to the gratification of an appetite whose cravings were insatiable and perpetual. Here was Flora's chosen seat; while with the most unwearied attention she would spend hour after hour in replacing the rod when it dropped from his hand; feeding him from time to time with the broken loaf-sugar which he particularly loved; or combing and parting his delicate hair, now arranging it in this way and now in another, as if she sought to revive the image of his former self, or to retrace in his features shadowy likenesses of the beautiful dead.

There was at this period a constant visiter at our house in the person of a young clergyman of a neighboring town, with whom my exchanges were frequent, and for whom we all entertained a lively regard. He was himself an orphan; and that circumstance alone, had he possessed far less moral attractions, would have given him a sure passport to Flora's sympathy. Gradually his calls became more frequent and his stay more protracted; till at length it was sufficiently apparent to us all that an influence of more than ordinary power drew him to our fire-side. By-and-by he was admitted with Flora into her brother's chamber; and seemed to feel no greater happiness than in sharing her services to the unfortunate object of her love, and entering into every feeling of her delicate and teeming heart. I could not but rejoice at the brightening prospect which was opening before my lovely charge, as I thought I discerned a change in her appearance which indicated that she had now found a precious comforter this side of heaven — one human friend, whose whisperings were sweet; to whom she could freely unbosom her sorrows, and who could understand and sympathize with and share them all. When therefore in due time my reverend brother declared to me his love for Flora, and expressed the hope that the offer which he had made to her, and which she had accepted, would meet my approbation,

I could only reply by an earnest grasp of his hand, and a burst of tears.

Their nuptials were soon after solemnized in my study; and Flora, with her husband and brother, and a few plants carefully potted from her parents' graves — under the auspices of the most heartfelt benedictions and silent prayers from us all — left the roof under which she had found all that love which she was calculated to inspire, to go and carry to another fire-side as much joy as virtue and beauty and pure affection can convey to an earthly home.

We all stood looking after the departing vehicle as it slowly ascended the hill, at a little distance on the road, until it fairly reached the summit. When all but myself, without a word having been spoken, entered the house. As I remained leaning upon the gate with a heart absorbed in prayer and thankfulness, wholly unconscious of every thing that was passing around me, I was suddenly startled from my reverie by a gentle touch upon my shoulder; and on looking up, I beheld Flora standing by my side. There was a tear in her eye; but her countenance beamed with one of her sweetest smiles. 'I could not leave you,' she said, 'without one more word. There is something within me which my heart bade come back and say, and which your kindness deserves to hear. *I am not an orphan now.* With you for my father, and Edward to divide my feelings of bereavement, and my parents *so* happy, and God blessing me as his own child; I should be ungrateful to think of orphanage. This,' she continued, pressing her lips to my cheek, 'was the sign of your sympathy when for the depth of my anguish you could not speak to me, and I could not have heard your words. Let this,' she added, putting her lips to mine, 'be the sign of my gratitude and my happiness now, which, believe me, are greater than I can tell.' The words were no sooner uttered than she turned to regain the carriage with a bounding step that I doubt not she intended should convey my thoughts back with the same light-winged motion over a long interval of sadness to the days when her heart was light.

I, THE grand-son, find carefully folded in the same envelope with the above simple tale, which certainly bears marks of being a narrative of facts, a manuscript delicately written, containing the following verses, which were probably the production of Flora, and as such carefully preserved by my grand-father :

WHEN the cup of joy is brimming,
  Daily at youth's glowing lips,
Not a shade the image dimming,
  That smiles back on him who sips :

E'er one precious link is riven
  From the chain of loving hearts,
Whose embrace a glow of heaven
  To our early days imparts :

When to-day smiles on to-morrow,
  And the light of bright hours gone
Gilds the fleecy mists of sorrow,
  As its misty wreaths, the morn :

When, her chart of hope unrolling,
  Fancy points to placid seas ;
While no knell of wreck is tolling
  In the music of the breeze :

When the pulse is calmly beating,
  Measuring life's gentle flow ;
And the truth that 'joy is fleeting'
  Is a truth we've yet to know :

Then, when love and bliss are waking
  All that's sweet and pure within ;
No unhallowed passion shaking —
  Checking every thought of sin :

Then, to give the heart to duty,
  And the heavenly word receive ;
Then, to wed immortal beauty,
  And the highest truths believe,

Costs no bitter strife of feeling,
  Needs no mightiness of will —
But obey GOD's gentlest dealing,
  He his own life doth instil.

But when sorrow's yoke is weighing
  Down to dust the noblest part,
And the sharpest pangs are preying
  On the bruised and fainting heart ;

When no friendly eye is smiling
  O'er the raging flood of grief,
And no kindly voice beguiling
  Nights, that then might seem more brief :

When the light of life seems clouded,
  And the Guiding Hand withdrawn ;
Love in dark pavilion shrouded ;
  Faith's last cheering signals gone :

When fierce doubts the soul are storming,
  Fighting with the power of prayer ;
And wild fears the lone heart swarming,
  Beckon onward dread despair :

Then, O, then, to be victorious ;
  To be all the times demand ;
Holding love and hope — is glorious ;
  Godlike, then, through Christ to stand !

c. B.

GRENADA AND THE ALHAMBRA.

BY REV. GEORGE B. CHEEVER.

NUMBER THREE.

The first gate-way through which you pass upward from the city to the Alhambra leads out of the 'Calle de Gomelez,' or street of the Gomelez, and was rebuilt by the Emperor Charles the Fifth. It bears the following inscription : *Jurisdiccion de la Fortaleza real del Alhambra;* 'Jurisdiction of the royal Fortress of the Alhambra;' and is at the top of the street, admitting you up the picturesque ravine that here divides the hill of the Alhambra into two high, and at the extremity, precipitous ridges. The lofty rows of houses on either side the 'Calle de Gomelez' terminate at the gate-way, and the banks suddenly rise almost perpendicularly to the right and left, the road passing upward in two branches, between luxuriant gardens and groves that fill the valley. Right before the gate-way is a stone fountain at which the people from the street without draw water; a sort of porter's lodge is near it. On the left, higher up the valley, beneath the towering walls of the Alhambra, a beautiful little waterfall supplied from a stream that has filled the fountains, baths, and gardens of the palaces, descends from the cliff, and rushes in a murmuring brook adown the declivity of the ravine. On the right of the gate-way rises the lofty 'Torre de Vermejas,' or Vermilion Tower, so called from the color of its materials. It is more ancient than the Alhambra, and indeed is probably the oldest work of art in the kingdom, being supposed to have been constructed by the Phœnicians before the Roman conquest. What mighty changes has it seen, while cities and palaces have sprung up and crumbled around it; and through what strange vicissitudes of uses itself must have passed ! Its original object is scarcely known, but it is now occupied as a pottery ! The view from it of the city, the vast plain, and the distant mountains, is one of the grandest and most extensive in the whole region.

Passing upward through the trees and gardens to the end and outlet of the valley, you find yourself on the open undulating surface of the hill outside the walls of the fortress; and turning westward you advance up a broad smooth road leading along the brow of the ravine you have been traversing, toward the first of the out-jutting towers of the Alhambra. Here you enter a magnificent Moorish gate-way composed of three successive arches, or compartments of the same massive arch, through the body of the tower, with a vaulted roof intermediate. Nothing can be more noble of the kind than this gateway, nor any thing finer than the approach to it; grand, lofty, and imposing; in every way befitting the entrance to so splendid a series of palaces. It is so lofty and majestic that it might seem built for the august introduction of supernatural beings, 'whose stature reached the sky.' It owes its effect upon the imagination not merely to the loftiness, symmetry and massive grandeur of the arch, but to the colossal proportions of the tower above and the great height to which it rises. On the outside is engraven on the key-stone, in the centre, the figure of a gigantic hand, and over the centre of the second arch in the middle of the tower the corresponding figure of a key. On the Mosaic tiling above, which measures nearly three feet and a half high, appears the inscription in Cusic characters: ' There is no conqueror but GOD.' The emblems of the key and the hand were significant of the national faith, and it was a traditional spell, wrought perhaps by some Arabian magician, that the gate and the palace should last till the gigantic hand on the outside could grasp the key within. The symbol of the hand was considered by the Arabians as a defence against infidels, and in certain postures as possessing the power of enchantment and miracles. When open, as in the ' Gate of Judgment,' they attributed to it the gift of weakening the strength of the enemy. It was also a designation of divine Providence, and with the fingers a prototype of the law, with its five fundamental precepts: 1. Faith in God and in Mahomet as his prophet; 2. Prayer, washing, and purification; 3. Alms; 4. Fasting; 5. A pilgrimage to Mecca and the Caaba. The key is well known as an oriental emblem of power, and in conjunction with the hand was sculptured by order of one of the monarchs in whose reign the fortress was constructed, to denote concord, or union and power together.

This majestic portal was called the ' Gate of Justice,' because within it sat the judges: and it was the popular tribunal where sentence was pronounced and judgment administered. In the inscription above it is called ' Gate of the Law;' and the inscription recording the name of Yusuf its monarch closes with these words: ' May heaven constitute it a protecting bulwark, and record it among the lasting acts of the righteous.' This custom of judgment in the gate among the Moslems was taken from the Hebrews; as were many other rites, and all that is beautiful in the Koran. When the people gathered around so noble a tribunal, and decisions of solemn importance were determined, the spectacle must have been in no slight degree imposing. It brings to mind several passages of scripture, as of the elders sitting in the gate; (Deut. xxv. 7;) the conduct of Absalom, (2 Samuel, xv. 2, 6,) when he stood beside the way of the gate to draw away the hearts of those who were coming with their controversies to the king for judgment. So also Solomon's designation of a fool, (Prov. xxiv. 17,) and perhaps Esther iv. 1, 9, Job, xxix. 7. The appellation ' Sublime Porte ' it is well known takes its origin in this custom.

From this grand gate-way and tower you pass along a narrow ascending lane between winding walls to the second great Moorish tower of entrance to the ' Plaza de los Algibes,' or Square of the Cisterns, the first esplanade within the walls of this palace-fortress. Beneath its surface were constructed the great reservoirs that still remain, supplied by a stream from the Sierra Nevada, which was through the whole extent of the palaces, from the ' Generalise ' or queen's summer palace above, to the court of the Lions, the ' Pateo del Agua,' and the waterfalls in the glen without the fortress, abundantly supplying the great fountains, baths, and wells, and watering the gardens. One of the cisterns in the Plaza is in its dimensions one hundred and two feet long by fifty-six broad, enclosed by a wall of six feet in thickness, overarched by a vault forty-seven inches high in the centre, and seventeen feet and five inches beneath the surface of the Plaza.

Following the westward course of the outer walls, you are next conducted into the Tower of the Bells, 'Torre de la Vela,' or campana; so called because the bells were rung to give the signal when the water-sluices were to be opened for the irrigation of the vega. This tower at present is used for a prison, and our approach to it was through a crowd of just such wild, fierce, wretched looking beings as fill the prison, and work upon the mole in Malaga. They were 'Carlistas,' taken prisoners near Auduxar. The tower of the bells is one of the loftiest in the whole fortress; and the view from it is beyond description grand, varied and delightful. West and southwest it overlooks the Albaycin, with its fortresses and churches, and the whole city of Grenada, with the mountain ranges toward Seville and Cordova. Southward it commands the immense luxuriant vega, studded with villages and dotted with groves, with the encircling sweep of sierras in the distance; on the east, directly at your feet, the 'Court of the Cisterns,' the palace of Charles the Fifth, the 'Tower of Judgment,' and beyond the hill, in the plain below, the Alameda of Grenada, the course of the Xeuil, and the distant romantic sweep of the Alpuxarra mountains; east and north the towers, palaces and courts of the Alhambra, the valley of the Darro, the palace and laurel gardens of the 'Generalise,' and above all, the magnificent snow-covered tops of the Sierra Nevada. It would be easy to spend an entire day on the summit of this tower alone, so crowded and magnificent is its prospect, and so great the interest added by the historical associations as they are brought before the mind. On the latter the guide points you to the winding route of the last unhappy king of Grenada, from the gate of the Alhambra to the 'Last Sigh of the Moor.' This is a distant point at the foot of the Alpuxarra mountains, the last point from which could be commanded a view of Grenada, and from which Boabdil cast back a lingering gaze upon its lost palaces and towers, and wept in the bitterness of his grief. 'Weep like a woman for thy kingdom,' said his mother, 'since thou couldst not keep it like a man.' Charles the Fifth is reported to have exclaimed, as he gazed from the tower of Comares in the Alhambra toward the distant heights of the Alpuxarras, 'I had rather have found a grave in a palace like this than a kingdom in yon rugged mountains.' You recollect that Boabdil surrendered Grenada with the condition of possessing a spot in the region whither Charles was gazing.

The palace of Charles himself is directly in front of the Plaza, the first object indeed which arrests your attention as you enter within the Alhambra fortress; a magnificent but unfinished structure, to make room for which he removed several quadrangles of the fortress, and tore down one of the finest portions of the palaces. With three splendid fronts to the south, east, and west, united on the north with the Alhambra, and being composed almost entirely of marble, it is quite worthy the greatness of its monarch; but its beauty is so entirely eclipsed by the interior splendor of the Alhambra palaces, that the visiter wishes it in any other place, and only despises the vanity and deplores the despotic taste which could destroy any portion of the Moorish structures for its sake. Outside it is a perfect square of two hundred feet; within, around the central court, it is an exact circle of one hundred and forty-four feet diameter, with a running Doric colonnade or circular portico of thirty-two marble columns, surmounted by an upper gallery or portico of the same number of marble pillars of the Ionic order. It was a splendid design; but the apartments were never roofed, and there it stands, an unfinished pile that in any other climate would long since have been a heap of ruins; and you walk around the flat verge of its lofty walls, amidst weeds and flowers growing from the crevices; admiring in it a monument of despotic luxury, vanity and caprice. From this position you overlook the Moorish palaces on the north; and if I were to sketch them now, it would be just the external description of a collection of gable-roofed and red earthen-tiled houses, united together like a little village, apparently without any order or design. So singular is the contrast between the eastern exterior and the inward aspect of that celebrated pile. At the same time the view from every point without the surrounding walls of the fortress is as truly regal and imposing as the inward ornaments are beautiful.

To the distant spectator the Alhambra wears the appearance of an antique regal city. From the Albaycin you behold a long line of lofty battlemented walls, flanked at intervals with high gigantic square towers, of a reddish gray tint; the whole rising as a diadem from the summit of a verdurous wall of hanging gardens, which seem as a green girdle to divide the region of palaces from the city below. Then also a range of green hills forms the back-ground of the palace of the 'Generalise;' and over all, the snowy bosom of the Sierra Nevada flashes in the sky — 'a kingly spirit throned among the hills.'

Let us now pass from the Tower of the Bells across the Plaza, and around the north-western angle of the imperial palace, through the first portal that admits us to the interior splendors of the Alhambra. From this moment the mind is filled with admiration and delight at the spectacle of oriental genius, refinement and luxury laid open to the view. It seems a spot for the habitation of etherial beings, Peris and fairies, lovely and chaste, to sport, converse and be happy; a fit abode of female sweetness, refinement and domestic elegance: and yet at the same time there are in it such ideas of nobleness and grandeur, that it seems a place for princes, sages and energetic minds; the abode of poets, philosophers and statesmen. A poet like Dante might have copied from it for some of the scenes of his 'Paradise.' We thought that our visit to that scene of Moorish magnificence was such an one as we would willingly cross the Atlantic to enjoy; nor can I describe to you the feelings of intense curiosity with which we gazed upon the exquisite fretted work of its halls and palaces. We might almost have believed that it was the work of fairy hands, so light, so delicate, so rich, so enchantingly beautiful; or that we had been transported within the walls of the palace built by the genii of Aladdin. So complete a realization of all my childish imaginations of oriental magnificence I never expected to behold. There is genius in these fretted walls; the impress of the romantic genius of the people.   Coleridge called the Gothic architecture AN IDEA.   I wish he could have visited the hall of the Abencerrages, and given a name to the fulness of its beauty.   The taste displayed in the ornamental work with which the whole of the palaces are covered is as pure and simple as it is beautiful.   There is nothing to offend the mind, or make it hesitate a moment to yield itself up to the impression of perfect symmetry and beauty.   That impression is involuntary, and without mixture; and when to this is added the romantic effect of the remembrance of the Moorish character and history, the feeling of delight and meditative pathos with which the stranger gazes upon it is extreme.

Your first step within this scene places you amidst the ' Court of the Alberca,' as our guide called it, or the ' Baths of the Communa,' or again, the ' Pateo del Agua,' as it has been termed.   It contains in the centre a sheet of water one hundred and twenty feet long by thirty broad, bordered with hedges of rose-trees.   At the sides and end of the pool, the court is paved with white marble, and at each end rise the graceful arches of the Moorish architecture upon slender columns, with ornamented alcoves within.   A fountain plays at each end, the stream running into the pond by a narrow marble projecting slab.   Connected with this court was the Moorish mosque or chapel of the palace, since converted into a church by the erection of an altar-piece at one end and a separation for the choir at the other.   I believe it was here that the first mass was performed after the conquest of the Alhambra, to purify the building from the pollution of the more simple rites of Mohammedanism, and to consecrate it for the use of the Roman Catholic denomination.   In spite of all intrusions, it is still a most beautiful apartment.   Its arabesques are well preserved, the usual inscriptions from the Koran running around the walls, and the roof resting upon them as lightly and solemnly as if it were a summer cloud.   The contrast in this hall between the simplicity of the Arabian architecture and the tawdry splendor with which the choir is constructed is very striking. The inscriptions also that ran around the walls in Arabic were infinitely more appropriate in their meaning than the ' Ave Marias ' and miraculous legends that fill the Roman Catholic churches.

This beautiful apartment, the former mosque and afterward the chapel of the palace, is now used as a store-house for meal ! — and while we were there a party of Spanish grain-merchants were weighing, buying and selling, the meal being spread in immense heaps over the floor.   This had never been the house of prayer amidst all its uses, and therefore the words of our Saviour in the temple could not be applied to its desecration, however it might be a den of thieves; but it was with vivid thoughts of the changes which had passed that I gazed upon the scene before me.   A portion of the most splendid palace in the world, which had been successively the theatre of the two most universal anti-christian denominations that have divided the world's religious empire, now converted, with its Popish altars on the one side and its Mohammedan inscriptions on the other still remaining, into a dusty store-house and meal-market for the fortress !

When Mr. Murphy visited the Alhambra, he transcribed from the walls of one of the alcoves of the court of the Alberca the following lines, which were written there in 1760; as just in their severity as they are elegant, save in the expression 'true worship.' If the writer had said 'fixed falser worship where the false prevailed,' it would have been nearer the truth than it now is. The lines are as follows:

> ' When these famed walls did pagan rites admit,
> Here reigned unrivalled breeding, science, wit.
> Christ's standard came, the prophet's flag assailed,
> And fixed true worship where the false prevailed;
> And such the zeal its pious followers bore,
> Wit, science, breeding, perished with the Moor.'

From the court and pool of the 'Pateo del Agua,' you pass through an arched and arabesqued passage in the northern side, and find yourself suddenly in a scene of splendor still more remarkable, in the far-famed 'Court of the Lions.' It is so named from the fountain in the centre, the immense richly-embossed marble basins of which rest upon twelve sculptured lions, the water rising in a central jet, and falling from basin to basin, to escape at length from the mouths of the statues into channels conducted through the fragrant parterres of the court. One of the inscriptions on the fountain is said to be as follows: 'The fair princess that walks in this garden covered with pearls, augments its beauty so much that you may doubt whether it be a fountain that flows or the tears of her admirers!' The forms of the lions are imperfectly carved, and I think were intentionally left in that state, like the Egyptian monuments; but the whole fountain is inimitably rich and perfect, an object of perpetual admiration. A Spanish writer, from whom Mr. Murphy obtained a collection of the poems inscribed in the Alhambra, has furnished several verses from the inscriptions on this fountain, of which the following are two: 'Is it in fact any other than a bright cloud, from which supplies are poured out abundantly to the lions? Resembling the extended hand of the Caliph, when engaged in imparting benefits to the furious Lions of War.' The court itself is an oblong square, one hundred feet in length by fifty in breath, and the colonnade, or pillared porch of arches that runs round it, is seven feet deep on the sides of the court, and ten at each end. At each extremity of the court a beautiful square portico of light marble pillars and arches exquisitely wrought projects from the colonnade toward the fountain in the centre, in the most perfect symmetry of proportion with the dimensions of the court, and the sweep of the surrounding corridors. Around each fretted arch runs a band of Arabic characters quoted from the Koran. Then there is a square of arabesques, and the corner spaces up and down from the pillars to the roof are covered with a sort of filagree work, a carved cornice at the top running round the whole. The marble columns of the corridors and porticos are slender and delicate, about nine feet in height, and disposed singly, or by two and sometimes three together; and the arches, which are of the width, above the pillars, of four and three feet alternately, spring from their capitals so airy and graceful, and with such rich and appropriate decorations, that they seem like a sweeping line of elms festooned together.

The stucco-work of the ceiling is very beautiful; and that of the vaulted roof in the porticos and corridors, as well as in the different halls and saloons of the palace, is wrought in the form of pendent stalactites, or triangular clusters of pyramidal divisions, with the point downward, enamelled with blue and gold in their innumerable projections, and arranged in crossing curvatures that spring from the tops of the marble pillars to the centre of the overhanging cupola. The effect of the combined frosting and painting, and embossed and embroidered work of the arabesques upon the walls, and the pendant canopies of the roof, is so rich and peculiar, that it seems like looking upward to the blue sky through an overhanging arch of the leafy boughs of trees. The appearance is such that I might compare it to that of the checkered moonlight admitted through an elmy overarching grove; or rather you may take these things as images rather than strict comparisons, by which the extreme beauty of the impression may be figured to your mind. Not only the vaulted roofs of the magnificent halls of the palace are thus adorned and composed of enamelled curvatures in pendent masses, but the pillared ends of the apartments, the recesses of the windows, the arched entrance-ways, the divisions of the porticos, and even the inclosures for the flights of steps, are each hung with their separate canopies of pendent stucco-work, elaborately wrought, while the walls in like manner are invariably enriched with arabesques, surrounded and intermingled at intervals with lines of Arabic inscriptions. The sound of 'leaves and fuming rills' in the green courts and fountains, with the fragrance of flowers, mingles with all this enchantment to render it perfect.

Passing now along the marble corridors around this splendid court, let us enter and admire the different halls at its sides and end. First, on your right at the south side of the court is the 'Hall of the Abencerrages.' But it is quite impossible to convey to your mind an adequate conception of its exquisite beauty; I may say without exaggeration, its radiancy of beauty; for it is as if you had entered into a tissued cloud of light interwoven with rainbows. You admire its symmetrical proportions, its roof, a grottoed canopy of stucco-work, enamelled with rich colors still distinguishable, the ornaments of its walls and ceiling, with their infinite variety of combinations, in lines running and returning, crossing and recrossing in a thousand forms, yet with perfect regularity, a lavishness of 'wanton heed and giddy cunning,' intermingled with borders of Arabic inscriptions executed with all the skill that you ever saw displayed in a copper-plate engraving of ornamental penmanship. As soon as you intermit your gaze of delight, the garrulous Matteo stoops down and wipes away the dust from the floor of the marble fountain, pointing you to its crimson stairs, which he assures you were imprinted when the fountain was made to run with the blood of the princes of the Abencerrages. That Boabdil secretly entrapped and beheaded in that hall a multitude of that noble tribe, enviously accused of treason, and one of them of illicit intercourse with the queen, there can be little doubt. Some say that thirty, some that eighty-six were murdered in one day. But whether the sanguinary stains were imbibed by the marble to remain to this day is not an article of inquisitorial faith. *Matteo credat;* but you are permitted to doubt.

Passing from this hall along the arched colonnade toward the western end of the court, you enter an open apartment, or oblong recess, called the 'Hall of the Judges;' so named from the curious old pictures with which the ceiling is covered, and which are supposed to be a representation of the Moorish lords of the council, or something similar. They are painted in their robes, turbans, beards, and swords, and the colors have remarkably preserved their freshness. In contiguous compartments are painted two similar pieces, one a representation of a boar-hunt, the other perhaps of the trial of the sultana.

On the northern side of the Court of the Lions you enter first the 'Anti-Sala,' or anti-chamber, and next the 'Sala de dos Hermanas,' or the 'Hall of the two Sisters,' an apartment almost equal in beauty to the Hall of the Abencerrages on the opposite side of the court. It derives its name from two magnificent slabs of marble contiguous in the floor, each fifteen feet long by seven and a half broad. A fountain played in the centre of this hall, the stream from which ran along the floor in a marble channel down across the Anti-Sala and the external corridor, and thence into the stream from the fountain of the Lions. Around this apartment the Mosaic of the walls exhibits a beautiful combination of gold, white, black, purple, blue and green. The arabesques here and elsewhere are equally beautiful, some of the figures being wrought in a diamond shape with an Arabic motto in the centre, and combined like the impressions of immense seals, five in a checkered square, and sometimes four in a diamond, with bands of Arabic letters running among them, as usual. This hall is provided with balconies above for musicians, and its windows look out into a portion of the gardens of the palace, left now to wildness and neglect. From the little myrtle-garden of the Linderaxa there was a communication with the baths of the palace, and a hall called the 'Hall of the Nymphs.' The baths are of the same pale white marble with the rest of the palace, time however having communicated to the whole an almost imperceptible pale ruddy tint, which makes it more beautiful. Their different apartments were covered with the richest arabesques, which are now partially removed, and were vaulted with stucco-work, with small circular passages in the roof, through which the light came down in a slanting direction, excluding the direct rays of the sun, and veiled and softened, so as to form a sort of subterranean twilight. With its costly furniture and incense-breathing perfumes it would be a picture to the life of the luxury of the harem of an oriental monarch.

A corridor near the garden of the Linderaxa runs from the hall of the 'Two Sisters,' communicating with several apartments built by Charles the Fifth; but without delaying in these, we will pass to what is unquestionably the grandest of all the apartments of the palace, the great Hall of the Ambassadors. It was entered from the front, through a noble outer hall, called the 'Anti-Sala of the Ambassadors,' from the centre of which you advance at once through a broad and richly arched entrance into the midst of this magnificent regal audience chamber. The height of this room from the floor to the centre of the ceiling is a little more than sixty feet. It is situated in the body of the tower of Comares, the loftiest and most colossal of all the towers, and its windows look out upon the west, north and south, commanding a series of landscapes of unrivalled beauty. The floor is partially inlaid

with Mosaic, and a Mosaic tiling of gold, silver, azure and purple
covers the walls to the height of three or four feet from the floor, to
the commencement of the arabesques, which are then continued in all
their variety and beauty up to the cornice at the first curving of the
lofty roof. Some of them are in circular relievos like immense medallion casts. Some are star-shaped, some like a diamond, others in different combinations of foliages; while amidst this beautiful variety of
embossed figures, no less than six separate lines of Arabic inscriptions
run in belts at regular intervals, some of them a foot broad, others
narrower, the ornamental characters fringing the ground-work and at
the same time mingling and harmonizing admirably with it. Sometimes the circular and starry embossings are composed almost entirely
of groups of Arabic letters, the Cusic character which is used being
susceptible of exquisitely beautiful combinations. As a specimen of
the general character of such inscriptions as are not drawn from the
Koran, take the following in a star-shaped ornament: 'Oh! how the
stars themselves desire a splendor equal to mine! If they had obtained
it, they would have fixed themselves, nor ever be seen wandering in the
hemispheres!' This boastful grandiloquence was very much the prevailing poetic taste of the Arabians; but the inscriptions from the Koran
are more simple. I may quote one runing round the arched entrance,
among the flowers and arabesques in stucco: 'By the sun and its
rising brightness; by the moon, when she followeth him; by the day,
when he showeth his splendors; by the night, when it covereth him with
darkness; by the heaven, and Him who created it; by the earth, and
Him who spread it forth; by the soul, and Him who completely formed
it — there is no other God but God.' Sometimes the letters are in
short inscriptions of 'Glory and honor to our lord Abdallah,' or the
reigning king. Mr. Murphy gives the following inscription in reference
to the roof, which he says is stuccoed in imitation of mother-of-pearl:
'This is the sublime Dome, and we (the other apartments) are her
daughters; but to me belong excellence and dignity above my kindred.
They (the other rooms) are the members of the body; but I am the
heart in the midst of it, and from the heart springs all the energy of
soul and life.' Again: 'My fellows are as the constellations of the
zodiac in the heaven of this structure, yet in me abides the preëminence
of the sun.' 'Yussuf has constituted me the throne of his empire, the
eminence of which is upheld by Him to whom belong divine glory
and the celestial throne.' The Hall of the Ambassadors was likewise
called the golden saloon.

The height, boldness and beauty of the dome of this apartment are
very striking. A cornice of dark wood richly carved separates between
the arabesques of the walls and the grottoed work of the ceiling, which
is most elaborately wrought, with an exceeding richness, delicacy and
symmetry. It is said to be of wood, keyed and fastened together in
such a manner 'that on pressing the feet on the centre of the summit,
the whole vibrates like a tight rope.' The beauty of the canopied
roofs in all the apartments of the palace is peculiarly distinguishable.
They are so exquisitely wrought that they seem to rise from the walls
and the marble pillars like a web of colored gossamer. I should have

mentioned before the niches of the wall on each side the arched entrance to the Hall of the Ambassadors, in which those who entered deposited their slippers, after taking them from the feet in token of reverence. The inscriptions in the window recesses of this hall may also be named, as indicating that beautiful basins stood in their centre, for the purposes of religious ablution by the Moors. Thus one of the poetical verses is as follows: ' The water basin which I enclose seems as a worshipper who stands in the *Kibla* of the sanctuary, performing his devotions.' In another recess is the following: ' I am the orna- mented seat of the bride, endowed with beauty and perfection.' These recesses were on one side fifteen feet deep, that being the immense thickness of the walls of the hall in the Tower of Comares. The grand entrance to this hall opened through its ' anti-sala' into an exter- nal range of marble columns, and thence into the great court of the Alberca, with its beautiful pool and fountains. Such was the distribu- tion of the apartments, with courts, fountains, gardens and columns intervening, and running into one another, that the effect is delightful; the variety and the extent delude you in such a way that you are almost lost in first traversing the pile.

From the north-eastern recess in this hall was a light open portico of marble pillars and Moorish arches along the verge of the outer battle- ment, to an apartment in the next tower, called the ' Tocador,' or ' Toilet of the Queen.' I speak of the battlement; and it must be borne in mind that on this side, the Alhambra rises with its massive walls and stupendous buttresses on a mountainous brow so steep as to be almost precipitous, looking down into the glen of the Darro, and across upon the opposite city.

The walls of this Tocador were once adorned with paintings wrought I believe in Charles the Fifth's time, though now greatly defaced. The windows look out from exquisitely-wrought recesses upon successive views as beautiful as those from the Hall of the Ambas- sadors. On the side toward the west, the Albaycin quarter of the city rises in a pile with its towers and gardens; on the south-west the eye roams across the wide vega to the distant mountains; on the north it commands the rising palace of the ' Generalise,' embosomed in ver- dure; and beyond, on the north-west, in a lovely situation, the extensive pile of the ' College of the Sacramonte,' with the course of the Darro winding around the base of the mountains. Nearer the palace, and directly beneath its overhanging towers, the eye looks down upon the gardens on the borders of the river, which runs in a deep glen over- shadowed with trees, that seem like a verdurous wall to girdle the foun- dations of the Alhambra.

It should be remembered that there are no windows except on this precipitous side, the apartments being lighted in the other direction by the open courts, so that all the prospects are vast, extensive and ele- vated. The points of observation for the different towers, with the windows looking from them, are chosen with great skill. Some of the inscriptions refer to the studied peculiarity of the palace being lighted from its courts; self-lighted, as it were, in the reflection of its own beauty, and without any thing to distract the attention from itself.

The light is abundant, diffused, like the open day, amidst pillars, halls, and arches; and the absence of any foreign outlet or point of observation gives an impression of unity to the whole pile, and a feeling of vastness, security and seclusion in wandering through the ranges of its apartments, which is very agreeable to the imagination.   One of the innumerable inscriptions runs thus : 'All the material and earthly stones employed in the construction of this palace draw their splendor from the light which the whole glory of the palace itself casts upon them.'   Another inscription is to this intent : 'My structure, the effect of an exquisite skill, has already passed into a proverb, and my praise is in all mouths.'   Well it might be, for its beauty is wonderful.   The architecture is so light and delicate, yet so rich and full of symmetry, so various from the simplest materials, so artless in its regularity, so chaste in its designs, and so pleasing in its combinations, that it seems as if Nature herself were here wantoning as in her prime, and 'pouring forth her virgin fancies, wild above rule or art.'   There never was a place exhibiting so much art with so much ease, so much magnificence with so much simplicity.   It is not the extent of the palace that arrests the mind's wonder, though its dimensions are not insignificant ; but the different halls and apartments, with the courts, fountains, gardens and balconies are so beautifully arranged, and so mingled on one side at least with the enjoyment of the splendid landscape scenery around them, that the sentiment of vastness is excluded by that of variety and loveliness. And yet, as it originally stood, the Alhambra was in itself almost a city of palaces.   Nearly thirty towers must have supported and crowned its walls, within whose circumference forty thousand men could be maintained as its garrison.   When we consider too that the Court of the Alberca is one hundred and thirty feet long, the Court of the Lions one hundred feet by fifty, and the audience hall nearly forty feet square, the actual extent of the palace as it now remains must appear noble.   The wondrous pile was in building under two long, successive and prosperous reigns, especially that of Yussuf Ben Ismael Ben Pharagi, surnamed Abul Hajji, and called an accomplished poet and scholar, as well as a lover of the fine arts.   He reigned from 1332 to 1354.   The founder of the palace was Aboa Abdallah Ben Nasser, the second sovereign of Grenada.   Yussuf erected the grand Gate of Justice, and in his days the palace was described as ' a silver vase filled with emeralds and jacinths.' For nearly a century and a half his descendants continued to reign, when the dominion passed from the crescent of the prophet to the standard of the pope.

The summer palace of the Alhambra rises high above the region we have been traversing, being situated northward at the base of a hill much loftier than the other, and nearer the Sierra Nevada.   Between the two ranges of palaces runs a winding gorge or ravine, descending abruptly to the valley of the Darro.   From a postern gate beneath one of the northern towers of the Alhambra, the princes of the Abencerrages were wont to pass across this wild glen, and upward to the gate of the summer palace, which was named the 'Generalise' or 'Palace of Pleasure.'   It is beautifully situated and arranged with its fountains, courts and gardens, commanding a prospect of great vastness and grandeur, whichever way the eye roves across the luxuriant vega to the distant mountains beyond. With a south-western exposure it overlooks the whole of the Alhambra, with its towers and terraces, and the deep wooded ravine of the Darro, with its alameda, a part of Grenada, and the tower-crested hill of the Albaycin beyond. A long portico runs along the front of the palace, divided into two by a central tower containing two apartments, which are hung with antique paintings of the Moors and christians. In one of them is the portrait of Boabdil, or El Rey Chico, and the Infanta of Grenada, with several princely Moors, who were baptized by christian names after their conquest. An antique tree of the generations of the kings of Cordova and Saragossa hangs at one end of the apartment. There are likewise two curious paintings representing a tower among the Alpuxarras, and a fight between two Moorish vessels of war, executed, though roughly, yet with much vigor, and a beauty of coloring which is still remarkable. In one of the garden courts of this palace are several gigantic cypresses, one of which is said to have been planted by the hand of the last unfortunate and beautiful sultana.

Above this court the gardens rise in terraces upon the hill-side, and you advance to the upper extremity of them through a thick shade of laurel trees, which in the month of June are a forest of fragrant blossoms. In the centre of the lowest of the garden terraces is a lofty circular bower in the shape of a dome, of so thick impervious foliage, as to be dark at noon-day, forming a beautiful summer retreat of twilight and coolness :

> —— ' The roof
> Of thickest covert was inwoven shade,
> Laurel and myrtle, and what higher grew
> Of firm and fragrant leaf; on either side
> Acanthus and each odorous bushy shrub
> Fenced up the verdant wall.'

Matteo cut for us a bit of fragrant bark from the sultana's cypress, and my beloved brother and myself each chose a laurel staff from the verdant gardens, deeming that we should consider a walking baton from the oriental groves of the Alhambra of far more value than those which we cut a few years ago in the ' Notch' of the White Mountains.

While we were in one of the courts of the Generalise, a party of Roman Catholic priests were there in their robes to administer the *Viaticum,* or extreme unction, to a dying old woman of the superintendent's family. The perspective of the priestly band in their gorgeous vestments, with their blazing tapers, as they emerged from the portico and wound their way downward, was very singular in itself and in its associations to our minds.

While wandering through these palaces, and while reading the description of them, if one would experience the full effect of the enchantment, for such it may almost be called, it is necessary to pause, and let the busy imagination people these halls with their first princely possessors, and figure them as furnished with a gorgeousness befitting their intrinsic splendors. ' A consideration of the various remains,' Mr. Murphy has well remarked, ' and of the recollected magnificence of the Arabian sovereigns, may enable us to judge what this palace had been in the zenith of regal power, with the courts and halls, baths and fountains, groves and gardens in perfection. Its possessors were sumptuously robed in fine linen, silk, and embroidery, glittering with gold and gems; they had costly furniture of citron, sandal, and aloes-wood, ornamented with ivory and mother-of-pearl intermingled with burnished gold and cerulean blue. They had vases of curious and costly workmanship, of porcelain and rock crystal, mosaic and sardonyx, with rich hanging flowery carpets, couches and pillows; and the whole was perfumed with the precious frankincense of Yemen.'

The whole scene must have been one of unparalleled magnificence; nor is it any wonder that it speedily passed into a proverb. I thought, while stepping from one silent court to another, and from one deserted fountain to another, and especially while wandering over the gardens of the summer palace, that when the pride of Moorish royalty was there, and the place was made the shrine of female delicacy and beauty, exquisite indeed must have been the aspect and the fragrance of these lovely retreats :

' Flowers of all hue, and without thorn the rose ; '

and over all attractions the strains of oriental music and poetry diffusing their romantic influence. The denizens of such a palace and city must have loved the spot and the region with an attachment indescribably strong. Indeed it is said that even now the Moors cherish a secret longing expectation, like that of the Jews towards Jerusalem, of one day revisiting and inheriting the possession of their fathers. When they were banished from the country its industry waned and its glory gradually departed, though for a season after the conquest of Grenada the Spanish monarchy was at its height of grandeur and prosperity; while the last of the royal Moorish possessors of Grenada had been utterly unworthy of the kingdom, and unable to maintain its independence or its power.

We traced the path which its conquered king had taken, from the 'Gate of the Tower of the Seven Vaults' downward to the little chapel near the banks of the Xeuil, where he formally delivered up the keys of Grenada and of the palace into the hands of Ferdinand the Conqueror. An inscription on the walls of the chapel commemorates the event.

If the spirit of the last king of the Moors was wrung with anguish when he took his melancholy way of banishment downward from the palace of his kingdom, with what sorrow must the princesses and maidens of the court have left the precincts of such an earthly paradise ! It was indeed a place more like the paradise of Milton than any earthly scene I ever expected to behold; so beautiful, that it is no wonder that the Moors should have placed above it, in that quarter of the heavens which overhung it, the seat of their celestial paradise of the faithful. Here, if it had been hallowed by the footsteps of a race who walked with God, the language of Eden's first possessor would well befit the beauty of the region :

> ' Here I could frequent
> With worship place by place where He vouchsafed
> Presence divine ; and to my sons relate
> ' On this mount he appeared ; under this tree
> Stood visible ; among these pines his voice
> I heard ; here with him at this fountain talked.
> So many grateful altars I would rear,
> Of grassy turf, and pile up every stone
> Of lustre from the brook in memory
> Or monument to ages ; and thereon
> Offer sweet-smelling gums and fruits and flowers.'

But it is a melancholy thought that neither then, when the region shone in all the fulness of its natural beauty and the palace in all its earliest magnificence ; nor now, when the one is falling to ruins and the other is left to the progress of nature's decay, have these scenes ever been the haunt of God's true worshippers. The mosques of the Moors rose in honor of the false Prophet, whose followers have contested the religious empire of the world with the legions of the Man of Sin. And the churches that now rise in their stead are dedicated to a worship quite as idolatrous and more superstitious in its ceremonies. Standing on the summit of one of those lofty hills, or on the terrace of one of those palace towers that commands a view so crowded and magnificent, the pathetic exclamation of our Saviour from the mountain that overhung Jerusalem comes forcibly upon the mind : ' How often would I have gathered thy children — but ye would not ! ' A city lies beneath me, whose inhabitants, nearly four centuries after the world has been shaken by the Reformation as by the new coming of Christianity, sleep almost as profoundly in the superstitious idolatry of popery, as they did when darkness covered the earth and gross darkness the people. And the heart almost sickens at the thought of the obstacles yet to be encountered, before this nation can be turned from their iniquities ; and this delightful region, rescued from the blight of infidelity, be pervaded with piety, knowledge and industry, and made to bud and blossom as the rose. Yet that blessed time shall come, and even now the signs are that the day is breaking.

RECORDS OF LIFE.

Cold Winter's snow-shroud is upon the hills —
His ice has hushed the music of the rills ;
The gorgeous flowers have bloomed and passed away,
The summer songsters and the vernal leaf ;
Each delicate being had its little day,
Then fled like human joys ; so bright, so frail, so brief !
Months have rolled over me, and I have spent
Long days and pleasant nights over the pages
Where are enshrined the radiant minds who lent
Lustre to classic shores and brilliant ages :
One all-important lesson have I stored
Within my heart ; the mercy of our Lord,
The boundless measure of a Saviour's love,
Which I can ne'er forget — which none can e'er remove.

January.   T.

The Rime of Sir Thopas.

DEDICATION.

To Sun, Moon, Stars, and lesser lights,
To planets, with their satellites,
To Saturn's Ring, and distant far,
To the Great Bear's tail, and canine star,
To the cream of all the Milky Way,
To the fixed stars, et cetera :
In short, to the whole universe
I dedicate my deathless verse ;
And in it I intend to show 'em
The way to write an Epic Poem.

PREFACE.

In olden time, historians tell us,
Poets were reckoned clever fellows:
Then yellow gold and good red wine,
With tender looks from ladies' eyne,
Were not too rich a boon to pay
For Troubadours' heroic lay.
But in these modern days, bald Science
Has to Apollo bid defiance ;
Politics, tales, newspaper trash,
Novels, love-ditties, balderdash
And prosy ratiocination
Are certainly the reigning fashion.
I, I alone am left to tell
Of ancient lore, of magic spell,
Of knights and dames and dragon-fights,
And all such out-of-date delights ;
And when they hear my wondrous song,
Shall male and female, old and young,
Learned and unlearned, agree to praise
The bard who sings the antique lays.

Soon as I get th' heroic stilt on,
I shall indulge my pen, like Milton,
In very picturesque profusion
Of learned and classical allusion.
But lest we yield to the temptation
Of coining lore to suit the occasion,
We 've Doctor ANTHON's Great Thesaurus
Open continually before us :
Yet I can't always have the patience
To make strict literal quotations ;
My author's quoted words must stand
Just put to suit the point in hand :
No matter if he never said it —
I 'll say it, and give him the credit.
As to bare facts, I do suspect
I mostly shall be incorrect.
For abstract truth I shall not stickle, or
About my statements be particular,

But make folk think and speak and do
Precisely what I wish them to.

And since great critics do maintain
No bard may epic laurels gain
Unless his private life shall be
An epic poem ta'en '*per se;*'
And since this life controlled by chance is,
And unexpected circumstances;
'T is clear our poem, to be true
To Nature, should be chance-led too:
Therefore we shall expend no thought
On a profound and labored plot.
Of modern epic heroes, some pass
Their blank-verse lives by rule and compass;
Must fall in love, fight, and get married,
Before of them their readers are rid.
Our hero nobly turns his back
On such a vulgar beaten track.
It cannot certainly be said
We 'll make him fall in love, or wed, }
Or eat, or drink, or go to bed;
For being nor seer nor prophet, we
Cannot discern futurity.
But know, he shall in our narration,
' Hoe his own row ' without dictation.

Now since I 've told you to a fraction
My principles and rules of action,
And you 're prepared to meet the worst,
I 'll eke begin with Canto First.

— . ---

CANTO I.

ARGUMENT.

Sir Thopas here is introduced
  As civilly as may be,
With some of his propensities
  While he was yet a baby;
And how his nurses tell that he
  Did often beat and scold them,
With divers other things which you
  . Will know when you are told them.

———

All ye who read what 's printed in
The Knickerbocker Magazine,
Whether in Gotham town or elsewhere,
Scattered 'mong country hills and dells, where
The small birds sing, and cool streams glide,
All, *all* attend — and more beside!
And distant o'er the Atlantic pond,
Old Europe, hark! — and, far beyond
The Pontic pool and Chersonese,
Thou realm where Prester John did sneeze!
While farther still, the great Celestial
Empire and Japan, with the rest, shall

List while I build a lofty rhyme
That shall survive the end of time,
And in heroic numbers tell
What once upon a time befel
A knight renowned throughout Európe, as
The fearless, peerless young SIR THOPAS.

Sir Thopas was a jolly knight;
The thing he loved best was to fight.
In infancy this trait ferocious
Appeared — for genius is precocious —
And ere young kittens' eyes are well ope'd
In him began to be developed.
For his old nurse has oft related,
(And to her credit be it stated,)
That he'd delight to draw the pin
From where his mother stuck it in;
Though honestly I should speak truer
By calling it a wooden skewer;
For, to our good mechanics' praise,
They had no pins in ancient days;
But with wooden pegs their clothes they put on,
As you would truss a leg of mutton.
This peg he used as mimic lance,
Laid it in rest: 'Retard!' 'Advance!'
And once, while at this exercise,
A fierce form met his fearless eyes;
All grimly black as Ethiop,
With thrice two legs, and burnished top,
With crooked jaws, yawning alway,
Ready to lacerate his prey;
Rapid he strode as the earth-born giants,
And all his bearing breathed defiance!
Undaunted infant Thopas viewed
The monster's threat'ning attitude;
He couched his peg. A deadly blow
Arrests the onward-rushing foe;
And prostrate by his prowess, lo!
The pismire prone in mid-career rolled —
And this ere he was half a year old!
A daring feat of high emprize,
And one just suited to his size.
But as our hero older grew,
He chose more noble weapons too:
And here, as in whatever more's said,
We take the account of Nurse aforesaid;
Who swears he oftened did provoke her
By beating her with tongs and poker,
And malgré all her cries and tears
Would lay the shovel 'bout her ears;
Whose hearty thumps and thwacks and bangs
Did cause her poor pate piteous pangs.

Perchance some critic, moved by spite,
May say it ill became a knight
In embryo, being masculine,
To strike his Nurse who's feminine.
But we can prove from precedents
Such critic lacks both wit and sense.
For many knights renowned and glorious
O'er females have been found victorious;
Whilst others 'generis ejusdem'
Very courageously abused 'em.

And many such like tales, which I
Have read in ancient history,
Are in my ready memory coming on
To justify our young phenomenon.
First take the case of Hercules,
Who, with his cronies, crossed the seas,
Where valiantly, or I have heard ill,
They slew a queen to get her girdle.
Yet ancient bards did never call it a
Cowardly deed to kill Hippolyta :
Nay, on the contrary, they have
So far agreed that it was brave,
They 've placed it, with right noble neighbors,
Among his twelve heroic labors.
And Cyrus, as we read in Homer, is
Said to have fought against Queen Tomyris,
Though a friend, who looks my proof-sheet o'er,
Maintains, and probably with more
Correctness than has been allotted *us*,
This story 's taken from Herodotus.
And that redoubted warrior,
Who, shipwrecked naked on the shore,
Plucked a green slender twig which hid well
The tender region round his middle,
Lest lovely virgins might have chosen
To catch him there without his clothes on ;
This man, this modest, coy Ulysses,
Who tasted Circe's sweetest kisses,
At first drew his cold iron trenchant,
Swearing he 'd give her every inch on 't,
And thereto added many a sore curse,
Because she changed his men to porkers.

Next take that valiant Guy of Warwick,
A famous name on page historic :
Did he not fight three days, I trow,
With an uncivil, great dun cow ?
And cows do mostly, I opine,
Belong to gender feminine.

What stronger cases could you find
To satisfy a candid mind ?
E'en Envy cannot but decide
That our young hero 's justified ;
And women, as a widower Judge held,
With sturdy broomstick may be cudgelled,
And vixens' crooked tempers righted,
Without endamaging one's knighthood.
So critic ass, thy cause give o'er,
And ope thy mouth to bray no more !

Much more have I to tell hereafter,
Which may afford fair food for laughter ;
Of Thopas, after he had been
A man with beard upon his chin,
And armed, like Shakspere's jolly Sir John,
With sword, and buckler, and habergeon.
Of his gray mare, so brisk and jaunty,
Whose boasted sire was Rosinante,
I 'll tell ; and of his doughty squire
Shall many gallant feats transpire ;
For beef and bumpers huge could he quell,
As shall be set forth in the sequel.

Thus far on foot and unattended
On my poetic way I 've wended;
No pinions that could be relied on
Had I, nor Pegasus to ride on.
He once was quite a colt of promise,
But over-driving's ta'en him from us!
Once a well-curried, dapper pony,
Now broken-winded, lean, and bony,
By poetasters sorely jaded!
By him unhelped, by Muse unaided;
And ah! the melancholy fact is
Of late I 'm somewhat out of practice!
No wonder, then, my powers I find
Flagging at last. So, reader kind,
To give the sweet repose I want, oh
Wait till next month for Second Canto.

THE QUOD CORRESPONDENCE.

The Attorney.

CHAPTER XVIII.

ABOUT nine o'clock one fine morning, Aaron walked deliberately into Mrs. Dow's little back parlor, in his shirt-sleeves, with a stiff brush under his arm. He paused in the middle of the room, rolled up his sleeves, took the brush from under his arm, and proceeded to polish a small mahogany table, particularly directing his strength against a yellow stain which had lately made its appearance in the wood.

'*He* did it — he! he!' muttered he, grating his teeth. 'That is the wery identical place where he sot down his tumbler. I seen him do it, and I knowed a spot would be the consequence. Never mind!' Here he shook his head in a manner indicating that he derived a slight degree of consolation from certain sources unknown to the world at large; and he continued polishing vehemently. It was not long however before the comfort derived from the unknown sources appeared to be exhausted; for he stopped again.

'I wish I had him here under this 'ere wery brush!' muttered he, pinching his lips tightly together, and concentrating the whole visual energy of two very irascible eyes on the stain with an expression of venom and hostility which might have had a powerful effect on any thing less obdurate than a spot in mahogany. 'I wish he was that spot, and I was the indiwidual that had the rubbing him out. This is what I 'd do!' In demonstration of his meaning, and under the agreeable delusion that he had Wilkins under treatment, and was rasping him down, Aaron put forth a degree of strength and vigor that completely annihilated the real object of his efforts long before the imaginary one had received what he deemed satisfactory attention at his hands.

'And *she!* a encouragin' him!' said he, casting a sullen look over his shoulder at his mistress, who sat in a pious frame of mind dozing over a tract in front of the fire. 'Sixty, if she 's a day; should 'nt wonder if she was seventy or even ninety. She looks every hour of it. If that 's the small beggar that rung yesterday, I 'll wallop him!'

The concluding part of his remark was called forth by a violent ring at the door, which interrupted the current of his thoughts, though it did not restore his good humor. Strong in his amiable resolution, he smoothed his hair over his forehead, laid his brush on the table, and proceeded to see who had favored him with this sudden summons.

On the side-walk stood a dwarfish boy in loose pantaloons, with a small cap perched on his head directly over his nose, and his hands thrust to the elbows in the pockets of the pantaloons just mentioned, where he jingled and rattled a number of small coins with great violence, at the same time looking up the street with an air of profound abstraction. On seeing the door open he walked gently back, ascended the steps with the leisurely air of a person who had plenty of time and a great aversion to violent exercise, and eyeing Aaron from head to foot, said :

'Hullo! old feller! Do you live here?'

The man-servant looked at the stunted marker (for he it was) for more than a minute; for having come out with the fixed determination of walloping a small beggar, and judging the stunted marker to be nearly of the same dimensions, out of his trowsers, and not having entirely resigned his intention, he was casting about in his mind as to the most approved mode of commencing, when he was taken aback by the abrupt salutation. A man of his years, addressed in such a tone by a small boy in loose trowsers! He had never met with such a thing in the whole course of his experience. Before he had time to recover from the shock produced by this unheard-of proceeding, the boy, who was growing impatient, said :

'Wake up! old beet-nose; you need n't stare so. I see your peepers; cussed ugly ones they are too; but you 've got a tongue as well as them, ha'n't you? Just rattle it; 'cos I can't stand here talking all day to a dumb youngster, if he *does* wear dirt-colored breeches.'

'It wo'n't do,' said Aaron drawing a long breath. And accordingly he woke up, and inquired what he wanted.

'Is there a young woman here by the name of Wiolet Dow? If there is, trot her out. I want to conwerse with her.'

'Mrs. Dow *does* live here,' replied Aaron; 'but ' ——

'She does, does she?' interrupted the boy. 'Well be spry. Young fellers like you should stir about lively, and leave it to old men like me to crawl. Speak quick, what you 've got to say.'

'But —' continued Aaron, as soon as the boy gave an opportunity to the current of his speech to ooze on; 'but ' ——

'But what?'

'She ain't a chicken.'

'Oh, ho! Past twenty?' said the marker, with an inquiring nod. Aaron winked a slow affirmative.

'Thirty — forty, fifty — sixty?' said the marker, just pausing sufficiently between each number to permit Aaron to perpetrate a deliberate assent to each.

'Oh! she's one of them vimmen as get gray, but wo'n't give up. I've seed 'em afore. They're quite common,' said the boy, dusting the sleeve of one arm with the cuff of the other.

Aaron's face brightened into a broad grin, and he began to feel sociably inclined toward the visiter, who proceeded to perch himself on the iron railing, where he sat swinging his feet to and fro.

'You are quite at home, young man,' said Aaron, leaning against the door post, as if he too had no intention of terminating the conversation.

'Of course, I are,' replied the boy : 'I 'spect to spend the morning on this 'ere very rail, unless I sees that voman to-once.'

'You're a strange boy. What's your name?'

'Charles Draddy,' replied the other, without hesitation, and swinging his feet with great violence. 'What's your'n?'

'Aaron.'

'Oh, ho!' again exclaimed the boy; 'then you're the man I want!' He placed his finger significantly at the side of his nose, and screwing up his mouth to a point, as if he had no very distant idea of perpetrating a whistle, he said : 'I came from Mr. Fisk, counsellor at law. Do you twig?'

Aaron's eyes brightened, and he nodded mysteriously.

'I want to see your young voman herself. No other young voman wo'n't do. Oh, no! I guess it wo'n't. I say, old feller,' said he, sinking his voice, and inserting two of his fingers in his jacket pocket, and making visible therefrom the end of a piece of paper; 'do you see that?'

Aaron nodded.

'Well, do you know what that is?'

'No, I don't.'

The boy leaned forward, and said in a low voice. "It's a *soopeeny!* One of them things as walks old vomen up into court whether they vant to or not, and squeezes the truth right straight out of 'em, jist like the juice out of a lemon.'

'Oh, ho!' said Aaron; 'is it about that Wilkins?'

'He's the man,' replied the other; 'but *this*,' said he, touching the paper, 'is for your old voman. Counsellor Fisk and I vants to clap the screws on her.'

Aaron favored the boy with a sagacious wink, as much as to say that he understood his meaning.

'You see,' continued the marker, 'the counsellor spoke to Mr. Rawley, a pertickler friend of mine; you know Mr. Rawley?'

Aaron answered in the affirmative.

'Well, Mr. Rawley knowed a good many of the witnesses what was wanted; and he was to ha' soopeenied 'em all; but he had n't time; so he sent me arter the vun as roosts in this 'ere dwellin.' Now my little feller, how 'll I find her? She ain't up to trap, is she?'

'Not she; not she! I'll fix that,' said Aaron; and he forthwith disappeared from the door, and proceeded to the back-parlor, where Mrs. Dow sat with her eyes still devoutly fixed on the tract, in which she had made but little progress, possibly from the fact that she held it in her hand upside down.

'A boy wants you at the door,' said Aaron bluntly.

'A boy!' exclaimed Mrs. Dow, instantly closing the book; 'did you say a boy?'

'Yes, I did.'

'Are you sure it's only a boy?' inquired Mrs. Dow, glancing nervously at the glass. 'Only a boy — not a man?'

'It's a boy,' replied Aaron; 'and a werry dirty one.'

'A boy!' repeated the relict of Mr. Dow, rising and coloring, 'and a dirty boy, too? Perhaps he's a small one, Aaron. Small boys do sometimes get dirty.'

'He *is* a small one,' said Aaron, 'but he's old. His years is got the start of his statur'.'

'Where can he come from!' exclaimed the widow. 'I've heard of boys who came to steal — especially dirty ones. Sometimes they bring letters. Those are generally nice boys; but nice boys will get dirty sometimes. I've been so myself occasionally; but I'll go and see him at once.'

In pursuance of this resolution Mrs. Dow sallied into the entry, followed by Aaron.

'How are you, young voman?' said the stunted marker, who had already found his way to the room door, without removing his cap, and looking her full in the eyes, and at the same time nodding sociably.

'Not very well,' replied Mrs. Dow, much mollified by a speech which insinuated that she still maintained an appearance of juvenility: 'I've got a bad cold; quite a bad cold;' and Mrs. Dow coughed very slightly by way of illustration. 'But I'm better now, thank you; much better, Sir.'

'Your 'spectable mother must feel werry glad; she must feel werry relieved, she must,' said the stunted marker, taking advantage of a momentary embarrassment on the part of the lady, to make a wry face at Aaron, which drove that worthy individual into a corner in strong convulsions, to the imminent danger of his suspenders.

'Oh! Sir, my mother, Sir: I ain't got no mother, Sir!' answered Mrs. Dow, simpering and coloring.

'Mrs. Wiolet Dow is the lady in question,' replied the boy gravely; at the same time looking inquiringly at Aaron, who nodded and winked with great vehemence.

'I'm Mrs. Dow,' said the relict.

'No! but you ain't though? Mrs. Wiolet Dow, Esq.?'

Mrs. Dow bowed.

'Then I soopeeny you!' exclaimed the boy, thrusting a dirty paper in one of her hands and a piece of money in the other; at the same time flourishing a paper before her eyes. 'You've got the copy, and the fee, and there's the 'riginal. You're in for it, old voman! Wo'n't you be salted when they get you into court? Wo'n't your affections be walked into? Oh! no; not a bit!'

Having displayed several extraordinary feats of agility in commemoration of the successful discharge of his task, and terminated them by turning heels overhead in the entry, a performance in which he was in no way impeded by the tightness of his garments, he gave a loud yell, and bolted out of the house as if shot from a cannon.

'A soopeny!' shrieked Mrs. Dow, holding the small piece of paper at arm's length in one hand and clutching the money convulsively in the other. 'What's the meaning of this, Aaron? What's it about, Aaron?'

'Perhaps you'd better open it and see,' said Aaron; 'it's a very mysterious business, out and out, *I* think.'

'Gracious me!' exclaimed the widow, following his advice. 'I'm *commanded* by all the people of the state of New-York to go to court! Me, a lone widow, to go to a court! — to be exposed to the licentious gaze of a crowded room of at least three hundred male men — without the judge! Bless me! and there's a penalty too! I'm to pay two hundred and fifty dollars! What will they do with me, Aaron? What do they do with witnesses?' demanded she, tugging with nervous violence at a brown handkerchief, the end of which appeared from the mouth of a side pocket.

'Axes 'em questions,' replied Aaron. 'The young gen'leman that just went out says they squeezes 'em just like they squeezes lemons; but I don't know nothin' about that.'

'*That* I never *will* submit to!' exclaimed the widow, indignantly; '*Never!* I'll die before I'll submit to *that!* Oh! Aaron!' said she, suddenly relapsing into the melting mood, as was indicated by her speaking in a broken voice, and blowing her nose with great force : 'nothing of the kind ever happened to me in the life-time of the late Mr. Dow; nothing! — and he had a great deal to do in law. He foreclosed three mortgages; sent two women to the penitentiary for stealing baby linen; and once went to see a man tried for running over three hens and a fat child, and I was never soopenied in all these — not once. If he had lived, this never would have happened. I'm sure of it.'

'I rather think so myself,' replied Aaron, gravely.

'Oh! no; I know it wouldn't!' repeated the widow, sobbing, and again making energetic use of her handkerchief. 'Something will happen! I know it! I feel it! I shall faint!' And in pursuance of this resolution she put the money in her pocket and the paper on a table; and sunk into the open arms of the man-servant, who gently deposited her in an arm-chair, where in the course of time she sobbed herself into a gentle slumber.

Just at the particular time that these things were going on in one part of the city, Higgs was walking sentimentally along in another with his hands under his coat-tails, indulging a low whistle, pausing thoughtfully at every corner, and looking up and down the streets as if he owned a house in each, and hadn't made up his mind which to visit first.

It was a fine soft day, glowing and warm for the season; and there was a feeling of luxury in idling about — now looking in a shop window, now pausing to read the signs over the doors, and now drifting along with the crowd — that just suited the taste of Mr. Higgs, and which he fully indulged until he had wandered off to a remote part of the city, where the small size of the dwellings and their mean and dilapidated condition denoted that the very poor had their homes.

There is not much amusement to be found in the haunts of the wretched; and this idea presenting itself with much force to the mind of Mr. Higgs, he had quietly reclined his person against a lamp-post in front of a mean-looking house, to make up his mind whither to direct his steps, when his attention was attracted to some one speaking in the house.

' Let it be a mahogany one,' said a plaintive voice, which seemed to come from a room on the ground floor. ' The best is not too good for him;' a low half-suppressed sob followed; ' and tell him,' continued the same voice, ' that he shall be paid soon, if I work my fingers to the bone.' All was quiet for a moment, and then Higgs heard, in a stifled voice: ' God bless you, my boy!—go!' and a thin sickly-looking lad came out of the house and ran off at the top of his speed.

It was not long before he returned, panting for breath, and went into the room.

' What do you think, mother?' said he, earnestly; ' he would n't let me have it!'

' Did you tell him all?' said the same sad voice which Higgs had heard before; ' what has happened, and how poor we were?'

' Yes, I did; and he said he would n't; there was no use in talking about it; that I might go to the poor-house for one; or for the matter of that, bury him without one. He said *that*,' continued the boy, sinking his voice so low that Higgs could scarcely hear him, and speaking as if the very idea startled him.

' Oh! no, no! he could not have meant *that!*' replied the mother. ' Bury my poor dead little boy in that way!'—and she sobbed as if her very heart would break.

Higgs' curiosity was excited by what he heard; and he rose and peeped cautiously in the room. It was very small, and every thing in it was wretched and poor. Near the window was a woman, yet young, but with whom sorrow and suffering had done the work of years; and at her side, with her hand clasped in her's, stood the boy who had just returned. They were both bending over a cot on which lay the dead body of a child apparently about two years of age. They were too poor to have done much for him, and the same little frock which he had worn when alive was his shroud now that he was dead. His light hair was parted over his forehead. There was a slight color in his cheek, and a smile around the small mouth, as if some angel had stolen away the spirit in an hour of happiness. All was like life; but the dark, sad eye of the mother, and the sorrowful look of the boy at her side, told their tale. The little fellow was resting in the long sleep which has no end; and his childish voice would never again gladden his mother's heart.

There are spots of gold even in the darkest character; and that bold bad man who shrank not from vice and crime, had strange feelings and recollections as he looked upon the face of the sinless child before him. Dreams of by-gone days and scenes and faces which he had long forgotten swept through his mind, softening his spirit. He wondered if he could ever have been young and innocent like *him*. He looked at the weeping mother, and it brought back to him a faintly-remembered face which had once hovered around him in dreams; but so long since that he could scarcely remember it; and then he thought of those who had played with him when they were boys together. Some had died then; some had grown up into youth, and then they too had died; some had gone he knew not whither; others had risen to wealth and respectability; and some had become stern, hardened men like himself.

Higgs drew back from the window, thrust his hand in his pocket, and walked directly into the house, and into the room where the child lay.

'*There!*' said he, placing a bill for a considerable amount on the table. 'Take that. Bury the boy as you want to. Think of me sometimes; and if you find it convenient, when you are saying your prayers, put in a good word for me: I need it.' Without waiting for an answer, he turned and left the house.

He had spent so much of the day in strolling about that he had not gone far when a clock sounded the hour of three in the afternoon. No sooner did he hear it than he changed his course and struck across to the eastern part of the city. His pace was now steady and rapid, like that of one who had a place of destination which he wished to reach without loss of time. In twenty minutes he stopped in front of a house more than a mile from where he set out. It was a small filthy tavern in the outskirts of the town. A sign had once hung over the door; but that had long since fallen to the ground, where it had been left to decay under the influence of time and storm.

Higgs however required no such indication to inform him where he was. He went through a passage with the air of a man perfectly at home; opened an inner door, and entered what appeared to be a kind of sitting-room for visiters. It was dark and gloomy, and redolent of gin and stale segars. The walls were discolored and stained; and from a pale yellow had gradually tanned into a deep snuff-color. Altogether, it was as cheerless and uncomfortable as might have been expected from the out-of-the-way part of the city and the wretched neighborhood in which the tavern stood. One or two old prints, blackened by smoke and time, hung against the wall; and a dirty sand-box filled with stumps of segars occupied the middle of the room, near a wooden table with a broken leg. A decrepit tongs and a shovel without a handle were lying together in the chimney-place, in the very centre of which sat a man in a rough great-coat, with his head bent forward, and his hands hanging listlessly over his knees, as he sat over a dim fire.

Mr. Higgs was at no loss to recognize Wilkins in this person. In truth it would seem that he expected to find him; for scarcely favoring him with a glance, he walked up, and slapped him between the shoulders, with a degree of friendly violence, which seemed to strike the person thus favored as quite unnecessary; for he requested him when next he addressed him, either to keep his hands off, or to lay them on with more tenderness.

'Why, what ails you?' demanded Higgs, abruptly; 'your flesh ain't eggs, is it? It wo'n't mash at a touch, will it?'

' What the devil brings you here ? what do you want ? ' demanded Wilkins in a surly tone. Without satisfying either of the interesting inquiries, Higgs went to the table, and looked successively into two small pitchers which stood on it; and having applied his nose to both of them, he took up the one-legged tongs and hammered lustily on the table.

' Hallo ! what 's the muss ? ' bellowed a voice from a small window; opening into an inner room; ' what you banging that there table for ? Do n't you see it 's weak in the j'ints ? Peg away at the floor, if you want to knock something; but when you come into a gen'leman's house do n't be a smashin' his furniter arter that fashion.'

In pursuance of this hint, Higgs shifted his blows from the table to the floor, and knocked with a force that soon brought a slip-shod girl, without stockings, and with remarkably red heels, to know what he wanted.

' Fill *them !* ' said Higgs, pointing to the pitchers. The girl took them up, eyed the inside very scrutinizingly, and disappearing, in a few minutes returned, and placed them foaming on the table. Higgs, pushing one of them toward Wilkins, buried his face in the other for some moments, then replaced the pitcher, with a sigh of satisfaction, and wiped his mouth on the back of his hand.

Wilkins had sat watching him in silence, until his thirst was satisfied, and then asked, in no very placable tone :

' What brings you here ? — what do you want ? Blast me ! if I do n't begin to suspect you. You never come near me now-a-days unless there 's something to be got out of me.'

Higgs looked at him for a moment, as if making up his mind what answer to make, and then said bluntly: ' Of *course* I want something. You do n't think I 'd come to this out-of-the-way, ungenteel little dram-hole, when there 's respectable places in the city, on purpose to find you, unless I wanted something, do you ? If you *do*, you do 'nt know me as well as I thought you did.'

' Well, then let 's know what it is,' said Wilkins; ' and do n't sit there, staring and gaping as if you had something in your mind you was afraid to tell. You have 'nt murdered any one, have you ? '

' Pish ! you know I have n't. What the devil ails you, man ? '

' No matter what,' replied Wilkins, not in the least mollified by the interest in his welfare denoted by the question ; and turning his back on the questioner, and stirring the fire.

Higgs, before going into the communication he had on hand, got up and shut the door. He then went to the small window opening into the other room and shut that, having first looked through it and satisfied himself that the apartment beyond was empty. He then returned, and drawing a chair so close to Wilkins that even a whisper could be heard, said: ' I 've come here to talk with you about that lawyer, Bolton ; and to let you into a small project I have on foot, before proposing it to him. I knew you were to be here at this hour.'

' Well, what about that man ? '

' You know that you and I and the lawyer are all in the same boat.'

Wilkins looked at him with a troubled glance, but said nothing.

'And you know he's a man that would'nt think twice before he put a halter round our necks, if we stood in his way.'

'Do'nt I know him?' said Wilkins, in a low, fierce voice: 'do'nt I know every corner of his black heart! I *ought* to. Well, go on.'

'If we were in his grasp,' continued Higgs, in the same subdued manner, 'and he could squeeze a few thousands out of us, and we could n't help ourselves, do you think he'd do it?'

There was something almost fiendish in the wild mocking laugh that preceded the response of Wilkins, as he said:

'*Do* it! He'd wring out the last drop of your heart's blood for *that*. Aye, he'd d — n you in this world and the next for *that!*'

'Then,' replied Higgs, in a stern determined voice, 'I'll show him that *two* can play at that game. This is what I mean. He has showed his hand to the girl; he has showed the will; he has let out that we are the witnesses to it. He's in for it; there's no back out for him. He admitted as much to me. *He can't go on without us!* But as yet *we* aint committed; for we have only stuck our names to the paper; we have proved nothing, sworn to nothing, and might be seized with a sudden loss of memory, and know nothing about it; or we might have done so only for the *purpose of preventing a fraud*, by blowing on him when we were called on as witnesses.

'Well,' said Wilkins, 'what's your drift?'

'Drift! It's plain enough,' replied Higgs; 'I've got a d — d bad memory; and I do n't believe any thing less than twenty thousand dollars will restore it, in this 'ere identical case. And I'd advise you to have as bad a one too.'

'But will he pay it?' demanded Wilkins, earnestly.

'Pshaw! what can he do? He can't stop. If he does he's d — d. If we do n't help him he's d — d. He *must* do it! Even then he will have a hundred and sixty thousand dollars for his share. He says the old man left two hundred thousand dollars.'

'My pay is n't money,' replied Wilkins, relapsing into his moody humor. 'He's to give me service for service.'

'Make him do that too,' replied Higgs. 'If he wo'n't come in to my proposition, I'll pay him back the five hundred dollars I've got, and withdraw from the service. This being flush is n't such great things after all. It's agreeable enough at first; but in the long run, it is n't half so exciting as going on tick, and knowing there's always some one to take an interest in your health. Curse me, how bad Mr. Quagley felt when I was near dying once, and owed him a small bill of forty dollars. His feelings was quite touched.'

Wilkins folded his arms and sat for some time in silent abstraction, giving no other indication of his being awake than by slightly drumming with his foot on the floor. At last he said:

'There's a good deal in what you say; yet I've sworn *not* to blow on him, but I have not sworn to stand by him.' Turning to the pitcher, he took a deep draught of the ale, which had hitherto stood neglected at his elbow. 'You shall know what I intend to do, before long.'

Higgs bowed in token of satisfaction ; and after a pause of some duration, crossed his legs, leaned back in the chair, and asked :
' What have you done about that divorce? I wish you 'd do something soon."

A change, as rapid as lightning, came over the face of Wilkins, as he replied :
' What 's it to *you* what I do, or when I do it? — or if I take six months or a year? — or if I never do it? What 's it to *you*, I say?' And he struck his clenched fist, which he had shaken at Higgs during these vehement questions, violently on the table.

' What 's it to *me* ?' inquired Higgs, with some surprise ; ' that 's a good one! Why, d — n it! I told you I intended to marry her myself.'

' By G — d! you shall die first !' exclaimed Wilkins, starting up and dashing his hat on the floor. ' You mus'n't come interfering between me and my plans. That girl I cast adrift because I intend to pay off the ill usage I 've had at her hands. She shall live and die alone ; wretched, in the very kennel ; and let me see you raise a finger to help her ! Marry her ! *No one* shall! Sooner than *that*, I 'd keep her in my own grasp ; and if I broke my own heart in doing so, I 'd break her's too.'

' It was agreed between us,' replied Higgs, earnestly, ' that I was to prove whatever you wanted ; you were to throw her off, and I was to take her. Honor! George, honor ! When a gentleman loses his honor he loses what 's precious ; ' and Mr. Higgs shook his head, as if he experienced feelings of the most poignant regret at the idea of such a dereliction on the part of his friend.

' I agreed to nothing,' replied Wilkins, in the same savage tone ; ' and if you attempt to cross me it will be the bitterest thing you ever did.'

Higgs's policy at present was not to exasperate Wilkins, lest he might in a fit of stubbornness come to the resolution of not obtaining the divorce. He therefore merely said : ' We wo'n't quarrel about it. If I was mistaken, I was — and there 's an end of it. I 've not lived to my age to fight about a petticoat. I must be off now. You know we 've got to go to the lawyer's to-night.'

Wilkins nodded sullenly.

' Eight o'clock is the hour,' said Higgs ; and without farther remark he arose and went out.

CHAPTER XIX.

IN the same office where he had hatched so much harm, the Attorney sat with his arms folded, his brows knit, and his amiable face gathered into a frown which bespoke any thing but mental tranquillity. On the table near him lay a note, written in the peculiar penmanship and worded with the elegance so characteristic of Mr. Higgs, in which, after informing the Attorney that he had strong misgivings that they were performing the rather incongruous acts of getting themselves in a box and into a pickle, he appointed that evening to see him, and to discuss their plans.   On this note the Attorney from time to time bent his eyes, now and then removing them to gaze abstractedly around the room.   His thin lips moved and twitched nervously, and at times he unfolded his arms, and clasping his long thin fingers about his knees, sat there motionless, looking wistfully in the smoking embers, and dreaming over plans which were corroding his heart, and which, even if successful, were dearly bought.   Once a voice reached his ear from the street, and he straightened himself up and listened ; but it sank suddenly into silence, and he relapsed into his old attitude.   One might have supposed him dead — for his features were pinched and pale, and had a rigid unearthly look — but for the brilliancy of those black, glittering eyes, and the low muttering which occasionally escaped him.

An hour or more had passed in this manner, when suddenly a step was heard in the passage below ; then one or two heavy jarring treads, as if a person had stumbled in ascending the stairs in the dark.   Bolton shook off his abstraction, turned to the table, snuffed the candles, thrust the note which was lying there in his pocket, drew one or two papers near him, and commenced writing.   In the mean time the stumbling continued, until the person had surmounted the stairs, and was heard coming through the upper entry.   Bolton did not raise his eyes from the paper as he entered ; but he knew, without doing so, that the tall, gaunt man who strode boldly in was Wilkins.   Without speaking, he threw his hat on a chair, and shaking his head to free his face from the long elf-locks which hung over it, drew a chair to the fire, seated himself opposite the Attorney, with the air of one who had every inclination, and only wanted an excuse, to give vent to a long-hoarded and abundant supply of ill humor.

Bolton wrote on, pretending not to notice him, until he could make up his mind how to meet him.   Wilkins, however, soon solved this difficulty, by demanding abruptly :

'What have you done in that business of mine?'

The Attorney raised his head.   'Ah ! Wilkins ! it's you ? So you've come ?   I wanted you.'

'What have you done in that business of mine?' repeated his visiter, taking no notice of the extended hand of the lawyer, which accompanied the remark.

'You mean that girl ? — your wife ? — the drab?'

'Come, none of that !' replied Wilkins, with an impatient gesture. 'I did n't come here to hear you call names.   She's no drab; and you know it.   All you 've got to do is to look to your work, and keep your tongue quiet.   What have you done ? I ask again.'

'As yet, nothing.'

'Then,' replied Wilkins, ' *do* nothing.   Our compact is at an end.'

Bolton laid down his pen ; his face became a shade paler, and his voice trembled slightly, as he asked :

'What now, Wilkins?   What do you mean?'

'Do n't I speak plain?' said Wilkins.   'You want something more, do you?   You shall have it; ay, to your heart's content.'

He rose, took his chair by the back, stamped it heavily on the floor within two feet of the Attorney, and sat down on it. ' *This* is what I mean. A certain lawyer was to get George Wilkins divorced from his wife ; and on condition of his doing so, George Wilkins was to prove a certain signature to a certain paper. Perhaps you understand that ? '

Bolton glanced nervously about the room ; for Wilkins spoke in a loud and excited key. ' Well,' said he, ' well ? '

' *Well !* ' echoed Wilkins with a bitter laugh ; ' *well !* A month went by. The lawyer was pushing his own business on finely ; but when Wilkins came to see what had been done in his, the answer was, ' Nothing yet ! '

There was something so unusual in the manner of his visiter, something so reckless and mocking, and withal so savage, that the Attorney fairly quailed. ' Now what I 've got to say is this,' continued Wilkins : ' I want nothing farther at your hands. I want no divorce ; and you, *you* who think of none but yourself ; who blight and curse and poison all who come in your path ; *you*, d — n you ! *you* may prove your will as you can ! May hell seize me, if I move a finger, stir a step, or utter a word to save you from the gallows ! *Now* you understand me ! '

' I do ! ' replied Bolton, whose hesitation vanished at the more imminent danger which threatened from this new resolution of his confederate. ' I *do* understand you,' repeated he, in that low, clear, calm tone, so often the voice of strong, concentrated purpose or of bitter wrath. ' No one could have spoken more plainly. Now hear *me*. You made a promise and confirmed it by an oath, that if I performed a certain service for you you would do the same for me. Relying on your good faith, I have taken steps which have compromised my safety beyond recal. I cannot retrace them. I cannot undo what is now done. There is no escape for me, except in going on. That will is already in the hands of the surrogate. Your name is to it as a witness ; and prove it you *shall !* Clench your fist if you will,' said he, grating his teeth, and shaking his thin finger at him ; ' I fear you not. I have you in my gripe. I can tie you neck and heels, and place you where you 'll rot. You 're mine, and prove that will you *shall.* There are but three cases in which the law will dispense with your testimony, and allow *your signature* to be proved.'

' What are they ? ' asked Wilkins, doggedly.

' You must be insane, which you are not, or you must leave the State.'

' Suppose I won't ? '

' *Then*,' said Bolton, leaning forward, and speaking slowly, ' to get along without your personal testimony, the *law* says you must be DEAD ! '

Wilkins sat opposite to him, eyeing him with a sullen, fixed stare, evincing neither surprise nor fear ; but seeming rather in deep and perplexed thought. At last he said :

' And so, Bolton, you would blow on an old comrade, who had stuck to you through thick and thin, because he had run you too hard once ? '

' I *would*, if he gave out at last,' replied the lawyer.

'And you would forget how often he had served you when none else would; and you would have him laid by the heels, and locked up, to rot and fester, and beat himself against his prison walls, and to lie there and rave, and curse the hour that he came into the world? — would you?'

'I would!'

'Or if you did n't, you'd send him to kingdom-come, off hand?'

'The *law* says that the witness must be *dead!*' repeated Bolton, sternly.

'But suppose the man was me, Bolton — your old tried friend?' said Wilkins earnestly, drawing his chair closer to the table, and leaning over it, and speaking rapidly; '*me*, who know so much of your dark doings? — who never turned my back on you till now?'

'The law makes no exception for friendship,' replied the lawyer.

Wilkins drew back. All trace of passion and excitement disappeared from his face. His features became cold, passionless, stone-like; and he spoke like one whose thoughts were far away, as he said:

'I said blood would come of it, some day; yes, I said it, or I dreamed it; but it's true!'

He thrust his hand half unconsciously in the breast of his coat, and then drew it out. 'Well, well!' said he, 'I'll wait — I'll wait. It may not come to it yet; but it will some day.'

He leaned his cheek on his hand, and gazed steadfastly in the fire, which flickered and smouldered in the grate, giving a wild, uncertain expression to his harsh features. At times he raised his head and looked with a troubled irresolute eye at the lawyer, and his lips moved as if he were speaking, but no sound came from them. How long a time might have elapsed in silence, is uncertain; for before it was broken, a quick step was heard coming up the stairs and through the entry. Then there was a sudden knock at the door, and before it could be answered, the door was flung open, and Mr. Higgs presented himself.

The excited looks of the two who already occupied the office did not escape the quick eye of the new-comer. He half suspected that a rupture had taken place between them, and by way of inducing an explanation, said:

'You look amiable, both of you. What's in the wind?'

Wilkins turned his back upon him and made no answer.

Higgs glanced an inquiring eye upon Bolton.

'He is faint-hearted, and would give out,' said he, with a slight sneer, and pointing to Wilkins.

Wilkins merely rolled his eyes up at him, but took no farther notice of him.

'Come, George,' said Higgs, going up to his friend, and placing his hand familiarly on his shoulder: 'What's the matter? Out with it, man.'

'Pshaw! — *you* know.'

'Ah! ah! I understand,' replied Mr. Higgs, into whose mind a ray of the truth flashed. Then turning to the lawyer, he said: 'It's a trifle — quite insignificant; merely this: Mr. Wilkins and myself, on having a small talk respecting this 'ere business, came to the conclusion that there was a great deal of risk and not a great deal of pay; which you know is quite as disproportioned as a very large dog with a very small tail, or any other figger that may suit the case.'

Mr. Higgs paused to observe the effect of his remark, and his very appropriate simile. Bolton merely bowed.

' And we thought,' continued he, ' that as the old gentleman had left a cool two hundred thousand, you might fork over to us a cool twenty thousand a piece ; quite a trifle, considering the risk, and the fight that the young woman is determined to make, which you know was altogether unlooked for, and not at all mentioned in the contract.'

' And suppose I refuse ? ' replied Bolton, impatiently.

' Then we abjures the proceeding, root and branch. I re-forks the five hundred which the old gentleman left me, a very little diminished, considering the respectability of my appearance for the last week or two ; and we wash our hands of the whole business, and gently retire, wishing you all success in your undertaking.'

' And this is what you will do ? '

' Most positively, and decidedly, and so forth,' replied Mr. Higgs, taking a seat, and crossing his legs.

' Well,' said the Attorney, after a long pause, ' will twenty thousand a piece clear me of all claims from both of you ? — and will you never make others ? — and will you carry this matter through in spite of all obstacles ? '

Both Wilkins and Higgs assented.

' I see no alternative. It 's yours. Do you want a written promise to that effect ? '

' No, thank you ; I prefer not,' said Mr. Higgs, quietly. ' I 'll find a way of enforcing the promise, if you should happen to forget it.'

Bolton attempted to laugh, but turned away, biting his lip with vexation ; for he felt that he was in the hands of one at least on whom he had no hold, and who neither feared him nor would abate one jot of his power over him, while there was an end of his own to be gained; but as he had already said, there was no alternative.

' Well,' said Mr. Higgs, ' now that that 's settled to our mutual satisfaction, let 's know what 's the most ticklish part of this business? What 's the spot as won't bear handling? That 's what we were to consult about.'

Bolton seated himself, and opening a small drawer in the table, took out a memorandum, and after running his eye over it, said :

' That old witness to the marriage. If he were out of the way, I 'd feel safe. I know of no other obstacle. He 's here day after day, on some pretext or other. I do n't know what to make of it. If we could get *him* out of the State —— '

' Or out of the world ? ' suggested Higgs.

Bolton looked steadily at him, but said not a word.

' Hist ! ' exclaimed he, at length. ' Some one is coming. I 'll shut this door, and meet him in the other room. Stay here quietly, till I send him off.' As he spoke, he went out, shutting the door, and was heard speaking to a person in the outer room. In a few moments he returned, with a face as pale as if there had been no blood in his frame. He shut the door after him tight, pushing it to again and again. Then he went up to Higgs and whispered :

'It's the very man ! — the old fellow ! — the witness to that marriage ! the *only* witness !'

His black eyes dilated until they seemed on fire, his lips compressed, and he trembled from head to foot.

'Well ?' said Higgs, looking up in his face.

'He's the *only witness to her legitimacy*,' said the lawyer; and he stopped again.   'He's in the other room — ALONE.'

'Well,' said Higgs, still looking at him; 'what of it ? You won't consent to — you know what ? You told me so yourself.'

Bolton, without heeding this remark, said : 'He came here to ask where he could find Miss Crawford. He came to me as an old friend of her father's. He thought perhaps I knew and would tell him. He's going there to-night, as *he wants to see her particularly.*'

He paused and cast a glance at Wilkins; but he sat with his head between his hands, and looking on the floor ; and then he and Higgs stood face to face.   Neither spoke, but the Attorney saw that the thin sharp features of his confederate were rigid and pinched; his jaws firmly set, as if screwed together, and his lip quivering with fierce emotion.

'Sit still, both of you !' said Higgs, in a hoarse whisper ; 'don't stir on your lives — neither of you. I've often risked my life for less than twenty thousand, and by G — d I'll do it now ! Your dirk, George ; but no ! — no blood ; a blow will be better.' As his hand reached the knob, Bolton's resolution failed him, and he sprang forward :

'Stop ! stop ! my God ! my God ! I cannot ! I dare not !'

'But *I* dare !' hissed out Higgs ; 'do n't balk me now, or by G — d ! you'll rue it !'

'What would you do ?' exclaimed the Attorney, wringing his hands.

'Talk to him ! *talk* to him ! *only* talk to him !' muttered he. 'Back, back, I say ! Keep the door shut ; tight — tight ! Ask no questions ; see nothing — hear nothing ; and do n't come in that room, or I'll cut your throat !'

He laid his hand on the door, and Bolton would again have interfered ; but Wilkins rose, seized him by the shoulders, and dashed him back on the floor as if he had been a child ; while Higgs flung open the door, and darted into the other room. But it was empty. The outer door was open, and the old man was gone.

A FRAGMENT

WRITTEN BY A COCKNEY ON THE DEATH OF GEORGE THE FOURTH.

How monarchs die is easily explained ;
  And thus it might upon the tomb be chiselled :
'As long as George the Fourth could *reign*, he reigned,
  And then he *mizzled*.'

THE APRIL SHOWER.

BY H. W. ROCKWELL.

I.

OH! swiftly the April-shower comes down
O'er hill and valley and snow-white town;
Swiftly it comes o'er the bright green meads,
With rain for the blossoms and scattered seeds,
And the weedy pools and the sprouting leaves,
And the wash-tubs waiting beneath the eaves!

II.

Darkening the air o'er the forest vast,
The large round drops are falling fast;
Merrily swinging the flowers that blow
Mid the boughs above and the weeds below,
And beading the bushes and springing grain
On the hill-side green and the distant plain.

III.

It comes! it comes! I hear it ring
And tinkle upon the running spring;
Gracefully stirring the reeds that look
In clusters down on the meadow-brook,
And dimpling the pools that darkly dyed,
Stand mid the grass by the highway side.

IV.

It comes like the pattering of angels' feet,
And the air of the forest grows fresh and sweet;
Softly and gently it glides away
From the setting light of the April day;
And dim in the smoky haze are seen
The waving trees and the mountains green.

V.

It passes away with a pleasant sound,
And voices awake in the fields around;
There's a chirping of insects amid the grass,
And a singing of birds as the rain-drops pass,
While over the woods on the upland height
Bursts forth in meek glory the evening light!

VI.

So passeth the terrors of death away
From the good old man on his dying day;
And thus when bitterest tears are shed,
And the heavy hours are dark with dread,
Brightening the gloom of his evening sky
Shall the sunlight stream on his aching eye.

PASSAGES FROM JEAN PAUL.

I.

NOTHING so moves man as the look of pardon. Our weaknesses are not purchased too dear by the hour of their forgiveness, and the angel who feels no resentment must envy the man who overcomes it. When thou forgivest, the man who wounds thy heart is like the sea-worm that perforates the oyster-shell, which closes up the wound with pearls.

II.

THE joy of sensitive men is modest. They show their wounds more readily than their raptures, because they do not think both are deserved, or they show both from behind the veil of a tear.

III.

WHEN a man remains modest not by praise but by censure, then is he truly modest.

IV.

BEGIN the cultivation of thy heart, not with the improvement of thy noble propensities, but with the bridling of thy perverse inclinations. When once the weeds are withered or plucked up, then will the noble flower raise its head and grow luxuriantly.

V.

ONE learns silence best among those who have none, and talkativeness best among those who are silent.

VI.

IN our age the decrease of stoicism and the increase of egotism are about equal. The stoic covers his treasures and buds with ice, the other is ice itself. So in physics; the mountains decrease while the glaciers increase.

VII.

WHEN one does not hold still at the sting of a bee or of fortune, the sting tears out and remains behind.

VIII.

SORROWFUL Earth, which three or four great men can make better or desolate! Thou art a real theatre. In the foreground are several fighting actors and linen tents, while the painted soldiers and tents crowd the back-ground.

IX.

STATES like diamonds when they have defects are divided into smaller; and men in great states and bees in great hives lose their courage and vigor, if they affix small lands to other small lands, like one colony-hive to another.

x.

MAN thinks his own affliction is that of humanity, as bees estimate the weather by the dryness of their hive, and although the sun shines, do not venture out for fear of the rain.

xi.

To man as to books there are before and behind two white empty covers — childhood and old age.

xii.

MEMORY is the only paradise from which we cannot be expelled. Even our first parents were not banished thence.

xiii.

VIRTUE itself gives no consolation when thou hast lost a friend; and the noble heart that friendship has pierced bleeds mortally, and all the balm of love cannot staunch it.

xiv.

IF thou hast completely separated from a friend, give him — not only out of philanthropy but out of hallowed reverence for departed friendship — no token, no leaf, and if it be possible, not a moment of thy presence; because the mementos of former attachment will but uselessly revive the pains of the breach. Man bears much easier the cold presence of an alienated lover than that of an alienated friend; for a lover can easily be replaced by others, but a friend never.

xv.

ONE seldom knows those who are happiest. The gentle zephyr of purest joy moves no metallic anemoscope, nor announces its noiseless flight from echoing towers.

xvi.

'WOULD that were the only greatness upon the earth which is innocent of evil!' we often exclaim; but the only man of this stamp was long since crucified; and still we, self-flatterers, give the name of greatness to princes and geniuses!

xvii.

A SLIGHT affliction makes us beside ourselves; a great one restores us. A bell with a slight crack sounds dead; but when the crack is wider it sounds clear again.

xviii.

EVERY friend is at the same time a sun and a sun-flower; he attracts and he follows.

xix.

SIN and the hedge-hog are both born without thorns; but we all know how they sting after birth. The most wretched man is he who feels regret before the deed, and commits a sin armed with teeth at the birth, whose bite shall deepen to the wounds of conscience's adder-fangs.

xx.

To look out of a window in a city gives one a humor for the epic; in a village only for the satire or the idyl.

xxi.

The griefs of wedded love unreciprocated, and the griefs of divorce, remind us of the teeth which pain us when they come and when they go.

xxii.

Suns rest behind suns in the remotest blue, whose beams have flown thousands of years toward our little earth without reaching it. But oh! thou milder, nearer God! Scarce does the human spirit open its little young eye, before thou shinest into it — Sun of suns and spirits!

xxiii.

Oh how immovable the bow of peace spans the furious storm of the water-fall! So God stands in the heavens, and the stream of time leaps and plunges, and above all its billows hovers the bow of His peace.

SLEEP.

Holy Sleep! They even compare thee with Death. In one moment thou pourest more oblivion over the troubled memory of afflicted man than the watchings of the longest day. And then thou coolest the feverish breast, and man rises again fresh as the morning sun. Be thou blessed, Sleep! until thy dreamless brother comes, and lulls me to a softer, wakeless repose!

FLOWERS ON THE COFFIN OF A MAIDEN.

Strew only flowers upon it, ye blooming companions! Formerly ye brought her flowers on the feast-day of her birth. Now you celebrate a greater festival; for the bier is the cradle of heaven.

A ROSE WITHERED IN THE SUN.

Pale withered rose! the sun gave thee thy color; the glowing orb has taken it again. Thou art like us. If the God who gave the human cheeks their glow comes down nearer and warmer to us, they also grow pale, and the man either dies or is transported.

POLITICAL SCIENCE.

It veils itself well; but it shows to the world her dead, her battle-fields and places of slaughter, and her new streams that flow with commingled blood and tears. So in Rome the brotherhood of the departed go muffled in white, while they carry the dead uncovered, and the mid-day sun shines upon the cold blind countenance.

THE OAK FOREST.

'FELL not my sacred oaks, O prince!' said the Dryad. 'I shall punish thee sorely!' but he cut them down. After many years the prince was brought to the scaffold. He looked on the execution-block and exclaimed: 'It is oak.'

MISAPPREHENSION ABOUT MEN OF GREAT DEEDS.

THEY stand raised in the ether-blue of time like mountains; but even on that account every thing which flies up to them from the multitude is reckoned as theirs. So the high mountains appear to smoke; but the appearance comes from the clouds that are drawn up and float around them. It is only the abyss that is foggy, and not the mountain.

THE GENIUS AND THE PRINCE.

THE people have the greatest admiration for both at two periods of their lives, when they commence and when they end their reigns. On their coronation and funeral days are they the most warmly eulogized. So a star sparkles twice most brilliantly, at its rising and setting; but the sun and every star appear smaller at their zenith, when they shed down their richest light over the earth.

HUMAN JOY.

THE pine-apple always ripens between two thistles; but our thorny present ripens between two pine-apples — memory and hope.

OLD MEN.

THEIR shadows are indeed long, and their evening sun lies cold upon the earth; but they point toward the morning.

THE FAIREST CHRISTIAN.

THINK you that the soul of woman who suffers much, but looks up with unshaken confidence in GOD; who though weeping and bleeding ever seems the picture of joy before men, and is neither shaken nor darkened by the rough storms of life; think you she has any where her emblem? In the heavens there stands the rainbow. The clouds and the winds shake it not; but it is radiant in the sun-light, and its drops glitter as it reposes on the sky like the sparkling morning dew of a summer day.

SHARP-SIGHTED UNBELIEVERS.

THEY direct their eyes with the telescope toward heaven, but it is dark and empty, and its solitudes immeasurable. O perverted ones! ye are wrong; ye hold the telescope inverted.

THE SUN-FLOWER AND THE NIGHT VIOLET.

'By day,' said the full-blown Sun-flower, 'Apollo shines, and I spread myself out. He wanders over the world, and I follow after him.' 'By night,' said the Violet, 'I am lowly and hidden, and bloom in the short night; but when Phœbus shines on me, then am I seen and plucked, and die on the breast of beauty.'

THE FLOWERS AND THE LEAVES.

AN APOLOGUE.

WHEN the Flowers withered in May, and pale and wan lay upon the earth, the Leaves exclaimed : 'What frail, useless things! Scarce born, and they sink into the earth! But we, the longer we remain in the summer heat, grow broader and smoother and fairer, and after a life of many months, when we have brought forth and given earth the finest fruits, then with variegated colors and amid the cannon-thunder of the storm, sink to rest.' But the fallen Flowers rejoined : 'We have indeed perished, but not before we had given birth to the fruits.'

Ye silent, unobserved, or soon-forgotten ones amid the common walks of life, in the counting-room; ye little esteemed masters of the school-room; ye noble benefactors without name in history ; and ye unknown mothers! despond not at the glitter and pomp of royalty, or the triumphal arches reared o'er the entombed victims of the battle-field — despond not! Ye are the flowers !

THE WANDERING AURORA.

WHEN man for the first time saw the morning light breaking in the heavens, he took it for the sun, and exclaimed: 'Hail, thou rose-robed Phœbus upon thy flaming car!' But soon the Sun-god himself arose out of the rose-bushes, and before the long flash of day the morning roses of Aurora faded.

But when it was evening, and Apollo's car descended into the waves of the ocean, and nothing remained in the heavens but Aurora's chariot full of roses, then man recurred to the error of the morning, and said : 'I know thee now, beautiful spring of the heavens! Thou art the harbinger of the sun, but not the sun himself.' And he waited for the sun, and thought the evening-star was the star of morning, and the evening breeze the breath of morning.

But he waited in vain. The star of Love did not ascend higher, but sank from cloud to cloud. The rosy chariot but just overtopped the ocean with a few pale buds, and swept down behind the earth, wading deep and sinking to cold midnight. Death-chills breathed up from her. 'Now I know thee for a robber of the dead!' said Man : 'Thou drivest Phœbus the beautiful youth before thee, through the ocean down to dark Orcus!' Weary and disheartened man closed his dark eye.

Awake! dreamer! and see in the blooming morning-heavens Aurora moving through her fields of roses, and the immortal youth Apollo striding behind her, with his hand full of the morning light!

And awake! thou deeper dreamer! who watchest the Aurora of human history in the west, and mistakest the evening twilight for the morning, and expectest the rising of the sun; and then art discouraged because it moves concealed around the north. Awake! for it comes again to its morning, and every time to a longer day.   x. x.

SONG OF THE TE-TOTALLER.

I.

Let others praise the ruby bright,
  In the red wine's sparkling glow,
Dearer to me is the diamond light
  Of the fountain's clearer flow:
The feet of earthly men have trod
  The juice from the bleeding vine,
But the stream comes pure from the hand of God
  To fill this cup of mine.
    Then give me the cup of cold water!
    The clear, sweet cup of cold water;
    For his arm is strong, though his toil be long,
    Who drinks but the clear cold water.

II.

The dew-drop lies in the floweret's cup,
  How rich is its perfume now!
And the fainting Earth with joy looks up,
  When Heaven sheds rain on her brow:
The brook goes forth with a pleasant voice
  To gladden the vale along,
And the bending trees on her banks rejoice,
  To hear her quiet song:
    Then give me the cup of cold water!
    The clear, sweet cup of cold water;
    For bright is his eye, and his spirit high,
    Who drinks but the clear cold water!

III.

The lark soars up with a lighter strain
  When the wave has washed her wing,
And the steed flings back his 'thundering mane'
  In might of the crystal spring:
This was the drink of Paradise,
  Ere blight on her beauty fell,
And the buried streams of her gladness rise
  In every moss-grown well:
    Then here's to the cup of cold water!
    The pure, sweet cup of cold water;
    For Nature gives to all that lives
    But a drink of the clear cold water.

Philadelphia, March, 1842.   GEORGE W. BETHUNE.

LITERARY NOTICES.

A COURSE OF LECTURES ON THE DOCTRINES OF THE NEW-JERUSALEM CHURCH, as revealed in the Theological Writings of EMANUEL SWEDENBORG. By B. F. BARRET, Pastor of the First Society of the New-Jerusalem Church in New-York. In one volume. pp. 443. New-York: JOHN ALLEN, at the Office of the KNICKERBOCKER: SAMUEL COLMAN, 14 John-street.

NEARLY one hundred years, as we gather from the volume before us, have elapsed since SWEDENBORG began to write; and although the world has ever since been steadily advancing in knowledge, it is alleged as a remarkable fact that his writings were never so much sought after nor so widely read at home and abroad as at the present moment. New editions of his works are in constant progress of publication, to satisfy a continually increasing demand; and men of piety and learning 'are known to read them extensively, and to take from them the very truths which gain for them their chief glory.' We propose therefore to devote a liberal space in this department to a sketch of the founder of the religion of the 'New-Jerusalem Church.' EMANUEL SWEDENBORG, the son of an eminently learned and pious Swedish bishop, was born at Stockholm in 1688. He was educated at the celebrated university of Upsal, and was even in youth remarkable for his attainments in philosophy, mathematics, natural history, chemistry and anatomy, and for his familiarity with the chief tongues of Europe and the East. When twenty-two years of age, he published a collection of Latin poems, of which a late edition was favorably reviewed in the July number of HERAUD's London Monthly Magazine. His next important writings were his 'Philosophical and Mineral Works,' 'The Animal Kingdom,' and 'Economy of the Animal Kingdom,' in Latin, which were published at Dresden, Leipsic, London and Amsterdam, and which immediately secured, by their profundity and comprehensiveness, the attention and admiration of the scientific world. At the age of twenty-eight years he was appointed by the famous Charles the Twelfth Assessor Extraordinary of the Board of Mines, a very important office in Sweden, whose metals are one of the principal sources of national wealth. In 1719 he was ennobled by Queen Ulrica, and took his seat thereafter as a member of the Diet of Sweden. In 1724 he was offered a professorship of Mathematics in the University of Upsal, which he declined. In 1729 he was by invitation admitted a member of the Royal Academy of Sciences at Stockholm; and was appointed a corresponding member of the Academy of Sciences at St. Petersburgh in 1734. Such in short was his reputation for talents and for learning, that he was honored with the friendship and esteem of the royal family and principal persons of his own country, while his acquaintance and correspondence were eagerly sought by the most distinguished scientific men of the age; among them KANT, WOLFF, FLAMSTEAD, DELAHIRE, and VARIGNAN. Nor was his moral character inferior to his intellectual. His conduct was regulated by the four following rules, which were frequently found interspersed among his manuscripts: I. To read often and meditate on the Word of the Lord. II. To submit every thing to the will of Divine Providence. III. To observe in every thing a propriety of behavior, and always to keep the conscience clear. IV. To discharge with fidelity the functions of his employment and the duties of his office, and to render himself in all things useful to society.

Count ANDREW VAN HOPKEN, Prime Minister of Sweden, who was himself eminent for talent and virtue, says of SWEDENBORG: 'I have been intimate with him for two-and-forty years, and I do not recollect to have known any man of more uniformly virtuous character. Always contented, never fretful or morose, although throughout his life his soul was occupied with sublime thoughts and speculations. He was a true philosopher, and lived like one. He was gifted with a most happy genius, and a fitness for every science, which made him shine in all those he embraced. He was without contradiction probably the most learned man in my country. In his youth he was a great poet. I have in my possession some remnants of his Latin poetry, which OVID would not have been ashamed to own. He was well acquainted with the Hebrew and Greek, and was an able and profound mathematician. If he had remained in his office his merits and talents would have entitled him to the highest dignity. He possessed a sound judgment upon all occasions; he saw every thing clearly, and expressed himself well on every subject. The most solid memorials, and best penned, at the Diet of 1751, on matters of finance, were presented by him.'

Such was EMANUEL SWEDENBORG, and such his character and qualifications, when in 1743 'he was chosen by the LORD as the instrument by which a new dispensation of divine truth was to be communicated to mankind, and a new church founded upon earth, in fulfilment of the prophecies in Revelations, which foretell the descent from heaven of the New Jerusalem.' We shall endeavor in a second notice of the volume before us to present a brief but clear synopsis of the more prominent doctrines of the church founded by this great and good man.

AN INTRODUCTION TO LATIN PROSE COMPOSITION, with a complete Course of Exercises, illustrative of all the important principles of Latin Syntax. By CHARLES ANTHON, LL. D. New-York: HARPER AND BROTHERS.

WE have many times before had occasion to speak of Mr. ANTHON's series of school classics, as deserving of especial commendation, and as an honor to the literature of America. This series has already — so great is the diligence of this unwearied scholar — extended to a considerable number of works, all certainly superior in method, clearness and correctness to any former school-books; and some, especially the Greek Prosody, as new as they were greatly needed. Another of these excellent little books now lies before us, in the shape of a Second Part of the Latin Grammar, or introduction to the composition of Latin Prose. There is nothing of which we are aware particularly new or original in the plan of this work; but like all Professor ANTHON's classics, it is a decided improvement on previous books of exercise, in clearness of arrangement, precision of language, conciseness and consistency. We can testify indeed with confidence to its great superiority. The rules of Latin Syntax are laid down very clearly; so much so that the youngest intellect can arrive readily at their true sense. All the rules on one subject are so arranged as to appear to spring as it were each from its last predecessor, as a natural and necessary consequence. The exercises appear to be admirably chosen, from pure and strictly classical authors, increasing in length and difficulty as the work advances, and constituting on the whole a very perfect means for the acquisition of a high degree both of accuracy and perfection in the composition of the Latin language. It will speedily be followed we learn by a similar work on the art of writing Greek; and with it will, we doubt not, be instantly reprinted and adopted in the schools of England. The paper, typography, and other externals, are worthy of the press from which it emanates. We mention this because the externals of school-books are with some publishers a matter of small consideration.

TECUMSEH: OR THE WEST THIRTY YEARS SINCE. By GEORGE H. COLTON. In one volume. New-York: WILEY AND PUTNAM.

WE alluded in a late number to the elaborate and finished production before us. We had read portions of it in manuscript, and are glad at length to hail its appearance in a volume whose beauty of execution must needs satisfy the most fastidious. We hazard little in saying that 'Tecumseh' is no common nor ephemeral effort. Essentially national in its design and spirit, embracing a field hitherto untrodden as we believe by fiction of any kind, and filled as it is with graphic description and pathetic sentiment, it can scarcely fail to command the attention of the friends of American literature and the American public at large. We propose at present to afford the reader a hasty outline of the poem, and to make a few remarks upon the first three cantos, reserving the consideration of the remainder for a subsequent number. It has evidently been our author's principal aim to give a full view of the wrongs, the struggles and the mournful decay of the Indian race. For this purpose he has wisely chosen a period of time so late as to leave all their history in the back-ground, and a hero embodying in himself all the sorrowful and indignant feelings of his race and name. This period is the last war, and this hero TECUMSEH — by all accounts a great and noble character. All the incidents, however, connected with his plans and efforts are effectively woven into an affecting story of love, danger and suffering — in itself sufficient to command the reader's interest. It is that of a maiden, through the villany of a white man taken captive by the Indians, while her family are slain and carried, first into the prairies and afterward along the northern lakes. The pursuit of the lover in quest of her forms the ground-work of the whole. The time is nearly two years, extending from TECUMSEH's great tour to consolidate the Indian league until his death in the battle of the Thames. The scenes are laid in the West, then an utter wilderness from the Ohio to Lake Superior, and though covering so great a space, they will be found to be skilfully connected. The regular characters are eight, of whom the boldest and perhaps the most natural is KEN-HAT-TA-WA, TECUMSEH's mortal foe; while his daughter OKEENA is TECUMSEH's inamorata. This peculiar relation forms in our opinion the great charm of the poem. But we must permit the author to speak for himself. The lines introductory to the several cantos are in the Spenserian measure; and to our conception they are among the finest passages in the volume. The poem opens as follows:

'My Country! if, unknown to fame, I dare
Amid the gathering years my voice upraise
For thee or thine in other tones than prayer,
Waking long-silent musings into praise
Of thee and of thy glories, let thy grace
Accord me pardon; since no master hand
Thy mighty themes on loftier lyre essays,
Which, treasured long in thought, my mind expand
And burn into my soul, O thou, my native land!

'What though no tower its ruined form uprears,
Nor blazoned heraldry, nor pictured hall,
Awake the 'memories of a thousand years;'
Yet may we many a glorious scene recall,
And deeds long cherished in the hearts of all
Who hail thee mother; yet from mountain gray
And forest green primeval shadows fall
O'er lake and plain. The journeying stars survey
No lovelier realm than thine, free-born Hesperia!'

The body of the poem is in the octo-syllabic of SCOTT, save that it is varied, and for the most part with decided effect, by a couplet of ten syllables at the close of a scene. The beginning is very impressive:

'A few years gone, the western star
On his lone evening watch surveyed
Through all his silent reign afar
But one interminable shade,
From precipice and mountain brown
And tangled forest darkling thrown;
Save where the blue lakes, inland seas,
Kissed lightly by the creeping breeze,
His beams, beyond unnumbered isles,
Glanced quivering o'er their dimpling smiles;
Or where, no tree or summit seen,
Unbrokenly a sea of green,
That wild low shores eternal laved,
The prairie's billowy verdure waved.

Nor ever might a sound be heard
Save warbling of the wild-wood bird,

Or some lone streamlet's sullen dash
In the deep forest, or the crash
Of ruined rock, chance-hurled from high,
Or swarthy Indian's battle-cry,
Whooped for revenge or victory.

'And through this wilderness of green,
Low banks or beetling rocks between,
Thro' rough and smooth, thro' fair and wild,
The still strange scenery of a dream,
By its enchanting power beguiled,
Birth of the rock, the mountain's child,
Th' Ohio rolled his sleepless stream,
From morn till evening, day by day
Urging his solitary way.
No nobler stream did ever glide
From fountain head to Ocean's tide!'

The first scene opens at sunset on this lordly river, with an Indian standing with three scalps in his belt. These are from the murdered family of the heroine, and this chief is KEN-HAT-TA-WA. Is not this description admirable?

'The beaded moccasins he wore
Were redder dyed in crimson gore;
The eagle's feather in his hair—
Drops of the bloody rain were there;
And on his wampum belt arrayed
Three scalps, sad trophies! were displayed;
An aged man's—the shrivelled skin
Still showed a few locks white and thin.
A woman's next—the tresses gray

Upon his thigh dishevelled lay;
And third, of all the saddest sight,
A child's fair curls in amber light
Hung trembling to the breeze of night.
The soft wind shakes their dewy wreath—
Alas! 't is not a mother's breath!
A beam of light upon them lies—
It is not for a mother's eyes!'

. . . .

As the night comes on, he brings the captive girl from a cave, thrusts her into his canoe, and with his young brother and a wretch named DE VERE descends the river, where its banks are lofty with rocks and forests. The moon rises, and the scenery is delightfully picturesque. The anapæstic measure, which is utterly worthless for powerful description, is admirably fitted for an hour like this:

'OH! softly and silently glides the boat,
As a cloud on the bosom of heaven afloat,
Which,fair Daughter of Ocean! hath risen in air,
And sails o'er as boundless an ocean there,
While she seeketh afar a home of rest,
Than the stormy place of her birth more blest!
The stars are out in the silent sky,
Mute sentinels of Eternity;
And low-voiced winds are hovering around
On their viewless wings, with a spirit-sound,
And the moon hath climbed with a pensive pace
And ever a sweet but mournful grace,
To behold from high heaven's loveliest daughter,
Her pale, fair face in the glassy water;
Which, far in the mirrored world below,
Allureth the gazer thither to go,
As often he pineth from earth to fly,

And dwell in her brighter home on high.
But now she looks down from her cold white throne
On a face as lovely and pale as her own;
For with sorrow and weariness, ceasing to weep,
The maiden hath sunk to a troubled sleep.
O'er bosom and forehead doth fitfully gleam
The changing light of a changing dream;
As now on her cheek a soft smile plays,
Till a burning blush drinks up its rays,
And her lips half utter a much-loved name;
Then an ashy hue for the flush of flame,
And a tear thro' her closed eye slowly strays.
O who is this fairer than heavenly vision,
Ideal seen, or in dreams elysian,
Thus breathlessly borne on her noiseless way,
Like a spirit passing from earth's decay!'

The author now proceeds to give the previous history of his heroine. Scorned by the girl, then living by the sweet Connecticut, De Vere had found means to beggar her father. He removes to the West. The following eulogium upon the Pioneers is not more just than beautiful :

'The noble, dauntless Pioneers,
 Journeying afar new homes to raise
In the lone woods with toil and tears,
Meeting with faith the coming years,
 Theirs be the highest meed of praise!
He who with cost and care and toil
Hath reared the vast enduring pile ;
He who hath crossed the ocean foam,
Strange lands for science' sake to roam ;
He who in danger and in death
Hath faced the spear, the cannon's breath,
Or borne the dungeon and the chain,
His country's rights to save or gain ;
He who amid the storms of state
Hath swayed the trembling scales of Fate
For her and Freedom, heeding nought
The scorn of hatred, sold or bought —
Are such not glorious ? Yet O deem
 Their being less heroical :
For mingling with it comes the dream
 And hope of Fame's bright coronal :

They see the light of years to come
Streaming around their silent tomb !
But those who leave the homes of love
And pass, by many a long remove,
Through the deep wilderness, to rear
In voiceless suffering and in fear
Not for themselves a resting place —
Their hope is only for their race,
For whom their lives of pain are given ;
Their light to cheer is light from Heaven ;
Nor look they, save to God, at last
For life's reward when life is past ;
But lay them down with years oppressed,
Beneath the patriarch woods to rest,
Without a thought Fame's wandering wing
One plume upon their graves shall fling :
Thus noiseless in their death as birth,
The best brave heroes of the earth !
While roll thy rivers, spreads thy sky,
Or rise thy lifted mountains high,
Hesperia ! guard their memory !'

The murder of the family and the captivity of the girl are the still farther fruits of the villain's revenge. As they float down the river, the young Indian is shot by the pursuing lover. On this incident turns the course of the poem. The conversation between Tecumseh and his brother in the beginning of the second canto is replete with mournful interest. Those portions relating to the wrongs of the red-man are, as they ought to be, the best of the poem. Our limits forbid long extracts ; but the following quiet picture of an Indian prairie-camp deserves to be cited :

'A motley scene the camp displayed.
Their simple wigwams, loosely made
Of skins and bark, and rudely graced
 With sylvan honors of the chase,
At scattered intervals were placed
 Beneath majestic trees — the race
Of other years ; while statelier reared
Alone and in their midst appeared
The lodge of council, honored most,
Yet unadorned with care or cost.
Their beaded leggins closely bound,
Their blankets wreathed their loins around,
Whence rose each neck and brawny breast
Like bust of bronze with tufted crest ;
Around, the forest-lords were seen,
Some old, with grave and guarded mien
High converse holding in the shade ;
Some idly on the green turf laid,
Or, girt with arms of varied name,
Repairing them for strife or game ;
Their dusky wives, from birth the while
Inured to care and silent toil,
Prepared the venison's savory food
And yellow corn, in sullen mood ;

Or sweetly to their infants sung,
Lightly in wicker-cradles swung
Upon the breeze-rocked boughs ; in play
Lithe urchins did their skill essay,
Beneath some chief's approving eye,
To launch the feathered arrow high,
The hatchet hurl, or through the air
Send the shrill whoop ; half robed or bare,
The youth would act war's mimic game,
Or strive their wild-born steeds to tame,
Perchance their captives scarce a day ;
Themselves untamed and wild as they.

And sat beneath the green leaves fading
Young maids, their checkered baskets braid-
 ing,
Whose merry laugh or silvery call
Oft rang most sweet and musical,
Whose glancing black eyes often stole
To view the worshipped of their soul :
And ever in th' invisible breeze
Waved solemnly those tall old trees,
And fleecy clouds, above the prairies flying,
Led the light shadows, chasing, chased and dying.'

We should be glad to quote the scene where the heroine is about to be put to death, when her lover is led in captive to take her place ; but our limits forbid. After years of absence, that meeting of one wild moment in so strange a place is touchingly drawn. The lover escapes from the gauntlet ; and there ensues a fearful race for life. This and the burning prairie with which it is connected are wrought out with great power. The third canto opens with three fine Spenserian stanzas, and is mostly taken up with Tecumseh's great tour from the Gulf of Mexico to the Rocky Mountains and the northern lakes. The whole of this journey is equal to any part of the poem ; and no extracts can do it justice. At the end comes the wildest scene of all — the burning by night of an Indian by the Prophet, TECUMSEH's brother.

We shall, as we have said, again revert to this volume; but in the mean time, if our metropolitan readers cannot even 'in these times' expend one poor dollar for such a book, we must say with DOGBERRY, they are 'not the men we took them to be.'

TRAVELS IN EUROPE AND THE EAST. By VALENTINE MOTT, M. D., President of the Medical Faculty of the University of New-York, Professor of Surgery, etc., etc. In one volume. pp. 452. New-York: HARPER AND BROTHERS.

UNPRETENDING and simple in its narrations, and printed evidently very much as written on the spur of the moment, the volume before us may not at first command that attention from the public which its merits demand; but having perused its pages with a pleasure that was not the less because almost unexpected, considering the hackneyed character for the most part of modern books of travel, we can confidently commend the work to our readers as containing much that is entertaining and more that is important for the information which it embodies. The tour made by Dr. MOTT was a very extensive one; embracing Great Britain, Ireland, France, Belgium, Holland, Prussia, Saxony, Bohemia, Austria, Bavaria, Switzerland, Lombardy, Tuscany, the Papal States, the Neapolitan Dominions, Malta, the Islands of the Archipelago, Greece, Egypt, Asia-Minor, Turkey, Moldavia, Wallachia and Hungary. These 'travels' were included in the years 1834, '35, '36, '37, '38, '39, '40 and '41; interesting periods on various accounts, and especially so to an observant American traveller. The first portion of the volume, comprising the themes of Great Britain, Ireland, France, Belgium, Holland, Germany, and Switzerland, is devoted almost exclusively to matters seldom dwelt upon by modern tourists, but which relate to medical science, and to interesting details of interviews with some of the more extraordinary individuals of the writer's own profession, and his visits to the most celebrated hospitals and medical schools. So many extracts have been made from this part of the book, by city and country journals, that we find our dog's-ears a nullity, and all our pencilled passages anticipated. The greater and concluding portion of the work is devoted mainly to those objects of interest in Italy, Greece, Egypt, Asia-Minor, and Turkey, which absorb and captivate all who make a pilgrimage thither, to mourn over the ruins of a land once adorned by the most powerful and polished nations that ever existed. 'At every step,' says our author, 'some vast edifice, some shattered column or mouldering temple, some pointed obelisk or towering pyramid, furnishes a theme for fruitful meditation, and admonishes us of the transitory duration of human glory. They foretell that the same sceptre of power and of civilization which has passed from the Pharaohs and the Ptolemies, from Cambyses and Xerxes, and Alexander and Titus, and the Cæsars and the Caliphs — which descended successively to the Egyptian, the Mede, the Persian, the Greek, and the Roman, and the Saracen, and ultimately into the possession of Northern and Western Europe — will in all probability continue its onward course to this other and American hemisphere, to whom, next to Western Europe, seems to be assigned the destiny to become the inheritors of the unextinguished and unextinguishable and Divine light of mental and of moral culture, but which may again depart from us to be revived once more in that benighted Eastern Asia, which was perhaps the first cradle of its existence.'

The 'Introduction' of the author is altogether worthy a true-souled *American*. We would gladly transfer it entire to our pages, but must content ourselves with the subjoined extract; the more willingly that it will be likely to stimulate the reader to an acquaintance with its context in the work whence it is taken :

"To my own beloved country I gladly and exultingly return, with attachments tenfold stronger, if possible, to her matchless institutions, than even those which I felt pressing and crowding around my thoughts as I lingered on the last crimson gleams of the twilight, fading behind the blue hills of the Neversink, and bade my native land adieu! I come back, if possible, a still better American than when I left; and, from the comparison I have made of the condition of the populations of other countries, feel still more deeply impressed with the conviction, that our own republican form of government is infinitely and immeasurably preferable to that of any other that has ever existed. That the blessings of liberty and equality, and of that bulwark and ark of our future hopes, *education* and the *freedom of the press*, are here alone prodigally and equally diffused, and alike shared and enjoyed by every citizen; that the laws under which we live are here enacted and enforced, and may be modified or abrogated by our own free-will and consent; that there are no hereditary classes, nor lordly castles, nor grasping nobles, nor mitred prelates, to arrogate to themselves a divine authority over their fellow-creatures, and the privilege to hold in bondage, and depredate upon the rights, the person, and the property of vassal serfs and peasantry. . . . Often in my travels in distant lands, when meditating upon the depths of human misery, and of moral and political degradation to which our fellow-creatures have been ground down under the iron hoof of oppression, have I turned with innate and shuddering horror from the contemplation of their majestic and magnificent ruins; because I could not help reading in them but the history of the accumulated wrongs and crimes which, for so many ages past, cruel and despotic forms of government have wantonly inflicted upon the great human family. . . . Whether amid the enchanting scenery of England, the gay vineyards of France, the gloomy fortresses of the Rhine; the snowy avalanches and gorges of Alpine Switzerland, the pageantry and splendors of the European capitals; the architectural ruins of the Roman empire; or the chaste monuments of fallen, unhappy Greece; the godlike Pyramids, scattered over the burning sands of wondrous and mysterious Egypt, or the mosques and minarets of the debased hordes of the Ottoman; the thought that this outward pomp conceals within it so vast and frightful an accumulation of human wretchedness, and that it is but the painted sepulchre or the funeral *cortége* in which the dearest rights of our fellow-creatures are consigned to a hopeless tomb, has dominated at times over every sentiment or association of a pleasing character with which, in the rapid change from place to place, I might otherwise have regarded them, and carried me forcibly and vividly back in my imagination to the substantial comforts, the inappreciable blessings, to that priceless treasure above all other treasures, HUMAN LIBERTY, allotted by Divine Providence to our own favored and happy people."

We must not forget to say a word in praise of the manner in which the publishers have fulfilled *their* part in the production of the volume. The type is large and clear, the paper white and thick, and the typographical execution is in the first rank of excellence.

POWER OF THE PASSIONS : AND OTHER POEMS. By KATHARINE AUGUSTA WARE. In one volume. pp. 148. London. WILLIAM PICKERING. New-York: WILEY AND PUTNAM.

WE have cordially to thank our old friend and correspondent for a copy of this exceedingly neat and tasteful volume. It has already made the tour of a wide family-circle, and wherever it has tarried it has gained admirers and 'made friends.' The poem from which the volume takes its main title was originally published in the KNICKERBOCKER, as indeed were several other shorter pieces, which we are glad to find embodied in so charming a collection. We remember, in reading the proof of 'The Power of the Passions,' being struck with the great beauty of a passage which we perceive has since excited the admiration of those 'whose judgment cries in the top of ours.' It is a picture which might serve for the 'divine FANNY' herself, and its moral too, belike·

'ANOTHER, too, in tinselled garb, is near,
Mid scenic splendor, like a thing of light —
With limbs scarce veiled, and gestures wild and strange,
She gaily bounds in the luscious dance,
Moving as if her element were air,
And music was the echo of her step.

> Around her bold unblushing brow are twined
> The deadly nightshade and the curling vine,
> Enwreathed with flowers luxuriant and fair,
> Yet poisonous as the UPAS in their breath.

Our gifted countrywoman very frequently produces lines of equal beauty with those which we have italicised above; and they occur so naturally as to assure the reader that in writing poetry she speaks but the natural language of her heart. The first stanza of the ' Visit to the Lunatic Asylum' may be cited as in point:

> ' I 've seen the wreck of loveliest things. I 've wept
> O'er youthful Beauty in her snowy shroud ;
> All cold and pale, *as when the moon hath slept*
> *In the white foldings of a wintry cloud.*'

It needs but a visit to the Asylum for the Insane at Blackwell's Island to convince the reader of the painful fidelity of the following, which concludes the poem we have indicated :

> ' I 'VE seen the wreck of glorious things : I 've sighed
> O'er sculptured temples in prostration laid ;
> Towers which the blast of ages had defied,
> Now mouldering beneath the ivy's shade.
>
> Yet oh ! there is a scene of deeper wo,
> To which the soul can never be resigned ;
> 'T is FRENZY's triumph, REASON's overthrow —
> The ruined structure of the Human Mind !
>
> Oh ! 't is a sight of paralyzing dread,
> To mark the rolling of the maniac's eye,
> From which the spark of intellect hath fled ;
> The laugh convulsive, and the deep-drawn sigh.
>
> To see Ambition, with his moonlight helm,
> Armed with the fancied panoply of war ;
> The mimic sovereign of a powerful realm,
> His shield a shadow, and his spear a straw !
>
> To see pale Beauty raise her dewy eyes,
> Toss her white arms, and beckon things of air ;
> As if she held communion with the skies,
> And all she loved and all she sought were there.
>
> To list the warring of unearthly sounds,
> Which wildly rise, like Ocean's distant swell ;
> Or spirits shrieking o'er enchanted grounds,
> Forth-rushing from dark Magic's secret cell.
>
> Oh ! never, never may such fate be mine !
> I 'd rather dwell in earth's remotest cave,
> So I my spirit calmly might resign
> To HIM who Reason's glorious blessing gave ! '

The ' Lines written in the Traveller's Book at the Hermitage on Mount Vesuvius' are not more forcible than felicitous ; and the stanzas addressed to a friend on finding a faded rose in a volume of BYRON are imbued with a touching tenderness, whose pathos is as simple as it is irresistible. We could fill this department of our Magazine with the excerpts which we had segregated from the volume before us, so pleasantly various is it ; here a pathetic picture, there an airy fancy sketch ; now a tribute of affection, and anon a quaint ballad or an amusing ' Address;' but we prefer to have the reader do our author the justice to read her effusions in the beautiful book in which she has gathered them together. We are well pleased to perceive, as we do by several of the English journals, that our fair author's talents are not unappreciated on the other side of the great water ; and we are not without the hope that the present work will be but the forerunner of another, from the same capable hand. ' So mote it be ! '

EDITOR'S TABLE.

THE PICTURESQUE IN THE CAREER OF NAPOLEON.—Sitting in our quiet *sanctum* a few evenings since, at that twilight period which is known of country conference-meeting-goers as the hour of 'early candle-lighting,' we were agreeably interrupted in the midst of a melancholy reverie (such as *will* steal upon the soul in the gloaming of early spring-time days) by a rap at the door, and the entrance of a rosy-cheeked lad, bearing in his hand a card of liberal dimensions, on which was inscribed the following:

Academy of Arts and Sciences.

TINNECUM LECTURES: NUMBER TEN.

The Picturesque

IN THE CAREER OF THE GREAT BONY-PART.

BY ONE OF HIS ADMIRERS.

ADMIT THE GENTLEMAN WITH THE LONG PIPE.

It is unnecessary to say that we at once accepted the invitation of our friend the historian of Tinnecum to be present on so momentous an occasion. The next ensuing Tuesday evening therefore found us seated in the 'Tinnecum Lectur' Room,' where Mr. PETER CRAM opened and closed his first and last singin'-school meeting, and where his rival Mr. JONAS WEATHERBY found such cause of gratulation and triumph. Previous to the appearance of the lecturer many of the prominent citizens were kindly presented to us by our companion; among them SQUIRE SHARKEY, a bland, courteous and honest villager; the Editor of the 'Tinnecum Gazette,' and the foreman in the printing-establishment of that eminent journal, Mr. DAWKINS. The musical but pugnacious Mr. WEATHERBY was pointed out to us; and Messrs. BRUFF and THWACKITT, who figured so conspicuously in the

'Serenade,' were also present. The room was oblong, and filled with long benches; and the brilliant tin reflectors which hung around it lighted up the faces of scores of lovely girls, whose glances must have been inspiration to the unpracticed speaker. A green-baize rostrum, decorated with four tallow-candles and a pair of iron snuffers, filled the eye at the end of the apartment; and —— But we forbear; remembering the words of Squire SHARKEY, who 'hoped if we *did* notice the lectur' in our 'KER-KNICKERBOCKER' that we would tread gingerly. 'There 's a tender feelin's here,' said he, 'and it ain't necessary to wownd 'em. It can be got along with without that. There is no difficul'.' A boy now ascended the tribune to trim the dimming dips, and expectation was on tiptoe for the 'admirer' of NAPOLEON; as was sufficiently manifested by the excitement among the audience. 'Come down out o' that *nostrum!* ' said the master of ceremonies, addressing the candle-snuffer; 'and I'd thank the boys on the high seats underneath the cornice not to talk so loud.' The lad had scarcely sat down, before the lecturer arose. He was a young man, apparently of some two-and-twenty years; of modest and at the outset even diffident demeanor; and before he had entered fully upon his task, we had begun to augur that the evening's entertainments were not to be of that order which we had been led to anticipate. But we were destined to be most agreeably disappointed; and were soon forced to join in the plaudits which followed the vivid pictures of the speaker, kindled as he had now become by the grandeur of his subject. No sooner had he concluded his task, and while the general hum of approbation was becoming *individualized* in little groups of commentators about the room, we repaired to the 'nostrum,' and craved a copy of the lecture, that it might be 'imprinted in this book' for the benefit of our readers. But the over-modest writer was for a long time intractably obstinate in his refusal to have any of it 'in print;' and he only reluctantly yielded at last to what he termed 'the official mandate of OLD SOIL KROUT himself,' so far as to permit an extract or two to be made for our pages; being thereto principally moved by a certain threat then and there made, that unless he complied, an imperfect sketch of some of the more striking passages, from a few rough notes in our possession, should take the place of the original.

Before presenting these extracts, however, we cannot resist the inclination to cite one or two of the lecturer's collateral remarks upon his great theme. In opening, he observed that it was only the thickening plot of a grand crisis which could have produced NAPOLEON; for it required not only the muster-roll of the great of many nations but many of *ages* to create such a man; and he then proceeded to sketch the throes and convulsions of revolution out of which the great Child of Destiny emerged to fashion and form the disorganized masses at his will. Speaking of the battle of Monte-Notte, which opened NAPOLEON's brilliant campaign, he said it was thence that the 'great Captain' dated the origin of his nobility; for he ever discarded the attempts of those who searched for his name among the musty records of old genealogies; and the bold answer which he gave to such is worthy of memory: 'I am *the first* of my family!' And truly, if a stream is worthy of celebrity, though miserably dwindled in volume and debased in purity, because it may be traced by long intervals and many a devious wan branch to a noble source, how much more honorable to be the very *fountain* of nobility!' 'We would not apologize,' continued the orator, in the same connexion, 'for the faults consequent upon the giddy eminence which BONAPARTE soon attained; but an impartial estimate of such a man as NAPOLEON is not to be derived from the writings of SIR WALTER SCOTT or any English writers. They are no more capable of doing justice to the character of BONAPARTE than to that of WASHINGTON. The guiltiness of that protracted warfare which disturbed Europe must be shared in a measure by the British cabinet, and by those men upon whom the mantle of PITT had fallen. It was owing to their implacable obstinacy that the several treaties of peace turned out so many armistices, mere moments of breathing-time, that the combatants might go more desperately at the work of carnage. They hated the principles which hastened from their triumphs in America to overturn the old despotisms of France; and they resolved in their solemn conclaves that no peace should be permanent which was not founded in acquiescence to the old order of things.' Leaving these thoughts to be pondered by the reader, we pass to the permitted passages to which we have alluded. The following succeeded an animated and graphic sketch of the assembling at Versailles of the gorgeous States-General Convention, and its striking contrast with the National Assembly, convened at the same time to frame a constitution for France:

'And then the curtain rose, and revealed the first scenes of that troubled drama, whose several acts were so many desperate orgies in which Blasphemy ruled the hour, and Impiety, assuming the most grotesque shapes, stalked abroad, and impatient Murder glutted itself in a more summary way than by the poignard of the assassin or by the executioner's dull axe. It was a time when Ignorance burst the bands which Despotism had thrown around it, and rushed to its own destruction, to purchase the freedom which it knew not yet to enjoy; when frantic men literally pledged themselves in goblets of blood and became drunken therewith; and the unimagined crimes and wickedness which shroud themselves in the darkness and recesses of a great capital, came forth to reveal themselves and to indulge in their fantastic revels, and to howl their vindictive triumphs in open day. It was the carnival of hideous merriment; full of tumultuous crowds and mock processions, maskings and heathen rites, got up with lavish tinsel, and emblematic pomp, and choral harmonies, of which the burden was: 'We bring you the baker, his wife and the little apprentice;' when laughter was never intermitted, but it was the laughter of fiends; and Frenzy lent inspiration to the music, and rioted in the dance, and the *Bals à la Victim*' went on, with full orchestra; when the majesty of kings and the grace of queens were transferred from the audience-chamber of royalty to the presence of regicides; and to the sight of the ruddy guillotine; and Beauty lifted up her streaming eyes on the scaffold and exclaimed: 'Oh, LIBERTY! what crimes are committed in thy name!''

We quoted not long since a passage from the writings of REV. ROBERT HALL, touching the invasion of Egypt by BONAPARTE. Our lecturer overlooks the moral view taken by that eloquent divine, but depicts the external features of this memorable expedition with equal force and beauty:

'There was a grandeur of conception in the conquest of Egypt, like all which emanated from the mind of the great NAPOLEON. A city with her lofty monuments lay before him, whose very name was enough to excite the most voluptuous dreams of ambition. Twenty centuries had passed away since the ashes of Alexander reposed in their urn at Babylon; and it was hither that he came from humbling the Persian, and whence he set out to find the world's limits, before the cords of his life were snapped in the stretching struggle after other worlds. Here was the great battle-ground where so many master-spirits had contended for victory, and never alleviated the cruel bondage of the sons of the soil; whither Pompey fled from Cæsar at Pharsalia, and where Cæsar received the head of Pompey, and wept; where Marc-Antony forgot the glory of Philippi, and Octavius wrested the laurels of Antony; where Ambition conquered Hate, and Love conquered Ambition, and Remorse preyed upon Love; and the asp gnawing upon that bosom was but the emblem of a land poisoned and stung to the quick. And now, after so many centuries, another master-spirit caught sight of Pompey's pillar; and as he leaped upon the strand, absorbed the inspiration of the conqueror and almost his identical schemes of grandeur. Already the full outline flashed upon his mind, and the dreams of the subaltern seemed ready to be fulfilled; that he would overturn the British dominion in India, penetrate to the Indus and the remote Ganges, and forgetful of France, establish an Oriental kingdom, and rule over it, the *Sultan Kebir* — THE KING OF FIRE. But a victory whither he had now gone seemed to have a reference not only to the whole living world and to the vast Future, but to be bringing into the grasp of his possession whatever was most splendid in the Past. For if time is but another word for the succession of events, then Egypt has no PRESENT. The mighty spirit of a by-gone age broods over the whole land. Her very gloom is but a species of eclipse occasioned by the far-stretching shade of her old monuments, intercepted by no objects in all the desert interval of time ; it is the Past, *the Past* casting its gigantic shadows over the Present!

'Napoleon led his army over the burning desert. Accustomed as they had been to the delicious clime of Italy, they were tortured by the insufferable agonies of heat and thirst, and his very officers were ready to trample their cockades in the dust. But presently they came within sight of the Pyramids and the encampment of the Mamelukes. Those tyrannous chieftains, having no home but the desert, and spending all their wealth on sumptuous trappings, and the fleetest horses which Arabia could boast, formed the most splendid cavalry in the world. As they came bounding on the full gallop to throw themselves with their impetuous bravery upon the serried and immovable columns of the French, it was then that Napoleon, uplifting his arm in the direction of the old monuments, addressed his soldiers in that sublime sentiment which only his mind could have conceived: 'Forty centuries are looking down upon you from the heights of the Pyramids!' And considering the system which he adopted in Italy and in Egypt, as no man ever asserted such a dominion over the Past, so the Past itself by strange omens and coincidences took cognizance of him. In his infancy he slept on ancient tapestry on which the heroes of the Iliad were pictured ; and while his camp was once digging in France, there were found medals of William the Conqueror ; at another time a battle-axe of the Roman army who invaded England ; and while he lay wearied on the hot desert, and moved the sands with his feet, he turned up a cameo of Julius Cæsar, of exquisite workmanship. Walking however within the sepulchral chamber of the great pyramid, the resting-place of the ashes of old kings, even he indulged in thoughts of his own littleness. He remembered that there is scarce a tenement on earth, however fragile, which does not remain a monument of the dead builders. Deep foundation, and lofty superstructure, fortress and tower, shaft and obelisk and pyramid, are often preserved in the balmy air, and may defy the storms of ages. And so the rivers flow on for ever, and the mountains are everlasting, and the trees of the forest may live a thousand years, and still bud and blossom, and expand into a more abundant comeliness. But proud man, fearfully, wonderfully made, aiming at all dominion, grasping at all science and all philosophy, is yet too short-lived to accomplish his own plans or to bring his own systems to perfection. We search painfully for his emblem among things which are themselves perishable ; and we can scarce discover it, unless it be in the summer rose, the early cloud, or the morning dew. The world with its forms of alluring beauty, the Past with its treasured wisdom, the Future with its endless stores, are open to his eager search. And what are these but the mockeries of life ? For Death comes at the instant of fruition, dashes from him the cup of pleasure, blots out the page of science, puts an end to his sublime discoveries, and mocks at his astronomy : *Pulvis et umbra sumus.*'

The passage of the Alps and the coronation of Napoleon as Emperor of the French are thus briefly but vividly sketched :

'In those regions of eternal snows where not a floweret is so brave as to endure the bitterness of the winters, nor a blade of grass appears on the scathed mountain-tops, nor the flutter of a bird's wing is heard, and where the stillness is unbroken except by the fall of an icicle, or the descent of an avalanche, or the sudden bound of a released torrent, suddenly the voices of a host of men are heard, and the high Alps are populated. Napoleon Bonaparte is there, high up above the nations of the earth over whom he lorded it ; and to have gazed at that array from an opposite Alp, one might have mistaken it for a grand tableau of his *apotheosis*, with his army and generals about him. That mountain-air had never echoed back the sound of war ; those pure snows had never been defiled by the blood of wholesale murder ; and now the trumpets which blow their blast for the battle-charge were heard, and the drums beat. But it was not yet to make an onset on men, but where the difficulties of the mountain seemed insurmountable, and the courage of the men must be reässured.' · · · 'We will contemplate another phase of his life, passing to that great day when he was crowned Emperor. It was in the church of Notre Dame. *Te Deum* resounded in those high arches in the temple of Religion which had been opened again after the days of terror and blood. The humbled Pope came there to consecrate the crown, but not to place it on brows. The same hand which had won it claimed the office of lifting it from the altar. All that was illustrious in the capital crowded into the temple and looked on in silence. And she too who had thus far shared a soldier's fortune, knelt down and received from his uxorious hand the imperial diadem. It glittered splendidly before her charmed eyes ; it was accepted with the grace which crowned all her actions ; it comported with a beauty which shone without gems ; but she lived to see it transferred to another, and that other to find it a crown of thorns. And when the first bitterness of her heart was over, she learned to delight less in its most brilliant gems than in deeds of charity at Malmaison.'

The burning of Moscow has often been described; but we do not remember ever to have encountered a more condensed yet glowing account of this sublime and awful spectacle than is contained in the few lines ensuing:

'The French entered into a deserted city. Only the vilest of its population remained. Swarming over its innumerable streets they began to plunder its churches and bazaars and magnificent palaces. But when the night came on, and the meanest soldier lay down wrapped in the costliest furs and drunken with the richest wines, the cry of ' Fire! fire!' burst like a knell of death upon the ranks. The flames shot upward, and their lurid light revealed a figure in the windows of the Kremlin palace. It was the Corsican. His hand grasped a pen, and he was writing by the light; and could any one have looked over him he would have beheld a letter indited to the Czar, and on its page was written 'peace.' The flames were extinguished; but the next night they broke out again in all quarters, spreading with such a rapid contagion that they involved at the same time the abodes of poverty and sumptuous palaces; monuments, and miracles of luxury and art. The very tombs were burnt up. In the midst of all, the equinoctial storm arose and raised the ocean of fire into great billows, which rolled and dashed against the Kremlin, and would not retreat at the bidding of him who stood upon the ramparts. In the midst of the howling of the storm and crackling of flames, the fall of massive structures and the explosion of combustible magazines, the rolling of drums and the sound of tocsins, the solemn peal of bells, and clocks striking their last hours, the revelry of the drunken and the shrieks of anguish, and all other sounds of a wild, exulting spectacle, were seen running through the streets the most squalid wretches that ever assumed the form of humanity; men and women with dishevelled hair, with torches in their hands and the aspect of demons revelling in their own pandemonium. NAPOLEON dashed out of the town on his charger, beneath the overarching columns of flame, and retired a league distant, where the heat of the fire pursued him. 'Oh!' exclaimed he, when he afterward described the scene at St. Helena; 'it was the grandest, the most awful, the most sublime spectacle which the world ever beheld!''

Scarcely less striking than the above is the picture drawn of the disastrous retreat of the Grand Army through Russia: but we pass to the final scene; well assured that our readers will thank us cordially for over-stepping the bounds prescribed by our friend:

'And now the clarion of war had ceased to resound, and those who had so long been spectators still held their eyes fixed intently upon the stage; but it was to behold the scene shifted. The personages who used to crowd it were all gone; the pomp and banners of innumerable armies are no longer there. That which was represented was no splendid capital; Paris or Vienna, Berlin or Milan, or Mantua; nor the lovely fields of Europe gleaming with tents; but a rocky rampart in the far-off sea, where high upon its eminence of frightful solitude, standing like a statue upon a pedestal, firm and compact as if defying all storms, a PRISONER OF STATE; deserted by his armies, stripped of his possessions; the suns of Toulon and of Austerlitz sunk in eternal night; the magic of his name fled, the charm broken; but not less great in captivity than at the summit of his fame; NAPOLEON BONAPARTE stands forth a spectacle to the world. It seemed as if the sublime was to be pictured forth in almost every attitude of his life; whether he led his army over the Alps, or stood in the palace of the Czars, or fought on frozen plains, or burning deserts, or beneath the shade of the pyramids; or when, discoursing of destiny, he looked forth from the place of his banishment over the lonely sea! They little understood him who thought that the climax of his crimes would be the ignominy of the suicide; that he who had faced death on a thousand fields, and plucked the standard from its bearer on the bridge of Arcola, would be too poor in spirit to endure the crisis of his fate, though it should exceed death in bitterness. They little studied the symmetry of his character, who believed that this alone was wanting to fill up that which remained, and that he would share the catastrophe of his grand story with the roué, or the common gambler who has forfeited the hazard of his last die. For greater than the spirit which endures thirst or hunger, or summer's heats or winter's bitterness, is the high bravery which stifles the birth of tears and murmurs, and wears its brow serene in adversity. If ever mental agonies were poignant, his must have been; for they were the agonies of the caged lion or the eagle beating his prison-bars in despair. He was suffocating for the vital air. But there was little occasion to anticipate that which came full soon. The plot was already filled up; the whole drama was evolved; it only remained to look upon the ending, and for the curtain to fall. Already had the tempest begun which was to herald forth his great soul; for as if prodigies were to go with him to the last, and Nature vindicated her watchfulness over great events, a high hurricane arose, howling around the island, and tearing up the trees, at the moment when the spirit of NAPOLEON was struggling to break its bonds. He heard the bursting of the storm without, but he mistook it for the sound of the rolling of the waves of battle; for the onset of his infantry, for the shock of the whirlwind of cavalry! He was on the field again, galloping along the lines on his charger. The charge, the recoil, the rally — he was presiding over all. It is uncertain what field he imagined it — whether Marengo, or Leipsic, or Wagram or Austerlitz; it might have been a confused mingling of something which appertained to all; a strange anachronism and irreconciliation of times; the eighteenth of June with the eighteenth Brumaire; with antagonist cries and acclamations of the multitudes, ' *Vive le Roi!* ' and ' *Vive le Empereur!* ' — a marvellous memory of the characteristics of all lands; solemn Egypt and gay France — the Danube and the river Nile; a Gothic cathedral and a snow-crowned Alp; a peasant's cottage and a pyramid; Rome and Elba, Corsica and St. Helena; St. Jean d'Acre and Malmaison; Jaffa, Ajaccio, and St. Cloud; with all contradictory characters that ever acted on the stage; Kleber and Toussaint; Duke d'Enghein, and Pichegru; Louis the Eighteenth and Pope Pius the Seventh; Bernadotte and Ney, Wellington and Labedoyère, Fox and Talleyrand; Melas and Murad Bey; Lord Nelson and Bruyes; Janizaries and Egyptians, and sun-burnt Syrians; cannonry and gleaming sabres, horses and camels and dromedaries; trappings and fantastic costumes and gay plumes; the high cap of the Austrian huzzar, the tri-color of France and the turban of the Mamelukes, mixed up in the confusion of that gorgeous delirium! Then he lifted his arm high in air, and with a triumphant voice which thrilled through every heart, exclaimed, ' *The d'armée!* ' ' The head of the army! — the head of the army!' His hand sunk down again; his voice was hushed in stillness; a seal was set upon his cold brow. He had *lost the battle* — he was overwhelmed with his last defeat!

' It is related by an eye-witness that at the taking of the town of Bard NAPOLEON pioneered the way for his soldiers, and succeeded in raising a cannon by a goat-path to the heights of Albasedo, when overcome by his immense exertions, he sunk down upon the rock and temporarily slept; and that each man as he passed by, paused and gazed at him for a moment as he lay, with a sort of mysterious awe. So now his few remaining followers, as he slept after life's fitful fever, looked on and wondered. Then they bore him to his grave beneath the willows in the valley of NAPOLEON at St. Helena, to a tomb which required no epitaph. It was very proper that he should be possessed of such a sepulchre; a solitary island, bristling with cannon at every aperture of the rocks at whose base the sea renewed his everlasting dirges; whither as the wayfaring man directed his gaze he would sever it from all association with the living, and think of it only as a tomb. It has been said that it would have been in better keeping had NAPOLEON's rest in St. Helena remained undisturbed:

> ' For little he 'd reck if they 'd let him sleep on,
> In the grave where the Briton had laid him.'

But his wanderings were not yet over; and it is but lately that a princely messenger went and returned upon his errand; and old memories were awakened, and a thrill of excitement ran through all France while a cry once more resounded in the capital: ' *The Emperor is coming!* ' But oh! how different the return from Elba and the return from St. Helena! The one full of the exultation of life and the acclaim of men worshipping as at the shrine of a demi-god; the other solemn and funereal. The Emperor *was* coming; but he came, not to take possession of the Tuilleries, or to strike terror into the heart of old royalty, but merely to reap the fulfilment of his last request: ' I wish my bones to repose on the banks of the Seine among the French people whom I have loved so well.'

' Years have passed away, and the blood which he might have been instrumental in shedding is dried up, and the groans of the families which supplied his conscriptions are no longer heard; and now when we calmly contemplate the character of NAPOLEON BONAPARTE, we cannot justly compare him either with Alexander or Hannibal or Cæsar, or any ancient or modern man, either for military genius, of brilliant achievement in arms; for the height of his elevation or for the depth of his fall. But it may be pardonable to allude to one, not to institute a comparison where the lines are too divergent to be forced into parallel, in whom a truer sublime is exhibited, because his great deeds, without dazzling by their sudden energy of completion, sprang from his matchless purity of soul:

> ' A conformation and a form indeed
> Where every god did seem to set his seal,
> To give the world assurance of A MAN.'

With him patriotism was not the cant-word of a revolution. No crown ever graced his temples; no regal wealth glittered in his hands or corrupted his heart. The nation never committed to him a boon which it could wish to recall. He has slept undisturbed in the sepulchre of his fathers; but wherever the boundaries of our country are, her rivers and mountains, her cataracts, and solemn groves, and fertile fields shall be associated to all time with the name of WASHINGTON. Still, we would look upon all master-spirits who have lived in the world, however they may differ in man's short-sighted estimate, as so many subordinate agents to carry out the designs of a great Providence, which will bring good out of evil, and make the darkness and miseries of war to be the harbingers of continued sunshine and of an eternal peace; and regarding all confusion as preceding a more permanent order, and all events as so many well-adapted parts in the harmony of a universal government, joyfully look forward to the day when the nations of the earth shall have other things to glory in than the exploits of their warriors or their fields of blood; and when RELIGION and JUSTICE and a true LIBERTY shall walk hand in hand over the world; and all annals shall be free from crimes; and England shall boast of even prouder memories than the name of WELLINGTON or the 'FIELD OF WATERLOO.'"

A new admiration of NAPOLEON appears just now to have been revived. We see his name oftener in the journals of the day, and books of all descriptions relating to him are announced. 'All this,' says a friend writing to us in deprecation of the 'Parallel' in a late number, 'is but the periodical budding forth of his luxuriant, magnificent, undying fame! And if we almost bow down in admiration of him, from merely reading of his great acts in imperfect and very partial chronicles, is it to be wondered at that the GRAND ARMY worshipped him with rapture, in whom was concentrated the whole glory of their host?' Having now, as we trust, 'satisfied the sentiment' in the eyes both of the friends and contemners of NAPOLEON, we leave the matter in the hands of a jury of forty thousand readers, in the freest and happiest country on earth.

HAP-HAZARD ENJOYMENTS. — There is a good deal of meaning in the common remark, that if we would 'look about us' in our daily walks we should find a thousand matters to interest or instruct us that to the thoughtless eye and the unobservant mind pass as things of nought. We were forcibly impressed with this trite truth the other day, as we stepped out of a rare repository of ancient books, fine paintings, rich prints, 'musical instruments and that of all sorts,' and nameless other articles of taste and *vertu;* and yet an establishment which is passed with indifference or inattention by crowds of persons every day, because *externally* it purports to be only an auction-and-commission-store. We were led to its pleasant precincts, as we were 'fetching a walk' in its vicinity, by a burst of ravishing harmony, issuing from the open door, and alternately swelling and dying upon the clear morning air; and having entered, we tarried two long hours, scarcely noting the flight of time; now listening to half a dozen overtures of the most renowned operas, played by an instrument that looked very like a private library-case, but which gave with wonderful fidelity, power and sweetness, a *fac simile,* so to speak, of a full orchestra; now following, in their order, an array of the largest and finest prints, suspended upon the walls; entranced meanwhile with the mingled notes of an exotic songster in its fanciful prison, and the rich tones of a musical-box, so capacious that it might have passed for an organ; and anon dwelling with delight upon the first black-letter edition of HOLLINGSHED's 'Historie of England and Scottish-lande,' with its crude but exceedingly expressive engravings; or examining a gold snuff-box, richly chased and ornamented, 'presented by His Majesty FREDERICK WILLIAM of Prussia, as a mark of His Royal Highness' approbation,' etc.; left to be sold, malgré all its honored associations, for the relief of its hereditary possessor. These are a few only of the objects which riveted our attention and won our admiration. At the north-east corner of Duane-street, reader, as you are passing up or down our wide and bustling Broadway, 'pause in your rapid career' for a moment, and ask those courteous gentlemen, Messrs. RIELL AND ABCULARIUS, to admit you to the rarer curiosities of their ever-teeming mart; and our word for it, if you have taste, imagination, or feeling, you will thank us (as we here thank them) for a view of the 'goodly shows' which they open to the public.

INTERNATIONAL COPY-RIGHT. — The publishers of '*Arcturus*' have issued a 'Speech' on International Copy-right, which was attempted to be delivered by one of the Editors of that Magazine on the occasion of the dinner recently given in honor of Mr. DICKENS at the City Hotel. We say '*attempted* to be delivered,' because the speaker arose in some embarrassment at a late period of the proceedings, while at least three fourths of the large number present were either engaged in unintermitted and noisy conversations at the tables, or walking about the lower end and sides of the hall; and the palpable inattention to the orator, through indifference concerning his theme or disapprobation of its untimely introduction, induced him to desist, and to arrive at his closing sentiment, an excellent one by the way, without 'delivering' a moiety of what now appears (as indeed it should, in justice to the writer) in a printed form. Our readers do not need to be told that we agree entirely with the author of this essay in relation to the justice of the proposed law. The advocacy of that measure was first commenced in these pages several years since by the late WILLIS GAYLORD CLARK, who did not confine his exertions to this medium, as Mr. CLAY will bear witness; and it has been continued in the KNICKERBOCKER at intervals by his own and other pens, including that of Mr. WASHINGTON IRVING, up to the present time. The cause of International Copyright is a righteous one, and must eventually and we trust at no distant day prevail; and we thank the author of the 'Speech' under notice for joining the fraternity of honest and disinterested 'agitators' in a matter of so much importance to our literature and to those transatlantic authors who, like Mr. DICKENS, are the unpaid and altogether unrewarded literary benefactors of thousands upon thousands in this mighty land. We must be permitted to doubt however whether a labored article like the one before us, even had it been delivered entire, and at a period so early that it might have been listened to with courteous patience, would have been appropriate to the social and convivial assemblage before whom it was attempted to be pronounced. The eminent guest himself must have been of this opinion; since if we are rightly informed he 'respectfully declined' an offer made at the time by a friend of the proposed law to speak in its favor on that occasion. The last 'Arcturus' pronounces the brief speeches of the Vice-presidents 'lethargic;' and adds, that in its own opinion its editor's 'Speech' was one of the only 'three *realities* of the evening.' But to our mind, the remarks of Mr HONE. (who closed with a most felicitous toast,) of Mr. KING, and Mr. DIVERSITTE OGDEN were admirably, and in far better keeping with the occasion that had brought the admirers of Mr. DICKENS together than would have been the sixteen pages of 'Speech' before us The Editor of 'Arcturus' in reporting them for the press has couched the introduction in such wise than an impression is conveyed that Mr. WASHINGTON IRVING '*proposed* the sentiment' in concert with the speaker, who at once 'rose to answer his summons;' whereas it was merely sent by some person to the chair, (Mr. IRVING,) who announced it, as he did several others which passed without remark, as a matter of course. Let us not be misunderstood. The writer of the 'Speech' before us is, as we have said, entirely with this Magazine in its advocacy of the great question which it was the first thoroughly to set before the American people; and while he shall aim to enforce its claims upon the public attention, he will deserve the thanks of all recognized 'authors' and of the country at large. At the same time we cannot resist the expression of our belief that the obtrusion of the subject at length — and in language not altogether free from affectation and offence — upon a convivial and social assemblage, like that convened to do honor to Mr. DICKENS, was in very questionable taste, to say the least, and little calculated moreover to make new converts to the good cause.

THE 'PHILOSOPHY OF FICTION.' — From some remarks upon the philosophy of fiction — incidental to a discriminating and highly commendatory notice of the works of Mr. DICKENS — in the last number of the Boston 'Christian Examiner,' we take the following eloquent passage. The writer is assuming the ground that the spirit of Christianity, evinced in the love of man for his brother, erring, sinful and depraved though he be, bids fair to supersede the old forms of romantic fiction, and to infuse a new and higher usefulness into the popular writings of the day:

'Christianity has not only a Paradise in the far-off past and a millennium in the far-off future, but a heaven near at hand, embracing the material world on every side; compassing the path and the lying down of mortals, though their eyes be holden that they see it not; a heaven into which the beloved have already gone, and from which there are well-known voices, saying, 'Come up hither;' a heaven, with which man may hold unceasing communion by that ever-flowing prayer, which needs no voice or sound. This past, this future, this unchanging present satisfies those aspirations and yearnings, which would otherwise prompt to the higher efforts of fiction. · · · Why should we invent, when there is every thing around us, for us to discover and to learn? Think what an exhaustless fund of poetry, what a boundless scope for the imagination there is in the actual. The idea of an infinite presence in all things seen; in the glad sun and the bright stars; in the glow of morning and the blush of evening; in the rushing wind and the flying cloud; how does it breathe new life into all the hues and forms of nature, load the air with harmonies, and crowd the most dreary scene with beauty! To think of every dew-drop and snow-flake, every ray of light, and breath of air, as a shrine of the Infinite One, how does it invest these material forms with an inexpressible grandeur and loveliness, impart a lofty dignity to life, shed a halo of glory over the most familiar scenes, and draw strains of adoring melody from God's least tuneful works! This present, this passing moment, how fast it flits by, how vapid as an idle tale does it seem to the sluggish spirit, that will not stay its flight, and analyze it, and trace the whence and the whither of its mystery of love! But immensity and twin eternities are enfolded beneath its wings. For this present moment the whole past has been a preparation day, and treasured mercies of the entire eternity that is gone are poured upon it, while the rays of an eternity to come light it up with hope and promise; nor is there an instant of that boundless past or that boundless future, which helps not to make the fleeting present blessed.'

We intended to have alluded to two or three other papers in the 'Examiner,' especially the one on the 'Reformation in Switzerland,' but we lack space for the present.

AMERICAN EMBASSY TO SPAIN. — The United States' government has conferred high honor upon itself in the selection of Mr. WASHINGTON IRVING as Minister to the Court of Spain. A more appropriate appointment could not possibly have been made; and it derives additional value to the eminent recipient from the fact that it was alike unsolicited and unexpected. 'His Excellency' can add nothing certainly to Mr. IRVING in the eyes of his friends; but the fact it indicates can and does add to the honor of the country. Health, prosperity and long life to GEOFFREY CRAYON! Mr. COGSWELL, who goes out with Mr. IRVING as Secretary of Legation, will confer honor upon his honorable station. He is a gentleman of tried integrity of character and great amenity of manners; and his rank as a scholar and man of letters is fully established. The 'New-York Review,' of which he has been the Editor since its first establishment, has made him widely and favorably known to his countrymen. Success then to the American embassy at Madrid! Our trust is, that neither of the gentlemen who compose it, and especially our distinguished correspondent, will find its duties so arduous but that he can indulge in old propensities with the pen. In this wish we are sure our readers will cordially join.

GOSSIP WITH READERS AND CORRESPONDENTS. — We have received the following earnest epistle from a grand-son of the good old 'GRAND-FATHER' whose 'Port-folio' has been opened for the edification of our readers. Our correspondent who lived for a time with a 'Deacon T.,' will perceive that he has mistaken his man:

'*To the calm and sagacious-looking gentleman with the bald head and small-clothes, who with pipe and pen in his hand sits musing in the antique chair* — MR. KNICKERBOCKER:

'RESPECTED SIR: Some 'friendly correspondent' has suggested that my good Grand-father was mistaken in his statement regarding the charity of Deacon T'; and to make good his opinion, gives you a very amusing story of 'a batch of extra-nice custard-pies' which he says were once made by the Deacon's discreet wife. Now I have no doubt that the anecdote itself is founded on fact. It has strong marks of authenticity. There is something which no story-teller could counterfeit in the circumstance of the nurse slyly tasting the custards, and also in the remarkable fact, that when the delicacies were consigned to the pig-sty, the occupant thereof should have 'come in immediately after.' It is very evident to me that your correspondent must have been familiarly acquainted with a Deacon T, whose character bore some resemblance to my Grand-father's church officer. But I can very easily prove to you that that man, his 'guardian,' the hero of the 'bad four-pence-ha'penny' was not the same worthy of whom my progenitor has written. Your correspondent informs you that the Deacon whom he has good reason to remember was blessed with a sympathizing help-meet by the name of HANNAH. I have searched the church records of the parish of P., and find that the wife of Deacon T. with whom he lived in holy union forty-five years, and who survived him about seven years, was christened as MEHITABLE. But your correspondent may slyly hint that perhaps she changed her name, as some others have done who have been ungratefully discontented with that which their parents selected for them. To be prepared for all cross-questioning, I have ascertained that she was admitted to the church as Mehitable, and buried as Mehitable; and farthermore that Mehitable is still preserved as a family name among her descendants, even to the third generation. I do freely confess that the coincidence between the two deacons in question are very remarkable; but facts are stubborn things, and church records are high authority. I like your correspondent's good story so well, that I wish you would ask him to turn over the pages of his book of remembrance once more, and see if he is not mistaken in the name of his Mrs. T. Is he sure that the Deacon did not say 'Go to *Mehitable*?' Your humble servant,

'MY GRAND-FATHER'S GRAND-SON.'

'*Thoughts suggested by the Rev. Mr. Parker's Lectures*' are not for our pages; and we are grieved to think that the writer should have considered himself 'encouraged' by any thing which he may have seen in the KNICKERBOCKER, to forward them to us for insertion. We have no sympathy with those, whoever they may be, who would reduce the inspired writings to a level with the ordinary compositions of men; who would take away the solace of religion from the undoubting believer, wearied with the cares and trials of life, or turning his eyes toward heaven from the bed of death. Some months ago a female friend and correspondent desired us to publish the annexed heart-felt and most touching stanzas; and she asked, we remember: 'Who can read these affecting lines, written by an English lady in the very depths of earthly affliction, and not feel that faith in CHRIST is a blessed thing, even though it were, what it cannot be, an illusion and a dream?' We commend the stanzas to our correspondent:

JESUS! I my cross have taken,
All to leave, and follow thee;
Naked, poor, despised, forsaken,
Thou from hence my all shalt be!
Perish every fond ambition —
All I 've sought, or hoped, or known;
Yet how rich is my condition —
God and heaven are all mine own!

Let the world despise and leave me,
They have left my SAVIOUR too;
Human hopes and looks deceive me,
Thou art not, like them, untrue;
And while Thou shalt smile upon me,
God of wisdom, love, and might!
Friends may hate and foes may scorn me,
Show thy face, and all is right.

Man may trouble and distress me —
'T will but drive me to thy breast;
Life with trials hard may press me —
'T will but bring me sweeter rest:
O, 't is not in Grief to harm me,
While my SAVIOUR's face I see;
It is not in Joy to charm me,
Were that Joy unmixed with Thee.

We shall have great pleasure in publishing the '*Fragmentary Memories of Actors and the New-York Stage*,' by a correspondent who has been 'an old stager here for the last thirty years,' and who incloses us the two following characteristic scraps, by way of sample: 1. 'In 1816, PHILLIPS the great singer first visited this country; and as the then theatre-goer must remember, eclipsed all who had preceded him. Poor old INCLEDON, who had arrived but a short time previously, was almost driven mad by his superior success, and at length in despair left the country. PHILLIPS in fact carried all before him, and played night after night to crowded houses; pocketing mean-time of course a large amount of money. He was noted for some peculiarities, conspicuous among which was his penuriousness. One or two instances I will relate. On one occasion he went to the store of Mrs. LEE, in Maiden Lane, (the widow of the celebrated Dr. LEE, of bilious-pill memory,) to obtain a box of her pills. 'How much are they?' inquired the singer. 'Half a dollar,' replied Mrs. LEE. 'Hm-m-m!' said PHILLIPS. 'Pray, Ma'am, how much are they *without the box?*' 'Well, Sir,' said the widow; 'we usually sell both together.' 'Ah, but I have no *need* of the box; I do n't *want* it.' 'Then I suppose you can have the pills *without the box* for three-and-sixpence.' 'Very good,' said the vocalist, taking out a piece of a play-bill and wrapping the pills in it. 'There 's three-and-sixpence. Good morning Ma'am.' On another occasion, a fine morning in May, he said to Mr. P——, a fine gentleman-like man, and the very antipodes of himself in this particular feature: 'Mr. P——, have you in this country such things as Woodstock gloves?' 'Oh, yes,' replied P——; 'I will take you to a store where you may obtain some of the very best quality. Away they went down Broadway to a fashionable dry-goods' store, P—— supposing as a matter of course that his friend would purchase a dozen pairs at least. They arrived at the store, and Mr. V——, its courteous proprietor, waited in person upon the two friends. 'How much are these?' asked PHILLIPS, examining a pair of real Woodstocks. 'Ten shillings,' replied Mr. V——. 'Oh, that 's too much; we can get them at 'ome for *two* shillings. However, I will take a pair if you will say *six* shillings.' After some little hesitation, Mr. V—— smilingly invited Mr. PHILLIPS behind the counter, and pointing to a seat, said: 'Well, Mr. PHILLIPS, just stand up there and sing 'Eveleen's Bower' for me, and you shall *have* the gloves for six shillings.' Mr. PHILLIPS did not sing; and his friend P—— never went with him again to buy gloves.' II. 'A Mr. W——, a gentleman who had the very bad habit of 'exasperating the haitch,' was often much bothered in consequence. One morning at the rehearsal of 'Alexander the Great,' in the third act, a pause was made in 'coming the apologetic' after the death of Clitus: 'When men shall hear how highly you were urged.' The gentleman who was to play Lysimachus, addressed Mr. W——: 'Well, Sir, that is your line.' 'Oh, no!' said W——; 'it is put down here (taking out his book) for Lysimachus; however, I'll speak it.' Accordingly at night he got his cue, and commenced: 'When men shall e'hear e'how e'highly you were *hurged.*' Mr. Clitus shook his sides lustily as he lay dead, and the living actors in the scene were not more decorous. Alexander among the rest.' · · · A little sense and a slight dash of grammar would greatly improve the ' *Reflections on the Death of the late M'Donald Clarke.*' The 'lessons' which the writer has prepared for 'the erratic sons of genius' would be thrown away upon most readers save those of his own calibre — and *they* are not included. We have ourselves however a word to say in passing, touching the sad life and sadder end of poor M'DONALD CLARKE. For the last ten years we have encountered him in the streets almost every day that we have been in town; and even now it seems strangely unnatural not to meet, as we were wont in our daily walks, the blue great-coat, navy-cap, red or blue neck-cloth, and silver-headed cane, which always announced the presence of the unfortunate being who may be said to have clothed them with a very specific individuality. His eyes were generally intently fixed on vacancy, as he wandered along the public ways, and he never obtruded his recognitions upon any of his acquaintances: but arrest his attention — *speak* to him — and his very heart rushed to his eyes, and a smile which a set of the most brilliant teeth rendered peculiarly sweet and winning, evinced his deep gladness that he was not altogether forgotten and unregarded. His was indeed a heart that 'leaped kindly back to kindness;' and lonely and desolate as he was, it was ever softened with a love of human kind. We have been informed that in early life his parents were rich, and that he himself was liberal to a fault; certain it is, that when in the depths of subsequent poverty he chanced to draw a large prize in the lottery, his generosity to the poor, with whom a similarity of condition had previously made him acquainted, knew no bounds, and his money was soon exhausted. He loved young children. We have frequently seen him with three or four rosy little people about him, listening with evident delight to their foolish, glad tattlement, as though it were reviving in his desultory mind a transient dream of the shadowy past. LOVE was his ruin — love, and the most cruel persecution of beings professing to be *men*, who used this emanation of the DEITY in him in furtherance of their heartless sport. CLARKE had always some 'angel-woman,' as he was wont to term her, to whom his whole heart went forth; but latterly and for many months his 'great affection' centred upon *one*, well known in this metropolis as a lady of fashion and fortune, for whose favor, unknown we may believe to her, he sighed, and sighed in vain. At length, however, through the base deceptions of unworthy persons, his simple heart was made to believe that his suit was accepted. The reality, the night which came down upon this mid-noon, drove him into a temporary insanity :

> 'Stern Fate transfixed with viewless dart
> The last pale hope that shivered at his heart ; '

and he was borne at night amid the driving rain and sleet of a February storm to a prison ; where instead of attempting to allay and ventilate his feverish, irritated feelings, he was thrust by the officers into a cold, dark cell, where he remained until the next day, when he was taken out, more dead than alive, and conveyed to a lunatic asylum — a place that to our eye has always 'a smack of Tartarus and the souls in bale ; ' where, after suffering the torments of the damned, he yielded up his blameless life, having fought with poverty and disappointment until Death made it a drawn battle. He was called 'the Mad Poet ; ' but there was brilliancy in his madness ; and bright gems often shone in his grotesque and fanciful settings. His thoughts like the gossamer stretched out, entangled without end, clinging to every casual object, flitting in the idle air, and glittering in the ray of a distempered fancy. But he has gone ! He has exchanged the dreams in which he walked on earth, for the long sleep and the sound in its peaceful bosom. And those who never raised a finger for his relief while he was living, and feeling, with an acuteness which only misery can give, the desolateness of his situation, now come with bastard sentimentality to drop crockodile tears over his cold ashes, emulous to engage in raising a monument to his memory ! What a transparent mockery ! · · · '*The Decay of Drinking in New-England*' follows the lament of COLERIDGE, that there is 'water, water every where,' but nothing else to drink. We should have published it entire, months ago, but that it struck us as being 'written to death.' Our correspondent stands right before his subject, which is an excellent one, and says, 'Hear me first ; ' and he goes on page after page to nullify all his efforts at fine writing by entirely over-doing the matter ; by jotting down every thing that passes through his mind, and lugging in ' by ear and horn ' incongruous similes and illustrations. The opening however is in better taste : 'Few of the changes which this innovating age has brought to pass come more sadly over the musing soul of one whose experience goes back to the last century, than the decay of good fellowship throughout our land. The pump and the tea-pot have put to flight a host of spirits, which, if they were devils, must at least be admitted to have been merry ones. Like some of the exorcised demons of former ages, they have demolished or taken with them in their flight many of the time-honored usages and habitudes which were to them as their local habitation. Their temples are deserted, their votaries few, their solemn ritual and high ceremonial services obsolete ; their priests dishonored, the vessels of their sacrifices desecrated, and perverted to vulgar and secular uses. The punch-bowl, our fathers' ' earliest visitation and their last at even,' is broken ! The mug, unconscious of flip, and stirred no more with the glowing logger-head or poker, is relegated to the regions of the ' oblivious cook.' The tankard foams no more with the generous strength of porter — destined to bear away upon his ample shoulders a load of cares — and now stands mournfully upon the marble table, the tame receptacle of our wives' or daughters' boquets of flowers. The brandy-bottle no longer smiles a welcome to the coming friend, or pours out a parting benediction upon the going guest. The mountain-dew rests ungathered upon its native hills ; its rare flavor, caught from the smouldering peat, no more transports us in imagination to the heathery Highlands of Scotland. Gin now only rectifies the marshy vapors which arise in a Dutch-man's brain. Even cider — sung of Pastoral PHILLIPS — New-England's former pride, scarcely ever gushes from the crushed veins of the apple. The parent orchards themselves have in too frequent instances bit the dust, and fed the oven.' · · · Will not ' P. R. S.,' of Hallowell, (Maine,) permit us to substitute for his collegiate prose performance the following lines upon the same identical theme ? They are from a late English periodical, and really seem to us to contain, in a very brief compass, the *spirit* of our correspondent's extended essay :

LIFE, DEATH, AND ETERNITY.

A shadow moving by one's side,	A gulf whose pathway never led
That would a substance seem,	To show the depth beneath ;
That is, yet is not, though described,	A thing we know not, yet we dread —
Like skies beneath the stream ;	That dreaded thing is Death.
A tree that 's ever in the bloom,	
Whose fruit is never ripe ;	
A wish for joys that never come —	
Such are the hopes of Life.	
A dark inevitable night,	
A blank that will remain ;	
A waiting for the morning light,	
Where waiting is in vain :	

The ' *Lay Sermons* ' of ' WHITFIELD, JR.' of Philadelphia are respectfully declined, for the reason that they are ungracefully written, too long, and quite too dull. The writer ' asks their publication with some confidence,' because several months since we commended the ' *Short Patent Sermons* ' of ' Dow JR.,' which he seems to think rather inferior to his own discourses. To our mind, however, there is more original humor in one of Dow's quaint, unique, irregular and often unequal essays, than in the entire five MS. numbers before us. There are *passages* in almost all of the Mercury's lay-preacher's ' sermons,' which having once read, it is very difficult to forget. There live in our memory at this moment a dozen scraps of philosophy, morality and humor, which may have been uttered a year or more ago by Mr. Dow. For example : ' Hope,' said he, in substance, in one of his discourses, ' goes it too strong on the credit-system ; always giving promissory notes, and extending them ninety days at a notch ; and the chances are ten to one that she does 'nt ' burst up ' at last, and leave her votary a bankrupt. Yet what a faithful companion she is ! How tenderly she watches over the fretful children of Toil and Care ! How kindly she journeys on with them, through weal and wo, in their pilgrimage to the grave ! Yes ; she lends man a staff when his knees begin to totter with age, and sits smiling with her pinions folded by the bed on which he lays him down to die ; and ere the vital spark has fled, she spreads them to the air, and takes her upward flight to prepare for him a heavenly home in a better land, and a house of many mansions.' In another sermon, speaking of the cloud under which all men walk, and their ignorance of themselves and the ' secret springs of eternal nature,' he made use, as near as we can remember, of the following striking and beautiful language : ' After GOD had called chaos to order, he scraped together a parcel of red dirt on the banks of the Euphrates, and caused the lump to rise with the leaven of life ; yet the being who was then formed knew no more how he became possessed of the powers of locomotion than a steam-engine. · · · But when this old body of mine shall have been reduced to a bushel of ashes, *I think* a spiritual spark will still linger in the pile unsmothered, ready to blaze forth in glory when the breath of OMNIPOTENCE shall re-kindle the fire that once burned upon the altar of life, and illumine the night of the grave with the light of a glorious resurrection.' We know not how such passages as these may impress others, but to us they seem imbued with spirit and beauty. It is true that thoughts like those we quote are often presented in singular juxtaposition with others of a different character ; but even this causes them to be remembered ; and thus a good inculcation is as it were *insinuated* to the heart, and the speaker is enabled successfully to ' patch up with the patent putty of preaching those windows of the moral understanding in which panes are wanting.' The subjoined from a late discourse is in another vein. The speaker is laying down the law to those who would be wise above what is written ; and is especially severe upon those humbugeous individuals who affect to be able to read the mysteries of the stars :

' My friends, what is an astrologer but a mere mortal, after all ? He is but a fellow-prisoner in the dark dungeon of Fate ; the chains of dependence hang heavily about his feet, and he can no more burst open the iron-barred doors of the Future, than one of our northern soft-shelled negroes can butt his head through a mill-stone. He may *pretend* to read your destiny upon the face of the moon ; ransack a ' house ' in some planet to find out who robbed a hen-roost upon earth ; and pump Venus to ascertain the issue of your love affairs. He may feel the pulses of the stars, to find out the why and wherefore of coughs, colds, agues, fevers, cholera, corns, head-ache, ear-ache, tooth-ache, dyspepsy, and bile ; tell what makes some men poor, some rich, some bashful, some brazen ; tell the cause of quarrels between lovers, husbands and wives ; make the stars confess how they intend to dispose of cities, towns and nations, and the lots of individuals. Yes, my friends, he may *pretend* to effect all this, but he knows no more about it than a pewter dog ; and there is just about as much dependence to be placed upon his predictions as there is upon the sign of a storm when an old ram stands with his tail to the north-east. No, my dear hearers, if you wish to know more about yourselves and your destinies than you do, you must *study yourselves*, as my friend POPE would recommend : read yourselves through every day ; peruse carefully your hearts and your inclinations ; discover your manifold faults, and learn how to correct them. Be content with what the present reveals, and do n't strain your intellectual optics by trying to peep into futurity.'

Without a doubt, ' *L. M. N.* ' would at this moment have us suppress the angry distribe against a Philadelphia contemporary, which he has sent us for insertion in the present number. We have ventured at least to *think* so ; and we take leave respectfully to commend to him the following advice of Dr. NOTT, once tendered to a friend who now fills the highest office in the gift of the Empire State : ' Never indulge in personalities ; never lose your temper, nor make an enemy if you can avoid it. Conquests may be made by conciliation and persuasion as certainly as by ridicule and sarcasm ; but in the one case the chains are silken and sit easy ; in the other iron, and gall the wearer. Though you point your arrows, never poison them ; and if the club of Hercules must be raised, let it be the naked club, not entwined with serpents.' · · · The obliging ' correspondent in a sister city ' to whom we were indebted for the capital anecdote in our last of the charitable deacon and economizing deaconess, has sent us the following, which was suggested, he tells us, by reading recently for the first time Mr. DICKENS' portrait of SIMEON TAPPERTIT in ' Barnaby Rudge.' This amusing personage, it should be premised for the benefit of any reader who may not have perused this latest work of ' Boz,' (a possible assumption, as the case of our correspondent leads us to believe,) had the scantest pattern of a leg and the most unchristian glance of an expressionless eye that it is possible to conceive ; yet he thought them both entirely irresistible, the latter especially, whence he was wont to twist out a look, ' a kind of ocular screw,' from which a blind pot-house comrade (who had a *feeling* admiration for his legs also, 'those twin invaders of domestic peace,') affected to screen his eyes, for the reason that, although he could n't *see* them, he felt them 'piercing him like gimlets.' This unique character, says our correspondent, 'reminds me forcibly of an individual whom I once knew in your good city of Gotham. He was a Scotchman by birth, and had without exception the ugliest face I ever saw on a man's shoulders; indeed I may add, on a monkey's. But by a perversity of taste not unusual in the world, the man made a complete hobby of his 'mug,' homely as it was; and was full of the conceit that on fit occasions he could summon to it a look of terrible and dignified sarcasm that was more efficacious than words or blows. He was rather insolent in his deportment, and was consequently continually getting into scrapes with some one or other, in which he invariably got worsted; because instead of lifting his hand and giving blow for blow, he always trusted to the efficacy of his 'look.' His various little mishaps he used to relate at meal-times to his fellow-boarders, always concluding his narrations with: 'But did n't I give the dirty rapscallions one of my 'looks!'' And then, twisting his 'ugly mug' into a shape that I sha'n't describe, he fancied he had convinced his hearers that his antagonists, whoever they were, would be in no hurry to meddle with him again. The last time I saw him, he was giving an account of an insult he had received the evening previous at a porter-house, where a little fellow, who was a perfect stranger to him, had insisted upon drinking at his expense, and who, when he refused to pay for the liquor, had not only abused him shamefully with his tongue, but had actually kicked him. 'Yes!' said the 'man with the face,' growing warm with the recital; 'the mither's deevil kicked me *here!*' — and he laid his hand over the part which had come in contact with the stranger's boot. 'And what did you say to *that?*' asked a listener. 'What did I *say* to that?' he replied, as if astonished that any one present should be ignorant of his invariable rejoinder to similar assaults — 'what did I *say?* I said nothing at all! The kick was but a soft one, at most, and the fellow that gave it but a wee bit of a jink-ma-doddy that I *could* have throttled with one hand on the spot. But I contented myself with jist giving him one of my *looks!*' And here Sawney 'defined his position' to the company, by giving them one of his awful glances. But this time he managed to convey an expression of ugliness and comicality so far beyond any thing he had ever called up before, that we could n't help thinking the kick he received must have been a great deal harder than he seemed willing to acknowledge.' · · · Will our Boston friend permit us to *publish* the '*Letter from a Friend in England*' describing among other things an interview with that gifted and shamefully-traduced lady, the Hon. Mrs. Norton? As it would violate no confidence, we *hope* so. One passage in particular throws a renewed interest around the lines written in the twilight of a wintry day, and addressed to the children from whom she had been cruelly severed, and whom she was not permitted to see:

'Where are ye, merry voices,
  Whose clear and bird-like tone,
Some other ear now blesses,
  Less anxious than my own?
Where are ye, steps of lightness,
  Which fell like blossom showers?
Where are ye, sounds of laughter,
  That cheered the pleasant hours?
Through the dim light slow declining,
  Where my wistful glances fall,
I can see your pictures hanging
  Against the silent wall;
They gleam athwart the darkness,
  With their sweet and changeless eyes,
But mute are ye, my children!
  No voice to mine replies.
Where are ye? Are ye playing
  By the stranger's blazing hearth;
Forgetting, in your gladness,
  Your old house 's former mirth?
Are ye dancing? Are ye singing?
  Are ye full of childish glee?

'Or do your light hearts sadden
  With the memory of me?
Round whom, oh! gentle darlings,
  Do your young arms fondly twine?
Does she press you to her bosom,
  Who hath taken you from mine?
Oh! boys, the twilight hour
  Such a heavy time hath grown,
It recalls with such deep anguish
  All I used to call my own,
That the harshest word that ever
  Was spoken to me there,
Would be trivial — would be *welcome*,
  In this depth of my despair.
Yet no! Despair shall *not*,
  While Life and Love remain;
Though the weary struggle haunt me,
  And my prayer be made in vain;
Though at times my spirit fail me,
  And the bitter tear-drops fall,
Though my lot be hard and lonely,
  Yet I hope — I *hope through all!*

We should like of all things to present a fac-simile of a letter from a highly respectable *business* firm in the 'Literary Emporium' *par excellence*, which a New-York friend has been kind enough to lay before us. We content ourselves, however, with an extract, which we beg to assure the reader is most 'faithfully rendered' from the *very* 'original.' Mr. Chawls Yellowplush doubtless thought he was spelling very nicely when, alluding to the various and contradictory treatment he received from his capricious mistress, he wrote: 'Sumtimes I get kisis, and sumtimes kix.' There are 'fax for the pepil' in such writing as the following, as well as in that of the literary London footman:

'we hav ben Expeted you to send the a mount of ower bill befor this time and hope it will be Convanant for you to send by the Return maile money is scirse with us or we should not Cauldon you for it for the present But we aire under the necesty of sow Duings we Persum you have got the bill of Lading Sum time a grow and you menshend in your Leter you woverd and when you Received a bit of Lading but we have not heaird from you yours Moast with Respet,' etc.

The long and elaborate paper upon 'Geology,' from a correspondent in Columbus, (Ohio,) would be more appropriate to SILLIMAN's 'Journal of Science' than to the KNICKERBOCKER. Several articles moreover from prominent native pens have already appeared in these pages upon this subject. Professor HITCHCOCK of Massachusetts, among others, has several times lent his distinguished aid to the cause, for the benefit of our readers. The theme is 'one of no small attraction,' certainly; and it is gaining new importance every day, by reason of the many hitherto-supposed facts with which its revelations clash. By the way, speaking of Geology: we observe that Dr. MOTT, in his graphic and glowing description of the pyramids of Egypt, mentions that the stones of those peerless monuments are filled with petrified shells and other marine indications. Now the pyramids are thought to be 'considerably old, if not older;' and the inquiry naturally arises, at what period of time were these shells deposited in the semi-fluid matériel that once composed the stones of which the gigantic Egyptian structures were formed?—how long a time must have elapsed before they became hardened and thoroughly imbedded in the stone itself?—and how long the stones had remained before they were employed in these time-lost erections? Verily, all this is a mystery and a marvel! The oldest art is a mushroom; Nature alone is antique; and 'day unto day uttereth speech' of her ancient wonders. It seems but a little while ago that we perused with surprise and eager curiosity the narrative of Captain ROSS's discoveries far in the frozen North; anon we find him at the *South* pole, making *there* the most wonderful revelations; of mountain peaks in a new and boundless land, so lofty that the voyager seems scarcely to approach them, though sailing directly toward them for many hours; peaks towering into the cold blue heights of a virgin heaven, covered with eternal snows, and sending out their glaciers for miles into the icy ocean that ever moans around their perpendicular cliffs; the whole magnificent view near and far only broken by the smoke and flame of a volcano twelve thousand feet above the level of the sea; at night sublimely lighting up this stupendous scene, which appeared to the new discoverer as if fresh from the hand of GOD! · · · In opening a recent series of lectures at Clinton Hall, Mr. J. N. BELLOWS avowed his determination to expose as he advanced the learned *humbugeousness* of the day; to remove the wigs and gowns from the solemn dunces who were disposed to clothe science and art with the mysterious and the unattainable, and to awe the common mind with abstruse terms, that expressed but the qualities of simple things. Some wag has sketched a spectacled scholar of this class, who is among other things an *antiquary.* He has picked up in the course of his walk an old crab-shell, which he presents to his favorite society, with a learned description and conjectures of great pith and moment. The relic is thus described: 'The body in question being like other bodies in a state of petrifaction, rendered inaccessible to the touch by the adscititious covering in which it is enveloped, can be considered in none of its natural or artificial conditions, beside those of form, color, and dimensions; all these, however, from the remarkable transparency of the hardened external fluid, are very perspicuously discernible. Its form, then, regarded laterally, or around its extremities, is a broad ellipse; and its superficies exhibits a figure either concave, or convex, according as one or the other of its faces may be turned to the eye of the spectator; so as, on the whole, to present immediately to the mind an image of the ancient *Testudo*, fabled to have been invented by Mercury. The color of this curious remain, being of a sub-fusc, or dusky green, (herein exactly agreeing with that of the sea-tortoise, or turtle, a creature sufficiently known to naturalists, *and others,*) is a further circumstance to be produced in behalf of my conjecture. I must not conceal a fact, however, which may seem to weaken its probability. The convex surface of the relic, though faintly marked in certain places by various indentations, is by no means distinctly portioned into those pentangular divisions which characterize the back of the *sea-tortoise,* which, as all authorities consent, was the basis of the genuine *Testudo*,' etc., etc. There is at least *one* of our readers who in looking over this gossiping corner of MAGA, will infer the decision intended to be conveyed by the above, touching this half-poetical, half philosophical, and wholly superficial essay. · · · The Boston 'Evening Transcript' corrects our correspondent Mr. CHEEVER for mistaking Good Friday for Easter, in his last number of 'Grenada and the Alhambra;' and not a few Catholics have reminded us that we are violating our polemical neutrality, in admitting his animadversions upon their faith. Not so, gentlemen. Our correspondent has a right to his own opinion; we do not indorse it. 'I am no Catholic,' writes one complainant, 'but I think there is an evident stepping out of the path to give the poor goat of Catholicism a kick. Why can't our travellers — our ministers at least — enjoy the good things of other lands, without lifting up their heels against that venerable religion to which they are indebted for almost every thing they see in the arts that is beautiful or magnificent? Your reverend correspondent asks continually what this or that place might not have been if it had only been peopled by protestants instead of Catholics and Moors? A steam cotton-factory or a tannery, most likely; or perhaps a Deacon Giles's Distillery!' We think Mr. CHEEVER must admit that our latest querist has 'got him there!' Aside from all this: there is, as it seems to us, something too much of asperity in the *denomi-*

national feeling of the day. It is to a good degree in this country as it was in England in the intolerant church-contentions so vehemently deplored by SIDNEY SMITH: 'I solemnly believe blue and red baboons,' says he, 'to be more popular here than Dissenters. They are more understood, and there is a greater disposition to do something for them. When a country squire hears of an ape, his first feeling is to give it nuts and apples; when he hears of a Dissenter, his immediate impulse is to commit it to the county jail, to shave its head, to alter its customary food, and to have it privately whipped!' · · · The '*New Readings of Shakspere*' will be acceptable, if there are not *too many of* them. They pall by repetition *en masse*. We could add one to the list of our correspondent. A verdant histrion, rather new to the stage, was playing Iago; who, it will be remembered, answers Othello's query concerning Michael Cassio, 'Dost thou believe that he is honest?' with 'damnable iteration:' '*Honest*, my lord?' Our Thespian altered the matter entirely: '*Honest?*' said he, with great vehemence; and then, as if giving vent to his intense wonder and surprise at such an idea, he exclaims: 'MY LORD!' The new reading 'took' like wildfire. · · · '*Yes*,' decidedly, to 'S.'s' proposition. We have listened a thousand times to the plaintive song of the '*Black Oat-Straw Man*.' His melancholy 'O-o-o-at St-r-r-aw!' always in the minor key, almost seems to us a moaning sound of Nature itself; and when a north-east storm is coming on, and the wind begins to howl over the rivers, and long waves of black smoke surge from steepled chimneys into the murky air, we always look to hear the voice of the 'Oat-Straw Man' amid the din; for on such occasions he revels in his time-honored vocation. · · · 'H. G. S.'s '*Scenes at the Old Custom-House*' shall appear — if possible, in the May number. Perhaps 'H. G. S.' will permit the insertion here of a remark (of which his revelations remind us) made by a New-York lad to his father, while recently looking through the interior of the massive and ungraceful structure now erecting in Boston for a new Custom-House. After having satisfied himself with gazing at the heavy stone-work, the boy turned to his father and inquired: 'What is it all *for*, father?' 'It's the Custom-House, my dear,' was the reply. 'What *is* a Custom-House?' rejoined the lad, persisting in his 'pursuit of knowledge under difficulties;' 'is it a *prison*, father?' 'Why y-e-s,' said the old gentleman, drily; it's a — a *sort* of a prison; *it's a place they put rogues in!* Past 'abequatulations' in various quarters probably suggested this luminous idea. 'Speaking of Custom-houses' — here is something that involves the good name of our own collector, Mr. EDWARD CURTIS. One of our State-senators is said to have created a good deal of private mirth among his friends by a recent incidental exposition of his igno-rance or 'rustiness' in classical matters. An opponent, speaking casually of Mr. VAN BUREN in debate, remarked, that on some particular occasion he had, like QUINTIUS CURTIUS, thrown himself into an abyss to save his country, 'or words to that effect, which this deponent does not more par-ticularly remember.' While he was yet speaking, our senator crossed over to a particular friend, and whispered in his ear: 'Does he mean CURTIS the New York Collector?' 'No, no!' was the reply; 'Quintius Curtius, the ancient.' The senator regained his seat, but presently returned, and again whispering in the ear of his friend, asked: '*What* did you say that CURTIS's first name was? — I've forgotten.' 'Quintius, *Quintius*,' rejoined the other, a little testily. The senator was in his place once more, and his adversary having concluded, he rose to respond. 'The gentleman,' said he, 'has instituted a comparison that wo'n't hold good — at any rate, not as *he* wants it. Unlike that respectable ancient, Mr. Quin — Mr. Quince — (and here he looked imploringly at his informant, but without result,) unlike him, Sir, Mr. VAN BUREN did not throw *himself* off a precipice to save his country, but his country threw *him* off, to save *itself!*' The effect of this retort, as the novelists say, 'may be more easily imagined than described.' As we are neutral in these pages, we must assign the joke part of this senatorial transcript to the Democrats, and the sarcasm to the Whigs. · · · Some dozen of correspondents, great admirers of Mr. QUOD, are impatient to know what is to become of the Attorney — of Higgs, and Wilkins, and poor Lucy. Restrain your curiosity, 'ladies and gentlemen;' all in due time. Perhaps you can perceive an evidence in the present issue that their intensely interesting history begins to 'appropinque an end.' Certain it is, that 'the wretch Higgs' will not now be deemed *utterly* unworthy. Read the affecting scene in the present number, friend 'P.' of Illinois, and withdraw 'that last remark o' your'n.' · · · We have often laughed at LAMB's idea, that his friend going to New-Zealand might find himself some pleasant day served up at table, 'not as a guest but as a meat.' The witty SIDNEY SMITH, lately chiding the new Bishop of New-Zealand for not doing more honor to his viands, has rather improved the idea. 'Come, my lord,' said he, 'this will not do in the Cannibal Islands. There you'll always find two co'rses, and a *cold man* on the side-board!' · · · · '*A Defence of the Pythagorean System*' evinces a good degree of ingenuity and humor, but there is *too much* of the theme. The reader would find himself more than '*slightly* interrogated' by its numerous queries. The belief of the *Shakers* partakes in some points of the Pythagorean shade. They believe in the immortality of animals as well as of men. They say that John saw horses in the world of spirits, as recorded in Revelations. They believe that all the ugly and venomous animals on earth are symbolical of the evil spirits that inhabit the lower regions of the invisible world, and that all the beautiful creatures, such as birds with gorgeous plumage, are symbolical of the good spirits in the mansions of bliss. · · · · 'Over-urgent Hospitality' shall appear. It is a well-written satire upon the over-doing in matters of hospitality, and especially in things edible and bibulous at country tables. We have seen this propensity illustrated in this way. Instead of saying : ' Do let me give you some more of this turtle ; ' ' I must insist upon your trying this nice melon,' etc., the language of truth should be : ' Do let me send you a little bilious head-ache ; ' ' Let me have the pleasure of helping you to a pain in the stomach,' etc. · · · · ' L. S. D.' is informed, that when Mr. DICKENS shall have found leisure to revise the ms. of his first paper for the KNICKERBOCKER, it will immediately appear. This (and it is by no means surprising) he has as yet found no moment to do. Mr. DICKENS has been solicited, as we learn from the ' Ladies' Companion,' to write for other American periodicals, but has been compelled peremptorily to decline. His pledge to us is specific and of some standing ; and it has recently been renewed with a generous courtesy that will reveal itself in a tangible shape to our readers before many weeks. · · · · ' Notice is hereby given' that love-poetry, strictly so called, must be rather good than otherwise, in order to gain admission into the ' OLD KNICK.' We have several tolerable amourettes on file ; but they are mostly of that class ' which we at the same time detest and praise.' One is very imaginative. The writer is exceedingly envious of a pair of ruby lips, the nether one round and pulpy, ' as if a bee had stung it newly,' because they are kissing each other all the while ; ' which, blessing still, themselves do kiss ! ' This, as the elder WELLER would say, is ' coming it rayther strong ! ' · · · A distinguished American gentleman now resident at Paris, and who has the entrée to the best society of the French capital, gives us in a recent letter the following sketch : ' Paris is full of Americans. Of the number, there are a few who lay some claim to aristocracy or fashion at home, and some four or five who are kind enough to admit each other to be ladies, but who turn up their noses at the rest. There is here indeed all the scandal of a little country village. Among all the crowd there are only two or three who go much into good French society ; and there are very many families, and those by far the best, who never have had a chance of setting their feet in a French house ; yet you shall find these to go homo full of praise of the Duchess This and the Princess That, who may possibly have elbowed them at some Charity-Ball. All are mad to return home, to sport their French dresses, which they have never found an opportunity of even airing here.' · · · · A correspondent inquires if the proceedings of the Dinner to Mr. DICKENS by the ' Novelties' Club ' are to be published ; to which we answer, No. The Club is a private one, and its proceedings, as a matter of course, are private also. It is sufficient to state, for the information of our friend, that in all respects the entertainment, physical and mental, was one long to be remembered. Nothing could exceed the admirable manner in which the externals were managed. The ASTON-HOUSE, that crowned king of all the American hotels, and not excelled by any in Europe, out-did itself on this occasion ; and although the great Master of Ceremonies, the capable 'Committee of One' on the Arrangements, Mr. JAMES STETSON, won laurels by the ' getting-up' of the PRINCE DE JOINVILLE dinner, he found, after the dinner to Mr. DICKENS, several additional sprigs in the wreath which he had previously won and worn. To say that the mental repast was ' in keeping' with all this, is the highest praise we can award it. · · · Among the articles filed for insertion or awaiting decision are the following: ' Lake Champlain ;' ' Ballad of Sir James the Ross ;' ' Leaves from the Basket of the Sans-souci Circle ;' ' Fragment from the mss. of CAGLIOSTRO ;' ' The Paradise upon Earth ;' ' Good Night ! ' from the German of Körner ; ' Letters from Rome,' Number Three ; ' Tawney Tom and Tabby Gray ;' ' The Skeleton Chief, a Prairie Legend ;' ' Father-Land ;' ' The Stars of Even ' and ' Stanzas,' by ' LEON ;' ' NAPOLEON's Death ;' ' Dream of the Dying Prophet ; ' ' The Review,' by the late Chief Justice MELLEN, of Maine, and ' Noor-Mahal, or the Light of the Harem,' both in type ; ' Burning of Danbury, Conn., from an Eye-Witness ;' ' American Naval Biography ;' Night, by ' H. H ;' ' The Buffalo-Hunter's Bride ;' ' Bird's-Eye Views of Florida, by ' T. J. S.' ' The Joys of the Stars ;' ' This to Thee, Lucy ;' ' The Fire-World ;' ' Stanzas to the Departed Poetess of Lake Champlain ;' ' My Sister ;' ' Windermere ;' ' Life's Seasons ;' ' The Free Rover ;' ' The Battle-Field,' etc.

LITERARY RECORD.

HISTORY OF NAPOLEON. — The first volume of Messrs. APPLETON's Pictorial History of BONAPARTE has already been noticed in the KNICKERBOCKER. The second is before us, and is in no respect inferior to its predecessor. The paper and typography are of the same order of excellence; and although some few of the engravings are more dim than we could wish, the mass of them serve a very useful and pleasing purpose, in illustrating the written pictures of the text. Although we have perhaps devoted space enough to NAPOLEON in the present issue, we shall be pardoned for citing a passage from his 'conversations' at St. Helena, wherein the renowned exile incidentally draws a comparison between himself and WASHINGTON.

'Look at the United States, where without any apparent force or effort every thing goes on prosperously; every one is happy and contented; and this is because the public wishes and interests are in fact the ruling power. Place the same government at variance with the will and interests of its inhabitants, and you would soon see what disturbance, trouble and confusion, and above all, what an increase of crime, would ensue. When I acquired the supreme direction of affairs, it was wished that I might become a WASHINGTON. Words cost nothing; and no doubt those who were so ready to express the wish, did so without any knowledge of times, places, persons, or things. Had I been in America, I would willingly have been a WASHINGTON, for I do not see how I could reasonably have acted otherwise. But had WASHINGTON been in France, exposed to discord within and invasion from without, I would have defied him to have been what he was in America; at least, he would have been a fool to attempt it, and would only have prolonged the existence of evil. For my own part, I could only have been a crowned WASHINGTON. It was only in a congress of Kings, yielding or subdued, that I could become so. There and there alone could I successfully display WASHINGTON's moderation, disinterestedness, and wisdom. I could not reasonably attain to this, but by means of the universal dictatorship. To this I aspired. Can that be thought a crime?'

NAPOLEON felt himself 'the world's cynosure' even amid the solitude and loneliness of his sea-girt rock. 'We have made, my dear LAS CASAS,' said he, 'to disappoint our tyrants. Our situation even here may have its charms. The eyes of the universe are fixed upon us! We are martyrs in an immortal cause. Millions of human beings are weeping for us; our Country sighs, and Glory mourns our fate!'

'THE CITY JOURNAL AND LADIES' GAZETTE' is the title of a new daily sheet, of a convenient medium size and very tastefully executed, recently commenced in this city by Messrs. BURLING AND MORRIS. It is to be devoted to literature, fashion, the fine arts, the drama, movements in fashionable life, the army and navy, and a general synopsis of the events of the day. It will aim at a more pleasant and nearer intimacy with the fair, and will seek a welcome to their firesides and parlors with matters expressly written and selected for their instruction and entertainment. The editorial direction of the publication is confided to experienced and competent hands; and arrangements have been made for the earliest receipt of Parisian fashions, and phases of fashion, together with all the choice periodicals of the French, English, and Scottish capitals. An extensive correspondence will also be maintained with the different cities, towns, watering-places, and other fashionable resorts of the Union, and eminent female pens, native and foreign, will enrich the columns of the work. Aside from these qualities, it will possess the characteristics of a literary journal of the first class. We predict for 'The Ladies' Gazette' a marked success.

LEGAL SCIENCE. — A very useful volume, and one which supplies an important desideratum in every citizen's library, has recently been issued by Mr. JOHN S. VOORHIES, Nassau-street. It is entitled 'An Introduction to Legal Science,' and is a concise and familiar treatise on such legal topics as are earliest read by the law-student, which should be generally taught in the higher seminaries of learning, and understood by every citizen as a part of a general and business education. A concise dictionary of law terms and phrases makes the volume complete. The author, SILAS JONES, Esq., has fully sustained his design, which was, to produce a book which could be both read and studied, not merely by those designed for the legal profession, but by those also who desire to give such attention to the leading topics of law as belong to general and business education. The writer has divested his work of adscititious technicality and dryness; has selected and arranged his subjects with care, and made the whole as general in its character as comported with accuracy and clearness. The book, in short, is an excellent one, and cannot fail to become widely disseminated.

THE POETS AND POETRY OF AMERICA. — By RUFUS W. GRISWOLD. Philadelphia: CAREY AND HART. This is one of the most splendid books ever published in the United States, both as regards its typography and its embellishments. It embraces selections from about eighty authors, whom Mr. GRISWOLD regards as POETS, with well-written and judicious biographical and critical notices, beside a large number of metrical compositions 'by various authors,' in an appendix, and an interesting historical introduction, in which are given specimens of the writings of the ante-revolutionary bards; the MATHERS, the WIGGLESWORTHS, the BYLES's, and their contemporaries, whose poems were as poetical as their names. The volume is a large octavo, of some five hundred and fifty pages, and is embellished with beautifully-engraved portraits of BRYANT, DANA, HALLECK, LONGFELLOW, and SPRAGUE, all from original pictures, recently painted by INMAN, EOTY, THOMPSON, VER BRYCK, and HARDING. 'The Poets and Poetry of America' must take its place in every well-selected library as a standard book. We shall speak of it more particularly hereafter.

AGRICULTURAL CHEMISTRY. — Eight Lectures on Agricultural Chemistry and Geology, delivered by JAMES F. W. JOHNSTON, Esq., before the Durham (England) Agricultural Society and Farmer's Club, have just been published in a neat volume from the press of Messrs. WILEY AND PUTNAM. The lectures treat of the organic and inorganic elements and parts of plants; the nature of manures; the results of vegetation, etc., etc. In the deeper interest which the noble science of agriculture is every where exciting among us, we foresee a flattering presage of the circulation and usefulness of this little volume.

NEW-YORK DEAF AND DUMB INSTITUTION.— We are indebted to the worthy Principal, Mr. PEET, for a copy of the Twenty-third Annual Report of the New-York Deaf and Dumb Institution, and rejoice to find that noble and philanthropic establishment in a most flourishing condition. Its numbers and its means have increased; mechanical pursuits diversify the employments and enjoyments of many of the pupils, while they add to the general health, and contribute to the wants of the institution; cheerful recreations are literally allowed; and yet the system of instruction is most advantageously pursued, as is clearly evident from the details before us, and especially from the extraordinary examples of improvement afforded in the uncorrected compositions of the scholars. We join cordially in the hope expressed by the board of directors that the time is not far distant when every deaf-mute in the State, of suitable age and capacity, will be placed in the institution; and that not one of these children of misfortune will be found growing up in the midst of a civilized and christian community, in ignorance of the laws of GOD and man.

'SCHMUCKER'S MENTAL PHILOSOPHY.'— The BROTHERS HARPER have published, in the enduring form of Mr. ANTHON's classics, a volume entitled 'Pachychology, or Elements of a new System of Mental Philosophy, on the Basis of Consciousness and Common Sense; designed for Colleges and Academies.' By S. S. SCHMUCKER, Professor of Christian Theology in the Theological Seminary, Gettysburg, Penn. We have not found leisure to peruse the volume, but the author, 'it is believed, has presented a more faithful and intelligible map of the human mind than those heretofore in use, and one which will tend to make perspicuous a subject hitherto proverbially abstruse and obscure, and which will exert a salutary influence upon the great interests of fundamental Christianity.' Such we may hope will be the result; but we would respectfully ask, what beneficial influence can be expected to result from the writings of a gentleman who comes before the public under the portentous name of SCHMUCKER!

DUTIES ON BOOKS.— We have received from an esteemed friend in the United States' Senate a copy of a 'Memorial' of FRANCIS LIEBER, praying a modification of the tariff in regard to the duties on books, which was ordered to be published by the committees on finance and printing. The grounds for the petition of the memorialist are so forcibly and succinctly put, that we shall avail ourselves of another occasion to do more elaborate justice to them than our leisure and limits will now permit. To our mind they are alike conclusive and irrefragible. We were struck with the truth of the following remark touching the influence of Magazines: 'They form,' says Mr. LIEBER, 'an important and characteristic element of our period, to which the future historian will be as assuredly obliged to turn, if he wishes truly to understand our age, as we must turn to the pamphlet in order to understand the times of CROMWELL. They furnish an opportunity for discussions too deep and serious for daily journals, and yet too short to cast them in the form of separate books. Their usefulness requires rapid and general diffusion.'

THE NEW WORLD: MR. ALDRICH.— JAMES ALDRICH, Esq. has become associated with Mr. PARK BENJAMIN, in the editorship of the 'New World.' Mr. ALDRICH is an accomplished poet, as our own pages have frequently borne witness; but our readers may not also be aware that he is an admirable prose writer and a judicious critic. He is both, however; and being so, can hardly fail to add largely even to the large attractions of the large 'New World.' One good thing has certainly already resulted from his connection with this journal. Without any lessening of its interest, the senior Editor has gained the necessary leisure to produce a most successful play at the Park Theatre, which has done more toward routing our metropolitan blue-devils out of house and home than any thing we have had since the days of 'poor POWER.' It has been a benevolent physical agent, that same 'Fiscal Agent' of Mr. BENJAMIN's.

THE 'MOTHERS' MONTHLY JOURNAL.'— We have already mentioned in terms of deserved praise the 'MOTHERS' MONTHLY JOURNAL,' published at Utica, (N. Y.,) and edited by Mrs. E. C. ALLEN; but the increasing merits of the work; the good taste, sound sense, and indefatigable exertions of the lady under whose charge it is placed; lead us again to say that this entertaining, useful, and withal cheap little publication deserves a wide acceptance at the hands of American mothers. The numbers for February and March have been read in a little family that we wot of, with unalloyed satisfaction and pleasure. 'Who are the Educated?' from the pen of the Editor, in the first-named issue, is a well-reasoned and effective essay. The writer will find her views strikingly enforced in the story of 'Edward Alford and his Play-fellow,' in the present number.

PARLOR MELODIES.— Messrs. HARPER AND BROTHERS and Mr. GEORGE A. PETERS have issued a large and well-printed quarto volume, containing music, original and selected, for the piano-forte and organ, with several tunes for the harp and guitar; adapted to a series of original, moral and religious songs, mainly from the pleasant pen of WILLIAM COTTER, Esq., the whole arranged and edited by Mrs. M. R. LLOYD and Miss M. E. BAILEY. These melodies are published with a special view to enlarge the hitherto limited stock of sacred or serious music for the piano-forte; and, with the 'Southern Harp,' an excellent work of a kindred description, will enable parents to place in the hands of their daughters at a small expense a great number of tunes, of standard excellence, with words adapted that are entirely unexceptionable in sentiment.

A NATIONAL BANK.— An old citizen, an older merchant, and a friend on whose judgment we have been long accustomed to place great reliance, has highly lauded to us a pamphlet which has been laid upon our table, from the press of Mr. W. E. DEAN, Ann-street, entitled 'A National Bank, or No Bank; an Appeal to the Common Sense of the People of the United States, especially of the Laboring Classes.' The author is Mr. JOHN R. HURD, of this city, a gentleman whose years and experience, not less than his evident ability, entitle him to be heard with no common attention upon the subjects of which he treats.

'THE VIGIL OF FAITH AND OTHER POEMS' is the title of a volume after the manner externally of LONGFELLOW's delightful and popular books, which has but recently appeared, from the pen of CHARLES F. HOFFMAN, Esq., and the press of Mr. SAMUEL COLMAN. The poem which gives the title to the work is an Indian tale of interest, and includes many graceful and beautiful limnings from nature, upon which the writer looks with the eye of a poet and a lover. The space we have elsewhere devoted to a similar work from another pen, is our apology for not lessening the variety of this department of the KNICKERBOCKER by a kindred notice of the volume before us. The 'other poems' of the collection have already appeared in print, and won the favorable suffrages of the public.

'CHAPTERS ON CHURCH-YARDS.' — Messrs. WILEY AND PUTNAM have published a very neat volume, containing the admirable 'Chapters upon Church-Yards' by Miss CAROLINE BOWLES, now Mrs. ROBERT SOUTHEY. We read them early in the month with great satisfaction, and *thought* our notes had been reduced to form for the present number; until, when it was too late, we ascertained that we had forgotten them altogether. We can therefore only warmly commend these 'Chapters' to our readers, without assigning more particularly the why and the wherefore.

'THOUGHTS ON MORAL AND SPIRITUAL CULTURE,' from the pen of Mr. R. C. WATERSTON, of Boston, will commend itself for many merits to our readers. It has received high praise from the 'North-American Review' and the 'Christian Examiner,' and deserves it all. We can only regret that the late hour at which we receive it prevents our rendering it elaborate justice. We may allude to it more at large in a subsequent issue. Messrs. CROCKER AND RUGGLES, and HILLIARD, GRAY AND COMPANY, are the Boston publishers.

THE LATE MISS LUCY HOOPER. — Mr. SAMUEL COLMAN, John-street, has in press and will soon publish a small volume containing choice selections from the writings of the gifted and lamented poetess, Miss LUCY HOOPER, accompanied by a brief memoir of her life. The work will find friends where the writer found them, and many more with the general public.

*** NOTICES of several books and other publications, including 'The Climate of the United States,' 'Philosophy of Mind,' 'The Lecturer,' etc., arrived too late for consideration in the present issue.

THE KNICKERBOCKER.

Vol. XIX.   MAY, 1842.   No. 5.

FRAGMENT FROM THE MSS. OF CAGLIOSTRO.

THE PARADISE UPON EARTH.

THE most profound wisdom and the habit of serious occupation cannot always preserve us from superstition, nor from those absurd illusions and singular fancies which are the result of this feebleness of the human understanding.   One of the most learned Italians of modern times was without doubt Doctor Romati, a man of an honorable and elevated character, and always distinguished for the most scrupulous veracity. I pray all his compatriots and mine to reconcile this if possible with the details of his adventure near Salerno, a recital which he has made to many persons worthy of faith, and of which I have taken notes under his own dictation.   One sees in it, if not a succession of marvellous facts, at least the effect of an illusion entirely inexplicable, and of a strange preöccupation of the mind.   It is worthy of notice that Doctor Romati has never varied in any details of the same history, and that during his residence at Naples he always alluded to it with the same air and tone of sorrowful resignation.   Here then is the doctor's recital, as he made it to me one day at the Palace Spinelli, in presence of Don Mario Caraffa de Moliterno, and of the Princess de Belmonte Pignatelli Née Spinellá, sister of the Duke of that name, and to the correctness of which these two illustrious persons will not refuse to attest if desired.

'You know,' said he, 'that I call myself Giulio Romati.   The Signor Don Marco Romati della Romata, my father, was unquestionably the most celebrated lawyer of Palermo, and consequently of all Sicily.   He was strongly attached as you may well believe to a profession which procured him honor and emolument at the same time ; but he loved not less the study of philosophy, to which he devoted all the time he could spare from his judicial occupations.

'I may say without boasting that I have followed in the footsteps of my father, for I was already doctor *in utroque* at the age of twenty. I do not tell you this out of vanity, but because having to relate to you a surprising adventure, I would not have you believe me an incapable or foolishly credulous man. I am so far from being superstitious, that magic, the cabalistic art, and astrology are perhaps the only sciences to which I have not cared to devote myself, while I applied to all others with such indefatigable ardor and such continued application as seriously to affect my health. In consequence, my father exacted from me a promise to travel, forbidding my return before the lapse of four years. I had a great deal of trouble to tear myself from my library, my laboratory and my observatory. But obedience was imperative; and I no sooner found myself *en route* than strength and appetite returned, and I already began to taste of the pleasure one experiences in viewing strange scenes for the first time.

'Many people know more of the entire world than they do of their own country. I would not that any one had to reproach me with such a contradiction; and I commenced by visiting the wonders which nature has spread in our isle with such profusion. Instead of following the usual route from Palermo to Messina, I passed by Castra Nuovo, Colsonizese, spent some time in traversing the mountain, and finally descended on the side of Catania.

'Thus far my journey had been but a party of pleasure; but at Reggio the enterprise assumed a more serious aspect. A famous bandit named Zambucco desolated Calabria, and the sea was covered with Tripolitan pirates. I knew not how to reach Naples; and if a feeling of shame had not deterred me, I would willingly have retraced my steps toward the *paterno nido*. I had been thus detained eight days at Reggio, when one evening, after having walked a long time upon the sands, I seated myself upon a piece of rock in a solitary place to meditate on my future proceedings. Here I was suddenly accosted by a man of noble figure, closely enveloped in a scarlet mantle, who seated himself by my side, and said abruptly: 'The Doctor Romati is doubtless occupied with some problem in algebra or alchemy.'

''Not at all,' I replied; 'Doctor Romati would go to Naples, and the problem which embarrasses him is to know how he can escape the band of Signor Zambucco.'

''Signor Don Giulio,' said the unknown, 'your talents already do honor to your country, and I doubt not you will become the glory of Sicily, when the travels you have undertaken shall have extended the sphere of your knowledge. Zambucco is too gallant a man to wish to arrest you in so noble an enterprise. Take these red plumes, put the largest in your hat, make your people wear the rest, and depart in security. He who speaks to you is that same Zambucco whom you fear so much; and that you may not doubt it, behold the symbols of my profession;' as he spoke he half opened his mantle and disclosed a belt filled with pistols and daggers. He then saluted me respectfully and disappeared.

'The well-known character of Zambucco inspired me with entire confidence in the assurances he had given me. I returned without inquietude to my inn, made all my preparations, and accompanied by an escort of muleteers left Reggio at day-break on the following morning. I was no sooner out of sight of the town, than I perceived at a distance a portion of Zambucco's band, who seemed to act as my escort, and who were relieved at regular intervals during the entire route; and you may well believe I could not retain any uneasiness.

'We were not more than two days' journey from Naples, when the fancy took me to turn from my road to pass by Salerno. This may appear to you a natural enough curiosity; but I am convinced that some unaccountable fatality drew me to make that unhappy excursion. In pursuance of this plan we quitted the high-way at Monte Brugio, and conducted by a villager entered into the most savage country that it is possible to imagine. Mountainous, rocky, and entirely barren, it seemed a fit abode for all manner of evil spirits; and if I had not been drawn onward by the fatality I have mentioned, its first aspect would have been sufficient to deter me. It was toward the close of the second day that I perceived upon the top of one of the mountains a vast edifice, which my guide informed me was called Lo Monto or Lo Castello by the neighboring villagers. He added that it was entirely ruined and tenantless, except by a few Franciscan monks, who had erected a sort of chapel with some cells in the interior; and he hinted mysteriously that strange stories were told about the ruins, and strange noises often heard there, which caused them to be shunned by all but their pious inhabitants. I asked if we passed near the chateau, and he said, 'Yes, within musket-shot of it.'

'During this conversation the sky had become covered with dark clouds, and toward nightfall a frightful storm burst upon us. Unhappily we found ourselves then upon a part of the mountain which afforded no shelter. The guide told me he knew of a cavern where we might be sheltered from the storm, but that the road to it was very difficult. However, I determined to venture; but hardly had we entered on a narrow path which scarcely left room for more than one to pass between the rocks and the precipice, when a heavy thunder-stroke startled my mule, and we rolled together a distance of several yards. I was able however to seize a branch of maple in my descent; and getting a firm hold, I shouted loudly for my travelling companions, but received no reply.

'The flashes of lightning succeeded each other with so much rapidity, that by their light I was enabled to distinguish the objects which surrounded me, and to advance by the aid of the wild vines and roots to a place of security. This was a cavern which, not bordering on any beaten track, I judged could not be the one to which my guide had had the intention of conducting me. The heavy rain, wind and thunder succeeded each other without interruption. I shivered under my wet clothes, and must have been some three hours in this disagreeable situation, when I suddenly caught sight of flambeaux wandering about in the bottom of the valley, and heard cries which I supposed came from my people. With all my remaining strength I shouted in answer; and after a short interval a young man of good appearance entered the cavern, followed by several valets, some of whom carried flambeaux and others bundles which seemed to contain clothes.

'The young man saluted me respectfully, and said: ' Signore Doctore, we belong to l'illustrissima Principessa di Monte Salerno. Your guide from Monte Brugio told us that you were lost in the mountains, and we seek for you by order of the Princess.   Put on these dry clothes, I pray you, and follow us to the chateau.'

''How!' replied I; 'would you make me pass the night in the midst of the rubbish and under the ruined vaults of that great chateau which is on the summit of the mountain?'

''Reässure yourself, Dr. Romati,' said the young man, smiling; 'you will see a superb palace.'

'Concluding that some Neapolitan princess had made her habitation in the mountains, I changed my clothes, and followed the young man who had been sent to guide me.

'To my surprise we arrived almost immediately before a portico of variegated marble, of which the architecture appeared to me to be in the style of Bramante; but as the flambeaux did not illuminate the rest of the edifice, I cannot give you any description of it.   The young man left me at the foot of a magnificent stair-case, which I ascended, and was received at the top by a lady of a fine and commanding figure, who said with an air of infinite politeness: 'Signor Romati, Madame la Princesse of Monte Salerno has charged me to make you welcome to her castle.'

'I replied to her that if one could judge of a princess by her lady of honor, I must have an exceedingly agreeable idea of that illustrious person.   The lady was indeed of a most perfect beauty, with something in her manners and physiognomy, a certain mixture of simplicity with a natural air of greatness and proud security, which induced me to imagine her at the first glance the princess herself.   I remarked that she was dressed in the style of the portraits of the sixteenth century, but concluded such might be the costume of the Neapolitan ladies.   I had learned from an Italian philosopher that in the case of costume nothing is entirely new, and I concluded that the elégantes of Naples had revived the ancient modes.

'We traversed first a vestibule, which appeared grand in its proportions and decorations; but all I could remark of it in passing through was the columns and pilasters of a single shaft, in the yellow variegated marble of Spain, with large vases, urns, groups of statues, and candelabras, in bronze of the most beautiful material and in the finest style. Loving architecture and all the linear arts with passion, the indifference or the precipitation of my conductress caused me great discomfort.   Still hurrying on, I caught a glimpse in the same way of a beautiful salle-du-dais, or saloon of the throne, which opened upon the same vestibule by means of a large and high-arched arcade, which was only closed by a barrier of gilded carving about breast-high.   Within the saloon, according to usage, was a throne of velvet, with its embroideries, its fringes and its plumes of feathers; a long suite of family portraits; coats-of-arms on the stained-glass windows; and trophies of armor, with banners and emblazoned pennons.

'After having again exchanged a few polite phrases with my beautiful companion, she introduced me into a saloon where all was in massive silver.   The pavement was formed of large octagonal slabs in silver, alternately frosted and burnished.   The walls were covered with tapestry of silver damask, of which the ground-work was polished and the figures in unwrought silver. The dome was sculptured in slabs corresponding to the pavement, and the silver lustres, the braziers, the perfuming pans, and all the other furniture were ornamented with the most rich and elaborate goldsmith's work. The uniformity of the metal was agreeably relieved by medals and medallions in the precious green-stone of Armenia, each representing one of the most famous personages that the territory of Salerno had produced.

''Signor Romati,' said the lady, ' why stop so long to examine this apartment, which is but an ante-chamber for the accommodation of the footmen, valets, and other livery-servants of the princess?' I could not conceal my surprise at the view of such magnificence, and we traversed yet another saloon, a little resembling the first, except that it was lined with silver-gilt in arabesques and flower-work of gold shaded in three colors.

''This apartment,' said the lady, ' is a first-saloon belonging to the servants of honor, the major-domo, the pages, the gentlemen and first officers of the chateau. You will not see much gold and silver in the apartments inhabited by the princess, and you can judge,' added she, smiling, ' of the purity, the elegance and simplicity of her taste, by the style and ornaments of her bed-chamber.'

'Before reaching the bed-chamber the lady opened a side-door, and I followed her into another apartment, entirely lined with flowered jasper. This was the dining-saloon of the palace. At two thirds of its height, extending entirely around, was a bas-relief of the most finished workmanship, and the material of which seemed to me to be the white Pentelic marble. This saloon was also adorned with magnificent buffets, covered with dishes, ewers, and large gilded basins, engraved with the arms of the city of Florence. Other cup-boards were loaded with vases and cups of oriental agate, aventurine and rock-crystal ; and all these precious monuments of the age of the Medicis were richly carved in Venetian goldsmith's work, or adorned with the admirable enamelled carvings of Benvenuto Cellini.

'On leaving this magnificent salle-à-manger, we reëntered the saloon of the officers, and from thence arrived at the hall of reception.

''Par example,' said the lady, ' it is permitted to remark the beauty of this chamber.'

My eyes had already fallen upon the pavement, and I could not withdraw them. The ground-work was of lapis-lazuli, incrusted with fine stones in mosaic of Florence, of which a single table has always cost several years of work and many millions of sequins. The general intention of the design was regular ; but in examining the compartments, one was surprised to see that the greatest variety in the details was not inconsistent with the perfect symmetry of the whole. In one compartment were flowers, in another, shells ; farther off, butterflies and birds ; while the most solid and brilliant materials were employed in the imitation of the most dazzling productions of nature. I remember that in the centre of this mosaic pavement was a represention of a casket filled with all kinds of precious stones, and ornamented with strings of pearl, the whole as boldly relieved and seemingly as real as in the most beautiful tables of the Pitti Palace.

' 'Dr. Romati,' said the lady, ' if you stop thus long at every step of this pavement, we shall never finish.'

'My eyes were now directed toward a picture which represented Hercules at the feet of Omphale. The figure of Hercules was assuredly by Michael Angelo, and in that of the female I recognized the pencil of Raphael. The other pictures of the same saloon seemed to me much more remarkable and more perfect than all the chefs-d'œuvres I had most admired until then. The tapestry, being velvet embroidered in gold, and of a sombre purple, displayed the paintings to the best advantage, and brought out the colors with inconceivable effect. I was in a state bordering on ecstacy while examining the antique statues which decorated the angles of this admirable saloon. One was truly the celebrated Cupid of Phidias, of which Pythagoras counselled the destruction; another the Faun of the same artist; a third the true Venus of Praxiteles, of which that of Medicis is but a copy; and the fourth the Ganymede, brought from the trenches of Salerno, and at present in the Cesarini palace. Around the saloon I perceived French furniture inlaid with boulle-work; but instead of being mounted with bronze, it was garnished with the beautiful gold inlaid work of India, and enriched with antique cameos. The cabinets contained sets of gold medals, caskets with collections of engraved stones, Roman trinkets, jewels of the middle ages, and Gothic manuscripts of the rarest kinds.

' 'It is here that the princess loves to pass her evenings,' said my charming cicerone; 'and this collection furnishes ample material for most interesting entertainments. Here is the bed-chamber of Madame la Princesse,' added she with an air of simplicity not altogether free from affectation.

The form of this chamber was octagonal, four of the sides forming alcoves, each containing a large bed. I saw neither ceiling nor floor, every part being elegantly covered with India muslin of such fineness that one might imagine it a light mist imprisoned and embroidered by the hand of Arachne herself.

' 'Why four beds?' demanded I of my conductress.

' 'That the princess may change when they become heated,' replied she; 'or when she finds herself unable to sleep.'

' 'But why are the beds so large?'

' 'It is,' replied the lady negligently, ' that the women of the princess may remain sometimes to talk with her before sleeping.' But let us pass into the bathing-room.

'This was a rotunda, the panels lined with mother-of-pearl, with carved borders of the same, the cornice and mouldings formed of glittering shells mixed with branches of coral and stalactites as white as alabaster. I remarked that this room received light from above only; the opening in the ceiling being filled by an immense glass globe containing myriads of the beautiful gold-fish of China. In the centre of the saloon, instead of a bath, was a circular basin, around which upon a circle of sea-moss were placed the most beautiful shells of the ocean, and prisms of precious stones mixed with the blood-red coral of Hindostan.

' So enchanted was I with the the wondrous magnificence of Monte

Salerno that I could not help exclaiming aloud : 'Paradise is outdone !
Paradise is no longer the most beautiful abode !'

' 'Paradise !' cried the lady, wildly ; 'who talks of Paradise ?   Here,
here ! — speak not, but follow me : let us go hence ; follow me !'

'I obeyed in wondering silence, and we found ourselves in an aviary
of which the wires were gold, filled with all the most splendid birds of
the tropics, and the finest singers of our own country.   We trod upon
a carpet of turf, fresh and green, and sprinkled with violets ; above and
around, clustering vines and flowering shrubs cast a grateful shade,
and filled the air with delicious fragrance ; while the pleasant sound of
falling water, as it trickled from a lion's mouth of green bronze and
filled a richly sculptured basin, mingled with the chants of the birds,
and made up a concert of ravishing harmony.   In the midst of this
charming spot a table was spread with every thing that could please
the sense and gratify the palate, and well provided with aliments prohibited during times of abstinence, which I determined not to touch.

' 'How can one dream of eating in an abode thus divine ?' said I to
my beautiful conductress.   'I cannot consent to partake of your hospitality, unless you will have the goodness to narrate to me the history of
the happy and noble possessor of so many marvels.'

'The lady smiled a gracious assent, and commenced as follows :
'I must first inform you, Signor Romati, that the princes of Monte
Salerno were issues of the sovereign counts of Salerno.   The last of
the title,' continued she, with a little air of self-sufficiency and satisfied
vanity, 'was grandee of Spain, at the creation of Charles the Fifth,
grand-admiral, grand-overseer of the high-ways, hereditary sword-bearer,
and holy standard-bearer of Sicily, beside uniting in his own person
almost all the grand offices of the crown of Naples.   Among the titled
officers in his service, the Marquis de Spinaverde, his captain of the
chase, possessed in common with his wife, tire-woman to the princess,
his most entire confidence.   The only daughter of the prince was
hardly ten years of age when her mother died.   At the same epoch the
Spinaverdes quitted the house of their master ; the husband to take the
management of some fiefs, and the wife to preside at Monte Salerno
over the education of Elfrida, the young princess ; and my first lesson
in self-control was an order to all the vassals as well as to the domestics of the house, to yield without resistance to all my wishes.'

' 'To all *your* wishes, Madame ?'

' 'Have the goodness not to interrupt me,' replied she, with some ill
humor.   'I put the submission of my women to all sorts of proof, by
giving contradictory orders of which they could never execute the half.
I punished them by striking, scratching, and sticking pins in their arms,
and they finished by flying from the chateau, while La Spinaverde
supplied me with others, who also deserted me in the same manner and
for the same cause.

' 'At this time the prince of Monte Salerno fell sick, and they conducted me to Naples.   I saw but little of him ; les Spinaverdes never
quitted him, and he died without having had time to dream of his
affairs of conscience.   By his will he had named the marquis as my
tutor and the administrator of all my possessions.   The funeral of the

prince occupied us during six weeks, and at the end of that time we returned to Monte Salerno, where I recommenced beating, scratching and pinching my women. Four years rolled rapidly away in these innocent amusements. The marquis assured me constantly that I was perfectly right; that all the world was made to obey me; and that those who did not obey me quick and well, merited all sorts of punishment.

''One evening, when all my women had left me one after the other, I found myself reduced to the necessity of being my own tire-woman, and wept with rage. 'Calm yourself, dear and sweet Princess!' said La Marquise; 'wipe your beautiful eyes. I will undress you this evening, and to-morrow you shall have five or six women, with whom I hope you will be better satisfied.

''The next day, on my awakening, my gouvernante introduced the new attendants, who were all very handsome but uncommonly large; and I experienced on seeing them a feeling of emotion for which I was utterly unable to account. There was in their faces an expression of courage, of energy and passion, which imposed upon me for the first time a species of restraint. However, I hastened to familiarize myself with them; I embraced them one after another; and promised them they should never be either scolded or beaten. Indeed, although they made many an awkward mistake in undressing me, and even disobeyed me, I had never the courage to anger myself about it.'

''But Madame,' said I to the princess, 'these grand persons were perhaps *boys*.'

'She replied with a tone of dignified coldness: 'Doctor Romati, I have requested you not to interrupt me, and it is your duty to remember it.' After some minutes of silence, she resumed with an affected air of innocent frankness and playful gayety: 'I remember that on the day I reached my sixteenth year, the Viceroy of the Two Sicilies, the Ambassador of Spain and the Count Duke de Guadarama came to pay me a visit; the latter to demand me in marriage, and the two others to support his pretensions. The young duke was very handsome, and I cannot deny that he appeared to me very agreeable. Toward evening they proposed a walk in the park. Hardly had we arrived there, when a furious bull rushed from a thicket and made directly toward us. The duke ran to meet him, holding in one hand his extended mantle and having his sword in the other. So furious was the animal's onset that he ran directly upon the extended weapon, which entered his heart, and he fell dead at my feet. I believed myself indebted for my life to the valor and dexterity of the young Spaniard; but the next day La Spinaverde assured me that the bull had been expressly posted there by the attendants of the duke, that he might have the opportunity of executing this piece of gallantry *à la mode de son pays*. I was highly indignant at the trick, and refused his hand.

''La Spinaverde appeared enchanted with my resolution, and seized this occasion to inspire me with the love of independence, and to expatiate on its advantages. I easily understood all I should hazard in giving myself a master; and to fortify my resolution and retain me at Monte Salerno, she caused to be brought from my palace at Naples and adjusted here all the beautiful things which you so much admire.'

"Ah!' cried I, 'she has perfectly succeeded, Madame, and this beautiful abode should be called the *Paradise* upon earth!'

'This time the princess rose hastily from her seat, saying: 'Romati, I ordered you not to make use of an expression which is insupportable to me. Paradise!' repeated she with a convulsive laugh; 'it is well to talk of Paradise! Yes, it is well; but you shall remember MY Paradise! And here she commenced pacing the apartment with an air of distraction, laughing convulsively, and uttering incoherent exclamations. This scene became painful, and caused me much embarrassment, since I was utterly at a loss to account for her emotion, or why so natural an expression should cause her so much distress. Thinking it best to remain silent however, I offered no apology, and this strange woman gradually recovered her self-possession. She then made a sign to me to follow her, which I did; and we passed through a massive door, which she opened with great effort and many expressions of impatience, into a species of vaulted gallery, where a most beautiful spectacle met my eye.

'Not far from the door, and arranged in a manner to be seen to the best advantage, were two peacocks of enamelled gold, the plumage formed of light slender sheaves of yellow brilliants, and the spread tails set with precious stones, suitable in color and size to the rich plumage of these birds. Parroquets and other South-American birds, of which the feathers were represented by minute emeralds, were placed amid the branches of trees of solid gold, while beautiful figures of slaves in black jasper, adorned with collars of pearl and hung round with the most beautiful gems of the Orient, presented on golden plates bouquets of diamonds, cherries of ruby, plums of topaz, and grapes sculptured from blocks of amethyst. Vases of porphyry were stationed around, filled to overflowing with golden money of every age and country, and a thousand other marvellous curiosities collected together in this new Elo Helias, the contemplation of which filled my mind with wonder almost amounting to stupefaction.

'The charming Elfrida had seated herself upon a pile of embroidered cushions, where she now invited me to place myself by her side. After having conversed with me for some time with surprising affability, she began to look at me with eyes so passionate, and to say such flattering things upon the beauty of my figure and the freshness of my complexion, that I could not help suspecting some trick, or that the princess wished to amuse herself at my expense. I soon found however that to ridicule me was not her intention, since she permitted herself to make use of singular familiarities, and I was utterly at a loss to account for her good opinion and my own good fortune. While conversing thus, I perceived that although she had perfectly white teeth, her gums and tongue were absolutely *black*, and I experienced a feeling of mysterious inquietude, a sort of unaccountable discomfort and disgust for my companion, which prevented me from responding in any way to her civilities. It must not be forgotten that it was the night of holy Thursday. Suddenly the idea entered my head to repeat once again the word which had produced such extraordinary effects on my companion, and it was my unhappy fate to yield to this improper curiosity, a weakness which you will see I was not long in repenting.

' ' Madame,' said I, in a tone of resolute determination, ' excuse me if I assure you once again, that you have shown me the heavens opened, and *Paradise* upon earth ! '

' To my astonishment the princess smiled upon me with the utmost mildness and benevolence. ' You are too good,' replied she ; ' and to put you in the way of knowing and appreciating more entirely the delights of Monte Salerno, I will make you acquainted with the six companions of whom I told you.'

' While saying this, she took from her side a key, and proceeded to open a large chest, covered with black velvet and bound with clasps of silver, which stood in a recess at the farthest extremity of the apartment. Hardly had she raised the cover, when to my horror and dismay an enormous skeleton leaped forth and threw itself toward me with a threatening air. Although it cleared in one bound the space which separated us, I had time to draw my sword and stand on the defensive ; but the skeleton tearing from himself his left arm, which made a formidable weapon, assailed me with inconceivable fury. The combat was fearful, I assure you. I defended myself with the pommel of my sword, in a way to break his carcass and utterly destroy the economy of his bones ! But just as I was flattering myself with the hope of victory, behold ! another skeleton rushed precipitately from the infernal chest, tore off a rib from his comrade, and commenced giving me most deadly blows upon the head ! While engaging with this new assailant, I saw a third creeping out with an air of perfidious precaution, and coming slyly round, he encircled me with his fleshless arms, which seemed to tighten and tighten around me until I could scarcely breathe, while he wreathed his head over my shoulder and gave me an abominable bite upon the right cheek ! Figure to yourself the agreeable sensation of seeing and feeling yourself bitten by a *death's-head !* I had seized him by the throat, or rather vertebra, which I pressed with all my force, with the intention of decapitating him. He was the largest, the strongest, and most treacherous, and he had caused me the most embarrassment ; I hoped therefore in conquering him to be relieved from a combat which had already deprived me of my strength ; but seeing the discomfiture of their brother, the three remaining skeletons came to join the party, and not hoping to escape with honor from such an osteologic controversy, I suddenly abandoned my hold of my adversary, and turning toward the miserable woman who stood calmly by, I exclaimed : ' *Misericorde ! au nom de Dieu !* '

' She made a sign to her abominable servants to retire, and then turning to me with an air of malice, said : ' Go, and never forget what you have seen this night ! ' At the same time she seized me by the left arm, when I felt a burning pain, and fainted.

' I cannot tell you exactly how long I remained insensible. When I recovered consciousness, I found myself in the midst of what appeared to be a vast ruin, and heard distant chanting as of monks engaged in their exercises of devotion. In exploring the place, as well as my weakness would permit me, I came gradually nearer these sounds, and finally found my way into a small chapel, where some monks were reciting the service of St. Francis. The superior received me kindly, and conducted me into his cell, where I narrated to him all that had befallen me during the night. The holy man examined the wound in my face, and asked me if I did not also carry some mark on that part of my arm which the phantom had seized. I raised my sleeve, and there indeed were the marks, resembling a burn, of the five fingers of the frightful princess. The superior then took from a box a large parchment sealed with a golden seal. ' Here, my son,' said he, ' is the deed of our foundation, which, if you will read, will explain to you the wonders and horrors of the past night. I unrolled this pontifical chart, and read what follows:

' ' To the profound affliction of the angels and our paternal heart, it became known to us, as well as to our venerable brothers the cardinals of the Holy Roman Church, that by a spirit of pride and blindness, inspired by hell, Elfrida Cesarini of Monte Salerno vaunted herself of having here below the enjoyment and possession of *Paradise;* declaring with words of blasphemy and horrible outrages against the saints, that she denied and disbelieved in and would renounce the participation in the true Paradise, as it is promised in eternal life. Nevertheless, to the eternal confusion of the spirit of evil, on the night of Holy Thursday, the year of Salvation, M. VC. III. Induction IX., and of our Pontificate the Sixth, an earthquake destroyed her palace, and this unhappy one was buried beneath the ruins, with the abettors of her debaucheries, and the accomplices of her impiety. Having been informed by our dear sons, the arch-priest and arch-deacon of the Cathedral of Salerno, that the site of this palace has become the haunt of Satan, where wicked spirits dare to beset by lamentable fascinations not only strange travellers who visit the ruins, but also the faithful christian inhabitants of Monte Salerno: We, Alexander VI., servant of the servants of God, etc., etc., etc., declare and authorize the foundation of a priory in the enclosure of these same ruins, having given this at Rome in our pontifical palace of Saint Ange, and having sealed it with the ring of the Pæheur.'

'The superior told me that the appearances had become less frequent, and that they were generally renewed on the night of Holy Thursday. He counselled me to have a mass said, *Deo profundis*, which I did, and left soon, to continue my travels. I have never been afraid either of ghosts or skeletons, and I am no longer an object of their mystification; but the things I saw and felt during that night at Monte Salerno have left an impression which can never be effaced.'

In saying this, Dr. Romati raised his sleeve and showed us his arm, where was distinctly visible the form of the fingers of the princess and the marks of burning.

LINES TO A PATRIOTIC SLATTERN.

You ' love your country's mother earth; '
  In this I cannot doubt you :
The soil is rich ; and from your birth
  You 've carried it about you !

THE BALLAD OF SIR JAMES THE ROSS.

The following ballad, as far as I can discover, has not appeared in any collection of old Scottish poetry; and I am not sufficiently versed in the national popular poetry of Caledonia to decide whether it be ancient, or a modern imitation; founded on fact or a pure fiction. What inclines me to believe the former however is, that allusion is made to MARGARET, queen of JAMES IV. of Scotland, and the battle of Flodden, which would bring the incident on which the ballad is founded to about the year 1514 or 1515. As to topography, the poet has been sufficiently exact; Earl Buchan's domains lying partly in Aberdeenshire and partly in that of Banff, while Ross county is on the other side of the kingdom, bordering on the western sea and the Isle of Skye; and the men in the latter place could certainly not defend their master while in the former. This ballad was taken down from the recitation of a Scotch carpenter, who learnt it from hearing his mother sing it at her spinning-wheel in his youth. But I must beg pardon of the antiquary for the mutilated copy I present to him. My reciter's memory was so defective that some stanzas made nonsense; others he could give me only in the form of improper fractions; things which ought to have no place in poetical numbers, however appropriate in arithmetical.

Of all the northern Scottish chiefs,
  Of high and warlike name,
The bravest was Sir James the Ross,
  The knight of mickle fame.

His form was like the lofty fir
  That crowns the mountain broad,
And waving o'er his shoulders wide
  His locks of yellow flowed.

The chieftain of the brave clan Ross,
  That firm undaunted band,
Five hundred warriors drew their swords
  Beneath his high command.

The bloody fight thrice had he stood,
  Against the English king,
Ere two-and-twenty opening springs
  This blooming youth had seen.

The fair Matilda dear he loved,
  The maid of beauty rare :
Even Margaret on the Scottish throne
  Was never half so fair.

Long time he wooed, long she refused,
  With seeming scorn and pride ;
Yet oft her faithful eyes confessed
  The love her tongue denied :

At last, pleased with his well-tried faith,
  She allowed his tender claim ;
And vowed to him her virgin heart,
  And owned an equal flame.

Her father Buchan, cruel lord !
  Her passion disapproves,
And bids her wed Sir John the Græm ;
  So here must end their loves !

' My father's will must be obeyed,
  Though cruel the command ;
Some fairer maid, in beauty's bloom,
  May bless you with her hand.

'Forget forlorn Matilda's name;
   To seek her hand forbear;
And may that happiness be thine
   Which I may never share!'

'What do I hear? Is this thy vow?'
   Sir James the Ross replied:
'And will Matilda wed the Graem,
   Though sworn to be my bride?

'My sword shall sooner pierce my heart
   Than thine averted eyes;
No cowardly Graem of all the name
   Deserves so dear a prize!'

' 'T was but to try thy love I spake,
   I 'll ne'er wed man but thee:
My grave shall be my bridal bed,
   Ere Graem my husband be!'

They part. The sun was set, and from
   Behind his golden light
The small stars one by one looked out
   Upon the silent night.

Up started listening Donald Graem
   From behind a bush of thorn;
'Ho! turn thee, turn thee, beardless youth!
   He cries with furious scorn.

Ere turned about the fearless chief,
   Or ere his sword he drew,
False Donald's blade before his breast
   Had pierced his tartans through.

'This for my brother's slighted love,
   His wrongs sit on your arm;'
Three paces back the chief retired,
   To save himself from harm.

With sudden hand he raised his brand,
   And ere his foe could move,
Down through his brains and crashing bones
   His sharp-edged weapon drove.

Without a groan his traitor soul
   Deserts its breathless clay:
'So fall my foes!' cried valiant Ross,
   And stately rode away.

On through the deep greenwood he hied,
   And to Lord Buchan's hall;
Where under fair Matilda's bower
   He soft began to call:

'Art thou asleep, Matilda dear?
   Awake, my love! awake!
In haste thy luckless lover comes,
   A long farewell to take.

'For I have slain young Donald Graem,
 His blood is on my sword;
And far and distant are my men
 For to defend their lord.

'Across the Sound to Skye I 'm bound
 Where my two brothers bide,
They 'll raise each man of the brave Ross' clan,
 To combat on my side.'

'Oh, fly not yet!—a little while
 With me, till morning, stay;
For dark and dreary is the night,
 And dangerous is the way.

'All night I 'll watch you in the park,
 And my little foot-page send
To run and raise the Ross' clan,
 Their master to defend.'

Beneath a bush he laid him down,
 And wrapped him in his plaid:
While trembling in the moonshine mild
 At distance stood the maid.

Swift ran the page o'er hill and dale,
 Till in a lonely glen
He met the craven Sir John Graem,
 With twenty of his men.

'Where goest thou, little page?' he said;
 'So late who did thee send?'
'I run to raise the Ross' clan,
 Their master to defend.

'For he has slain young Donald Graem,
 His blood is on his sword;
And far and distant are his men
 For to assist their lord.'

'Oh say, where is he, my little page,
 I will thee well reward.'
'He sleeps within lord Buchan's park—
 Matilda is his guard.'

They pricked their steeds in furious mood,
 And scoured along the lea;
The rich lord Buchan's lofty towers
 Ere dawn of day they see.

Matilda stood without the gate;
 'Ah! lovely maiden! say,
Saw ye Sir James the Ross last night,
 Or did he pass this way?'

''T was yesterday noon,' Matilda said,
 Sir James the Ross passed by;
He pricked his swift steed furiously,
 And onward fast did hie.

'By this time he 's at Edinboro' town,
  If man and horse hold good ; '
'Your page then lied, who said he was
  Now sleeping in the wood.'

She wrung her hands, she tore her hair,
  'Oh, Ross ! thou art betrayed ! '
From the dewy grass uprose the Ross,
  And drew his bloody blade.

'Your sword last night my brother slew,
  His blood yet dims its shine ;
Before the rising of the sun
  Your blood shall reek on mine ! '

'You word it well,' the chief replied,
  'But deeds approve the man ;
Set by your men, and hand to hand
  We 'll try what valor can ! '

'Your boasting hides a coward heart,
  My weighty sword you fear,
Which shone in front at Flodden field,
  When yours kept in the rear.'

Forward the fearless chieftain strode,
  And dared him to the fight ;
The Graem gave back ; he feared his arm,
  For well he knew its might.

'On ! on ! my merry-men ! ' said the Graem,
  'Lay at him one and all ;
Here 's fifty pounds of the silver white
  For him that makes him fall ! '

'Neath Ross' arm the bravest four
  With their blood their tartans died ;
When behind him came the cowardly Graem,
  And stabbed him in the side.

'Alas ! ' cried he, 'that e'er a chief
  Of the bold clan Ross should rest
In a soldier's grave, with a wound behind,
  And no scar on his breast ! '

'Gainst seventeen armed men what could
  A single maiden do ?
The sword, yet warm, from his left side
  With frantic hand she drew.

She leaned the hilt upon the ground,
  She bared her snowy breast,
And side by side on the ruddy sod
  Ross and Matilda rest.

'Four of my men are gone,' said Graem,
  'And I 've lost a wealthy bride !
But Ross is dead — and that lucky stroke
  Saved fifty pounds beside ! '

Burlington, (Vt.,) March, 1842.   J. Rhyn Pierson.

LETTERS FROM ROME.

BY GEORGE WASHINGTON GREENE.

LETTER FIFTH.

THERE is perhaps no part of Rome which bears so impressive a record of the singular destiny of this wonderful city, as the walls. Of the original fortifications of its founder, not a vestige remains. There are but a few scattered fragments of the great work of Serverus; and although the line of the modern walls is the same with that which had been marked out by Aurelian, but a small portion of the walls themselves can be assigned with certainty to that emperor. It was in a moment of doubt and dismay that this line was drawn around the fabrics of the imperial city; and degraded as her citizens were, it must have been with a feeling of deep humiliation that they gave this fatal testimony to the withered majesty of the Roman name:

> —— 'Roma, Roma!
> Non sei più qual eri prima,'

was the melancholy strain that greeted the ears of Byron as he rode around the walls of Rome; and surely there is no spot where you feel so deeply the touching simplicity of this lament. On one side vineyards and gardens, here and there a villa, and from some higher points a glimpse of the Campagna and the solemn, unchanged mountains beyond; on the other, an unbroken circle of walls and gates and towers. In parts you can trace, in the firm regularity of the materials and construction, the age of Aurelian; a more careless hand betrays the hurried restoration of Honorius; and in the violated sanctity of tombs and monuments you read the triumph of a new religion. Some towers have fallen from age, and a screen of moss and ivy shades their dilapidated remains. Others were shaken by the battering-ram or overthrown in the first shock of a successful assault: and when the tempest of war had passed, a new defence was raised upon the foundation of the original structure. Then come the proofs of greater haste and an emergency yet more trying; shattered architraves, the rich volutes of a capital intermingled with blocks of square stone and broken bricks and tiles, hastily gathered and piled with trembling and unskilful hands. They are the work of Belisarius; the old and the young, women and children joining in the labor, and a Gothic army upon the heights of Tivoli ready to spring upon them before half of their fragile defence could be completed. Next follow the middle ages, century by century, in dark succession, each leaving some record of its passions and their unbridled license, till the milder rule of the pontiffs began a new series of repairs and inscriptions, from the rough initials of Nicholas the Fifth to the unrecorded labors of the reigning sovereign.

All the public acts of the ancients were consecrated by their connection with religious rites. Of peculiar solemnity were those observed upon the building of a new city. The leader of the colony held with his own hand the sacred plough. The coulter was of brass. It was drawn by an ox and a cow, and the colonists following the furrow, carefully turned inward the broken clods. At the spots designed for gates, the plough was raised and the ground left unbroken. A space on each side of the furrow distinguished by *cippi*, or blocks of stone or marble, was held sacred, and from its relative situation to the walk received the name of Pomærium. Within this, the augurs took their observations, and no profane hand dared to pollute it by building thereon. But although the original limits of the Pomærium were fixed by the line of the walls, this sacred circle might be enlarged upon the accession of new territories; and thus we find that while the walls of the city were left unchanged from the reign of Servius to that of Aurelian, the pomœeium was enlarged by several of those distinguished generals who by the success of their arms had extended the limits of the empire.

Such were the rites observed by Romulus in the foundation of Rome. Tacitus has preserved the current tradition of his own times upon the starting point and course of the founder, and modern archaiologists have established to their individual satisfaction the number and position of the original gates. The first wall of Romulus was confined to the Palatine, one only, and with the exception of the Capitoline the smallest, of the seven hills. The rapid increase of population during his own reign and under that of his immediate successors required a proportional enlargement of the fortifications of the city; and when Servius Tullius ascended the throne in the year 175 from the foundation, the greater part of the seven hills and intervening valleys were already covered with buildings. To protect these and give to the capital of his dominions a form and an aspect suited to its warlike character and increasing power, he enclosed it with new walls, and added upon the side most open to hostile aggression that celebrated rampart which still preserves his name. As these walls continued until the third century of the Christian era to form the sole defence of Rome, I trust that I shall not be accused of too great a propensity to dwell upon minute details, if I attempt to trace their course with as much accuracy as the nature of the subject will permit.

The description of Dyonissius must be the basis of every such attempt. Fortunately the point of view under which he has considered them is purely military, and hence his description is couched in terms which would seem to leave but little room for disputation. On one side a natural barrier was formed by the rapid current of the Tiber. It was on the banks of the river therefore that the line of the walls began; and their object being defence, they were carried along the crests of the hills, and wherever the nature of the ground permitted it, built upon rocks and precipices. On one side only this natural protection failed them, and there the want was supplied by the erection of a massive mound surmounted by a wall, and defended by a ditch thirty feet deep and one hundred wide in its narrowest parts. This gigantic barrier still remaining, the number of the hills enclosed being known, and their general characteristics, from the nature of the rocks of which they are composed, having suffered no material variation, the only question to be decided in order to establish their course with certainty is the question of their extent. This also is supplied by a passage of Dyonissius and confirmed by the corrected text of Pliny; the former giving us an approximative estimate of more than seven and a half miles, the latter fixing it positively at eight thousand two hundred paces,

With these data the question becomes as simple as a question of localities can be made. The theatres of Marcellus and Foro Olitorio are known to have been without the walls; the Ponte Rotto (Palatino) within. The course of the walls from the river to the capitol is thus ascertained: for it must have begun between the river and the bridge, and followed a line which our knowledge of the situation of the Foro Olitorio makes it easy to trace. In this short space there were three gates; the Flumertana near the river; the Carmentale at the foot of the capitol; and between them the Triumphalis. The direction of the streets, which has probably been subject to little or no change in this part of the city, assists in establishing the position both of the gates and the walls. Ascending the side of the Capitoline the wall wound around its summit, acquiring additional strength from the rocky and precipitous nature of the hill. A fragment of this primitive work may yet be seen behind the stables of the Caffarelli palace. The tomb of Bibulus upon the opposite side of the Capitoline marks the limits of the enclosure in this direction; for by a law of the twelve tables no tomb could be erected within the walls. Here too it is evident that an ancient street must have passed, and accordingly this is the spot near which archaiologists have agreed to place the Porta Ratumena. Traversing the valley now occupied by the imposing remains of the Forum of Trajan, they ascended the Quirinal close to the structures which were erected by that emperor as an ornament for his forum and a support for the hill. Their course along a large portion of the Quirinal is indicated by the foundations in the gardens of the Colonna and the northern walls of those of the Pope. The palace of the Prince Barberini stands upon the site of the Circus of Flora, which was without the walls; and here again the nature of the ground, with constant reference to the outline of Dyonissius, enables us to follow them as far as the gardens of Sallust, where another fragment intermingled with the pompous fabrics of the luxurious historian gives a positive proof of the correctness of our conjectures. Two gates, the Sanguale at the head of the actual ascent to the square of the Quirinal and the Salutare at that of the four fountains, preserved the communication with the Campus Martius, and country on this side. We now come to the 'Agger of Tullius,' which carries us round a large portion of the circumference, and one which, but for the preservation of this invaluable monument, could never have been ascertained. The position of Porta Collina, through which the Gauls made their fatal entry, is established by an opening near the commencement of the Agger, and that of the Esquilina is known to have been near its termination on the Esquiline Hill.

Mid-way between these extremities was another gate, which likewise took its name from the hill on which it stood, and was called the Viminal.

The next tract of wall, by which the Esquiline was united to the Cœlian, has given rise to some discussion, the nature of the ground admitting of the adoption of two lines of different extent. The variation however is but small, and later writers are nearly agreed even in the details. It is agreed also that in the valley between the Esquiline and Cœlian there must have been a gate, for the form of the ground testifies to its original use as an access to the city. Both Nibby and Canina concur in placing it near the church of S. S. Marcellino e Pietro, and giving it the name of Luerquentulana. But upon issuing from this valley and beginning the ascent of the Cœlian, we find it impossible to decide between the two antiquaries, one of whom comprehends the space now covered by the Basilica of St. Giovanni within his plan, while the other is no less positive in rejecting it. Following the crest of the Cœlian to St. Stefano Rotondo and Villa Mattei, we meet numerous traces of ancient works, some of which are supposed to have actually formed a part of the walls. Descending thence to the narrowest point of the valley that separates the Cœlian from the Aventine, we reach the spot marked out as the position of the Porta Capena. In their passage over the Aventine they passed the portion occupied by the church of S. Balbina; and here we again meet among fragments of more recent date some parts which may justly be assigned to the original wall. Other remains are found between S. Sabba and S. Prisca, near the valley that separates the false from the real Aventine; and at this point, climbing once more to the summit, they followed the brow of the hill to the modern Salara, girding it with a bulwark, which rising above the natural precipices would seem to have rendered that portion of the city impregnable. I have omitted to mention the gates of this line. The position of many of them is uncertain, and it is to positive and well ascertained facts that I wish as far as it is practicable to confine my attention. The porta Trigemina however is an exception, and is allowed to have stood upon the banks of the river not far from the Ponte Sublicio, thus occupying a position which corresponded to that of the Porta Flumentana upon the opposite side of the city.

Upon the right bank of the river, two curtains, ascending the steep side of the Janiculum, united the citadel of Æneus Martius to the fortifications of the city. An artificial dell behind the fountain of Aqua Paola shows with how much labor this fortress was separated from the rest of the hill, and how well that work was done which twenty-five hundred years of change have not been able to efface. A garden scented with perfumes of the clime covers a portion of the space marked out for blood and strife; and fronting the city, where the signal standard was displayed in full sight to the watchful multitude of the Campus Martius, the waters of an aqueduct rush through three broad canals with the deafening roar of a cataract.   o. w. o.

Via del Quirinale, 49, }
  July 21, 1841.   }

MY SISTER'S GRAVE.

I.

I sat beside my sister's grave,
Upon a grassy knoll,
And many cherished memories
Came crowding on my soul.
I saw her playing round the door
Of our own cottage home,
And heard her laugh; 't was long ago,
Ere I had learned to roam.

II.

Few were the summers she had seen,
That little sister fair,
But she was bright and beautiful —
Her glad heart free as air;
The world was but just opening then
In freshness to her sight,
And every flower and leaf she deemed
As lovely as the light.

III.

And often would she question me :
'Who made the trees, the earth?
Who colored all the flowers so well,
And gave the birds their birth?
Who made the grass grow by the brook,
Where many feet have trod?'
''T was God, my sister; He made all : '
' Well, brother, who made God?'

IV.

Ah! would I could go back again,
To play as once I played,
To laugh as I once laughed with her
Beneath the maple's shade !
But I have sadly changed since then ;
This jaded heart hath felt
Too much of bitterness since we
Beside our mother knelt!

V.

She rests: but oh! she rests not here !
This cold grave could not keep
A spirit that was pure as her's ;
Below she does not sleep !
I would not call her back ; she 's free
From all of care or pain :
I would not call her back to earth,
'T would still an angel-strain !

Auburn, N. Y., March, 1842.

E. S. KEENEY.

NOOR MAHAL: OR THE LIGHT OF THE HAREM.

BY A NEW CONTRIBUTOR.

ON the right bank of the Jumna, near the rich and beautiful gardens of Rambaugh, stands the far-famed mausoleum of Ulha-ma-Dowlah, the revered parent of the Noor Mahal. At the death of her father the inconsolable daughter proposed, as a proof of her affection and a memorial of her magnificence, to perpetuate his memory by a monument of solid silver. Dissuaded from this, she erected a noble fabric of marble, which still stands in the city of Agra, a lasting memento of a daughter's affection, and a beautiful specimen of oriental architecture.

From the top of this monumental edifice may be seen the blue waters of the Jumna winding through a rich champaign country, with gardens stretching down on either side to the rippling current. Opposite, the city of Agra, with its bastioned fort, its marble palaces, splendid cupolas, and broad ghauts, intermixed with trees, stands in all the pomp of eastern architecture; below, in silvery pride, the lustrous Taaj-Mahal is seen; and far as the eye can reach, country-houses decorated with light pavilions springing close to the margin of the stream, diversify the landscape.

This sepulchral monument, a splendid relic of the house of the immortal Timour, and a lasting memorial of the once august dynasty of the great Moguls, is here selected to introduce to the reader one of the most remarkable personages that ever wielded the sceptre of India. She did not wield the sceptre directly. She enjoyed a convenient medium in the person of her imperial husband. And here let me remind the reader, as he peruses the character and history of this extraordinary woman, that she lived in an age and in a country in which her sex are by prejudice, by custom and religion, doomed to a state of ignorance and degradation, from which humanity recoils and over which Christianity weeps. Woman is there deemed incapable of mental improvement, unworthy the companionship of the other sex, and wholly unfit to share in the counsels and transactions of state. She is indeed a blank in society; and doomed to drag out a life of animal existence in blind subserviency to the 'lords of creation,' and ministering only to the grosser appetites of human nature.

Under such inauspicious circumstances the heroine of our tale appeared at the imperial city. It was about the year 1585. The renowned Akbar, surnamed the Great, then swayed the sceptre over the vast Mohammedan empire in India. Selim was his only son. At the death of his father he came to the throne in the year 1605, under the modest title of Noor-ul-Deen Mohammed Jehanjire, 'Mohammed, the Light of the Faith and Conqueror of the World.' He was the husband of the singular personage whose history we shall now attempt briefly to trace. We shall avail ourselves of the authority of the Persian historian, who is almost the only chronicler that has transmitted to us records of those semi-barbarous but intensely interesting times.

Chaja Aiass was a native of Tartary. He was descended from an ancient and noble family, which had by the various revolutions of fortune at this time fallen into decay. Hence he left his country to try his fortune in Hindostan. A good education was his whole patrimony. Falling in love with a young woman as poor as himself, he married, but soon found great difficulty in providing for his wife even the necessaries of life. Reduced to the last extremity, he turned his thoughts to India, the usual resource of the needy Tartars of the north. He clandestinely set out for a foreign country, leaving behind him friends who either could not or would not afford him relief. His whole resources consisted of one sorry horse and a very small sum of money. Placing his wife on the animal, which was already laden with a sack containing articles of food and a few cooking utensils, with a sleeping mattrass, he walked by her side. She could ill endure so long a journey, for she was about to become a mother. Their scanty pittance of money was soon exhausted. When they arrived on the confines of the great solitudes which separate Tartary from the dominions of the Grand Mogul, they had already subsisted several days on charity. No house was there to cover them from the inclemency of the weather; no hand to relieve their wants. To return was certain misery; to proceed, apparent destruction.

They had fasted three days; and to complete their misfortunes, the wife of Aiass was seized with the pains of labor. She began to reproach her husband for leaving his native country at an unfortunate hour; for exchanging a quiet though a poor life for the ideal prospect of wealth in a distant land. In this distressed situation she became the mother of a daughter. Here they remained for several hours, in the vain hope that travellers might pass that way. They were disappointed. Human feet seldom tread these deserts. The sun declined apace, and they feared the approach of night. The place was the haunt of wild beasts; and should they escape their hunger, they must fall by their own. In this extremity the husband placed his wife on the horse, but found himself so much exhausted that he could scarcely move. To carry the child was impossible; the mother could not even support herself on the animal. An agonizing contest now began between parental affection and necessity. The latter prevailed; and they agreed to expose the child by the high-way. The infant, covered with leaves, was placed under a tree, and the disconsolate parents proceeded in tears.

When they had advanced about a mile, the eyes of the mother could no longer distinguish the solitary tree under which she had left her first-born; she gave way to grief; and throwing herself from the horse, exclaimed, 'My child! my child!' She endeavored to raise herself; but she had no strength to return. Aiass was pierced to the heart. He prevailed on his wife to sit down, promising to bring the child. He approached the spot, and as his eye caught the infant, he stood petrified with horror. A black snake was coiled around it; and Aiass fancied that he beheld him extend his fatal jaws to devour it. The father rushed forward. The serpent, alarmed, retired into the hollow tree.

He took up his daughter unhurt and brought her to her mother; and as he was relating the wonderful escape, some travellers appeared and kindly relieved their wants. They proceeded gradually, and came to Lahore, where the emperor then held his court.

Asiph Khan then attended the presence. He was a distant relative of Aiass, and one of the monarch's omrahs. He received his kinsman with attention and kindness, and to employ him, made him his private secretary. Aiass soon recommended himself to Asiph; and by some happy accident his diligence and ability attracted the notice of the emperor, who raised him to the command of a thousand horse. He became in process of time master of the household; and his genius being still greater than even his good fortune, he raised himself to the office and title of Actimâd-ul-Dowla, or 'High Treasurer of the Empire.' Thus he, who had almost perished through mere want in the desert, became in the space of a few years the first subject in India.

This daughter of desert-birth received, soon after her arrival at Lahore, the name of Mher-ul-Nissa, or the 'Sun of Women.' She had some right to the appellation; for in beauty she excelled all the ladies of the East. She was educated with the utmost care and attention. In music, in dancing, in poetry, in painting, she had no equal among her sex. Her disposition was volatile; her wit lively and satirical; her spirit lofty and uncontrolled. Selim the prince-royal one day visited her father. When the public entertainment was over, and all but the principal guests had withdrawn, the ladies according to custom were introduced in their veils.

The ambition of Mher-ul-Nissa aspired to the conquest of the prince. She sang; he was in raptures. She danced; he could hardly be restrained by the conventional rules to his place. Her stature, her shape, her gait, had raised his conceptions of her beauty to the highest pitch. When his eyes seemed to devour her, she as if by accident dropped her veil, and shone full upon him in all her charms. Her timid eye by stealth fell on the prince and kindled all his soul to love. He was silent the remainder of the evening. She endeavored to confirm by her wit the conquest which the charms of her person had made.

Mher-ul-Nissa had been betrothed by her father to Shere Afkun, a Turkomanian nobleman of great renown. Selim, distracted with his passion, knew not what course to take. He applied to his imperial father; but he refused to do such an act of injustice, though in favor of the heir to his throne. The prince retired abashed. Mher-ul-Nissa became the wife of Shere Afkun. Selim, though chagrined, dared make no open attack on his fortunate rival during the life of his father. Shere Afkun however suffered severely on this account at court, and retired in disgust. Selim mounted the throne of India. His passion for Mher-ul-Nissa, which had been repressed from respect and fear for his father, now returned with redoubled violence. He was now absolute. No subject could thwart his will or his pleasure. He recalled Shere Afkun from his retreat. Still he was too much restrained by public opinion directly to seize the wife of the omrah. Shere was inflexible. No man of honor in India can relinquish his wife without disgrace. He was naturally high-spirited and proud; his incredible strength and bravery had rendered him extremely popular; and it was not to be expected that he would yield to public indignity. His family and his former reputation were high. He had served in Persia with renown, and during the reign of the illustrious Akbar had distinguished himself in the field, and shared the highest honors of the court.

Shere Afkun was called to the presence, received graciously, and loaded with new honors. Naturally open and ingenuous, he suspected not the emperor's intentions. Time he hoped had erased from his mind the memory of Mher-ul-Nissa. He was deceived. The monarch was still resolved to remove his rival. He appointed a day for hunting, and ordered the haunt of an enormous tiger to be explored. This animal is said to have carried off the largest oxen. The monster was discovered in the forest. The emperor, attended by Shere Afkun and several thousand of his principal officers with their trains, directed thither his march. Having according to the custom of the Tartars surrounded the ground, they moved toward the centre. The tiger was roused. His roaring was heard in all quarters; and the emperor hastened to the spot.

'Who among you will advance singly and attack this tiger?' cried Dehanjire to his nobles. They were silent. All eyes were turned on Shere Afkun. He spoke not, imagining that none durst attempt a deed so dangerous. After the refusal of the nobles, he hoped the honor of the enterprise would devolve on him. Three however offered themselves for the combat. Not to be outdone, (as the emperor had rightly judged,) Shere at length addressed the presence: 'O Monarch of the World and Light of the Holy Faith, to attack an animal with weapons is both unmanly and unfair. God has given to man limbs and sinews as well as to tigers; he has added reason to the former to conduct his strength.' The omrahs objected in vain, 'that all men were inferior to the tiger in strength, and that he could be overcome only with steel.' 'I will convince you of your mistake,' replied Shere Afkun; and throwing down his sword and shield, he prepared to advance unarmed.

The emperor, secretly pleased, made a show of dissuading him from so dangerous an enterprise. Shere however was determined; and the monarch with feigned reluctance yielded. After a long and obstinate struggle, the intrepid warrior, mangled with wounds, laid the savage beast at his feet. His fame was increased, and the base designs of the emperor defeated. But the determined cruelty of the latter did not stop here. Other devices of death were formed against the unfortunate Shere. Again he appeared at court, and again caressed by the emperor, he suspected no guile. But fresh machinations of his imperial rival awaited him. Orders were at one time secretly given to an elephant-rider to crush him to death in his palanquin, as he passed through a narrow street; and at another, forty ruffians were employed by the viceroy of Bengal, whither he had now retired, to dispatch him in his bed. He overcame the elephant with his sword, and dispersed the ruffians with the most prodigious deeds of daring.

The fame of the last exploit resounded through the empire. The populace thronged around him on every side, and shouted his praises. He retired to Burdwan, where he hoped to live in obscurity and safety with his beautiful and beloved Mher-ul-Nissa. He was again deceived. The viceroy of Bengal had received his government on condition of removing the emperor's rival, and he was not unfaithful to his trust. Under pretence of visiting the dependent provinces, he came to Burdwan. He made no secret of his design to his chief officers. The brave and persecuted Shere met him as a friend with only two attendants. The mercenary viceroy feigned politeness; but his bloody designs soon became apparent. Shere was insulted by a pikeman; swords were drawn; our hero had no time to lose. He spurred his horse up to the elephant on which the viceroy sat, broke down the amari, or castee, and cut him in two. He turned his sword on his officers. First fell Aba Khan, an omrah of five thousand horse. Four other nobles shared the same fate. A death attended every blow. The other chiefs, astonished and affrighted, fled to a distance, and formed a circle around him. They galled him with arrows; they fired with their muskets; his horse fell under him. Reduced to the last extremity, he challenged his foes severally to single combat, but in vain. He had received several wounds, and now plainly saw his approaching fate. Turning his face toward Mecca, he took up some dust in his hand, and for want of water, threw it by way of ablution on his head. He then stood up seemingly unconcerned. Six balls entered his body before he fell. His enemies had scarcely courage to come near, till they saw him in the last agonies of death. They extolled his valor to the skies, though in adding to his reputation they detracted from their own.

Mher-ul-Nissa received the intelligence of the fatal combat with fortitude and resignation. She was sent with all possible care to Delhi, where Jehanjire then held his court. Though kindly received by Rokia Sultana Begum, the emperor's mother, Jehanjire refused to see her. Whether his mind was now fixed on another object, or remorse had stung his soul, authors do not agree. He gave orders to shut her up in one of the worst apartments of the seraglio; and contrary to his usual munificence to women, he allowed her but fourteen annas, about forty cents, per day, for the subsistence of herself and several female slaves. Such coldness to a woman whom he passionately loved when not in his power was unaccountable and absurd. The haughty Mher-ul-Nissa could not brook it. She had no remedy. She gave herself up to grief as for the death of her husband. The hope of an opportunity to rekindle the emperor's former love at length reconciled her to her condition. She trusted to the astonishing power of her beauty, which to conquer required only to be seen. An expedient soon offered.

To raise her own reputation in the seraglio, and to support herself and her servants with more decency, she called forth her invention and taste in working some admirable pieces of tapestry and embroidery, in painting silks with exquisite delicacy, and inventing female ornaments of every kind. These articles were carried by her servants to the different squares of the royal seraglio and to the harems of the great officers of the empire. The inventions of Mher-ul-Nissa so much excelled every thing of their kind that nothing was in high esteem among the ladies of Agra and Delhi but the work of her hand. By these means she accumulated a considerable sum of money, with which she repaired and beautified her apartments, and clothed her slaves in the richest tissues and brocades, while she herself affected a very plain and simple dress.

In this situation the widow of Shere continued four years without once having seen the emperor. Her fame reached his ears from every part of the seraglio. Curiosity at length vanquished his resolution, and he determined to be an eye-witness of what he had so often heard. He resolved to surprise Mher-ul-Nissa; and communicating his purpose to no one, he suddenly entered her apartments, when he was struck with amazement to find every thing so neat and elegant But the greatest ornament of all was Mher-ul-Nissa herself. She lay half reclined on an embroidered sofa, in a plain muslin dress. Her slaves sat in a circle around her, at their work, attired in rich brocades. She slowly arose, in manifest confusion; and received the emperor with the usual ceremony of touching first the ground, then her forehead, with her right hand. She uttered not a word, but stood with her eyes fixed on the ground. Jehanjire remained for some time silent. He admired her shape, her stature, her beauty, her grace, and that inexpressible voluptuousness of mein which it is impossible to resist.

Having recovered from his confusion, Jehanjire at length sat down on the sofa, and requested Mher-ul-Nissa to sit by his side. Astonished at the simplicity of her dress, the first question he asked her was: ' Why this difference between Mher-ul-Nissa and her slaves?' She very shrewdly replied : ' Those born to servitude must dress as shall please those whom they serve. These are my servants; and I alleviate the burden of bondage by every indulgence in my power. But I that am your slave, O Emperor of the Moguls! must dress according to your pleasure, and not my own.' Though a sarcasm on his conduct, this answer was so pertinent and well turned that it greatly pleased Jehanjire. He took her at once in his arms. His former affection returned with all its violence; and the very next day public orders were issued to prepare a magnificent festival for the celebration of his nuptials with Mher-ul-Nissa. Her name was also changed by an edict into Noor Mahal, or the Light of the Harem. The emperor's former favorites vanished before her; and during the rest of the reign of Jehanjire she bore the chief sway in all the affairs of the empire.

Her adroit management for her family was scarcely less remarkable than that for herself. Her father was raised to the first office in the empire; her brothers were made nobles; and a numerous train of relations poured in from Tartary to share in the good fortune of the family of Aiass. All were gratified with lucrative employments ; some with high ones. No family ever rose to rank and eminence more suddenly or more deservedly. The charms of the new sultana estranged the mind of the emperor from all public affairs. Easy in his temper, and naturally voluptuous, the powers of his soul were locked-up in the pleasing enthusiasm of love by the engaging conversation and the extraordinary beauty of Noor Mahal. She for the most part ruled over him with absolute sway : sometimes his spirit broke forth from her control. An edict was issued again to change her name from Noor Mahal, the Light of the Harem, to Noor Jehan, the Light of the World.

To distinguish her from the wives of the emperor she was always addressed by the title of Shahe, or empress.　Her name was joined with that of the emperor on the current coin.　She was the spring which moved the great machine of the state.　Her family took rank immediately after the princes of the blood.　They were admitted at all hours into the presence; nor were they excluded from the most secret parts of the seraglio.　Indeed she exercised a complete control over the mind of the emperor.　He dared attempt nothing without her concurrence.　She disposed of the highest offices at pleasure, and the greatest honors were conferred at her nod.　The magnificence of the favorite sultana was beyond all bounds.　Expensive pageants, sumptuous entertainments, were the whole business of the court.　The voice of music never ceased by day in the streets; the sky was brightened at night by fire-works and illuminations.　The magnificent gardens and the rich and stately palaces of Agra and Delhi were alternately vocal with the festivity and joy of a most voluptuous court.

Agra, the imperial city, now displayed all the beauty and splendor which eastern wealth, despotism and luxuriance could so readily bestow. The imperial palace, built of the richest white marble, with its spacious hall of audience ceiled with silver, and hung with the most costly tapestry, and adorned with embroidered sofas, gay ottomans, and furniture of the richest description; with its many suites of marble apartments, decorated with Mosaics of flowers executed in many-colored agates and cornelians, overlooking the beautiful waters of the Jumna, was the centre of magnificence and beauty.　The tomb of Akbar; the fort, with its lofty walls and turrets; the mausoleum of Aiass, already mentioned; the Mootee Musjid, or the pearl mosque, rivalling in beauty and splendor the Taaj Mahal itself; with gardens, fountains, noblemen's palaces, and the towering domes of a hundred mosques, combined to form the glory of the once renowned seat of Moslem power.

It was at this period that the English ambassadors first appeared at the court of the Great Mogul.　On several occasions they witnessed the full pomp of this luxurious court.　They represent the splendor and extravagance of the court as almost incredible.　Precious stones and jewels appeared in the greatest profusion.　The person of the emperor on state occasions was not only covered but laden with pearls, rubies and diamonds; and his elephants, with gilded trappings, had their heads ornamented with valuable jewels.　Nothing astonished the foreigners more than the grandeur of the royal encampment when the emperor had taken the field.　The imperial tents were surrounded by a wall half a mile in circuit; and the tents of his nobles exhibited the most elegant shapes and brilliant variety of colors.　The whole vale in which they were collected resembled a beautiful city.　Mighty monarchs!　Unrivalled beauty and magnificence!　Where are they?　The haughty race of Timour have passed away like a morning cloud.　The peacock-throne is deserted; the proud city has fallen; stately palaces, tombs and mosques are crumbling to the dust.　Only a few marble monuments remain to tell how great, how little — how strong, how weak — how vain the moslems were!

Two centuries have passed, and yet Agra still presents some of the noblests specimens of human art; the sad relics of Mohammedan wealth and greatness. On surveying the ruins of Agra, and contemplating the marble palaces and mausoleums which still remain, a modern traveller, the writer of 'Scenes and Characteristics in Hindostan,' says: 'The delights of my childhood rushed to my soul; those magic tales, from which, rather than from the veritable pages of history, I had gathered my knowledge of eastern arts and arms, arose in all their original vividness. I felt indeed that I was in the land of genii, and that the gorgeous palaces, the flowery labyrinths, the oriental gems and glittering thrones, so long classed with ideal splendors, were not the fictitious offspring of romance. · · · Here the reader of eastern romance may realize his dreams of fairy land, and contemplate those wondrous scenes so faithfully delineated in the brilliant pages of the Arabian Nights.'

But to return to the favorite sultana. She had now completed her ascendency over the mind of the emperor. Her influence at court was supreme. Nothing could stand before her. Her caprices were law; her intrigues for her children for a long period distracted the whole empire, and she never failed to take signal vengeance on all who sought to thwart her wishes. Mohabet Khan, a loyal omrah and faithful adviser of the emperor, at length unhappily crossed the path of this ambitious woman. The machinations of her evil genius were now awakened to remove the troublesome nobleman; for she could revenge as well as fascinate. So powerfully had she wrought on the mind of a weak and credulous prince that she soon procured his recall from an important foreign service, under the suspicion of conspiracy. He came, found the emperor encamped on the banks of the Jumna, and immediately formed the bold design of seizing his person. He entered the imperial tent with five hundred brave rajpoots and bore away the imperial spoil. Noor Jehan was with the main army on the opposite side of the river. Enraged at the disaster which had befallen her royal spouse, the fair sultana resolved to make one desperate effort to rescue the emperor. The river was to be forded in the face of the hostile rajpoots. Mounted on an elephant the 'Light of the Harem' first plunged into the river with her daughter by her side. She exposed herself to the hottest of the battle, and emptied four quivers of arrows on the enemy. The young lady was wounded in the arm, but the mother pressed on. Three of her elephant-drivers were successively killed, and her elephant was severely wounded. The rajpoots rushed into the river to seize her; but the master of her household, mounting an elephant, saved her from their hands.

The battle was long, desperate and bloody. Complete victory remained to Mohabet and his invincible rajpoots. The emperor was retained a prisoner; and the flickering 'Light of the world,' with diminished rays, retired to Lahore. She was soon recalled by stratagem to the presence of her fallen lord; accused of treason; and her own husband compelled to sign her death-warrant. The dreadful message was delivered to the sultana. She heard it without emotion. 'Imprisoned sovereigns,' said she, 'lose their right to life with their freedom; but permit me once more to see the emperor, and to bathe with my tears the hand that has fixed the seal to the warrant of death.'

Mohabet consented to the interview on condition that it should be in his presence. She entered. She uttered not a word. Her beauty shone with additional lustre through her sorrow. Jehanjire burst into tears. 'Will you not spare this woman, Mohabet?' said the emperor; 'you see how she weeps.' 'The Emperor of the Moguls,' replied Mohabet, 'should never ask in vain.' The guards retired from her at the wave of his hand; and she was restored that instant to her former attendants.

The noble Mohabet, having vindicated his character and reduced the emperor to the necessity of granting his own terms, generously liberated his royal prisoners. But the vindictive empress, once chagrined and humbled, ceased not to pursue the man who had spared her life when in his power, till he was reduced to the condition of a fugitive and a beggar. She again governed the empire without control.

But the meridian was passed; our eastern luminary was sinking beneath her horizon. 'The Sun of Women,' 'the Light of the World' continued to wane, till in the death of Jehanjire she set to rise no more. Shah Jehan mounted the throne. Another favorite sultana irradiated the harem; and the once beautiful Mher-ul-Nissa, whose charms and brilliant wit and diplomatic intrigue had for many years swayed the most powerful court of which the world could then boast, now ruined in all her schemes of ambition, remained a prisoner at large in the imperial palace at Lahore.

In the mean time the court at Agra shone in all the splendor of oriental magnificence. New palaces were erected; new and more stately gardens formed; and new inventions of pleasure and new pomp and show marked the reign of this extravagant prince. Even the gorgeous shows and the brilliant festivals of the favorite sultana of the late reign are said to have vanished in the superior grandeur of those exhibited at the court of Shah Jehan. Having assassinated his elder brother and exterminated every male of the house of Timour, he had assumed the royal umbrella under the pompous titles of 'THE STAR OF THE TRUE FAITH; THE SECOND LORD OF THE HAPPY CONJUNCTIONS; MOHAMMED, THE KING OF THE WORLD!'

A single instance will serve as a specimen of the vanity and splendor of the imperial court at this time. On a festive occasion, the birth of a son to the heir-apparent to his empire, the emperor mounted a new throne formed of pure solid gold, embossed with various figures, and studded with precious stones. This throne had been seven years in preparing; and the expense of the jewels only amounted to one million two hundred and fifty thousand pounds sterling! It was distinguished by the name of the Tuckt-Taous, or the peacock-throne, from having the figures of two peacocks standing behind it with their tails spread, which were studded with jewels of various colors to represent life. Between the peacocks stood a parrot of the ordinary size cut out of one emerald. The finest jewel in the throne was a ruby which fell into the hands of Timour among the rich spoils of Delhi.

'The Sun of Women' must at length sink from our view. 'The Light of the Harem' was extinguished. Noor Mahal died in her palace-prison at Lahore in the year 1645. Her power had ceased with the death of her husband; and she was afterward too proud even to speak of public affairs, and therefore she devoted her remaining days to study, retirement and ease.

In beauty and grace she excelled all the women of the East; nor was she less extraordinary in the peculiar features of her mind. She rendered herself absolute in a government in which women are thought incapable of participating. Their power, it is true, is sometimes exerted in the harem; but like the virtues of the magnet it is there silent and unperceived. Noor Mahal stood forth in public; she broke through all restraint and custom; and acquired power by her own address more than by the weakness of Jehanjire. Ambitious, passionate, insinuating, cunning, bold and vindictive, yet her character was never stained with cruelty; and she maintained the reputation of chastity, when no restraint but virtue remained. Her passions were indeed too masculine. When we see her acting the part of a soldier, she excites our ridicule more than admiration. It seems to detract from the soft charms of the captivating Mher-ul-Nissa, and transcends that goal of feminine delicacy beyond which her sex ceases to please.

THE REVIEW.

THE following lines were penned by the late CHIEF JUSTICE MELLEN, of Maine, a short time before he was seized with the illness that terminated in his death. They bespeak a heart at ease with the world and at peace with itself; and are an emanation of that kind, benignant spirit which made the writer so beloved while living and lamented when dead. — ED. KNICKERBOCKER.

How calm the closing day! The tempest-clouds
Are passing on their journey, and the roar
Of distant thunder, which so lately burst
In majesty and terror o'er me, now
Is faintly sinking in the distance; while
The breeze is breathing softness and perfume,
And Earth, with all its countless charms, receives
The Sun's mild radiance and his farewell beams.
See in the east, displayed in beauteous hues,
GOD's own bright bow of promise! All serene
The gradual Evening spreads her brooding wings,
And wearied Nature seeks her loved repose.

Now is the hour of thoughtfulness; for all
Around me and above me lifts the heart
From scenes of earth-born interest, and awakes
The song of gratitude for countless joys
Along life's blooming vista; and the voice
Of sorrow too for blessings thrown away,
Time unimproved, and treasures unemployed!

Sweet is the memory of departed years!
It gives us back, in beautiful review,
Ten thousand joys of youth and innocence
In varied, glad succession; while the heart
Feels new pulsations in the fond recall
Of sunny skies, and babbling streams, and shades,

And loved retirement in poetic bowers,
And Nature robed in all her simple charms.
'Tis true the scene may call the heart to mourn
Beside the graves of buried comforts: there
To read their epitaphs afresh in tears,
And sigh for consolation! Happy those
Who 'talk with wisdom' in this lone retreat,
And leave its precincts more prepared to join
The world around them in its busy walks,
By love of duty guarded, and with hearts
By sorrow softened, and affections raised
To purity and peace and heavenly joy.

Come then, dear Memory! give me back the scenes
Which have so long, by sunshine and by smiles,
By cheerfulness and hope, been richly crowned.
The morning of my days was bright and fair:
Kind hearts and dear affections hovered round
My childish years, and taught me where to find
The lovely paths of safety, mid the cares,
The passions, and the perils of the world.
My heart was buoyant in my varied course:
The tears of sorrow, and the sighs of 'hope
Deferred,' and withering in despair and gloom,
Were never then my portion. Health and joy
Margined my way with flowers, and spread around
A balmy fragrance. Yet, though years have passed;
Though scenes have changed, and autumn-chills have laid
The verdure of the forest in its grave,
And winter clothed the earth in nature's shroud;
The social circle, and the thousand ties
Of friendship and its family of joys
Have never lost their balsam or their charm.

The summer feelings of my cheerful heart
Have lived in sympathetic fellowship
With those which leaped and broke in youthful joy
And bounding gratulation from the founts
Of virtuous feeling; while the beaming eye
And sparkling intellect of WOMAN shed
New lustre and new interest o'er the scene.
The garden's flowers, the grotto, and the vale
Of wild romantic beauty, seem as fair
As Tempe's in its loveliness: and *now*
The rose is sweet as ever, and the song
Of joy and gladness still delights mine ear;
And music in its soft and zephyr-strains
Dissolves the soul in tenderness: and when
In thunders of hosanna HANDEL calls,
' Let the bright seraphim, in burning row,
Their loud, uplifted angel-trumpets blow !'
Amid the bursting harmonies all hearts
Are lost in wonder, gratitude and praise;
Such joys as these now glad life's evening years.

But thorns as well as roses in our path
Oft wound us in the garden of our hopes.
O! I have seen my darling child resign
Young life to HIM who gave it, ere the world
Her purity had tarnished; and her eyes
Closing in peace, while mine were drowned in tears.
Long has she slumbered in her narrow bed !

Again the summons came ; and he whose hopes
Dressed him in smiles, awakened him to joy,
And led him onward in life's garden ; he
Went down to darkness and the worm! Awhile
He loved the pencil and the muse ; but death
Performed his sad, sad office ! Here I found
A lesson on mortality, and learned
The fleeting nature of all earthly hopes ;
Of youth, of health, of prospects, and the pride
Of all our airy castles. Still the smiles
And blessings of our Heavenly Father claimed
Our gratitude, and healed each wounded heart.
Love, hope and joy now gladdened our abode,
And all their promises spread out to view
Delightful landscapes, and on these we gazed.

The patron of my life — my trust, my stay,
My cherished consolation — where is she !
The couch on which she lay in sweet repose
And peaceful dreams of purity, in one
Short hour became her death-bed, and a scene
Of wailing and of wo. But she is gone !
And I, and those who in her life she loved,
Guided and guarded still in virtue's path,
Are left — the monuments of mercy still !
Let me learn wisdom, and prepare to meet
My final summons !

What cause for gratitude and praise to HIM,
The fountain of all good, still, still remains ;
Who spreads before us and invites us all
To enjoy the banquet of his love ; to inhale
The breezes fresh and pure of moral health ;
To wake to life the affections of the heart,
Diffusing wide their influence on our lives,
While journeying on through sunshine and through shade,
By the still waters and the verdant fields
Of peaceful life, or mid the thousand cares
That mark our progress through a busy world !

But though my home so oft has been the scene
Of blighted hopes and deep distress ; and though
The evening clouds of life have lost the bright
And golden beauty which they erst displayed
In Hope's prophetic glass ; yet all around
Is full of deep instruction. I am taught
More readily to find the 'narrow path'
That leads to heaven ; to learn the soothing truth,
That in the cup of sorrow and the bowl
Of human joys — in both — may Wisdom find
Still a corrective medicine ; designed
To purify our hearts ; to add new strength
To all our better purposes ; t' improve
Health, happiness, and all the smiling group
Of social virtues, and the precious calm
Of home and its endearments : thus to feel
As ' blessings in disguise ' the wounded heart,
The 'cup of trembling,' and the day of gloom ;
The house of mourning, dear departed joys,
Flowers withered in their infancy and bloom,
The alarm of conscience, and repentant tears.

SENEX.

EDWARD ALFORD AND HIS PLAY-FELLOW.

BY THE AUTHOR OF 'WILSON CONWORTH.'

CHAPTER THIRD.

'I am unwilling to throw out any remarks that should have a tendency to damp a hopeful genius; but I must not in fairness conceal from you that you have much to do. . . . You are in the condition of a traveller that has all his journey to begin. And again, you are worse off than the traveller which I have supposed, for you have already lost your way.' — ELIA: 'LETTER TO AN OLD GENTLEMAN WHOSE EDUCATION HAS BEEN NEGLECTED.'

THIRTY years ago a college education was thought essential to success in professional and literary life. A man who in those days aspired to be thought a scholar without knowing Latin and Greek, was considered a kind of quack or pretender. It is not so now. Sheepskins have become dog-cheap. Colleges have so multiplied in our country, so many have had the opportunity of whatever advantage they can afford, that the world is beginning to find out that a mere knowledge of languages, a smattering of the sciences, are not the only nor the best foundation for the intellectual structure. It is at length discovered that a man may go through college and write A. B. after his name, and even A. M., and be no great things either. Science and learning are no longer confined to the professions. Many mechanics and merchants are as well educated as many college-bred men. A memory full of learned phrases and scientific terms is not valued so highly as the knowledge of the very things those terms stand for. When learning was rare, pedantry could play its tricks before the world without fear of discovery. Then was the golden harvest of medical men. The simplest prescriptions were accompanied with an ominous shake of the head or a mysterious silence, which the uninitiated mistook for an almost miraculous gift at healing. The law flourished not a little by the same humbuggery; and the divine owed no small part of his influence to his knowledge of Greek and Hebrew — tongues in which were supposed to be hidden the decrees of God and the future destiny of man.

The evil cured itself; fairly run itself out, in the multiplication of books and the continued use of terms which at last got to be generally understood. The boy pedant now talks of ' perforating the convex extremity of the egg' which he wishes to cleanse for preservation, ' and also overcoming the attraction of cohesion at the corresponding apex, and propelling into the last aperture, by means of the labial organs, some of that fluid compounded of oxygen and nitrogen, vulgarly called air.' His grandmother lifts up her hands and eyes in astonishment, and exclaims: ' La! how much the children do know now-a-days! when I was a gal we used to break a hole in both eends and blow in it!'

Before we proceed with the particulars of our story, we hope the reader will pardon us if we consider what is the true value of a college education, as compared with that practical training the young man may

obtain in the actual duties of life.   And it may be stated that the usual
way in which young men treat their college advantages, fits them not
half as well for the serious duties of fathers, voters and citizens, as
some trade or actual work would fit them.   The lounging manner in
which most of our young men pass through college generally unfits
them for all valuable exertion in after life.   While their youth lasts and
their spirits are fresh, they are agreeable companions and objects of
hope; and youth itself, whether in a young man or maiden, is a charming object to look upon, even when full of errors and follies.   It is the
youth we love; it is what they may be if they choose, that we admire;
and not their waste of time and pursuit of vain amusements.   Still the
advantages of a college education are great; and we are sorry to see
that there is an increasing disposition to give up one of the most valuable parts of college training; we refer to the discredit into which the
study of the dead languages is passing.   It is said that this study is
useless waste of time.   Now if the end of such study is only to enable
one to talk learned jargon, or if it be asserted that such a course is
necessary in order to understand what is in ancient literature, both of
these reasons are inadequate to the labor of their acquisition.   But if
it be said that the study of the classics is a ' discipline of humanity;'
that they teach us ' to prefer honor to ease, and glory to riches;' that
they convince us that there is something 'permanent in the world,
surviving all shocks of accident and fluctuations of opinion;' that they
furnish the best training for the mind, and lead to the most full developement of all the intellectual powers, at the same time refining the
taste; giving us in the clearest manner the philosophy of language, the
nice distinctions in the meanings of words which the man of one
language considers as synonymous; making us familiar beside with
the allusions of the best English writers who formed themselves upon
them as models; then surely there are sufficient reasons why they
should not be dispensed with.   And to add the argument of experience,
the highest of any, it may be said that the brightest ornaments of the
English senate, the leaders at the English bar, the divines, the wits, the
orators and poets, those men who make the eighteenth century a galaxy
of talent such as the world never saw before, were trained almost
exclusively in the study of Latin and Greek, at the schools of Westminster and Eton, and at the colleges of Oxford and Cambridge.
    The truth is, that the object of a college-life has been overrated by
people at large and by the college-bred man himself.   It has been
thought that a degree completed the education, and that after that little
could be done; while every student who gains the most from college
that can be gained, knows that after he has been graduated he has
only just begun to learn, having by his college discipline but learned
how to study.   This is the great object of education, to learn how to
study; how to think; what use to make of the thousand facts daily
occurring in the walk of every individual; to put the mind in a condition to receive that knowledge.   It is like the ploughing of the land,
the working of the soil, to fit it for the seed.   God giveth the increase
here too, by his providences; by the wonders he from time to time
unfolds in the natural world; by spiritual impressions and noble

impulses, which carry forward the man in knowledge and intellectual power beyond what ever could be gained from books.

This is the difference between the trained scholar and the self-taught inquirer ; the one knows how to go work at once upon a subject; where the doors and entrances and passages lie; while the last, guided by no rule, but relying on instinct and chance, spends much time in knowing how to begin.   When this shall be acknowledged, that early education and all school and college education is but the discipline of the intellect, as a main object, the course of study by which this can be best effected will be judiciously decided.   But a course which embraces modern languages, (excluding the ancient classics,) the sciences and rhetoric, carrying the student over so wide a collection of books that he can know no one well, must produce a habit of mind which nothing but necessity can chain to the careful examination of any subject.

The voluntary system, as it is called, by which each student now studies what he pleases, there being a few exceptions to this rule, seems to do away with one of the highest advantages of a college course.   For if a young man needs any instruction at all, it is in knowing what to study; and though under the present plan he may have advice if he asks it, it is to be feared that prejudice, his own laziness or zeal, will oftener decide for him than a regard for distant future good.   Now we contend that the mind is more strengthened by the diligent study of a branch of learning which may at first be distasteful to it, but which it pursues from a sense of duty and by an exertion of the will, than by ever so much time employed in subjects congenial to the taste.   Is not the object of education to prepare for life ? and is life a series of duties and investigations in which we sail along as over a summer sea ?   The mind must be made familiar with difficulty; must learn to act from better motives than ease and love of pleasure. Beside, the adoption of the voluntary system is a tacit acknowledgment that study at college is not disciplinary in its main object; or if it is so, that one course is as disciplinary as another, a position at war with the opinions and practice of the best scholars of the past and present.

It is not wonderful that in the age of steam-boats and rail-roads, men should be seeking short cuts to intellectual strength, an easy way up the Parnassian heights; but they will find out that the steep is too large an angle with the horizon to admit of any ascent except by the old paths.

It was fortunate for Edward that he entered college at a time when the old system was in full force.   Latin, Greek, and Mathematics, were the chief studies of the two first years.   They laid the foundation for an understanding of the mental and natural philosophy of the subsequent time.   They formed the mind to habits of analysis, and then might be, and often were, thrown aside for ever, while moral and mental philosophy and the natural sciences furnished facts and data from which to reason.

The discipline of Edward at school had not been very strict, as we have seen, but here he was under no restraint at all, except to be present at prayers and attend recitation regularly. Established in a handsomely-furnished room, arranged by the taste of his mother; with plenty of pocket money; for beside the allowance from his father he had received an extra supply from his too tender mother; with good health and good physical habits, our hero started on his college career under great advantages, as he himself thought, and as every body thought. How much greater the chance of that poorly-clad student on the seat next him, at the examination! His name, Timothy Blossom; a pale, light-haired, slender boy of seventeen, who the day before had walked thirty miles, with his books tied up in a cotton handkerchief, to be present at the examination for admission. Timothy was the son of a farmer of moderate means. He had fitted himself for college with the occasional assistance of the village clergyman. With what different feelings did these two boys go to their first recitation! The one was thinking of his dress, his appearance, the set of his shirt-collar, his style; the other, of his lesson, his hopes of an education, future use-fulness, perhaps fame. We say how much higher his chance for honor, improvement and success in life, with only a change of linen, and his one suit of clothes and meagre fare, than that of the favored son of wealth who had nothing left to wish for!

And where is Tom Towley all this time? That boy, clad in a leather apron, brushing the flies off the horse that is being shod, is he. The horse is one of the coach-horses of Mr. Alford; for Edward came out with his mother in the carriage. The horse cast a shoe, and Tom is happy enough to see even a familiar brute. He brushes him tenderly and pats his neck now and then, while a tear stands in his eye as he thinks of his home and his toiling parents. He takes up a corner of his new apron and wipes the tear away, and neither Tom nor the apron is the worse for it.

The blacksmith, with whom he is learning his trade, is a kind-hearted man, and he means to do all the good he can to the boy whose open manners and ingenuous countenance won him from the first.

'And now tell me boy,' said Robert Nailer, the blacksmith, to Tom, when he first came to the shop, 'what you have learned at school?'

'I can read, Sir,' said Tom, 'and folks say I can write pretty well. I can keep accounts and cast interest too; and beside what our master Mr. Wickliff taught me, father taught me how to work a garden and how to speak the truth always.'

'That's good learning,' said Robert; 'no blacksmith ever should tell a lie. The man who works iron and handles a sledge-hammer as easily as the baby throws his penny toy, would look pretty, would n't he? in telling a mean lie? I can show you how to use the hammer and how to drive a nail into a horse's foot. But you must practice upon my horse first. We do n't spoil other people's horses here teaching boys their trade. A horse's foot is a tender thing, and many a fine beast has been spoiled by the hammer of a boy. Yes, you shall shoe my horse by and by; and I'll make a man of you as fast as I can.'

'Thank 'ye, Sir; I want to be a man very soon, so that I can help mother.'

'Well, do as I tell you, and do n't be in a hurry. Make haste slowly;

strike when the iron's hot, but don't snatch it out of the fire before it is heated, for you see, then you lose time.'

'That's almost equal to Mr. Wickliff,' thought Tom. Robert Nailer was already quite a sage in his opinion. 'I'll do as well as I can; and how happy mother will be when I have a shop of my own!' So to work he went, in patient drudgery, with the great object of having a snug blacksmith's-shop, where he could toil and sweat on his own account.

With less fuss than is usual for very rich people when they make any movement, whether to take a ride, prepare for dinner or a party, or place a son at college, Edward got settled in his new quarters and went to his work also. But less happy than his play-fellow, for he worked with no definite object. His present position seemed to him a matter of course; one of the laws of nature, rather than any peculiarly good fortune which he was called upon to improve. Many were the ordeals the young freshman had to pass through.

From time immemorial a playful animosity has existed between the freshman and sophomore classes; and the feeling is carried up into the higher classes, the juniors and seniors. The junior class is the natural ally of the freshman class; and the senior of the sophomore class. Indeed this is as true a feeling, and about as hearty as that between the political parties in our country; it only breaks out on great occasions and at times stated by custom, while it slumbers like fire buried in ashes, until by concert it is raked open and kindled into a blaze for fun, frolic and excitement. In old days, and we believe the custom still obtains, the first point of dispute is the respective strength of the feet and legs of each class, a question that is settled by a game of foot-ball in the delta, a large enclosure near the college, fenced in the shape of the Greek letter of that name, thus : Δ. We consider this a remarkable instance of the perversity of youth; that they who profess to be seeking intellectual eminence, the powers of the head, should upon the earliest opportunity fall to disputing about the superiority of heels. So it is. The younger class generally occupy the upper angle of the delta, and the sophs are ranged at the base of it; for this gives the freshman class a little advantage, having a smaller goal to protect, while their opponents have a wider space to guard. The game often becomes highly exciting, and many a little freshman measures his length upon the classic ground. Nor does the tall soph. always escape a similar catastrophe. The short, squabby little man from the hills of New England, bringing his whole muscular power, in the shape of a ball, in a direct line with the long legs of some youth who in the last year has shot up like a poplar sapling, cuts down his opponent as the sythe of the mower reaps the tall clover-heads in the meadow. What the record says we do not know, but we strongly suspect the freshman is as often victorious as the sophomore; for the first comes fresh from school sports, and is not yet enervated by late study. Beside, he cares little about the derangement of his dress, a matter of prime consequence with the newly-created soph., but throws his whole soul into the game. However, we have in this instance to record the overthrow of the freshman. The game was lost by the carelessness or apathy of Alford, who being left as guard of the goal had turned at that moment to say a word to Tom, who was looking through the fence at the sport.

'Home!' cried the victorious class.

'We are beat!' responded a red-faced little freshman. 'Ned Alford! where did you learn to kick foot-ball? Why did n't you throw your dandy hat at it, if you were afraid of spoiling your boots?' A shout of laughter followed this smart sally. Edward blushed scarlet; he was too proud to exculpate himself, but not too proud to jump over the fence and take Tom by the arm and walk off.

'Who is that,' asked one of his class, 'that Alford has gone off with?'

'That? oh that 's the black-smith boy. I saw him to-day in Bob Nailer's shop.'

'What! does Alford keep such company? We must cut him!' cried one. 'What a black-guard!' cried another.

'They were school-mates,' said some one, 'and Alford is perfectly right to notice him. How do we know but he may be a fine fellow, even if he is a mechanic? I for one like Alford all the better for his kindness to an old friend.'

Some of the young gentlemen of Alford's class called at his room, on their way home, and found him alone and in tears. 'They had called,' they said, 'to tell him, as friends, that he must cut his old acquaintance; for it would never do for him to be seen about the college in the company of mechanics.'

They reasoned and argued the matter with that skill and good sense common to spoiled children, who become young aristocrats in a republican country without knowing why; and whose assumptions are the more disgusting, because unaccompanied with any intellectual merit, but depending almost entirely upon the amount of wealth which is or has been possessed by those from whom they happen to be descended.

Now Edward Alford was naturally a just-minded boy, and by no means agreed with his friends about Tom Towley. Still he was too weak to follow his own convictions in the face of college opinion. Indeed when the matter was urged home upon him, and an appeal was made to his family pride and character as a gentleman, he did yield so far as to say that he would break off his intimacy with his play-fellow.

The foot-ball affair being decided, there was a cessation of hostilities between the younger classes. It is matter of policy with the sophs to wait a little before they begin their large practical jokes upon the freshmen. For the school-boy comes to college with his eyes wide open, expecting a quiz at every step. The last few months of his school-days have been filled with stories and speculations about what was done to this freshman and that; so that it is necessary to allay these fears in the first place.

Quiet had reigned for a week or more, and the new class had been unmolested. No key-hole had been stuffed with putty; no rancid butter thrown into suddenly-opened doors; no hideous noises were heard at night along the entries; for a great ceremony was about to take place in the college, a ceremony that could only occur once in a century. All were on the tiptoe of expectation. The sophs, taking advantage of this event, chose the largest and most dignified members of their class as a committee to visit the rooms of the freshmen as tutors, to summon them to appear before University Hall after prayers for the purpose of preparing for the procession on the coming occasion; that they might become familiar with the evolutions, marches, openings to the right and left, etc. A visit from a tutor is always matter of awe to a freshman, and in fact it never takes place unless from some mock tutor, except there is outrageous noise and riot in some room in the college. Too much overcome to look up at the awful personage, with downcast eyes and trembling limbs, a ready acquiescence was given, and at the appointed time nearly all the class were present. Here, after being arranged by the pretended tutors they were marched about the college-yard to the great amusement of the whole college. And it has been strongly suspected that some of the tutors and real bonâ fide proctors were eye-witnesses of the joke, the blinds of their rooms being carefully closed.

Stately and proudly did they march with expansive nostril and swelling breasts. At length they were drawn up in as solid a body as possible beneath the windows of some wily sophs, for the purpose of hearing some final general instructions regarding their behavior and dress upon the great day; and while attentively listening to such words, a deluge of water fell suddenly upon them. The mock tutors escaped in the confusion that followed, and the half-drowned freshmen scattered to their rooms looking like chickens caught out in a shower.

The success of this stratagem seemed to satisfy the sophs for a long time. They felt that by this act they had paid off all they owed somebody, for the trials of their own freshman year. The college relapsed into quiet, and the hard study began in good earnest, as it always does in this college, where competition and struggle for 'parts' are such prevailing motives.

The first year passed rapidly away. Alford had as yet taken no rank as a scholar. He was too poorly fitted for that. The gentleness of his manners and refined appearance saved him many a 'screwing.' He was not asked questions he could not answer, and his case was fully understood by his instructers. How much better it would be if none were admitted to the institution without being fully prepared! But Mammon will have a finger in every pie. The pecuniary interest of the college, the size of the catalogue, will be thought of. The numerical force of the students must be on the increase by some means; and so many are admitted every year to whom the hour of recitation is torture, because they cannot get the lessons.

The form of Edward was slender and graceful. His delicate features and curling locks would better have belonged to a girl than a young man. His habits of late hours and luxurious living; riding when he should have walked; dancing when he should have been asleep and sleeping when he should have been awake; so outraged dame Nature that she paid him in poor health and lassitude of body. He ceased to be a boy without becoming a man.

Our young mechanic Tom worked early in the morning, and his sleep was sweet. His frame expanded with the invigorating exercise of the shop. His eye was brighter than ever, and he swung his hammer with the strength of a man. All intercourse between the boys ceased. Edward passed his play-fellow once or twice without recognition, and after that Tom ceased to expect his notice.

He mentioned the fact to his master : 'Edward wo'n't speak to me in the street and when he passes the shop, as he used to do.'

'Well, what of that ? Do you suppose he wants to take one of your blackened hands between his kid gloves ? He do n't speak to me neither,' said Robert, 'but his betters do.'

'But,' said Tom, 'he might pass the time of day with an old play-mate. Why master we are just of an age, and were born almost under the same roof. I love him almost like a brother.'

'You 've a great deal to learn about the gentry, Tom. Now there's the president of the college, he always says : 'How do ye do, Mister Nailer ?' and I say, 'Pretty well, Mr. President ; ' but he do n't invite me to dine with him, and I should be a fool to expect it. If I should go and see him in his parlor without any business but to pass the time of day, he would no longer say, 'How do ye do, Mister Nailer ?' Oh no! he would pass along then, as your Master Alford does, pretending to be in a deep study. You see, Tom, it would n't do, no how. Men that work must keep company with men that work. Those that have the same occupations can talk together with some pleasure. But what could I say to the President in his parlor ? Why I should feel like a cat in a strange garret.'

Robert had evidently thought the matter all out to his satisfaction, and was glad to utter himself. 'Just take that iron out of the fire. There, a little more that way.' Tom placed it on the anvil. Down came the hammer with a vengeance. 'Do you think the President could do that ?' In a short time he had turned out a horse-shoe. 'The President makes books and I make horse-shoes. Now unless he wants to talk to me about his horses or repairing the locks on the doors that some of those wild students break in their frolics, what can we have to talk about together ?'

'Why master,' said Tom, 'can't you talk politics ?'

'No, boy, I never talk politics. There 's too much of that done now by other people. They 're always talking and never doing any thing. They jabber, jabber, and make long speeches, when the country is suffering for want of good laws.'

'Then you might talk religion with him, Sir. I 'm sure they must know a great deal about it in the college, for they 're most all ministers; mother said so.'

Robert here struck a harder blow than ever ; and wiping the sweat from his face with his shirt-sleeve, said : 'I found it all out there, too, Tom. I never talk religion neither. There 's no place where people talk so much religion as in the taverns. When men get half drunk they 're always bent upon talking politics ; and when they get so they can hardly sit up straight, they begin to talk religion.'

'Yes, Sir ; I recollect Mr. Wickliff used to tell us that we must do good acts, as well as say good thoughts,' said Tom. 'That Mr. Wickliff was a sensible man,' continued Robert ; 'I wish we had him here to teach our school this winter. I once thought religion was all talk, but now I know better. I say there's religion in working up good iron into shoes, and doing all our work well. A man may be religious enough for me, who tries never to do any wrong to any body.'

'So I think,' said Tom.

'You must n't be uneasy, Tom, if rich folks who have plenty of money do n't treat you just as if you were one of themselves. It is n't nature. We have our rights and they have theirs. The man who works and earns his bread, and is honest and true to his fellow men and obeys the laws of God, is as good as any body; but he is n't like every body. I 'm as good as the President of the college or the President of the United States, but we should n't take any great pleasure in eating and sitting together; he in his clean and rich clothes and I in my leather apron. He would be uncomfortable and so should I; but I rather think he would feel the worst of the two. Some of the working men say hard things of rich people, and call those who wish them well by hard names; and all because they happen to be brought up in a different way. This, Tom, is the whole of it; we are equal, but we are different. If there is any first about it, I have as good a right to say I am first and they are second, as the other way.'

Under such instructions did our friend Tom Towley thrive; and while learning his trade, such lessons were sinking into his heart. Robert did not call himself a philosopher, nor think himself one; but his plain good sense and practical wisdom lost none of their virtue, because they were not given forth in a cap and gown and with a sounding name to attract attention. His young apprentice wrought with his heart now as well as with his hands. He did not consider himself a drudge, an inferior being in creation, as some of our working men do. Under the influence of such a man as Robert Nailer he began to have right views of his relations to those born to a more easy, perhaps not more fortunate condition. A feeling of pity, instead of mortification, pervaded him, as his old play-mate whirled by him in his gig, or passed him in the street in the company of his gay companions. Tom saw his thin form and pale face with commiseration, and observed a languor and feebleness of step, which no aids of dress or affectation of spirits could hide.

Let not the reader suppose that our young mechanic had no opportunity of cultivating his mind. The good master, as a matter of self-interest, will attend to this with his apprentices. He had time to read; he kept the accounts of the shop; wrote letters for Robert; and his companions in the town, finding out how expert he was with his pen, got him to indite many a letter, and some of a tender nature too. Beside he belonged to the village lyceum and had a chance to hear all the lectures of the season; for it was a part of Robert Nailer's plan of life to encourage public instruction. 'The man who works with his hands,' said Robert, 'who handles the things of the world, is the very man to understand theories about them. Now I 've worked in iron all my life, and though I never had more than a year's schooling, I presume to say I understood more of Professor Black's lecture on the metals than any of the book-men there. Some of his long words puzzled me a good deal at first, but I soon found him out. To be sure he said what we call 'rust' was an oxyde; and he said steel was a carburet of iron; and much more such lingo, which I suppose is all right enough for scholars; but when men lecture to the people they ought to try to make their hearers understand them, and not be carried away with the desire of showing how much they know. Now when Mr. Black took hold of his experiments and made the things talk in their natural language, for iron never tells any lies, why I understood him as well as he did himself.'

How happy it would have made the blacksmith could he have fore-seen the hopeful tokens of these times, when poets and scholars are turning their faces to the fields, not to find flowers and rivulets there, but the rich harvest of corn and grain! Yes, looking at labor in the land and in the work-shop as the true school for the intellect and the soul; returning to the simplicity of innocence and natural habits by the discipline of a high refinement of the manners and cultivation of the mind. Extremes meet; and the poet and scholar are now doing from choice, by arguments drawn from experience and thought, what the husbandman does by the promptings of necessity, the calls of hun-ger, and the sense of self-preservation. It is not difficult to see what effect this must have upon the sons of labor in our land; what a new value will be given to the employments of manual labor; what spring and sinew will be infused into the limbs of the laborer; when he finds the gifted, the cultivated, the rich and refined, coming back to repose upon the bosom of a mother they had begun to scorn! His labor will be lightened, not by requiring less physical exertion, but because his heart will be in it; it will be cheerful, respectable in his own eyes, from such companionship. He will no longer consider himself as doomed to a hard life, as the serf of the soil, but as leading the true life ordained by Providence for man.

A great poem may result from this at some future time. When this battle now going on between the true and the false, the artificial cus-toms and natural impulses shall be ended, and the question settled, some Homer will arise to tell the story of a great revolution. The shame the scholar now suffers who advocates new doctrines may be his great glory; that he is able to withstand the temptation of a small present possession, for a great future good to his race. Like Peter of Russia, he may leave his throne for a while to work at the bench of the mechanic; and so be able to build a monument for himself of materials that will not perish with time.

A celebrated divine has been preaching for many years of the dignity of human nature; the elevation and grandeur of all human condition, however humble, because informed with the soul. 'I honor not a man,' were his words upon one occasion, ' because he is a shoemaker, or a laborer in any calling, but because he is a man.' And another divine, younger and less experienced, but not less earnest, nor less con-fident in the truth of his theme, says: 'The glory of man, that which distinguishes him from the brutes, is his capacity of being indefinitely educable. This belongs to the highest and the lowest, and all are equal in this great privilege.' It would occupy too much space to state all the fine things that have been said about the dignity of man and the dignity of labor; but it is impossible not to conclude how much more eloquent are they who have taken it upon themselves to verify this new doctrine; to preach it in their lives, and who have begun to show the world that they are willing to do something more than merely state the principle.

But we must return to poor Edward Alford. We call him *poor* because the situation of his parents was so prosperous in one sense as to shut him out from all participation in those noble feelings which made Tom, the black-smith boy, so happy and hopeful. Term after term passed away, and he had made progress in language, in science, and his physical man grew also; but there was wanting to him an object. His heart burned not within him for any great cause. Humanity had no place in his interest. He loved his parents, his companions and intimates; was generous and open, truthful and obliging; but he was not moved to act, to study, to work by any principle of usefulness. How could learning, poetry and eloquence find any sympathy in such a mind? If he could have made up his mind to study for a 'part,' to be graduated with high honor, it would been have better than nothing to study for; and but little too. But Alford was too rich and fashionable to enter into competition with the herd of students; and beside, feeling his own incompetency, he made a virtue of necessity, and pretended to despise what he could not obtain. Honor was his watchword, but not college honor.

Behold him now a senior; cold, distant and polite, having arrived by great care and study at an appearance of indifference to every thing; unmoved and unexcited, with studiously slow pace, dressed after the highest fashion, he is seen moving to lecture. Prayers he has cut, to the extent of a 'public;' and now only attends as few as possible and avoid disgrace. At this period of his college life, our hero met with a severe mortification. A cousin of his, James Alford, a student at Hanover College, in New Hampshire, visited him at his rooms, (for a senior *has rooms*,) and it being vacation with him, proposed to himself a glance at college life in Cambridge. He held the first rank in the senior class at Hanover, and came not a little swollen with ideas of his consequence. Edward was glad to see his cousin; indeed he came by his invitation, and introduced him to his friends, the gay and fashionable men of his class. The manners of James were very offensive: he was a boaster, an egotist, vain of a person without beauty, and he was talkative without wit. Among other insulting things, he remarked one evening at a supper at Edward's room, that a Cambridge senior would find it hard work to enter the junior class at Hanover. Now every body knows the fact is exactly the reverse. This was an insult that quickly spread, and a plan was laid for signal vengeance.

The students vied in the attentions showered upon the distinguished stranger. Suppers, rides, compliments, deference of the most marked respect, quite turned what little common sense the 'first scholar of Hanover' possessed, away from him. After his suspicions were sufficiently lulled, and Edward's too, for he was not in the secret, a grand entertainment was given in one of the conspirator's rooms. The wine

circulated freely, and James as usual made some insulting boast to th e
student next him by design. High words followed, and a blow w s
received by the Cambridge man. The party broke up in confusio ,
for their purpose was answered.

The consequence was a challenge next morning, which Edwar d
would not allow his cousin to refuse. His words were: 'The famil y
blood, Sir, requires you to fight.' James was for setting off for home ;
but no, that could not be allowed; fight he could and should. At las t
by persuasive representations that his antagonist was no shot, etc., he
accepted the challenge. The time and place were agreed upon by
Edward and the second of the aggrieved party. There was a difficulty, Edward being one of the seconds, in having the pistols loaded
without balls; but this was managed. Trembling for his life, James
Alford raised his pistol at the signal and fired. As was preconcerted,
his opponent fell, as if shot. A surgeon was at hand, and pronounced
him beyond hope. The ball had penetrated his heart. Some chicken's
blood from a phial poured on his white vest was sufficient evidence to
James of the horrible work he had done.

A chaise in waiting carried him quickly from town. He was pursued, brought back, and imprisoned in a room in one of the colleges,
to which he was led blinded and hand-cuffed. He was told that the
government had jurisdiction, even life and death, over all offences committed within its grounds. He was examined by a mock justice and
committed for trial, which would take place immediately.

The pursuit and capture of his cousin were unbeknown to Edward.
He verily thought him guilty of the death of his class-mate, and that
he had escaped. He kept his room in fear and anxiety.

One of the large halls of the college was obtained from the government, as is usual, ostensibly for some society meeting. The law-
students were let into the secret, and applied to for aid to conduct the
trial. Every thing was arranged in perfect order. There were the
judges, the jury, the counsel, the officers of justice with their poles.
The prisoner, at evening, was led into the criminal box to be tried for
his life. In due form, in solemn mummery, the culprit was brought
in guilty. The judge rose to pronounce sentence, and James Alford,
'first scholar of Hanover,' fainted.

When he recovered he found himself in a chaise on his way to
intercept the stage for New-Hampshire. His luggage had been cared
for and funds provided. As he parted from persons who told him he
had been rescued and hurried off, a letter was put into his hands which
he solemnly promised to deliver to the 'second scholar' in his class,
immediately on his arrival. He did so. The contents ran thus:

'The students of the senior class, Cambridge, to the honorable
seniors of Hanover, greeting:

'We return you your 'first scholar' quizzed. Adieu!'

Whether the government ever found out this frolic is doubtful. The
man who was shot was seen at prayers next morning with a more joyful countenance than usual. Edward stood aghast for a moment when
he saw him; but the truth flashed upon him, and his face became as

red in degree as it had been pale.   After this Edward became moody and distant.   His pride had received a festering wound.   He took his degree on the same day that Tom Towley raised his sign in a neighboring village :

THOMAS   TOWLEY.
Black-Smith.

His father and mother were present, and so was Robert Nailer, with his pretty daughter Mary, to witness the ceremony.

John Towley and Jane, by their careful deposits in the Savings-Bank, that blessing to the laborious poor, had now become able to buy a small place in the same village where Tom had determined to settle. They had enough beside for neat and comfortable furniture; and he owned a horse and wagon with which to transport his vegetables to market. Tom was to board with his parents, and now we see him restored to his loving mother, who was as proud of her son as any lady in the land could be of a child taking his first degree with honor at the first institution in the country.   He was indeed taking his degree in the school of action.   Robert said, 'few men could shoe a horse better; that he was honest, industrious and moral, and never had deserved a harsh word during his whole apprenticeship.'   If this is not a *degree*, we should like to know what is.

The sign-raising was celebrated by a neat supper in John's cottage. Tom sat next to Mary Nailer, a pretty girl of seventeen, whom he had all along treated like a sister ; but now when he was about to part with his master's family, he felt something was the matter with him ; what, he did not know.   At supper he began to look sorrowful, and had hard work to keep in his tears ; he could but eat but little, and thought he would give worlds to be alone.

Mary sat smiling and happy, the joy of her father and the admiration of Tom's parents.   These tokens in Tom rather increased than lowered her spirits.   She had more color than usual, and studiously avoided looking the apprentice in the face.   The fact is, the thought that Tom liked her as well and in the way that she liked him, had just become a strong hope in her heart.   As Tom helped her into the chaise when the time of parting came, that hope became assurance, as she felt a slight pressure of her hand, and saw that the words, 'Good-by !' were choking him.

'Good-by ! Tom,' said Robert ; 'when you have time you will come and see us.   We shall always have a place for you.'

'You wo'n't have to ask him twice,' said Jane, with an arch look at her husband.

It requires a woman to see into these nice matters of the heart. Robert knew not what the speaker meant.   The daughter was quicker, and jogging her father, said : ' I fear we shall be late home, Sir.'   ' True enough, Mary.'   As the chaise moved away, Tom stood gazing after it long after it was out of sight, and forgot for the moment father, mother, his new shop, his freedom, and every thing but sweet Mary the black-smith's daughter.

The splendid dinner in Ned Alford's rooms was the talk of the next fashionable party in the city. The fine oration of Timothy Blossom was the delight of the audience on commencement day. Whether Edward had a 'part' or not was not inquired about; and indeed it was a matter of little consequence; but the fact of his not deserving one was not of so small moment, as the progress of our story will show.

THE FREE ROVER.

BY W. H. CARPENTER.

I.

A HORSEMAN! a horseman! he travels with speed
The fathomless wave on a marvellous steed,
And the wind as it whistles his raven locks through
But dashes his cheek with a ruddier hue;
And the rain-storm and lightning, though fierce they be,
Are co-mates and play-mates he loves to see!

II.

The tempest, the tempest! what recks he its wrath?
O'er mountains' storm lifted he holds on his path;
Though the heavens are black with the murkiest rack,
And the foam and the spray hiss around on his track,
He calls for a beaker and fills to the brim,
For the danger to others is pastime to him!

III.

A monarch, a monarch! he standeth alone,
The ocean his kingdom, a good ship his throne;
With rude swarthy vassals who wait his command
To ravage with fire or harry with brand,
Or gather in tribute whence tribute is due,
Of silks from the Indies, or gold from Peru.

IV.

A vessel, a vessel is cleaving the brine!
An oath swore the Rover, and washed it with wine:
'Who races with me must be sparing of breath;
If he fly, if he fight, he but wrestles with death!
And the white-livered coward despatched with a blow
But ushers the fate of the sturdier foe!'

V.

A praying, a cursing are borne on the blast—
A moment are heard, in a moment are past;
A surge, and a shriek, and the waters roll over
The pale fools who dared to dispute with the Rover:
'Ho! ho!' quoth the monarch, in blood to his knee,
'More food for the maw of the ravenous sea!'

MY GRAND-FATHER'S PORT-FOLIO.

NUMBER FIVE.

AUNTS SUSAN AND BETSEY.

I never could sympathize with the common depreciation of 'old maids;' perhaps because it has been my good fortune to be conversant only with the better specimens of the sister-hood. A maiden aunt supplied to me the place of a mother from my second year; discharging the arduous duties of that delicate situation with a fidelity to which every good quality I possess bears testimony, and with a tenderness for which I can never be sufficiently grateful. She was a pattern of disinterestedness. Had I been her own child she could not have loved me more, been more patient with my infirmities, or more indefatigable in her discipline of my character. Bless her memory! I could not find it in my power to speak slightingly of the class to which she belonged, were it only for her sake.

But I have other reasons for holding the sister-hood in high esteem. Even while I am writing, there is my own sister Jane in my wife's chamber, ministering to her in her confinement; or perhaps down in the kitchen, superintending the affairs of the household, which under her administration always go on most systematically. Why! what should I have been, and what should I now be, had not a kind Providence appointed the holy estate of single blessedness? Society could not get on otherwise. Without some spare members of the gentler sex to step into the vacant places of dilapidated wives and failing mothers, the whole social machinery would be out of joint. What would become of many old fathers and mothers, did it not generally happen that some one of their daughters, more filial, more disinterested or more homely than the rest, rejecting all thoughts of matrimony, dedicates her affections to them, and *weds* herself to her parents? And how desolate would be the homes of many brothers, whose wives have been taken away from their infant families, were it not for some sister, or other near female relative, whom God has kept in reserve to supply the otherwise irremediable deficiency?

I know that there *are* old maids, who have become so sorely against their inclinations, who have met their fate with exceeding contrariness, and have sustained their lot with perpetual discontent, and to the grievous annoyance of all their kinsfolk and acquaintance. A more disagreeable class than they compose cannot well be conceived of. But such are comparatively few. The number is far greater of those who, having taken the vow deliberately and voluntarily, that they 'may attend upon the Lord without distraction,' and discharge offices of affection and virtue to their friends without constraint, wear the white robe of their virginity with meekness and content, richly meriting esteem.

We have, however, but few of this respectable class in P., for our young women are renowned no less for their comeliness than for other more substantial qualifications of good wives. Indeed many of my jewels now shine in the most respectable circles of Boston and New-York, and our own young men are forced to be expeditious in their selection of a partner, or some stranger of distinction is sure to step in and take our village beauties away. Moreover, from motives of policy, as well as from my conviction of the good moral effects of such an arrangement, I have come to be a strenuous advocate of early marriages; especially when the parties have been intimate from childhood, and are disposed to settle down in the midst of their mutual friends. And if I have sometimes practiced a little slyness in fostering the attachment of two young hearts, when they have appeared mutually fitted for a permanent union, I hope I may be pardoned for it. At any rate, I have good reason to be satisfied with all the matches I have helped to make; and I should be cold-hearted indeed if I could forbear to enter into sympathy with the little children of my flock, whom I have baptized and watched from their infancy, when their hearts begin to glow under the influence of the tender passion. This ever has been and I trust ever will be one of the sweetest of my enjoyments. It is thus I keep the affections of my old heart always green. It is thus I live over again some of the happiest experiences of my youth. I am thus continually reminded of my own first love, and all that pure, sweet passion revives. Again I take those twilight walks with my gentle Mary, the blushing maid of seventeen. Again I knock timidly at her father's door. Again I sit with her soft hand in mine, dreaming of future bliss. Again I watch for her fairy-like form as it emerges from the front gate at the ringing of the church-bell. Again I look across the aisles toward her pew, and think of her when the prayers are said. Again I seek through the meadows for her favorite flowers. Again I sue. Again I read the answer of her tear. Again my whole frame thrills with the rapture of that first kiss. And if my Mary of seventy ever feels, as I believe she does, that she would not exchange her lot for that of the Mary of seventeen, she may thank the young lovers of to-day for the greater part of her happiness. But all this has very little to do with Aunts Susan and Betsey.

They are, or rather *were* until within a few months, for now they are not of the earth, two of the most respectable of my parishioners; daughters of my predecessor in the ministry, and his only children. They inherited from their father a good estate, homely faces, devout sentiments, strong aristocratic tendencies, a rigid formality of manners, and great eccentricity. They occupied the same house in which they were born, which is decidedly the most imposing and venerable mansion in P., situated on the summit of ' Meeting-house Hill,' and not more than a stone's throw from the parish church. They took pride in retaining every thing within and around the house precisely as it was before their orphanage. There was all the old-fashioned furniture carefully bestowed in the same position and order in which it was distributed forty years ago. Old John, their man-of-all-work, and Ruthy their maid, were the same staid and faithful domestics who served the family for not less than half a century. Their curricle was brought over from the 'old country' before their remembrance; and if the quiet steed that drew it about a year ago was not their father's Tom, he was so like him in every particular as greatly to lighten their distress at the necessary innovation. The two ancient portraits that hung in the parlor appeared perfectly at home amidst the relics of other days. Beneath them were the very chairs in which the originals used to sit; between them was the same stand to which they were accustomed to draw up at evening; supporting the same old family Bible which was so often in use, and the same tall silver candlesticks from which its sacred pages were illuminated.

Leaning against the corner in the entry was their father's heavy cane, and above it hung his hat, exactly where he left them when he laid them by for the last time. In the closet in his study were his dressing-gown and shoes, his decanter and wine-glass, his mirror and wash-stand, his wig and hair-powder, as if waiting for him to come back and use them again. On the table were his ink-stand, bristling with shrivelled pens, and his silver snuff-box not quite full. By the fire-side his poker stood ready to be thrust into the coals once more, on a winter evening, to sizzle in the tankard of beer, which John never waited to be asked to bring, when 'Master' was at home, punctually as the clock struck nine. On the mantel-piece were the long pipes and the capacious tobacco-box, which were often in demand to help the studious mind in its weekly preparations for the pulpit. Not a book on the populous shelves had changed its neighborhood since the hand of its owner put it up. Indeed, if the shades of departed worthies are permitted to revisit the familiar scenes of their earthly employment, when that of Doctor S. comes back to his study it can find nothing to mar its happiness.

Aunt Susan, though the younger of the sisters, was by universal consent allowed the priority whenever their names were coupled together. This honor was given to her from the circumstance of her intellectual superiority, and because her character was the more prominent and impressive. Moreover, she was in fact the mistress of the mansion, and always took it upon her to do the honors of the family. She was a perfect lady of the old school; of small stature, fond of rich dresses; of pleasing though formal manners; very precise in the use of language, inclined to criticism, really witty, and prone to indulge in sarcasm, which always received a peculiar pointedness from the sharpness of her tones and the emphasis of her quick and abrupt nod. There was no subject upon which she could not converse, no new book of any value that she did not read, and no measure in politics which she could not and did not discuss with great sagacity and warmth. She was the literary oracle of the town. Her *ipse dixit* was authority beyond appeal in all matters of taste. Her fund of conversation was never exhausted, her tongue never wearied, her invention was never at fault; and he must have been quick-witted and extensively read, who was not made to feel abashed in the course of a long interview with her.

She was at the head of the aristocracy of the town, whether of literature, of wealth, of rank, or of virtue. Her fire-side was accessible only to the most intelligent and refined, or to such as had the claims of real merit. She was particularly jealous of all *new* men and new women; putting them down most effectually by her cold reserve, and keeping every body in his proper place, almost as if she were some fairy to whom had been committed the disposition of the spheres of our town's-people. It did not matter how much her neighbors rebelled against her authority, or who showed signs of an insurrectionary spirit; she swayed her wand like an empress, and always with success. Those whom she slighted, struggled vainly to hold up their heads in the first society; and those who were admitted to her favor were by that circumstance alone stamped, in the eye of the world, as persons of undoubted respectability and sterling worth.

If there was a modest young girl in the town, whose poverty was the only bar to her advancement, Aunt Susan was sure to spy her out, and one or two airings with her in her curricle, or one or two invitations to a select party at her house, with the present of a new bonnet now and then, served effectually to remove the incumbrance. Or if there was a lad at our school of promising parts and virtuous behavior, she would borrow his arm for a walk, lend him her books, place his themes upon her table, take him under her patronage, and if his parents could not bear the expense of his liberal education, pay half of his college bills from her ample purse. In fine, many loved her; many called her proud; a few feared and hated her; but all respected her in their hearts.

Aunt Betsey, who was some five or six years' older, was a lady of a very different stamp. Her figure was tall and corpulent. Her face, which was homely to a proverb, was full and rosy; and though generally seen in repose, as if the soul within were placid and well nigh passionless, yet occasionally lighted up with a smile so full of sweetness as to make the beholder not only forget the irregularity of the features, but even wonder how any thing so beautiful could be produced by such unhandsome instruments. That smile! No beauty in woman's face was ever so winning to me. Its sunshine lingers on my heart and will linger there till I see it again. For why may I not? It was wholly an emanation of the spirit, and I am sure that her spiritual body can borrow from a brighter world no more beautiful expression.

She was studious of plainness — almost careless in her attire. She was usually taciturn, as if to give full scope to her sister's brilliant conversational powers. When she did speak however it was to a good purpose, her remarks being always indicative of sound sense and genuine kindness. She was a most interested listener to aunt Susan, drinking in with undisguised avidity every syllable she uttered; watching every look and gesture with evident tokens of admiration; often looking round upon the faces of their guests to see what impression had been made upon them, and to enjoy their manifestations of approval and delight; habitually coinciding with every sentiment, and never interrupting her, except to qualify her sarcasm when it assumed as it sometimes did a tone of unjustifiable bitterness.

All the affairs of the household, external to the parlor and the drawing-room, devolved upon her, and were managed with singular energy and neatness. In the culinary department her skill was unrivalled; as every Saturday's good pie and pudding which John delivered up with a profound reverence and a masterly flourish of the white napkin at my door, and also my wife's jelly-closet, abundantly testified.   Those Indian puddings, so beautifully red and clear, all shaking but never crumbling in the yellow dish which greeted my appetite every Sunday at dinner, and those deep pumpkin pies which so often graced our tea-table!— I never could have believed that I should miss them as I do. My sister Jane has tried her best a hundred times, and strictly followed the very same recipe; but, mortifying as it is to her to confess it, she acknowledges that she cannot equal them.

Never were two sisters more unlike in appearance and disposition, or more devotedly attached to each other.   They seemed to have but one will and one heart.   They never addressed or looked at one another except with the tenderness of lovers.   There was a child-like fondness in their intercourse that was irresistibly charming, and to strangers sometimes almost ludicrous.   Each was as provident of the other's health and comfort as a mother could be of a delicate child; and often has it excited a titter among our young folk to see them adjusting each other's shawls and pinning an extra handkerchief around the neck, or to hear them interchanging over and over their mutual injunctions to be careful of the cold or the evening dews when they were returning home from a neighbor's house. 'Betsey, are you comfortable?' has long been a by-word with our children.   I have often smiled to hear it passing from one group of the young girls to another in an evening walk; and more than once have joined them in their hearty laugh as the answer came back like a countersign :   'Yes, Susan dear, but I am afraid *you'll* take cold.'

About a year ago, when Aunt Susan was in her eightieth year and Aunt Betsey nearly eighty-five, while the former was riding back under the guidance of old John from the 'middle of the town,' whither she had been to purchase the last new book that had made its appearance, which was a somewhat rare occurrence on the counter of our little book-store, it chanced that in descending a hill one of the fore-wheels of the curricle became suddenly detached, and John and his mistress were both thrown out.   The former received no material injury, but the latter was so stunned and bruised as to render it doubtful whether life was not already extinct.   Assistance was immediately rendered, and she was carefully conveyed home.   Doctor H. being fortunately at hand was soon at her bedside, using every possible means for her resuscitation.

For a long time all his skill proved ineffectual; but at length to the unspeakable gratification of Aunt Betsey the poor woman opened her eyes and looked about her as if waking from a painful dream.   Her glance wandering for a moment gradually became fixed upon the countenance of her sister; at first with a faint smile, as if she was glad to see her once more, but soon with an expression of pity as if she was thinking how distressing it must be to her to see her sufferings. Perceiving that her senses had fully returned, I took the doctor by the hand and beckoning to the rest to follow us, led him out of the room, and left the sisters to indulge their feelings as they might for a little while alone.

During several weeks the patient continued to suffer greatly and with less and less prospect of recovery. Her sister remained constantly in the chamber, from which no entreaties could prevail upon her to be absent for an hour. She ministered at her bed-side with almost as much activity and interest as if she were in the prime of life. At length however, when it became evident to her that her sister would never amend, the old nurse would occasionally steal away while she slept, to give vent in secret to her grief, but quickly return to have ready when she should awake that same placid countenance which she knew was so pleasant to the invalid.

'Betsey, dear,' she heard her say one morning, when she had just finished reading to her a favorite Psalm — and she came nearer to catch the almost inaudible whisper in which she spoke — 'bring me our parents' pictures. I wish to see those venerated faces once more before I die. I feel that my hour has come. They smiled upon us at our birth; I wish to realize that they are smiling upon me while I die.' The portraits were brought and placed opposite to her at the foot of the bed. 'Sweet! sweet!' she murmured; 'thus ——.' The remainder of the sentence was lost. 'Love · · · near · · · all · · · God · · · good · · · peace · · · praise · · · glory · · · home!' These detached words, parts evidently of connected sentences which she had not strength to articulate, fell at intervals upon her sister's ear and mine, as we bent over her. They were evidently visions of the heavenly world which she was striving to reveal to us. Her lips moved till with a deep sigh the spirit and the body separated from their mysterious union.

Aunt Betsey, as we all expected, survived but a few days; but those were any thing but days of mourning. 'How beautifully she died!' she repeated over and over. There never had been any selfishness in her feelings; and to think that her sister had been so happy, and that she should so soon meet her again, seemed to quiet every pang of bereavement that in other circumstances she might have felt.

'Let the pictures remain where they are,' she said to Ruthy after the funeral was over, which she had been too feeble to attend. Early that evening she lay down upon her sister's pillow and never left it till she died. A day or two after, a gentle stupor stole over her senses, and the same veil of placid repose which had so often covered from observation her deep and rich feelings during her life-time, shrouded whatever sweet experiences her spirit may have been permitted to enjoy in its passage to heaven.

There was something characteristic as well as commendable in the manner in which the sisters left their property. They had entered into an agreement several years before their death that at the decease of either, the whole of their estate, which they held in common, should accrue to the survivor; and that upon her demise it should be distributed as follows: Old John and Ruthy were to remain tenants of the mansion, under the care of such trusty person or persons as I might select, as long as they lived. Every thing upon the premises was to remain unaltered, with the exception of their father's library, which was bequeathed to myself, with the privilege of transferring it to my study whenever it might suit my convenience. When both these trusty domestics should have followed their mistresses to the 'Jerusalem that is free,' the whole of the real estate was to come into the possession of the town of P., to be used for the benefit of its poor. After sundry legacies to individuals and a liberal bequest to the church had been paid, the remainder of their personal property was to be devoted to the establishment of a fund for the support of the schools of the town and the collegiate education of indigent young men.

The library I could not bear to have removed while every thing else remained untouched. So there remain the old books and manuscripts awaiting the general revolution which will succeed the death of Ruthy and John. Meanwhile I often amuse myself by sitting in the old doctor's chair and turning over the pages which so often ruffled at the touch of his patient finger. Some of the works are ancient and curious, and I am anticipating a rich treat in examining them at my own fire-side.

Among the manuscripts I have found one which purports to be a 'Journal of a Voyage from New-England to Barbadoes, on board the Thomas and Eliza, of four hundred and fifty tons, twenty-four guns and forty men, Henry Sherburne, commander; begun on the eve of March 29, 1709, from Scarlet-Wharf in Boston, in company with the Dolphin, of two hundred and fifty tons, sixteen guns and twenty men, Nathaniel Green, commander, and my good friend Mr. John Russel, surgeon.' In the beginning of this Journal the writer remarks: 'To fill up the vacant spaces I shall transcribe pleasant popular songs, and such scraps of verse as hit my fancy, from books and from my own memory.' The voyage was continued to London. The good gentleman sailed in the capacity of chaplain. The armed ships were for the protection of a fleet of merchant vessels.

I have just returned from a visit to his study, where I have copied for my own amusement the following 'scraps of verse' that have 'hit *my* fancy:'

THREE POETICAL FRAGMENTS

FROM A BOOK ENTITLED 'POEMS ON SEVERAL OCCASIONS,' BY THE AUTHOR OF 'CENSURE OF THE ROTA,' 1675.

I.

INSECTS.

WHAT skill is in the frame of insects shown!
How fine the threads in their small textures spun!
How close those instruments and engines knit,
That motion and their slender sense transmit!
Like *living watches*, each of them conceals
A thousand springs of life and moving wheels:
Each ligature a lab'rinth seems; each part
All wonder is, all workmanship, all art!

II.

HEARING A DRUM.

GREAT talkers, that with all their din,
Nothing of solid have within;
Who make a noise, and promise fair,
But yet examined are but air,
When to *performances* they come,
Prove louder nothings, like a drum.

III.

FAME.

HOLLOW and empty things alone are found
As empty air, to yield and spread a sound :
And none but such as hollow places ring
With sounds that still from hollow causes spring.
So void of substance is an airy *fame* ;
So vain is he that doth that nothing claim ;
So vain the hollow world that still employs
Its empty echoes to return the noise.

———

KING CHARLES THE SECOND,

ON THE PARLIAMENT'S BRINGING IN THE BILL OF EXCLUSION IN JANUARY, MDCLXXX. — XXXI.

UNDER five hundred kings three kingdoms groan ;
Go FINCH," dissolve them — CHARLES is on the throne,
And by the grace of GOD will reign alone.

What would the Commons have ?   The royal line
Heaven doth dispose of — 't is not theirs nor mine ;
But 't is by God kings reign and are divine.

I represent the King of kings, who gave
The crown, the sword, the sceptre that I have :
I am God's servant, not the people's slave.

Bid them be gone,† Finch, they are d—d uncivil,
To dare to drag me with them to the devil :
To save three kingdoms I will not do evil.

The Presbyterians, sick of too much freedom,
High ripe for Bedlam ! 't is full time to bleed 'em ;
The SECOND CHARLES doth neither fear nor need 'em.

———

AN EPITAPH

ON THE LATE REVEREND DR. SH——, DEAN OF SAINT PAUL'S.

HERE lies within this holy place,
　　The Lord have mercy on him !
A weasel in a wooden case,
Exempt from human plagues, unless
　　You lay his wife upon him.

---

* Lord Chancellor.　　† Dissolved January 18, 1680—1.

Some people think if this were done,
  Though dead, he would be ready
To rise before his time, and run
The Lord knows where, again to shun
  That termagant, his lady !

Since he is gone, 't is hard that she
  Should be so long deserted.
Why, Death, should 'st thou so partial be ?
Since all good people do agree
  'T is pity they are parted.

Pray bid her, when she comes, not prate,
  But cease her teasing nonsense :
For if the weasel smell a rat,
He 'll fly his wife, I 'll tell you that,
  As once he did his conscience.

ON THE DEATH OF PRINCE RUPERT, MDCLXXXIII.

Utinam Viveres.

BY MR. FLATMAN.

MAN surely is not what he seems to be !
  Surely ourselves we overrate !
Forgetting that, like other creatures, we
  Must bend our heads to fate.

' Lord of the whole creation, Man ! '
  (How big the title shows !)
Trifles away a few uncertain years,
Cheated with hopes and racked with fears,
  Through all life's little span —
Then down to silence and to darkness goes !

And when he dies, the crowd that trembling stood
Ere while struck with the terror of a nod,
Shake off their wonted reverence with his claims,
And at their pleasure use his poor remains.

LINES

ON BISHOP ATTERBURY'S BURYING THE DUKE OF BUCKINGHAM, A DEBAUCHEE AND DEIST.

' *I have no hope!* ' the Duke declares, and dies ;
' *In sure and certain hope,* ' the prelate cries.
Of these two learned peers I pri'thee say man,
Which is the lying knave, the priest or layman ?

The Duke departs an *infidel* confest :
He 's ' our dear brother,' says the lordly priest.
The Duke, though knave, still ' brother dear ' he cries :
And who can say the reverend prelate lies ?

THE FUNERAL OF WILLIAM THE CONQUEROR.

THE corpse of the Conqueror being carried into the church of St. Stephens, and the services begun, one ARTHUR FITZ ASCELIN, a Vavasor, pressing through the crowd and standing upon a high stone, called in a loud voice to the prelates, forbidding them to inter the body in that place, which was the area of his father's house, unjustly seized by the Conqueror, whom he summoned before the Divine Tribunal for that act of oppression. The bishops immediately inquired into the truth of the charge, and finding the allegation just, agreed to pay the demand. The ceremony was then suffered to proceed.

THROUGH fair St. Stephen's spacious aisle the funeral train advance,
Each nodding plume is thrown aside — reversed each burnished lance;
A gallant host for prowess famed, they come in sad array,
To mingle with its kindred dust their chieftain's lifeless clay.

Through the tall casement's tinted panes the parting sunbeams fall,
And paint with bars of rainbow light the chancel's sculptured wall;
O'er blazoned tomb and fretted vault a flood of brilliance shed,
And gild with golden drapery the scutcheons of the dead.

And sacred Music lends its aid to solemnize the hour,
And bind the rugged warrior's soul in spells of mystic power;
Now rising high, like ocean's roar, its swelling peal is heard,
Now breathing low yet mildly sweet, like song of woodland bird.

The glimming day-light fades away, the holy tapers glare,
And incense borne in curling wreaths perfumes the twilight air;
The white-robed priest on bended knee, with deep pathetic tone
Pours forth a thrilling homily to Heaven's eternal throne.

'For him, the valiant Conqueror, whose form of stalwart might
Was foremost in the battle-fray — the hero of the fight;
The boast of Norman chivalry, fair England's bounteous lord,
From stately dome and cottage-hearth be sorrowing dirges poured!

'See! where embowered mid ancient trees our cloistered abbeys stand!
Those massive piles were reared aloft by his creative hand;
Such noble deeds of pious zeal and deep devoted love,
Approved by Heaven's propitious glance, are registered above.

'His spirit long shall linger o'er the scenes his presence blest,
And long shall sorrowing Friendship's voice bewail the absent guest:
From baron's hall and peasant's hut the sounds of grief ascend,
And wrinkled Age and smiling Youth demand their common friend.

'Almighty GOD! before whose throne the haughtiest heads must bow,
With blighted hopes and contrite hearts we kneel before thee now;
To crave for him whose mighty soul hath burst its bonds of clay,
A brighter crown in realms above, undimmed by earth's decay!'

The priest his anthems ceased; before the marble altar's base,
With downcast eye and visage sad, the regal pall they place;
When hark! a voice amid the crowd demands in accents dread:
'Why do ye gild with honeyed lies the memory of the dead?

'The very spot whereon ye stand, each foot of earth is mine!
My rights, contemned by tyrant pride, I never will resign;
Your robber-chief, whose praise ye chant in Flattery's servile strains,
Must seek some kindlier resting-place to shroud his cold remains!

' A brother's blood in battle shed here crimsoned the green sod —
Methinks 't would rise from out yon grave in vengeance-cries to God ;
A father's ashes rest in peace where yonder altar stands —
I ne'er will see his dust disturbed by strangers' impious hands.

' My fertile fields despoiled and waste, to glut your despot's pride,
My cheerful hearth defaced and sad, with kindred blood-drops dyed,
Shall plead before the righteous Judge who hears the mourner's prayer,
And slighteth not the lowliest voice that supplicates His care ! '

In each rude beating bosom these unwonted feelings glowed,
While from the dauntless speaker's lips his stern remonstrance flowed ;
Then counting forth the glistening coin, large store of gold they gave,
And *bought*, with Mammon's treasured hoards, their chief's appointed grave.

LIFE IN HAYTI.

NUMBER SIX.

THE government of Hayti is called ' republican.' The chief magistrate bears the title of President, but then he is president *for life*, and nominates his successor. They have a senate, the members of which are elected for the term of nine years; but then the candidates are selected *by the president*, who sends three names to the legislature, from which they elect one to fill a vacancy. They have also a chamber of representatives who are elected from the people; but not by universal suffrage, there being more restrictions upon this point than comports with a true republican form of government. Since the consolidation of the government up to 1840, more than twenty years, there has been very little interest displayed by the people in their elections, and the representatives are usually chosen in a quiet, matter-of-fact way, not one in five of the electors going to the polls. I saw only one contested election; and in this case the commotion was entirely confined to the two candidates, which resulted, after months of provocation and outrage on each side, in the death of one by the hand of the other, and the escape of the murderer from the country. He fled to New-York and thence to the Windward Islands, where he now resides with a sentence of outlawry on his head.

A peculiar feature in the election of representatives is, that a *substitute* is always chosen together with the regular member to take the latter's place ' en cas d' accident.'

| LIBERTÉ, | | EGALITÉ. |
| RÉPUBLIQUE | | D'HAITI. |

Thus are ostentatiously headed all state papers, proclamations, and other public documents. The blank space in the centre is filled with the coat of arms, a palm-tree, beneath which repose piles of cannon-balls, and guns, drums, swords and standards. Such a motto looks one in the face from every coin and ' billet de caissé,' and the important maxim heads every stamped paper employed in commerce or in law; while even the journal of the trader cannot prove a debt unless the book is first sent to the treasurer at the capital and by him stamped on every page at an expense to the owner of six cents for each impression. These stamps were to me interesting from the part they played in the progress of the American revolution. They are on common writing paper, each sheet bearing three impressions, one of which is the above-mentioned arms of Hayti, in printing ink, the second is the value or price of the sheet (varying from six cents to four dollars) in red ink, and the third is in raised letters, ' Chambre des Comptes,'signifying that the account has been taken in that department. These are distributed to the sub-treasurers in the different ' communes,' by them sold to the people, and thus bring in a considerable amount annually to the public purse. They are required to be used for all bills brought into law for notes, contracts, government bills for duties, and many other purposes. They are not however exacted by persons engaged in trade in their daily intercourse with each other under ordinary circumstances; therefore the great mass of business-paper, as bills of goods, receipts, etc., have not passed through the operation of the 'timbre.'

With the name and nature of his government thus constantly before his eyes in a variety of ways, the Haytien becomes fully imbued with the important rank which he fancies his country holds in the scale of nations, and moreover that he is the citizen of a *bonâ fide* republic. To be sure he is jostled at every step by an impudent soldier, and the roll of the drum or the clatter of muskets is continually grating upon his ears; and there are sundry little matters beside the presence of a standing army which do not exactly tally with some people's ideas of a republican form of government; but what of that? He reads every hour in the day (if read he can) 'Liberté, Egalité, Republique d' Haiti;' and what all the world says must be true, his own convictions or experience to the contrary notwithstanding. In the words of an infantile philosopher, yclept 'Chicken Little,' 'How can he *help* knowing it? He sees it with his eyes and he hears it with his ears;' and would it not be rank skepticism to doubt such authorities?

JEAN PIERRE BOYER, who is now president of Hayti, was nominated to that station by his predecessor, the popular and lamented ALEXANDRE PETION, who died in 1818. Boyer was then a general commanding the arrondissement of Port-au-Prince. He is not far from sixty-five years of age, in complexion a mulatto of the ordinary brown hue; his hair is curly, but his features have nothing of the negro expression. His eyes are black and sparkling, nose long and face thin. Though of spare figure and middling height, yet an air of dignity and self-possession is never wanting. His administration of the affairs of state proves him a man of remarkable talents and sagacity; and he is probably as sincere a friend of his country as that country has ever known.

I am aware that a party is now arrayed in more or less open opposition to Boyer, and it is to be feared that his day of popularity may pass away; I say *feared*, because I consider that his death or abdication would be a great misfortune to the country. Possessing great skill and judgment in preserving a balance between the blacks and mixed bloods, keeping down their jealousy of each other by incessant watchfulness and timely appointments to office or promotions from one class or the other, as circumstances may seem to demand, he is in this single talent alone of the greatest benefit in preserving tranquillity and mutual good feeling. Though possessing almost unlimited power as the commander-in-chief, and having as boundless authority over the civil officers, yet no one can tax him with ever having shown a disposition to play the tyrant. I have never heard an act of cruelty laid at his door during the twenty-four years of his administration, although he is sometimes energetic and perhaps arbitrary in his proceedings. When he has displayed the latter quality I believe it has been more from a conviction that the public weal demanded such action than from any desire to injure others or benefit himself. Could the writer address a word of advice to the people at this time, he would warn them to beware of quarrelling with their chief magistrate. That man should be cherished, under whose wise government they have lived in peace so many years. His wisdom consolidated that government by conciliating the royalists of the north, while by his valor he reduced the Maroons of the south. His loss would very probably be followed by a renewed struggle between the colors, at the anticipation of which every Haytien, who knows any thing of his country's history, should fear and tremble. They should beware how they rouse this sleeping animosity. They should beware of the turbulent spirit of a fierce and impoverished soldiery, who will thirst for more blood when blood once begins to flow. They should reflect, either that a black president must succeed, who to ingratiate his color may oppress or even massacre the other race, or that another mulatto will take the reins, who without the coolness and experience and impartiality of Boyer, will soon lose his balance amid the multifarious minutiæ of the administration which he is obliged to watch and control. It seems as if scarcely a sergeant was promoted from the ranks or a clerk appointed in a custom-house, that Boyer did not first know all the circumstances of the case, and decide whether the choice fell upon suitable individuals. Not only has he to choose individuals of proper capacity, but he must also have them of the proper *color.* In every department, whether it be a company of soldiers or a treasury office, there must be a judicious proportion of yellow and black officers.

There is for instance a functionary called the 'Grand Judge,' the head of the law, a sort of grand-mufti who resides at the capital. To prove to the blacks that they may expect even-handed justice in law-matters, Boyer has vested this high office in a huge black, named VOLTAIRE, who is I believe a very worthy sort of man. The public weigher of Port-au-Prince, who is brought into constant collision with the laborers and cartmen of that city, (a set of ruffians who are inconceivably lawless and insolent) is as black as the ace of spades; and the same is the complexion of Colonel Victor, the commandant of the place, who is a most active and meritorious officer, a perfect Fouché in ferreting out criminals of every description. Herein is displayed the good judgment of the Executive. Let him put a mulatto at the head of the police of the city, and straightway there are tumults and quarrels on every hand ; but with a smart black to take his own color in hand, quiet reigns at once, wherever his presence is to be feared. The other instances named above are analogous in their bearings. There are also scattered throughout the island many black officers, civil and military, of high rank, generals commanding whole districts, and judges of the different courts. Thus we see, that beside the ordinary cares and demands made by a country upon its rulers, we have here a new and grave matter of domestic economy, namely, the preservation of the equilibrium of color. This is doubtless the great source of trouble in the South-American states, which occasions so incessantly the building up and the pulling down of governments, the binding together and the severing of states. The chief who sweeps over the mountains of Guatemala, leading hordes of desperadoes to conquest and rapine, the bold and cruel Carréra, is a full-blooded Indian ; and how the Spaniards crouch and shrink away from his presence! Will my country ever see the day when part of her policy must be to conciliate and sue for the suffrages of a now despised race? When one of the questions to be answered of a political aspirant must be : 'What is his *color* ?' Who will dare to grapple with this stupendous question? During the past winter the law prohibiting intermarriage between whites and blacks was very near being repealed in the legislature of Massachusetts. Let this and a thousand other signs of the times be consulted before any one shall undertake lightly to consider it as the vagary of a wild fancy.

There are various complaints against the administration of Boyer from those who perhaps think a change of rulers will change the habits of the people. The ' hard times,' that old hobby-horse for malecontents to ride, is a fertile cause of murmuring. The indolence of the country people and their irregular, debauched habits, making a wilderness of what should be a garden, are doubtless crying evils. But how would they remedy them? Would they have another Christophe to make men answer with their lives for petty offences? If they could find another black chief who would acquire such an ascendency over his color as to induce them to admit such rigor, would he not be likely to follow the example of Christophe in his treatment of the colored population also? Would he not aim too, as did the black king, at their *extermination?* The fable of the ' Frogs desiring a King' suggests itself forcibly in the contemplation of such a state of things. But the only reason of the blacks submitting so slavishly to Christophe was their confidence in his ability to protect them from a still more dreaded enemy — the French. Without such influence continually operating in his favor, no man could compel them to labor as he did. Habits of industry with a nation, as with an individual, must be grounded on a better foundation than that of despotism. Industry and thrift must prevail from a knowledge of the *blessings* which accompany them, and not from the mandate of a king; otherwise they will be as short-lived as the frowns of the despot himself. Is there any individual in the country who, if raised to Boyer's place, could induce the cultivators to perform more labor than they now do? If it is their wish to do their best, they have an excellent opportunity under the present administration; at least those who do not belong to the army; and if it is not in the negro character to be from choice prudent, thrifty, and diligent, it certainly is not in the power of any ruler, black, white or yellow, to alter that nature.

The slave is industrious not by nature but by fear of the whip; and if he shakes off the fetters of a white master to wear those of a black one, he is far from improving his condition in any respect. To this day the name of their Emperor DESSALINES is pronounced beneath the breath. This savage, who wore the imperial purple for a few years, having previously been a general under Toussaint and Christophe, exceeded the latter in ferocity. When any unfortunate wretch fell under his suspicion or incurred his displeasure, he would order him into his presence; and after the interview it was a common custom for him to point with his bony finger to his victim, and cry to his soldiers: ' *Couper moi tête Mouchee, (Monsieur), la!* ' in a squeaking voice and clumsy dialect, which he brought from the coast of Africa, for he was an imported slave. He it was, who hearing of disaffection in a distant quarter, swore as he mounted his horse that ' he would ride to his saddle-girths in blood ' — not of white men but of his own color! He was killed on his route by a party lying in wait for him at a place called ' Le Pont Rouge,' which from the glorious deed done there has become the most famous locality in the island. The fearful reign of Dessalines resembles more that of Jenghis Khan or Timour the Tartar than that of any despot of more recent date. If a cultivator was pointed out as very indolent, he buried him alive in presence of all his neighbors! Such a fear pervaded every individual, that immense crops were forced from the soil, particularly on those plantations belonging to himself or his friends, which comprised all the best in the vicinity. What then did the blacks gain by changing the yoke of French masters for that of this monster? Let the Haytiens destroy their President Boyer and they may find another Emperor Dessalines. There is many a soldier and officer in the army who might prove good imitators. I could point out a hundred such men.

Another cause of complaint against the government is the late treaty with France. Of this it is only necessary to say, that the French admiral had a powerful fleet to back his demands, and if the people had been disposed to resist them, why did they not signify as much through their representatives? On the contrary, the whole country was filled with joy on the occasion. Upon the ratification of the treaty a new financial policy was adopted. The import duties which before were paid in currency was ordered to be paid in gold and silver, and without any material reduction on the former tariff. This of course inflicted a heavy but to the mass an imperceptible tax upon the people, and the money was consecrated to the payment of the instalments due the French government. It will be seen that by this operation the country lost one of its most important sources of revenue, from which it had previously met the expenditures. But the expenditure was not lessened, for causes mentioned below. How then continue to meet them? In the first place there was a radical reform in the custom houses. Severe laws were enacted against frauds on the revenue', and vigilant officers appointed to enforce them. Here doubtless there was a great saving made to the nation, both in the import and export duties. But still the deficiency was not made up. The only resource left was the manufacture of paper money. But the mere signing of names to pieces of paper does not create wealth; and accordingly the currency has steadily declined since the treaty, as well as previously; and in this month of March, 1842, Spanish doubloons are quoted in Port-au-Prince at forty-six dollars, showing a premium of nearly three hundred per cent. In 1823 they were at par; in 1826 they had risen to twenty-four dollars; in 1830, to thirty dollars; in 1832, back to twenty-four dollars; in 1838, (the year of the treaty,) thirty-six dollars; in 1842, forty-six dollars.

If the French indemnity agreed upon is too high, it is so from the *habits* and not from the *capacity* of the people to meet it. If such is the case, there must follow one of three results: a reduction, a war, or national bankruptcy. And in any event, I do not see that the responsibility should be thrown upon the President. The ultimatum of France was a treaty or a war; and Boyer was obliged to make the best terms he could under the circumstances. If the French find the government making honest efforts to satisfy their terms, they will not be disposed to be severe in their exactions; but they will doubtless insist that the finances be managed with all possible economy. This demand brings up an inquiry whether the expenditure is not *needlessly large?* Is there no point where retrenchment may be made? Where for example is the necessity of a standing army, forty thousand strong, with no enemy to attack or resist? The soldiers are paid six dollars the 'pay,' equal to a dollar a week; including the officers and a suit of clothes furnished each soldier annually. The pay of the army alone costs the country some twenty-five hundred thousand dollars per annum. About one third of the troops appear on parade every Sunday in their several districts, and on pay-day, once in six weeks, every man is expected to make his appearance. At other times, excepting only when on guard duty, which service requires perhaps sixty or eighty men from each regiment, they are masters of their own time; but they have just enough of military life to disgust them with labor and to render their homes irksome and unattractive. The lounging, dissipated habits contracted in useless garrisons and parades render them a worthless portion of the population, and a baneful example to all around them. There are however exceptions to this remark, there being many individuals who when not on military duty are industrious and exemplary in their habits.

Can this army be disbanded, or greatly reduced, and the sword and spear be exchanged for more useful implements? This important measure every intelligent native has long desired to see accomplished, as the only one which can restore general prosperity. Before the treaty it would not have been a popular measure, when a French fleet might land a hostile army upon their shores at any moment; but this danger removed, there seemed no longer any reason for maintaining such a force, unless it might be to promote any ambitious designs entertained by the Executive, or to strengthen him against revolution. That President Boyer has no ambitious designs, he has proved by his official conduct for a quarter of a century.

From the day of the first revolt in the plain of Cape François in 1791 to the conclusion of the treaty in 1838, the island had been in a constant state of excitement connected with the movements or designs of France. There was a constant apprehension that fresh attempts would be made to bring the island under the dominion of its old masters. Every slave felt that his liberty was not complete, and that he might be called upon at any moment to defend it. At last an amicable and definite arrangement is made, and there is every prospect of an undisturbed peace spreading its blessings over the land. The people are congratulating themselves upon the dawn of a proclaimed and certain liberty which has opened upon them. Already the subject of disbanding or greatly reducing 'the Janissaries,' as they have been called, is mooted in a thousand circles; and strong hopes are entertained that the brutal soldiery may be transformed into quiet agriculturists. Much now depended upon the President. Would he be willing or would he *dare* to disband an army which had always existed since the first outbreak of the revolution? Would he dare to encounter the intrigues and hatred of the officers, who would thus be thrown out of service and deprived of a comfortable living? Would he be willing to give up the protection of a body of troops whose officers for the most part he had himself put in commission?

These were grave topics, demanding sound judgment; but no time was allowed the government to mature any new plans or adopt any new policy. Revolutionary movements began to develope themselves. A black officer of rank revolted at Cape François, but was defeated and shot by the troops who remained true to their allegiance. Before the excitement arising from this affair had subsided, a blow was struck nearer home. On a certain night, General Inginæ, the secretary of state, and prime adviser and minister of the President, was at his plantation near Léogane, some twenty miles from the capital, when a horseman rode up to the door at midnight and demanded to see to him. Madame Inginæ, suspecting mischief at such an untimely hour, endeavored to dissuade her husband from going to the door. He however persisted, and sallying forth asked his visiter's business. 'Despatches,' said the man, touching his hat, 'from the city.' He took the pretended papers and turning about to enter the house, the assassin drew a pistol and stretched him nearly lifeless before his own threshold; and uttering a malediction upon both his victim and his master, he galloped away. Medical aid was procured without delay, and as soon as possible the general was conveyed to Port-au-Prince. My friend Dr. S., from New-York, his physician, informed me that the ball struck him in the back of the neck, went straight through and came out of his mouth, taking two teeth with it; but his lips being parted at the instant were not touched. This story may seem rather of the 'Munchausen' order, but I was at Port-au-Prince at the time, and am desirous of confining myself strictly to the truth in these remarks. But there is a sequel to the adventure: Inginæ, though advanced in life, *survived* the wound, and still lives to be, what he has been for thirty years, the Haytien

Talleyrand, with no other faculty injured save that of speech. He is a tall, portly quadroon, of a fair ruddy complexion. His countenance bears a pleasant expression, and in his own house he is cheerful and affable to those about him. His large round head, covered with curling locks of snowy whiteness, is often seen at mass, and on other important occasions. With an inquisitive and watchful mind, penetrating into the most distant and the most (apparently) trifling affairs of the country, visited by every person of any note who comes to the capital, from whom he extracts all possible information — many paying their court to him by giving all the intelligence from their respective districts which they possess — having the ear and the confidence of the President, and universally acknowledged to be a man of superior talents, it will be seen that General Inginæ is a most important personage.

The day succeeding the attempt upon his life, it was found that the blacks in the neighboring hills were in a state of insurrection, when troops were instantly sent against them from Léogane, and they were subdued without difficulty. Six of the ring-leaders were captured, one of whom was the assassin, and proved to be a mulatto residing on the estate of the man whom he attempted to murder, and from whom he had received many favors. The negroes had been falsely made to believe that there was to be a general rising throughout the island, though for what purpose does not plainly appear. It is perhaps merely an illustration of the old saw, that the devil will find work for those who have none. The prisoners were executed in Port-au-Prince a few days after, and thus died this attempt. With such threatenings of a coming storm, of course all thoughts, if any had existed, of reducing the army, were abandoned, as there was a prospect that their services might be demanded ere long to sustain the government.

Meanwhile came trouble in the House of Representatives. Certain members arrayed themselves in open opposition to the President. A demand was made by them, that an account should be rendered to that body of the disposition of the public funds, or a certain portion of them, for some years past. This was resisted by the government party, who had as usual an overwhelming majority. In fact there has never been but one party, though occasionally some *erratic* spirit would wander far enough out of the beaten track to show that opposition *might* exist, to a certain extent, at any rate. But now, in the session I think of 1839, the liberals, as they designated themselves, came out bold and furious. Their leader was Dumesle, a black lawyer, representing Aux Cayes, which district by the way has the largest proportion of colored population of any in the island. He is said to be very eloquent. I can vouch for his tremendous voice and well-oiled tongue, though I never heard him plead before 'listening senates,' or in a court of law. He has been a vexer of the 'powers that be' for several years.

Another bone which he and his friends had to pick with the President, was on the occasion of the choice of certain senators. The constitution requires that the President send in three names to the legislature, from which they elect one to that station. There were five senators to be chosen, and there were not furnished as many names as the law required. How Boyer explained his conduct here, I do not know, but he was sustained and the senators chosen. The violence or contumacy of the rebellious representatives continued, until one fine day a stop was put to their want of politeness by expelling the whole of them from the house by a vote of the ' collared' members; and the next morning, when they went up to take their seats, they received a modest hint from the gentleman in a soldier's coat at the door, that ' they were not wanted.' Finding them unwilling to take his *ipse dixit* on so important a matter, he stepped back and presenting his bayonet, soon convinced them by that potent argument that he did not speak without book. The expunged gentlemen walked quietly away, and were soon off to their districts and constituents. How one of them was received will hereafter be shown. These members were from Aux Cayes, Aquia, Jeremie, and one from the capital itself.

The fact of the President not sending in as many names as are required by law is not so arbitrary an act as it may at first appear; he of course will give no other names than those of his friends, and it can make but little difference whether he furnishes ten or twenty candidates. The matter of the public accounts is more serious. Doubtless it is a grave political offence to refuse to account to the people for the distribution of the revenue; but it seems incredible that the head of the state can have been a peculator when he is exposed at any moment to be called to an account; for though the representatives may defend him to-day they may desert him to-morrow. But there is a far better reason for believing Boyer to be honest in financial matters, and that is, his general character for integrity. At all events there cannot have been any great *surplus* in former years; and if there had been, nothing seems more easy than to detect any chicanery, as the financial machinery is extremely simple.

In Port au Prince resides an officer called the Treasurer General, from whose department issues all the money which forms the circulation of the country, both paper and metallic, when it is first put out by government. A sub-treasurer resides in each town, at whose office are paid all duties and other monies to government, and he pays the sums required for the troops and other expenses. If he has a surplus, it is held until drawn for, for some other district, and if he is short, he forthwith despatches a barge with a guard of soldiers to the capital for a supply. The accounts are made up monthly and sent to the treasurer-general; and a defalcation on the part of these officers has seldom taken place — the prisons of Hayti being most dismal places of abode. . Sᴛ. Cʀᴏɪx.

HOPE OF HEAVEN.

Say not there is no hope for thee,
    That guilt will cling to thee for ever;
That all thy lot is misery,
    And peace and joy shall cheer thee never.
In that bright heaven where shine the stars,
    Where the fair moon rides gloriously,
Where nought its bliss and beauty mars,
        There 's hope for thee!   c.

WINDERMERE.

I 've floated o'er thee, Windermere !
   When Spring, arrayed in smiles,
Had kissed thy flashing waves to sleep,
   And garlanded thine isles :
Beneath the flood its image fair
   To each green islet clung,
And quivering there in liquid light
   The mirrored mountains hung !

I see them now ! And on the hills
   That gird the beauteous scene,
I see the streams with silver feet
   Dance down the sloping green ;
Like children in a joyous race
   The struggling wavelets hie,
Until into thy stainless breast
   They leap, and murmuring die.

Full well I know those sparkling streams,
   In noon's unclouded glow ;
And shimmering in the moon's mild beams,
   I 've seen them foam and flow.
Ay, every burn and torrent there
   I wandered by so long,
That blindfold I could tell them all,
   Each by its own sweet song.

But not alone, bright Windermere !
   Does this fair landscape stand
Among the memory-pictured scenes
   Of that enchanted land :
How should it ?   When each lake's green shores,
   Each dell and field I 've trod,
Where WORDSWORTH linked to deathless verse
   The lowliest works of GOD !

Those fields — I 've read ' The Daisy ' there,
   Until the simple lay
Seemed gushing from the milk-white cups
   That beautified my way.
While ' LUCY's ' music-breathing face
   Beset my waking dreams,
Now peeping through the wild-rose hedge,
   Now smiling in the streams.

And well might Fancy weave her spells
   Where Poesy had taught
How pictures in immortal words
   By Genius could be wrought ;
Where WORDSWORTH in his youthful soul
   Her sweet revealings stored,
And COLERIDGE, borne upon her wings,
   Amid the thunder soared.

For this the shores of England's lakes
  Are hallowed ground to me ;
This, and the beauty God has showered
  On mountain, wave and tree ;
Till Memory, steward of the Past,
  Has lost the power to bring
Back from the deepening gloom of years
  The scenes of which I sing ;
Though paths as green my feet may tread
  Where nobler waters roll,
Those silvan haunts shall be to me
  The Garden of the Soul !

                                          J. M.

THE QUOD CORRESPONDENCE.

The Attorney.

CHAPTER XX.

It needed but a glance at the excited features of Higgs, as he broke from the grasp of the Attorney and rushed into the outer office, to see that his mind was made up for murder ; but when he found the apartment empty, and his victim gone, its very quiet and air of desertion brought with it a reäction. It was so hushed, so dim and gloomy ! A faint blaze flickered up from the crumbling fire, and fantastic shadows leaped along the dusky halls, whirling and flitting about like spectres at revel, and apparently beckoning him on. Higgs was a man of little imagination, and not prone to weak fancies ; but for a moment he yielded to a feeling of misgiving. This irresolution however was transient ; for the next instant he turned and warning the Attorney back, sprang through the door, darting along the dark passage and down the tottering stairs, utterly reckless of life and limb in his headlong haste. He heard the echo of retreating footsteps in front of him, but when he reached the street he lost them, nor was there a soul in sight.

It was very dark ; for although the night was clear, there was no moon. The house stood in a neighborhood where none cared to linger after night-fall ; a lone, dreary spot, of bad repute, where a blow might be struck or a stab given, and the last cry of the victim be echoed through the deserted rooms of ruined houses ; or if heard, heard only by those too much accustomed to sounds of suffering and despair to heed them. In such a place Higgs feared no interruption to any act of violence. Whatever he did, he knew that few would be the wiser. Perhaps after a time this man might be missed ; his body found ; a bustle created at first, and a search made ; but soon, amid the never-ending stir and excitement of this vast city, the matter would blow over, and both the murderer and his victim be forgotten.

With thoughts like these flashing through his mind, he hurried up the street, looking into the houses. The doors of many were wide open ; some because they were deserted and tenantless, others because their occupants were too wretchedly poor to offer temptation for theft or burglary. In one he thought he saw the dim outline of a human figure shrinking back as he approached ; but at length entering and groping about in the dark, he found he was mistaken. It was only a door swinging idly in the wind. Feeling his way out, he resumed his search without success. He saw but one person ; a man as savage and reckless as himself, who half paused and eyed him as if he were on no peaceable errand ; and then went on, hesitating and looking back until the darkness hid him. Finding his task a fruitless one, Higgs turned on his heel and walked slowly back, endeavoring to solve in his mind the somewhat uncertain problem whether the abrupt departure of the old man was in any manner connected with the conversation which had taken place between Bolton and himself, or was the result of accident.

' A vigorous old boy he must have been, or he could n't have hobbled off so fast ! The pettifogger was wrong. There 's no use-up about his trotters,' muttered he, as he stood at the door of the building, straining his eyes to penetrate the gloom which enveloped every thing about him, and which, in the shadows formed by the irregular angles of its architecture, assumed a pitchy blackness. ' He might easily be poked away in this ragged old piece of brick-work. A dozen men might skulk yonder,' said he, leaning over an area whose darkness made it seem deeper than it really was. After a vain attempt to carry on his investigations in that quarter, he detached a stone from the crumbling wall and threw it in. A sullen splash followed. ' The house is built over a swamp, I remember. He can't be there. Pah ! the smell of the stagnant water is enough to choke one ! '

He turned away and stood for a moment with his hand on the doorpost ; and then apparently relinquishing the search, went in, his slow deliberate tread jarring heavily along the empty hall. No sooner had it died away and the door of the office closed after him, than the one which communicated with the street was thrown so wide open that it touched the entry wall ; it was gently pushed forward and a head thrust from behind it. After casting a quick, hurried glance about him, the old witness darted out. Half wild with a vague fear of he knew not what, he dashed through the street ; now running, now tottering and reeling from age and debility ; ever and anon casting a terrified look behind him, as if in momentary dread of pursuit ; but still pushing on as if death and delay went hand in hand ; and as eager to save the few days of decrepitude which would sum up his span of existence as if his life were in its morning, and his frame full of health and strength. He did not pause nor slacken his pace until he found himself in a wide street where there was a throng of people moving to and fro. When once there he began to feel secure, and stopped to breathe and to look for some one whom he knew. Hundreds passed him ; singly, or in knots of four or five ; persons of all classes ; some pushing along in haste ; others sauntering idly on. And with what varied expression !

There was the gay glad eye of the young and the happy; the buoyant step of hope; and the slow, shuffling gait, the wandering, vacant look, the hollow cheek, and the moody expression of wretchedness and despair. Night is the season when misery stalks forth, and squalid figures that during the noon-day cower in hiding-places which the light of the sun never cheers, then come forth with the bats and owls, and are seen gliding like spectres through the gloomy streets.

The old man saw much to sicken his heart; but the saddest of all was what he could not find — the face of a friend or acquaintance. He had hoped for that. It was an idle hope; for he had been away many long years; and those whom he had left young were gray-headed now; and all was strange where once all had been familiar. He should have gone to the church-yard and looked over the grass-grown grave-stones, and he would have seen there old and long-cherished names; for most of those whom he now thought of, and whom he had not heard of for years, had laid their heads there, and were sleeping undisturbed by the hum and turmoil of the moving thousands above their resting-places.

He stood for some time leaning on his stick, and watching the varying crowds. Then shaking his head sadly, he joined in and drifted on in the living current. Now that he was once more amid the stir of life, he began to wonder what had caused his sudden alarm. He could not tell. The Attorney it was true had seemed much agitated when he spoke with him; had left him abruptly; had gone into another room, from which had issued the sound of voices in high dispute. Hearing this, he had skulked off; and that was all. He had heard nothing more. A man had come out, and had even gone into the street to look after him, apparently surprised at his abrupt departure. It was quite natural that he should be; and he was an old fool.' So thought the witness as he went on; growing courageous as he left the danger behind him. 'Yet it *was* strange too that he should have been seized with such unaccountable terror — for he was no coward; no, he knew he was n't;' and he clutched his stick, struck it fiercely against a post, straightened himself up, and endeavored to feel young and bold as he had once done. But he was old now, and young feelings will no more come to an old frame than young hopes to an old heart. His fatigue and fright had been too much for him; and after going a short distance he leaned against a railing, resting his cheek upon the cold iron. He remained there so long and seemed so much exhausted that he attracted the attention of a man who was standing on the opposite corner, whistling to himself, and with a small rattan beating time to his music on a pile of empty boxes, without seeming to know that he did so. Whatever might have been his object in waiting, he gave it up, and crossing to where the witness was, he walked slowly past him without speaking, but whistling as before. At last he went up to him and said :

'You seem ill, my good fellow, or tired; what ails you?'

'I 'm old,' replied the other. 'Old age is a sickness which has no cure, young man; no cure — no cure! You 'll find it out some day, if you live long enough.'

'Perhaps I may,' said the stranger, a man whose powerful and well-knit frame seemed built to bid defiance to time for many years to come.

'Perhaps I may, and perhaps I may find a home in the ground before that. Who knows?'

'Who knows, indeed!' muttered the other. And repeating these words, he prepared to resume his walk, when the stranger continued:

'I am going your way, if that's it?' He pointed with his stick up the street. 'And as you seem tired, if you choose you may lean on my arm as far as you go. I'm strong, and it won't trouble me.'

The old man thanked him, took his arm without hesitation, and they walked on, he talking of the city as it had been when he was young; how it had changed; how the green fields with their waving grass and bright flowers had given place to massive and gloomy piles of brick and mortar; how the quiet shady lanes which he had haunted when a boy were now narrow streets, with tall houses frowning down on them from each side. How close and pent up the air seemed to him! He wondered at it too; for he had been used to the city when he was a child; but it was not now what it was then. He had gathered apples in what was now the very heart of this great throbbing metropolis; and where they now were was then far out of town. Things were greatly altered; but he had been absent twenty years, and of course he must expect it; but still it *did* look very strange to come back and find it so changed, and the faces of all about you changed, and no one whom you knew; all dead, or gone off—very few left. God bless me! how full the church-yard must be! How the dead must crowd each other! Ay, and the living too; how *they* crowd and cluster together; so close that one cannot find even an old friend. I've been looking for a man for some days,' said he, breaking off in his rambling conversation; 'perhaps you know him?—a Mr. Crawford?'

'It's a common name,' said the other. 'What was his first name?'

'I've forgotten—I've forgotten. The lawyer knows; but he did not tell me. If I could recollect that, I could find him without trouble.'

'It will not be easy without knowing that,' said the stranger. 'There are many of the name; still it can be done. I am going in here,' said he, stopping in front of an eating-house and pointing in the door. 'I have a keen appetite; and late as it is, have not yet dined. So I'll bid you good-by.'

'I'm scarcely less hungry than you are,' replied the old man, looking at the house. It was a tempting place, snug and old-fashioned. There was a flood of light within, and through the half-opened door came the flashing blaze of a fire. Every thing about it had a cheerful and comfortable appearance; while the street was dark and cheerless, and though crowded with living souls, was lonely to one to whom they were all strangers. A companion was a pleasant thing to him; and so without much reflection, and somewhat to the surprise of his new acquaintance, he followed him in, and seating himself, cast an investigating eye toward a table which stood in the middle of the room, covered with viands of various descriptions; serving both as a bill of fare and as a temptation to the appetite. At one end of the apartment, on a small stool, sat a red-faced lady with a large head and a small cap on the top of it, a little the worse for wear. But the wearer was of an amplitude which spoke well for the nutritious qualities of the larder, and fully atoned for any deficiency in the dimensions of her head-gear. On seeing the visiters, by a sudden motion of her feet she caused herself to revolve rapidly on the stool, and looking very hard through a small door, which opened into a dark depository, she called: 'Tim!'

'Hallo!' responded Tim.

'Two gen'lemen's waitin' to be sarved.'

'Oh!' said Tim; and he forthwith appeared in the shape of a large boy, with an uncombed head and his shirt-sleeves tucked up. Having received the orders of the two visiters, he with equal alacrity communicated those orders to his mistress, and she with a celerity quite remarkable in a person of her size, set about fulfilling them, so that but a short time had elapsed before a dish of smoking meat was on the table before them, and they both fell to; one with the high relish of youth, and the other with the keen appetite of long abstinence.

'Ha!' said the old man, plying his knife and fork vigorously, and occasionally pausing to wipe his mouth on the end of the table-cloth; 'once taste the food and appetite comes. Yet not half an hour ago I had a fright which I could well-nigh have sworn would have kept me without one for a month. Well, well; man is a strange animal!' And as if the arriving at this conclusion was a settlement of all his difficulties, he thrust his fork into the dish and ate with unabated vigor for some time.

His companion, who had been equally busy, with the difference that he did not speak at all, at last laid down his knife and fork, and pushing his plate from him as if he had finished, inquired what had frightened him.

'Ay, you may well ask! you may well ask!' said the old man, shaking his head gravely; 'for I can scarcely tell myself. When I was young like you, I would not have turned for a troop of mounted horsemen; but I am old now, young man, and old age is shadowed by care, and fear, and suspicion. When the ability to resist danger leaves one, the fear of it becomes stronger. Timidity and decrepitude come together. And *he*,' said he, half speaking to himself, 'is a man one does n't like to be alone with; and it's a dark old place that he lives in; and he *did* look strangely when I spoke to him to-night — indeed he did! He was so white, and his hands shook, and his voice was husky, and his eyes glassy. No, no! It was n't *all* fancy; and he slunk off with a slow, stealthy step, like a cat when she steals on a mouse. No, no! — it was n't for nothing that I was frightened.'

'I'm all in the dark,' said the stranger, who sat listening with no great appearance of interest, but still amused at the earnest manner of his companion. 'Who was the man that scared you? and what was it all about? Tell me — come.'

'I told you before,' said the other, 'that I was looking for a Mr. Crawford. Did n't I?'

The stranger nodded.

'Well, it was about him. I lived with him many a long year ago, when he was young — before he was married. A gay young fellow he was too; ay, and I was at his wedding; a runaway match — his friends never knew it. There was only I and Daniel Ripley; poor fellow! but he's dead; and the parson's dead, and Crawford's dead, and his wife's dead — all dead but me! It's very strange! But I suppose my turn will come soon. Well, they were married, and shortly after I went away, and have been gone twenty long years. I came back two weeks ago. I went to inquire where Mr. Crawford lived, for I wanted to see him. I found that a man had been looking for me, and asking whether I was alive or dead. He said that he was an old friend of Mr. Crawford's, and his name was Bolton; a lawyer — Reuben Bolton.'

'Ha!' exclaimed his listener, who had hitherto been leaning back in his chair, with his eyes fixed on the old man's face, for no other purpose than that of giving him an opportunity of indulging his garrulity: 'ha! what did you say the lawyer's name was?'

'I told you that before — Reuben Bolton. He knew where Mr. Crawford lived; so I went to him to ask, and he questioned me as to what I wanted, and about *him*, and about his marriage; and then he told me he was dead, and he believed had left no children.'

'Well, go on!' said the other, now listening with keen attention. 'He said he had left no children, did he? What then?'

'Yes, he said so; but he said he'd ask, and let me know. I told him I had a longing to see any one of the old man's kin. I loved him, for he was kind to me years ago; and although I had forgotten his first name, I had not forgotten that. But names never will stay in my head. My memory fails,' said he, tapping his wrinkled forehead, and shaking his head; 'it shows I'm growing old.'

'Well, did you see him?'

'Yes, I went there; and he said Mr. Crawford was dead, and had left no children.'

'The liar!' muttered the stranger, between his teeth. 'Well, go on.'

'He told me *that*, and that he never had *had* any; but I knew better,' continued he, rubbing his hands with much apparent glee. 'I knew he *had* a daughter; and I told him so. And I did n't believe the rest. He seemed vexed and uneasy at having been misinformed, and said he'd ask again, and wished me to come to-day.'

'Did you go?' inquired the other.

'Yes, I did. It's a very dreary place at night, and I felt a strange sinking of the heart as I was going up the stairs; and I thought I heard something whispering in my ear to keep away. It was very dismal; and the old house moaned and seemed like an old ghost, so that when I got to his room I was nearly frightened to death; and when he stepped out and met me, I thought the devil himself had come. There he stood twisting his fingers; his eyes on fire; his lips quivering and trembling as if he had an ague fit; and at last he stole into the inner room, and there was something in his eye so devilish that I grew faint-hearted, and hurried out without waiting for him to come back. You see I'm old now, *very* old. I would not have done so many years ago; but I am easily frightened now, and I heard men quarrelling and whispering in the back room, and a struggle. There might have been a murder doing there. I do n't know — I do n't know; but there might have been — there *might* have been. I've heard of such things.'

' Is that all?' said the young man.

' That 's all.   I was coming away when I met you.'

' Well,' said the stranger, ' I can help you to what you want.   The man's name was John Crawford.   He is dead, and has left a daughter, who is now alive, and no doubt will be glad to see you.   Her father died a few weeks since, and by his will gave all his property to this Bolton, and to his daughter — nothing.'

' I do n't believe it!' exclaimed the old man, positively.   ' I do n't believe it!   I 'll go to her and tell her so.'

' Well, you can do as you like,' said his companion ; and taking a piece of paper from his pocket, he wrote a few words upon it.

' There's the name of the street and the number where she lives; and there,' said he, ' if you want at any time to make farther inquiries of me, is my name and address.'   As he spoke, he added something to the bottom of the paper.   ' I must leave you now, for I have overstayed my time, and am to meet a man on business.'

' Thank you, my young friend,' said the old man, taking his hand ; ' you 've been very kind to me.   The young do n't often think of the old; but *you* have, and I thank you for it.   I 'll rest here awhile, and then go on.   God bless you!'

The young man turned his frank, good-humored face toward him, and bidding him good night with a merry voice and a warm shake of his hand, he called the servant, paid his reckoning, and went out.

When he was gone, the old man drew a candle close to him, put on a pair of old iron spectacles, held the paper to the light to ascertain the name of his new friend, and read the words : ' JOHN PHILLIPS, No. 96, —— Street.'

CHAPTER XXI.

LATE that night Phillips sat in his own room, pondering over the words of the old man whom he had so oddly encountered.   The more he thought them over, the more weight they seemed to have.   Could it be that he knew more than he had expressed, when he so boldly denied his belief that Mr. Crawford had disinherited his daughter?   And was it possible that Lucy was right, when in her interview with him she had declared that will to be a forgery?

' It must be so!' exclaimed he, starting from his chair, and pacing the room ; ' and I have been duped by that scoundrel Higgs.   I might have known that truth never came from such a source as that.   Lucy was right.   She spoke positively ; it was no vague suspicion ; she said she knew it and could *prove it.*   The lawyer too, he trifles with the old man ; he lies to him, to keep him from seeing Miss Crawford.   He was *afraid* that they should meet — that was it!   What *could* have frightened that gray-headed old man to-night?   His *look* — what was there in that?'   He stopped in the middle of his walk, in deep thought: ' That might have been fancy.   It *must* have been ; for he would not dare to ——   Well, well,' continued he, breaking off in his musing; ' I 'll see Lucy to-morrow.   Poor girl! she must think me lukewarm, indeed.'

Phillips was one of those who earn their bread by the sweat of their brow; and it was not until the following afternoon that he was able to leave the place where he had spent the early part of the day in toil, and direct his steps toward Miss Crawford's residence. His way lay past the office of the Attorney; and as he looked up at the crumbling walls he could not help cursing them in his heart, and wishing that they might some day fall to the ground and crush in their ruins the dark schemer who had his nest there.

Just at the hour that Phillips was on his way to the house where Lucy had her home, a female figure might have been seen walking slowly along a narrow street in the upper part of the city. This female was Lucy; but Lucy sadly altered — feeble and wasted; her frame worn down by sorrow and anxiety. She paused frequently to rest, and looked listlessly about her, as if her thoughts were far away. None paused to notice her; for there was little in the outward appearance of the meanly-dressed girl to attract attention. A loiterer, as he passed, might glance at her frail figure, and at the lustrous eyes, so deep and dark that it seemed as if the very soul were looking out of them, and wonder who she was and what she did in the streets, when she should have been where kind hands could minister to her wants; whether she would live through the winter, or whether the spring flowers would blossom on her grave; and his eye might even sadden for a moment; but that was all. Before he had reached the next street the poor girl was forgotten.

But if they thought not of her, she thought as little of them. She had but one motive of action now — but one thought. And that was an intense burning desire to extricate her husband from the influence of Bolton. The fear of what might happen to him, and that she might not be successful in foiling the Attorney, had made the havoc of years in her appearance; had robbed her of her look of youth; and had impressed upon her brow that expression of deep and sad thought which time alone should bring.

If she was feeble when we last saw her, she was far feebler now. Her breath was short and labored; her cheek pale, transparent and colorless, except a single bright spot in it, brilliant and glowing, as if the last rays of life were lingering there before they departed for ever. She tottered as she walked; but still there was something so restless and earnest about her manner, that it seemed as if an eager, powerful will were taxing her debilitated frame beyond its strength. She never murmured; but there was something painful in her sad smile as she surveyed her own attenuated form, when she was obliged to pause from fatigue. She felt that in all else than earnest devotion of heart and fixedness of purpose, she was not the same that she had been but a short time since, when she spent the whole day in search of her husband. Her heart was very heavy now; for she had no hope of his love to cheer her on: no, no; he had crushed that! Her strength too was gone; but what of that? She could move about, and while she could do that, something might yet be done for him. She knew that at times a strange sensation of sinking came over her whole system; but that would soon wear off; she knew it would, and she had no other ailment. She was still young; her eye was not heavy, and her cheek was very bright. And so she dreamed on, forgetting herself, thinking only of Wilkins; and in her plans and schemes for his welfare, unconscious of the cloud that was gradually covering her with its dark shadow.

It was a work of time for her to reach her point of destination, which was no other than Bolton's office; for thither she had resolved to go, to see the lawyer himself; to use tears, entreaties, arguments, and if necessary even menaces, to effect her object; and she thought that she knew enough to bend him to her will. At all events, it was worth the trial.

As she went on, engrossed in her own thoughts, she did not observe that for some distance she had been followed by a man who kept her always in sight, loitering slowly after her, and retarding his own steps to keep pace with hers; and it was not until she came in sight of the house in which the lawyer's office was, that he walked up to her and touched her gently on the shoulder.

'Lucy!'

The girl started; a slight flush passed over her face, as she looked up and saw who it was; and a faint smile flickered about her mouth; but it went as soon as it came.

'Ah! Jack!' said she, her lips trembling as she spoke, 'you see I hav n't given up yet. I'm going *there!*' She pointed to the dilapidated building which loomed up against the sky. 'I will see the lawyer myself; and perhaps when he hears what I have to say, and knows that I am *his* wife, and that my heart is breaking, he will find some means of extricating George sooner than have my death at his door. They say he is a skilful lawyer, and perhaps he will do that. I can but try, you know,' said she, with a faint smile; 'and if I succeed, I feel as if I should be quite well, though I am very faint now, and a very little wearies me.' As she spoke, she pressed her hand against her side, and her breath came quick and fluttering, like that of a wounded bird.

'Let me go with you, Lucy,' said Phillips, earnestly; 'let me go with you to protect you from insult; for believe me, you will need protection. *Do*, Lucy; dear Lucy, *do!* I will not open my lips unless he treats you ill. You shall do every thing, and say every thing. Only let me be with you; and let him see that you have at least one friend left. It will obtain for you a milder answer and a more patient hearing. I will not say a single word. I will stand only as your protector. Will you, Lucy?'

The girl shook her head. 'No, Jack, it cannot be. You know why, already. You know what suspicions are in George's mind respecting you and me; and God forbid that I should do aught to give even color to them. No, Jack, I thank you; from the bottom of my heart I thank you; and under other circumstances I would gladly accept your offer. But now I cannot. I must go alone; and whatever is in store for me I must meet — and God give me strength to do so with a good heart! Good by, Jack; I'm wasting time. God bless you!' She made a slight motion of her hand, as if bidding him farewell, and attempted to smile; but her lips trembled, and the tears gushed in her eyes as she left him.

Bolton was sitting at a table, engaged in examining a bundle of papers, when the door opened and Lucy entered.   He had never seen her, except on the night at Mr. Crawford's, and did not now recognize her.   Observing only a meanly-dressed female, he might have made some uncourteous answer to her question whether he was at leisure, for the poor were not welcome visiters at his door; but he observed that she was exceedingly beautiful, so he told her to take a seat.

Lucy merely bowed, and although she grew deadly pale, she remained standing.   Bolton paused, and looked at her as if to inquire what she wanted.

' My name is Wilkins,' she said, with some effort; ' Mrs. George Wilkins.'

Bolton's face became a shade whiter, and it might have been that his eye grew a little troubled; but his manner was calm.

' I have the pleasure of knowing your husband.   I am happy to make the acquaintance of Mrs. Wilkins also.'

He said nothing more; being resolved not to aid her, in any communication that she might have to make.

' I presume,' said Lucy, after a pause, ' that you do not recollect having seen me before ? '

Bolton looked at her earnestly, and ran over in his mind a long list of those whom he had ruined and beggared.   Her husband was one of them; but Lucy he had never seen; and he shook his head as he said: ' I do not.'

' And yet you *have* seen me,' said Lucy, quietly.

Again the lawyer fixed his eye on that wasted face, and dreamed over the past.   It well might have belonged to one of his victims; but he could not remember it; and he asked where it was.

' At Miss Crawford's,' said Lucy, firmly.   ' You may recollect the evening you first brought a will there.'

Bolton looked suspiciously at her; but whatever emotion he might have experienced, he evinced none, and said nothing.

' A will,' continued she, ' which gave you all Miss Crawford's property, and left her nothing.'

' I remember its contents,' said the lawyer, quickly.   ' Well ? '

' Who made that will ? ' demanded Lucy.

Bolton moved uneasily in his chair, and asked : ' What 's this will to you ? '

' Much ! ' replied Lucy, ' much !   I wish to God that it was not! Will you answer my question ? '

' My good woman,' said Bolton, coldly, ' my friendship for your husband would lead me to treat you with all due respect.   But as this is a matter which does not concern you, I must decline speaking on the subject.   I am not in the habit of making my own private affairs the subject of conversation with strangers, especially strange women.'

Lucy's heart beat violently, and she grasped the top of a chair to support herself, as she said :

' I came here to perform a duty; and perform it I will, if I die!'

The paleness which overspread her face seemed reflected in that of the lawyer, as he sat watching every word.

' That will was signed by Mr. John Crawford,' said Lucy, in a clear, distinct voice; 'and it was witnessed by my husband and one William Higgs. Is not that what you say?'

The Attorney made no reply.

'Be it so!' said Lucy; 'whether you speak or are silent, the facts are the same. That will is a forged one. I *know* it to be so. I can *prove* it; and I came here to tell you so, before you or my husband were gone too far for your own safety.'

'Words! words!—idle words!' said the Attorney. 'What wild phantasies women *will* get in their heads! Miss Crawford, without the slightest reason, calls this will a forgery, and sends you to echo her cry; as if a woman's din could frighten me, or a repetition of the cry of 'forgery' could prove an authentic instrument a counterfeit! If this is all you have to say, you may save your time and breath.'

'And is it so?' said Lucy, earnestly. 'You *will* go on in this criminal transaction! You have already involved my husband in ruin, and will sink him yet deeper. Will nothing induce you to spare him? Oh! think of what he was and what he now is—a poor, wretched, broken-down man; and do not make him worse. Do not make him one who cannot look his fellow-men in the face. You have blighted him already. For God's sake leave him a quiet conscience! I will be as secret as the grave. I'll never breathe what I know to a human being; and I will bless you and pray for you; you, who have been a curse to him and me; if you will but let him escape this last and greatest sin of all!'

'So you've come to entreaties at last,' said Bolton, with a sneer: 'I expected it. But you waste breath,' continued he, sternly. 'That will shall be proved; but at the same time I tell you that it is authentic.'

'And *I* tell *you*,' exclaimed Lucy, in a clear loud tone, 'it is *not*. I tell you that it is forged, and bears its falsity on its very face.'

She leaned forward and whispered in the ear of the lawyer. He made no reply, but sat as if frozen; not a muscle moved. His face became ghastly and livid; his eyes opened and glared wildly from their sockets, and his hand rested listlessly on the table, but it did not stir.

Lucy was frightened and ran to the door to call for help. This brought the Attorney to himself. Starting to his feet he caught her arm.

'Come back!'' said he, sternly; 'come back! I say. You shall not leave this room till I have heard more. Is what you have told me true?' demanded he, fiercely; 'true, by the God of heaven?'

'It is.'

'And who can prove it?'

'There are fifty at least,' said Lucy. 'Will you go on now?'

'I *must!* Do you hear *that*, woman? I MUST! Hell is before me and hell is behind me! Fifty can prove it; but it may never reach their ears. *You* alone are ready to do so; and you—*you dare not!*'

'Indeed, for my husband's sake, I dare do any thing.'

'For his sake, for *his* sake, you dare not!' exclaimed Bolton; 'for by G—d! you'll condemn *him* if you do! He is an accomplice in the fraud, and will go to the state's-prison for ten years. That's screening him with a vengeance!—screening *him*, who at this very moment is contriving the shortest mode of getting you out of his way, except by cutting your throat. Ha! ha! it makes me laugh!' and the Attorney laughed so wildly that it made the poor girl shudder. But there was something in his last words that startled her more than all else; and she waited till he was more composed, and then asked his meaning.

'Simply this,' replied Bolton, with a sneer: 'I have received instructions from your husband to commence proceedings against you in the Court of Chancery, to obtain a divorce, on the ground of adultery on your part with one John Phillips.'

Lucy shrank as if blighted. Her fingers worked convulsively, and she closed her eyes as if to shut out some painful light, and then she asked in a whisper:

'Is this true?'

'True as you live,' replied Bolton, coldly.

'And will you swear to it?'

'I will,' replied Bolton. 'Do you wish farther proof?'

'No, no! I 've heard enough.' The next moment the lawyer was alone.

She stole out of the room and down the stairs, like a cowed and guilty thing. Jack Phillips met her at the door and spoke to her; but she did not notice him. Her face was like the face of one without life, and her step was irregular and unsteady; and it seemed every moment that she would fall. He joined her, and walked at her side; and she did not forbid him, nor did she seem to be aware of his presence. He spoke to her; but she made no answer. Once or twice she paused to gain breath, and looked him full in the face, and there was so much agony there, that he dared not inquire farther; but he drew her arm in his, and in silence accompanied her until they came to Miss Crawford's house. Here he stopped.

'One word, Lucy,' said he; 'you know I would do any thing for you, and I feel as deeply interested in your welfare as if you were my own sister — indeed I do. Tell me what success you had with the lawyer. Is there any hope?'

'Only in heaven! — only in heaven!' exclaimed she wildly; and without saying any thing farther, she left him and entered the house.

SONNET.

Voice of the world! which speakest solemnly
　　From meadows and from vales; from herbs and flowers;
　　From pathless forests, Nature's primal bowers;
From out the bosom of the rolling sea,
Imaged eternal; from the giant breast
　　Of the sky-gazing mountain, and the womb
　　Of red volcanoes! Thou dost speak the doom
Of Nature, and of Man — the idle guest
Of this quick-passing globe! Thy thrilling tone
　　Is heard unto the stars, and rings along
The distant pathway of bright worlds unknown,
　　And dieth in the heavens to a song:
Time *was* and *is;* but yet shall find his doom,
The last, eternal conquered, in a tomb!

x. x.

T I M E.

BY MRS. R. S. NICHOLS.

I.

O, TIME is a grave old man!
His form is bent with the weight of years,
Years that are laden with human fears,
    For ah ! do not *all* dread Time?
The locks on his brow are thin and gray,
While his sharp, shrill voice doth seem to say :
    ' A solemn old man is Time ! '

II.

O, Time is a gay old man !
He has his ivied marble halls,
Where the lizard sports, and owlet calls
    Through the night, a weary time !
A powerful lord, of wide domains,
Where ivies creep ; and the mildew stains —
    How they work for gay old Time !

III.

Ah, Time is a fierce old man !
He breathes, and lo ! on the fairy brow
The white dews of Eld are sprinkled now,
    And he laughs, doth fierce old Time !
The light hath passed from the brilliant eye,
Mourners are tramping steadily by :
    List ! 't is the march of old Time !

IV.

Time is a lonely old man :
Nor kindred, friend, nor lover hath he,
But like a rock in a dreary sea,
    Alone, all alone is Time !
Wherever he lists he builds a home,
And there the lone wind is sure to come,
    And sing, and sing to old Time !

V.

Time is a wrathful old man !
He treads down the graves and levels the tombs,
And loves, when the deadly night-shade blooms,
    To garland his brow, old Time !
He loves the shriek at the charnel gate,
And stalks 'mong the dead, with step elate,
    As who should say, ' I am Time ! '

VI.

O, Time is a kind old man :
He speaks of peace to the weary breast,
And folds the broken-hearted to rest :
    A healing spirit hath Time.
He whispers : ' Come to the quiet grave,
Smoothly thy bark shall sail on the wave,
    The kindliest wave of Time ! '

LITERARY NOTICES.

SECOND NOTICE OF 'A COURSE OF LECTURES ON THE DOCTRINES OF THE NEW-JERUSALEM CHURCH, as Revealed in the Theological Writings of EMANUEL SWEDENBORG.' By B. F. BARRET, Pastor of the First Society of the New-Jerusalem Church in New-York. In one volume. pp 443. New-York: JOHN ALLEN, at the Office of the KNICKERBOCKER: SAMUEL COLMAN, 14 John-Street.

WE promised in our last number to present in a subsequent issue a brief exposition of some of the more prominent doctrines of the 'New-Jerusalem Church,' held by the followers of EMANUEL SWEDENBORG. They are mainly as follow: GOD the creator and preserver of heaven and earth is essential love and essential wisdom — essential good and essential truth. He is one, both in essence and in person, in whom nevertheless is a divine trinity, consisting of Father, Son, and Holy Spirit, like soul, body, and operation in man. The Lord and Saviour JESUS CHRIST is that God who came down from heaven as Divine Truth, and took upon him human nature, for the purpose of subduing the powers of hell, of restoring the spiritual world to order, of preparing the way for a New Church upon earth, to be founded on the new commandment of charity. Thus it was that the great work of redemption was to be accomplished ; and thus the Saviour, by enduring suffering and temptation, glorified his humanity, by uniting it with his essential divinity. Thereby he established an eternal medium of accommodation to, and conjunction with, his fallen creatures. Those who, possessing the divine revelation, believe in Him with the understanding from the heart, and live accordingly, will be saved : and those without the church, who live in conformity with the best light they enjoy, will *also* be saved, being equally admitted to the benefits of redemption.

The sacred Scripture, or Word of God, is the very Divine Truth, and contains beside the literal sense a celestial and spiritual one, wherein is Divine Truth in its fulness, sanctity and power ; so that it is accommodated to the apprehension both of angels and men. The spiritual and natural senses of the Word are united by correspondences which make one, as the soul and body. The science of correspondences between natural and spiritual things was in some degree known to many of the most ancient nations, particularly to the Egyptians, whose hieroglyphics are based upon and can be explained by it. It was lost to the world however for many thousand years, when it was revealed, as is alleged, by the LORD to SWEDENBORG, as a key to unlock the sacred treasures of love and wisdom contained in the Word. The earth is eternal, and the passages of Scripture which appear to predict its destruction are misunderstood. They merely foretell the end of the church, instituted by the LORD at His first advent; which end, in consequence of evils of life and errors of doctrine, was accomplished during the eighteenth century, when immorality and infidelity were at their height in Christendom; when HUME, GIBBON, SHAFTESBURY, BOLINGBROKE, VOLTAIRE, ROUSSEAU, D'ALEMBERT, and MIRABEAU were the intellectual, and WALPOLE, LOUIS the Fifteenth, FREDERICK the Great, and CATHARINE the Second, the political rulers of the age. The revival and extension of religion within the last fifty years are caused by the descent of the 'New Jerusalem,' and the unacknowledged influence of the New Church doctrines. The second coming of the LORD is not a coming in person as at first, but is merely the new revelation or dispensation of His divine truth communicated to the world through SWEDENBORG. The New Jerusalem is not a city, but a *church* from heaven. The last judgment occurred in 1757 in the spiritual world : the subjects of it were the spirits who had been accumulating there since the first advent. Hence there will be no general resurrection, but at death man's spiritual body is separated for ever from the natural, and finds itself in the world of spirits, an intermediate state between heaven and hell. In that world man's true character is speedily developed to himself and others ; and if it be evil, he joins the evil spirits, whose association constitutes hell; if it be good, he joins good spirits, whose association constitutes heaven. GOD however, who is Love itself, does not condemn or punish the wicked, nor does he, strictly speaking, reward the good. Misery and happiness in the other world are but the natural and necessary consequences of the society we have chosen to prepare ourselves for in this life. He who is good merely from the expectation of being rewarded by the joys of heaven will find himself wofully mistaken.

All evils, whether of affection, of thought, or of life, ought to be shunned as sins against GOD, because they proceed from infernal spirits, who in the aggregate are called *the Devil*, and who destroy in man the capacity to enjoy the happiness of heaven : but on the other hand, good affections, good thoughts and good actions ought to be cherished and performed because they are of GOD and from GOD ; and every act of love and charity should be done by man as of himself, but under the acknowledgment and belief that it is really from the LORD. Charity, faith, and good works are unitedly necessary for man's salvation ; since charity without faith is not spiritual but natural, and faith without charity is not living but dead ; and both charity and faith, without good works, are merely perishable things, because they are without use or fixedness ; nevertheless charity, faith and good works are not of man but of the LORD. Man, during his abode in the world, is kept in a spiritual equilibrium between heaven and hell ; enjoying free-will in spiritual things, and possessing the capacity either of turning himself to the Lord and His kingdom, or of separating himself from both, and joining the powers of darkness ; and by virtue of this faculty, man ought to do the work of repentance for the remission of sins, since by the remission of sins is meant their removal from man by the LORD ; but the LORD cannot remove sins unless man explores them in his own heart, and by actual repentance makes them hateful to himself. He cannot enter into the kingdom of heaven unless he be regenerated or created anew ; and he is regenerated by the LORD, so far as he does the work of repentance, receives the truths of faith, and conjoins them with charity and a good life. Every event or occurrence in human life, whether of prosperity or adversity, is under the immediate superintendence of the Divine Providence ; and nothing does or can befall man either in his collective or individual capacity which is not (in the most minute as well as in the most important circumstances attending it) made to contribute to his final benefit and advantage.

Such are some of the main features in the doctrines held by the 'New-Jerusalem Church.' From the illumination in 1743 of its illustrious founder until his death at London in 1772, he remained in quiet obscurity, occupied solely in writing and publishing his numerous and voluminous theological works. He never attempted personally to make proselytes, but his works were read and his doctrines received to some extent throughout Europe, and in this country. We are indebted to a friend for the following lines written by PHILIP FRENEAU more than seventy years ago, on reading SWEDENBORG's 'Universal Theology.' In opening, the writer speaks of the work as developing a 'noble system to reform mankind,' although skeptics had denied and others perverted and derided its great truths:

' Here, truths divine in heavenly visions grow
From the vast influx on our word below ;
Here, like the blaze of our material sun,
Enlightened reason proves that GOD is ONE.
As that, concentred in itself, a sphere
Illumes all nature with its radiance here ;
Bids tow'rd itself all trees and plants aspire,
Awakes the winds, impels the seeds of fire,
And, still subservient to th' Almighty plan,
Warms into life the changeful race of man ;
So, like that sun, in heaven's bright realms we trace
One power of LOVE, that fills unbounded space ;
Existing always by no borrowed aid,
Before all worlds, eternal, and not made ;
To that indebted, stars and comets burn,
Owe their first movement and to that return ;
Prime source of wisdom ! all contriving mind !
First spring of reason that this globe designed,
Parent of ORDER ! whose unwearied hand
Upholds the fabric that his wisdom planned,
And its due course assigned to every sphere,
Revolves the seasons and sustains the year ;
Pure light of TRUTH ! where'er thy rays combine
Thou art the substance of the power divine !

Nought else on earth that full resemblance bears,
No sun that lights us through our circling years,
No stars that through yon heavenly mansions stray,
No moon that glads us with her evening ray,
No seas that o'er their gloomy mansions flow,
No forms beyond us and no shapes below.

Then slight, ah ! slight not this instructive page,
For the low follies of a thoughtless age ;
Here to the truth by Reason's aid aspire,
Here the gay visions of the blest admire ;
Behold that heaven, in these neglected lines,
In whose vast space perpetual day-light shines ;
Where streams of joy through plains of pleasure run,
And night is banished from so bright a sun.
Where parted souls with kindred spirits meet,
Rapt to the bloom of beauty, all complete ;
In that celestial, vast, unbounded sphere,
Nought there exists but has its image here !
All there is MIND ! that intellectual flame,
From whose vast depth Platonic visions came,
In which creation, ended and began,
Flows to this abject world, and beams on man !'

The state of the 'New-Jerusalem Church ' in this country we should judge to be very flourishing. Only twenty-five years have elapsed since the first society for the dissemination of SWEDENBORG's writings was organized at Philadelphia, and the number of those who then received his doctrines did not amount to more than an hundred. Upward of four thousand believers are now counted, who support three magazines for the dissemination of their religious views, thirty-eight licensed ministers, and several depositaries in the Atlantic and inland cities for the sale of their books and periodicals. The Lectures under notice are receiving a wide and general sale; a practical proof of the gradual extension of the doctrines of the ' New-Jerusalem Church.'

AHASUERUS: A POEM. By A VIRGINIAN. New-York: HARPER AND BROTHERS.

THE production of a good poem is perhaps the highest evidence that can be given of the possession of genius. There is nothing that combines so essentially profound thought with discursive fancy, and high-toned sentiment with wild passion; nothing indeed that affords such free scope for the whole soul of man as poetry. If the heart be swelling with tender emotions, the fancy glowing with splendid images, or the mind teeming with lofty thought, how naturally is the rich oblation poured forth upon the altar of genius through the medium of verse! How naturally does the young enthusiast of nature come glowing from the sight of the beauties of the external world; from the life-giving breeze, from the redolent air;

from the green earth with its many-colored flowers, and from the blue sky with its fleecy and rose-tinted clouds; and breathe forth in poetry; perhaps rudely and unskilfully constructed, the new and delightful thoughts and emotions that *will* have expression, and *will* imprint themselves *somewhere*, as freely and as vividly as the bright conceptions of the painter rush out upon the canvass. We may say with AKENSIDE:

> ' From Heaven descends
> The flame of genius to the human breast,
> And love and beauty and poetic joy,
> And inspiration.'

Yet it is the beautiful things of earth, and the sympathies which they excite, that feed this sacred flame, and nourish it in our heart of hearts. It is when these emotions are fresh; when the 'gaze of young astonishment' is cast upon all things with its earliest intensity; that enthusiastic minds express themselves in effusions which the severe critic may not find faultless, but toward which we are always inclined on that very account to be indulgent. We love the natural spring gushing out pure and bright from the foot of the mountain, far better than the artificial well, though constructed with vast labor and built with consummate care and skill.

We have before us the poem of a young and inexperienced writer, who has written from promptings such as we have attempted briefly to describe. The author of ' Ahasuerus ' comes before the public not only under the disadvantage above alluded to, but, as he is understood to be connected with a distinguished political personage, he is subjected to the additional disadvantage of being judged by political bias, without reference to real merit. We shall endeavor to sustain the impartiality we feel, by evidence from the work itself.

The subject of the poem is the *Wandering Jew*, who, under the mysterious mandate of our Saviour, ' Tarry till I come,' is supposed to be still dragging out a fearful and wretched existence, and is carried in the poem to the final catastrophe of all things. The subject is one of thought and not of action; it is perhaps on this account less interesting but more profound; and tasks more severely the genius of the writer who attempts to handle it. The mission of our Saviour is first mentioned, and in the following extract, his gentle office is certainly happily described:

> ' Such was the office, such the mission pure
> Of Him who died for man, by man reviled :
> And like a happy stream that gently flows
> With breezy current through some arid plain,
> A comfort and a glory to those shores
> Where flowers of loveliest dyes may sweetly
> 　　bloom,
> And lave their pure brows in its cooling tide ;
> Where the tall tree in healthy grace may rise,
> Fed by the gushing waters of the stream ;
> Where birds may build and pass their happy
> 　　lives,
> And rear their young, and teach them how to fly
> In the blue air that God has made for all ;
> And teach them how to sing at morn and eve,
> When sunbeams kindle or when twilight weeps,
>
> Delicious thrice from their instinctive breasts,
> The praise and glory of Eternal Power ;
> Yon, like the south wind, like the summer's sun,
> Filling the land with song and odors sweet ;
> Like a white fleecy cloud in azure skies,
> Whose innocence invites a smile from heaven,
> Bright link of joy between this rosy earth
> And happy spheres above, where angels live ;
> Like evening's twilight star, whose pearly orb
> Seems fixed in fields of never-fading bliss,
> Whose melting light sinks through the enrap-
> 　　tured soul,
> And fills the mind with visions from on high,
> Where Love supreme reigns o'er eternal life :
> Such to the man of faith the Saviour seemed,
> And where he walked the earth itself rejoiced.'

The Saviour is crucified; the envious Jew gloats over the sacrifice of the Lamb of God :

> ' Behold that Jew in sacerdotal robes :
> Dark curses dye his livid lips with rage.
> How bold his daring eye ! His granite front
> Looks like a mount o'er which a storm-cloud
> 　　towers.
> His brawny arms might lift the city's gates :
> His firm, full lips speak of audacious thoughts ;
> Audacious thoughts that owned no moral sense,
> That sought the eternal secrets of the world,
>
> And finding naught but dust and ashes there
> (For fruit nor flower the eye of sin can see,)
> He in his heart the chain that bound him cursed,
> Cursed in his heart his impotence of will,
> Cursed in his heart the virtues of his race,
> Cursed in his heart the God who gave him life,
> Cursed in his heart the very life he owned,
> And mid the poisons of his venom soul
> Nursed thoughts of hate and malice to mankind.'

The Saviour dies; the dome of the Temple is rent in twain, and man is in despair:

> 'Each smote his fellow with a maniac hand,
> Or, baring to the steel their raging breasts,
> Quenched fear and madness both in their own blood.'

The shadow of the dark deed passes off from the earth, and all is again bright and beautiful. Man, illuminated by light from Heaven, acquires new dignity and loftier powers: and his improved condition is described in a beautiful rhapsody, from which we have room but for the following extract:

> 'All that we see in ocean, earth, or air,
> Our being, life, our upright form, and step
> That proudly spurns the dust the serpent breathes;
> The eye, that views the beauties of the earth,
> Then wanders up to heaven, and gazes there
> Till moon, and suns, and stars, and angels bright
> Become our fellows in the realms of thought,
> And mortal taint is lost, and we are gods:
>
> The cheek, whose flood or ebbing tide proclaims
> The proud heart's triumph or its crushing woes;
> The brow, the ivory throne of thought, whose light,
> More dazzling than the day, strikes Falsehood blind,
> Whose frown is blacker than night's starless void:
> These are our birthright and our empire wide,
> O'er which we wave our sceptre as a king.'

The out-cast partakes not of this elevation — knows nothing of these joys; but lives on, till the earth has outlived them itself, till

> 'Crestless and surgeless the untravelled seas,
> No longer moved by tide or lifting breeze,
> Slept dark and stagnant on their unwashed sands.
> The thick and inky element stood still,
>
> No more to sing in triumph to the gale,
> No more to bear swift o'er its briny foam
> The white-winged bird, the eagle of the sea;
> In the wide basin of the unfathomed deep
> Waveless and black the bitter waters rest.'

He, the accursed Wanderer, the last form in which nature has life or motion, drags his withered and weary frame to

> 'A huge rock that reared its hoary crest,
> Close by the ebbless margin of the sea,'

and looking out upon the fearful void around him, his memory recurs to the still more fearful moral desolation of the past, the result of his blasphemy at the crucifixion. This part of the poem is very spirited and vigorous, and evinces poetical powers of a high order. We cannot do it justice without extracting more than we have room for, in an article of this kind; and we give only the conclusion, in which the author has most happily depicted the influence of repentance, and the 'quality of mercy' that 'droppeth as the gentle rain from heaven':

> 'When thus the Fated spake, in fear, in faith,
> In heartfelt penitence, he bowed his head,
> And at his feet, upon the thirsty ground,
> The sacred tear of sorrow gently fell;
> And softer then than human thought conceives,
> Softer and clearer than the sweetest note
> That spring's light breeze or summer bird o'er sang,
> Yet swelling like the thunder's volumed tone,
> Glided a voice into his listening ear;
> While Universe through all her shining spheres
> Ceased her loud music then, and trembling heard:
> Hush! 't is the voice of the Almighty God!
> Across the skies a dazzling radiance sweeps,
> The clouds roll back, and earth is bathed in light;
> The sea leaps up unchained through all his depths,
> And laves his shores with amaranthine waves:
>
> Down from their sources rush the volumed tides,
> And rivers sparkle in the heavenly beams,
> And lakes reflect the dimpling smiles of morn;
> The sod puts forth its turf, the tree its leaf,
> And flowers spring up from the sweet, fragrant soil,
> Enamelling the land; and Spring's soft winds
> Bear to the violet the rose's breath,
> And clouds of perfume fill the amber air.
> Hush! 't is the voice of the Almighty God!
> A crown of mercy circles his calm brow,
> And sad Ahasuerus sleeps at last.
> Upward on wings of penitence his soul
> Hath sought the pure realms of eternal rest;
> And with the bow of glory set on high,
> With flashing seas and smiling azure skies,
> With purple mists and golden-bannered clouds,
> Millennium comes, and Earth, harmonious all,
> Rolls slowly through her silver-beaming sphere,
> And swells the music of the choral stars!'

We are not disposed, after reading lines like these, to ferret out trivial errors, which are liable to drop from the pen of genius, as scratches may have carelessly fallen from the chisel of PRAXITELES. As a first effort, we consider 'Ahasuerus' as uncommonly free from errors, and exhibiting more than usual artistical skill. But it possesses all the essential elements of a good poem ; vigorous thought, lively imagery, and harmonious diction. We have pleasure therefore in cordially commending this work to our readers ; and we shall gladly welcome the author to the higher walks of literature, in which he can scarcely fail to win an honorable distinction.

Tecumseh : or the West Thirty Years Since. By George H. Colton. In one volume. New-York : Wiley and Putnam.

We mentioned in our last number that we should again advert to this rather corpulent but exceedingly neat and tasteful volume ; and we now proceed to a hasty fulfilment of our promise. The poem, it must not be disguised, has many faults ; but it possesses as undeniably surpassing merit. The work is now before the public ; and we leave the reader to judge of the justice of the few direct remarks which we propose to make upon its execution. It should be premised, that 'Tecumseh' ought not to be judged by the common rules of narrative poetry. To thus judge, would be perhaps to condemn the story, which although abundantly exciting, is so frequently broken by matter more or less extrinsic, as to appear to lack condensation and continuity. But the poem strikes us as peculiar in this, that while it is cast in the mould of mere narrative fiction, it yet borders upon the epic. The subject is not the captivity of the maiden and the lover's long pursuit. These form only the *colorings* of the story ; but the bold outline and entire back-ground are the vast schemes and efforts of Tecumseh to regain the inheritance of his race ; and this belongs as truly to the field of the epic as did ever the founding of the Latin empire or the recovery of Jerusalem. Considered in this light, the hero's great tour, which would otherwise, by its extent in the book, mar the interest of the story, becomes a feature of great beauty. Indeed, we know not where to look for a nobler spectacle than that solitary savage, traversing unmeasured regions, by lonely streams and forests and unknown wastes, for the sole purpose of banding together the wild tribes of his race against the encroachments of the white man. All this Mr. Colton has depicted with a masterly hand. The battle of the Wabash, the naval conflict of Erie, and the subsequent great Indian council, break the thread of the mere narrative ; but all these were intimately connected with the failure of Tecumseh's plan, and are something loftier than mere fiction. Whenever the narrative is broken, it is only that the epic may come in with renewed power.

A wild and terrific scene succeeds the description of the tour, in the burning of an Indian chief. The writer here successfully tasks his powers to produce a startling and fearful picture. The fourth canto opens with a fine tribute to the lamented Harrison, which, now that he belongs to history, will be read by all parties with pleasure. True and simple pathos is displayed in a scene which ensues — the search of an Indian mother for her wounded boy. The introduction of the battle which follows is not less felicitous than original. First comes a spirited soldier's song ; then, in the midst of the joyous chorus, the wild war-whoop, the onset and the clash of arms, and last the rapid and vigorous battle. In the fifth canto, the sketch of the old pioneer and his log cabin, of the feverish Ebed, and the lovers' touching interview with the Indian boy, will arrest the reader's attention and win his admiration. The chieftain's courtship of his foeman's daughter will not be likely to be overlooked ; for it has originality, simplicity, and truthfulness to recommend it. We regret that we cannot notice in detail the hero's noble soliloquy by the shores of Huron, the voyage through Saint Mary's river, and along the shores of Lake Superior, which the writer describes with the spirit and enthusiasm of a true lover of nature. At times indeed he seems to be enraptured; as when he breaks forth, for example, with these stirring lines :

> 'O Nature! mighty Nature! thee
> Obey the earth, the sky, the sea!
> At thy immortal balmy breath
> Each morn awakes the world from death;
> And by thy power, unchanged, unworn,
> The universe is hourly born,
> As ever on, from sphere to sphere,
> Circleth round the eternal year!'

The passage describing the Pictured Rocks, the Grand Sable, the storm, and the dusky crew crossing the calm lake by starlight, are admirably contrasted pictures. But for these and many others, which we lack both leisure and space more particularly to indicate, we must refer the reader to the volume itself, which we cordially and confidentially commend to his acceptance. 'The author,' says the 'American Biblical Repository,' 'although young and 'unknown to fame,' has exhibited an elevation and strength of conception, and a boldness and beauty of imagery, which would do honor to a much more practiced hand.'

ZANONI. By the Author of ' Night and Morning,' ' Rienzi,' etc. In two volumes, 12mo. New-York : HARPER AND BROTHERS.

ON the broad wings of the 'mammoth sheets' from the weekly press, as well as in the form of the volumes before us, this latest work of the first novelist of the age will have been borne to the farthest corner of the United States, before these pages will reach the eyes of our readers. And as we sit down to say a few words touching the impression which this last creation of the writer's genius has made upon our mind, we cannot help thinking what an enviable power a popular author like Mr. BULWER wields. In town, as you walk the streets, you behold in every second window 'Zanoni' in the hands of the staid matron, the blooming girl, the prim bachelor, and eke the gray-haired sire. Through half-opened store-doors, the dapper clerk is seen intent upon the newspaper edition, unmindful of his customers; and those who take their ease in inns, and milliners' apprentices, and carmen in their frocks, awaiting calls, are at the same employment. This too is but one aspect. On steam-boats and in rail-cars, journeying every where, circulate the same pages; and at the same moment, in town, village, country, are kindred readers, from the Bay of Fundy to the Rocky Mountains! And this is the triumph of genius! Since we have drawn no ideal picture, we shall not have the temerity to attempt a criticism of what nine in ten of our readers have perused and admired for themselves. We published several months since a series of papers upon the Rosicrucian philosophy; and in these the reader will have found a full description of one of the most prominent peculiarities of the very effective matériel of the romance under notice. Passing this feature, therefore, we would only record our verdict in favor of the deep interest which 'Zanoni' excites; of the curiosity awakened, stimulated, enhanced to almost painful excitement; of the portraiture of character — the stern and mysterious, the loving and gentle, in humanity; of the pictures of nature, and the external adjuncts of the narrative — scenes depicted as by the pencil of a painter, who superadds to his divine art the skilful machinery of a panorama, moving before the eye of the deceived spectator. We hope hereafter to elaborate the pencil-notes which we made as we read, into a commentary that shall at least do justice to the impressions which 'Zanoni' made upon our own mind; to the thoughts rare and precious awakened by the splendid conceptions and beautiful diction of the author.

EDITOR'S TABLE.

AMERICAN REVIEWS FOR THE APRIL QUARTER. — We have read several of the articles, and glanced cursorily through others, contained in the 'New-York' and 'North-American' Reviews for the present quarter. Without (as we hope) any undue sectional bias, we must pronounce our own Quarterly to be in this instance quite superior in spirit and variety to its elder contemporary. The 'Biographies of Great Men,' the 'History of Modern Art in Germany,' the review of CAMPBELL'S 'Life of PETRARCH,' but above these and above all the other papers in the number, the article on 'The United States and England,' will abundantly justify our preference, as well as the warm commendation of every true-minded American. From this well-reasoned and matter-full paper we have selected two or three passages for the gratification of our readers. The reviewer, in speaking of the causes of ill-feeling which have operated between the two countries, alludes to and pointedly rebukes, not less the petulant, querulous English tourist in 'the States' than those pencilling Americans who have gone into British society and made records of conversations and incidents of unrestrained social life, for the purpose of making them public in print, in violation of that trust which good breeding always recognizes but never proclaims or exacts. Great injury, it is justly contended, has thus been done to those who came after in a better spirit, and with no covert or ulterior intentions. We were forcibly impressed with the following remarks upon the bad policy, not to say injustice, of one nation interfering, collectively or individually, with the government, laws, or religion of another: 'We should reflect how justly sensitive *we* are to all foreign interference in our domestic policy. In all such matters it would well become every right-minded American to turn with dutiful facility to the wisdom of WASHINGTON — that simple, manly, honest, upright wisdom, so plain in these few words, and so instructive, alike to governments and individuals: 'My politics are plain and simple. I think every nation has a right to establish that form of government under which it conceives it may live most happy, provided it infracts no right or is not dangerous to others; and that no people ought to interfere with the internal concerns of another, except for the security of what is due to themselves.'

How true is this passage, touching a flashy, showy, talkative national vanity, sometimes exhibited among us by a nervous apprehension of a danger of American opinions and sentiments sinking into a kind of vassalage to British habits of thought and feeling: 'It seems to betray an unworthy distrust of ourselves, when persons declaim, for instance, about setting up an independent American literature — arraying it in an unmeaning contrast with British literature. If we were disposed to judge harshly of this way of talking, which may be heard occasionally, it might be looked on as a device to secure an extrinsic and undue consideration for the least deserving efforts of our literature — flimsy novels and rickety trage- dies. The spirit of our best authors, those who have done most for our literature, utterly repudiates any such appliances to help them to their popularity. In this respect, we may allude to WASHINGTON IRVING's career as an honorable and instructive example of American authorship, showing how true feeling for his own country may be perfectly reconciled with good feeling to the old country.' The allusion here to 'flimsy novels and rickety tragedies' is as just as it is candid and severe ; as many an American publisher can bear witness.

The admiration for NAPOLEON our reviewer considers an incongruous and unnatural element in the breast of an American ; and moreover as not without its influence in having created an additional feeling against England :

'What did the cause of freedom gain at NAPOLEON's hands? What the cause of humanity? or rather what did they not all suffer? · · · The most instructive lessons, in many respects, which modern history teaches, is the contrast between WASHINGTON and NAPOLEON. When, to take only a single point of this contrast, when the ill-clad remnant of the American army was huddling together in the wretched winter-quarters of Valley-Forge, where was their chief? Clinging to his fellow-soldiers, cheering them and suffering with them ; holding together the fragments of an army, in spite of the discontent and reproaches of those in authority who opposed his policy, by his presence and participation in the gloomy fortunes of those who obeyed him. When winter smote the armed hosts of France, where was _their_ chief, and where his devoted legions? He whose reproach was never the want of physical courage, the foremost in the flight ; they, abandoned, forsaken as victims to the avenging Cossack's spear, or the fiercer fury of famine and a Siberian winter ; the instruments of his ambition left to perish pitiably upon ' the snowy plains of frozen Muscovy.'

Among the 'Critical Notices' we are well pleased to see one which confirms our own judgment of COLTON's 'Tecumseh,' and which moreover will serve, we trust, to disabuse those who have hinted that our pages were 'open to enhance the repu- tation of a near relative, while they were closed to the claims of other young writers, equally if not far more deserving of its kindly interest.' 'As the produc- tion,' says the reviewer, 'of a very young man, just freed as it were from college, 'Tecumseh' must be regarded as one of uncommon excellence and great promise. It abounds in unequivocal marks of high poetic power, while its defects are such as greater maturity of years and more practice will be sure to remedy.'

In the 'North-American,' we have found leisure only to peruse the articles upon CATLIN's 'North-American Indians,' the 'Early History of New-York,' WASHING- TON ALLSTON's 'Monaldi,' and 'Spanish Popular Poetry,' together with a few of the briefer critical notices. The last-named paper is a very interesting one, aside from its exposure of the numerous and glaring liberties which Mr. LOCKHART has taken with the authors of his 'Spanish Ballads.' We perceive, as we think, the hand of Prof. LONGFELLOW in the fine taste and critical commentary of this arti- cle. In the seventh paper justice is rendered to the 'Monaldi' of our eminent poet-painter, which has already been noticed in the KNICKERBOCKER. One of the most entertaining articles in the number, especially to readers in this meridian, will be found the review of Mr. FOLSOM's 'Collections of the New-York Historical Society,' to which we have heretofore alluded. In referring a few months since to the 'Ordinances of the Burgomasters and Schepens of Niew-Nederlands in 1653-4,' we cited proofs of the unquestionable authenticity of KNICKERBOCKER's renowned history. Our reviewer fully sustains this position : 'IRVING's History of New-York, by DIEDRICH KNICKERBOCKER, has greater foundation in fact than people generally suppose. The charm resulting from the happy manner in which the facts are arranged, and the witty style in which they are related, have induced the almost general belief that it is entirely a work of imagination. Who would suppose that the Dutch Governor, using his knife or tobacco-box as a warrant for the apprehension of an offender, or to bring a debtor before him for judgment, had precedent to sustain it? Nevertheless, such is the truth, extraordinary as it may seem at first blush.' And who, we may add, would have believed that the dispute ‘concerning a sow with pigs' could have been settled as it was by the Burgomasters and Schepens in 1653, if he had not seen it solemnly recorded in the ‘Ordinances' of that remote period?

‘MR. CHAWLS YELLOWPLUSH' AS A CRITIC. — Messrs. WILEY AND PUTNAM have favored us with the perusal of two volumes, recently from the London press, entitled, ‘ Comic Tales and Sketches; edited and illustrated by MICHAEL ANGELO TITMARSH, author of the ‘ Paris Sketch-Book,' etc. ‘ Mr. TITMARSH ' is the *nom de plume* of Mr. THACKERAY, whose ‘ *Yellowplush Correspondence*' is included in the work before us, with the addition, which we have never before encountered, of a criticism by the accomplished London footman upon Mr. BULWER's play of ‘ The Sea-Captain.' The opening, descriptive of the reception of SIR EDWARD and his scientific companion, now in this country, at a dinner to which they had been invited, is in Mr. YELLOWPLUSH's best vein:

‘ Well, being a Wig, it's the fashn, as you know, to reseave littery pipple ; and accordingly, at dinner t'uther day, whose name do you think I had to hollar out on the fust landing-place about a wick ago? After sevral dukes and markises had been enounced, a very gentell fly drives up to our door, and out steps two genlemn ; one was pail, and wor spektickles, a wig, and a white neckcloth. The other was slim, with a hook nose, a pail face, a small waist, a pare of falling shoulders, a tight coat, and a catarack of black satting tumbling out of his busm, and falling into a gilt velvet weskit. The little genlmn settled his wigg, and pulled out his ribbins ; the younger one fluffed the dust off his shoos, looked at his wiskers in a little pockit-glass, settled his crevatt, and they both mounted up stairs.
‘‘ What name, Sir ?' says I, to the old genlmn.
‘‘ Name ! — a ! No, you thief o' the wurrld,' says he, ‘ do you pretind not to know *me* ? Say it's the Cabinet Cyclopé—— No, I mane the Litherary Chran—— Pshaw ! Bluthanoune ! Say it's Doctor Dioclesian Larner. I think he 'll know me *now* — a, Nid?' But the genlmn called Nid was at the botm of the stare, and pretended to be very busy with his shoe-string. So the little genlmn went up stares alone.
‘‘ Doctor Dioclesius Larner !' says I.
‘‘ *Doctor Athanasius Lardner !*' says Greville Fitz-Roy, our secknd footman, on the fust landing-place.
‘‘ DOCTOR IGNATIUS LOYOLA !' says the groom of the chambers, who pretends to be a scholler ; and in the litle genlmn went. When safely housed, the other chap cum ; and when I asked him his name, he said, in a thick, gobbling kind of voice :
‘‘ Sawedwadgeorgearllittnbulwig !'
‘‘ Sir *what* ?' says I, quite agast at the name.
‘‘ Sawedwad—— No, I mean *Mistaw*-edwad Lyttn Bullwig.'
‘ My neas trembled under me, my i's fild with tiers, my voice shook, as I past up the venrabble name to the other footman, and saw this fust of English writers go up to the drawing-room !
‘ It's needles to mention the names of the rest of the compny, or to dizcribe the suckmstansies of the dinner. Suffise to say, that the two littery genlmn behaved very well, and seamed to have good appytights ; ispecially the little Irishman in the whig, who et, drunk, and talked as much as ¼ a duzn. He told how he 'd been presented at cort by his friend Mr. Bullwig, and how the queen had received 'em both with a dignaty undizcribable ; and how her blessid Majisty asked what was the bony fidy sale of the Cabinit Cyclopædy, and how he (Doctor LARNER) told her that, on his honer, it was under ten thousand.
‘ You may gess that the Doctor, when he made this speach, was pretty far gone. The fact *is*, that wether it was the cornation or the goodness of the wine (cappitfe it is in our house, *I* can tell you,) or the natral propensuties of the gests assembled, wich made them so ispecially jolly, I dont know ; but they had kep up the meeting pretty late, and our poar butler was quite tired with the perpechual baskits of clarrit wich he 'd been called upon to bring up. So that, about leven oclock, if I was to say they wer merry, I should use a mild term ; if I wer to say they wer intansicated, I should use an igspreshn more near to the truth, but less rispeckful in one of my situashn.'

Previous to the dinner-party in question, Mr. YELLOWPLUSH had written a criticism upon Mr. BULWER's play of ‘ *The Sea-Captain*,' in commencing which he frankly advises the author : ‘ I propose, honrabble Barnet, to cumsider camly this play and the prephiz, and to speak of boath with that honesty witch, in the pantry or studdy, I 've been always phamous for.' It should be mentioned, that in the preface alluded to, Mr. BULWER had complained of injustice at the hands of his critics, and defended the 'principles' by which he had been governed in the composition of his play :

'One may objeck to an immence deal of your writings, witch, betwigst you and me, contain more sham sentiment, sham morullaty, and sham potry, than you 'd like to own ; but in spite of this, there 's the *stuf* in you : you 've a kind and loyal heart in your buzm, Barnet — a trifle deboshed, praps ; a kean i, igspecially for what 's comic, (as for your tradgady, it 's mighty flatchulent,) and a roady, plesst pen. The man who says you are an As is an As himself. Do n't believe him, Barnet ; not that I suppose you will ; for if I 've formed a correck apinion of you from your wucks, you think your small-beear us good as most men's. Every man does — and why not ? We brew, and we love our own tap — amen ; but the pint betwigst us, is this steupid, absudd way of crying out, because the pubhc do n't like it too. Why *should* thay, my dear Barnet ? You may vow that they are fools ; or that the critix are your enemies ; or that the wuld should judge your poams by your criticle rules, and not their own ; you may beat your brest and vow you are a marter, but you won't mend the matter. Take heart, man ! You're not so misrabble, after all ; your spirits need n't be so cast down. You are not so *very* badly paid. I 'd lay a wager now, that you make, with one thing or another — plays, novvles, pamphlicks, and little odd jobbs here and there — your three thousand a year. There 's many a man, dear Bulwig, that works for less, and lives content.'

After these 'general remarks,' our critic-footman takes up the subject of style, and argues with a good deal of ingenuity and force in favor of simplicity and terseness, especially in a performance like 'The Sea-Captain :'

'Sea-captings should not be eternly spowting and invoking gods, hevns, starzs, angles, and other silestial influences. We can all do it, Barnet ; nothing in life is easier. I can compare my flivry buttons to the stars, or the clouds of my backopipe to the dark vollums that ishew from Mount Hetna ; or I can say that angles are looking down from them, and the tobaco-silf, like a happy soil released, is circling round and upwards, and shaking sweetness down. All this is as esy as to drink ; but it 's not poatry, Barnet, nor natral. Pipple, when their mothers recoknize them, do n't howl about the suck-umambient air, and paws to think of the happy leaves a rustling ; leastways, one misstrusts them if they do.' . . . 'Look at the neat grammaticle twist of Lady Arundel's spitch too, who in the cors of three lines, has made her son a prince, a lion with a sword and coronal, and a star. Why gumble and shenk up matafers in this way, Barnet ? One simily is quite enuff in the best of sentences ; and I pershume I koeedn't tell you that it 's as well to have it *like*, when you are about it. Take my advise, honrabble Sir ; listen to a humble footman ; it 's genrally best in poatry to understand puffickly what you mean yourself, and to igspress your meaning clearly afterwards ; the simpler the words, the better praps. You may, for instans, call a coronet an 'ancestral coronal,' if you like, as you might call a hat a 'swart sombréro,' a glossy four-and-nine, 'a silken helm, to storm impermeable, and light-some as the breezy gossamer ;' but in the long run it 's as well to call it a hat. It *is* a hat, and that name is quite as poeticle as another.'

The remarks of Mr. YELLOWPLUSH upon some of the segregated passages are amusing enough. Take the following, for example :

> '' Girl, beware !
> The love that trifles round the charm it gilds,
> Oft ruins while it shines.'

'Igsplane this, men and angles ! I 've tried every way ; backards, forards, and in all sorts of trancepositions :

> The love that ruins round the charm it shines,
> Gilds while it trifles oft ;

Or :

> The charm that gilds around the love it ruins,
> Oft trifles while it shines ;

Or :

> The ruins that love gilds and shines around,
> Oft trifles while it charms ;

Or :

> Love while it charms, shines round and ruins oft
> The trifles that it gilds ;

Or :

> The love that trifles, gilds and ruins oft
> While round the charm it shines ;

'All witch are as sensable as the fust passadge.'

Before the literary guests depart, the noble host is incidentally informed that he has in his service the celebrated CHAWLS YELLOWPLUSH; 'and nothink to do but he must be brot up from the kitching.' After a little mock-compliment his master addresses him as follows. The ' littery footman's ' reply is also annexed :

' With all my admiration for your talents, Mr. YELLOWPLUSH, I still am confident that many of your friends in the servant's hall will clean my boots a great deal better than a gentleman of your genius can ever be expected to do. It is for this purpose that I employ footmen, and not that they may write articles in magazeens. But you need n't look so red ; I do n't wish to throw you upon the world without means of a livelihood ; and have made interest for a little place which you will have under government, and which will give you an income of eighty pounds a year, which you can double I presume by your literary labors.'

' Sir,' says I, clasping my hands and busting into tiers, ' do not, for Heving's sake, do not think of anythink of the sort, or drive me from your suvvice because I have been fool enough to write in magazeens ! Glans but one moment at your honor's plate ; every spoon is as bright as a mirror: condysend to igsamine your shoos ; your honor may see refiekted in them the fases of every one in the compny. If occasionally I 've forgot the footman in the littery man, and committed to paper my remindicencies of fashnabble life, it was from a sincere desire to do good and promote nollitch ; and I appeal to your honor — I lay my hand on my busm, and in the fase of this noble compny beg you to say — When you rung your bell, who come to you fust ? When you stopt out till morning, who sot up for you ? When you was ill, who forgot the natral dignities of his station, and answered the two-pair bell? O Sir,' says I, ' I knows what 's what ; do n't send me away ! I know them littery chaps, and b' leave me, I'd rather be a footman. The work 's not so hard — the pay is better — the vittels incompyrably supearor. I 've but to clean my things and run my errints, and you put clothes on my back, and meat in my mouth. Sir! Mr. Bullwig! an't I right? Shall I quit my station and sink — that is to say rise — to yours?'

Chief among the remaining ' comic tales and sketches ' of these pleasant volumes, are a series of laughable adventures, entitled, '*Some Passages in the Life of Major Gahagan*.' They embody a forcible and truthful satire upon a very common species of military Irishman, whose impudence is only equalled by his bragadocio spirit and pretension. In the present instance, if we may credit the redoubtable Major, he received the most marked and familiar compliments while dining at the Tuilleries with LOUIS PHILLIPPE, the Duchess of Orleans, the Queen of the Belgians, etc. Our hero was possessed of a very captivating person, as may be gathered from the following, doubtless too partial portrait, drawn by himself: ' I am six feet four inches in height, and of matchless symmetry and proportion. My hair and beard are of the most brilliant auburn — so bright indeed as scarcely to be distinguished at a distance from scarlet. My eyes are bright blue, overshadowed by bushy eye-brows of the same color as my hair ; and a terrific gash of the deepest purple, which goes over the forehead, the eyelid and the cheek, and finishes at the ear, gives my face a more strictly military appearance than can well be conceived. When I 've been drinking, as is pretty often the case, this gash becomes ruby bright ; and as I have another which took off a piece of my under lip and shows five of my front teeth, I leave the reader to imagine, that ' seldom lighted on the earth '—as the monster BURKE (the Major mistakes the London murderer for the celebrated statesman) remarked of one of his unhappy victims — ' a more extraordinary vision.' The feats of our handsome hero in love and war are equally astonishing — nay, tremendous. In the latter department they are ' illustrated by our victories at Ahmednugger, where I slew with my own sword twenty-six matchlock men and cut a dromedary in two ; and at Assaye, where WELLINGTON would have lost the battle but for me. I headed nineteen charges of cavalry, and took (aided by only four of my troop) seventeen field-pieces, killing the scoundrelly French artillerymen. On that day I had eleven elephants shot under me ; and I carried away the Prince Scindia's nose-ring with a pistol-ball. I was daily on guard and in the batteries for seventeen hours out of the twenty-four, with fourteen severe wounds, and seven musket-balls in my body !' A curious circumstance happened here to the Major. His gold repeater was shot into his stomach, and at the hour of twelve it struck *thirteen,* in its fleshly prison : 'a remarkable fact!' It is quite certain that he does not overstep the modesty of his nature, when he says, with equal correctness and self-distrust :

> ' I dare do all that may become a man ;
> Who dares do more is neither more nor less! '

The Major called upon NAPOLEON at St. Helena, in returning from one of his foreign murderous expeditions ; and a ludicrous picture is given of the little exiled Emperor looking up to the portentous ' brave,' and listening with an air of intense interest to a narrative of his marvellous exploits, which he interrupts occasionally with expressions of the most profound admiration. But ' enough! ' exclaims the reader. Very good. Cordially commending Mr. TITMARSH then to his numerous American friends, we take a reluctant leave of his agreeable and mirth-moving volumes.

A CONCERT OF THE POETS. — Some twenty years ago a waggish contributor to BLACKWOOD'S Magazine fell asleep in his arm-chair one sunny summer's afternoon, ' and as he slept he dreamed a dream.' He fancied that all the then reigning poets were convened in a concert-room, where they were to play on such instruments as each had chosen. The reader will recognize, we think, in the character of the individual performances and the instruments by which they are produced, an unique but forcible criticism upon the poetical styles of each of the visionary musicians. Lord BYRON commenced with a solo on the serpent. 'Such playing,' says the dreamer, ' I never heard ! He seemed to have such command over the strange instrument that he could make it almost as soft and melancholy as a flute ; and the depth and beautiful inflection of his lower tones were miraculous. I sometimes couldn't help feeling a mistiness about the eyes, and a heavy palpitation of the heart, as he proceeded.' CAMPBELL gave a sonata on the violin, which he played very scientifically, though he seemed very timorous, and played a weak bow. However, he received plenty of applause, both from his companions and the spectators in the gallery. WORDSWORTH, a grave, plain-looking man, with a sort of absent air, his hair combed smoothly over his forehead, something like a Methodist preacher, next came forward. He would have neither music-book nor music-stand, nor did the writer see any instrument he had ; when presently to his astonishment he overheard somebody whisper: ' WORDSWORTH 's going to give us a grand concerto on the Jew's-harp which he bought last week of a philosophical Jew pedler !' And so he did ; and what is more, the concerto was well worth the hearing. ' You wouldn't believe what tones he brought out of his gew-gaw. He got thunders of applause ; though I could see that some laughed and some few sneered. WORDSWORTH turned away in a pet and walked into a corner, where stood a very antique-looking, magnificent organ, to which he sat down. The name of ' MILTON,' in gilt letters, was on the front; and WORDSWORTH struck a bar or two in such grand Miltonic style that he immediately silenced the laughers. SOUTHEY gave a grand master's flourish on a bruised trumpet, which he had taken up late in life, but which had been used ever since Queen Elizabeth's time, in the coronation of English sovereigns. He concluded in the midst of great plaudits. COLERIDGE, after an eloquent dissertation upon the powers of his novel and simple instrument, sat down to play a *fantasia* with a skewer upon a gridiron, which he called the ' dulcimer of nature.' The applause was immense ; and when it had subsided he proceeded to favor the company with a specimen of his manner of playing the Æolian harp, which he did by breathing into it. He soon played himself to sleep, and presently produced a most capital bass accompaniment in the way of a snore. When he awaked, which he did in about ten minutes, he proceeded to maintain that ' a hair and a cinder ' was one of the finest instruments that human wit ever invented ; and to prove it he played a rhapsody upon it with no small effect. After the applause had subsided, he informed the audience, in a rather transcendental tone, that the cinder came from a subterranean fire in Abyssinia, and the hair from the tail of a black horse with green eyes, of a mysterious breed, preserved by a certain German baron, a friend of his, and a descendant of Dr. FAUSTUS, on his domain in the Hartz Mountains. MOORE, who was universally called upon, played an exquisite old Irish air on the flute, with a pathos that brought tears to the eyes of all listeners. He then attempted a grand Turkish march, with the aid of Turkish bells, which he jingled as an accompaniment. This did not accord with the genius of his instrument ; and seizing a dancing-master's fiddle, he rattled off a humorous divertimento with infinite spirit. Elated with the success of this piece of gayety, he produced a small coach-horn, and proceeded to amuse the audience with a burlesque of Mr. SOUTHEY's grand trumpet-flourish, in which he at last got so personal as to raise quite a tumult. SHELLEY horrified the company with some most terrific passages upon the trombone, which became at last perfectly disagreeable. SCOTT made all ring again with a most spirited reveillée on the patent bugle ; and again he won enthusiastic applause by his execution upon a pair of huge old bagpipes, dusty and neglected, which had belonged to ALLAN RAMSAY. ' We were now interrupted,' says the writer, ' by a wonderfully striking, expressive, and even sweet ditty, which on turning round I found to proceed from an elderly electrical-looking personage, who was playing on the hurdy-gurdy. When I saw it was Mr. CRABBE, I was not surprised at the pleasure which even this monotonous, not to say vulgar instrument afforded me. But what cannot genius do ?' Several other poetical performers, of an inferior grade of merit, brought the imaginary concert to a close ; and the voices of the various instruments in the sleeper's dreaming ear melted away.

PUNISHMENT BY DEATH. — We noticed briefly a few months ago, and in terms of commendation, a legislative report of Mr. O'SULLIVAN in favor of abolishing capital punishment. The variety and amount of argument brought together — in a manner however which we remember to have been sufficiently miscellaneous and desultory — certainly impressed us favorably with the views entertained by the compiler, especially as their tendency was in consonance with the humane improvements of the age. A recent work however from the pen of Rev. Mr. CHEEVER, upon the authority and expediency of punishment by death, we are free to confess has changed our views upon this subject, and induced the firm belief that the abolition of capital punishment would be productive of great evil without a counterbalancing good. Mr. CHEEVER makes of course a strong argument from Scripture ; but he presents as we think even a still stronger argument from expediency. Imprisonment for life it has been argued is preferable to punishment by death, because it gives the murderer time to repent ; but Mr. CHEEVER shows that this very grant of time will be likely to keep him from repenting at all, by fixing that habit of procrastination which evil courses have incorporated in his very nature. ' Because sentence against an evil work is not executed speedily,' his heart will be fully set in him to do evil. A very forcible argument against making the punishment for murder the same as for highway robbery is given in the tenth chapter. When in Pennsylvania this latter crime was punishable by death, murder was more frequent ; because if the robber must be hung for the lesser crime he could but suffer the same penalty for committing the greater, and by committing it he might escape conviction. On the other hand, by putting murder on a level with other crimes, ' we tempt men to commit it for the same inducements; we make murderers out of common thieves and robbers; since if a man must be imprisoned for robbery, his punishment will be no worse for murder, by committing which he may entirely escape!' Is not this setting as it were a premium upon the crime of murder? Is it not protecting the murderer's life, while it leaves that of his victim at his mercy? Who would be the keeper of a state's-prison, when men who have no additional punishment to dread, must continually be tempted to put him out of the way that they may gain their freedom? These arguments against the abolishment of capital punishment, and the substitution of imprisonment for life, strike us as altogether irrefragable. We agree fully with the 'New-York Review,' that 'it is true piety and humanity that call for the most deliberate consideration of the question, both as to duty and expediency, before the awful denunciation against him that sheddeth man's blood be erased from our statute-book.'

GOSSIP WITH READERS AND CORRESPONDENTS. — We have found great pleasure lately in reading a memoir of GALT, contained in the first volume of BLACKWOOD's new edition of his works. We shall take another occasion to present a few passages from this eventful history of the life of genius. It is a little remarkable that the last articles that Mr. GALT and Hogg the Ettrick Shepherd ever wrote were penned for the KNICKERBOCKER. The 'Auld Wife of Altrive,' by the latter, was sent to us, but being blindly directed, failed of its destination, and was re-mailed to the author from Liverpool. The former commenced and forwarded to us 'a romance on an American theme,' for our pages; but he never lived to continue it. 'When in America,' said he, in the letter which accompanied it, 'I was sensible of having obtained many new ideas; and perhaps it may now and then be thought that one who has seen as much of the world as most men, may have seen some things in your 'woody land' not quite in the same light as other travellers from this island.' Indeed, Mr. GALT always spoke in his letters to us in the warmest terms of Americans, and of four or five of our own citizens in particular; and especially of Mr. PHILIP HONE, 'an accomplished gentleman, with a warm, true heart,' to whom he was desirous of dedicating his romance. We cannot resist an inclination to present here an extract from a note of Mr. HONE, to whom we had sent the Memoir in question:

'I happened to be in Edinburgh when the 'Annals of the Parish' was published, and got one of the first copies from BLACKWOOD's office, which after reading I sent out to my family. Mr. GALT's intellect was then 'towering in its pride of place;' his health had experienced none of those shocks which toward the close of his life brought his manly frame to the lowest level of poor humanity; nor had the troubles of the world and the collisions of his fellow-men disturbed the brightness of his imagination nor the equanimity of his temper.

'My acquaintance with Mr. GALT commenced at a later period, when he passed through New-York on his first visit to Canada; and after his return home I was occasionally favored with a letter from him. I wish I could lay my hand upon the last one I received, that I might send you a copy. It contained a touching and affecting description of his helpless condition, bound hand and foot in the iron grasp of paralysis, but still afforded evidence that his 'bosom's lord' had not deserted his 'throne.'

'I am struck with the force of the following remark of his biographer in the volume before me: 'Perhaps the great drawback to Mr. GALT's prosperity and happiness, was the multitude of his resources, and from his being equally fitted for a student and man of the world. As the old proverb hath it, 'The rolling stone gathers no fog;' so in the transition from one occupation and employment to another he expended those powers which if long concentrated on any particular object must have produced great results.'

'It is highly probable that a mind roaming in the fields of fancy, and studying realities only as the material for fiction, would find it difficult to settle down to the mere technical business of surveying lands and laying out lots; and it is not unlikely that the force of his writings may have been impaired by the interference of his other pursuits; but it has been well said of his sketches of Scottish life, that 'no one either among the living or the dead could have written them but himself.'

Is it not a strange thing, this recent discovery of the Mesmeric influences? — that surprising phenomena, by which man, even while in the bonds of corporeal existence, may rise above organization, and be more or less free from time and space? How wonderful have been many of its developements! Marvellous, yet true, if we may believe those whom we know to be alike incapable of delusion and deception. Mystery of mysteries! — that mind should link with mind in unspoken, unwritten union, and go whither we list on far journeys, bringing back faithful records! — the very air seeming, even as BYRON thought, to be a part of us and of our souls! BULWER has this fine passage, touching upon a cognate spiritual theme:

'In the small as in the vast, God is equally profuse of life. The traveller looks upon the tree, and fancies its boughs were formed for his shelter in the summer sun or his fuel in the winter frosts. But in each leaf of these boughs the Creator has made a world: it swarms with innumerable races. Each drop of the water in yon moat is an orb more populous than a kingdom is of men. Everywhere in this immense design, science brings new life to light. Life is the one-pervading principle, and even the thing that seems to die and to putrefy, but engenders new life, and changes to fresh forms of matter. Reasoning then by evident analogy if not a leaf, if not a drop of water but is, no less than yonder star, a habitable and breathing world ; nay, if even man himself is a world to other lives, and millions and myriads dwell in the rivers of his blood, and inhabit his frame, as man inhabits earth, common sense (if your schoolmen had it) would suffice to teach that the circumfluent Infinite which you call space — the boundless Impalpable which divides earth from the moon and stars — is filled also with its correspondent and appropriate life. Is it not a visible absurdity to suppose that Being is crowded upon every leaf, and yet absent from the immensities of space ? The law of the great system forbids the waste even of an atom ; it knows no spot where something of life does not breathe. In the very charnel-house is the nursery of production and animation. Is that true ? Then can you conceive that space, which is the Infinite itself, is alone a waste, is alone lifeless, is less useful to the one design of universal being than the dead carcass of a dog, than the peopled leaf, than the swarming globule ? The microscope shows you the creatures on the leaf ; no mechanical tube is yet invented to discover the nobler and more gifted things that hover in the illimitable air. Yet between these last and man is a mysterious and terrible affinity.'

—

We do not know when we have laughed more heartily — when our usually quiet sanctum has resounded with a more irresistible guffaw — than when we perused the ' cramp piece of penmanship,' which records the following capital anecdote. The narrator may be assured that we cannot hear from him too often :

THE TWO VIRTUOSOS.

Not many years ago there lived in the little town of R——, a suburb of one of our Atlantic cities, an individual known as Dr. Q——, who was noted for three remarkable ' manifestations of the passion of love,' as Mr. Tapistro would classify them. These were, the love of money, the love of science, and the love of Bologna sausages. The first he inherited with his estate from his father ; the second he caught by inoculation from a near neighbor, Professor Z., formerly of some eastern college ; and the third probably grew out of the first, as it is well known that Bologna, *American* Bologna sausages, when eaten sufficiently sparingly, are the most economical food that can be procured. Dr. Q—— had attached to his mansion at R—— a large room, which he called his ' museum,' filled with pictures and all manner of curiosities and articles of *virtu.* The walls were ornamented with numerous paintings of every size and shape ; some of them landscapes of a peculiarly dirty and smoky appearance, and which in consequence had been pronounced by friendly connoisseurs to be the genuine works of Teniers, Claude and Ruysdael ; others were portraits of ancient ladies and gentlemen, with glaring red and white cheeks, and stony blue eyes that at the first glance chilled through the gazer like an east wind. These were all veritable ' Titians,' ' Vandykes,' and ' Raphaels,' supposed so probably from the fact that they looked as little like the works of those immortal artists as it was possible for a bad painter with bad materials to make them. In addition to these invaluable paintings, our Doctor's museum was filled with stuffed birds, striped snakes, ring-tailed monkeys, and every kind of flying and creeping thing, as well as all manner of unknown and unknowable curiosities from the four quarters of the world, including of course that article indispensable to all museums, ' the identical club with which the renowned Captain Cook was killed at Owyhee.' All the Doctor's friends and every little boy and girl in the village were laid under contribution to furnish additions to this rare collection, for which they generally received a ' Thank 'ee,' and sometimes, if the donation happened to be unusually dirty and unclassifiable, the ' thank 'ees ' extended to two or three. Now the Doctor had a nephew, the son of a widowed sister-in-law, a lad of some fifteen or sixteen years, who had been unusually active in securing rubbish for his uncle's collection ; which by the way he must have done from sheer love of science, as he never received any remuneration for his pains, excepting the ever-lasting ' Thank 'ee,' and a free admittance to the museum, which he enjoyed in common with the other acquaintance of his uncle.

Ned Wilson, (the nephew,) having after much importunity prevailed upon his mother to let him go to sea, had accordingly procured a voyage, and one morning presented himself in the breakfast-room of his uncle, to take leave of his rich relative previous to sailing. The Doctor was at first surprised and then delighted ; surprised when his nephew announced his purpose, and delighted when he learned that his destination was the Mediterranean, and that it was his intention if possible to visit the ruins of Herculaneum and Pompeii. ' Of course, Ned,' said he, ' you will not forget your old habits when there ! What vast fields for the industrious and patient explorer are those two buried cities ! Every house a museum in itself, and every street strewed with the curiosities of a former age ! You 've been a good boy, Ned, at home, and you must n't forget your uncle when at Pompeii ! And,' suddenly recollecting himself, ' your uncle must n't forget you neither ! ' And then turning to his wife, he inquired whether she could n't think of some little present that would be acceptable to their clever relative. Now it happened that on the morning in question the Doctor had had his favorite dish of Bolognas on the table ; but they did n't relish very well. He thought they were rather ' hurt,' as the term is ; his wife thought so too ; and the cook, who had been called in, pronounced them the ' werry worst kind of tastin' things she ever see.' They were accordingly rejected, and now stood on the side-board. ' What can we do for Ned ? ' the Doctor repeated, as he began to pace the room, for there was a struggle going on in his breast between his innate meanness and a desire to do a little something for a lad who had done so much for him, and from whom he expected a great deal more. He kept walking to and fro, occasionally repeating ' Give him — give him ——' but he could n't make up his mind what, until he accidentally cast his eye on the discarded Bolognas, when he finished the sentence : ' Give him a — a — Bologna sausage, Hetty ! Nothing can be more delicious on board a ship.' And drawing a long breath, his mind seemed relieved of an immense load. The sausage was accordingly wrapped in an old newspaper and given to Ned, with many almost paternal benedictions, and not a few injunctions to remember his uncle ; and the nephew quitted the splendid mansion of his relative with a swelling breast, and a not very exalted opinion of his liberality.

Three years passed away, and Ned Wilson returned to the village of R——, having in the mean time visited nearly every port in the Mediterranean. One morning, a few days after his return, he made his appearance at Dr. Q ——'s mansion, having under his arm a small tin box. The first greetings over, his uncle, who had not for a moment lost sight of the little tin box, led his nephew into the museum. 'And now, Ned, what have you got in the box, eh? Something rare, I'll warrant.' 'It is something rare,' said the nephew, 'but what, I can't tell. I picked it up in Pompeii, but nobody there knew what it was.' And he handed the box to the Doctor, who received it as eagerly as if it had been filled with mortgages. 'But stop!' said he, laying the box on the table, 'we must have professor Z —— here;' and ringing the bell, he sent a message after his brother virtuoso. In a few moments the Professor made his appearance; and the men of science proceeded to examine the contents of the box, which after undoing sundry wrappers, they found to consist of one article only. Throwing his spectacles over his forehead, which he always did when about to look sharply at any thing, the Doctor commenced the examination. He turned the curiosity over and over, and looked at it on every side, and in every position of light, until his eyes ached and began to grow dim; but he could make nothing of it; and then, his spectacles suddenly dropping in their place unnoticed, he handed the article to the Professor, protesting that looking at it had made him nearly stone blind. The Professor examined it as closely as the Doctor. 'The *form* is familiar to me,' said he; 'it looks very much like a *sausage*.' 'So it does — it *does!*' chimed in the Doctor; 'do n't go, Ned,' turning to his nephew, who had his hand on the latch of the door. 'Do n't go; we shall soon know what it is!' 'It *looks* like a *sausage*,' repeated the Professor solemnly; 'and,' putting it to his nose, 'it *smells* like a *sausage*.' And then, having tasted it, he threw it from him as if it had been a rattlesnake, exclaiming: 'And by G——d! Doctor, it *is* a *sausage* — a Bologna; and a d——d bad one too!' The truth flashed on the uncle. He stood irresolute a moment, and then seizing the club that had killed Captain Cook, he turned suddenly round —— But his graceless nephew had just closed the street door behind him.

, READER, as you walk by country-roads, with Nature bursting into bloom all around you, and listen to the myriad voices of the glad awakening Spring; or as you traverse the city's streets, and amid their dust and din catch passing glimpses of reviving green on distant slopes across the broad river or spreading bay; is it given you, in God's providence, to think of those who, early lost and vanished from this blessed earth, shall never gaze upon these scenes again? — of one perchance who looked upon each opening season with a poet's calm delight; the soft April shower; the pale green of the fresh-budding willow; the darker verdure of the springing grass; who with a full heart and wistful eye pursued the setting sun, until twilight came down upon the earth, and the evening star went up upon its watch? Precious in the solemn spring-time are the memories of the dead!

LINES

ON THE DEATH OF WILLIS GAYLORD CLARK.

UP to the Spirit-land! — the unfinished song
Still on thy lip — the breathing lyre
Warm in thy tuneful hand;
A spell-bound throng
Intently listening to its thrilling wire:
Thou, early called by the unerring Sire,
Up to the Spirit-land!

Up to the Spirit-land! whose soul inwrought
To harmony, that naught could move;
Not earth's dense atmosphere, nor jarring thought,
Nor the crushed vase of love,
Scarce could they weave a thread of mournful dies
Into thy woof of song;
For sunbeams kissed it from the sky,
Till finely blent, and healthfully,
Its colors moved along.

Up to the Spirit-land!
Though we thy music ill can spare,
That charmed away our care,
Up! up! — *her* she is there,
O'er whom thy breaking heart-strings rang,
Whose image lingered still, to soothe thy latest pang;
She gives to thee her angel hand.

Go, Minstrel, go!
Though well we love to hear thy numbers flow,
Though still we need
In thy pure life to read
The sweet example of a truthful soul
Calm in its own communings with the skies,
We, o'er whose heads the sand-clouds roll,
The siroca of our desert-way,
Whelming us, when we fain would rise
To reach the living lay:
Yet, Minstrel, go
To thy divine employ;
Leave us to mourn: Earth's lot is wo,
And Heaven's is joy!

L. H. SIGOURNEY.

'I scarcely know how,' says our esteemed friend and correspondent, 'to explain why the foregoing lines have not earlier been sent you. They have however been much on my mind; and although at this late hour, I hope you will accept them as a sincere tribute to the memory of one equally loved and lamented.'

WE have received a dozen communications, some denying and others confirming the truth of the remarks of a correspondent in our last number, touching the manner in which Americans deport themselves in Paris ; the ' really small figure they cut in the French metropolis, and the superabundant pretension thereanent, which they display on their return to the United States.' We have only to repeat, that our correspondent has the entrée to the best society in Paris, and to add, that he is incapable of misrepresenting the truth. The following well describes the condition of numbers of our young American bloods, who carry their brains in their pockets, and are hence unable to appreciate the advantages they possess : ' Unsuited by their tastes — unprepared by previous information — deeming a passport and a letter of credit all-sufficient for their purpose — they set out upon their continental travels. From their ignorance of a foreign language, their journey is one of difficulty and embarrassment at every step. They understand little of what they see, nothing of what they hear. The discomforts of foreign life have no palliation, by their being enabled to reason on and draw inferences from them. All the sources of information are hermetically sealed against them, and their tour has nothing to compensate for its fatigue and expense, save the absurd detail of adventure to which their ignorance has exposed them.' · · · We take our old and favored correspondent ' M.' at his word ! Let him at once, within a month of the date hereof, excogitate, concoct, write, indite, and clerkly deliver into our hands one of those tragi-comic essays which used to set so many to reading us with unsated eyes ; ' to devouring us with unwearied jaws ; to swallowing us down with immeasurable throat.' ' Do it !' · · · We shall not be so indiscreet as to name the popular clergyman against whom a correspondent inveighs bitterly, in that, ' having heard great things of him, he went to hear him, and came away dis — appointed.' The subjoined lines are quoted at the conclusion of our correspondent's commentary, as ' expressing exactly what the writer desired to describe.' If the limning be faithful, the divine must have won the suffrages of those who affect ' interesting preachers : '

' O ye ruling Powers
Of Poesy sublime, give me to sing
The splendors of that sermon ! The bold a-hem !
The look sublime, that beamed with confidence,
The three wipes with the cambric handkerchief ;
The strut — the bob — and the impressive thump
Upon the Holy Book !
                    ' No notes were there ;
No, not a scrap. All was intuitive,
Pouring like water from a flashing fountain,
With current unexhausted. Now the lips
Protruded, and the eye-brows lowered amain,
Like Kean's in dark Othello.

' But let us hear
Somewhat of this same grand and flowery sermon.
Aha ! there comes the rub ! 'T was made of scraps !
Sketches from Nature ; from old Johnson some,
And some from Joseph Addison and Goldsmith ;
Blair, William Shakspere, Young's Night Thoughts,
    The Grave ;
Gillespie on the Seasons ; even the plain
Bold energy of Andrew Thompson here
Was pressed into the jumble. Plan or system
Had it none : no gleam of mind or aim ;
' A thing of shreds and patches !' Yet the blare
Went on for fifteen minutes, haply more.'

' My Uncle's Will' is a good story, but it is upon a time-worn theme. The incidents are very like those of ' The Sprout Family,' heretofore quoted in the KNICKERBOCKER. The disinterested anxiety of the widow-aunt reminds us of a complaint made by JEAN JACQUES, who tells us that when his wife died, every farmer in the neighborhood offered to console him by one of their daughters ; but that a few weeks afterward his cow having shared the same fate, no one ever thought of replacing his loss by the offer of another ; thereby proving the different value people set upon their cows and children ! · · · The gentle and kind spirit, whoever he may be, to whom we are indebted for the little essay upon ' Kite-Flying,' will take our ' warm right hand.' He could not have touched upon a theme so full of delightful boyish remembrances. We once thought — and we are not sure that the impression is not pretty strong within us still — that there could scarcely be a more pleasant thing than to hold a kite-string in the gloaming of a warm spring day, and watch the spiritual toy far up in the soft mild air, taking the dying sunlight on its breast, and wagging its tail as if for very joy. We can never be sad when the air is full of kites ; and sometimes it is, for city sports are always contagious. Little kite-flying citizens may confidently count upon our assistance at all times in untangling their lines and adjusting their tails ; and we are rejoiced to find that there is one staid denizen ' in populous city pent ' who can sympathize with our sympathy, and whose thoughts go back with ours to the past, from the busy, bustling present. ' Let us pray ever,' says a recent foreign essayist, ' that as we still move on in life, travelling as of necessity we must gradually and imperceptibly, day by day, farther from the freshness, the joyousness, and the romantic ardor of our youth, that we may be privileged to carry with us the remembrance at least, if not a single vestige, of our bright experience ; so shall we be blessings to the young ; neither churlish nor discontented ourselves, nor a source of uneasiness to others. Let us bear in our years only that knowledge of our youth that will suffice to save the elder from becoming the envier of the young ; for what is that incessant evil-eyeing of the amusements of early life — those surly, fretful, and over-hasty complainings at its pleasures — but envy, the most malignant, the most odious, and the most unprofitable ? Yes, let us pray that our sunset may be streaked with the memories and shadows only of the brilliant dawn.'

We are indebted to a kind correspondent — himself a writer of distinction, with whom we hope ere long to make our readers better acquainted — for the following original sonnet by the lamented JOHN G. C. BRAINARD. It is placed in type from the departed poet's own manuscript, and has never before been published:

MEETING AND PARTING.

WE met and parted on an Autumn eve,
　When moonlight with its beauty steeped the vale,
Silent, and not a cloud was seen to sail
Athwart the azure firmament. Believe,
　Ye who have felt the ecstasies of love,
What were my feelings when I gazed on her,
Whom — absent — life had nothing to confer;
　Whose presence rendered earth like heaven above !
Upon a rock, above the murmuring sea,
　Linked arm in arm, in thoughtfulness we stood ;
And, as I marked our shadows on the flood,
I dreamed that Fate intended us to be
　United always — 't was a dream ; and lo !
Between us mountains rise and oceans flow !

' *The Littérateur's Lament* ' is ingenious ; but we are not yet *quite* reduced to the admission of a disguised *nostrum-puff* into this department of our Magazine. We commend to our suffering ' Littérateur ' a reduction of the following ' domestic medicines ' into an essay for some of our contemporaries. Possibly he may be more successful with them in disguising his ' benevolent object : '

' A stick o' brimstone wore in the pocket is good for them as has cramps.
' A loadstone put on the place where the pains is, is beautiful in the rheumatiz.
' When babies is troubled with worms, the leastest drop o' gin give to 'em mornin's fasting will — kill 'em !
' For a cold : a basin o' water-gruel, with half a quartern o' old rum in it, or a quartern, if partic'lar bad, with lots o' brown sugar, going to bed.
' If you 've got the hiccups, pinch one of your wrists, and hold your breath while you count sixty — or *get somebody to make you jump !*
' The ear-ach. Put an ing'un in your ear — after it 's well roasted.'

The ' *Tale of Terror* ' may be ' one of remarkable interest and thrilling to a delirious pitch,' as the writer modestly states ; but the total indifference of the public to similar hackneyed scenes — that of the *Beauchampe Murder* for example, lately reproduced, with revolting adjuncts, in a ' native romance ' that has been

　　　　　 ——' neither damned nor blamed,
　　　　 But very quietly *dismissed*,'

would ' give us pause,' even had we no taste of our own in the premises. . . . . ' I remember,' says a recent writer, ' to have been very much struck with the death-scene of a celebrated romance-writer in Germany, who up to the very last persuaded himself that he should get well, and who spent some of his latest moments in dictating the pages of a new novel which he was composing. ' Only life !' was his exclamation ; ' this sweet life ! — life at any price ! — life even with suffering ! — Only life, life, life !' Mrs. NORTON, in ' *The Child of Earth*,' has beautifully illustrated the tenacity with which poor humanity clings to this shadowy existence :

FAINTER her slow step falls from day to day ;
　Death's hand is heavy on her darkening brow !
Yet doth she fondly cling to earth, and say :
　' I am content to die — but oh, not now !
Not while the blossoms of the joyous spring
　Make the warm air such luxury to breathe ;
Not while bright flowers around my footsteps wreathe.
Spare me, great GOD ! — lift up my drooping brow :
I am content to die — but oh, not now !'

The spring hath ripened into summer-time —
　The season's viewless boundary is past ;
The glorious sun hath reached his burning prime :
　' Oh ! must this glimpse of beauty be the last ?
Let me not perish while o'er land and sea
　With silent steps the Lord of light moves on ;
Nor while the murmur of the mountain-bee
　Greets my dull ear, with music in its tone.
Pale sickness dims my eye and clouds my brow —
I am content to die ! — but oh ! not now !'

Summer is gone ; and Autumn's soberer hues
　Tint the ripe fruits and gild the waving corn ;
The huntsman swift the flying game pursues,
　Shouts the halloo, and winds his eager horn.
' Spare me awhile, to wander forth and gaze
　On the broad meadows and the quiet stream ;
To watch in silence while the evening rays
　Slant through the fading trees with ruddy gleam :
Cooler the breezes play around my brow —
I 'm content to die ! but oh, not now !'

The bleak wind whistles ; snow-showers far and near,
　Drift without echo to the whitening ground ;
Autumn hath passed away, and cold and drear,
　Winter stalks on, with frozen mantle bound ;
Yet still that prayer ascends : ' Oh ! laughingly
　My little brothers round the warm hearth crowd ;
Our home-fire blazes broad and bright and high,
　And the roof rings with voices light and loud ;
Spare me awhile — raise up my drooping brow !
I am content to die ! but oh ! not now !'

We suspect ' *Jeffrey, Jr.*' must have fallen a victim to the criticisms of some one of the small and spirited newspapers. He calls the editors ' Two-penny Dips,' because, as he alleges, they only dip into a book, and then condemn or praise it, as the case may be, without perusal. Our correspondent may be right in some isolated case — his own perhaps ; but usually the brief judgments of the daily press, when well considered, have as much weight with the mass as the long, elaborately dull dissertations which pass with small commentators for the only veritable criticism. . . . '*A Widower*' has sent us for publication the following fragment, in one of the most touching yet sententious letters we ever read. As we might infract an implied obligation of privacy, we reluctantly suppress the note. There is a tender affection in the lines which we have rarely seen surpassed:

> ' MY little girl sleeps on my arm all night,
> And seldom stirs, save when with playful wile
> I bid her rise and press her lips to mine,
> Which in her sleep she does. And sometimes then,
> Half muttered in her slumbers, she affirms
> Her love for me is boundless. And I take
> The little bud and close her in my arms ;
> Assure her by my action — for my lips
> Yield me no utterance then — that in my heart
> She is the treasured jewel. Tenderly,
> Hour after hour, without desire of sleep,
> I watch above that large amount of hope,
> Until the stars wane, and the yellow moon
> Walks forth into the night.'

'*M.*' has humor, but his taste is naught. Nevertheless he exhibits great promise; and we *do* ' say the word : ' *Go on.*' Only remember this ; discriminate styles with more caution and better judgment. One comparison in the chapter on ' *American Novelists*' reminds us of the Dutchman's ' big house, dat always shtood right py de side of a little yellow dog.' . . . Our port-folio actually *teems* with articles in prose and verse, many of them of a high order of excellence, and including several for which we had hoped to the last to find a place in the present number. The following are either filed for immediate insertion, or under ' believing' consideration : ' An Audience with SULTAN ABDUL MEJID,' by an American ; ' The Battle Ground,' by ' R. S. C.' ; ' Domestic Servitude,' by ' H. F.' ; A ' Fishing Excursion in Boston Harbor ;' ' Frank Upton ;' ' Snarleyhead, the Reformer ;' ' The Vision of CADMAN the Saxon ;' ' The Infant's Miniature,' by Mrs. E. CLEMENTINE KINNEY ; ' You ask Me why I look Grave,' and ' Lines written during the Illness of a Friend ;' ' Letters from Rome ;' ' Stanzas ' by ' LEON ;' ' Reduplicate Forms in English ;' ' A New Phrenological Idea,' by ' C. R.,' Boston ; ' Life's Seasons ;' ' To the Departed Poetess of Lake Champlain ;' ' Tawney Tom and Tabby Gray ;' ' The Joy of the Stars.' The alterations indicated by ' J. O. W.' will be attended to.

' THE DIAL.' — This publication, as we learn from the April number, has passed into the hands of the editors, by whom it will hereafter be published. Many things have appeared in ' The Dial ' to which we have awarded honest commendation ; and we have no shadow of prejudice against a periodical whose aim is to ' seek truth and pursue it.' But we implore the editors to shut out from its pages such solemn, elaborate humbugs as Mr. A. BRONSON ALCOTT, who has the place of honor in the present issue. Why was he not permitted to withdraw his MS.? He inclined to do so, saying : ' The Dial prefers a thought and diction, not mine. A fit organ for such as myself is not yet, but is to be.' Ah ! what a pity ! We commend the transcendental soothsayer to a *hand-organ.* Doubtless he might obtain some relief for the poverty of which he complains, by repeating his Orphic ' scriptures ' in the by-streets of Boston, accompanied by appropriate music on a ' fit organ for such as himself.' Seriously, is it not amusing to behold a horned-owl pretending to peer deep down into a mill-stone ? — or in other words, to see a man like Mr. ALCOTT pretending to such great light, that all his contemporaries are in the dark in comparison ? — who fancies indeed that he is a martyr ' whom his age despises ;' the said age not knowing that he is ' making his way through the gate of obloquy and shame to the temple of renown.' Like MAWWORM, he ' *loves* to be despised.' And in the mean-time he ' waits with a calm patience for the souls that shall make organs for him, in which his ' scriptures may take body,' and the ' privatest life of virtue and genius be made public,' since ' nor gods nor true persons have secrets.' We have in the ' Diary '-extracts to which we have alluded some admirable examples of Mr. ALCOTT's style. Neither GOLDSMITH, ADDISON, nor STEELE could have penned such ' scriptures ' as the following, even if they had had a dozen ' organs.' How Mr. ALCOTT must pity them ! They *had* good parts, certainly, which were capable of transcendental improvement : ' Piety is unconscious, vascular, vital. Like breathing, it *is* — and is, *because* it is !' . . . ' Childhood! Time stretches backward into the period whence it proceeded, and forward to its return therein, yet dates not thy genesis, thine advent, nor ascension. Nature thou art not, but of thee she is the show. Matter is thy shadow, as thou runnest on thy behests.' Mr. ALCOTT thus apostrophizes this dim and ignorant present : ' O Age ! thou Believest nothing of this divine lore, but deemest it all moonshine, madness, wild fanaticism, or witless dream ! GOD has ebbed clean from thy heart, and left thee loveless and blind. But lo ! he is rushing in full flood into the souls of thy youth, and thy sons and daughters (this last allusion is probably intended for ABBY FOLSOM,) driven from the sanctuaries of wisdom and piety, shall prophesy soon with cloven tongues of fire to thy discomfort and shame; for thy priests are godless, and thou art a slave to the gauds of sense!' Our Orphic expostulator should take heart. His 'divine lore' and his pellucid style are finding admirers and imitators. Witness the following advertising 'scripture' of one Mr. PARSONS, who proposes to take Daguerreotype portraits of the Bostonians:

'When we reflect that it is but a few years since not any thing but the vague representation of Photography floated on the brain of the imagination and before the eye, but now it is found long hid in the quarry of nature's philosophy, that beauteous art and science, which is no less the herald or the expressive messenger of the past, under many associating, pleasing reflections and enjoyments in youthful pleasures. The realizer and proclaimer of all that is the most endearing in children. Their prattle of the present; their hopeful promise of their future enjoyments, of the delighted parents in the future completion and final comfort and bliss of all their anxieties and toils, (although much to be regretted,) of their past, present and future hopes of their lives, no wonder that we are ready to embrace all that can come within our power to enjoy of such endearing scenes, that we are immediately transported with the views of the society of heaven, while on earth; such views are not very dissimilarly presented in the Photographic reflection; also, that they may be enjoyed for a mere bagatelle expense. LIKENESSES FULL, will be given, or no payment will be received. They are got up under such style as to suit the present exigence of the times, at his Rooms in Gloucester, Rockport, West Parish, Squam,' etc., etc.

The above is not the less transcendental because its grammar is a little lax. That is 'a part of the system.' Mr. ALCOTT says in one passage of his diary: 'I planted my seeds and wed my currants and strawberries.' If he should 'wed' a young crook-necked squash or a small feminine potato, it would be 'a good match.' We must forego allusion to the other contents of 'The Dial.' The forty-six pages of 'Marie Van Osterwich,' from the French, looked at first as though they might require an ostrich to digest them; but the story is a good one, and very agreeably disappointed us. The 'Entwicklungsgeschichte,' etc., of VON DORNER we have not as yet found leisure to peruse.

SOUTHERN PERIODICALS. — The deserved success of the Richmond (Va.) '*Messenger*' Magazine — which, while it is the organ *par excellence* of the best periodical contributions of the South, is yet, like the KNICKERBOCKER, necessarily indebted to writers from *all* sections of the country for its reputation — has given rise to other Southern publications, some of which (from out the number of those that must needs ere long expire) bid fair to emulate its merit, and to earn a like popularity. Chief among these, it is easy to perceive, will be 'THE ORION,' a very neatly printed, well supplied, and admirably embellished monthly Magazine, under the care of Mr. RICHARDS, late editor of 'Georgia Illustrated;' and 'THE CHICORA, OR MESSENGER OF THE SOUTH,' published weekly in Charleston, (S. C.,) and edited by our accomplished correspondent, N. S. DODGE, Esq., and B. R. CARROLL, Esq., a gentleman of fine literary attainments. Our respected contemporaries, we may reasonably assume, will be found too sensible to indulge in invective against the literature of the North and East in contradistinction to that of the South; a matter always sufficiently harmless, certainly, and sometimes particularly amusing, especially to those who are in the secret, and know why 'the grumblers grumble.'

TRANSLATION OF BERNARD'S 'GERFAUT.' — We gave in a late number one or two spirited passages from a translation of 'Gerfaut,' from the French of BERNARD, by Oscar COLES, Esq., of this city. It was rendered from the original in a most faithful and spirited manner, and was entirely prepared for the press, when the translator discovered that in 'The Lover and Husband,' recently published by Messrs. CAREY AND HART, Philadelphia, Mrs. GORE of England had so far anticipated him, as to present in the above-named work a mutilated and altered copy of the stirring French romance in question. We hope that some of our publishers will do themselves and the reading public a favor by presenting *the* translation to the American public. It could scarcely fail of the amplest success.

. AMONG the works which we have been unable adequately to notice in the present number, are the comprehensive and well-digested 'Discourse' of Dr. FRANCIS, at the opening of the Lyceum of Natural History; 'Ambrosio de Letinez,' the first Texian novel; CONN's excellent New Spelling-Book; 'Ideals,' etc., by 'ALGERNON;' LYELL's Geological Lectures; 'Homœopathy,' etc., by O. W. HOLMES, M. D.; the 'Cyclopedia Indanensis' of SCHOOLCRAFT; and 'The Fame and Glory of England Vindicated.' 'Dramatic Doings and On Dits,' and the subjoined 'LITERARY RECORD' articles were in type for the present issue, and are in type for the next: 'Gunderode;' 'The Zicali;' 'Short Stories;' 'Daughters of England;' 'Devotional Melodies;' and 'The Crofton Boys.'

PORTRAIT OF MISS CLIFTON. — The admirers of this popular American actress have now an opportunity of obtaining a most admirable and faithful likeness of her, from a drawing on stone by Mr. M'DOUGALL, No. 11 Park Place. We do not remember ever to have seen a more finished and tasteful specimen of this species of art. Mr. M'DOUGALL may fairly 'divide the honors' between successful miniature painting and lithographic execution — for he excels in both.

THE KNICKERBOCKER.

VOL. XIX.   JUNE, 1842.   No. 6.

AN AUDIENCE WITH SULTAN ABDUL MEJID.

BY AN AMERICAN.

IN 1840, being at Constantinople, Commodore PORTER, then newly appointed Minister Resident of the United States to the Sublime Porte, was so kind as to attach me to his legation, and to permit me to witness the presentation of his credentials to the young Sultan, ABDUL MEJID. Although our government had been represented by him at the Porte since 1831, as its Chargé d'Affaires, that rank did not qualify him for a public reception by the Sultan; and as all eastern nations judge of the importance of foreign powers by the rank of their representative, an increased grade was necessary to elevate our great republic, in the minds of the Ottomans, above the very smallest and most insignificant powers of the old world. The government at Washington, seeing the propriety of the measure, offered to our veteran public servant, Commodore PORTER, then in the United States on leave of absence, the increased rank of Minister Resident to the Sublime Porte, which he accepted, and returned to his residence at Constantinople. He being therefore the first minister our country has had accredited to the Sultan, and this his first audience, I thought it would perhaps interest the readers of the KNICKERBOCKER to know something about his reception; and with this view I now do myself the pleasure of sending you a copy of the notes which I made at the time in my journal.

Before the Minister's credentials were perfectly valid, he made visits to two of the higher officers of the Sublime Porte; but I will commence with that to MAJESTY itself, and mention the others in regular succession. The first step taken was by the Dragoman of the legation, who made a translation into Turkish of the letter of the President to the Sultan, from a copy which, as is usual on such occasions, was sent for the Minister of foreign affairs. On handing it to him, the Dragoman requested for his Minister an audience with His Majesty, to present the original. The office of the Minister of Foreign Affairs is held in a great building in the heart of Constantinople, called in the Turkish language

Deri-alich, or the Sublime Porte, where we were afterward received by him. The Minister replied that he would make known the request to His Majesty, and give his answer on the following day. This was on Monday, and on Tuesday it was learned that the Sultan had appointed Thursday, May 23d, at eleven o'clock, for the audience. In the mean time a very important preliminary was under execution; that of the preparation of a bag or sack to contain the President's letter to the Sultan. It was made of rose-colored satin, richly embroidered in gold five-pointed stars, lined with white satin, and closed with a gold cord, having a golden tassel at its end; the whole bearing a remarkable contrast with the simple but appropriate style of the contents of the letter. I only got a glimpse of the envelope of the great document, and distinctly remember that it was addressed in a fair legible hand: '*To our Great and Good Friend*, SULTAN ABDUL MEJID KHAN, *Emperor of the Ottoman Empire.*'

Each foreign legation at the Porte has a barge of four, six, or eight pair of oars, according to the rank of the representative, in form much like the picturesque models of the smaller caïques of the Bosphorus and the Golden Horn. They draw but little water, and glide over it with noiseless speed; are painted with the national colors of the legation, and the bargemen, or *caïquejees*, as they are denominated at Constantinople, are dressed in colors to match. That of ours is of course blue and red, and agreeable to the established usage and the rank of the Minister, is pulled by six men, over whom at the bow floated the striped bunting flag of the United States.

The Sultan at this season, the month of May, resides in the magnificent new palace of Tcharagian, erected by his late father Sultan Mahmoud II., on the European side of the Bosphorus, about two miles from the mouth of the Golden Horn. Sultan Mahmoud died suddenly before it was completed; and as it was to have been the most splendid of all his edifices, the most costly, and the one about which he always evinced the greatest interest and anxiety, it now bears with it to reflective minds the forcible moral that in our most heart-felt and eager enterprises we may be called away with but a moment's warning. I was told that he had for many years — almost from his accession to the throne, in 1808 — acted upon a feeling of superstition, that so long as he was engaged in erecting public edifices, the affairs of his empire would be prosperous. The greater part of the palaces and kiosks on the Bosphorus, his favorite stream, were built by him; where he doubtless spent many hours of enjoyment in his youth, before troubles overcame him, and the fairest portions of his empire were reft from him by the hand of the infidel. Tcharagian is built on the site of a pacha's *Yali*, or summer residence, in which some years ago a splendid nocturnal fête was given to Sultan Mahmoud by its owner; when the building and gardens attached to it were brilliantly illuminated. The latter were filled with the most beautiful flowers of Constantinople, and the Sultan in his walks among them was attended by the fairest Circassians that could be found in his capitol, dancing round him, and singing praise-songs to his delighted ear. The fête made so agreeable an impression on his mind, that it induced him to erect the present magnificent palace and gardens in the place of the more humble *Yali*, and give it the name of 'Tcharagian Seray,' or 'the Palace of Lights.'

I return from my digression. About half-past ten o'clock, A. M., the Minister Resident, Dragoman, Consul, and Attaché, with guards and servants, seated in the stern sheets of the barge, might be seen issuing out of the Golden Horn, to follow the numerous windings of the Bosphorus, and proceeding along its shores, (which in the month of May are decked with the most beautiful verdure and flowers,) to approach the palace of the Sultan.

Before I introduce the reader to the presence of His Majesty, who by his subjects is called in their figurative language, the 'Centre of the Universe,' and the 'Refuge of the World,' the 'Orbit of Majesty,' and the 'Sovereign of the two Worlds;' in the latter title probably meaning the present and the world to come, for it dates antecedent to the discovery of our own Yankee land; I say, before I bring you within reach of the 'Blood-Letter,' the 'Possessor of Men's Necks,' and the 'Owner of the Two-edged Sword,' allow me to recall to memory an audience with Sultan Mahmoud in his younger days, and before reform had been introduced into his empire.

The author of 'Constantinople and its Environs,' whom I have invariably found to be correct, in speaking of the old palace of the Sultans, situated on the site of ancient Byzantium, and called by Europeans by the exclusive name of 'the Seraglio,' says : 'Another ceremony of the Divan, is the reception of ministers of foreign powers, who come here to be duly made fit for reception by the Sultan. On the day appointed, they and their suites assemble at an early hour in the morning, and all the process of deciding cases, distributing money, and running for pilaff,' (referring to scenes which occured within the inner gates in the presence of the Grand Vizier and other imperial ministers, highly dishonorable and degrading to the ambassador,) 'is ostensibly displayed before them, in order to dazzle, astonish, and impress on those stranger-infidels a high opinion of Turkish superiority. They are allowed to enter the Divan seemingly as spectators, and are left standing in the crowd without notice or respect. On rare occasions, the tried ambassador, if he be from a favored nation, is allowed a joint-stool to sit on; but such an indulgence is not permitted to the rest; secretaries of legation, dragomans, consuls, attachés, etc., are kept standing for several hours, till the whole of the exhibition is displayed. It is then notified to the Sultan that some Giaours are in the Divan, and on inquiry into their business, that they humbly crave to be admitted into his sublime presence, to prostrate themselves before him. It is now that orders are given to feed, wash, and clothe them; and it is notified that when they are fit to be seen they will be admitted, and this is done accordingly. Joint-stools are brought in, on which are placed metal trays, without cloth, knife or fork, and every one helps himself with his fingers, including the ambassador. After this scrambling and tumultuous refreshment, water is poured on the smeared and greasy persons who partake of it. They are then led forth to a large tree in the court, where a heap of pelisses of various qualities lie on the pavement, shaken out of bags in which they were brought. From this every person to be admitted to the presence takes one, and having wrapped himself in it, he is seized by the collar and dragged into the presence of the Sultan, where he is held during the very few moments that the ambassador is permitted to pass in presenting his credentials,' etc.

This was the ceremony of an audience with the Sultan as late as 1808; but civilization has made great changes at the Sublime Porte. The school-master is abroad among the Turks, and the preceding is now only quoted to show the difference between that period and the present.

On this occasion, the Minister's barge, after gaining the point on which the winter palace of *Dolma-Baktcha* is situated, crossed over to the Asiatic shore, and continuing along its banks as far as the village of *Tchengel-kieny*, suddenly turned its prow again toward the more civilized continent of Europe, and aided as much by the current as the oars, neared the white marble stair-case of Tcharagian. The author from whose pages I have borrowed the account of an audience under the *ancient régime*, in speaking of this palace says: ' It consists of a centre with two extensive wings. The long façade presents, not foundation walls of rude masonry supporting a barbarous superstructure of wood, with windows darkened by dense blinds, like the older imperial palaces on the opposite shore; but a Doric colonnade of marble is approached by spacious flights of steps of the same material; these elevate stately fronts of sculptured stone, pierced by cornices and balustrades. The centre is a superb entrance of six Corinthian pillars, crowned by a noble pediment, enclosing a sculptured tympanum. This central portion is the residence of the Sultan; the left wing contains the harem of his establishment, and the right the various offices of his household. The edifice stands on a quay of hewn granite, and forms the most noble and novel object of all the buildings that line the shores of the Bosphorus.'

I will only add, that to the right of the palace, though within the enclosure of the walls which surround it, is a plain building, two stories high, occupied by the great chamberlain and commander of the imperial guard, Reza Pacha; in front of which, as we approached, a captain's guard was drawn up, presenting arms, and having by their side the band of music of the palace. On the quay at the landing stood Reza Pacha with Ali Effendi, then dragoman of the Porte, now Ottoman minister at London; the Sultan's secretary, Teofik Bey, and several pages and other officers of the household, ready to receive the Minister. After the barge was grappled to the quay, the Minister stepped on shore, followed by his suite in full uniform and attendants. The Pacha, after shaking hands with him in the European style, assisted him to enter his office and ascend the stairs. Leading him into a comfortable but plainly-furnished apartment, he was presented to S. E. Rechid Pacha, then minister of foreign affairs, and now ambassador at Paris, the projector of the famous Hatti-Sherif of Gul Khaneh, (the 'Magna Charta Liberatum of the Turks;') Achmet Pacha, minister of commerce; Said Pacha, Capondan Pacha, both brothers-in-law of the Sultan; Mustapha Nouri Pacha, minister of war; and Kimal Pacha, minister of finances; all wearing the diamond insignia of their respective grades on their breasts. They were all standing as he entered the room, an attitude assumed for the purpose of not being compelled by civility to rise on the reception of an infidel, even though in the character of an ambassador; and after each had saluted him, they all seated themselves, Rechid Pacha sitting near the Minister.

As soon as his health had been inquired after, coffee was handed round in small cups not much larger than half an egg-shell, supported by rich silver forms of elaborate workmanship; then a lighted pipe was presented to each, varying in length, richness and beauty, according to the grade of the individual. The coffee no doubt was of the purest Mocha, for I would not suspect the Sultan's officers of drinking any other; but not being used to its superior flavor, I thought I never had tasted any thing half so bitter and ungrateful in all my life. Fortunately the cup contained but a thimble-full in quantity, so I swallowed it as well as I could. The tobacco however was really delicious, preferable in my humble opinion to either Virginian, Maryland, or even Cuba; and while the Minister and his Dragoman were engaged in conversation, letting theirs go out, I smoked mine until not another puff could be got out of it.

Within the room stood about a dozen officers, evidently attendant on the several pachas, and as many pages of the palace, ready to take away the cups or renew the pipes if necessary, at a moment's warning. They held their arms crossed before them, and in their movements and personal appearance were as genteel and neat as the best drilled *valets* of Versailles. After the pipes were taken away, they brought to each of us a delicious goblet of sherbet made of pomegranate juice scented with rose-water. While the Minister and the pachas were engaged in some desultory conversation through the intermediation of the Dragoman of the legation, an officer hastily entering the apartment, informed Rechid Pacha that the Sultan was ready to receive the Minister.

At the invitation of the Pacha, we all arose and followed him and the Minister and pachas down the stair-case, and through a neat flower-garden leading to the entrance of that part of the palace where the Sultan awaited our arrival; the Dragoman bearing in his hand, neatly folded in a white satin envelope, the gold-embroidered sack containing the letter of the President. Rechid Pacha, with the gentlemanly kindness for which he is so remarkable, assisted the Minister to ascend the lofty stair-case which brought us to the apartment of the audience, and we and the other pachas followed them *pêle-mêle*, with little regard to rank or file. The Dragoman of the Porte, a fine young Turkish gentleman, having observed that none of the members of the legation were decorated with orders, asked me in French if the Constitution of the United States forbade it. He had one on *his* breast as large as the palm of my hand, brilliant in rich and lustrous diamonds. When I answered in the affirmative, he observed: ' C'est donc une véritable République ! '

Of the interior of the palace we saw but little; the stairs were well made, supported on one side by mahogany balusters, lighted on the other by lofty windows; and it being spring, were only covered with matting. Suddenly we found ourselves at the entrance of a great apartment, the distant windows of which looked out upon the Bosphorus. Its furniture was wholly European, consisting of settees, chairs, mirrors, and side-tables, and carpeted with fine white Egyptian straw matting. A few persons stood here and there, scattered as if by chance through the room, but all having their faces turned toward its centre. At the bottom of the room, opposite the door through which we entered, near the windows, the young Sultan was seen seated on a settee, his person partly covered with a light cloth cloak, closed at the throat with a diamond clasp. He held himself erect, was apparently near five and a half or five and three fourths feet in height when standing; his face rather long and pale, embellished with a short black beard and mustaches; his eyes small and black, and his nose aquiline. His countenance, lit up as it was with a smile of dignified benevolence, seemed to me highly intelligent, bearing a strong resemblance to his late father. His form is delicate, and his movement graceful and dignified.

As we approached his Majesty we all made a profound reverence, repeating it as we came nearer to his person. The pachas, who attended the Minister to do him honor, all at once stooped low, and bending forward, put each their right hand near the floor, then raised it to their mouths and their heads, signifying by the act that they gathered the dust of his feet, kissed it, and strewed it on their heads in humility and respect. This they did three times. Seeing that the Minister was aged and fatigued, the young Sultan beckoned to him to be seated. This act of consideration on his part, worthy of the good feelings that inspired it, was perhaps never shown to any other Minister at his court. It was not taken advantage of, though properly acknowledged and esteemed; and taking from the Dragoman of the legation 'the letter of the President, Commodore Porter presented it to his Majesty, who received and laid it on the settee by his side. The Commodore at the same moment commenced a short complimentary speech, such as is usual on similar occasions, which the Dragoman translated, and was repeated by Rechid Pacha to the Sultan. His Majesty answered him in a very neat address, nobly and gracefully receiving him as Resident Minister of the United States, etc., etc., and expressive of the desire which he entertained of cherishing the good feeling and friendship which then existed between his Sublime Porte and the government of the United States.

So soon as this was translated to the Minister, Rechid Pacha turned as if to depart, and making a low obeisance to his Majesty, we all backed out of the imperial presence, accompanied by the same individuals who had borne us company into it. All the Pachas took leave of the Minister at the front of the great stair-case, to return to the Sultan, with the exception of Reza Pacha and the Dragoman of the Porte; they and the pages attending him through the garden to his barge. There they bade him adieu, the guard presented arms, and as we departed down the Bosphorus for Pera, the band played a lively air in compliment.

Having got through the most important part of the instalment, I will now *carry* you (as we say in Virginia) to the Sublime Porte, where a few days after the audience of the Sultan, the Minister paid a visit to the Grand Vizier and the Ottoman Minister of Foreign Affairs.

The 'Sublime Porte,' properly speaking, was a large building near the walls of the Seraglio, but in 1838 it accidentally took fire and burned down. Since then the offices of the Grand Vizier and the other Turkish ministers have been held in the *Konak,* or winter residence of a late Vizier, now deceased, situated near the Hippodrome, and the great mosque of Sultan Achmet. It is a large frame building surrounded by a high stone wall. Its entrance is guarded by a sentry at either side, attended by a corporal in the new uniform, who presents arms to the ministers or other high functionaries when they pass. The façade is rectilineal, with a wing projecting at each extremity in straight lines, leaving the intermediate space for carriages and horses. Projecting from the middle of the basement is a demi-circular platform with a roof supported by wooden columns, and joined to the main building. On this the officers of the Porte dismount from their carriages and horses. The building is three stories high, the first being a ground floor occupied only as stables for horses and their grooms, many of whom remain here from morning till night, waiting their masters. The second story is upheld by a row of wooden columns in front, and is reached by a flight of stairs some twenty steps in height, at the foot of which stands a sentry, and a man to receive over-shoes and boots, with which no one is allowed to ascend. All the officers of the Porte have at least one servant in attendance on them, who takes charge of his master's over-shoes, cloak, and pipe. From this story, every part of the Porte is covered with straw matting, and the rooms or apartments of the Ministers are carpeted with fine Brussels carpets, which now are preferred by the Turks to their own thick carpets of Asia Minor.

On this floor the Minister of Justice holds his office, and the great hall or vestibule in front of it is generally thronged with people of both sexes waiting to have their complaints examined. There, and indeed throughout the whole of this vast building, prevails the greatest order, silence, and circumspection; every one speaks in an under-tone of voice, and quarrels and altercations are never heard. The Dragoman of the Porte, who may be called an under secretary of state, holds his office also on this floor, having near it a bureau for translations under his superintendence. The dragomans of the foreign legations have two apartments here, from which they visit the officers of the Porte. Above this, on the third story, are the offices of the Grand Vizier, the Minister of foreign affairs, the Minister of the interior, the great Auditor of accounts, the Counsellors of State, the heads of Bureaux, and finally the bureaux themselves, consisting of long apartments where the clerks in files, perhaps more than a hundred in number, with a director at their head, are all seated on the floor. I noticed on a subsequent visit to the Porte, that over the door of each room, or suspended on the wall, was a verse in Turkish, framed. These, I was told, were moral aphorisms, placed there by order of the Sultan to remind his officers not to neglect or put off their respective duties. That over the door of the Grand Vizier was translated for me, and is as follows:

' Defer not the poor man's case until to-morrow,
For thou knowest not what you (thee and he) may be then.'

In a government like that of Turkey, where there have been many instances of Viziers being hurled in the space of a day from their charge of absolute power, and a person comparatively insignificant elevated to it in their stead, this seems to be an appropriate and significant warning.

On the Saturday of the same week in which we visited the Sultan, the legation landed from its barge at a quay of Constantinople, called *Baktchecapouson*, where the Minister found the carriage of the Minister of Foreign Affairs and several of his horses, waiting to convey him and his suite to the Sublime Porte. The Minister and Dragoman entered the carriage, whilst the rest of the cortége, among them myself of course, mounted the animals, some of which no doubt were pure Arabian, though indeed I never backed a less spirited horse in my life than the one I bestrode. The carriage was English, drawn by two German horses of good mettle, and like my own, those of my companions were all dull and too fat for much active service. Winding up through steep, narrow, and often very dirty streets, we suddenly perceived the carriage enter a lofty gate, beside which stood a guard of soldiers, drawn up and presenting arms. We all dismounted on the platform, and before ascending the first stair-case, pulled each a pair of thin Turkish leather slippers over our boots, to prevent them from soiling the mats and carpets of our hosts. Imagine my feelings when after a violent exertion, which (in my eagerness not to delay the Minister, who kindly waited a minute for me) made the perspiration start out on my forehead, I discovered that mine were too small to conceal properly my soiled boots! Finding my efforts to pull them on of no avail, my anxiety settled down in calm desperation, and was only relieved by the voice of a considerate old Mussulman, who, shuffling into his own slippers with perfect ease, told me not to trouble myself farther, but wear mine just as they were — half on, half off. No sooner said than done; and mounting the steps, passing through a crowd of Cavasses, soldiers, and people in ordinary, drawn up on either side of the way, we reached the door of the foreign Minister's apartment, where he received the Minister with the polished politeness of a Frenchman. He was quite alone, except attended by a few domestics, who, so soon as we were all seated, served each with a cup of coffee and a pipe.

We remained with him for some twenty minutes, he occasionally addressing each one of us in French, which language he spoke fluently. Afterward, he informed the Minister that he would accompany him to the Grand Vizier, who waited to receive him. Leading the way, we all followed him to the opposite wing of the building, where the Sultan's lieutenant of absolute power held his court. As we passed, I noticed several officers of rank, waiting to see him; a soldier stood sentry at his door; and as the Perdadar raised the curtain which hung before the entrance, we were ushered into the presence of the great man.

The Vizier was seated on a broad sofa which extended along the angle of the room opposite the door, and did not rise as we entered, but bade the Minister and his suite welcome, with a smile and wave of the hand, motioning to the former to be seated at his left hand. His name is Raouf Pacha, and I learned that he then filled the chair of lieutenant for the third time. He was of short stature, with dark features and beard, the latter intermixed with some white hairs; his face was somewhat wrinkled with care, his eyes small and sparkling, and altogether he had the appearance of a mild and benevolent old gentleman, not much disposed to cut off people's heads, nor have their feet bastinadoed into jelly, which I was told he had full power to do whenever he chose. In the course of conversation, he said he had often heard of the Minister, but until then had never had the pleasure of seeing him, etc.; that he desired much to become acquainted with him and his country — calling the latter the 'New World.' The usual refreshments of coffee, pipes, and sherbet were handed round, and we made a longer visit here than any where else; the good old Vizier treating us all in the most cordial and friendly manner; and he seemed by his conversation well informed, particularly on the subject of *Mania-Americana* — rail-roads and canals.

After an half hour's stay the Minister took his leave, and was accompanied to the head of the stairs by the Minister of Foreign Affairs. There they separated, and returning to the water's edge, the Minister in his carriage and we on the same horses which brought us, we entered the barge of the legation and returned to Pera.   D.

LIFE'S SEASONS.

THE YOUTH WOULD KNOW OF THE OLD MAN LIFE'S HAPPIEST TIME.

Thou who art bending here, thoughtful and sage,
Tell, since thou know'st it, Life's happiest age:
Is it of Childhood the various dream,
While the boat scarcely rocks on the perilous stream;
While the milk of the mother runs cool through the blood,
And the passions are folded like leaves in the bud?
Thou art shaking thy white locks; then is there a time
More golden and fragrant than that lovely prime?

'T is the day then when Nature first startles the boy
With whispers mysterious of terror or joy;
When she calls from the hill-side or breathes through the wood,
Or murmurs her wooings from fountain and flood;
Till the youth in his transport scarce calls it a dream,
That fond worship in Hellas of laurel and stream.
Thou art looking denial: old man, thou hast not
The birth of young love in thy bosom forgot?

Thou wouldst tell me that life has no happier hour
Than the one when we light on that paradise-flower
Wherewith we create the lost Eden anew,
And a world without sin, shame, or sorrow renew;
A world which we furnish from pictures within,
Which shall last like that lost one, till tainted by sin:
There 's a tear in thine eye — there 's a cloud on thy brow;
Nay, speak not, old man — thou hast answered me now!

LINES

WRITTEN DURING THE SEVERE ILLNESS OF A FRIEND.

I.

Now in the twilight, when the hush of night
  Is falling gently on the misty earth,
And the far day-beam's slowly sinking light
  Fadeth away before the dim star's birth;
When deep'ning shadows gather close around,
  And not a human eye is near to see —
Father in heaven! I bow me to the ground,
  And humbly lift my soul in prayer to Thee!

II.

Thou, who can'st give the wounded spirit rest,
  Send down thy peace upon my wearied heart:
Aid me to still the tumult of my breast,
  And calmly bear with my allotted part;
O, bear me, Father! hear thine erring child!
  Gird me with strength to meet this chast'ning blow;
Let not my heart, so passionate and wild,
  Sink down beneath its heavy weight of wo.

III.

I know that I have given to *human* love
  The early freshness of my young heart's flow,
And turned away from sparkling founts above,
  To fill my cup with bitterness below;
Yet now in dust is laid my sinful pride;
  My Father! crush me not beneath thy hand:
O let me in some *other* way be tried,
  And do not thou this sacrifice demand!

IV.

Let me be spared *this* anguish; let my heart
  With holier love still to its idol cling;
I could not see his gasping breath depart,
  I could not watch his wrestling soul take wing;
Oh! spare, in mercy spare him! — do not say
  He must go down in all his life's young bloom,
To that dark place of never-coming day,
  That voiceless prison-house, the silent tomb!

V.

But if thy holy wisdom hath decreed
  My dearest hopes when grasped should from me glide,
Let not thy strong sustaining arm recede;
  Uphold me, or I sink beneath the tide!
Lead me to thank thee that from dreams I woke,
  Which led my straying soul so far from Thee;
Lead me to meekly bow before thy stroke,
  And humbly bless thee for my misery!

FRANK UPTON.

'SI MOLLUM POST LIMINIUM.'

'WHO IS DEAD?' I think it was the younger Godwin who had the credit of ringing many mournful and soul-stirring changes on this inquiry, many years ago in Blackwood. Who is dead? It is a full theme; so full, I must not fear trenching on the designs of so powerful a limner as has spoken it and dwelt upon it before. How many stories stranger than romance lie in it! How it stirs the current of our own years, and sets up tide-marks along the desolate waste of domestic memoirs! What a knell in those three Saxon words — *who is dead?* Who is dead? — a father; who is dead? — a husband; who is dead? — a son. What a touching picture of their bereavements, in those short questions and answers of the duchess, the queen of the murdered Edward, and the children of poor Clarence:

ELIZABETH.	What stay had I but Edward's, and he 's gone.
CHILDREN.	What stay had we but Clarence, and he 's gone.
DUCHESS.	What stays had I but they, and they are gone.

But the question has force in busy life, apart from domestic ties. Who is dead? Your debtor, and you are ruined; your creditor, and you have lost his indulgence; destitution stares you in the face; your employer, and you are adrift again on the world; your friend, that had supplied the place of father, mother, wife — and you are alone; your school-boy companion, that wrestled with you on the green-sward, and recollections flow swift again far from the distant years. Who is dead? — a class-mate, and you stay to think how fast the months fly; you lose yourself in dim, pleasure-bearing remembrances, while he, the dead one, grows smaller in the eye of memory, a beam, a very mote, that fades with the hour for ever!

Not so of thee, poor UPTON! — not so of thee. Thou wilt fill a large space in back-going thoughts, till 'Who is dead?' shall be answered by many a grave-stone name, singled from our lessening company.

Never stirred healthier blood than leaped in the ninety stout hearts that went out from college-cloisters, ten or more years agone. How unthinkingly we planned our future meetings! I can hardly realize that we were all alike in condition, when we agreed a twelvemonth before our leave to meet together every tenth year so long as we should remain unmarried. The company is smaller than it was. There was Strong, a stout bachelor. I should say it was he that proposed the resolve; and now there are at the very least, as I hear, some five or six little Strongs — girls and boys. There was Tom Boswell, who I thought a man of strong judgment; he writes me that his wife 'is as lovely as a June day, and their child, not a month old, as bright as a spot of June-day sun-shine on the grass.'

But to return. We supped together last autumn, a shattered remnant. Not a moiety sat down that festal night at our table; but the old buoyancy came up, the old blood stirred, and we catalogued the dead ones with scarce a sigh, for they were deaths of old date, till some one down the table asked: 'What has become of Upton?'

'Dead!' said Kennedy, in a low tone.

'WHO IS DEAD?' exclaimed half-a-dozen voices at the upper end of the table.

'Upton,' returned Kennedy.

'What! Frank Upton, that married Caroline Murray?'

'The same,' said Kennedy.

'Frank Upton dead!'

There was a pause for more than a minute. 'Rat-tat-tat' went Rodney's knife, who (Rodney I mean) was placed by common consent at the head of the board, and rising, he gave in his calm, solemn tone: 'The memory of Francis Upton, erewhile a member of our brotherhood!'

There was an audible sigh as one and all rose and drank to the bottom. Frank Upton had been loved — the term is not too strong — he had been *loved* by us, and he was dead. I take occasion of the pause and the stifled whisperings that followed this unexpected announcement, to bring down the history of the subject of my sketch to the time of his leaving college.

Frank Upton entered in advance, joining us about the middle of sophomore year, being somewhere near the age of nineteen, I should judge, from my recollection of his form and countenance. His father, who held a considerable place in the army of '75, drew a small pension up to his death — the year Frank joined us. His mother died after he had been with us a couple of years, under circumstances I may hereafter notice. His entrée to our companionship was characterized by a singular modesty, which was the more remarkable from the self-sufficiency which at that period of our course there was scarce a man of us but possessed to a marvellous degree. By some accident he retained a room in the attic of Old South College for a couple of years. He had no chum, and his habits of estrangement kept him very constantly within his own study. He was certainly the most sensitive man I ever knew. He seemed to dread a contact with the world, lest his innocence should contract a stain. Though easily persuaded to ordinary courses of action, he yet shrunk from the sensual indulgences that were the life of many of us in those days of juvenile folly; and it was the sensitiveness of his nature, rather than the strength of his principles, that saved his pliant disposition from ruin. I leave to the moralist the question of his merit. Still he was meritorious in his generosity — above all, in charity; but this from natural bestowments. His parents had I fancy much of the world's morality without its essence. Hence his principles were instincts; yet his instincts were delicately wrought and intimately conjoined with his whole being. They could be directed but not torn from him; he could be duped to second baseness, but the tempter had to play upon his goodness. Had he been ungenerous he would have become the dupe of many; but as he was generous, all loved him. Yet beyond or back of this exquisite sensitiveness there was strung a stronger chord; there was a noble sense of honor, a high regard for personal dignity, that claimed and gained our esteem. A wrong of a superior in college life — how inimitably he treated it! His was not a thought of brute opposition; there came not nigh him so gross a sentiment; but the look of mingled pity and scorn and indignation convinced me that the elastic and ever-living mind had been touched, rudely touched, but had given in return its native tone, undisturbed by a single corporeal affection. I occupied a room for a long time immediately beneath him; and I can easily fancy, at this distance of time, that I hear the patter of his step upon the stairs, or see him seated in the broken-backed chair — the only one I had for strangers; his eye the very soul of benevolence, and his smile ready for my saddest jokes. For a long time he held himself aloof from society, but family friends (sad, sad acquaintances for a man at college!) at length drew him into the vortex, and he was swept away! I don't know that he manifested a particular fondness for society, or the contrary.

The Murrays, who boarded in Temple-street, were notorious flirts. They were strangers in the place, but brought pretensions of great respectability. Col. Murray had been shot — some said by the Indians, some said in a duel; howbeit, he was shot, and his widow was left his reputation, a small income, and two unmarried daughters. These latter she established in our town. The elder, say a girl of twenty odd years, was inveterate in her flirtations, and during our stay contracted with a bachelor lieutenant, of a couple of scores, who was slightly bald and stuttered somewhat, but *per contra* owned a snug little property in the country and danced well; so that upon the whole Mrs. Murray was satisfied with the match; and Isabel, that was the bride's name, decamped, though not until she had become, as I said at the first, notorious; (a very bad word to be applied to a marriageable woman.) The younger, perhaps eighteen, was a brunette — the true color for a coquette; but had a remarkably little foot, a sparkling eye, and a most voluble tongue. She seemed artless. I cannot speak positively of this matter even at this time; the mother was ever the prime mover in the negotiations of both.

These Murrays, I have said, or should say, lived in handsome style at one of the *ton* boarding-houses; saw visiters in the best parlor, and received 'especials' in their sitting-room up stairs. Among those who found their way to this theatre of feminine tact, Upton, poor fellow! by some chance fell. Caroline, if I have not already intimated as much, was pretty — very pretty. She wore her hair in the Madonna style (how else should she?) parted on the brow; but not content with this fashioning above, it fell from beneath a gold circlet into long wavy tresses. Boxall has painted a picture of Lolah of the Harem, that if you allow for a little more fulness of form and face, is very like her as she was twelve years ago. Frank saw her first at disadvantage, considering his sensitive temperament. She had been weeping over the leave of Isabel after long years of sisterhood.

Upton was reputed rich, and the game was high. Both dame and daughter were stimulated to unwonted effort; yet it was many weeks before the iron had entered his soul. Mean-time his cheerfulness seemed upon the wane, and the excess of his one love swallowed up as it were the thousand little out-going streamlets of generosity, which had so characterized my neighbor of the attic. It is ever thus with sensitive minds. The heart's affection they so far refine as to deem it gross in its multiplication; and they feed its fondness on a central object, which imbibes the whole strength of the soul's love. It is only the gay and hilarious that can laugh and be glad when they have found their heart's worship. But I am astray again. Upton drew within himself more and more — too much for the healthy action of any part of him. He could not disavow his affections for us; he could not forestall the charities that went out from among us. He was more alone; we loved him none the less for that; rumor said that his mother lay dying, and sympathy besieged our affection for him. Not a suspicion lay in the right quarter for a long time. A twelvemonth did not reveal the secret fully. True there began to be sly tales of an engagement between our friend and the belle of the hour. But none passed the joke upon him. He was not the man to joke with in a matter of the heart's concernment: as soon joke a father upon the frailties of the mother of his child.

Matters were in this state, when on coming toward the close of the second senior term, I took a stroll with Upton before the night-service. He was unusually sad. He had heard of his mother's threatening illness; he was not the one to let her die without an inward struggle. He spoke fearfully of his hopes, all withered from boyhood; of his family cut down like the grass — yea, the flowers withered! If I remember rightly, my poor inexperience tried to dictate encouragement to him; but though he had been my neighbor, his was such a soul as joyed in such sorrows, and philosophy was freezing as an iceberg. How heartily I condemn my folly, as I call to mind the pleasantry I sought to intermix with consolation, and spoke of more endearing connections than he had hitherto known to kill griefs! I will not recall the interruption I met with there: it silenced me. I know the full force of it now. We sat together that evening in the chapel. The service is now as fresh in my mind as if the chapter, the hymn, and the prayer were uttered yester-night. That impassioned complaint of Job was read which closes in this wise: ' *I was not in safety, neither had I rest, neither was I quiet; yet trouble came.*' Frank was thoughtful; sad almost to tears, during the exercises. We rose to go; but the tide was checked. The President rose in the desk. Upton's form quivered; so did mine, though I could not tell why. I fancied his emotion was equally involuntary: the sequel showed. ' I am compelled to announce,' commenced the President, in his tremulous, venerable tones, ' that Francis Upton, having contracted marriage, is no longer a member of this institution! '

A titter went round the lower classes, and some among us could hardly restrain a smile at what they innocently thought a good joke. The truth rushed upon me in an instant; for to him beside me it was a thunder-bolt. As the declaration was read, his features were as if

chiselled. They changed not even at the close, and amid the tormenting murmur of suppressed laughter, I rose to escape the stifling
atmosphere. Was it pride that made me sidle away from the object of
attention as the throng hurried out? Then I renounce it for ever!
And he went out alone; and he needed not a friend, though a hundred
hearts were leaping to pour their balm into his injured soul; not one
but knew their utter inefficacy to restore genial life. There was not
one on-looker but knew his own sensibilities, however touched, would
miserably contrast with the fineness of those whose sufferings alone
gave them a voice. Not at this day, reckoning all I have seen of
mental agony in the busy eddies of life's fluctuations, can I compare
any or all with Frank Upton's feelings that night. Yet a stranger
could not have pointed me out the man in that whispering throng. So
proud his indignation, so intense his sense of dignity sacrificed. That
he, so retiring, so charitable, so beyond his years in his views of personal dignity, and withal having a heart bleeding sorely at domestic
sorrows; that he should be aggrieved by a stroke his soul so loathed,
was it not a quick comment on the text: '*I was not in safety, neither
had I rest, neither was I quiet; yet trouble came?*'

I was Upton's executor: he left town the next day. He left his wife
behind him, but not without a promise to find her a home. Caroline
Murray flirted no longer, for a time; public sentiment, that sustains
half the vices of the age, would sustain her no longer. Sadness was
the result, and the most charitable construed it into sympathy for
poor Frank. His story even now is not told up to the narrative of our supper. Evils come not single-handed. Shakspere has
worded the sentiment rather better, but I may miss his words though I
stop to recall them. A letter of the morning after the evening jour-
nalled above, came to Frank, black-sealed. Yet his mother's death,
long expected, was a short grief to the intelligence that she had died
insolvent. He who was born for money; who was born to humor the
delicacy of a refined taste; to exercise benevolence, and to relieve the
yearnings of a heart keenly alive to pity; was become a pauper! The
family that nourished him was utterly gone; he had lost the last relative that loved him tenderly; he had lost the companionship of us, his
loving friends, for a couple of years; he had lost his triumphant independence of other's wealth; he had gained — a wife! Let not the
married impute to me the claim of logical sequence of these events as
they are written down, or the converse; he had gained a wife, and had
lost all else. We (meaning our brotherhood) are neither wedded to
wives nor dogmatism.

I shift the narrative here to the eager inquiries that followed after
the lapse of a few months, Kennedy's unlooked-for announcement at
our table.

' Where did he die?'
' When?'
' Poor Upton!'
' And his wife?'
' Poor Isabel!'
' And she, the —— '

' An East-Indiaman ? '

' Before the mast ! '

Why these inquiries followed in such a connection, and how Kennedy revealed the story, I must tell in my own words. True, more than true, that I cannot improve upon the glowing narrative that Kennedy gave us, eager listeners that night, even with my laboring pen; but memory is so weak that should I attempt to give the occasional outbreaks of passion, the strong exclamations that interluded his *telling*, I should spoil the perspective of poor Upton's history, without atoning for it by the spirit of the fore-ground. First however I will try out of my own benevolence to make clear some points, which I doubt not are hanging most perplexingly on the reader's mind.

How came Upton to marry as he did ? All I can say is, they, the mother and daughter, with an eagerness I cannot realize, and therefore cannot describe, would secure their prize. They discovered his weak points, and assailed them vigorously, and by weapons to which he ever yielded : they did not subdue him, but led him into self-subjugation. Such is human foresight ! The world-wise mother, like many another one, was pushed on by a zeal that ' o'er-leaped itself.' Had she triumphed in patience, and found his wealth a bubble, the mother and child would — not have broken his heart ; I will not believe it — but steeled his affections, seared as with a hot iron susceptibilities too strong, and left him a living man, active beside us now !

But how came he, the gentle, the fastidious, the refined, to love the hoyden Caroline Murray ? It is beyond my art to answer. There are, it is said, deeper matters in these social connections than philosophy has dreamed of. Frank Upton's case has almost made me a convert to the faith. One while, as I reflected on it, I thought I saw clearly the developement of the attachment ; I thought I traced it logically from his idiosyncracies of character ; but alas for my logic ! there was a link, a chain wanting, when I brought plainly the sensitiveness of my friend to bear upon the popular belle, ' the prostitute to common fame.' Reader, I cannot tell how my quondam neighbor ever found it in his heart to love that piece of flesh, Caroline Murray.

But how bore they the news of Frank's destitution ? As every heartless woman and daughter of the world would bear it. You have seen a young bird caged in spring-time, struggling with the pent air, and beating the wires till beak and wings and tiny feet ached ; and you have seen the bird-mother sorrowing in the confinement of that she loved, and her earnest desires (brute sorrows, loves, and desires) to free her offspring ; then discarding if you can all the ideas of innocence which plumed vesture may bring up, you have before you in these beaked strugglers Mrs. Murray and her daughter Caroline, when the astounding intelligence first came upon them that Upton was penniless.

———

MEAN-TIME Frank buried his dead mother — she lies yet without a tomb-stone — and set off for the glorious west ; the retriever of wealth, the ruiner of health, the theatre for mediocre talent, the asylum of all.

Is any modest young man laboring under the delusion that mere mental abilities will prove the shibboleth of greatness in the American
states? Let him take lesson from the fate of my friend, and be wise in
season. *Confidence, boldness, activity* — in these three words have I
catalogued the whole system of means for attaining power in our western world. The patriot may mourn over it, the scholar may deride,
the political economist may question — it is so. Alas for the extravagant closet-hopes that went with that high-beating American heart of
Frank Upton, to achieve a name! They withered in a season. For
why? He·saw the meagre in mind, the stinted in ability, rising like
mushrooms into favor, and he *disdained* competition. (Young man,
be careful; be careful of that leviathan — pride!) He *was not rich
enough to disdain it.* What should he do? Discard his refinements;
' duck with French nods;' mingle with the worthless; trumpet his
name before him — and yet what hope but the brayings of those beside
him, as they scented the thistles in the wind, would be louder than his?
What should he do? Here was one of those pages opened in the book
of destiny that are so inscrutable. He who had been born into the
world to erect himself on circumstances, found circumstances crushed
and crumbling beneath his weight. More strange than this, Justice,
that his mind had fancied immutable, was a subordinate in the great
court of the world's appeal — a creature of hire — of prostitution!
When such discoveries of what the world in fact is, crowd on a man,
do they not make him, if any thing does, plead inwardly, though by no
outward token, for the presence and aid of the eternal God, who piled
up the mountains and lifted the clouds above them?

But what Frank Upton *did* do, will be a more acceptable problem to
my story-readers than what he should do. He did then strive to make
men treat him fair; he did yearn in the loftiness of his pride to win
opinions golden, or at least gilded; he did shake off, much as in him
lay to do, the modesty which had hung like a mantle over him; he did
measure his sensitive mind with those who derided his refinements;
he did array his power of learning with the noise of the tavern
declaimer. All this — was it for the love of his unborn child, for his
self-pride, for his avarice, or all the heart's affections cynosured yet
where they had begun to be? Let us look. Will it lessen the respect
I ought to maintain for my hero, when I tell my reader, on the authority
of Kennedy, who received it from Upton himself, that he (Frank) was
all this while laboring under the deep, the maddening delusion, that Caroline Murray, his wedded wife, loved him? That she ought to have
loved him, his worth and her frailties should have taught her; but
there is a species of woman — far be it from me to say how large a
space they occupy in the order *femina* — who are not capable of love;
love of a worthy object. The deep fountains of the heart that poets
have sung prettily of, seems in them (I hazard the beauty of the sentiment
for its truth's sake) to be a cracked cistern, filling not from self-derived
copiousness, but the over-abundance of others, which evaporates fast
in the elements by which they live. But, as I was saying, Frank was
laboring under a deep delusion; so deep, that when a letter addressed

to a friend of his was shown him, which ran in this wise, he did not cease to 'take up arms against a sea of troubles:'

'Poor Upton — do n't for Heaven's sake let him know his error! — is lost by his love for a heartless woman. You will recollect that there was an opinion against her for a time, but hydra-hearted society has received her again to its lascivious embrace. Last evening she waltzed for the third time with Capt. E——. You know his character! Poor Frank! my heart bleeds for him.'

But this — did this weaken his resolve? No. 'I will be rich; she shall have the wealth whose loss has so shattered her anticipations; and I shall be proud of my new independence, and shall love my pride, and she shall love me!' It is so; it is so. There are times when reason restrains not, and woman makes man an idiot, 'talking sound and fury,' when most he should be wise.

Years rolled away before Upton's energies, put to task by pride, had found such a home as he blushed not to offer to those he had left. Caroline came; her mother came. Various reasons induced their compliance. Younger belles (alas, that little girls should ever put off their modest innocence, for the mockery of fashion's life!) were coming on the stage to mar Caroline's success. Her child was a burden amid the varied calls of dissipation. But enough — they came; and were disappointed. For what alternative? Upton to build himself a maintenance had renounced his tastes, and numbered among his acquaintance the illiterate and vulgar; what alternative, I ask? Must not he who would successfully serve Mammon, be one with Mammon's servants? Must he not, to slake their fiery jealousies, renounce the upliftings of a cultivated mind? Caroline was disappointed; a disappointment that melted not in tears. She could not forego the refinements that had dallied with her young years; she could not, she said she could not, give up her child to the associations of the vulgar.

How turned it then with Frank? Do you ask — his wife and child and education upon the one side, with the wordy mouthings of the money-seeking multitude upon the other? Mark the result of his determination. The reputation in whose pursuit fondest desires had been blasted, and whose possession had fed daintily his ambition, vanished like a day-dream. Riches took wings. Once, twice he plunged in the gulf of speculation, and came up unscathed from its desolating waters. A third time he entered with success; his anxiety called him to the scene of so many triumphs away from his home. A twelve-month he tarried, and with the titles to unbounded wealth turned heart-ward; that he might make a joy of bitterness in the breast of her whose soul was pride and whose affection was interest.

It was the middle of an August afternoon that he came in sight of the village where his heart lay. Never had it looked so lovely. The green grass springing anew from the destroying sythe, glittered in the sun-light; the clouds were all resting, white and fleecy, and grand in their tranquillity. The twin spires that rose and lay like threads of light on the blue hills beyond, were as if they had ever pointed to the same sky and could never change. But was it so? and was the heart of the town mirrored in the world? No. *There* were men full of words and anxiety; hundreds came daily to throng the pent ways. Brick houses and churches without spires rose with their assumed ornateness; coaches rattled along the half-paved streets; and boats dragged over the great sluice-way of the north, flanked London-styled squares with metropolitan ware-rooms. Marriage ceremonies were heard in the churches nightly, and black hearses picked their way among drays and wagons, with not so much as a startled looker-on to pause and ask, 'Who is dead?' But just before you entered the town, though it has now submerged it, there stood and yet stands a cottage — apart from business then! Upton built it for his wife.

On the afternoon of which I am speaking, a travelling carriage was at the door. It was not Frank's, and he observed it with some surprise, not unmingled with apprehension, as he passed in. He met a servant at the door; and did he not misunderstand him, or was in truth his Caroline to leave with a gentleman that afternoon for the East? He threw open the parlor door; there was his guilty wife, bustling for departure; there was his child too, that had frolicked in his dreams, who ran to him now, with words thrilling as a man's tones:

'Father, you will not leave me!' and she laid her little white hand in his, and kissed it softly, tears flowing on it.

'My child — my child!'

The full heart of the father, how did it yearn in that brief utterance! Pride, indignation, love, scorn, were agonizing in his bosom; not a word of explanation with his silent wife; or she, the mother, the cause of his woes. He knew he had that within his hand which would seduce both to allegiance, and yet pride mastered his soul, and he said not a word. They passed out, and the door closed *for ever* on the heartless mother of the child! Was it a desolate night that — after an absence of a year and a day — in his own home, for Frank Upton and his gentle Isabel? Are you a father, a husband, a child? Oh say, was it a desolate night for the lone parent and the lonely child? 'Ah!' said Upton, as he gave the story to Kennedy, a short week after, 'there was a deeper lesson in the wakeful silence of that night than in the whole concourse of years that had rolled it up! The world — its emptiness; time — its fleetness; eternity — its strength; I felt; and religion, which had been but a passion, became almost a living principle. Again and again had an ecstacy of joy lifted my heart in indescribable beatitude to the Creator of its bliss; thoughts the while crowding up too deep for utterance, and tears struggling as a sweet relief to the soul that could not tell the half its feelings; sorrow too had robed its seductive sensibilities in the same bright garment of heavenly up-looking; but till that night the Tempter dashed them all to the ground. 'For what mind,' whispered he to me, (a Satanic whisper,) 'can think of God, the great, the good, the immortal, the parent of earth, and its myriad forms of being; of God spreading the green tree, the limner of the floral leaflet, and feel a part of his spirit throbbing within, and beating restlessly up and up, and ever up to the skies, without the heart running over in tenderness — native, untaught, unspiritual, undevotional tenderness?'

But did I not say Shakspere had put in the mouths of some of his creations (the Duchess of Gloster for instance) the sentiment: ' Grief boundeth when it falls ? ' and again by the lips of the Dane-king:

> ' When sorrows come, they come not single spies,
> But in battalions.'

Upton rose next morning, after the events cited, to find his fortune a wreck. Not his domestic fortune; that had foundered the night before. The bubble of speculation had burst, and men every where wanted bread! He came to the metropolis; 't was there he told his story to Kennedy; 't was there he assured him that his child Isabel should have wealth; should riot in indulgence; the monomania clave to him. She shall have wealth; the want of it, the beastly craving for it, shall never debase *her* soul!' He placed that motherless child in the hands of his only relative; he obtained a divorce; he engaged service before the mast of an Indiaman, to make riches over the water; and ' a month out of port,' said Kennedy, in a nervous, quick tone, that spoke his grief, ' they threw his body to the sharks!'

Before we broke up that evening, a subscription went round the table for Isabel Upton, and the amount was generous.

' But what has become of the wife, the widow ? ' said the voice down the table, that had introduced the inquiries.

' Married,' said Kennedy; ' she married a widower of threescore, reputed exceedingly wealthy. They live yet in L——.'

Whereupon was proposed by the voice down the table, that resolutions expressing the deep regrets of our brotherhood, at the death of Francis Upton, Esquire, and our unfeigned testimonials to his public and private worth, be transmitted to Mrs. M'Farlane of Louisiana.

' M'Farlane!' said half-a-dozen voices.

The voice at the bottom of the table, whose was it ? It belonged to the only son of the rich widower! And he might have told us, but he did not, that he found pride festering in his old father's heart, stirred by cankerous desires, and left him and his young wife alone. What an ebb and flow belong to the life-tide of Americans!

My story is told and — true. Upton, who was made to love and to be loved deeply, reverently; to make home happy and his country blessed; lies, if indeed the case that held his noble heart be not torn piece-meal, a hundred fathoms under the green waters. And she, Caroline, his thoughtless murderer, yet gloats upon the dissolute pleasures of fashion's world; and pays the worldly price of her unmasked presumption, in enduring the irritable sallies of a weak, vain old man; and she, the gay, the beautiful, the fair-haired Isabel, who should have nestled in a mother's caress, and chased the wrinkles from a father's brow, has become the orphan *protegé* of our little company of ' childless men.'

Shall I add the moral ? You who hope in joy, stop here. You whose young life is bright, with whom the honey-moon is lingering, though Cynthia has clove the sky, and rolled up the tides once and again, stop — nay, read not a line farther. But I must unburden my own conscience : *Is matrimony always a blessing ?*

TAWNEY TOM AND TABBY GRAY.

AN ACTUAL OCCURRENCE.

THERE dwelt two cats in our town,
  In a garret loft so gay;
The name of the one was TAWNEY TOM,
  Of the other, TABBY GRAY.

For years had they together lived
  In mutual love, and spent
Their peaceful span of days in calm
  Connubial content.

But lo! one day the family
  A mournful change espies,
And in full many a bosom fair
  Did anxious thoughts arise.

The kitchen-maid began to note,
  That Tabby ne'er was seen,
And Tom's — like angels' — visits were
  But few and far between.

The mice soon smelt a rat, and round
  The pantry 'gan to play:
What *was* become of Tawney Tom,
  And what of Tabby Gray?

Ah! Death spares none, from kings to cats:
  And 't was one Saturday
That he laid his bony hand upon
  The back of Tabby Gray!

Now see the strength of Tommy's love!
  E'en cold Death could not sever
The heart-strings which for years had bound
  This loving pair together.

By day and night, with sleepless eye,
  He watched by Tabby's side;
And if Tom-cats have tears to shed,
  I could swear that Tommy cried.

Now though true love has power to blunt
  The nose of a true lover,
Yet other noses could not fail
  The secret to discover.

With cruel hands from Tommy's side
    They snatched his Tabby Gray;
And some held wailing Tom at home,
    While she was ta'en away.

In vain, poor Tom! thy tender love!
    In vain thy piteous wail!
Far off into a stony field
    They 've swung her by the tail!

How could they treat her dear remains
    With such indignity?
'T was well for thee, poor Tawney Tom!
    Thou wast not there to see:

Far keener would have been thy pangs,
    Deeper thy woful bale,
To have seen them into that stony field
    Swing *thy* Tabby by her tail!

Nor meat nor milk Tom's whiskers passed,
    But still the live-long day
In his lone loft, disconsolate
    And motionless he lay.

The leaves had now began to fall,
    Upon the wooded hill,
And the Autumn nights, though long and clear,
    Were growing very chill.

Yet when the mellow moon-light rose
    Upon the grassy plain,
Poor Tawney Tom went out to bring
    His Tabby home again.

And ever and anon he cried,
    As cats are wont to cry;
A dull and distant echo — not
    His Tabby — made reply.

O'er hill and dale he wandered far,
    It was a weary way;
Until at length he found the field
    Where poor dead Tabby lay.

He put his paw upon her breast,
    And turned her body o'er;
And then he gave a long, long howl
    More piteous than before:

For in her soft and tender side,
    That he stroked so smooth at morn,
He saw a sharp and ugly stone,
    A cruel gash had torn!

He took her up, and carried her
  A rod across the heath;
Then stopped, for he was lean and weak,
  And panted hard for breath.

There, there he stood, beneath the moon,
  He with the dead, alone!
He laid him down upon her breast,
  And gave a piteous groan.

He carried her another rod,
  Then laid her down and groaned;
He carried her another rod,
  Then stopped again and groaned.

He labored thus the live-long night,
  And he had brought her far,
When brightening o'er the eastern hills
  Up rose the morning star.

The moon grew pale — the little stars
  Each closed his sleepy eye,
And soon long gleams of rosy light
  Adorned the eastern sky.

With hastening toil, poor Tawney Tom
  His Tabby gently bears;
With the loved load he stands at last
  Below the garret stairs:

Up the steep stairs he carried her,
  With weary steps and soft,
And when at last he gained the top,
  He laid her in the loft.

Beside his faithful mate then down
  He sat ' in dule and sorrow,'
And in cat-language thus did he
  Lament ' his winsome marrow : '

' Miow! miow! Ah, wo is me,
  That I 'm bereaved of her!
No more I 'll hear her moonlight voice,
  No more shall hear her pur.

' In love we lived together, like
  A sister and a brother;
And when one caught a rat or mouse,
  He shared it with the other.

' From the same bowl we lapped our milk;
  And every one might see,
When the cook gave her a bit of meat,
  She gave the half to me.

'But now I 'll lap my milk alone;
  Alone I 'll eat my mice;
And bid farewell, since you are gone,
  To sweet connubial joys.

'There 's none in the cold winter nights,
  Dear Puss! to keep me warm;
Even now, about the garret roof,
  I hear the howling storm!

'Thou 'rt in that happy clime where skies
  With storms are never rough;
Where mice are fatter far than here,
  And rats are never tough.

'While I must linger here in grief;
  Miow! miow! miow!
Till death shall bring my soul relief:
  Miow! miow! miow!'

The morning dawned.   But 't was not long
  After the sun did rise,
Ere all the noses in the house
  Declared hostilities.

Tom's requiem sounded from the loft,
  Quick to the loft they sped;
And there they found poor Tawney Tom,
  Sitting by Tabby dead.

They took her up, though Tommy howled;
  The howl reëchoed round!
They took her down, and buried her
  Four feet deep in the ground.

But Tom, poor Tom, poor starving Tom,
  Oh! tell what was his fate?
Did he lap his milk, and catch his mice,
  And take another mate?

Oh, no! Roaming by day and night,
  He searched the country round;
But not in barn, nor loft, nor yard,
  Nor field, was Tabby found.

For two long weeks, forlorn, he sought her,
  Nor sleep nor food he found;
But bootless were his wanderings — she
  Was deep down in the ground!

With wasted form, and broken heart,
  Poor Tommy homeward hied;
Crept to his solitary loft,
  There mew'd, laid down, and died!

Burlington, (Vt.,) March, 1842.   J. BRETH PIERSON.

DOMESTIC SERVITUDE.

BY A SUFFERER.

In England the great topic of conversation is the scarcity of bread-stuffs ; at least the current literature that reaches us from the other side compels us to this conclusion ; but with us, the one unvarying subject among housekeepers is the scarcity of good servants. Every calling is over-stocked with professors, and if you advertise for a book-keeper or for an agent of any kind, candidates will present themselves in hosts ; but if you want a cook or a chamber-maid you must go about looking for one, not like Diogenes with a lantern, but like an ambassador with a bribe. Good servants cannot be found ; neither love nor money will buy them. And in truth how can they be looked for in a country where good fat land can be purchased for ten York shillings an acre ? It is absurd to expect them, and indeed almost wicked to wish for them. If we would be well served we must learn to serve ourselves. But this is an idea for which fashionable society is hardly prepared ; so we must flounder on until the world grows wiser and better, and continue to find fault with silly women who will not consent to act as servants when they can set up for mistresses as well.

Miss Sedgwick has related an incident quite *outré* even for fiction, in one of her well-meaning little domestic stories, which startled me not a little when I read it. A cross-tempered termagant, who had consented to act in the capacity of cook in a gentleman's family, was one morning brought to her bearings, as a sailor would say, by her mistress sending her a bottle of congress-water when she complained of the mullygrubs. 'What a jewel of a cook !' thought I, 'to be mollified by an aperient, while I am making presents of silk dresses to the ladies in my kitchen with the delusory hope of being rewarded with a cup of clear coffee or a well-broiled steak ! 'Sure such a cook was *never* seen.' The conclusion was harsh but unavoidable. I had been a house-keeper some fifteen years, and had never met with such a gentle creature : how then could I believe in her ?

My own experience in servants had been something of a ' caution ' it is true ; but on comparing notes with my neighbors, I found that I had only shared in the common lot. We had a good deal of difficulty in the beginning to prevail upon any body to listen to an offer ; but after feeing two or three intelligence-offices we felt ourselves peculiarly fortunate in securing the services of two ladies who consented to aid as chamber-maid and cook in our little household. We were determined to gain the good-will of our servants if it were possible to do so by gentle treatment ; trusting that sympathy would beget sympathy, and that kindness would insure good service, if money would not. But we had to contend with the prejudices of caste, of country, and of religion ; and these could not be conciliated ; so we had nothing to do but to pay high wages, and resolve not to murmur at any thing short of being turned out of our own doors. Mrs. Mary McLaughlin having been duly inducted into the chair of the stew-pan professorship, and Miss Bridget McLaflin having assumed the charge of the broom-handle and duster, every thing went smoothly for an entire fortnight; but at the close of this period, Mrs. Mac. gave formal notice that she would not remain another hour under the same roof with 'such' a chambermaid; and before my wife could inquire into the particulars of the disturbance, Miss Mac. announced her intention of quitting the house, if 'such a creature' should be allowed to remain in it. It so happened that my wife had invited a small party of friends to sup with us, and there was no time to send them an apology, so she tried to reconcile the two ladies to each other: but she might have tried to reconcile the north and south winds with as much chance of success. Mrs. Mac. had allowed herself to insinuate ungentle things against a certain 'young man,' and reconciliation was out of the question. It was an awkward affair, but the cook's services were indispensable; so the chamber-maid was discharged; but no sooner had she quitted the house with her band-box and her wages, than Mrs. Mac. remembered that she had engaged to go to a christening in Cannon-street at her cousin's 'that very evening as ever was,' and she begged to be excused 'for that wonst,' for she 'would n't disappoint her cousin upon no consideration.' My wife was struck with amazement at this unreasonable request, and begged Mrs. Mac. to be more considerate. But Mrs. Mac. was not the person to disappoint her cousin; go she would and go she did; and when our company came, we had to treat them to the story of our woes instead of the supper that we had intended to set before them. This was bad, you will readily confess; but the sequel was worse.

It was a full hour after sun-rise when Mrs. Mac. returned from the christening at her cousin's; and as I had not entirely slept away the memory of my wrongs, I endeavored to impress upon her mind the enormity of her guilt; but she was in no mood for reproof; and as she bestowed an indiscriminate load of epithets on me and mine in return, I was compelled from self-respect to give the lady her discharge on the spot, and pay her a month's wages for a fortnight's services. There was no alternative after this but to assist my wife in preparing breakfast, a task by no means unpleasant, if the usages of society would only allow of it. The great Alfred baked the cakes for a peasant's supper, although it must be acknowledged that he made but an indifferent cook; and why should so humble an individual as myself hesitate to prepare his own breakfast?

I had scarcely swallowed my first cup of coffee, and was complimenting my wife's skill in broiling a mackerel, when a fierce ring at the hall-door introduced me to the bearer of a polite note from Patrick McShannon, Esq., attorney-at-law, No. 65 Spruce-street, inviting me to call at his office and settle for an assault-and-battery committed upon the person of Mistress Mary McLaughlin. I read my fate as clearly as though I had been in a magnetic slumber; and to save myself the mortification of being tried for assaulting a woman upon whose person

I had never put the weight of a feather, I compounded with her legal adviser by paying him fifty dollars in full.

The next day we had the rare good fortune to engage the services of an English protestant as a general servant. Her most remarkable point was her piety. She refused to go to the pump on the Sabbath, because she was principled against it; and I chid my wife for objecting to her strict construction of the fourth commandment; if it was an error it leaned to the right side, and gave good promise of something better. But the next day my wife, having been tempted by the fine weather to stroll down Broadway, on her return found our pious 'help' in as happy a condition as gin could help her to. This was any thing but *the* thing; and the world was once more before us and we had once more to choose, but our choice was Hobsonian. A servant who lived with a neighbor heard of our destitution, and came to recommend her cousin, who was every thing that she should be or that we could wish for. She was of Milesian origin, and her name was Margaret — Margaret Mahony. Margaret is a sweet name; there is to me a tone of melancholy tenderness in the sound of it; and I felt a prejudice in the new candidate for our favor before I had seen her. But her appearance was even more prepossessing than her name. She was rather slender, and her hair and complexion were of a different quality from what we generally see in females of her class; while her large black melancholy eyes gave an expression to her face that ill suited with her condition. We pitied her, and were resolved if she did not prove unworthy, to better her situation in life. She performed her duties to a charm, and we were delighted. Those who have suffered as we had, will know how to understand our feelings. She had been with us a month, when sitting down to breakfast one morning, upon removing the cover to what I supposed to be a dish of wet toast, a pair of corsets and a dirty night-cap revealed themselves to our astonished eyes! My wife took hold of the coffee-pot and discovered that it contained a pair of shoe-brushes and half a dozen tallow candles! Margaret was immediately called upon for an explanation. Poor girl! I can see her now! She came creeping into the room pale as ashes, and her coal-black hair hanging wildly about her shoulders. She crossed her hands deprecatingly upon her breast, and said, in a voice that went to my heart, ' Do n't murder me!' One glance was enough. The poor creature was a maniac. Upon inquiry, it appeared that she had left the insane hospital only the day before we took her; and as was supposed, perfectly well. She had come over from Ireland about two years before with the expectation of being married upon her arrival to a young Irishman, to whom she had been betrothed some years; but the first news that greeted her when she landed, was an account of her lover's marriage to another, and of his having removed to one of the western states with his wife. The shock deprived her almost instantly of her reason; but a course of judicious treatment at the asylum where she was taken had, it was thought, restored her to her right mind; and her cousin had given us no hint of her condition, being fearful that she would be objected to if her story were known. She was taken back to the hospital, and in less than a month poor Margaret was no more.

It was several days before we succeeded in securing the services of another servant. But experience had made us cautious; and we would take no one without a written recommendation. At last a young lady presented herself who bade fair to fill all our expectations. She brought with her the following testimonials of her ability:

NUMBER ONE.

'THIS is to sertify Mary Jan Jinkins is lived with me long wile is gud woshur an iremur wants hier wagis wich cant afford to giv, but hav guv 600 six dollars is reason she leves me.
S. DEMERITT.'

NUMBER TWO.

'THE bearer of this, Mary Jane Jenkins, has lived in my family as a servant and leaves me of her own will. I believe her to be honest. ELIZABETH MARTIN.'

NUMBER THREE.

' *To all whom it may concern:*
'This is to certify that Miss Mary Jane Jenkins has lived as an assistant in my family for the last six weeks, and has proved herself all that a young lady in her situation should be. She is an American by birth, and a highly respectable and exemplary protestant. Her ancestors were revolutionary patriots, and her mother is the author of several beautiful poems which have appeared in the Swampville Mirror. She is an excellent washer, and in the preparation of buck-wheats her superior is not to be found in the wide expanse of this occidental world. Her disposition is extremely child-like and gentle, and the *tout ensemble* of her character exhibits a rare combination of the *suaviter in modo* with the *fortiter in re.* Although she excels in plain cookery, she is great in mince and pumpkin pies. Although possessed of a very superior bringing-up, she is not one of your stock-up flirts, but is always very willing to do any thing that she is requested to do, in reason.
(Signed,) JULIET HICKS,
Pr. G. WASHINGTON ATKINS, Att'y.'

My wife was quite overcome with this last missive; and as she did not understand all the expressions, she submitted it to my inspection before she closed with the bearer of it. I was compelled to confess that the recommendation was a very eloquent production, although strictly considered, the style might be deemed a shade too ambitious. But the facts it set forth gave it great importance; and as a native-born white servant was a novelty, I was decidedly in favor of employing Miss Jenkins at her own price.

The first week our new 'help' fully equalled our wishes. Her buck-wheat cakes were equal to the praises of her last employer; but an unlucky accident well-nigh deprived us of her valuable services. My wife in calling to her omitted her second name, upon which she flared up and threatened to take her discharge if the omission should be made again. My wife promised of course to take good care for the future, and the young lady appeared satisfied. But Miss Mary Jenkins, the descendant of revolutionary sires and the daughter of a poetess, proved a perfect phenomenon in the consumption of food. Her performances in this regard were a subject of continual wonder to Mrs. F., who could never count upon any thing eatable unless it were under lock-and-key; and what particularly excited her astonishment was the fact that the girl's appetite through the day was quite delicate, but at supper she disposed of a quantity of food that was really astounding; cold turkies, rounds of beef, pots of jellies and pumpkin-pies disappeared under circumstances of great mystery; until one evening my wife happening to make her appearance unexpectedly in the kitchen, she discovered that Mary Jane had not been making a solitary meal, although the only evidence of a visiter was an extra plate on the table which happened to have been abandoned at a moment's notice.   A clearing up of the mystery immediately followed.   Miss Jenkins did not deny that she had been entertaining company, but ingenuously confessed herself a ' courted gal ; ' and that her lover, no less a person than G. Washington Atkins, Esq., was at that moment secreted in the pantry ; and she insisted on her right to be courted and to feed her beau, as her peculiar and inalienable privilege.   Mrs. F. however differed in opinion with her ; and having released Mr. Atkins, she requested that learned gentleman to remain a few moments until Miss Jenkins should be ready to accompany him ; but he excused himself on the ground of his having an appointment with one of his clients ; and he left the basement-door just as I began to descend the kitchen stairs — a circumstance that I have regretted ever since, as it would have given me no small satisfaction to have made his acquaintance under such peculiar circumstances.

These were among our first experiences ; but a score or two of others followed, similar in effect, although differing in kind and degree ; but the charm of novelty being gone, their peculiarities did not stand out in such bold relief as those that I have related.   But all that we had ever endured from unfaithful servants was a mere jest compared with the sufferings of an Englishman whom I overheard in a stage-coach a few weeks since, while journeying in New-Jersey, making his complaints to a neighbor :

' My missis is bad enough, Mum,' said the gentleman ; ' nothink was ever like it.   She caught the fever, and she shakes like anythink.   And there is Mary, our servant, she won't work unless she likes, and she knows nothink at all about cooking a joint of meat.   I am blessed if her missis do n't get up and get breakfast for her every morning ; and if the coffee is cold when she comes down, she grumbles like everythink ; and that 's what vexes me more than all.   But the worst of it is, she wears off my good woman's best clothes ; and only last week she spoilt her new silk pelisse by going off to a ball with it ; and when her missis talked to her about it, do n't you think she threatened to leave us !   Upon my soul she did !   And there 's John, he won't do anythink 'ither.   I pay him the highest wages going, but he won't work unless he likes.   There he sits over the stove, and he won't move only to his dinner, and he eats like everythink.   One day last month his missis wanted some water, but John would n't go to the well, because he had got the chills on him, and Mary would n't go because it was n't her place ; so I went myself ; and do n't you think, as soon as ever he eats his supper he dresses himself up in my best blue suit, as cost me five pounds in England, and off he goes to the tavern to a ball ; and I was forced to sit up for him until almost day-light !   Ah ! I and my missis have both wished ourselves back in the old country times enough ! '

This may be thought an extreme case, but it was real nevertheless ; or at least the conversation was real, and the gentleman who related it appeared like any thing but an imaginative person.

Good servants at small wages are unquestionably very good things ; but it should be borne in mind that these cannot be had except in countries where bread is scarce and labor plenty ; and where our fellow beings are degraded by want to the condition of slaves. God be praised, we live in a land where men must learn to be their own servants, since every man can and will be his own master. The day is coming when servitude will not be disgraceful, because labor will be honorable. So far then from exacting servants being a just cause of complaint, they should be looked upon as indications of a happy and prosperous condition of human affairs.

m. f.

THE JOY OF THE STARS.

I.

GAZE on yon heaven!
Methinks that each dim-twinkling, distant star
Feels deeper joy, e'en in its home afar,
Than e'er was given
To thee, vain-glorious man!
Thou toilest through thy threescore years and ten,
For love, ambition, and for riches; then
The ruthless fan
That Death, stern winnower! bears,
Sweeps thee, like chaff upon the threshing-floor
Away, and ended then for ever more
Are all thy cares.

II.

But for a few brief years
Thou art remembered by thy fellows; they
Forget thee, and unheeding wipe away
Earth's transient tears:
But still perchance thy fate
May be upon the glittering page of fame
Enrolled, and men may still record thy name
Among the great.
And what were this to thee
(Poor worm! by fellow-worms long preyed upon
In the cold tomb, where sun-light never shone,)
But vanity?

III.

But round the pole
That star through all eternity shall wheel,
Its influence through each generation steal
Into man's soul:
And it shall tell
Eternity of being, time and space,
And with a pen impalpable shall trace
A soothing spell,
A spell to purify
Man's heart, and bid it hope when life is o'er,
When e'en this moving world shall be no more,
For endless joy!

Cambridge, March, 1842.

j. o. w.

MY FIRST AND LAST SEA-FISHING.

BY A BOSTONIAN.

DOWN THE HARBOR.

ON one of the loveliest mornings of June, the loveliest month of the year, the pleasure-boat 'Skimmer of the Seas' swung from her moorings at Granite-wharf, Boston, and proceeded down the harbor on a fishing excursion. The party on board consisted of twelve individuals, exclusive of the Skipper and his mate. The most prominent of these were Mr. Philemon Scissors, a man who had 'been to sea' in his youth, but who was now the 'talented' editor of the Blueberry Weekly Gazette, and a very lively and witty fellow in his way, as we shall prove in the sequel, and his affianced, Miss Amanda Flirtle; Mr. Charles Dawdle, a dry-goods' clerk, and *his* intended, Miss Babara Huckins, a young lady of ample dimensions, who supposing a fishing-party a sort of drawing-room affair, presented herself in all her ball-room finery, including a pair of clocked rose-colored silk stockings and a splendid new challey dress 'got up expressly for the occasion;' Mr. Simeon Huckins, brother to Barbara, and Miss Angeline Amelia Stubbs; Mr. Bobby Rhubarb, an apothecary's apprentice, and Miss Chlorinde Ophelia Tartar — or rather Miss Cream O'Tartar, as Bobby used to call her — a young lady just from a country boarding-school, and as untamed and uneducated as an ass's colt. These individuals were the 'life of the party,' the others being but just so much ballast, which served to keep the hilarity of their more mercurial companions in proper trim.

It was early morn. The broad sun having for a moment 'pillowed his chin upon the orient wave,' had taken his upward course; and his yellow beams, piercing the morning mist which they tinged the while with their own golden hue, and even at that early hour falling warmly on brow and cheek, gave promise of a scorching noon. The slanting rays lit up the glassy waters with matchless splendor; and as the gallant boat drifted with the tide full in the face of the rising luminary, she seemed gliding down a long level path of golden light that extended from her prow to the very verge of the eastern horizon. A dead calm lay all around, save that now and then a slight cat's-paw crept warm and sultry from shoreward, swelling the sails into momentary life, and dying away again and leaving them as helpless as before. The stillness of the scene and the novelty of the situation to most of the party — for the greater number of them had never been on the water before — gave a saddening hue to their thoughts, as they sat silently looking at the slowly-receding city of their home. That exquisitely mournful feeling which will creep over the stoutest heart as it views from seaward for the last time for months and perhaps years the faint blue outline of its native hills still sharply defined against the splendor of the setting sun, will also steal, though perhaps in a more subdued tone, over the voyagers of a single day. For how many hearts as young and as joyous as their own, who had left their homes on a morning as bright and with hopes as high, and trusted themselves in a treacherous bark in anticipation of the enjoyments of but a single day, had sunk ere night beneath the remorseless waves, and in the very sight of shore! Thoughts like these kept our party silent for some time; and even the volatile Mr. Scissors drooped under their influence, as he gazed pensively through his whiskers at the gilded spires of the city now flashing in the bright rays of the glowing sun, and at the blue jets of smoke that crept lazily upward on the morning air.

The craft soon drifted beyond the shelter of the city, and a fresh gale from the hills sweeping across the bay, her white canvass bellied to the welcome visitant, and leaning to the pressure, the 'Skimmer of the Seas' soon began to leave the city in the distance. First the tall spars of the multitude of shipping at the wharves melted and mingled in one confused, interminable mass of light tracery-work; then long blocks of substantial warehouses of brick and granite gradually lost their individuality; then spire after spire faded from view, until but two or three of the loftiest could be distinguished above the black masses by which they were surrounded; and then, last of all, the eye identified only the tall dark obelisk of Bunker's-Hill looming up on the city's right, and the drab-colored dome of the new state-house, that like a huge Quaker hat settled down over its summit.

As the city was gradually shut out from view, signs of life began to be manifested on board the Skimmer. Fort Independence had already been left behind, and the boat was fast nearing Long-Island Head, when Mr. Scissors, suddenly starting up as if he had forgotten something very important, gave a stretch and a loud yawn, and descended into the cabin. In a few moments he returned with a flushed countenance and a slight twinkle in the eye, which made Miss Amanda Flirtle whisper to Miss Barbara Huckins that 'Phil' had got something in his noddle, and that she would 'see presently.' And now Mr. Bobby Rhubarb followed in the footsteps of the illustrious Mr. Scissors; Mr. Dawdle followed Mr. Rhubarb; and then the others followed Mr. Dawdle; not one, however, staying a moment longer than the talented editor, and what was very remarkable, all returning with faces equally flushed. Some of the young ladies of the party wondered at all this; but Miss Huckins, who was older and more experienced, whispered something in their ears which undoubtedly gave perfect satisfaction, as no farther wonderment was manifested on the subject.

The boat was now hugging Long-Island Head closely, when Mr. Dawdle, who had never been 'to sea' before, suddenly woke out of a day-dream, and inquired of Mr. Scissors the name of the country they were then passing?

Mr. Scissors scratched with the forefinger of his right hand the pendent part of one of his long ears — a trick he always performed when puzzled, as well as when about to say something smart — he scratched his ear, but nothing came of it. 'Really,' said he, 'I can't 'zactly remember at this moment. How strange! I've seen it a hundred times at sea, and know it just as — well! It's an inland country; Cape — Cape — something —'

'Cape Hatteras,' suggested the boarding-school Miss, lispingly.

'Ah! yes! — yes, that's it!' exclaimed Scissors, rubbing his hands in great glee. 'Now I recollect all about it! It *is* Cape Hatteras; and that up there is the light-'us; and that black night-cap thing on the top is the lantun; and down there is the light-'us man;' and he pointed to a man digging clams on the beach.

'Lawk! how natural!' exclaimed Miss Barbara; 'and is the lantern lit up now?'

'Oh no,' replied Mr. Scissors, scratching his ear; 'it's never lit up a-day-times except Sundays; and only in dark nights, so that the sailors can see to go a-courting.'

Miss Flirtle cast an intelligent glance at Miss Barbara Huckins, as much as to say, 'Did n't I tell you so?' and then leaning over, she whispered in her ear: 'You do n't know, Barbara, what critturs them sailors is. They say they has gals on the land and gals on the sea.'

'I've read all about 'em in books,' replied her friend Barbara. 'Mermaids they calls 'em — a sort of confabulous crittur; half woman half fish.'

'Jus' so,' said Amanda; 'but what a drefful taste sailors must have! For my part, if *I* was one, I think I should prefer ——'

What she would have preferred in the supposed case however will probably never be known, for just at this moment a new source of interest appeared on the other side of the boat, and Miss Amanda's preference was nipt in the conception. The object which now attracted attention was a large clumsily-built schooner which had anchored in the outer harbor, waiting for a favorable wind and tide to take her up to the city. All hands gazed at her for a moment, when Mr. Charles Dawdle, thinking it full time that he should do something for the amusement of the company, declared his intention of hailing the strange craft. Accordingly, springing upon the companion-way and placing both hands to his mouth, he shouted through them: 'I say, Skipper! what o'clock is it?'

'You be d — d!' replied a gruff voice, issuing from what had until now appeared to be a large mop rolling about on the bulwarks of the schooner. Dawdle seemed a little frightened and sat down.

'That's because you did n't do it right, Dawdle,' said Mr. Scissors. 'There's a nottical way of doing such things, which is very effective. I've been to sea, and know. Mark how quick I'll bring a civil answer.' And then mounting the companion-way, he made a speaking trumpet of his hands as Dawdle had done before him, and shouted: 'Schooner ahoy! Where from? How many days? Where bound?'

'Go to h — ll!' answered the same gruff voice over the stern-boards.

Scissors looked puzzled, and scratched his ear for a long time. 'That's the strangest craft I ever saw,' said he; 'and I've seen a great many in my day — at sea. Skipper! what do you think of her?'

And he turned to the boatman, who, one eye shut, was squinting with the other at the editor's glossy and well-turned whiskers, and wondering what kind of a soft fish they belonged to. 'What do you think, Skipper?' repeated Mr. Scissors; 'do you suppose she's a pirate, eh?'

'Not 'zactly,' replied the Skipper, luffing a little; 'that 'ere aint a pirate build.'

'Do you 'spose she's armed?'

'Guess not. Why?'

''Cause if I thought she was armed, I'd put about and board her. But if she aint got no small arms it's no kind of use. Them sailors would beat us like the devil with their fists!'

The schooner however was soon left a long way behind. Scissors now suddenly diving down the companion-way as mysteriously as at first, again returned after an absence of about the same length, and with a countenance a little more flushed even than before. Dawdle and the other gentlemen went through the same mysterious manoeuvre in turn; and then they one and all declared themselves ripe for fun of all sorts.

Scissors, spitting on his hands and rubbing them briskly together, announced his intention of going aloft to 'look out;' and springing upon the crotch of the main-boom he began to 'shin up' the mast.

'Oh dear! dear! Philemon! Philemon!' screamed Miss Amanda Flirtle, jumping up and catching her lover by the legs; 'do — *do* come down! — Philemon! for *my* sake come down.'

Philemon slid down again, for the reason that he could hold on no longer; protesting however that 'climbing up them masts was just nothing at all. Many and many a time,' said he, 'at sea, on the darkest and murkiest and blackest nights that ever was, I've clomb to a ship's top-mast-head and remained there for hours together, on 'the look-out!'

But this assurance didn't soothe the fears of the amiable Miss Amanda, who pressing her open hand to her bosom, drew a long breath. 'He's so ventur'som'!' said she, as soon as she could find words; 'he's so ventur'som', he's ollers a doin' somethin' to frighten me. He'll be the death of me yet, I know he will!' And then drawing a handkerchief from her side-pocket she blew her nose with profound sorrow. At this moment a slight squall struck the sails, and the boat careening, gave them all a sudden start. Mr. Scissors who happened to be standing at the moment, and a little off his balance withal, made a most formidable pitch, and would have gone overboard head-first if the Skipper had not caught him by the tail of his coat and saved him. If he *had* gone over in the manner in which he started, he would never have lived to verify Miss Amanda's murderous prophecy; for going to the bottom like lead, and his head acting as a sinker, it would have been impossible for him ever to rise again.

A new object of interest now hove in sight. 'What's that?' inquired Miss Cream O'Tartar, pointing to a low mound of stones rising out of the waves.

'Nix's Mate,' replied Mr. Scissors.

'How queer!' exclaimed Miss Angeline Stubbs. 'It looks just like the monuments at Mount Auburn! I wonder who's buried there?'

'There aint nobody buried there,' answered Scissors; 'but somebody was hung there, though.'

'Ah! I know!' interrupted Mr. Rhubarb; 'I've read all about it in books. It was Old Nick's wife; she *is* buried there, and them's the stones he put over her to keep her down.'

'She must have been an awful crittur!' remarked Miss Huckins; and then the conversation flagged again.

THE FISHING-GROUND.

THE boat had now arrived at a spot where were seen numerous other small craft; some riding quietly at anchor; others tacking about and shifting their positions; and some who like themselves had just arrived. In a word, they were on the FISHING-GROUND. The Skipper having selected a spot which he assured the company was the best for catching all sorts of fish—which in fact however was altogether too shallow, but the only place where his shortened cable would fetch bottom—the 'killick' was dropped over the prow, in a moment after the boat lost her head-way, her stern swung slowly round with the ebbing tide, and the 'Skimmer of the Seas' sat motionless on the bosom of the water.

Preparations were now made for fishing. First the Skipper drew up from the hold a bucket of live clams, and set it in the broiling sun; at which those testaceous creatures manifested their displeasure by uttering sundry very audible '*pishes*,' which frightened the ladies not a little, and then by throwing up several jets of water, which frightened them still more. Then the gentlemen of the party became quite lively and active; lines were examined critically, sinkers and hooks adjusted and baited, and every thing made ready for throwing them overboard all at the same moment, when one of the company suggested that in order to make the pastime 'interesting,' a purse should be made up of a contribution of one cent all round; the stakes to fall to the individual who should catch the first fish. This was instantly acceded to by all except Mr. Scissors, who declared he would have nothing to do with it, and that he considered gambling a very vicious vice indeed; that he had never countenanced it and never would, even in its lowest and apparently most innocent shape; that he had opposed it in public and in private, both by precept and example; and also with the utmost vigor of his pen through the columns of the Blueberry Gazette. This threw a damper on the proposition for a moment; but Miss Amanda Flirtle, taking from her breast-pocket a cent of the newest stamp, declared that *she* meant to wager one, gambling or no gambling; upon which Miss Stubbs and the other ladies did the same. The gentlemen of course could do no less than follow the example of the ladies, and the sum of eleven cents soon lay together in a heap, to which Mr. Scissors readily added the twelfth, and then proposed to double the stakes, which was unanimously acceded to. But here a knotty question arose, as to what should be considered a fish within the meaning of the bet. It was finally decided that a cod and nothing but a cod should be entitled to the prize. This decision being strictly conformable to the general rule of the fishing-ground, was acquiesced in, and the signal being given, the lines were silently let down into the deep. And now another difficulty was suggested. Who was to decide what was a cod and what a haddock?

'For my part,' said Dawdle, 'I do n't know one from 't other!'

'Nor I either,' echoed Stubbs.

'Well, I knows 'em like a book,' said Scissors. 'I 've seen whole ship-loads of 'em at sea. The cod 's of an entirely different species ——'

But his scientific explanation was here cut short by a sudden scream from Miss Amanda Flirtle, who letting her line drop overboard and falling back into the arms of Miss Huckins, seemed about to go into a fit of hystericks.

'Oh dear!—dear!' she exclaimed; 'oh dear! I—I 've had a bite!'

'A bite!' cried Mr. Huckins, springing to her assistance; 'where? what did you do with it?'

'I let it go, line and all!' replied the young lady. 'Oh!'

'Let it go!' shouted Huckins, with a look of profound astonishment.

'Yes, to be sure!' replied Miss Amanda sharply. 'What should I have done? Do you suppose I was going to let the crittur' run away with me?'

'No,' said Mr. H.; 'but you might have pulled up ——'

A slight flush passed over Miss Flirtle's countenance, and she pursed her little mouth into the shape of a wedding-ring, but said nothing; instead however she cast an intelligent glance at her lover, who in turn glared fiercely at Huckins. There 's no knowing what fatal consequences might have followed this scene, if a new incident had not attracted the attention of the parties. This was no less than the capture of a Skulpin; one of those big-headed, little-tailed devils which people can always catch when they can catch nothing else. This specimen of an unamiable and I do n't know but deservedly much-abused fish, in performing the very foolish feat of swallowing a whole clam belonging to the apothecary's apprentice, had unfortunately taken down a large cod-hook attached to the line of the same young gentleman, and in punishment of his temerity he now lay gasping on the hot deck of the 'Skimmer of the Seas.' The hook probably did n't set well in his stomach, for he appeared very ill at ease. He beat the deck with his tail, chasséed right and left several times, yawned once or twice hugely, and then puffing himself up like a bladder, turned some half-dozen summersets with an agility that was truly wonderful considering the precarious state of his inwards. Then as he lay quiet for a moment, a consultation was held by his captors as to the best method of making him disgorge the hook. Skulpins are ugly customers any how ; and this one happened to be particularly so. Various plans were suggested ; but at last that proposed by Mr. Scissors was agreed upon and immediately put in execution. First Mr. Huckins, being the heavier man, planted the heel of his boot on the skulpin's tail ; Messrs. Dawdle and Scissors each grasped an ear to keep his head still ; and then the apothecary prepared to extract the hook by main force. But before commencing the torture upon his captive's body, Mr. Rhubarb, with a worldly disposition hardly to have been expected in one so young, determined to inflict a little wholesome torture upon his feelings in the shape of a moral lecture. ' You ugly sea-devil ! ' he commenced, something after the manner of Launcelot to his dog ; ' you young deformity ! I 'll learn you to go swimming about and stealing other people's clams ! What do you think of yourself ? Where 's your morality ? Who brought you up ? And did n't you know better than to go for to swallow a 'potecary's bait arter this fashion ? ' The captive, looking hard at Rhubarb, winked several times in rapid succession and worked his huge jaws convulsively, as signifying that he heard and understood perfectly every word that was said to him, but that being dumb, it was utterly impossible for him to make that reply which the extremity of his case as well as the respectability of the querist seemed to demand. He next tried to wag his tail, but could n't, for the heel of Huckins' boot held it like a vice ; then to shake his head, but equally in vain, for Dawdle and Scissors were on their guard, especially the latter gentleman, who said he had seen millions of 'em at sea, and that he was up to all their tricks and knew just how to handle them. Rhubarb now began to wind the line round his hand to assist him in the operation, the skulpin staring at him the while with his large gray eyes, and saying as plainly as eyes could speak, ' Do it gently, Bobby ! ' In a moment more, the prisoner was relieved by ejectment of his disagreeable tenant, and immediately began a grave Shaker dance about the deck, and to exhibit various other marks of solemn joy at his deliverance, to the no small terror of his captors, who mistaking these antics for demonstrations of rage, scampered out of his way as quickly as possible, clearing the whole quarter-deck as an arena for his gymnastics. The skulpin, who was evidently of a social disposition, did n't like this desertion on the part of his captors ; and accordingly, after cutting some few pigeon-wings with his tail, and promenading all round, he suddenly sidled up to the ladies, and managed by a dexterous summerset to throw himself plump into the lap of Miss Barbara Huckins. Great was the consternation produced by this unexpected movement. The ladies shrank back and screamed in terror ; the gentlemen stood irresolute and afraid to attack the monster, and were about to call in the aid of the Skipper, when the fish throwing another lofty back summerset into the sea, disappeared for ever. And thus came and went their first and last fish ! It was a long time before the party got over their fright, especially Miss Huckins, who declared she should never forget it, and that her new challey dress was utterly ruined.

THE STORM.

It was now some time past meridian, and the sun, which all the morning had poured down a scorching heat, suddenly became enveloped in clouds, that gradually spreading over the horizon indicated a shower near at hand. The Skipper called the attention of the party to the fact, and proposed putting in to Long-Island for shelter. This suggestion was thought reasonable by all except Mr. Scissors, who laughed at the cautious fears of the Skipper. He had been at sea too often to be deceived or frightened by a few black clouds at noon-day. 'There!' said he, lifting his long delicate hand and pointing to a strip of blue just over the eastern horizon; 'when you see a patch of clear sky off there, you may be sure of dry weather for the next forty-eight hours at least.' As he spoke, a large drop of rain pattered down on his hand; he lifted his face and another dropped on his nose; then another followed, and another; then the rain descended thick and fast; and finally, by the time the party were safely stowed away in the little cabin, it poured down in torrents, and sea and sky appeared like one vast sheet of water. The crackling thunder bowled along seemingly on the very surface of the sea, and the sharp lightning flashed its way even into the close-shut cabin of the Skimmer of the Seas, where the party, huddled together, crouched in terror and dismay. Scissors turned pale as a sheet, and the contrast of his thin lily-white cheeks with the fierce coal-black whiskers that bordered them, which now curled tighter than ever with affright, was very striking; as Bobby Rhubarb afterward remarked, they together looked like a pictur' of thunder and lightnin'. No one dared to utter a syllable except Miss Huckins, who ever now and then struck up a low lament over her new challey dress, which she was sure would never be fit to wear again — never!

But in the mean-time the Skipper and his mate, two of the toughest sea-dogs that ever floated, were not idle. Every thing had been made tight and fast; the killick raised, and the stiff little sea-boat, her sails bellying to a smacking breeze, was streaking along like a gray-hound for Long-Island Head. A half hour's such sailing brought them side by side with the landing-place, and leaving the boat, the party wended their way through the rain to the only house of entertainment on the island. On their arrival they found it crowded with company; for some dozen other parties, who fortunately not having had any one among their number who had been to sea and could prognosticate all about the weather had wisely started in season to escape the shower, were now stowed away about the premises, occupying every inch of available room from cellar to garret. But there was a snug, clean barn, the landlord said, filled with the sweetest June hay, in which they might make themselves very comfortable if they chose. This was declared by one and all to be just the thing.

'It will be so romantic!' said the boarding-school Miss.

'And so ——' responded Miss Angeline Stubbs.

''Zactly! — 'zactly!' exclaimed Mr. Scissors, almost dancing with delight. And the party followed the landlord into the barn.

Their place of refuge was indeed clean and neat, as the landlord had represented it; and the sweet-scented hay in the loft looked cool and inviting.   But the ascent to it was by a ladder of some twenty rounds, which made it a very awkward affair.   The men indeed could mount easily enough; but the thing was not so practicable with the ladies — in the presence of their admirers.   However, Mr. Scissors, the spokesman on all occasions, proposed that the ladies should mount first, in which operation they could be materially assisted by the gentlemen. This he declared was the only proper as well as the only practicable mode, as precedence in every thing should always be accorded to the gentler sex.

To this proposition however Miss Huckins, notwithstanding her well-turned ancles and rose-colored stockings, gave a decided dissent. ' No!' she said, shaking her head oracularly :   ' The ladies takes the precedent in every thing 'cept goin' up stairs.   *Them* the gen'lemen ollers mounts fust.   *Ollers!'*   And she again shook her head.

' But this ain't a pair of stairs,' suggested Scissors, scratching his ear ; ' it 's only a ladder.'

' It 's all the same,' responded Miss Barbara ; ' they both on 'em goes *up*.   It 's all the same, 'zactly, only a great deal worser.'

The dispute was finally settled by the gallant Scissors, who gaily mounting the ladder first, was followed by the other gentlemen, and then one by one the ladies were drawn up and safely deposited on the hay-mow.   The party then dispersed themselves about the loft in couples ' to suit ;' and an order was given the landlord to send in an abundance of his best cheer.   In a few minutes after, a huge basket filled with edibles made its appearance at the top of the ladder, moving upward apparently by some mysterious agency ; then a pair of large goggle eyes, and a nose and mouth and chin succeeded the basket; then followed a short round, dumpy body, in shape not unlike a soda fountain ; and lastly a pair of drum-stick legs stepped upon the platform, and the servant-of-all-work of the inn stood before them, with the refreshments ordered for their entertainment.   This supply was soon fast disappearing before the sharp trencher-work of the party, whom the sea-air and long-fasting had made voracious.   During the interesting performance scarcely a word was spoken by any body except Miss Barbara Huckins, who seemed to be unusually restless.   She hitched nervously about on the mow ; moved an inch or two one way, and then as far over the other ; once or twice partly arose and then sat down again ; muttering the while to herself, and acting in fact just as a thousand people do when ' something 's the matter — they do n't know what.'

Presently a small boy, the landlord's son, made his appearance on the hay-mow, to see if any thing more were wanting from the house. But no sooner had he cast his eyes on Miss Huckins than he uttered a loud exclamation, and pointing toward her, stood for a moment speechless.

' What 's the matter, boy ? ' inquired a half-dozen voices at once.

' Oh! that 'ere voman!' he cried, still pointing with his finger ; ' she 's a settin' — a settin' ———'   And here he gasped for breath.

'Well! we know she's a setting,' said Scissors, scratching his ear; 'we *know* she's a setting, and we 'spect she 'll *hatch* soon.'

'But she *is* a hatchin' — *now!* ' screamed the boy louder than before; 'she's a settin' on a whole heap of aigs!'

Miss Barbara jumped up in terror. It was too true! In the twilight of the hay-loft she had innocently sat down on a pile of nest-eggs, and some dozen or two of incipient chickens had been crushed out of a prospective existence by the warm pressure. She put her hand behind her:

'Oh dear!' she exclaimed, 'what have I done? Poor little things! And my new challey!'

But order was soon restored; Miss Barbara's nerves again quieted; and several hours spent in hilarity, in which Mr. Scissors outshone all others, and fully established his claim to the compliment bestowed upon him by the doting Amanda, that he was the 'tip-top life of the party.'

The storm which drove them to the shelter of the barn now began gradually to abate. The rain pattered less forcibly against the roof and sides of the building; in a moment more, the sound grew fainter and fainter still; then only a few large drops fell at intervals; and finally it ceased altogether, and the bright sun-beams came glancing through crack and crevice, streaking the hay-mow with long lines of golden light. Chanticleer in the barn-yard was the first to welcome the change. Shaking the rain-drops from his wings, and hugging them close to his sides, he gave a shrill scream that set every feathered inhabitant of the island in motion, not excepting Mr. Scissors in the hay-loft, who starting as at a trumpet-call, lifted up his voice and returned the summons with a yell so natural and cockerel-like, that Mr. Huckins declared he could almost see his spurs. Even chanticleer himself was deceived, and with every feather ruffled and in motion, came bustling into the barn to see what formidable rival had usurped his throne. But finding it was only Scissors, who flattered by the success of his first essay was at the moment issuing a second edition, the cockerel turned on his heel contemptuously, and strode away.

THE RETURN.

THE party now made preparation for a return, when a new difficulty sprung up in their path. The gentlemen's ascent of the ladder in advance of the ladies was a matter of propriety; their descent in the same order now seemed one of necessity. For how were the ladies to get down at all unless their gallants were below to assist them? It was awkward, but there seemed no alternative; and Scissors leading the way, they soon stood on the ground floor. Then began a contention among the ladies as to who should descend first and form a cover for the remainder. One of them proposed that Miss Barbara should lead the van, because being the bulkiest she would form the most effectual screen for those who followed. To this proposition Barbara accorded a peremptory refusal. She said she would stay on the hay-mow till the cockerel picked her eyes out, before she'd do it! The others also showed signs of obstinacy, notwithstanding the urgent solicitations of the gentlemen, who all at once appeared to be in a great hurry about the affair. At last Miss Cream O'Tartar, vowing she was n't the least afraid, stepped forward to the edge of the loft. Here she hesitated a moment, and putting her right foot forward, withdrew it again, and advanced the left; but finding that contrive it as she would, she could n't descend the ladder without pushing her ancles beyond the protection of her petticoats, Chlorinde chivalrously threw herself upon the honor of the gentlemen, and boldly took the 'first step,' the others following in close succession. A gust of wind which blew in the door at the moment giving buoyancy to her dress, she floated down like a zephyr, and sprang, all blushes, into the 'wide embrace' of Mr. Bobby Rhubarb, who stood ready to receive her, repaying his gallantry with a sly pinch on the arm, and declaring at the same time that he was a little Satan, and she would never speak to him again.

And now they are once more in the open air, and gaily wending their way to the sea-shore. Gaily — all but Miss Barbara, who happened to be particularly displeased with her mishap in the hay-loft. Her temper was ruffled not a little; but her new challey dress had been the greatest sufferer by the accident; for beside a very marked addition of coloring matter by no means of the most fashionable shade, it had acquired a stiffness also in the hinder breadths that caused no small bustle and 'rumpus' as she walked sulkily yet loftily along.

Scissors however was still all life; and on the way to the boat he performed many wonderful feats of a gymnastic and ventriloquistic nature. At one moment, springing from the ground, he grasped with his right hand the limb of a tree, and swayed to and fro in the air, like a monkey; dropping again, he leaped over in succession some half dozen stones a foot high, clearing them all one by one with the most surprising agility; then rising on his toes and clapping his hands thrice to his hips he again crowed lustily like the lord of the hen-roost; and finally, in attempting to throw a summerset in imitation of the skulpin of the sea, he unfortunately slipped — and the editor of the Blueberry Gazette lay sprawling where but a moment before a cow had passed.

In a short time our little party were again collected on the deck of the Skimmer of the Seas, and floating on their homeward path. But, as in the early morn, a dead calm pervaded sea and sky; a stillness so profound that the winnowing of the air by the sea-bird's wing was heard distinctly on board their little craft. The sun too was nearly down, and they were seven long miles from home, and not a breath of wind to waft them there. Luckily the tide was setting in, and leaving the boat to glide slowly upward on the bosom of the young flood, the party gradually sunk down in a dreamy thoughtfulness. Twilight came on with its deep mysterious silence, broken only by the sharp cry of restless watch-dog in some anchored ship, or the soft chime of bells from Christ-church steeple that floated through the moist sea-air in tones of dirge-like melody; and then the dark shades of night gradually closed around them. Jaded and tired and anxious to reach the shore, a sullen silence was kept up on board, except that now and then a word or two from one brought a monosyllabic answer from another, and then all were dumb again. Even the mercurial Scissors had yielded to the general torpor, and with his head resting on Miss Amanda's lap, he lay gazing at the young moon that glittered in the deep azure above, who in turn stared down at him with all her eyes, wondering what in the devil's name the fellow could be looking at.

'A penny for your thoughts,' said Miss Cream O'Tartar to Scissors, in a desperate attempt to 'make talk.'

Scissors rolled his large black eye from the sky to Chlorinde and from Chlorinde to the sky again; and then parting his thin lips just enough to let his small pearly teeth glitter in the moon-light, he smiled — but said nothing. Amanda however spoke for him. 'Hist!' said she, laying a finger on her rosy lips; 'he's a thinking — poetry!' Whatever was the subject of his waking thoughts, however, they were of short duration; for after the lapse of a few minutes his eye-lids gradually closed, his under-jaw fell, and overcome by the fatigue of being the 'life of the party,' Philemon Scissors slept and — snored; while the gentle Amanda, pillowing his heavy head, gazed down upon him with emotions of pride that he was all her own.

No farther attempt was made to break the monotonous silence, which lasted until the boat reached the wharf, and the party were wending their homeward way, when they once more found their speech; especially Miss Barbara, whose tongue wagged eloquently about her various mishaps. Among other things, she had learnt this: Never to go a fishing in a new challey dress and rose-colored silk stockings.

'What luck to-day?' inquired a brother skipper of the captain of the Skimmer of the Seas, as the latter chained his boat to the moorings.

'Not a d — d fish!' replied the Skipper, sulkily; ''less you call a skulpin a fish — the hornéd critturs!'

TO THE POLAR STAR.

BY HANS VON SPIEGEL.

Lone star that watchest o'er the frozen sea,
   With ray resplendent yet serenely cold,
Full of deep meaning comes thy light to me,
   As on life's dreary voyage my way I hold.
For linked with thee in memory is one,
   Most tender, beautiful, and good withal,
Whom I had fondly pictured as a sun,
   That with its radiance bright might cheer my soul
While gliding onward to that bourne of rest,
   The silent grave. But now, ah me! I weep,
And shrine pale Sorrow in my aching breast
   With ceaseless worship, while I wake or sleep.
And I shall *alway* cherish this *first love* —
My heart the sea, and that the star above!

Utica, April, 1842.

THE BATTLE-GROUND.

BY M. E. CHILTON.

When Morn her golden eye first opes,
　It rests upon this field of grass,
Whose wavy bosom gently slopes
　To where yon silent waters pass:
And here the yellow sun-beams sleep
　Throughout the long and sunny day,
Till twilight's dusky shadows creep,
　To chase the golden hues away.

How sweetly doth each rural sound,
　Mellowed by distance, strike the ear!
While peace breathes from the very ground,
　That seems to slumber gently here.
Not such the scene in days gone by,
　When Earth's fair bosom, drenched with gore,
Threw up to yon o'er-arching sky
　The black-mouthed cannon's deafening roar.

Here raged the battle fiercest; here
　The crimson life-blood thickest ran
From many a sturdy musqueteer,
　From many a hardy rifleman;
Changing from summer's green to red
　The dull and spiky grass, that stood
Untrampled by the soldier's tread,
　Like bristling bayonets dashed with blood.

As hissed the bullet o'er the ground,
　Bidding the heart's warm current start,
Through many a deep and ragged wound
　From the expiring patriot's heart;
So many an eye with anger fired,
　Its quick, dark glance of hate would throw,
Till closed in death, its light expired,
　That pioneered the deadly blow.

While thick and fast the bullets streamed,
　And through the smoky battle-cloud
The musket's dull red flashes gleamed
　Like lightnings through their misty shroud,
The wounded soldier from the plain
　Crept to the cooling river's side,
Till, madly writhing in his pain,
　Clutching the warm wet earth — he died!

But hushed the sound of battle-fray;
　No more o'er fields of trampled grain
The slashing sabre cleaves its way,
　Gashing the hot and dizzied brain:
A gentle peace succeeds; a still
　And calm profound; no sound is heard,
Save low of cattle on the hill,
　Or merry lay of forest bird.

The river sparkles in the light —
　　Its bright face wrinkled, as with mirth,
By gentle airs, that day and night
　　Chase one another round the earth ;
The black-bird sits upon the stalk,
　　Or sings amid the ripened grain,
While high in air the wheeling hawk
　　Describes his circle o'er the plain.

A lovely scene ! — ah ! never more
　　Be heard War's wild and mingled shout
Among these hills, that old and hoar
　　Lie calm and peacefully about :
May never aught but plough or spade
　　Disturb these fields of bearded grain ;
Nor aught but twilight's sombre shade
　　Darken these solitudes again !

L I F E   I N   H A Y T I.

NUMBER SEVEN.

THE paper money of Hayti is printed with common type, upon common French writing paper. The bills are of the denomination of one, two, five and ten, and are about twice the size of an American bank-note. They bear upon the face a 'promise to pay' on the part of government to the bearer, and are signed by some half-dozen individuals high in station, consisting, I think, of the Treasurer-General, the Secretary of State and sundry other officers of the 'Chamber des Comptes,' et cetera. The signatures are nearly all at one end of the bills on a blank space, and with one or two exceptions resemble very closely the frantic efforts of some luckless fly just escaped from an ink-bottle. There being however some method in their madness, the *effect* produced is precisely the same in all the notes, and sets at naught the respectable attempts of counterfeiters ; for while the round and clerk-like signature of Senator Rouanez is easily imitated, the attempts upon those of Cupédon and others are signal failures ; and no wonder, for it would puzzle any but the most ardent imagination to tell where they commence or where they end their fantastic flourishes. The gentlemen whose signatures are thus appended have been bred to the camp, and wield the broad-sword with more grace than the goose-quill.

But not one in twenty of the country people can *read* ; how then distinguish between a two and a five? The difficulty is obviated with as much simplicity as ingenuity ; the tens have four black lines running in a diamond thus ◇ across the entire face of the bill, while the others have as many little squares printed upon them as they represent dollars ; thus a *two* has two, □ □, which he who runs may read, without the aid of the alphabet. The metallic currency is in dollars,

halves, quarters, eighths, and sixteenths, like the Spanish, and the
' color of the money ' is that of silver, and it contains doubtless some
of this precious commodity; *how much*, is known only to the higher
powers and the mint-master ; probably it amounts to forty or fifty per
cent.   The coin itself is about half the size of the legitimate piece ; that
is, a Haytien half-dollar is of the size of a Spanish quarter.   Copper
coin were not used until within a few years ; they are half the ' size of
life,' and represent one and two cents.   The shop-keepers were very
sorry to see them, and complained very much that they sold for penny-
worths half the time, whereas before there was no such insignificant
trade.   The country people prefer very much the metallic to the paper
money, (though there is no intrinsic value in the former unless submitted to the crucible,) and in consequence of this fancy, the former
bears a premium over the other, sometimes as high as five per cent.
There is one great piece of stupidity exercised by the money-makers
at the capital, and that is, that they make a very large proportion of the
paper in ten-dollar notes.   The agriculturalists have a still greater aversion to these than to the small bills ; and the consequence is again, that
small bills are worth more than tens — a premium of two or three per
cent.
   The coffee-dealer on contracting with the merchant for a quantity of
coffee, stipulates for his pay in a certain proportion of large and small
paper, and a proportion of coin.   The merchant finding nothing in his
strong box but the large bills, is obliged to go to the retailers and buy
the other kinds at the high premiums mentioned above, and is thus
fleeced (either through the ignorance or laziness of those whose duty
it is to attend to these matters) of large sums.   One reason of the
country people preferring the coin to the paper is, that they are in the
habit of burying it for safe-keeping.   It is singular that this fancy has
prevailed frequently in this island ; first among the Flibustiers, or Free-
booters, then by the French, when revolutionary times prevailed, and
now by the blacks themselves, who like their predecessors consider
mother earth to be the only safe office of deposite.
   The greatest exploit of this kind is that recorded of Christophe,
who is reported to have sent an immense treasure, which fell into his
hands after the sack of Cape François, some leagues into the interior
under a military escort, who buried it at a given spot.   On their way
back to the city they were every man shot by an ambuscade placed by
orders of the black tyrant, and he thus remained sole master of his
secret.   It is farther said also that he died without revealing it, as he
perished by his own hand in a sudden fit of despair.   Another current
' on dit' is that the late Stephen Girard, at that epoch doing business
at the Cape, assisted to save quantities of valuables from the insatiate
maws of the rebels, the owners of which were more or less fortunate
in making their escape afterward.   The West-India planters in those
days were enormously rich, as can well be imagined from the prices
which they obtained for all their products.   With a servile insurrection
suddenly breaking out, they had no other means of saving their gold
than to bury it in the earth ; and as thousands of them were slain, root
and branch, the soil still holds the precious hoards.   A young woman

of a decent but poor family, built a house costing three or four thousand dollars; how she came possessed of the means was a mystery, and the matter afforded food for gossip for some time. At last it was ascertained that on a day when she was walking among the hills immediately behind the town, she observed a piece of iron protruding from the bank; loosing the earth around it, she extricated a small cast-iron pot filled with coin.

Government has passed a law by which they have a claim of one third upon all 'trésor-trouvé,' and the finder is not usually too well-disposed to publish his good luck. A very intelligent and worthy acquaintance of mine was present on his land when one of the negroes was digging out a yam, which was of very large size. On taking it out of the ground, there appeared at the bottom of the cavity a ' carreau,' or thin square brick, which the French in former times made great use of. His curiosity being roused, he continued to dig, and found after going down several feet, another 'carreau;' this last was of white marble some twelve inches square. It lay flat like the former, and across the face was drawn a diagonal line. Doubtless this line pointed in the direction of the spot where the planter had buried his valuables; but whether he had escaped the general massacre and had come back for them (and such an attempt would have been at great peril) did not appear to be known. Monsieur —— had no doubt of the meaning of the signs he discovered; but the place being distant from town, he went home without any farther scrutiny, and with true Creole apathy never made another effort to discover what perhaps would have made him independent for life. A Yankee, under such circumstances, would have dug over his whole farm; or what is as likely, would have sold it to a company on speculation.

Two spots have been pointed out to me, where at different times large holes have been excavated during the night. One of these was amid the ruins of a large and apparently an elegant house in the centre of the town; the other was a solitary spot on the sea-shore. No doubt existed among the citizens, that in both instances a treasure had been taken away by persons who had been furnished with ground-plans, and came to the Island, probably from France, (though many of the exiled French went to Cuba and the southern states,) for the purpose. At all events, no other explanation has ever been given of the making the holes, which were large enough to bury a man. They were not done in joke, to set the people on the *qui vive*, for in a country like Hayti, with ignorant and savage soldiers at every point, and patrolling through every street, such a pastime would have been at the imminent peril of life; or if they should take the trouble of arresting the wag without shooting him first, he would labor under a ban of suspicion never to be shaken off or forgotten. No Haytien ever dreamed of any thing in either case but of bona-fide prizes successfully carried off.

In repairing an old building in the centre of the town, quantities of earth were removed from the premises, and such quantities of Spanish coin were found to be scattered promiscuously about, that the laborers, some twenty in number, made more by their good fortune than their daily wages for several weeks. How such seed came to be sown there broad-cast, was more than we could understand. It was amusing to see the men sift the earth from their spades into the carts, as if they expected diamonds would appear next.   These little facts seem to show that if gold is a rare commodity in Hayti at the present day, such has not always been the case.

A person who has not lived some time within the Tropics, forms rather an incorrect notion of the climate.   It is not (excepting at midsummer) like the hot summer air of the north, which produces languor and oppression even in the deep shade of the woods ; it is rather like the softest, balmiest days of spring, when vegetation in more northern climes is bursting into life, and every living thing seems to rejoice in the new principle which pervades the air.   Notwithstanding that he came from the leafy groves of Spain, the great Navigator named one of the first spots he visited in Hayti, ' The Vale of Paradise ; ' thereby forcibly expressing his delight with his newly-found world, where seemed indeed to centre the beauties of Eden.   I have a vivid remembrance of the exquisite odors which were wafted from the shores each time I approached them, and which were a continued delight after landing, for several days.   Nothing is more natural than that the air should be perfumed, where the soil produces abundantly the fragrant orange and coffee blossoms, and even when left to nature, still spreads out to the sunny eye of day a rich embroidery of buds and flowers and bloom, whose fragrance, mingling and combining together in the pure laboratory of the surrounding atmosphere, produces that aroma which the French have sought to embody under the title of ' Mille-Fleurs,' but which can be prepared by no mortal hand.

In Cuba these luxuriant domains of Flora have been turned to good account.   Millions of little artisans are employed to extract from their painted receptacles the stores of wax and honey.   Thousands of tapers which burn before the shrines of Catholic saints are furnished by the busy bees of Cuba, and the honey which they produce, to be consumed in less flowery lands, amounts to thousands of barrels annually.   The quantity produced in Hayti, compared to the capacity of the Island for furnishing it, is exceedingly small, as is the case with all other of its products.   It would seem that the very bees indulged too much in the ' *dolcé far niente*,' or mayhap their sagacity teaches them that in a land of perpetual summer there is no necessity for hoarding up that of which there is an unfailing supply, amid the thousand

> ——— ' banks whereon the wild thyme blows,
> Where cow-slips and the nodding violet grows ;
> Quite over-canopied with luscious woodbine,
> With sweet musk-roses and with eglantine.
>   MIDSUMMER NIGHT'S DREAM.

But the delightful odors of the woods and fields are not enough for the Creoles, and essences and pommades form important items in the toilets of every beau and belle of Hayti.   The Parisian manufacturers find here a large market for these and various other ' friandises ; ' and the scent of musk and lavender with which their handkerchiefs and dresses are redolent mingle with the perfumes of the pommades with which the quadroons and the blacks dress their long tresses or crispy locks on church and gala days. On such occasions are to be seen constantly passing men of every hue, wearing dress-coats of black broadcloth of a quality worn only by the rich in more civilized lands, and which in many instances must require weeks of hard labor to pay for. This passion for a coat of the finest French cloth is rather peculiar, pervading as it does all classes; and the principle seems to be, if they cannot get either cash or credit for a *superfine* article, to go without any.

A good coat necessarily implies a good tailor, and this is a trade which flourishes among a people who dress usually in thin garments, and who rarely think after the garment is once on their bodies, of ' a stich in time' to save it from impending rents, which therefore grow apace without let or hinderance. There are good shoe-makers, though this trade finds competitors in the United States. There is some peculiarity in the *understanding* of the blacks which makes them very partial to wearing their shoes ' *en pentoufle.*' Whether this is because the said understandings cover a greater space than common, or whether they have so much heel of their own that they can dispense with any in their shoes, or whether it is the climate, or that peculiar fancy which some people have of being continually ' down at the heel,' I will not undertake to say; especially as the reader is probably sufficiently well acquainted with negro conformation to be able to satisfy his own mind on this important point.

Such however is the fact; and thus when the black citizen buys a pair of shoes, the probability is that he will wear them slip-shod before he has had them twenty-four hours. He thinks it vulgar to go bare-footed; but if he bears about on the extremities of his toes a pair of dilapidated slippers, his dignity is safe: there may be innumerable apertures, cruel rents and gaps, but the sole of his foot must have *something* between itself and the ground. Nothing is more ludicrous than to see men whose occupations require activity, shuffling about in this clumsy manner; carpenters and masons repairing houses, cartmen running after their horses, all slip-shod! Boys go to school slip-shod, women promenade the streets slip-shod, country people bring in their produce and soldiers go to parade, slip-shod; and though they all get over the ground in an unaccountable manner with slippers dangling from the tips of their toes, yet such a slip-shod nation can never, in the American meaning of the term, ' go ahead.' Now this may appear absurd, and yet there is some show of reason in it. In this country such miserable apologies would look as if the owner had been scouring the gutters for them; but there, where all his fellows wear the same, there are none thrown away, and *par consequence* none to pick up. The conclusion therefore is inevitable, that the owner of the ragged slippers was once the owner of a pair of new shoes; and the same feelings which lead you to respect the time-worn vestments of an unfortunate, as evincing the past of better times, lead you also to respect the *pentoufles* of the Haytien negro. He has two powerful reasons why he should shuffle through life in a pair of old shoes. In the first place shoes cost money, and money signifies work. In the second place ' an old shoe' is easy, to a proverb. To be sure, this exposure to the irritations of gravel-stones does not please all tastes;

but '*de gustibus,*' etc.   And now if we have been able to 'point a moral' in this treatise on the slip-shod, we hope it may benefit the reader.   Our countrymen however are not disposed to go slip-shod. They are much more inclined to wear seven-league boots.

The articles which draw oftenest upon the purse-strings of the Creole women are the handkerchiefs for the head.   Of these the most costly is the Madras, which as its name imports is of East-India manufacture, and reaches Hayti usually through the United States, in which latter country it is seldom used, unless occasionally by gentlemen as a cravat.   The figure is a plaid of different sizes and colors, principally bright yellow, green and red, of various shades.   They cost the wearer from three to six dollars each.   The Ventapollam, also from the other side of the Cape of Good Hope, is the next in value, and is the common head-dress of the better class of people, the Madras being reserved for full dress when attending mass, or on other like occasions.   These are both made I believe of the bark of a tree, and are of exceedingly strong and fine fabric.   The variety in the plaids both in size and hue is so great that hardly any two are alike; and the females having each her peculiar mode of wearing them, their costume assumes a character from this article alone.   The manner of wearing is to fold it into a triangle; the doubled edge being placed against the forehead, the ends are carried round the head and tied in a small knot behind or on the side.   The different modes of wearing are given by the shape of the part above the head; for the handkerchief being highly starched, it remains in any position in which it is adjusted. The corners too, which hang down on the back of the neck or over the right or left shoulder, have as many different *airs* as there are wearers, though a man can hardly conceive of the corners of a handkerchief being endowed with so much expression.   Let him recollect how many ways the ladies have of wearing their bonnets and shawls; or is he so unobserving as to think that there is no skill in such matters?

There are of late years imported from England large quantities of handkerchiefs made of our great Southern staple, in imitation of the more expensive India articles; and as the country grows poorer or the people more prudent, they may supersede in a great degree the others. India handkerchiefs are almost the only things which the women preserve with care.   It is very common for them to have several hundreds folded nicely away in their 'armoires,' and to which large stock they make additions constantly; and they must have very little vanity who have not several dozens.   Importers have to watch very narrowly the prevailing taste in the colors and designs.   At one time green was considered outrageous in a Madras, and a year or two after it was all the rage.   Blue is voted vulgar beyond endurance.   The favorite tints are a delicate straw-color mixed with chocolate and crimson.   A house in Philadelphia (now I believe not in existence) had the reputation of getting out the most splendid India handkerchiefs for the Haytien market, they making a business to send favorite patterns to those remote countries, after which they were colored.   The die is perfect, never losing its brilliancy or delicacy as long as the fabric holds together.   The dresses usually worn are English calicoes manufactured expressly for the market. The designs are various. A very common one is a ground of some bright color, as red, yellow, or blue, on which is a sprig or leaf, of goodly size. Many goods are also brought from France and Germany. A very quaint and old-fashioned article for ladies' dresses, and an expensive one, which was in vogue a few years since, has entirely disappeared, more apparently from a falling off in the manufacture than from a change of taste. This is the East-India seersucker, made perhaps of the same material as the handkerchiefs: the figure in all I have seen is a stripe, wide or narrow.

The negroes in the country wear frocks and pantaloons of coarse German or English ' collette,' while the females are dressed in cheap linen or checks. As has been before observed, the great market-days are on Saturday and Sunday. Then the shops are brought out of doors, and every possible temptation in the shape of gaudy calicoes and handkerchiefs is spread before the admiring eyes of the country people. Some of the people are on horseback, some on mules, some drive asses before them laden with produce; others are dragging the same useful little beast by his halter. Here passes a string of beasts each bearing a couple of bags of coffee balancing each other, and then a dozen men and women following in single file with a huge basket of beans or bananas on their heads. The motley procession is through a pageantry of cottons in which are all the colors of the rainbow. Such a spectacle would delight the eyes of Leeds and Manchester. Think of England clothing so many nations of the earth, and who can wonder at the vast amount of her manufactures, or at the thousand shiploads of cotton which we send to furnish them? What did people wear before England built her mills and America raised cotton? Think too and rejoice, ye men of Manchester! that the stitch in time rarely saves nine to these unthrifty mortals; for when the rent begins it runs riot through the length and breadth of the garment.

American fabrics are not used to any extent, the quality of our goods being altogether too good to compete with the ' open-work ' of the British mills. When American goods *are* imported, they are sought with great advidity by the sellers; but they will not pay for them any more than for the English article of the same *name.* The strong sheetings and shirtings of Lowell and Providence cannot compete with those which are manufactured expressly for this and similar markets, which are exceedingly coarse, but are covered with a size which gives them the appearance of nice white paper, and effectually conceals the *net-work* from the unskilled eyes of the rude purchasers. The printed goods, such as handkerchiefs, cottons, and the finer descriptions of ladies' dresses, are made after patterns furnished by the merchants; and the changes of the fashions must be watched very closely, since the caprice of the ladies is as uncertain and rapid in its changes as in Paris itself. At one time, for example, the height of the vogue is a bright ground on which is a leaf, or a French muslin (for high dress) with silver sprigs. Then again the figure must be in stripes or squares.

Bonnets are entirely unknown, unless upon the head of some European lady, and the effect is certainly awkward compared to the easy Madras. Brilliant parasols of yellow and red silk, sometimes richly embroidered, are always used. There has grown of late years a fashion among the fair sex of dispensing with the handkerchief (this is an awkward word for a head-dress, but there is no other for the French 'mouchoir') and of going to church with no other shelter from the sun than the parasol. This is a mode eminently aristocratic; a rule of 'caste;' for the black ladies find it decidedly difficult to follow the example of their lighter-complexioned country-women in dressing the hair. The latter twist their long black massy tresses into any shape which pleases them, while the great anxiety of the others is to get the twist out, and comb it into some semblance of straightness, so that it may be tied in a knot; and thus, proud to be able to follow in the footsteps of the arbitrary Goddess whose sway is equally potent in Paris or in Timbuctoo, they go to church without the adventitious aid of a '*mouchoir de téte.*'

ST. CROIX.

THE FIRE-WORLD.

'While I was musing the fire burned.' — PSALM XXXIX.

I DEARLY love to sit and gaze
  Into the glowing grate,
And fancy that its flickering blaze
  Is not inanimate.

How human-like it strives to soar
  High from its place of birth,
Then falls and seems to know once more
  Its origin of earth!

And in its murmuring I hear
  A city's busy hum,
As distantly and then more near
  Its concourse seems to come.

Full many a sound of joy and wo
  May in that murmur be;
The stream of life may onward flow
  E'en there invisibly.

And in that silvery, crackling sound
  I hear of bells the peal,
E'en there perhaps may hearts be found
  That love like ours may feel.

I fancy there the marriage bell
  And two young hearts united,
And there I hear the funeral knell
  Of hopes forever blighted.

Then wonder not that thus I sit
  And wish not company,
For there within that glowing grate
  I have a world with me.

Cambridge, March, 1842.

J. O. WILLIAMS.

EDWARD ALFORD AND HIS PLAY-FELLOW.

BY THE AUTHOR OF 'WILSON CONWORTH'

CHAPTER FOURTH.

'THE most improper things we commit in the conduct of our lives we are led into by the force of fashion. Instances might be given in which a prevailing custom makes us act against the rules of nature, law and common sense.'
SPECTATOR.

A FEW days after the event recorded in our last chapter, a well-dressed set of men and women had assembled to eat dinner in Pearl-street, where the town house of Mr. Charles Alford was located. The hour was about two o'clock; but let not the late-diner raise his hands and eyes in horror at this announcement. Unless we greatly mistake, two o'clock is still the usual dinner-hour in New-England cities. There was a time when this important crisis happened at one, and even at half-past twelve; such were the simple and natural habits of the people. It has always been very hard work to engraft *very* fashionable habits upon New-Englanders. There is yet too much of the blood of the Puritans circulating in their veins, to allow them to be very pliant pupils in schools of folly and outrages of nature. Even among those who aim to be thought uncommonly fine, there is a measure of reason left. Still it cannot be denied that among the Yankees there is a proneness to imitate the Europeans. Neither will we dispute the fact that some how or other the time when people dine is considered a kind of test of their gentility. But only one ceremony there was at Mr. Alford's, unknown at this day, and not of foreign growth. The gentlemen, previous to sitting down to table, drank the health of their host in a glass of spirits and water; this by way of an appetite. Young Alford took wine with one of his young friends. The conversation, from some mysterious cause, became very animated; hands were shaken with cordiality; smiles were interchanged about nothing. The ladies thought the gentlemen grew silly. The gentlemen thought the ladies grew handsome and they themselves very wise. The viands were eaten, not in moderation; the wine was drunk in no small measure. The ladies withdrew to the drawing-room; the green cloth was removed, and fresh glasses and cigars were placed upon the table.

A very fat old lady, the wife of a sea-captain, was talking to Mrs. Alford as Edward entered the drawing-room, redolent of wine and cigar-smoke:

'Indeed Ma'am, your son is quite a wonder; to be so tall, and you so young-looking! I think he looks like Byron; such a corsair look about him.'

'I think I shall make somebody *cor-* (*heart*) *sair*,' said the youth to his mother, brushing his fingers through his hair.

The old lady did not understand Latin, but concluded that in this wretched attempt at a pun he had said something very fine.

'Edward, my love, this is Mrs. Gross,' said his mother; and thus escaped from flatteries which were becoming nauseous.

'And so you are just out of college, Mr. Alford?' said the lady.

'O yes Ma'am, some time ago; that is, last week.'

'Mr. Gross is going to send our Philip to be educated soon.   Did you have your washing done to home?'

'My *what*, Ma'am?' said Edward, hardly believing his ears.

'Your washing,' said the fat lady, in a louder voice.   'Do n't you look after your clothes?   Why my husband sows on all his own buttons; mends his own stockings, and knows how to do every thing.   He l'arnt how when he went cabin-boy.'

'I fear my education has been much neglected, Madam,' said Edward; 'for I never touched a needle but once, and then I pricked my fingers;' and he left her, quite unceremoniously.

'I declare!' said the fat lady to Mrs. Alford, 'your son do n't know nothing about his things; do tell me what you pay your cook a week?'

'O, the house-keeper attends to that, Mrs. Gross; my health has been so poor that I really have no spirits to attend to the bargains.'

'And do n't you know *your* own business either?' said the lady, as Mrs. Alford left her again.   'I declare Philip sha'n't go to college.'

Now such scenes were not rare, if they are yet, in a state of society where wealth *was* the criterion of respectability, rather than education and refinement.   Mr. Gross had been a sea-faring man; had made good voyages, and at last became a ship-owner and had a large store on India wharf.   He lived in a large house, and kept a carriage.   His wife and daughters dressed richly.   And this will account for the appearance of his wife at Mr. Alford's.   The woman was a good soul, by whose aid and thrift Mr. Gross made his early savings and laid the foundation of his fortune.   They were both from Cape Cod, where all the girls are brought up in habits of industry.   Among people educated like herself, Mrs. Gross would have been happy and respectable; in her present condition she was ridiculous and useless, and possessed too much simplicity and honesty to see the cause of her own predicament.

Miss Delia Gross was urged to take her seat at the piano.   She was one of two sisters present; short, fat girls, with coarse features and large feet and hands, so deeply laden with French capes and flounces as to resemble a small brig under a crowd of sail.

'Edward, my darling,' whispered the mother to the son, 'do be polite to the Misses Gross; your father and I quite expect it; they are very rich people, and I have particular reasons; *do*, that's a dear.'

Miss Delia yielded to the solicitations of Edward, and sang 'Come rest in this Bosom,' in a style that she thought must reach his heart. The fat lady reconsidered her decision about Philip, and said emphatically to herself: 'Yes, he shall go to college.'

The older gentlemen at this point came in from the dining-room, having exhausted all the politics of the country, with much of the stock of imported wines in their host's cellar.   They drank like patriotic citizens, feeling that at the death of every bottle they added so much to the revenue of the country; not considering that for the sake of paying Uncle Sam thirty cents they wasted fifty upon a gross appetite, and in fact impoverished the country to the amount of eighty cents for every bottle. It was upon this principle that the old Federalists wore English hats and broadcloths, and did all they could to encourage the use of English manufactures. They were accused by the Democrats of loving England, of favoring a monarchical form of government. The fact was far otherwise. They only loved themselves better than they did the country. When Federalism was at its height, Boston was the chief importing city of the Union. The merchants made their money in navigation. They opposed the last war because it interrupted their trade. They opposed a tariff when they had no manufactures, always having reference to self. The war in behalf of the rights of impressed American citizens they denounced, because it obliged their ships to be idle or be turned into privateers. The Federalists never loved England. The charge is false. They only loved themselves.

The dinner party broke up about the time a more modern dinner begins. The sleek and fat citizens waddled home, along the orderly streets, at eight o'clock. By ten, the young Misses Gross were fast asleep, Delia dreaming of the handsome graduate; while the youth himself was tossing feverishly on his bed, dreaming of trying to drink soda-water, while the fat lady kept withdrawing the cup and drinking it herself, as fast as it was filled; saying that he should not have any, unless he would tell her what he paid for his washing.

――――

CHAPTER FIFTH.

' And let us linger in this place for an instant, to remark that if ever household affections and loves are graceful things, they are graceful in the poor.'　　　　MASTER HUMPHREY'S CLOCK.

WHEN we left the young black-smith, he was looking after the chaise that conveyed away from him Mary Nailer and her father. If he could have heard the conversation that passed in that vehicle on their way, not so heavy of heart would he have felt. It is unnecessary to tell the reader, we presume, that Thomas Towley had a warm heart in his bosom, and that now that heart beat quickly for the love of his master's daughter. But a certain degree of despondency belongs to love: it is almost an element of its existence. 'The course of true love never did run smooth.' Certain trials are necessary to fix it; to ripen an affection into love. The seed of the vigorous plant, when it is buried in the earth, in its passage to the surface meets with obstacles that demand energy and life to overcome them. It is all the firmer and surer rooted because of them. What is easily gained is carelessly lost. As Heaven intended love as the bond between the sexes, it has appointed a certain course of discipline to it, as it has to the seedling; hence when 'true' it is never 'smooth in its course.'

When the pure heart of a young man first wakes to love (for the impure cannot love) the object seems unattainable from its very excellence. He is modest of his own merits; and not feeling any admiration for his own humble qualities, he cannot imagine himself capable of exciting any in another. That he should be loved as devotedly as he loves, seems an impossibility to him. He desponds and becomes melancholy; raises imaginary difficulties in his own way; grows more and more humble and mistrustful of his claims, till having passed through the necessary stages of this training, when on the brink of despair, he is accepted, and rewarded with an assurance of affection. The fair one herself has noted the whole progress of the matter in his demeanor. With the true instincts of her sex, she has seen, with throbbing interest, the growth of something in his heart that will repay her quicker but more wary passion. Not without reason was it that the knight was obliged to perform deeds of valor before he dared to ask the hand of his lady-love. His capacity, his faith, his constancy were tested, before he could receive the precious gift. He must pass through dangers with fortitude, through reverses with patience; he must be generous as a victor and be undaunted by defeat; to such high qualities alone was successful love the reward. By a different test in these modern days is the youth tried, to gain the heart of the maiden; for no true woman gives away herself merely for the asking.

The highly-educated and refined are apt to think that love, impassioned and romantic love, does not dwell in the hearts of the humble and unlearned. They hear of the marriages of their servants and dependents, of the husbandmen and laborers of the land, as originating in some coarser motive than the same event among themselves. It is not so. If there be any difference, the grosser passion is felt by the luxurious; by those with whom love and flirtation have been a pastime and amusement from their early years; who have become so hackneyed in affairs of the heart, that their feelings have lost much of their original freshness and not a little of their purity. The affections of the poor and laborious are their chief sources of happiness. They cherish in secret, as a hidden treasure, down deep in their hearts, feelings they hardly dare to breathe to themselves. Of the humble village maiden, rather than the daughter of wealth, it may be said, that if unfortunate in her attachment, 'her heart is like some fortress that has been sacked and abandoned and left desolate.'

'Tom is a nice fellow, according to my way of thinking,' said Robert Nailer to his daughter, after a long silence.

'Yes father; that is, you think so.'

'Think so! why yes, did n't I say so?' and Robert turned round and took hold of the bonnet of his child and peered into her face, as if to satisfy himself of some sudden conjecture. Now if Mary had said 'O yes, father,' Robert would have thought nothing more about it, than a mere assent to his remark; but her attempt to hide her opinion of Tom, or rather not to express it, shed more light into the old man's mind than she intended.

'You 've been brought up together, as it were, Mary; I love him like a son, and should n't wonder if you liked him better than a brother.'

'*I*, father? O yes, Sir, I like Tom. He is always kind to every body; all the people like him. All the girls in the village are glad to have him for a gallant home from lecture; but he always used to go with Sarah Brown. I think he liked her best.'

'No he do n't, Mary. Sarah has no father nor brother; she lives a

long way from the village, and Tom used to see her home out of real
kindness.   You know I always look after you myself.'

'Well, father, I guess it was so,' said Mary, with evident satisfaction.

They rode on in silence, each absorbed in their own reflections.   The
country through which they passed was suited to inspire thoughts of
domestic love and happiness.   The suburbs of Boston are one great
garden.   In no part of the world dwell a more orderly, industrious, and
simple-hearted people.   The farms are small and highly cultivated;
every where are marks of that respect for religion and education which
was the rich legacy left them by their fathers.   The evening was calm
and soft; the trees were loaded with fruit, that gave a delicious odor to
the air; the chaise wheels gave forth that easy creak that betokens a
comfortable gait to the beast that drew them; all of which circumstances inspired Robert to think first, and then to speak to his dear child.

'I've been to you, Mary, for many years, both father and mother; for
your other parent was taken from me when you were a little thing.   She
looked, at your age, just like you.   I courted her when I was a 'pren-
tice in her father's shop, and I have always thought I should like you
to marry a mechanic.'

'Indeed, Sir, we've time enough, by and by, to think of that.'

'No we have n't.   You was eighteen the twenty-third day of last
December, early in the morning.   If your mother was alive I should
leave this talk to her, but as it is, I must take it upon myself.'

'No, father, I sha n't marry any body and leave you,' said Mary, seriously; for the sincerity and almost solemnity with which her father
spoke, repressed her girlish diffidence and prepared her to throw off all
disguise.

'I do n't intend you shall leave me, Mary; that's the very thing I'm
aiming at.   All young women do think of marrying, and if they do n't
they ought to.   It is as much their nature to marry as for a man to
labor.   If they do n't think of marrying, there's something wrong about
them.   But you may depend upon it *they do*.   The worst of it is, they
are too apt to want to marry out of their place.   Now I would n't have
you marry one of those gay fellows in the college, for nothing.   I do n't
want a son that's ashamed of his father-in-law.   No, Mary, you must,
to please me, take a companion from your own walk in life, and you
may be just as much of a lady as you please.'

Robert turned to look at his daughter to see the effect of his words,
and Mary's eyes were upon the ground.   The horse was jogging on at
his own pace, and the reins hung dangling at his sides.   Swiftly by a
cross-road came a carriage in which were seated a lady and gentleman.
The driver, thinking to frighten the plain people in the chaise, came
closer to them than he intended and, running against the wheel, upset
Robert and Mary, and cast loose their horse.   Robert received no injury.
Not so his daughter; she was taken up insensible; her head had struck
a stone by the road-side.

The carriage was stopped, and out issued Mr. Edward Alford and his
mother.   He recognized Robert; expressed the sorrow he really felt for
the accident, and severely reprimanded the coachman.   Fortunately

they were but a mile from Robert's house.   Mrs. Alford insisted upon taking Mary home, and she was lifted into the carriage.   Robert gathered up the wreck of his vehicle, and preferred to walk with his horse.

Tenderly did mother and son support the fair girl to her dwelling. When there arrived, Edward ran for a physician, and his mother stayed by her bed-side while she was bled.   No bones were broken, but the doctor said it might have been a great deal worse, without saying what was really the matter, which amounted to a stunning blow, from the effects of which a few hours relieved her, excepting a slight head-ache.

Mrs. Alford was anxious to recompense Robert for the breaking of his chaise, and would have paid him for the carelessness of her coachman ; but Robert said : ' No Ma'am, you need not give yourself concern about it ; it is a trifle I can soon repair with my own hands.   You must not suffer for the fault of your English driver ; and if this accident causes you to give employment to some sober man among your own countrymen, I shall be glad.'

Asking leave of Robert to call on the next day to inquire after his daughter, Edward and his mother took their leave ; the former wondering he had never found out so pretty a girl as Mary, dwelling so near the college.

But we have kept the reader in suspense as to the person of the black-smith's daughter, a pain we must no longer inflict.

Mary was rather short and of a slender figure, with large blue eyes and light hair.   Her nose was aquiline enough to denote energy, and not so much so as to evince love of authority.   Her lips, teeth, and complexion were faultless ; but the crown of her appearance was the modesty and graceful neatness of her attire.   She had obtained her education at the town schools of her native village ; and though Robert was able to send her to a boarding-school, he had sense enough to keep her away from those seminaries of accomplishments, from which young ladies bring home to the plain dwellings of their parents such ultra notions of dress and gentility — seminaries taught by foreign women of elegant manners and unexceptionable morals, but who cannot be supposed to have any deep sympathy with republican principles and habits. Mary had escaped all such training, and was all the simpler and more interesting for it.

Edward called the next day after the accident of the upset, without his mother ; apologized for her absence on the score of ill health, and without affectation showed great interest, in his looks and words.

Robert being absent at his work, Mary had the task of entertaining her visiter alone, in which she so well succeeded that he staid nearly an hour.   This call was followed by another and another, which we may well suppose were not matters of indifference to a young woman of eighteen, who had seen but little of society, and who must have been very insensible not to have admired the polished address of so elegant a young man as Edward Alford.   Beside, his visits were made in no improper spirit.   If we hate those we have injured, we are prone to love whom we benefit ; and we have seen that it was a real occasion that threw Mary in his way.   Being a great admirer of beauty, and being struck with her want of affectation and her open, unsuspecting manner, he came as near to loving her at first sight as could be and escape such a bewilderment. When he compared her with Delia Gross and her sister Sophia, the Misses Armor and the Misses Faddle, all young ladies of fashion in the city, educated out of town at French boarding-schools, and whose subsequent reading consisted of the deaths and marriages in the newspapers, the dry goods advertisements and the latest novels, how infinitely superior she appeared! Here was a piece of fresh nature, there an attempt at art; here form, color, teeth and hair were realities, matters of certainty and sense; there these attributes of humanity were perhaps unreal, matters of uncertainty and painful conjecture. How mortifying, after committing one's self in passing judgment upon a fine form, to find that the credit of it belongs to the lady's dress-maker!

But what surprised Edward more than any thing else was the superior mind and information of Mary. He had been taught to look down with contempt upon mechanics, as unfit society for a gentleman; but here he found a young girl without a mother to control her, presiding over her father's household, and yet finding time to cultivate her mind to such a degree, that he, a graduated gentleman, feared not a little her pertinent questions; for Mary had in common with many others the idea that a graduate from college must know almost every thing — such is the respect of the public mind for what education, especially college education, ought to be. But we must no longer keep the reader in the dark concerning our friend Tom, who while Edward was reaping this rich enjoyment from Mary's society, was winning if not golden yet good iron opinions from all sorts of people.

The young black-smith went to work in earnest and like the man that he was. Early in the morning the sound of his hammer was heard in the village where he newly resided. He took two of his brothers lately arrived from England into the shop with him to learn the trade, and endeavored to do by them much after the fashion his old master had taught him. He retailed out to them Robert's sage counsels, but took care not to give them too much republicanism at a dose, lest they should doubt him; for they had been ground in the English mill, and knew the actual pangs of hunger on the soil of the most boastful nation in the world.

Jane sometimes doubted if her situation was real; with all her children about her, in a cottage of her own, and her son the master of a trade with his name in full upon a sign. John took matters more coolly; smoked his pipe and drank his pint of ale at evening, with the air of a man who deserves prosperity. From the gravity of his manners and a growing habit of reading newspapers, (for he had learned to read for the pleasure of reading Tom's sign,) one might have suspected him of aiming to become a politician, preparatory to getting an office.

And was Mary forgotten in this new station and amid this family happiness, by the young man? By no means. The thought of her gave vigor to his arm. His father and mother, his brothers and sisters were provided for, and in a fair way of earning their bread; and Tom, having thought the matter all over, felt he had a right to work for the prize chance and a kind Providence had placed within his reach. He said nothing about her even to his mother, much less to his brothers; and Jane had too much to think of, in her own children, to trouble him upon the subject; but he thought the more of his master's daughter and loved her the more ardently for loving her in secret; for the tender passion thrives best when concealed, as plants grow fastest in the night, and the tears and sighs of absence nourish it as the dews and warm south winds cherish the young seedling. The weeks flew by swiftly, as they always do to the industrious; and Tom having occasion to purchase some stock, concluded to take Robert Nailer's house in his way to town. He did not make his intention known to any one any farther than that he was going to the city. Arrayed in a plain but handsome dress, the fruit of his own industry, after an absence of two months he approached Cambridge. Never was the sun brighter, the air so pleasant to Tom, though it was late in the fall of the year. The warmth of his feelings, hope, and love made every thing look beautiful to him. The very animals by the road-side looked happy, as if enjoying unusual satisfaction, and the horse he rode pricked up his ears as if intent upon important business.

As he approached nearer to the town, his heart beat quick. The house is in sight; he sees the short, broken column of smoke from the chimney of the forge; and the lover hurries on. When within thirty rods of the house, he saw a chaise drive to the door and a gentleman alight, when a servant drove the vehicle away. There was no mistaking that form. Tom recognized in the young man who entered the person of his play-fellow. He had stopped his horse, and sat like a statue in the middle of the street. The laugh of some students, who mistook him for a countryman who had lost his reckoning, recalled him to himself; and turning his horse's head he dashed off on the road to the city.

CHAPTER SIXTH.

'Be still, sad heart! and cease repining,
Behind the clouds is the sun still shining.'   LONGFELLOW.

THE violent rate at which the jealous lover rode gave him no time for reflection. The sudden pang that shot through his heart to find himself too late in securing the attention of Mary had for a moment deprived the youth of his sober senses. His imagination had supplied a tissue of circumstances the most unfavorable to himself. He would be neglected and spurned and miserable for life; while his more fortunate rival, his superior in address, wealth and beauty, was leading the being his heart doated on to the altar. All this passed through his mind in half the time we have taken to describe it.

Arrived in the city, and bethinking what he was there for, he went directly about transacting his business. He made his purchases, and performed some office for his mother; and this little employment gave steadiness to his feelings and prepared him to take a rational view of his conduct. 'Why should he be vexed that Edward Alford visited Mary? What particular claim had he upon her time? Had he any right to select her associates? Perhaps he had called on business; to pay for some work, or to engage some.' A few such queries and reflections convinced Tom that he had acted like a fool. He was confident none of the family had seen him, and therefore proposed to call on his return, and say nothing of what had happened.

He rode slowly over the bridge, and kept as cool as he well could. Summoning up his courage and hope, he got, in a tolerably calm condition, nearly into the town, when a lady and gentleman passed him in the very chaise he had seen at Robert Nailer's door in the morning; and though he had but a glance at the persons, he concluded they were no other than Edward and Mary. Without pausing to reflect upon a probable mistake or going to Robert's to satisfy himself of the truth of his conjecture, he continued on his way, and stopped not until he reached home, in a frame of mind by no means to be envied.

It requires but little to fan a jealous spark into a flame. Some have contended that a spice of it is necessary to love. It certainly very commonly afflicts lovers. If we are sincere in our admiration of a person, what is more natural than to suppose others feel the same? — and if we see others seek their society, is it not reasonable to suppose they do so with similar motives to ourselves? Many persons are so confident of their own attractions, that their lack of jealousy is more the result of their vanity than their reason. Some are too cold to be jealous; some too blind; but the most have pride enough to conceal it.

The condition of Tom when he got home was as fair a case of jealousy as Shakspere ever noted. He had the regular symptoms; loss of appetite, a frowning countenance, and struck his anvil as if he was slaying a giant. At one moment his heart was dissolved in tenderness, and the next his eye burned with anger. Poor Tom! he was too much a novice to know what was the matter with himself. His imagination got completely the ascendency, and one suspicion only excited another. He even spoke sharply to his mother, and laughed no more at the happy gayety of his brothers and sister. If Tom had been a scholar, he would in those days have taken to reading Byron, who had a ready sympathy with all doubters who had no faith in man or woman; with whom life was a jest; love, the refinement of an animal instinct, and marriage a mere convenience; who embarked in his Grecian expedition for what that nation had been rather than what they were;

> ‘ Who lived in worship of a wild ideal,
> And quite forgot that any thing was real ; ’

such a poet he would probably have read, accompanying his studies with cigars. As he had never heard of Byron and never learned to smoke, he went to work harder than ever, and was glad when night came, and his tired limbs and anxious heart found rest in the sweet sleep that toil only begets.

Tom was a marked man in the Plains by this time. His excellent work and industrious habits were often mentioned by the old men, as they collected together before and after meeting on Sunday, on the steps of the meeting-house, the Yankee farmers' 'change; there his character and habits and prices were canvassed, and it was concluded that he was a fine young man, and ought to be encouraged, especially as he worked as cheap and a great deal better than Robert Simons, who was a candidate for the general court, and had taken to drinking rum by the quart; whereas they and their fathers never exceeded a pint a day. 'Squire Barker had a yoke of oxen that wanted shoeing and two daughters who wanted husbands. During the prayer and sermon of one service he had devised an attack upon Tom, and settled the whole matter in his mind. He would put off his daughter Sally upon Tom; sell him his gray mare, and get the start of all his neighbors; and for all these advantages to himself, for the mare was a kicking jade, and Sally was not much better when she was crossed, he would give him the job of shoeing a yoke of cattle for him.

On Monday morning 'Squire Barker, in his usual farmer's dress, topped off with his Sunday hat, a broad-brimmed, long-napped beaver, which usually hung on a peg in the sitting-room for six days in the week, as much unthought of as the meeting-house or the minister, in that abode, took his way to Mr. Towley's shop. The hat, intended to make amends for the deficiences of his other attire, only made his boots and frock look a thousand times more uncouth and dirty. If he had been going to offer his cattle for sale, that Sunday hat would have said as clear as day-light to a real yankee that he wanted to sell. It made no impression on Tom, any way. 'Good morning, Mr. Towley.' The salutation caused Tom to turn to the speaker, who went on to tell him what he very well knew: 'Fine weather for the fall, Sir; thought I'd give you a lift.'

'Good morning, Sir,' said Tom, going to the door of his shop. 'Glad of the chance; what may it be?'

'Why you see I'm going to draw some wood, and I want my cattles' feet tinkered a little. That off ox is a slippery dog; I'm a feared of the ice, and I think it looks like snow. The nigh one could stand up and draw a load on skates. That ox, Mr. Towley, came from my brindle cow, that my darter Sally has milked night and morning ever since her first calf. She's a whopper I tell you, for milk and calves; I raise all her calves. Sally could n't hardly bring in the pail, she gave such a mess: but then she was little; she's stout enough now, I tell you.'

This was an introduction worthy of the 'cutest lawyer in the country, as the 'Squire thought. At the first fire he had told his errand, praised his ox and cow, and let the young black-smith into the merits of his Sally; for he estimated women by their weight and capacity to work, very much as he did his oxen. 'Shall be glad to shoe your cattle,' said Tom: 'come boys!' and he called his brothers; 'lend us a hand.' But the 'Squire was in no hurry; beside, he could not bear to have a job done with so little talk.

'Fine sermon yesterday, Mister Towley,' he continued; 'I think the morning discourse one of the best we've had from Parson Greaves this many a day.' Much he knew about it, truly!

'Excellent,' said Tom. 'I believe it was upon the government of the thoughts. But I liked the afternoon one quite as well, Mr. —— what may I call your name?'

'O, my name's Barker; people call me 'Squire Barker; but Ephraim is my given-name — Ephraim Barker. The folks thought I was old enough to be a justice, and talked about making me one; but I never set; but since, they *do* call me 'Squire — 'Squire Barker.'

'Well, 'Squire Barker, the afternoon sermon was as good if not better than the morning. Can you tell me the text? Mother and I were talking about it, and could n't recollect it.'

'Really I forget where it was; but I 'll ask Sally. *She 'll* know, I warrant you. What a memory that gal has! Before she was ten, she could say the whole catechism right through without missing a word. But I shall have to lose her some day, good as she is; some of you young sparks will catch her up I suppose, though she is n't spoke for yet.'

This set Tom a-thinking, not about Sally, but his late expedition to Boston. He stood leaning against the door-post, and a tear actually did gather in the corner of his eye and roll down his cheek. He wiped it off with his apron.

'You sweat easy, Mr. Towley,' observed the 'Squire. 'I 'll call for my cattle by and by;' and thinking he had done enough for one assault, he shouldered his whip-stock and departed.

While Tom was engaged in shoeing the cattle, a well-known voice struck his ear, which startled him like a thunder-clap. The speaker was no other than Robert Nailer himself.

'How are you, my boy?' said he, as he grasped the hand of Tom with a pressure that would have broken the bones of a gentleman's soft hand; but here it was Greek to Greek: 'where have you been? — at work, eh? That 's right! I thought I 'd just see how you come on.'

'Thank 'ee, Sir; very well, Sir; how do you do? and how 's ——— ' he would have said Mary, but the word choked him: 'how 's the folks?'

'Pretty well; no they aint neither: Mary's dumpish of late, and I 'm getting old and stiff. Young man,' said Robert turning to one of the brothers, setting a shoe on one of the oxen, 'you are putting that iron on too far for'ard;' and taking hold he put it on himself, as if he was still the master.

Robert was evidently in quite a fever. His task was a new one for him, but he was too honest to leave Tom long in doubt as to the nature of his visit. He took him aside and said:

'You see, Tom, we 've been wanting to see you down at home. Every day we thought you 'd come. You know; no, you do n't know; but we got upset going home from your sign-raising, by that drunken coachman that drives Mrs. Alford about. Young Edward was with his mother at the time. They took Mary home, not much hurt to be sure; but ever since, he 's been often to see my daughter, and is turning her head with novels and fine talk. The young man is well enough, for all I know; but he is 'nt one of our sort of folks, and it 's all fol-de-rol for him to be making love to a plain man's daughter. I see it all through from first to last. Now why have n't you been to see us?'

'Perhaps the visits of Mr. Edward are more agreeable to Mary than you think for, Sir,' said Tom.

'Agreeable! to be sure they are. All the girls like to have beaux; the more the better; it 's their weakness; it 's all the honors they have, poor things! They like compliments as well as a politician likes votes, without being very particular where they come from.'

'Well, Sir, to tell you the truth, I did start to make you a visit;

and —— and I met Mary riding out with a young man I took to be Mr. Edward.'

' It was n't so ; Mary has never been to ride with any body, to my knowledge. Young Alford has acquaintances, near neighbors to us, whom he often rides with.'

' I 've got to go to the city again, soon,' said Tom, ' and you may be sure I shall take Cambridge in my way.'

' Do ; you 'll always find us at home ;' and Robert, having accomplished the object of his visit, took his leave. Tom returned to his shop, light of heart. Again the sparks of wit flew about among the brothers, as the sparks flew from the anvil ; and the young men wondered what could be the reason that five minutes' talk with his old master had so lighted up Tom's countenance.

We must defer the particulars which gave occasion to Robert's visit to another chapter.

THE VISION OF CÆDMAN THE SAXON.

BY S. D. DAKIN.

THE venerable BEDE says that CÆDMAN the Saxon did not dream that he was a sublime poet ; and whenever the circling harp, that ' wood of joy,' as the Saxon glee-men have called it, was offered to his hand, all unskilled, the peasant, stung with shame, would hurry homeward Once in a dream the apparition of a strange man greeted him : ' CÆDMAN, sing some song to me.' The cow-herd modestly urged that he was mute and unmusical. ' Nevertheless thou shalt sing,' retorted the Apparition. ' What shall I sing ?' rejoined the minstrel. ' Sing the origin of things.' The peasant amazed, found his tongue loosened, and listened to his own voice ; a voice that was to reach posterity. D'ISRAELI.

I.

BRIGHTLY to the page of heaven
The stars their words of light had given,
Studied and loved from age to age,
By poet, lover, shepherd, sage,
But never more adored than now,
By Cædman of the mystic brow ;
 The Saxon seer, the spirit-taught,
The child of song, around whose soul
 Glow the effulgent beams of thought,
As northern lights flash round the pole ;
 Wandering with joyous harp and phrenzied eye,
At the sad noon of night, through Druid grove,
 Where moonbeams on stern horrors sweetly lie,
Struggling 'mong frowning rocks with looks of love.

II.

HE leaned against a pillar rude,
In musing melancholy mood ;
And streamed his white and glossy hair,
Like a soft cloud, upon the air ;

And beamed his deep prophetic eye,
Clear as the glowing stars on high,
Both burning with the fires intense
That human destiny dispense ;
And gathering all the mystic lore
In Heaven's blue depths they brightly bore,
He swept the harp-strings to the midnight wind,
While the dim aisles of rocks and woods combined,
Rang with the echoes of his sounding lyre,
And glowed with forms his fancy clothed with fire !

III.

THE triumphs of his race he sings —
Of Saxon blood and Saxon deeds ;
From them what lofty glory springs,
And all of ancient times exceeds ;
How Barons seize with mailéd hand
A charter for their sea-girt land,
And sturdy Commons in their turn
With the same lofty ardor burn,
And grasp with hands could keener feel,
Hardened by labor than by steel,
    The sacred scroll, on which in words of flame,
Nature delights the rights of man to trace ;
    That scroll, which Time assaults with fruitless aim,
And servile Ignorance seeks in vain to efface ;
And shall be ever banner-like unfurled,
The guide, the light, the glory of the world !

IV.

HE sweeps the strings with bolder hand,
And glow his eyes with fiercer joy ;
The Saxons in another land
His burning fancy now employ.
He bends his head with eager gaze
To catch the vision's glorious maze,
While winds among the harp-strings bear
The sleet-storm of his streaming hair.
Sudden the Druid grove expands,
A forest spread o'er boundless lands ;
Then mountains, streams, and a vast chain of seas,
Gleaming with sun-beams, quivering in the breeze,
And, by their borders, temples, cities, rise,
New worlds of splendor to his wondering eyes ;
And man, the lord, from his own glorious race,
Walks these proud regions worthy of his place,
Freed from the bigot's rage, and tyrant's rod,
Controlled by nought but nature and his God ;
With thoughts that from his bosom spring as free,
As from the harp the minstrel's melody !
And lo ! 't is FREEDOM leads him on,
A radiance from the heavenly throne ;
No idol such as Rome adored,
And frantic France in blood restored,
With casque of steel and iron tread,
An icy shape, a shadowy dread,
Reckless of human wo or weal,
Grinding the many with its heel ;

While the mad few it wildly calls,
To bacchanal in gorgeous halls,
And drugs their cups that they may be
Drunk with an insane liberty !
But taught by those harmonious spheres
Whose song in heaven had rapt her ears,
The circling powers she gently sways,
  That orb-like, self-adjusting, move,
Self-governed through their star-like maze,
  By inward principles of love,
Making for man those homes so bright,
That shine on all with equal light ;
And, gathering all in one fraternal band,
  She calls them to the festival of soul,
Where moon-light paths of peace and love expand,
  And Thought surrounds them with its star-lit scroll !

v.

ILLUSTRIOUS seer ! now ravish forth
From yielding strings the loftiest praise ;
A spirit comes of noblest worth,
In form of light before your gaze ;
A man, that holds the lightning of his soul,
Like Jove his thunder, at his own control,
Calm not because the less intense its fires,
But that he wields the reins of its desires ;
Bright is his brow with all the light of love,
Yet stern with lofty aim and firm resolve ;
He grasps the sword at freedom's trumpet-call,
Nor shrinks, though each support around him fall ;
Unfaltering still, though at his bleeding heart
His country's woes hang like a barbed dart :
Trampling the envious, croaking harpies down
Would pluck the proud leaves from his laurel crown,
O'er the sad mounds of prostrate hopes he springs,
To crush the bulwarks of a line of kings,
While prudent Valor is his chariot-guide,
Till Victory mounts triumphant at his side !
      Sure 'tis more than mortal mind,
        That guides the step, the act, the will,
      Where majesty and love combined
        The world with generous wonder fill ;
            His lofty soul
            Spurns the control
Alike of his own passions and the sway
            Of tyrant power
            That dares to lower
O'er all his native land in that sad day ;
            And striking down
            From tyrant's crown
Its proudest gem, he sets it in the skies,
            First in the galaxy
            Of star-bright liberty,
The cynosure for all up-looking eyes ;
And then, his mighty mission done, behold !
How from the loftiest height e'er man attained,
The golden skies his god-like form enfold,   •
Leaving all eyes like thine with sorrow stained,
While pride and grief divide the public heart,
To see the glory of the world depart !

VI.

RAISE your drooping eyes again,
Brush off the tears of dark despair;
Strike yet a bold triumphant strain;
The vision peoples still the air!
See how is spread from pole to pole
The blood that beats in Saxon hearts;
Their surest shield, a lofty soul,
To quench the fatal fiery darts,
From Power's strong quiver madly sent,
Or sterner Fate's, that 's never spent.
Old forests own the master mind,
And fly in ashes on the wind;
Rude mountains, unsubdued before,
Smooth their rough sides and summits hoar,
To speed th' all-conquering victors on
In bloodless triumphs nobly won;
          And the bright flood
          Of Saxon blood
Quickly absorbs and whelms all meaner streams;
          As in that land
          A river grand,
That through a continent in splendor beams,
Draws to its rapid and o'erwhelming tide
The tinkling rills from farthest mountain side,
And rushing streams from valleys broad and deep,
To increase the grandeur of its mighty sweep!

VII.

Sound on the ' wood of joy ' the strings,
Once more, thou seer, whom angels send
To sing the origin of things —
Now boldly sing the glorious end.
Back from the land the vision shows,
A tide of light intensely flows,
And o'er the old world brightly glows,
          Swift surging wide and far,
Mingling with Snowdon's silver light,
And proud Mont Blanc's rose-tinted height,
And flames that rage with fitful might
          In Etna's hellish war;
Kindles on Himmalaya's granite spires,
A far more sacred light than Ghebres' fires;
And on Mount Sinai burns with holy flame,
Bright as when God did there his laws proclaim;
Glancing o'er every sea such beams as threw
O'er waves at Salamis their lustrous hue;
Flashing the evil demons of the earth
In terror back to dens that gave them birth,
Doomed there in dungeons of their native night
To gnaw at their own chains with harmless spite;
While all bright spirits that the earth has known,
And some whose glory never there had shone,
Lured by the lustre of the heavenly sheen,
As clouds speed shining to a sky serene,
Lead forth from valley and from mountain side,
All the glad millions she now counts with pride,
To join the happy sports and pleasing toil,
That ring on every breeze and bless her soil!

New-York, May, 1842.

THE QUOD CORRESPONDENCE.

The Attorney.

CHAPTER XXII.

THE Attorney stood like a statue, as Lucy went out, neither moving nor speaking to interrupt her. He heard her faint steps as she went down the stairs. He even counted them; for his sense of hearing seemed to have gained ten-fold acuteness; but at last she was out of hearing, and he had nothing left but his own thoughts. Still he remained in the same posture of intense attention; but the words which dropped from his lips showed that his mind was running on the one engrossing scheme of his present life.

' Fool! dolt! that I was, to have committed such a short-sighted blunder! Why, the veriest ass that knocks his head against a law-book, and calls himself a lawyer, could not have made a fouler one. To be balked too by a girl; a mere *girl*, like the , she which that old man has left behind him! To see her in possession of all his property! and myself— where? God only knows! And all by my own cursed folly! It will drive me mad!'

The Attorney fairly gnashed his teeth, as he strode up and down the room, after this last out-break of chagrin.

' She would have me grovelling in the very dust; crushed, blasted; a thing for the world to hiss at; my name a by-word for all that is vile and hateful; myself pointed out, as the plotting, scheming, shallow-headed fool, who had not brains enough to outwit a girl in her teens! Pah! it sickens me!'

All violent feelings wear themselves out, and so it was in this case. For a long time Bolton paced that room, scourged by the very demons which his own fears had raised; and then he set to work to see if there was no escape from the evil which threatened him.

The fact which Lucy had communicated, and which had so startled him that in the first moment of wild apprehension he had betrayed his plans, was this: The will was dated on the tenth of August; and of course purported, unless the contrary was shown, to be executed on the same day. But during the whole of that month both Higgs and Wilkins were absent from the city, and consequently could not have witnessed its execution.

' It's too late to alter the date,' muttered Bolton; ' for that is already known. They must swear that it was signed on some other day; and we'll contrive some way to account for the discrepancy between the date and execution. Such a variation, with a plausible reason for it, will not affect the validity of the will.'

He went to a shelf, took down a number of books, turned over the leaves of several of them, and was soon engrossed in deep study. ' I 'm safe on that point,' said he at last, throwing the book which he was reading from him ; but even as he spoke the color fled from his cheek, and his look of satisfaction was succeeded by one of the most sickening fear. He muttered in a whisper so low that he seemed almost afraid to breathe it to himself : ' Can I have told any one that it was executed on the tenth of August ? If so, God help me, or I 'm lost ! '

It was a strange appeal, from such a man, in such a cause. Every conversation which he had ever had respecting that will returned to his memory, as clearly and distinctly as if it had taken place but an hour before. Many had spoken to him about it, for it was noised abroad that the rich Mr. Crawford had disinherited his only child to give his property to a stranger. The world had its say ; and people shrugged their shoulders, and shook their heads ; but the Attorney was a man whom few liked to grapple with ; so they kept their thoughts to themselves.

Every word, every person who had ever alluded to this matter with him, the lawyer heard and saw in his mind as palpably as if each were standing before him, flesh, bone and blood. Some had jested with him ; some had congratulated him ; and not a few had listened to his tale with down-cast eyes, and had left him without a word. He was surprised that every thing presented itself to him so distinctly ; for trifles hitherto unheeded sprang up, like phantoms of the dead from burial-places where they had long lain forgotten.

He had said much which it would have been better for his cause that he should never have uttered ; but he had not thought so at the time ; for he had resolved to show no apprehension on the subject of the will ; and although he never introduced it, he never shrank from it when others did. He remembered too that he had mentioned the fact which he so much dreaded to several ; but he had done it in a casual manner ; and he hoped that it was forgotten by those who had heard it. The only time that he had boldly and unequivocally asserted it was on the night that he produced the will at Miss Crawford's house. None were present then except herself and Lucy. The first could not be a witness — the last *would* not, lest she might blast the character of her husband by doing so. Then he remembered what he had told her respecting Wilkins' intentions toward her ; and a fear crossed him, that this might change her feelings toward her husband into one of hate. If so, and she appeared as a witness, and told what she knew, and what she had that day seen and heard, he felt that his ruin was certain. But that was a risk which could not be avoided. All others could ; and he determined to shut his eyes to his danger, and to apply himself to guard those points which could be defended. It is scarcely necessary to trace his course, or to detail particularly the nature of the conferences which he had with Higgs and Wilkins, in arranging his plans.

Before the day for proving the will arrived, he received a notice that Mr. Fisk had been retained as proctor, on the part of Miss Crawford. Unwilling to trust to himself alone, in a matter where he ran so much risk, he engaged the professional services of Mr. Whitman, a man of eminent legal abilities, and of unimpeachable integrity. There was policy in this; for Bolton, although reckless and unprincipled, knew full well the influence which a fair name has with the world at large, and that the very fact of having such a man as Whitman enlisted on his side would tell strongly in his favor. He fabricated a specious tale of his case, which completely enlisted the legal sympathies of the lawyer, who although he might have regretted that a young girl had been stripped to enrich a man like Bolton, still felt that Bolton had rights which ought to be protected. All that his case admitted of, Bolton had done : and he now awaited the result with a degree of calmness in which there was a strong mixture of desperation.

The day appointed for the trial at last arrived. It was a bright golden morning, and all the world which thronged the streets seemed gay and glad ; far unlike the gaunt spectre-like man who sat in the back office of the crumbling house already so often mentioned. Mental anxiety had done its work on the Attorney. Thin he always was ; but he had become so meagre and lank, that his flesh seemed to have been starved away, until his skin covered only a skeleton. Although there was a daring concentration of purpose in the burning eyes which glared from beneath his black brows, yet on that day at intervals a feeling of terror, the most abject and paralyzing, overwhelmed him, crushing him to the very earth, and sweeping before it every trace of hope and resolution. The next moment came a reäction ; and he sprang up — erect ; his eyes flashing, his brow knit, and undaunted in purpose. After one of these fits of temporary weakness, he walked up and down the room until he was perfectly calm. He stopped and laid his hand on his heart. Its pulsations were slow and regular. He took up a small looking-glass which hung in a corner, and examined his own face in it. It was wasted, and even ghastly. He looked into his eyes, and smiled. ‘ No cowardice *there* at least !’ said he. He was never more collected. He turned over his papers, examined them, ran his eye over some relating to other matters than the will ; paused to correct them; made a few trifling alterations in the punctuation ; and then carefully tied them up and laid them on the table. There was a speck of dust on his coat. He got up, reached a brush and brushed it off. He was surprised at his own composure, for he felt that it certainly was a most momentous day for him. At times his mind wandered off ; but he felt no alarm ; for he was thinking of things far away. There was a glass of water on the table ; and he caught himself shaking it, and watching the wizard circles made by its reflection on the ceiling. He wished that the hour for proving the will would come. He threw himself back in his chair, and drew out his watch. Ten o’clock was the time, and it was now but nine. The minutes lagged heavily until half-past nine, and then Higgs and Wilkins made their appearance. He had already drilled them in their part, so that there was nothing to be done. He conversed with them on indifferent subjects, while he was putting on his hat and coat. He felt uncommonly merry, and jested as they went into the street. The matter-of-fact appearance of every thing there however gradually recalled him to a more natural state of feeling. His apathy wore off; his mind recovered a more healthful though a less comfortable tone ; and it was with burning anxiety that he found himself in the surrogate’s office.

The office of the surrogate consisted of two rooms, with thick massive walls, connected together by a small door. The floor was of stone, scantily covered with straw matting, and strewed with torn papers. On shelves against the wall were rows of heavy volumes, in which were registered the last wishes of thousands who had long since died and were forgotten. Documents of various kinds — bonds, blank letters of administration, old wills, and fragments of paper, were scattered over the desks and tables, at one of which sat an old man in spectacles, with a frizzled wig, copying a ragged will in a large book with a red cover. As they entered, he rubbed his eye with the knuckle of his fore-finger, at the same time opening his mouth to facilitate the operation, and took no farther notice of them than to point with the feather end of his quill to the inner office, in which a number of persons were already collected. In the middle of this room was a round-table covered with green baize, with a small platform behind it, on which stood an arm-chair. In the arm-chair sat Mr. Jagger, the surrogate. He was a short fat man, with a head so void of hair that it looked like the egg of an ostrich, and a beetle-brow, beneath which glowed a pair of red-rimmed, wrathful eyes, that seemed to nourish a grudge against every one, and dead men in particular.

Bolton arrived before the time; yet he had scarcely entered the office, when his proctor made his appearance. He was a tall man, with a dark cadaverous face, and loosely made, as if hung together at the joints with hooks-and-eyes. He had a nervous habit of twitching at his watch-chain when much excited, and of gnawing the end of his quill. He was constitutionally irritable; but had his temper so much under control that at a trial of a cause few would have perceived this failing; although an unlucky witness, during his cross-examinations, would occasionally find the air of a court room to be very oppressive and extremely conducive to profuse perspiration. But with all his irritability, he was a good-hearted man, and rigidly correct in conduct.

He walked quietly across the room, bowed to the surrogate, and taking a seat in one corner, thrust his hand in a pocket of immeasurable depth, and drew out a bundle of papers tied together with red tape. Untying these, he carefully selected one, and commenced reading, taking no farther notice of any one.

As it grew close upon the hour of ten, Bolton became more nervous and restless. He got up, walked to and fro, stopped suddenly, took out his papers, fingered them over, as if looking for a particular one; then laid them down, without having seen one of them, and crossed over to where Mr. Whitman was sitting, whispered a joke in his ear, laughed loud, and turned suddenly away and took a seat. Mr. Whitman looked at him sternly and inquisitively. He liked not the man; but he supposed his cause to be legally a just one, and therefore waived all personal feeling. There was something strange in the manner of Bolton; but he knew that he had much at stake, and attributed his eccentricity to that. After staring at him for a moment or two, he again turned his attention to his papers.

Just then the door opened, and Mr Rawley walked gravely in, and close at his heels stalked Wommut. Both seated themselves, the one on a chair, the other on the floor directly in front of the surrogate. Mr. Jagger looked at the dog with the solemn eye of a surrogate, and shook his head as only a surrogate can shake it.

' Are you one of the witnesses ? ' inquired he of the dog's master.

' I am, Sir,' replied Mr. Rawley. ' I was subpœnaed to testify ; and here 's the document.' As he spoke, he laid upon the table a paper which from having been several days in that gentleman's pocket, had faded from white into a snuff-color, and was particularly crumpled.

' What 's that animal doing here ? ' demanded the surrogate.

' He has 'nt had time to do any thing,' replied Mr. Rawley. ' He comes when I come. He goes when I goes. He 's a peeler.'

' The animal must leave the court. It 's contempt of court to bring him here,' said Mr. Jagger, angrily. ' Remove him instantly.'

Mr. Rawley had frequently been in attendance at the police courts, and once or twice had had a slight taste of the sessions ; so that he was not as much struck with the surrogate as he otherwise would have been ; and he replied :

'I make no opposition, Sir ; and shall not move a finger to perwent it. There 's the animal ; and any officer as pleases may remove him. I say nuffin' ag'in it. I knows what a contempt of court is ; and that aint one.' And Mr. Rawley threw himself amiably back in his chair.

' Mr. Slagg ! ' said the surrogate to the man with a frizzled wig who sat in the outer room ; ' remove the dog.'

Mr. Slagg laid down his pen, took off his spectacles, went up to the dog and told him to get out ; to which Wommut replied by snapping at his fingers, as he attempted to touch him. Mr. Rawley was staring intensely out of the window. The dog looked up at him for instructions ; and receiving none, supposed that snapping at a scrivener's fingers was perfectly correct, and resumed his pleasant expression toward that functionary, occasionally casting a lowering eye at the surrogate, as if deliberating whether to include him in his demonstrations of anger.

' Slagg, have you removed the dog ? ' said Mr. Jagger, who, the dog being under his very nose, saw that he had not.

' No Sir. He resists the court,' replied Mr. Slagg.

' Call Walker to assist you,' said Mr. Jagger, sternly.

Walker, a small man in drabs, had anticipated something of the kind, and had accidentally withdrawn as soon as he saw that there was a prospect of difficulty ; so that the whole court was set at defiance by the dog.

' Witness ! ' said Mr. Jagger.

' Sir ! ' exclaimed a thin man in the corner, who had been subpœnaed, to his own great terror, and who at that particular moment had an idea that he was the only witness in the world, starting to his feet, under the vague impression that he was to be sworn on the spot, and thoroughly convinced that testifying and committing perjury were only different names for the same thing.

' Not you — the man with a dog.'

Mr. Rawley looked the court full in the face.

' Will you oblige the court by removing that animal ? ' said Mr. Jagger, mildly.

'Certingly, Sir,' said Mr. Rawley. 'Wommut, go home.' Wommut rose stiffly and went out, first casting a glance at the man with a wig, for the purpose of being able to identify him on some future occasion : and having comforted himself by a ferocious attack on a small dog belonging to the surrogate, whom he encountered in the entry, was seen from the window walking solemnly up the street.

This matter being disposed of, the court scratched its nose with the end of a pen, and looked impatiently at a clock which hung over the door, as much as to ask how it dared to keep a surrogate waiting. At last he said :

'Mr. Whitman, do you know whether Mr. Fisk ever intends to come ?'

'I presume he does,' replied Mr. Whitman. 'It's not time yet;' and without farther reply he went on reading, while the surrogate looked out of the window.

A slight beckoning motion of Higgs' finger at that moment brought Bolton to his side.

'What's the meaning of that fellow's being here ?' said he, indicating Rawley by a scarcely perceptible jerk of the head, who sat watching Mr. Whitman with a look of profound and mysterious import. 'I do 'nt want him here. It bodes us no good.'

'Who is he ?' inquired the lawyer, nervously.

'Rawley,' replied Higgs, bluntly. '*He knows us.* Till within a week or two we've been at his place daily. He can tell a good deal that I 'd like to have kept close.'

Bolton attempted to smile, but his lip quivered and twitched, and the expression of his face became perfectly ghastly.

'Be a man! will you ?' muttered Higgs, savagely. 'No nonsense now. If you betray *us*, you 'll have to reckon with *me*. Your lawyer's looking at you ; and you say he 's not in the plot. Laugh, man, laugh ! I believe he half suspects something wrong.'

A glance showed Bolton that although Mr. Whitman seemed engaged in perusing the paper which he held in his hand, he was in reality watching him. He muttered a few incoherent words to Higgs, and walked off with a loud laugh. As he did so he met Mr. Fisk, who at that moment entered the office with Mr. Cutbill at his heels, carrying two law-books under his arm and a pen over his ear. Mr. Fisk glanced at Bolton, and passed on without speaking to him ; and so did Mr. Cutbill. Mr. Fisk nodded to the surrogate, who answered it by an inclination of the head ; and Mr. Cutbill, being in doubt whether he might venture on the same familiarity with a surrogate, bowed to the man with a frizzled wig. Mr. Fisk placed his hat on the table, and threw in it a bundle of papers, which he had in his hand, and then nodded to Mr. Rawley. Mr. Cutbill thereupon placed *his* hat on the table ; laid his two law-books by the side of it, and advanced and shook hands with Mr. Rawley sociably ; and finding that Mr. Fisk had seated himself, he immediately followed his example.

'If you are ready, gentlemen, we will proceed,' said Mr. Jagger.

'I am ready, Sir,' said Mr. Fisk, untying his papers and spreading them on the table. Mr. Cutbill forthwith made three pens, tote several sheets of paper in halves, and prepared to take voluminous notes. Mr. Whitman, after a few moments spent in looking over a paper which he held in his hand, rose on the opposite side of the table, and said that he appeared on the part of Reuben Bolton, to ask that the last will and testament of John Crawford, late of this city, deceased, be admitted to probate, and letters testamentary granted to him, as the executor named in it. The proper order, he said, had already been entered, on a petition heretofore made by the executor, who at that time had furnished due proof of the death of the testator. The testator, he continued, had left but one child, a daughter, surviving him; who could properly come neither under the head of heir-at-law, nor next of kin, she being illegitimate. A citation had nevertheless been served on her, notifying her of the time appointed for probate of the will; so that she might appear in court and make any opposition which she thought fit. He understood that it was her intention to resist this application of the executor; but of the position assumed by her in such opposition he was ignorant. He would proceed to prove due service of the summons, and would then produce witnesses to show the execution of the will.

After reading an affidavit, proving the service of the summons, he sat down, and whispered a few moments with Bolton, who was seated at his elbow, and called William Higgs.

It was a moment of intense anxiety to Bolton, when Higgs took his stand. He fixed a keen hawk-eye on him, as the oath was administered to him. But there was nothing to fear; for Higgs was a man whose nerves were of iron; and of the two, the Attorney was the most agitated. Higgs seemed to be of the same opinion; for as his eye wandered around the room, it fell on that of Bolton with a look full of stern warning and menace. It was but a glance; the next instant it was gone. But the Attorney understood it; and leaning his head forward, to hide his face, he pretended to be engaged in reading.

'What's your name?' asked Mr. Jagger, drawing a sheet of paper to him, and dipping his pen in a large stone ink-stand.

'William Higgs,' replied the witness.

The surrogate took it down. 'Gentlemen, proceed.'

Mr. Whitman rose and taking the will, unfolded it and placed it in Higgs' hands. He then walked deliberately back to his seat, put on his spectacles, took up a pen, and prepared to make notes of the answers of the witness.

'In whose hand-writing is the second signature to the attestation-clause of that will, and by whom was it put there?' said he.

'It is mine, and I wrote it,' replied Higgs.

'On what occasion?' asked Mr. Whitman, without raising his eyes from the paper on which he was writing.

'At the time that the will was signed by Mr. Crawford,' replied Higgs, in a firm, clear voice.

'Be good enough to state to the court the manner in which it was executed, and how you came to attest it. Raise your voice.'

Higgs paused a moment, and then stated that he together with Wilkins had gone to the office of Bolton to transact some business of their own. On arriving, they found Mr. Crawford also there with Bolton.

He was reading a paper which he afterward informed them was his will. When he had completed the perusal of it, he was desirous of executing it on the spot, and proposed to Wilkins and himself to become the witnesses to its execution. On their assenting, he declared it to be his last will and testament, subscribed it in their presence, and they witnessed it in his.

'Not so fast,' interrupted Mr. Fisk, who was taking down the testimony as rapidly as his pen could fly over the paper. 'Repeat what you last said.'

Higgs did so.

'Very well; go on.'

'Were you acquainted with Mr. Crawford?' asked Mr. Whitman.

'Very slightly. I had talked with him, and knew him to be Mr. Crawford.'

'Was he present when the will was attested?'

'He was. He held the paper open while we signed it.'

A few questions were asked as to the mental capacity of the testator, and these being satisfactorily answered, Mr. Whitman paused, leaned his head on his hand, and whispered a few words to Bolton; after which he said: 'Mr. Fisk, the witness is yours.'

Mr. Fisk paused to nib a pen, and then with a pleasant smile on his face, and in a quiet, friendly tone, inquired: 'What's your age?'

'About forty.'

'Where do you reside?'

'In this city,' replied Mr. Higgs.

'What's your occupation?'

'I have none at present. I'm a gentleman at large.'

'A pleasant profession,' said Mr. Fisk, in an amiable tone. 'When did you first begin to be a gentleman at large?'

'I have always been one,' returned Higgs, not altogether seeing the dangerous tendency of the questions, while Bolton sat upon thorns, vainly endeavoring to catch his eye.

'I suppose you have property?'

'I'm rather snug at present; more so than I have been. I inherited something lately.'

'From whom?' demanded Mr. Fisk, pausing in his writing, and looking up; though Mr. Cutbill did not for a moment suffer his pen to stop.

'From a deceased uncle,' replied Higgs, beginning to feel a little uneasy at the turn the examination was taking.

'What was his name?'

Higgs hesitated, but it was only for a moment. He caught the eye of Bolton, and saw the half-triumphant smile of Fisk, and his hesitation vanished.

'His name was the same as mine, William Higgs.'

'If your honor please,' said Mr. Whitman, rising, 'I object to these questions, as altogether irrelevant. They have no bearing on the case, and only consume the time of the court and counsel, without profiting any one.'

Down he sat, and up got Mr. Fisk. 'The counsel,' he said, 'was as well aware as he was, of the object of these questions ; and as he had no wish to let the witness see his hand, nor to place him on his guard, he hoped that the court would permit him to continue his examination, without compelling him to state its immediate object.   If in his progress he should ask any question which the laws of evidence prohibited, of course the court would stop him ; but until he did so, he claimed the right to elicit any information from the witness which would benefit his client.

Mr. Whitman replied, and the questions were ruled to be proper. Mr. Fisk then continued his examination.

' When did this relative die ? '

Mr. Higgs, after a slight process of mental arithmetic, calculated the time, and replied : ' A fortnight since.'

' What property did he leave ? ' said Mr. Fisk, with a smile which would have been more agreeable had the question been less embarrassing.

' The amount was not very large,' replied Higgs ; ' a few thousands or so.'

Again Whitman rose and objected, and the court supported the objection, unless Mr. Fisk would state the object of the examination.

Fisk then said that it was his intention to show that the witness was a man of a notoriously infamous character ; that he had led a vagabond life for many years past ; that he had never possessed, nor gained by his own industry, nor inherited property of any description ; and that all his means of support were derived from Bolton ; furnished no doubt on the understanding that he was to lend his assistance in establishing this will.   *That* he said was the object of his questions ; an object which, now that he had been compelled to mention it, he presumed it would be impossible for him to attain ; as the witness being warned would be careful so to frame his replies as to baffle all farther inquiries.'

He sat down, dipped his pen spitefully in the ink-stand, and violently assaulted a corn on Mr. Cutbill's left foot with the heel of his boot.

The surrogate rubbed his chin, and said that he thought the party had a right to draw from the witness any facts which would tend to show what credit might be given to his testimony.   He permitted the question to be put.   Mr. Whitman requested the court to note his exception ; and Mr. Fisk continued his examination by a series of short but pertinent inquiries which, had they been answered as he wished them to be, would have gone far to shake the credibility of Higgs. But that gentleman was now on his guard ; and although the skilful attorney varied his mode of attack and shifted his ground, and from time to time returned and renewed his efforts unexpectedly on various points where he thought the witness was most assailable, he was still completely baffled ; for Higgs' resources increased with his risk ; and he fabricated with a facility and ingenuity truly wonderful.   At length Mr. Fisk turned to him, and looking him steadily in the face, demanded :

' Have you at any time received money from Mr. Bolton ? '

' No ! ' replied Higgs, bluntly.

' Did you ever receive a cheque from him ? '

'No.'

'Are you positive?'

'I am.'

'What is that?' asked Mr. Fisk, extending toward him a paid cheque, the very one which Bolton had given him in his office, and which he had got cashed at the bank. 'Have you ever seen that before?'

'I have,' replied Higgs, with unruffled composure.

'Did you ever get the money for it?'

'I did,' said he, without looking at Bolton, who sat with a blanched face, and the perspiration standing on his forehead. 'I was going to the lower part of the city; Mr. Bolton wanted some money, and asked me as I passed the bank to stop and get the cheque cashed for him. I did so, and handed the money to him.'

A close observer might have observed that Bolton drew a long breath as Higgs gave this plausible reply, like a man suddenly relieved from some great pressure.

Fisk cross-examined him severely; but he drew nothing from him. He then took up the cross-examination as to the will.

'Were you present at the execution of that will?' inquired he.

'I was.'

'Who signed it?'

'Mr. Crawford, the testator.'

'When was it?'

'Some time in the month of September last. I don't recollect the day.'

Mr. Fisk's countenance fell, and Mr. Cutbill looked absolutely miserable.

'Are you sure that it was in September?' asked Fisk, going on with his notes; although it was a moment of intense anxiety.

'I am.'

Fisk rose and took the will from the witness.

'The will is dated August 10th, and purports to be executed on that day,' said he, handing it to the surrogate. 'Here's a strange discrepancy between the date and execution.'

'How do you account for that, Sir?' said Mr. Jagger, looking very profoundly at him.

'I don't pretend to account for it,' replied Higgs. 'All I know is, that I put my signature to that paper at the request of Mr. Crawford, and it must have been in September; for Mr. Wilkins and myself were both absent from the city during the month of August, and did not return until September. It was shortly after our return. I think within a week. I can't swear to the day of the month; but it was from the fifth to the tenth of September. If that will states that we witnessed it in August, it's wrong.'

There was a look of triumph on the face of Bolton when Fisk, after a long and fruitless cross-examination, told the witness that he might go. Mr. Whitman then called George Wilkins.

His testimony was substantially the same as that of Higgs; and he sustained a very severe cross-examination without the slightest flinching. He was blunt and even savage in his manner; but his testimony was direct and clear; and when examined as to the date of the execution of the will, he swore positively that it was on the fifth or sixth of September, he did not recollect which; but he was sure it was one or the other. He was present; knew Mr. Crawford, and saw him sign the paper. It was in Bolton's office. He also swore to the capacity of the testator.

' We have done with the witness,' said Whitman, leaning back in his chair.

Again Fisk tried cross-examining; but at last he threw down his pen, after having exhausted every effort to impair his testimony without success. He felt that the day was against him. His manner was unconstrained; his smile pleasant; but both of the lawyers opposed to him were too well acquainted with his manner not to be satisfied that he was greatly disappointed, as he dismissed the witness.

Probate of the will was then requested; but Mr. Fisk mentioned that it was his intention to introduce witnesses on the part of the heir-at-law, and the surrogate declined giving a decision until they had been heard.

The whole morning had been consumed in the examination of Higgs and Wilkins, and in skirmishes between the lawyers as to points of law and the admissibility of evidence, the detail of which has been in a great measure omitted. As soon as they had got through, Mr. Jagger drew out a large watch, looked at the hour, compared it with the clock over the door, held it to his ear, adjourned the court for two hours, and without the loss of time jumped up, put on his hat, and walked directly out of the office, looking neither to the right nor left, and speaking to no one.

His example was followed by the others, who gradually dropped off, until the man in the frizzled wig, who was quietly slumbering behind his spectacles, with his pen in his hand and a large blot on the page where he had intermitted his labors, was the sole occupant of the office.

CHAPTER XXIII.

THE interval of adjournment was passed by the Attorney and his two confederates in Bolton's office. The long-legged clerk was sent off on some unimportant errand, to get him out of the way; for many matters were to be discussed which the Attorney thought it wise to keep from his ears.

The haggard, unnatural look which during the early part of the day had pinched his face almost out of human semblance was succeeded by one of high excitement; for the trial thus far had gone off well; and he was proportionably sanguine. Higgs seemed to participate in his feelings, and gave vent to a variety of demonstrations of satisfaction which were peculiar to himself; such as throwing his hat with great violence across the room; waving his hands in divers hitherto unheard-of and fantastic manners, and whistling with tremenduous force. But

Wilkins, from the time that he had delivered his testimony, had become moody and sullen, taking no share in the conversation, and scarcely deigning to answer when spoken to.

'We managed it well,' said the Attorney, rubbing his hands together with an appearance of keen satisfaction. 'We shall beat them. Fisk has given up. His looks show it.'

Wilkins raised his eyes from the floor, which he had been contemplating, and said in a gloomy tone: 'You'll gain your end; and to help you do it, I've damned myself, body and soul. I'll never hold up my head again. It is the first time I ever committed perjury.'

Higgs placed his hand on his shoulder, and said: 'Psha! George, don't be a woman. Think of the twenty thousand.'

'I do think of it,' answered the wretched man; 'and I would count down every dollar of it on this very spot, to the man that could make me even the miserable outcast that I was before I crossed the threshold of that office. I sha'n't go there again. The air of that blasted room chokes me; and when I think of the curse that I have drawn down upon myself in that very room, and see those big books on the shelves about its walls, and know that on each leaf of them is written the last wishes of a man who was once living like myself, but has gone to his last account, it makes me shudder. I can't go there again. It's torture. I wo'n't! — I *swear* I wo'n't! I'll keep *that* oath, if I have broken another.'

'Well, George, I did not expect this from you,' said Higgs, taking his hand. 'Why, who used to be the wildest and most daring of our set? Who led us on when there was mischief in the wind? Who always cheered the faint-hearted and encouraged the hot-headed? Who but you? My dear fellow, do n't give up now! All looks fair. Do n't it Bolton?'

'Fairer than we could hope,' replied the lawyer. 'We must win. You are safe; nor is it necessary that you should go to the surrogate's office again. But do n't lose heart.'

Wilkins shook his head. 'I do n't know how it is,' said he, 'but I am as frightened as a child to-day. I feel as if some great evil was hanging over me; and I think that at times I can see its shadow, but I look up, and nothing is there but the blue sky. I know that it's all fancy — a kind of dream; and I try to shake it off; and it leaves me for a time, but it soon comes back. I hope it's no omen of evil. I should like to live to see the twenty thousand. I've done your business,' said he to Bolton abruptly; 'you must do without me now; for to gain the half of this city I would n't go into that room and swear again to what I swore this morning.'

All attempts to change his resolution were fruitless: and the hour to which the court had adjourned being nigh at hand, they left him sitting in the office, and once more directed their steps to the surrogate's office.

When they arrived there, the room was filled with witnesses, and with those whose curiosity had led them thither. Among the last, in a conspicuous position, sat Mr. Quagley, with the stunted marker at his side. Presently the surrogate came in, hung his hat on a peg, and took his seat. In a few moments Mr. Cutbill made his appearance, leading in Mrs. Dow, who after courtesying nervously to every body, and growing very red in the face, sat down and smiled incessantly, as if she wished to impress it upon those present that she considered being subpœnaed as a witness one of the most agreeable things in the world.

Bolton experienced a slight feeling of trepidation as he ran his eye over the array of witnesses; but more particularly when it fell on a man with white hair, who was sitting behind the rest, with his chin resting on his hands, which were crossed over the top of his cane, and watching those about him with deep interest. It was the old witness. Bolton felt that a supporting column of his fabric was knocked away. The proof of the legitimacy of Miss Crawford would throw a shadow of fraud upon the will which it would be difficult to remove. Still it would be suspicion only, and the will might be valid; but would the court so decide? He dared not answer his own question; and he sat down in a dream-like stupor, paying attention to nothing until Mr. Fisk rose to speak.

He stated briefly that he appeared there to contest the instrument offered for probate, and which purported to be the last will and testament of John Crawford deceased, on the part of the HEIR-AT-LAW. As he said this, he turned and looked significantly at Bolton. He said that he would prove beyond a doubt the marriage of Eliza Jones to John Crawford, and the subsequent birth of a daughter, Helen Crawford, who was the party opposing the will. He would also show to the court that the character of the witnesses to that instrument was such that they could not be believed under oath; that they were men whose very means of subsistence were obtained by crime, and to whose testimony no weight whatever could be attached. Declarations of Reuben Bolton as to the time of the execution of that paper would also be offered in evidence; declarations totally at variance with the sworn evidence of the witnesses, who by their own account attested the paper in his office and in his presence. He would also offer in evidence declarations of the testator, made shortly previous to his death, and since the time at which that will was pretended to have been executed, that he had made a will, naming his daughter Helen Crawford therein as his sole devisee; and lastly, he would show that at the very time this pretended will was sworn to have been subscribed by the testator in the office of Bolton, Mr. Crawford was absent from the city; had been so for several weeks, and did not return until two months afterward. He cast a triumphant glance at the Attorney; but Bolton had recovered his composure. Mr. Fisk sat down, and called John Hastings.

This was the old witness. He gave his evidence in a clear straightforward manner. He proved the marriage; gave the name of the clergyman, and of those present at the ceremony, and mentioned the place at which it was performed. The book in which it was registered by the officiating clergyman was also produced, and his hand-writing and the identity of the book were proved beyond a doubt; for the information obtained from this witness had enabled the friends of Miss Crawford to discover the name of the person who had performed the nuptial ceremony, and the proper place at which to search for the record of the marriage.   He also gave a detailed account of his recent visits to the office of the Attorney for the purpose of ascertaining the residence of Mr. Crawford, and of the manner in which Bolton had deceived him from time to time, and of his strange behavior on the night of his last visit to his office.   His manner was so simple yet earnest and truthful that his evidence told terribly against Bolton.   Mr. Whitman cross-examined him, and attacked and harassed him in every possible manner; but the story was still the same.   There was no variation, no contradiction; and at last he was told that he might go.

As he sat down Mr. Whitman turned furiously to Bolton, and asked in a whisper: 'What's the meaning of this, Sir?   It's proved beyond a doubt.   There's no doubt as to her legitimacy.'

'I can't understand it.   It's *false*,' replied Bolton in a faint voice. 'Perhaps there's subornation.   I suspect foul play.'

'*So do I*,' said Mr. Whitman, looking at him with a lowering eye. 'If Fisk makes out his case there will be no doubt of the d — dest villany *somewhere* that ever was perpetrated; and be the perpetrator who he may, he shall pay the penalty, if there's law in the land.   As he said this, he turned savagely away to take down the answers of the next witness, who was no other than the relict of the late Mr. Dow. Mr. Fisk handed her to a chair near the surrogate.

'What's your name?' demanded Mr. Jagger.

'Mrs. Dow — Mrs. Wiolet Dow,' replied the witness.

The surrogate took it down, and then extended the Bible toward her. 'Put your hand on the book.'

Mrs. Dow did so.

'Are you left-handed?' inquired Mr. Jagger, gruffly.

'O! no Sir; my husband was, but *I* ain't.'

'Then put your right hand on the Bible, and listen to the oath. Stand up.   You solemnly swear that the evidence which you shall give in the matter of proving the last will and testament of John Crawford deceased shall be the truth, the whole truth, and nothing but the truth, so help you GOD.'

'Of course it shall be, Mr. Surrogate.   Of course it shall,' said Mrs. Dow, courtesying; 'I always tell the truth.'

'Kiss the book!' interrupted Mr. Jagger, at the same time extending to her a remarkably dirty Bible, which in due form of law had submitted to the embraces of every witness he had had for the last ten years.

Mrs. Dow kissed the book; and after a few preliminary rufflings settled herself down, and looked very earnestly at Mr. Fisk, at the same time pulling her gloves off and putting them on again with rather an unnecessary degree of frequency.

'Where do you reside, Mrs. Dow?'

'In the Bowery, three doors from S —— street, on the north side; a small brick house with a yellow door.'

'No matter for that,' interrupted Mr. Fisk.   'You reside in the city?'

'Oh yes, Sir; I do.'

'What is your age?' inquired Mr. Fisk.

Mrs. Dow reddened, and hesitated.   'My age, Sir?   Is that very material?'

' No. You are past twenty, are you not?' said Mr. Fisk.

' I object to that question as leading,' said Mr. Whitman, a grim smile crossing his face for the first time that day.

' Put it yourself,' replied Mr. Fisk, looking up from his writing.

' I will. Are you past sixty or seventy, Madam?'

' Seventy! gracious me!' exclaimed Mrs. Dow, extremely agitated.

Here the mirth of the stunted marker, who had been watching the trial with great interest, became exceedingly uproarious, and was cut short by Mr. Quagley, who quietly applied his knuckles in a single hard knock upon the top of his head.

Mr. Jagger looked sternly at the stunted marker, and said something about committing him, but altered his mind; he scratched his nose with his little finger, and told Mr. Fisk to proceed.

' You need not answer the question,' said Mr. Fisk. ' It's unimportant, and I withdraw it. Are you acquainted with a man by the name of George Wilkins?'

' O yes, Sir, I think I am — I ought to be.' And Mrs. Dow looked as if she could say a great deal more if it was necessary.

' Then you are acquainted with him?' said Mr. Fisk.

' O! yes Sir, quite acquainted.'

' Did he ever make to you a proposition of marriage?'

Mrs. Dow became overwhelmed with confusion. Mr. Fisk repeated the question; and amid various flourishes of an article which had once been a handkerchief, the lady admitted that he had ' *once;* ' and thereupon she hid her face and her blushes in the article before mentioned.

' Did he ever write to you when he was absent from the city?' demanded the counsel.

Again the handkerchief was flourished in the air, and again the lady buried her face in it, while an affirmative escaped from among its folds.

' What was the nature of those letters?'

' If your Honor please,' interrupted the opposite counsel, gradually unfolding himself until he stood on his feet, ' I object to these questions. It appears to me that the family history of the witness has little to do with the case. Her matrimonial arrangements may be matters of deep interest to herself; but I must confess I do not participate in that feeling; and unless the learned counsel can show some very good reason why the time of the court should be taken up in listening to the amatory adventures of an old woman of seventy, I shall move that all farther detail of the throes and agonies of her susceptible heart be excluded.'

As he sat down, no part of Mrs. Dow's face was visible except a peppery eye, and that gleamed at him over one end of the handkerchief in glances of fire.

Mr. Fisk rose to reply. ' Since the gentleman is so very desirous of knowing what I intend to prove by this witness, I will tell him. The paper which he has produced in court, and which he wishes to establish as a will of real and personal estate, *purports* to have been attested by two persons, George Wilkins and William Higgs. It is my intention, by the testimony of this witness, to show the character of the first of these two men; to prove him what he is, a man void of principle, who would lend himself to any transaction, however foul, provided he found it to his interest to do so. The object of the particular questions to which the learned counsel objected is to prove that this same George Wilkins has made to this lady an offer of marriage; is in the habit of corresponding with her as his affianced wife; and is at this very moment under a solemn pledge of marriage to her, when he has a wife living and residing in this city at this very time.'

Mr. Fisk's remarks were brought to a sudden termination by a loud sound between a hiccough, a laugh, and a scream, emanating from Mrs. Dow. The next moment, after several violent flourishes of her arms and feet, in which latter performance there was rather an unnecessary display of red flannel under-clothes, Mrs. Dow fell flat on the floor, carrying with her a pile of law-books which she had unconsciously grasped in her descent, to the great annoyance of a deaf witness, who was sleeping in the corner, and whose foot formed the receptacle of one of the last-named articles.

Mrs. Dow was not a very bulky specimen of her sex, and the man with a frizzled wig, with the assistance of a far-from-vigorous bystander, had very little difficulty in transferring her from the room to the open air. A slight bustle was created by this occurrence; but in a few minutes it was announced that the lady was reviving; and Mr. Fisk said he would trouble her no farther, as he could prove all that was necessary by other witnesses, whose nerves were less sensitive.

It is scarcely necessary to trace him through the gradual developement of his case. Witness after witness was produced. The character of both Higgs and Wilkins was painted in its true light; vilest even where all were vile, callous, hardened, and reckless. Even Higgs, indifferent as he usually was to the opinion of those about him, slunk into a corner away from the eye of the crowd, and leaned down his head so that none could see his face. Bolton still sat where he had stationed himself at the beginning of the cause; but his face, usually so pale, became flushed. He dared not look at his own lawyer; for he felt that every now and then the piercing eyes of Mr. Whitman were flashing on him in glances of fire, and that while he was laboring to the utmost in his cause, his mind was filled with suspicion.

'A d — d pretty pair of witnesses you had to that will!' said he at last, in a snappish whisper.

'I never vouched for their character,' replied Bolton, with apparent coolness. 'You know how they happened to witness it. A man has all sorts of men among his clients.'

Mr. Whitman turned his back on him; and Mr. Fisk went on with his case. A witness was produced to prove assertions of Bolton that the will had been executed on the tenth of August. On the cross-examination however he became confused, and eventually contradicted all that he had said in his direct examination; and when he got out of Mr. Whitman's hands his testimony amounted to nothing. Still Fisk produced witness after witness; some proving one thing, some another, but all materially strengthening his case. With the exception just mentioned, the case looked unfavorable to the Attorney. Persons of unimpeachable character swore to declarations made by the testator subsequent to the time at which the forged will was sworn to have been executed, that he had left all his property to his daughter. Cross-examination had no effect on their testimony. The facts remained the same; uncontradicted, unshaken. Again Whitman cast a stern inquiring glance at Bolton.

'It may be as they say,' whispered Bolton in reply to the look; 'but I know nothing of it. If there's a later will, let them produce it. Until they *do*, this one is the *last*, and stands.'

Again Whitman turned away, baffled in his suspicions, and again the Attorney felt himself relieved as that stern, searching eye was removed from his face.

There was a great deal of quiet confidence in the manner of Fisk, as he called his last witness. As he did so, he whispered a few words in a pleasant tone in the ear of Mr. Cutbill, who laughed convulsively. The witness had been an upper-servant in the house of Mr. Crawford. He swore that Mr. Crawford went in the country in the month of August, and was absent until late in the month of November following; that he lived with Mr. Crawford at the time, and knew when he left the city and when he returned. All went on smoothly during the direct examination. Fisk grew very confident, the surrogate frowned at Bolton, and Mr. Cutbill laid down his pen, and in the excess of his delight cracked the knuckles of ten fingers at once.

'The witness is yours, Mr. Whitman.'

Before commencing the cross-examination, a long and earnest conversation was carried on in an undertone between Bolton and his proctor, who turned to the witness and asked:

'At what time in the month of August last did Mr. Crawford leave the city?'

'About the fifteenth,' replied the man.

'How long was he absent?'

'Until the end of the month of November following.'

'You are certain?'

The witness answered in the affirmative.

'Did he not at any time return to the city between the fifteenth of August and the end of November?'

'I think not. I'm positive that he did not.'

Mr. Fisk here whispered something to Mr. Cutbill, who laughed in a subdued but violent manner. Mr. Whitman looked up at them; and there was a smile on his face which Fisk did not relish.

'Were you in the habit of carrying letters from Mr. Crawford to Mr. Bolton's office?'

'I was, frequently.'

'Do you recollect on one occasion taking a note containing a large sum of money, which you dropped in the outer entry?'

'I do,' replied the witness.

'Who gave you that letter?'

'Mr. Crawford.'

'Where was he when he gave it to you?'

'At his own house.'

' Did he send any message with the letter ? '

' He told me to tell Mr. Bolton that he would call there himself in an hour, and that he particularly wished him not to go out till he came.'

' Did he state to you the nature of the business which he expected to transact with Mr. Bolton.'

' He did not.'

' Do you recollect that you mentioned to Mr. Bolton what you supposed the nature of that business to be ? '

The witness paused for the moment, and said that he remembered having told Mr. Bolton that he suspected the old gentleman wanted to make his will.

' Why did you suppose so ? '

' Because, while Mr. Crawford was speaking to me and giving me directions to go to Mr. Bolton's office, there was a paper lying folded up on the table near him ; and on it was written in large letters, that it was Mr. Crawford's will ; and before I left the room he put it in his pocket.'

Mr. Whitman got up, handed him the forged will, and showed him the endorsement on it. ' Was that the paper ? ' said he.

The witness examined it carefully, and said that he did not know. It certainly *looked* very like it. It was folded that way, the writing on the back of it was in the same hand, and put on in the same manner. He did not know. He thought it was, but he could not swear to it.

' Now,' said Mr. Whitman, laying down his pen and looking the witness full in the face, ' when was that ? '

The man stood for some time, running the matter over in his mind ; then he grew exceedingly red, hesitated and stammered, and at last said, he recollected that it was the month of September last ; he had forgotten it, when he answered at first ; he had intended to tell the truth — indeed he had.

' Don't be frightened, my good fellow,' said Mr. Whitman, soothingly. ' I have no doubt of it ; and the object of my asking those previous questions was to recall it to your recollection. Now try if you can tell me what was the day of the month ? '

The witness paused, and at last swore positively that it was the sixth. He knew it because his wages had become due on that day, and Mr. Crawford had paid them before going out of town, which he did the same afternoon. He mentioned a number of other reasons for his being certain as to the day. He was positive as to the date. A few more questions were asked ; and Mr. Whitman told him that he was done with him.

It was in vain that Mr. Fisk endeavored to alter his testimony, by renewing his direct examination. The fact, luckily for Bolton, was as the witness had sworn ; and Fisk dismissed the man with the strong conviction that the tide was against him.

' Have you any more witnesses, gentlemen ? ' said the surrogate.

' None ! ' replied Mr. Fisk.

' Have you any more testimony to offer ? ' said he, turning to Mr. Whitman.

Mr. Whitman replied in the negative.

'If you have any remarks to make before submitting this matter to the decision of the court, I will hear them.' Mr. Jagger thrust his thumbs in his waist-coat pockets, and frowned at the opposite wall, by way of showing that he was preparing to listen intently; and Mr. Fisk, after running his eye over his notes, arose. In his speech he contended that the discrepancy between the date of the will and the time when it was proved to have been executed; the notoriously bad character of the attesting witnesses; the ample proof of the legitimacy of Miss Crawford, and the declarations of the testator as to the disposition which he had made of his property; were facts too overwhelming to be withstood, and he proved that the will was a fraudulent one, beyond even the shadow of doubt. He supported his position by powerful and plausible argument. He cited cases; read extracts from some, and called the attention of the surrogate to others, which went to strengthen those previously read. His speech, which lasted more than two hours, was able, vigorous, and exceedingly bitter, sparing neither Bolton nor his confederates.

Mr. Whitman was one of those men who take a long time to get started; and it was not until he had spoken for fifteen or twenty minutes, that his strength began to show itself. He said that the facts relating to the date of the will, which appeared so very mysterious to the opposite counsel, were simply these. The testator had caused his will to be drawn up, had intended to have executed it on the tenth of August, and had inserted the date in his own hand-writing on that day. For some reason, he had neglected to do so; and went from the city, leaving the will incomplete. In the month of September he returned for the purpose of attending to other business; and while in the city, thought of his will, and that it had not been executed. He sent word to the lawyer, as was proved by the testimony of one of their own witnesses, on whom therefore there could rest no suspicion of bias in favor of his client, at the same time taking his will with him. He went to the office of Mr. Bolton and executed the paper. He had no time to spare, as he intended leaving town by the boat which was to start in the afternoon. Higgs and Wilkins, whom he knew from having frequently met them in the lawyer's office, and who also knew him in the same manner, happened to be there at the time; and he requested them to attest the will. They did so. The will was left with Bolton, and in an hour Mr. Crawford was on his way up the Hudson. This he said was the solution of this very profound mystery. To his declarations that he had left a will in favor of his daughter, he had nothing to say. If there was one, on its being produced this will would be a mere dead-letter; but until it *was* produced this will stood. The gentleman made a great argument of his calling his daughter illegitimate in his will, when she was not so; and on that ground declared the present will to be forged. He believed it was not the first time that people had made misrepresentations in their wills when they wished to justify any act which they supposed the world would censure, which wills nevertheless had stood. It might be a ground for attacking the mental capacity of the testator; but it was the first time in the whole course of his experience that he ever had heard that because the testator in making his will had misrepresented a fact, that therefore the will was a forged one.'   The evidence of his opponent was pulled to pieces, while the facts in his own case were presented in the most favorable point of view, and the law bearing on them was applied in the most masterly manner.   Nothing could be more clear, forcible, and apparently conclusive; and when he sat down, although Mr. Jagger looked as earnestly as ever at the opposite wall, and seemed perfectly impervious to speeches of all kinds, the feelings of the less experienced of the audience were with Bolton.

The two counsel then gathered up their papers; and Mr. Jagger said that he would examine the case, and give his decision as soon as possible.   He then adjourned the court.

'What's the meaning of what that last fellow swore to about the will?' said Higgs, as soon as they were clear of the building.   'Was he bought?'

'No; what he said was true,' replied Bolton.   'Crawford did come to my office on that day, and he *did* bring a will; but he never executed it.   He wanted to consult me about it, suggested some alterations, and went out of town, leaving it in my possession until his return.   I have it in my office now.   It was a lucky coincidence with what you and Wilkins swore to.   I had forgotten it.   It flashed across me as soon as Fisk called the fellow; and I happened to have a memorandum in my pocket-book, made by Crawford, and dated by him; so that I was sure of the time before I broke the matter to Whitman, who is as suspicious as the very devil.   He managed the fellow finely.   His summing up was not bad.'

'But those assertions of the old man, that he had made another will?' suggested Higgs.

'I suppose he referred to this one.   He must have forgotten that he did not execute it.   He left every thing to *her* in that one.'

'You'll gain the cause,' said Higgs, quietly.   'When will you be ready to plank up?   You'll not hang fire?   If you *do*, you'll be sorry for it!'

'I'll be ready on the very day,' said Bolton.

'That's enough.'   And Higgs left him, and made the best of his way to one of his old haunts.

STANZAS.

It may be we have loved too much,
    Too fondly for our own repose;
That 't was unwise, dear girl! for such
    As we to pluck love's thorny rose.

But though our hearts oft feel the sting,
    While peace forsakes her calm abode,
As often love a balm doth bring,
    To heal the wounds itself bestowed.   Lees.

LITERARY NOTICES.

THE FAME AND GLORY OF ENGLAND VINDICATED. Being an Answer to 'The Glory and Shame of England.' By LIBERTAS. In one volume. pp. 306. New-York and London: WILEY AND PUTNAM.

WE shall pass — as natural to a writer in defending the mother country from the charges of an unscrupulous assailant — many things in this volume which as Americans we could not approve, that we may at the outset yield the author our hearty thanks for his timely exposure of a *concoctor*, against whose elaborate fabrications we have already twice cautioned our readers. Rev. C. EDWARDS LESTER is here exhibited to the American public as a writer utterly unworthy of credit, and as one of the most inveterate and voluminous plagiarists of which there is any modern record. His antagonist seems to leave him 'without excuse.' He has arranged in parallel columns the originals from which it is contended our reverend plagiarist obtained much of his matériel with the same passages as contained in the work of which he declared himself the author. MEDWYN's 'Conversations of Lord BYRON' and GRANT's 'Great Metropolis' it should seem were especially favored; and several additional portions are signalized as being too well written to have proceeded from Mr. LESTER's pen; to say nothing of their vivid familiarity to the mind of our censor, who is unquestionably a man of parts and of no small research. Taking the evident misrepresentations, the probable 'whids,' the puling sentimentalities, and the alledged plagiarisms into account, we must consider Mr. LESTER, 'by virtue of his office,' as placed in a situation wherein he should take counsel of shame, and retire to some obscure quarter, where he may blush out the remainder of his literary life. We dismiss him, as game not worth the candle. Some illiberality we have at the hands of 'LIBERTAS;' but this, as we have said, we shall pass unnoticed, since the 'moving why' is sufficiently transparent in the purpose of an avenger. On the other hand, our censor puts some pungent and pregnant queries to the affected sympathizer, whose statements, when not altogether fabricated, he declares to be founded upon rare and extreme cases:

"What would be thought of the man who should come over from Britain, land in New-York, and at once proceed to an examination of the worst houses in the Five Points or Anthony-street; and having met some beggars in the street, should set up a cry that there was no injustice and oppression equal to that of the government of the United States; that there was no place so wicked as America, and nothing so good as his own fertile plains of Cheshire or Devonshire. · · · Why do you confine all your sympathy to one class of the community? Why not extend it to others of a higher class, who are suffering from the pressure of the times? Do you think that those who have been more highly educated, and those who have been accustomed to more comforts, feel the pressure of privation less when it visits them? Cast your eyes on that respectable-looking individual who is just closing the doors of his counting-house in Liverpool. See the anguish depicted on his countenance. He has been long a merchant, and by honest industry had realized a respectable competency. He was about to retire from business, and spend the remainder of his days with his attached family in peace and tranquillity, on a small property he had bought in the adjoining county of Chester. Some months ago he had been advised by his banker to purchase foreign bonds to the extent of £40,000, expecting to draw the dividend and to sell off a part of the principal, to pay his remaining obligations, and thus to wind up his business. But alas! the State that issued these Bonds has refused to pay either interest or principal. It is known that his whole fortune is embarked in them, his credit is broken, all his savings must go, and his property must be sold. He retires from business penniless. Follow him home, and witness the distress of his family. If he had lost his all by the ordinary transactions of business, the blow would have been sufficiently heavy; but in this way it is doubly severe."

'LIBERTAS' may well ask Mr. LESTER if he has no sympathy with *this* sufferer — not by a 'proud and haughty English aristocracy,' but only the cotton aristocracy of the 'high and chivalrous South' — and with thousands who are laboring under distress from the same source? We commend 'The Glory and Fame of England Vindicated' to all who have read the discreditable work to which it is a reply. 'LIBERTAS' is not unknown to us. We gave his name to his publisher before reading thirty of his pages. His incognito however is safe with us; and we only allude to it to say that our readers will find that whatever subject he may touch, neither the argument nor the interest will 'come scantly off.'

THE POETS AND POETRY OF AMERICA. With an Historical Introduction. By RUFUS WILLMOT GRISWOLD. In one volume. pp. 468. Philadelphia: CAREY AND HART.

THIS important work, as our readers have been advised, has been several months in press, and high hopes have been formed of its excellence by those who were acquainted with the peculiar qualifications of Mr. GRISWOLD for the very responsible task he had undertaken, and with the zealous and patient care he had devoted to its preparation. We doubt whether there be another man in America so well fitted by his studies and his tastes for precisely such a work as this, as the Rev. RUFUS W. GRISWOLD. The researches of years have made him acquainted with all the literature of our colonial era, and especially with the lives and the writings of our earlier poets; for strange as it may appear to the general reader, we too have our 'poets of the olden time,' whose grotesque yet not wholly contemptible productions can only be found by an antiquarian toil not unlike that which is at once a passion and a profession in the Old World. With the lives and characters of most of our living poets, personal acquaintance has made him familiar; and the materials thus bountifully provided have been subjected to the examination of a fearless critical taste. The book is a monument to his own ability and diligence, and confers abundant honor on the national literature it was designed to illustrate. It is neatly and appropriately dedicated 'to WASHINGTON ALLSTON, the eldest of the living Poets of America, and the most illustrious of her Painters.' After a brief and well-written 'Address to the Reader,' in which the importance of an International Copy-right is not forgotten, the volume opens with an 'Historical Introduction,' in which are traced the earliest efforts of the American Muse in the rhymes of MORRELL, WELDE, MATHER, FOLGER, WIGGLESWORTH, BRADSTREET, and many others, whose names are now almost unknown. It abounds in personal anecdote, and forms one of the most interesting portions of the volume. With regard to the productions of that day Mr. GRISWOLD remarks, aptly and with truth, that 'the bar to progress was that spirit of bigotry, at length broken down by the stronger spirit of freedom, which prevented the cultivation of elegant learning and regarded as the fruits of profane desire the poet's glowing utterance, strong feeling, delicate fancy, and glowing imagination. Our fathers,' he continues, 'were like the laborers of an architect; they planted deep and strong in religious virtue and useful science the foundations of an edifice, not dreaming how great and magnificent it was to become. They did well their part; it was not meet for them to fashion the capitals and adorn the arches of the temple.'

The next and main division of the work comprises biographical sketches of the eighty-six writers deemed worthy a place among American poets — with as copious selections from the choicest and most enduring of their productions as four hundred and thirty-two large octavo pages with double columns and fine type would allow. These are accompanied by critical remarks, characterized by a clear and judicious taste, and above all by a fearless and independent candor. In a few cases nearly all they have written is included in the collection; in others only a small part, but that always the best, is presented. To JOEL BARLOW seven pages are assigned; to PIERPONT eight; to ALLSTON seven; to DANA eleven; to BRYANT twelve; to SPRAGUE seventeen; to PERCIVAL eleven; to WILLIS nine; to BRAINARD seven; to DRAKE eight; to Mrs. SIGOURNEY seven; to LONGFELLOW five; to WHITTIER nineteen; to HOLMES six; to WILLIS GAYLORD CLARK six, etc. This, by far the most responsible part of the work, has been exceedingly well done. We can think of but one or two poems which we should have desired to see here that we do not find; and these we learn were excluded by copy-right. A severer judgment and a taste which paid more close regard to the strict demands of Art might have been less liberal; and for sundry songs and especially sonnets upon which the eye now falls, we are sure we should have sought in vain; for they never can sink into the heart of the nation and abide as permanent portions of American literature. But the instances where this occurs are so rare and so well compensated by the general spirit and excellent taste of the work, that we are by no means disposed to complain. The volume closes with thirty-six pages of selections from sixty-seven other writers, who are not generally known as poets, but who have still written occasional verses well worthy of preservation. Such are EVERETT, J. Q. ADAMS, BETHUNE, WOODWORTH, MORRIS, and many others.

This is by far the most satisfactory and in every way the best collection of American poetry that has ever been made. Previous compilations by BRYANT and others, and even that by Rev. GEORGE B. CHEEVER, by far the best of them all, had no claim to the completeness and value of this by Mr. GRISWOLD. Nor can we omit farther allusion to the just honor it reflects upon American poetry. No critic, however cynical, can turn over its leaves and say that we have no literature. There is no similar collection of English verse that for varied excellence can compare with it. Setting aside, as belonging to eternity rather than time, and as therefore precluding all comparison and all thought of envy, SHAKSPERE, SPENSER, and MILTON, the choicest collection of British gems could scarcely outshine this from the newly-opened mines of the New World's boundless wealth. There are poems here which would honor the names of WORDSWORTH, COWPER, BYRON, or any other English poet; and in all the elements of poetic worth; in power of imagination, in calm philosophic musing, in light, playful fancy, in solemn harmonies, in festal songs and in the strong, high sweep of a free, unfettered spirit; bright as is the splendor of England's stars, they do not rival the light of BRYANT, DANA, DRAKE, LONGFELLOW, and WHITTIER. As Americans then we feel a just pride in the book before us. It will give to those abroad a more just opinion of our merits, and will become incorporated into the permanent undying literature of our age and nation.

It was our intention to have made several selections from the writings of many of our best poets, which are less familiar to the public; and this we shall hope to do hereafter. In the mean-time we are loath to omit the following characteristic lines from 'The Music-Grinders' which with various other extracts that we have not before encountered, is already in type:

'THERE are three ways in which men take
　One's money from his purse,
And very hard it is to tell
　Which of the three is worse:
But all of them are bad enough
　To make a body curse.

'You 're riding out some pleasant day,
　And counting up your gains,
A fellow jumps from out a bush
　And takes your horse's reins;
Another hints some words about
　A bullet in your brains.

'It 's hard to meet such pressing friends,
　In such a lonely spot;
It 's very hard to lose our cash
　But harder to be shot;
And so you take your wallet out,
　Though you would rather not.

'Perhaps you 're going out to dine:
　Some filthy creature begs
You 'll hear about the cannon ball
　That carried off his pegs,
And says it is a dreadful thing
　For men to lose their legs.

'He tells you of his starving wife,
　His children to be fed:
Poor, little, lovely innocents,
　All clamorous for bread;
And so you kindly help to put
　A bachelor to bed.

'You 're sitting on your window-seat
　Beneath a cloudless moon;
You hear a sound that seems to wear
　The semblance of a tune,
As if a broken fife should strive
　To drown a cracked bassoon.

'And nearer, nearer still the tide
　Of music seems to come,
There 's something like a human voice,

And something like a drum;
You sit in speechless agony,
　Until your ear is numb.

'Poor 'Home, sweet Home!' should seem
　A very dismal place:　　　　　　[to be
Your 'Auld acquaintance' all at once,
　Is altered in the face;　　　　[MOORE,
Their discords sting through Brass and
　Like hedge-hogs dressed in lace.

'You think they are crusaders, sent
　From some infernal clime,
To pluck the eyes of Sentiment
　And dock the tail of Rhyme,
To crack the voice of Melody
　And break the legs of Time.

'But hark! the air again is still,
　The music all is ground,
And silence, like a poultice, comes
　To heal the blows of sound;
It cannot be — it is — it is!
　A hat is going round!

'No! pay the dentist when he leaves
　A fracture in your jaw,
And pay the owner of the bear
　That stunned you with his paw,
And buy the lobster that has had
　Your knuckles in his claw:

'But if your are a portly man,
　Put on your fiercest frown,
And talk about a constable
　To turn them out of town;
Then close your sentence with an oath,
　And shut your window down!

'And if you are a slender man,
　Not big enough for that,
Or if you cannot make a speech
　Because you are a flat,
Go very quietly and drop
　A button in the hat!'

THE TWO ADMIRALS. A TALE. By the Author of 'The Pilot,' 'Red Rover,' 'Water-Witch,' etc. In two volumes 12mo. pp. 483. Philadelphia: LEA AND BLANCHARD.

AGAIN we are called upon to make Mr. COOPER welcome to a field, the 'salt sea-field,' in which he has neither living superior nor equal. 'The Two Admirals,' our author tells us, is the first, among all the sea-tales that the last twenty years have produced, in which the evolutions of *fleets* have formed any material feature; every writer of nautical romances having carefully abstained from dealing with the profession on a large scale, himself among the number; partly from a sense of incompetency, but more from a desire, in writing of ships, to write as much as possible under the American flag. We are glad however to find Mr. COOPER rebuking, as Mr. WASHINGTON IRVING has already done in these pages, that maudlin patriotism which holds that works of fiction must be written solely in reference to the country of one's birth; a sentiment unworthy. a nation of confirmed character and enlarged views. Mr. Cooper adds, with playfulness but just satire, that even had he been disposed to write about admirals and fleets, he would have been compelled to desert our flag; for it has never yet waved over a fleet or signalled an admiral. This a hint which we hope will not be lost upon our government, when legislating for the honor and dignity of the American navy. We have not the leisure, nor we may add the inclination, to present a review in detail of 'The Two Admirals;' not because it would not be a pleasant task enough and sufficiently easy withal; since the main scenes are few and distinct, and the love-story simply interwoven; but for the reason that we desire our readers to partake of the enjoyment which we have derived from a perusal of these volumes; not by devouring them piece-meal, with curiosity half sated by partial revealments in 'thrilling' extracts, but by taking up the work and reading it deliberately through to the end; thus insuring a full appreciation of the artistical contrasts of scene and character, and of the power of our gifted countryman to awaken and stimulate the interest of his readers. With these brief remarks, we cordially commend 'The Two Admirals' to all who may have found cause, during years of familiar literary intercourse, to place faith in our critical tastes and opinions.

SKETCHES OF FOREIGN TRAVEL AND LIFE AT SEA. Including a Cruise on board a Man-of-War, as also a Visit to Spain, Portugal, the South of France, Italy, Sicily, Malta, the Ionian Islands, Continental Greece, Liberia, and Brazil; and a Treatise on the Navy of the United States. By Rev. CHARLES ROCKWELL, late of the United States' Navy. In two volumes. pp. 841. Boston: TAPPAN AND DENNET. New-York: D. APPLETON AND COMPANY.

THE above extended title bespeaks at once the prominent characteristics of the volumes before us. We cannot conscientiously affirm that among the various works of a kindred description they supply any very important desideratum; still their details are never altogether without interest, and they are often not only exciting but exceedingly instructive. Familiar with the prevalent languages of Southern Europe, the writer was enabled, during a prolonged stay in ports adjacent to its most interesting sections, by frequent inland excursions to obtain the latest and most accurate information in relation to the matters which he has recorded. He leisurely crossed Spain and Portugal in different directions, resided for a time in the capitals, and visited the most important cities of the two kingdoms. He resorted to almost every possible means of conveyance; became familiar with various classes of society, and learned from original sources the disclosures resulting from the then recent suppression of the convents; 'now travelling with smugglers through wild and unfrequented paths, and now rolling in the stately diligence along the royal high-way; one day roaming through princely palaces, and the next a captive to lawless robbers.' He spent some time also on the western coast of Africa, where he visited the settlements of the colored colonists from the United States, and the villages of the native tribes. He has devoted much labor to the preparation of an account of the natural resources of Central and Western Africa, their trade and commerce, state of the slave-trade, the influence of the colonies on that traffic, etc., etc. In short, cut off from all who spoke his own language, and domesticated among those of other tongues, our author met with many singular incidents, and acquired much interesting and useful information, which the public we think will welcome to their libraries and fire-sides, the number of apparently similar works from native authors to the contrary notwithstanding.

EDITOR'S TABLE.

NATIONAL ACADEMY OF DESIGN. — It is always with pleasure that we notice the annual exhibitions of this institution. It is now some seventeen years since it was first established, and its successful progress is the result of the exertions of the artists themselves, aided by the funds derived from their annual exhibitions. This speaks well for the artists, and as well for the public. We are aware that it is the impression of many that when they see the annual collection of paintings and sculpture, they see *all*; but such, we are happy to inform them, is not the fact; for beside possessing a library containing some of the most rare and costly works on the arts, they have a large and valuable collection of casts and models from antique statuaries; and in addition to their antique school, a *life*-school is established, where subjects are introduced for the study of anatomy and expression. To furnish all these advantages a heavy expenditure has necessarily been incurred, yet not a dollar has been received by way of donation or patronage. The whole has been derived from the proceeds of the annual exhibitions. It will therefore be perceived, that from these exhibitions the academy draws its sole sustenance and support; furnishing to its students instruction without charge, and to the public an intellectual gratification for a very trifling sum. And is the mere intellectual gratification to the public *all?* Who that has watched the growth of taste and the establishment of correct feeling among us for the arts, within the past fifteen years, can fail to perceive how much of it belongs to these annual exhibitions? The public then should continue to rally around these yearly presentations, and by its countenance and support contribute to build up and sustain so meritorious an institution. But our business is more particularly with the exhibition itself. The public have performed their duty very well, and we have no doubt will continue to do it; and we entertain a like belief that the artists will continue to do theirs.

Notices and criticisms of the works of the artists in these exhibitions, when rendered with kindness and discrimination, are of great service to the academy and to the artists; but when conceived in a spirit of fault-finding and written without judgment, the effect is far otherwise. For ourselves, we propose to make a few remarks on several of the paintings which we deem especially worthy of notice, reserving the consideration of others for a future occasion. Fearing that we might at times be wrong in our judgment, we have freely sought the opinions of those whose knowledge and taste in the arts are well known to many of our readers; 'all which is respectfully submitted.' In the present large collection there are unquestionably many inferior works; many that the council would have done well to have left off the walls; but in so doing they would have given offence; by yielding them a place they have allowed the public to judge for itself; and the exhibitors will consequently have the benefit of a verdict. Works of this kind we shall pass by; and many portraits interesting only to their possessors we shall also omit to notice.

We desire to make a passing remark here to visiters who wish to form a correct judgment on the works of the artists; and that is, never decide on the merits or demerits of a picture on a single examination. There is always more or less of novelty in a painting, and the effect of this novelty should be allowed to wear off before a decision is given. A superficial picture will be the first to win the eye, while a work of real but unobtrusive merit may be overlooked. On a subsequent examination, we may discover our mistake, and recur to that very picture with satisfaction and delight.

MR. TALBOT. — Two of the most prominent landscapes, on entering the room, are by this artist, Nos. 54 and 84. They possess considerable merit. No. 54, 'Indian Hunting Ground' is very clever in parts, particularly the *bluff* in the middle-ground and the water beneath it. The latter is transparent and liquid, and does Mr. TALBOT great credit. We should like to see a little more lightness and apparent activity in his clouds, and looseness in his foliage. No. 84, 'View on the Saco River,' is inferior to the other. The great fault in both pictures is a poorly-executed fore-ground. With the exception of the trunk of one or two old trees, the fore-ground is stiff and clumsily drawn. Mr. TALBOT however is comparatively a new beginner, and has arrived at his present excellence by the most untiring industry. With the same continued application, we may predict that he will paint some few years hence far better pictures than either of those we have noticed.

A. B. DURAND. — Mr. DURAND has lately returned from Europe, where he has been spending several months in studying the works of the old masters; and some of the pictures in the present exhibition have been painted since his return. The most attractive is No. 199: 'View in the Valley of Oberhasel.' This is certainly a picture of great merit. The subject is from a sketch made on the spot. The distant mountains covered with their eternal snows, lighted up with the broad glare of the sun, contrasted with the nearer mountains, which are shaded by the dark intervening clouds, is a very happy arrangement of effect; and in color (if we may be allowed to deduct for a too free use of yellow and brown in the fore-ground) it is unequalled. We have rarely seen mountain scenery painted with so much skill; for while we have all the airy indistinctness as a whole, we see each minor part finished in the most careful manner. No. 26, 'View: Castle Blonnai, Lake of Geneva,' is another Swiss view, but under a different aspect. The distance and sky are Claude-like, and the warm mellow tone of the middle ground full of truth and beauty. But a little positive green in the foliage would assist amazingly in giving it force. No. 89, 'Portrait of a Turk,' is another good picture, but to our eye inferior to his No. 22, 'Il Pappagallo,' or 'The Girl and Parrot.' This is a fine picture, and has a tone throughout which we rarely see in modern productions. In examining it, we feel the influence of the artist's study of TITIAN, and must hold it up to our artists as worthy of their study. There are several other pictures by Mr. DURAND in the exhibition, which we should be glad to notice, but our limits forbid.

MR. GRAY has advanced his reputation this year. No. 158, 'Rosalia,' from WASHINGTON ALLSTON's 'Monaldi,' is certainly a clever performance. There is very great expression in the countenance, and the attitude of the figure is extremely graceful. The arrangement of color is also well suited to the subject. The picture is in good keeping with the character. The coloring in No. 148, 'The Artist's

Sister,' by the same artist, differs from the preceding, being light and lively. It is most sweetly and attractively painted. The expression of the countenance is worthy of great praise. In this latter particular we think Mr. GRAY excels many of his young brethren. We are also much pleased with the subdued tone of his pictures — a rare beauty in modern works. Mr. GRAY has talents of a high order, and we are convinced that he has before him a bright career.

MR. AGATE'S picture of 'The Ascension,' No. 107, is a very happy conception, and is managed with much skill. The effect is pleasing. The head of the apostle, on which is thrown the greatest mass of light, is very expressive and exceedingly well drawn. The coloring, with the exception of a too great prevalence of *red*, is in keeping with the rest of the picture. We should like to see Mr. AGATE enlarge this picture to life size; and we hope some of our Catholic churches may be induced to give him a commission for it as an altar-piece. Mr. AGATE has several other works in the exhibition, chiefly portraits.

W. ODDIE has a landscape with which we are much pleased. It has great breadth and clearness; and what is rare for this artist, it is generally well drawn.

V. G. AUDUBON has also a landscape, No. 167, which we like for its great simplicity and truth. He has made it attractive without any labor for effect or powerful color. The fore-ground is perhaps a little monotonous and somewhat tame; but take it all in all, it is just such a picture as we could wish to be more frequently painted from American scenery.

W. S. MOUNT'S 'Scene in a Long-Island Farm-Yard,' No. 184, has much of the humor and point of this artist. No painter has illustrated familiar scenes of a rustic character with more fidelity, at least so far as drawing and expression go, than Mr. MOUNT. Yet we cannot say that we always admire his *execution*. His coloring is too frequently hard and monotonous, and his drapery lacks looseness and ease. To a person standing a few feet from this picture, the porker, the man, the barn-yard, and all else save the sky, has a reddish hue, which is unpleasing to the eye. Mr. MOUNT we think ought to go abroad. He would derive great advantage by studying carefully the Dutch masters. He is wanting in nothing to become a very *great* painter in his peculiar line, but a more thorough acquaintance with the mechanical part of the art. His brush is too apparent in every part of the picture. A study of the best masters would teach him to hide this defect.

MR. CLONNEY. — 'Jonathan's Introduction into Good Society,' No. 140. We are disposed to be angry with this artist. He has painted a picture which conveys a slur upon the arts themselves. We Americans too frequently carry our notions of what *is* and of what is *not* indelicate to a degree of fastidiousness that is ridiculous and absurd. At one time ladies are seen shunning as a pestilence the sight of the 'Venus de Medici;' while at another, churches and Sunday-schools, matrons and maids, are all rushing to see the naked figures of a French barber and chambermaid, because forsooth they are called the 'great moral picture of Adam and Eve.' Mr. CLONNEY's picture has the effect to encourage this vitiated taste and ridiculous affectation. The picture has some good points about it, although it is defective in composition, and the *red* colors too strongly predominate.

MR. INMAN has a most sweet picture in No. 227, 'Mumble the Peg.' It is very carefully and neatly finished, and we think is one of the best he has lately painted. It is good in all things; in effect, in color, and in drawing. The boys evince great earnestness in their play, and we feel inclined to fling ourselves down beside them, to participate in their sport and enjoy the beautiful landscape which surrounds them. Mr. INMAN has also a portrait in his usual excellent style.

Mr. Page. — The style and character of Mr. Page's works were recently elaborately treated in these pages. We forbear therefore to 'repeat ourselves.' It may suffice to say, that the two portraits, Nos. 231 and 242, by this distinguished artist, command general admiration.

Mr. Weir, we believe, has but one picture, No. 62, 'The Counsellor;' but that is a very remarkable one. It is carefully and beautifully painted; and we presume is designed to show us the importance of a single feature to the human countenance. At all events, no one can fail to be struck with its impressiveness; and without removing the cap, we think we know what kind of a face the *nose* belongs to.

Mr. Ingham has several portraits in the collection. No. 165 is the most distinguished. It is astonishing with what care and minuteness this artist finishes up his work. There are scarcely any of the old Dutch masters who excel him in this particular. It is usual with artists and critics to condemn Mr. Ingham's works for being too hard and marble-like; but in our judgment his heads will be as highly prized fifty years hence as those of any of his contemporaries.

S. B. Waugh has two pictures, Nos. 113 and 14. We understand that Mr. Waugh has just returned from Italy, where he has been spending the last five years in the study of his art. Our readers have seen him spoken of by our American correspondents abroad as having obtained considerable reputation in Rome and Naples, particularly among the English residents of these cities. His style is after the English school; very free and effective, but too florid for our taste. We shall look for better things from him hereafter.

F. W. Edmonds has two pictures in this exhibition, No. 130, 'Italian Mendicants,' and No. 214, 'The Bashful Cousin.' Although the 'Bashful Cousin' is the more elaborate work, the 'Italian Mendicants' pleases us most. In this picture we discover that the artist has availed himself of his trip abroad to improve his style. Those who have travelled in Italy have noticed and been annoyed by the swarms of beggars that people that classic land, and have been struck with their apostle-like appearance as exhibited in the works of the old masters; their long beards and sun-burnt countenances. Mr. Edmonds has given us a very faithful pictures of one of these characters, accompanied by his daughter. There is a brightness and clearness in the whole picture perfectly in keeping with the subject; for Italy with all her wretchedness still wears a cheerful aspect, and her mendicants, though begging with a doleful countenance at one moment, are the next dancing with light hearts and lively steps to a mountaineer's pipe. Mr. Edmond's pictures please us for their correct composition, great breadth of light and shade, and judicious arrangement of color. The visiter will notice the entire dissimilarity of style as exhibited in the two paintings. We observe with pleasure the great care Mr. Edmonds bestows on the detail of his pictures.

Regis Gignoux. — No. 209; 'View taken in New Jersey.' We are glad to see foreigners of talent come among us. This artist has but one picture in the exhibition, but this shows a practiced hand. It is somewhat sketchy, but nevertheless well arranged and very effective. The trunk of the tree on the left hand side of the picture is masterly drawn. The water would have appeared to better advantage, if more reflection had been permitted to flicker around it. We perceive that it is for sale. It should not long lack a purchaser.

Mr. Flagg. — 'Judith and Holofernes,' No. 27. Mr. Flagg has had the courage to paint a large picture on canvass eight feet square. We expected therefore something above mediocrity; but there is nothing in this picture to justify that expectation. A scriptural piece of this kind and size should be classic in its design, drawing, and execution generally; but to our eyes every thing about it is modern. Had we not been otherwise informed by the catalogue, we should have taken it to be the portrait of a wife by the bed-side of a sick husband. Mr. FLAGG has we believe been abroad, and must have frequently seen how this same subject has been managed by the old masters. He will understand therefore what we mean when we say his is not a classical picture.

Mr. WHITEHORNE has several portraits in this exhibition. Most of them we have no doubt are very good likenesses, but none of them are distinguished for remarkable coloring, or any great expression of character. Mr. WHITEHORNE, like many other of our portrait painters, has to paint for a livelihood, and has therefore but little time to labor for distinction or renown.

Mr. HUNTINGTON has also a number of portraits and one or two landscapes that please us. His portraits are all good, but no one particularly prominent over the others. We regret to learn that ill health has prevented him from presenting at this exhibition works of a more elaborate character.

T. W. BURNHAM has in No. 21, 'Boys playing Paw,' given us a picture which deserves attention. The characters of the three boys are well expressed; and had the coloring been more pleasing, and the *lights* and *darks* more decided, it would have equalled some of MOUNT's favorite works.

F. FINK is a young artist pursuing his studies abroad. He has sent for the exhibition two pictures, both of them painted in Paris. No. 185, 'Head of an old Man' is very rich in color, and is boldly and vigorously drawn. We look for a great improvement in this artist before his return.

J. JAURE: No. 138; 'Interior of St. Peter's' at Rome. We have here another new name, we presume a foreigner. St. Peters! Master-piece of modern art! the perfection of all that is sublime in architecture; the temple alike of Catholic and Protestant, of saint and savage! Poet, sculptor and painter — all meet to worship here; all have a common right to mingle in their devotions, their admiration, their wonder. This is a most capital picture, very correctly painted; and the labor bestowed upon it is immense. To those who have never stood within the walls of that mighty cathedral, we have only to remark, on competent authority, that it is the most perfect representation that has ever been seen of it, *out* of it. We commend it to the attention and examination of all, but especially to those who may never hope to visit its sacred precincts.

S. A. MOUNT has several pictures. Nos. 61 and 68, 'Fish,' are remarkably well painted. We are pleased to notice the progressive improvement exhibited by this artist.

A. SMITH, JR. has a very good half-length picture styled the 'Epicure,' the still-life of, which is very carefully and accurately painted. The 'Cook' also is well done, particularly the hands and arms; but the old man's head is hard and unnatural. Mr. SMITH would have improved his picture materially had he disposed of his still-life better. As it is, the objects seem confused.

R. HAVELL., No. 3, 'View on the North River,' is a very correct perspective view near Sing Sing. The distance is well preserved, but the fore-ground, particularly the foliage, is somewhat *mannerish*.

T. DOUGHTY. — No. 29, a Landscape, would be a very fine picture if it did not want what this artist's pictures always lack, boldness and strength in the foreground.

The catalogue embraces some three hundred and fifty pictures, beside several works of the chisel. Some of these we shall take another occasion to notice. We recognize the portraits of several of the busts, but are unable at present to speak of their general merits. There is also a large number of miniatures. Those by CUMMINGS and SHUMWAY impressed us favorably; the former by their delicacy, and the latter by their force. Mr. McDOUGALL has also a frame of miniatures that does credit to his talent and improvement.

On the whole, the exhibition is a satisfactory one. We are convinced that the Arts are not declining; but we must frankly confess, that there is not that decided progress and evidence of improvement which we hoped to find on first entering the doors. There are too many portraits and too few landscapes and pieces of an historical character. This to be sure is more the fault of the public than of the artists; but as we have already observed, the taste for these things is forming; the seed is planted, and in good time we doubt not the fruit will ripen and yield an hundred fold.

DRAMATIC DOINGS. — At the PARK THEATRE, opera has been in the ascendant, and the SEGUIN and MANVERS *troupe* have acquitted themselves with their accustomed honor and to the acceptance of unwonted audiences. Miss CUSHMAN's new Theatre is placed as we learn beyond the contingency of failure. A large portion of the stock was speedily subscribed, and the edifice will ere long assume a tangible theatrical aspect. Of Mr. HAMBLIN's new metropolitan establishment the same may be said. This gentleman has brought forward strong claims upon the New-York public for their liberal support; and we have always observed that he never appeals to his friends in vain. We shall have occasion hereafter to allude more at length to these new candidates for public favor.

WARM SEA-BATHING. — We have frequently heard our literary brethren and gentlemen of other sedentary pursuits, complain of occasional lassitude, of depression, etc., and marvel what among all the infallible nostrums of the day would tend most to alleviate the feeling. Gentlemen, *Eureka!* The remedy is in *warm salt-water bathing.* Its immediate efficacy may be easily tested by a visit to the new and beautiful warm baths of Mr. HENRY RABINEAU, at the foot of Desbrosses-street. Diverse 'complainants' have found occasion to thank us for the private information which we now have pleasure in making public.

A NEW BOOK-STORE. — Mr. LOCKWOOD, late of the firm of LOCKWOOD AND SMITH, and formerly very favorably known by his association with the house of Messrs. WILEY AND PUTNAM, has opened a beautiful establishment in John-street near Broadway, where he will have at all times choice supplies of the literary rarities of the English and American markets, including all the varieties of rare stationery, prints, etc. We take pleasure in commending Mr. LOCKWOOD's accessible and well-filled establishment to the patronage of our literary friends and readers, who may have occasion to 'shop' in his vicinity.

A NEW WORK BY 'MARY CLAVERS.' — We understand that a new work in two volumes, from the pen of Mrs. MARY CLAVERS, author of 'A New Home, Who'll Follow?' will be issued from the press of Mr. C. S. FRANCIS on or near the first of June instant. The mere announcement of the fact will insure the ready attention of the public. We shall notice it at large in our next.

GOSSIP WITH READERS AND CORRESPONDENTS. — An allusion to the old black ' Oat-straw Man' in a late 'Gossip' has called out a welcome contributor, who has illustrated some of our New-York cries, and recorded the impression which they first made upon his mind. The subjoined includes a fair specimen of the ' sinking in poetry ' so common to young imaginations : ' Among the multiplicity of cries with which the good people of Gotham are familiar, there are many which are rather pleasing than otherwise to the musical ear. Among these may be noted the clear voice of the charcoal-vender, and of the ' Fine fat porgies, here they go-o!' man in the morning ; the deep, rich bass of the Rockaway clam-merchant in the evening ; and above all others, the low, melancholy drone of the old black, crying ' Fresh o-oat stra-a-w!' under your window at midnight. The latter possesses an exquisitely mournful tone ; made doubly so to me from a notion I once got in my head and could n't get rid of, that he was a man who never went home o' nights. But to the tuned ear, the shrill cry of many of our strawberry-women is almost insupportable. A friend at my elbow tells me, that before making his first visit to New-York, he had formed some very extravagant notions of our strawberry-girls, and painted one so vividly on his mind's eye that he fell desperately in love with the ideal. The following is a copy of the fancy portrait : She might be about seventeen years of age ; neither short nor tall, but just the height ' one likes one,' which by the way, as the world runs, includes the varying heights of nearly all of human kind, for there is no army-standard in love ; complexion nut-brown ; eyes black, lustrous and mellow ; pouting lips, red and tempting as her own berries ; a voice rich and full-throated as the robin's ; bust prominent, and swelling with the strong tide of health and juvenility ; in a word, a form and features that ' gave the world assurance of a' *woman*, ' rich, ripe and real,' and without any of those little drawbacks which the experienced are so well acquainted with. This creature of the brain he had clothed (rather scantily, I must confess) in a petticoat of blue or green, he cared not which, very short both at top and bottom, with here and there a rent made by some envious briar, the accident of the morning ; a round gipsey-hat of the scantest pattern ; and no stockings ; for he had a theory that a white and well-turned ancle — one of God's handiest works — and and — how shall I word it ? — the graceful swell that rises just above it, should never be hidden by garniture of coarse cotton or still coarser woollen. Such was his ideal strawberry-girl. How sadly was he disappointed by the reality ! One morning, soon after his first visit to our city, he sauntered up Broadway, in search of the counterpart to this creature of his brain. It was one of those moist, yellow days of early June, when the dew lies long in the streets, giving a fresher and cooler look to all around, and every thing lovely wears a lovelier hue. The prisoned birds shook their useless wings and sang melodiously at the open windows, as if to them the free air and green fields and leafy trees were things uncared for or unknown. Full of the inspiration of the hour, my friend sauntered on, not doubting but that he should encounter his ideal beloved, for he had long felt that it would be on just such a lovely morning that his destiny would lead him to her presence. He had already passed Bleecker, and was just crossing the head of Amity-street, when a harsh voice broke on his ear. ' Straw-*brees!*' it shrieked, and the sound pierced his head like a knitting-needle, for he was ' fine-eared.' ' Straw-*bre-e-s!*' it repeated, in a still shriller key, with a shake on the last syllable that made the needle wriggle its tail as it passed through his ear a second time. He turned his head and caught one glimpse of his long-sought-for. It was enough, and he passed on. His ideal faded away like a dream ; and he felt like one who in sleep presses lip to ruby lip, and clasps a lovely and yielding form that suddenly changes to some wrinkled beldame, who lifting a long skinny hand, threatens to tear his eyes out for the ' lib'ties he 's a-takin'!' · · · We chanced lately to encounter the following beautiful passage in our note-book, where it stands credited to BULWER : ' It cannot be that earth is man's only abiding-place. It cannot be that our life is a bubble, cast up by the ocean of eternity to float a moment upon its waves, and sink into nothingness. Else why is it that the high and glorious aspirations which leap like angels from the temple of our hearts are forever wandering about unsatisfied? Why is it that the rainbow and the cloud come over us with a beauty that is not of earth, and then pass off and leave us to muse upon their faded loveliness ? Why is it that the stars which hold their festival around the midnight throne are set above the grasp of our limited faculties ; forever mocking us with their unapproachable glory? And finally, why is it that bright forms of human beauty are presented to our view, and then taken from us ; leaving the thousand streams of our affections to flow back in an Alpine torrent upon our hearts? We are born for a higher destiny than that of earth! There is a realm where the rainbow never fades ; where the stars will be spread out before us like islands that slumber on the ocean ; and where the beautiful beings which here pass before us like shadows will stay in our presence for ever.' Now we can only say that if this was written by Mr. BULWER, somebody wrote something very much like it in good blank verse, twenty-five years ago, in BLACKWOOD's Magazine. The theme of the lines was a young girl, radiant with grace and beauty, whom the writer once encountered in a ball-room, and never afterward ceased to remember with rapture:

'. . . . .

'It cannot be that for abiding-place
This earth alone is ours; it cannot be
That for a fleeting span of checkered years,
Of broken sunshine, cloudiness and storm,
We tread this sublunary scene — and die,
Like winds that wail amid a dreary wood,

To silence and to nothingness; like waves
That murmur on the sea-beach and dissolve.
Why then from out the temple of our hearts
Do aspirations spring, that o'erleap
The barriers of our mortal destiny,
And chain us to the very gates of Heaven?
Why does the beauty of a vernal morn,
When Earth, exulting from her wintry tomb,
Breaks forth with early flowers and song of birds,
Strike on our hearts, as ominous, and say,
Surely man's fate is such? At summer eve,
Why do the faery, unsubstantial clouds,
Tricked out in rainbow-garments, glimmer forth,
To mock us with their loveliness, and tell
That earth hath not of these? The tiny stars,
That gem in countless crowds the midnight sky,
Why were they placed so far beyond the grasp
Of sight and comprehension, so beyond
The expansion of our limited faculties,
If one day, like the isles that speck the main,
These worlds shall spread not open to our view?
Why do the mountain-steeps their solitudes
Expand? — or roaring down the dizzy rocks,
The mighty cataracts descend in foam?
Is it to show our insignificance?
To tell us we are nought? And finally,
If born not to behold supernal things,
Why have we glimpses of beatitude —
Have images of majesty and beauty
Presented to our gaze — and taken from us!'

We must not be understood to hint that Mr. BULWER plagiarised from this poem. It is more probable that some other English writer paraphrased the lines for his own purposes, and that the extreme beauty of the language has caused them to be attributed to the eminent novelist. . . . 'The Comet' is too long to flirt its tail in our pages; moreover it is more opaque than its subject. We propose to let this celestial traveller as well as the 'Spots on the Sun' alone. Mr. MAPES' excellent 'Repertory' is the organ for these papers. The 'Man in the Moon' complains of the planet-gazers, and says that the people in his quarter take us earthites 'a deuced deal more easily, and give themselves very little trouble to make out the size and character of our spots.' The first-named communication was disposed of as directed. The other is at the desk of the publication office. . . . The following pathetic and simple lines were written more than eighty years ago, under the title of 'The African's Complaint on board a Slave-ship.' A correspondent sends them to us, with the remark, that 'a recent account of the taking of a slaver full of stolen men has brought them very forcibly to his mind; and that never having seen them in print, he is tempted to send them for insertion in the KNICKERBOCKER:'

'TREMBLING, naked, wounded, sighing,
   On dis winged house I stand,
 Dat with poor black-man is flying
   Far away from his own land.

'Fearful water all around me!
   Strange de sight on every hand,
 Hurry, noise, and shouts confound me,
   When I look for Negro-land.

'Every ting I see affright me,
   Noting I can understand;
 Wilt de scourges white man fight me —
   None of dis in Negro-land.

'Here de white man beat de black man,
   Till he 's sick and cannot stand;
 Sure de black if beat by white man,
   Will not go to white-man land!

'Here in chains poor black man lying,
   But so tick dey on us stand,
 Ah! with heat and smells we 're dying:
   'T was not so in Negro-land!

'Dere we 've room, and air, and freedom,
   Dere our little dwellings stand;
 Families, and rice to feed 'em —
   Oh I weep for Negro-land!

'Joyful dere before de doors
   Play our children hand in hand;
 Fresh de fields, and sweet de flowers,
   Green de hills, in Negro-land.

'Dere I often go when sleeping,
   See my kindred round me stand;
 Hear 'em talk — den wake in weeping,
   Dat I 've lost my Negro-land!

'Dere my black-love arms were round me,
   De whole night — not like dis band!
 Close dey held, but did not wound me;
   Oh I die for Negro-land!

'De bad traders stole and sold me,
   Den was put in iron band:
 When I 'm dead dey cannot hold me —
   Soon I 'll be in black-man land!'

We like to encounter a correspondent who jots down in the postscript of a friendly, familiar epistle such little matters as have afforded himself amusement. The subjoined is a pleasant example: 'A near friend of mine told me a story last evening, which is too good to be kept private. I was patting his little boy's head, and talking playfully of his phrenological developements. This led my friend to remark, that a few months ago — feeling rather discouraged by the many symptoms of perverseness which had manifested themselves rather suddenly in his child's behavior, and partly for the sake of amusing the lad for an afternoon while his mother was suffering from the head-ache — he had taken him to a Phrenologist to have his cranium examined. The boy was told that he was going to see a man who professed to be able to tell *what was in folk's heads* and what sort of a man he would make. It seemed necessary that his curiosity and reverence should be somewhat excited, in order that he might be kept quiet during the operation, for he was usually as restless as a miller. Upon entering the room, and seeing the skulls upon the shelves and table, the little urchin was found to be as subdued and reverential as his father could desire. He took his seat with great solemnity, and gave his head to the man of skill without opposition. His eyes were seen to be fixed with a wondering gaze upon the table, where lay an unfinished bust, a human skull, and a fork in juxtaposition to a large bowl containing some liquid plaster, and a large spoon. All these strange appearances the child put together in his mind, with evident indications of being puzzled to find a reasonable cause for the phenomena. At length, when the Phrenologist paused for an instant and went to the other side of the room to get a small treatise upon his favorite science for the father to read, the little fellow significantly beckoned to the latter to approach, and pointing to the objects which had elicited his curiosity, cautiously whispered: 'Look, father! have n't they been *eating* a man?' · · · Our friend 'P. L.' of Vermont will find '*The Dignity of Labor*' well set forth and illustrated in the domestic tale of 'Edward Alford and his Play-fellow,' now in progress of publication in these pages. The theme is a fruitful one. We have often thought, on seeing of a calm summer morning a knot of clear-headed master-mechanics around a noble edifice arising by their labor and skill, what a contrast they presented as *effective citizens*, to the moustached, be-padded, and altogether artificial exquisites, numbers of *which* may be seen on a sunny day lounging listlessly along Broadway; devoid alike of sense and occupation; doing no service to themselves nor to others; but frittering away an existence, a 'holy human life that GOD gave,' without doing the *slightest* good in their day and generation. How such bipeds appear in the country! — where in the peaceful pursuits of agriculture the farmer sows his seed, or swings his scythe and turns his hay, or gathers in his plentiful harvests! Very much out of place is a fashionable exquisite amid the impressive works of GOD, and among honest men in his image, in the quiet country. Indeed he is out of place *anywhere*. Nature disowns him:

> 'Some say there 's nothing made in vain,
> While others the reverse maintain,
> And prove it, very handy,
> By citing animals like these,
> Musquitoes, bed-bugs, crickets, fleas —
> And worse than all — A DANDY.'

'*My Experience of Old Maids*,' from one who 'at the same time admires and doubts the picture transferred to the KNICKERBOCKER from the good old 'GRANDFATHER's Port-folio,' is at hand. We shall not print it. The writer wrongs the great sisterhood of spinsters. That his 'experiences' are rare, we cannot doubt. He says that *his* beau-ideal of an old maid was well hit off by a recent Yankee lecturer. At sixty, she had n't given up the idea of getting married; and 'when her hair was gray as a rat, and but one dark-yellow tooth stood a solitary sentinel at the falling door-way of her cavernous mouth, she was heard to say, in reply to an inquiry as to her age: 'Well, I 'm getting a little old *now*; but I 've *seen* the time when I was as good as ever I was!' · · · We are sincerely obliged to 'P. D. S.' for his suggestions; and by some of them we shall assuredly profit. We affect no superior 'gift' in our professional labors, and confess ourselves open both to instruction and reproof. We leave to new Magazinists, over-wise in their own conceit, to announce, as LORREQUER expresses it, 'what literary miracles it is their intention to perform; how they shall fill up all the deficiencies observable in other periodicals; how smart will be their witty contributors, how deep their learned ones; what soundness will characterize their general 'views;' by what acumen and impartiality their criticisms will be distinguished; in short, what poor, barren, empty productions other magazines are; and how, by some strange fatality, every clever writer had permitted his wits to lie fallow, until they were to be called forth by the great 'periodical reformer.' We have seen scores of such fine Magazines on paper '*flourish*, fade, and fall,' and go down unwept in 'Time's wallet for oblivion.' · · · *Ethil*'s lines are 'shocking, positively shocking!' We hope we shall be pardoned for 'speaking plain,' since we are four times requested to do so, in the letter accompanying the stanzas. We have a lover for 'ETHIL,' who will take the place of her discarded swain. He is a poet moreover — at least he *is* a rhymer of her own school:

> 'Oh! once I loved another girl,
> Her name it was MARIA;
> But POLLY dear, my love for you
> Is forty-five times higher!'

We fully appreciate the condition and sympathize with the annoyances of the friend who has so feelingly depicted the '*Horrors of May-Day in Gotham*.' He was removed on a feather-bed, and overheard the doctor tell the landlady that he could n't possibly live through it; 'but *I did live through* it,' he writes, ' and through my doctor's bill too — (a man who ' mixed drugs of which he knew little, to pour into a body of which he knew less, to cure a disease of which he knew nothing ') — which was a worse infliction than the fever.' The families who ' live and move, and have their being ' in a continuous turmoil of three or four weeks in May, have a very forcible ante-past of purgatory. Oh ! for the long-domiciled habits of the English people ! Was n't it JOHNSON who said that he never could see a post removed, without a feeling of regret ? Our ' habitativeness ' partakes of this feeling. Residing for years in one mansion, we had come to love it as though it were a living thing. Our sanctum had become sacred. There was a precious past in it. Looking around it at any time, we could recall by its familiar features the forms and voices of the many contributors and friends who have forgathered with us there in pleasant hours ; the good GEOFFREY CRAYON ; the kindly-spirited and refined JOHN WATERS ; our own chief Bard of Nature, and his graceful brother of Cambridge ; the pleasant COUNTRY DOCTOR ; OLLAPOD, now no more ; and the beloved biographer of Mr. PICKWICK and dear little NELL ; these and ' nameless numbers moe,' arose at will, as we sat alone, and pausing now and then from our labors, looked listlessly about the apartment. May our new sanctum become as fruitful in thoughtful and pleasurable reminiscences ! · · · There is a good degree of humor in the sudden contrast of sentiment and language exhibited in the subjoined stanzas, which we take from a tragi-comic poetical tale of a deserted sailor-wife, who with her baby in her arms comes often to a rock that overlooks the main, to catch if possible a glimpse of a returning sail. At length in despair she throws her infant into the sea :

' A gush of tears fell fast and warm,
    As she cried, with dread emotion,
Rest, baby ! rest that fairy form
    Beneath the rush of Ocean ;
'T is calmer than the world's rude storm,
    And kinder — I 've a notion !

· · · · ·

' Now oft the simple country folk
    To this sad spot repair,
When wearied with their weekly yoke
    They steal an hour from care ;
And they that have a pipe to smoke,
    They go and smoke it there.

' When soon a little pearly bark
    Skims o'er the level brine,
Whose sails — when it is not too dark —
    With misty brightness shine ;
(Though they who these strange visions mark
    Have sharper eyes than mine.)

' And beauteous as the morn is seen
    A baby on the prow,
Decked in a robe of silver sheen,
    With corals round his brow —
A style of head-dress not, I ween,
    Much worn by babies now.'

In ' *London Assurance* ' there is a character called ' *Cool*,' and his part is one which might be well filled by Mr. JOHN NEAL ; a victim of the *cacoethes scribendi*, who has contributed more spoiled paper to line trunks and singe fowls than any other writer in the United States. A friend has called our attention to an insinuation in one of his late crazy communications to a city journal, that he had declined heretofore to write for the KNICKERBOCKER, because he was fearful that he should not be sufficiently rewarded for his pains ; as two of our favorite correspondents (whose very last brief communications to these pages brought to the one twenty-five and to the other fifteen dollars) had advised him of old DIEDRICH's defalcation in their case ! Now we desire explicitly to say, in justice to our reputation for a respectable taste, that we never in our lives saw an article from the pen of Mr. JOHN NEAL, in prose or verse, with which we would have encumbered the pages of the KNICKERBOCKER, even had we been *paid* for so doing ; that we never invited him to write a line for our Magazine, nor has his name ever been mentioned or alluded to in any way as one of our contributors. We have been once or twice asked indeed by a friend (and doubtless at Mr. NEAL's own instance) to solicit his contributions ; but sharing the indifference of the public to his be-dashed, inflated, and affected ' tattlements,' or rather *twattlements*, we always very respectfully declined the proposition. · · · It *was* ' a beautiful sight ' to behold the crowds of Sunday-school children in the blossoming Park, on a fine forenoon in May ; countless girls and boys in their beauty and bloom, looking

———— ' as happy as if spring
Lodged in their innocent bosoms, and the spirit
Of the rejoicing morning were their own : '

but the occasion was one, we are sorry to say, to which our right-feeling contributor ' P. C. A.' has not done justice. · · · We have heretofore spoken of the *inherent* idea of might and power which the Chinese celestials entertain of themselves, and which is so amusingly manifested in their special edicts to the ' outside barbarians.' Prof. KIDD, in his late work on China, gives us another curious illustration of their indomitable conceit. The Deluge it seems was cleared away and ' got under ' through the aid of a long-tailed celestial, named YU. The annexed is part of a dialogue between YU and YAOU, taken from ' *The Shoo-king.*' The Emperor says : ' Approach the imperial presence ; you have abundant communications to make.' YU worshipped and said : ' May it please your Majesty, how can I speak ? My thoughts were unweariedly and incessantly employed day by day. The deluge rose high and spread wide as the spacious vault of heaven ; buried the hills and covered the mountains with its waters, into which the common people astonished to stupefaction sank. I travelled on dry land in a chariot, on water in a boat, in many places on a sledge, and climbed the sides of hills by means of spikes in my shoes. I went from mountain to mountain, felling trees, fed the people with raw food, formed a passage for the waters to the sea in every part of the empire, by cutting nine distinct beds, and preparing channels to conduct them to the rivers. The waters having subsided, I taught the people to plough and sow, who, while the devastating effects of the flood continued, were obliged to eat uncooked food. I urged them to barter such things as they could spare for others of which they stood in need!' Now who but a Chinese would ever have preferred such a claim as this upon the credulity of a nation? . . . Owing to a preparation for the 'moving accidents' of May-day, as well as for our advent in a new and beautiful dress, the present number was sent several days earlier to press than is our usual custom. This fact will account for an omission to notice in the present issue many books, pamphlets, and communications, received at a later hour. They will receive attention in our next.

LITERARY RECORD.

'BIOGRAPHICAL STORIES.'— A greater than PETER PARLEY has appeared. Of all the writers for the young, in England or America, commend us to NATHANIEL HAWTHORNE. Here are six biographical stories, all revolving round a pathetic domestic tale of a poor blind boy, which we, hackneyed as we are in the perusal of books of kindred *intention*, could not lay aside till we had read every line, from title-page to colophon. The brief biographies of BENJAMIN WEST, NEWTON, Dr. JOHNSON, CROMWELL, FRANKLIN, and Queen CHRISTINA are imbued with a new interest, and rendered as attractive and exciting as the most adroitly-managed fiction. We make but one extract, and that we take from that part of the sketch of Dr. JOHNSON which represents him as atoning for an unkind refusal in his boyhood to take his father's place at his book-stall, when the old gentleman was ill:

'Well, my children, fifty years had passed away, since young Sam Johnson had shown himself so hard-hearted toward his father. It was now market-day in the village of Uttoxeter.

'In the street of the village, you might see cattle-dealers with cows and oxen for sale, and pig-drovers, with herds of squeaking swine, and farmers with cart-loads of cabbages, turnips, onions, and all other produce of the soil. Now and then a farmer's red-faced wife trotted along on horseback, with butter and cheese in two large panniers. The people of the village with country squires and other visiters from the neighborhood, walked hither and thither, trading, jesting, quarrelling, and making just such a bustle as their fathers and grand-fathers had made half a century before.

'In one part of the street there was a puppet-show, with a ridiculous Merry Andrew, who kept both grown people and children in a roar of laughter. On the opposite side was the old stone church of Uttoxeter, with ivy climbing up its walls, and partly obscuring its gothic windows.

'There was a clock in the gray tower of the ancient church; and the hands on the dial-plate had now almost reached the hour of noon. At this busiest hour of the market, a strange old gentleman was seen making his way among the crowd. He was very tall and bulky, and wore a brown coat and small-clothes, with black worsted stockings and buckled shoes. On his head was a three-cornered hat, beneath which a bushy gray wig thrust itself out, all in disorder. The old gentleman elbowed the people aside, and forced his way through the midst of them, with a singular kind of gait, rolling his body hither and thither, so that he needed twice as much room as any other person there.

' 'Make way, sir!' he would cry out, in a loud harsh voice, when somebody happened to interrupt his progress. 'Sir, you intrude your person into the public thoroughfare!'

' 'What a queer old fellow this is!' muttered the people among themselves, hardly knowing whether to laugh or to be angry.

'But, when they looked into the venerable stranger's face, not the most thoughtless among them dared to offer him the least impertinence. Though his features were scarred and distorted with the scrofula, and though his eyes were dim and bleared, yet there was something of authority and wisdom in his look, which impressed them all with awe. So they stood aside to let him pass; and the old gentleman made his way across the market-place, and paused near the corner of the ivy-mantled church. Just as he reached it, the clock struck twelve.

'On the very spot of ground where the stranger now stood, some aged people remembered that old Michael Johnson had formerly kept his book-stall. The little children, who had once bought picture-books of him, were grand-fathers now.

' 'Yes; here is the very spot!' muttered the old gentleman to himself.

'There this unknown personage took his stand, and removed the three-cornered hat from his head. It was the busiest hour of the day. What with the hum of human voices, the lowing of cattle, the squeaking of pigs, and the laughter caused by the Merry-Andrew, the market-place was in very great confusion. But the stranger seemed not to notice it, any more than if the silence of a desert were around him. He was wrapt in his own thoughts. Sometimes he raised his furrowed brow to heaven, as if in prayer; sometimes he bent his head, as if an insupportable weight of sorrow were upon him. It increased the awfulness of his aspect, that there was a motion of his head, and an almost continual tremor throughout his frame, with singular twitchings and contortions of his features.

'The hot sun blazed upon his unprotected head; but he seemed not to feel its fervor. A dark cloud swept across the sky, and rain-drops pattered into the market-place; but the stranger heeded not the shower. The people began to gaze at the mysterious old gentleman with superstitious fear and wonder. Who could he be? Whence did he come? Wherefore was he standing bare-headed in the market-place? Even the school-boys left the Merry-Andrew, and came to gaze, with wide-open eyes, at this tall, strange-looking old man.

'There was a cattle-drover in the village, who had recently made a journey to the Smithfield market, in London. No sooner had this man thrust his way through the throng, and taken a look at the unknown personage, than he whispered to one of his acquaintances:

' 'I say, neighbor Hutchins, would ye like to know who this old gentleman is?'

' 'Ay, that I would,' replied neighbor Hutchins; 'for a queerer chap I never saw in my life! Somehow, it makes me feel small to look at him. He's more than a common man.'

' 'You may well say so,' answered the cattle-drover. 'Why, that's the famous Doctor Samuel Johnson, who they say is the greatest and learnedest man in England. I saw him in London streets, walking with one Mr. Boswell.'

' 'Yes; the poor boy — the friendless Sam — with whom we began our story, had become the famous Doctor Samuel Johnson! He was universally acknowledged as the wisest man and greatest writer in all England. He had given shape and permanence to his native language, by his Dictionary. Thousands upon thousands of people had read the Idler, his Rambler, and his Rasselas. Noble and wealthy men, and beautiful ladies, deemed it their highest privilege to be his companions. Even the King of Great Britain had sought his acquaintance, and told him what an honor he considered it that such a man had been born in his dominions. He was now at the summit of literary renown.

' But all his fame could not extinguish the bitter remembrance which had tormented him through life. Never, never, had he forgotten his father's sorrowful and upbraiding look. Never — though the old man's troubles had been over so many years — had he forgiven himself for inflicting such a pang upon his heart. And now, in his own old age, he had come hither to do penance, by standing at noon-day in the market-place of Uttoxeter, on the very spot where Michael Johnson had once kept his book-stall.'

This delightful picture is but a fair example of Mr. HAWTHORNE's manner of writing for his little people. We trust the juvenile public will not permit his graphic pen to remain idle for a moment. Messrs. TAPPAN AND DENNET, Boston, are his publishers.

WALKER ON PATHOLOGY: HOMŒOPATHY. — The volumes of Mr. ALEXANDER WALKER upon ' Intermarriage,' ' Woman,' ' Beauty,' etc., have made his name widely and favorably known to the English and American public; and will cause his last production, now before us, to be sought after with avidity. It is from the press of the Messrs. LANGLEY, and is entitled ' Pathology, founded on the natural system of Anatomy and Physiology; a Philosophical Sketch; in which the natural classification of diseases, and the distinction between morbid and curative symptoms, afforded by pain or its absence, are pointed out; as well as the errors of Homœopathy and other hypotheses.' OLIVER WENDELL HOLMES, M. D., of Boston, as good a son of the Muses as he is of GALEN, has also taken up the subject of this latter ' delusion,' as he terms it, and in two lectures before us, deals out to the followers of HAHNEMAN several mixed doses of argument and satire, to be taken, we may suppose, with many wry faces by the parties interested. We purpose to keep our pages free from the farther discussion of the character and claims of the Homœopathic system; still we are bound to say, that within our own circle of acquaintance, we are aware of some most remarkable cures, and among them one or two of confirmed consumption, by the alledged influence of this method of treatment. *Was* it the treatment or was it the effect of the patient's imagination? This latter is Dr. HOLMES' hypothesis.

LIFE OF PETER VAN SCHAACK. — We find on our table from the press of the Messrs. APPLETON a large and well-printed volume, entitled ' The Life of PETER VAN SCHAACK, LL. D.; embracing selections from his Correspondence and other Writings, during the American Revolution, and his exile in England. By his son, HENRY C. VAN SCHAACK.' This is a biography of an eminent American, of elevated character, of high integrity, and of honorable association, who in sentiment was opposed to taking up arms in the American Revolution. We had the pleasure to peruse the work in manuscript, and to present some extracts from it in these pages. Much of the matériel of the volume, being at once autobiographical and historical, will be found to possess intrinsic value. We could wish that the compiler had omitted some of the mere journalizing passages, since subsequent works have made their brief records so familiar to American readers, that they must needs now seem somewhat hacknied. The letters, however, of Mr. VAN SCHAACK, and the light which they thrown upon the events of a distant and fruitful era, will be found to well repay perusal and preservation.

' GUNDERODE.' — There are several passages in the letters of BETTINE and GUNDERODE, two young spiritual German girls, which would justify the trouble of translating into English, but nothing which deserves to elicit the extravagant praise awarded to the writers in the preface to the little volume of their correspondence, for a copy of which we are indebted to the publisher, Miss E. P. PEABODY, of Boston. We were struck with a beautiful picture of the character of our Saviour, drawn by a Franciscan priest, and quoted in an epistle of GUNDERODE's; and pleased with another drawn by BETTINE, of a cavalier who entered a ball-room in a round-about-jacket, which he had put on in the dark. Some lady-friends observed his mistake, and manœuvred to have him retire before ' showing the full front of his back ' to the company; but not understanding their whispers, he turns to be enlightened, and thus frustrates their benevolent intentions. ' Günderode ' is well enough; but is really not so very remarkable as to justify the extatics of the editor.

THE MILLENNIUM OF THE APOCALYPSE. — This is a work from the pen of Prof. BUSH, of the New-York University, upon a theme of interest to most readers. The writer assumes the ground that the *Millennium*, strictly so called, is *past*; but he adds, that he has not been led to embrace or utter this opinion merely from a perverse love of paradox, and that he has no disposition ruthlessly to pluck from the Christian or the philanthropist so fond and sacred a hope as that of a coming age of light and glory to the church, without offering any thing to compensate the spoliation. ' Instead of robbing the treasury of Christian hope of a gem so precious, and of abstracting from benevolent effort so mighty a motive, his view of the futurities of Zion, admitting the Millennium to be past, opens to the eye of Faith a still more cheering prospect — a lengthened vista of richer and brighter beatitudes.' We think this volume will find many readers. It is neatly produced by the publisher, Mr. JOHN P. JEWETT, of Salem, (Mass.,) and is on sale in this city at Messrs. DAYTON AND NEWMAN's.

'CYCLOPEDIA INDIANENSIS.' — We argue well for the interest and value of this forthcoming publication of Mr. SCHOOLCRAFT, from a specimen which has been laid before us by the publishers, Messrs. PLATT AND PETERS. The work will contain a general description of the Indian tribes of North and South America, comprising their origin, history, biography, manners and customs, language and religion; their numbers and divisions into tribes, their ethnographical affinities, territorial possessions, and geographical and proper names; their antiquities and monumental remains, their mythology, hieroglyphics, and picture-writing; their allegories, oral tales, and traditions; their civil polity, arts, employments and amusements, and other traits of their character and condition, past and present; together with a comprehensive lexicon of Indian words and phrases; the whole alphabetically arranged. This is a wide field of illustration and research; and we hazard nothing in saying that there is no man in the United States so competent to its complete occupation as Mr. HENRY R. SCHOOLCRAFT. As an old correspondent of the KNICKERBOCKER, our readers do not need to be informed that he holds the pen of a ready and graceful writer; nor will they require any commendation of ours to secure its records, when 'clothed upon' with paper and types.

LYELL'S LECTURES ON GEOLOGY. — The eight Lectures on Geology recently delivered with such marked acceptance at the Tabernacle by Mr. LYELL, the eminent President of the London Geological Society, have been issued in a neat pamphlet from the office of the 'New-York Tribune.' They were reported with remarkable accuracy by the able associate-editor of that popular journal, H. J. RAYMOND, Esq., and are upon the following subjects, or divisions of the main theme: Fresh Water formations of Auvergne; Extinct Volcanoes of successive Periods; Structure of Ætna; Origin of Granite Rocks; Changes in the organic World; Upheaval and Subsidence of the Earth's crust; Submergence and Reёlevation of the Temple of Serapis; Origin of Coral Reefs, and Theory of their Circular Form; Coraline Limestone of various Geological Ages; Nature and Origin of Coal; Period of its Formation; Foot-marks of Fossil Animals; The Niagara District; Chirotherium organic remains of the most ancient Rocks; Recession of the Falls of Niagara; Boulder Formation; Transporting Power of Ice; Action of Glaziers and Icebergs.

HOUSE OF REFUGE. — We have before us the Sixteenth Annual Report of the Managers of the New-York House of Refuge for Juvenile Delinquents; and are surprised at the amount of good which its benevolent operations have effected. Since the introduction of this admirable system of reformation, the number of juvenile convicts, as appears from official returns, has diminished by nearly one half, and in some years beyond even this; and of those once discharged from the confinement of the House of Refuge, very few are ever re-committed. Indeed, we find in the appendix ample evidence that a great majority of those who leave the walls of the institution subsequently become valuable members of society. Their pride of character is preserved; for they have no prison-taint upon their name; and the 'delinquencies' for which they have been rather admonished than punished are swallowed up in their confirmed reformation — a 'newness of life,' morally speaking, which serves as a 'mantle of oblivion' to the past.

HISTORY OF ITALY. — The last three numbers of HARPER'S invaluable 'Family Library' are devoted to a 'History of Italy and the Italian Islands, from the earliest ages to the present time. By WILLIAM SPALDING, Esq., Professor of Rhetoric in the University of Edinburgh.' The plan of the work is founded upon that of the Edinburgh Cabinet Library. The history of the revolutions, political, social, and intellectual, through which the Italians have passed, in ancient as well as modern times, is combined with a description of the antiquities, the scenery, and the physical peculiarities of the interesting region which they inhabit. The writer resided for a considerable period in Italy, and brought to his task an enthusiasm and unwearied research, that have resulted in a more popular survey of the country, embracing all its relations, than we remember before to have encountered. The volumes are illustrated by numerous engravings, maps, plans, etc.

NATURAL HISTORY. — The Discourse delivered by Dr. JOHN W. FRANCIS of this city, upon the opening of the new Hall of the New-York Lyceum of Natural History, has recently been published. The accomplished author modestly states that the Address is 'merely a general and hasty view of some of the objects to which the scientific institution, by whose request it was written, are devoted;' but we must be permitted to add, that it is much more. It is in fact a comprehensive and well-arranged synopsis of all the prominent themes of natural history, interspersed with collateral allusions and suggestions, which show that they proceed from a full mind, that can both reason and illustrate its reasonings in a manner equally clear and eloquent. The Address is very neatly executed by its publisher, Mr. LUDWIG, Vesey-street.

'THE ZICALI, OR GIPSEYS OF SPAIN.' — We have been greatly entertained and instructed by a perusal of this work from the press of Messrs. WILEY AND PUTNAM. The singular race of which it treats, long an especial study of the author in the various countries which they inhabit, are minutely presented to the reader, in their habits, manners, and modes of existence; matters which have often formed a prominent feature in much of the poetry and romance of Europe. We were surprised to learn that in Russia, and especially in Moscow, the beautiful gipsey-women are often allied in marriage with some of the noblest families in the empire; and that they frequently acquire immense wealth by the exercise of their vocal powers, which are described as being of the highest order of excellence. We commend 'The Zicali' to the reader as a work concerning which there can be 'no mistake,' as touching the interest it excites and the instruction it imparts.

'THE IDEAL MAN.' — This is the chief title of a small volume of 'Conversations between two Friends, upon the Beautiful, the Good, and the True, as manifested in actual life.' The purpose of the writer is certainly an excellent one; and judging from a cursory perusal, he would seem to have successfully executed it. His remarks upon the fine arts, on the management of children, and on the influence of domestic affection, are admirable; and other themes are glanced at with scarcely less force of argument and grace of style. We commend especially to our bachelor and spinster readers the observations upon matrimony, and the picture which is presented of the comparative blessings of the double and single state. We predict that the 'Ideal Man' will prove a most potent match-maker; and if his readers follow his inculcations, we doubt not they will find his matches to have been made in heaven.

STERLING'S POEMS. — We are right glad to welcome the handsome edition of the poetical works of JOHN STERLING, recently published by Mr. HERMAN HOOKER, Philadelphia. Our readers can hardly fail to remember 'The Sexton's Daughter' of this charming poet, as well as his various 'Hymns of a Hermit' in BLACKWOOD'S Magazine. The London Quarterly Review pronounces STERLING'S poems to be 'full of tenderness, fancy, and truth, and especially to be recommended for correct versification and good English. They have the pleasing tone of WORDSWORTH without the mannerism of phrase and imagery by which the *imitators* of that poet are marked and distinguished.' Beside 'The Sexton's Daughter' and 'Hymns of a Hermit,' the present volume embraces many superior poems by the same author, which we lack space to particularize.

THE BLIND BOY. — OLIVER DITSON of Boston, late PARKER AND DITSON, one of the first musical publishers in the United States, as regards taste in the selection and neatness in the execution of the ballads which bear his imprint, has just issued Miss GOULD'S pathetic song of 'The Blind Boy,' with DEMPSTER'S music. With the chaste beauty, feeling, and expression which distinguish this production, we have long been acquainted; and we are glad that it has been wedded to music which corresponds perfectly to the sentiment it embodies. No musical composer has succeeded better than DEMPSTER in the composition of those touching melodies which go home to the heart; and we think in the present instance he has been eminently successful. 'The Blind Boy' has become a general favorite, having already reached a goodly number of editions.

'SHORT STORIES' is the appropriate title of two little volumes from the press of BIXBY AND COMPANY, Park-Row. Without possessing any supernatural feature, or any thing indeed that could be termed 'thrilling,' these short stories will yet be found to repay perusal as well as more ambitious and more popular sketches. They are for the most part evidently founded on fact, and many of their incidents are derived from the personal observation and experience of the writer. A friend at our elbow characterizes these two volumes as books likely to be very take-up-able on board a steam-boat or rail-road car, or take-down-able from a shelf in one's library.

THE DAUGHTERS OF ENGLAND. — Mrs. ELLIS, whose 'Women of England' was most favorably received, has been encouraged to treat the theme more at large, and to follow out the minuter details of individual, domestic, and social duty. She proposes to divide the main subject into three parts, in which will be separately considered the character and situation of the Daughters, Wives and Mothers of England. The 'Daughters' form the subject of the volume before us; and the social and domestic duties of the middling ranks are more especially set forth and illustrated. The series can hardly fail to be productive of great good to 'those of the sex who think.' Messrs. APPLETON AND COMPANY are the publishers.

GOETHE'S 'EGMONT.' — Messrs. JAMES MUNROE AND COMPANY, Boston, have issued in a handsome form the tragedy of 'Egmont,' one of the finest of the plays of GOETHE. Mrs. JAMIESON, it will be remembered, alludes in terms of warm commendation in her 'Winter Studies and Summer Rambles' to this production ; and the two scenes from it contained in Mrs. AUSTIN's 'Fragments from German Prose Writers' will form an additional inducement to a perusal of the entire performance. For ourselves we may say that we have read 'Egmont' with increasing interest to the end, and can promise its readers a similar enjoyment.

'DEVOTIONAL MELODIES.' — Thus is entitled a thin and miserably-executed book, containing sundry moral and religious hymns, by CHARLES M. F. DEEMS, A. B. We are bound to believe the writer 'a good man,' in the sense of Neighbor VARGES, at least. His poetry, though very poor is very pious, and sufficiently original ; but his design of giving devotional words to favorite airs has been anticipated by more capable pens. Mrs. DANA's 'Southern Harp' will more creditably supply the desideratum of which our sacred bard complains. Mr. DEEMS does not seem to anticipate the circulation of his volume, save among his personal friends. He will not be disappointed.

'IDEALS AND OTHER POEMS.' — We think we recognize in 'ALGERNON,' the author of this tasteful little volume, a poetical correspondent of the KNICKERBOCKER. The work contains two or three felicitous translations from the German, and several original effusions of merit. Those of the latter which impress us the most favorably are 'A New Year's Chime,' 'The Departed,' and the pleasant paraphrase of the celebrated 'wolf story' of Gen. PUTNAM. The externals of the volume are creditable to the care of the publisher, Mr. HENRY PERKINS, Philadelphia.

'THE CROFTON BOYS.' — Miss MARTINEAU is turning her talents to good account in the production of entertaining and useful little volumes for youth. We have already had occasion, in noticing the Messrs. APPLETON's series of 'Tales for the People and their Children,' to mention several works of this character from her pen ; as the 'Peasant and Prince,' 'Feats on the Fiord,' etc. The book before us we thought not to have read ; but dipping into it, we found it so interesting that we read it through at a sitting which was not so long as it was pleasant.

Our New Volume.

ON the first day of July next will be published the first number of the TWENTIETH VOLUME of the KNICKERBOCKER MAGAZINE. It will appear upon entirely new type throughout, of the most tasteful kinds, and will be printed in a style of unsurpassed excellence. It will also be embellished with an illustrative engraving, designed and executed expressly for the work. In relation to its literary attractions, it will be deemed sufficient to say that it will not only fully sustain its past character in this regard, but that its intellectual claims will be enhanced by numerous contributions, already in hand, from eminent and popular pens, in various sections of our country, and from distinguished trans-Atlantic writers. In short, we may truly affirm that we never before entered upon a new volume with so many good things in store for our numerous readers. We ask but *promptitude* on the part of our subscribers, to insure them a monthly *mélange* as various and entertaining as can be found on either side the great water.

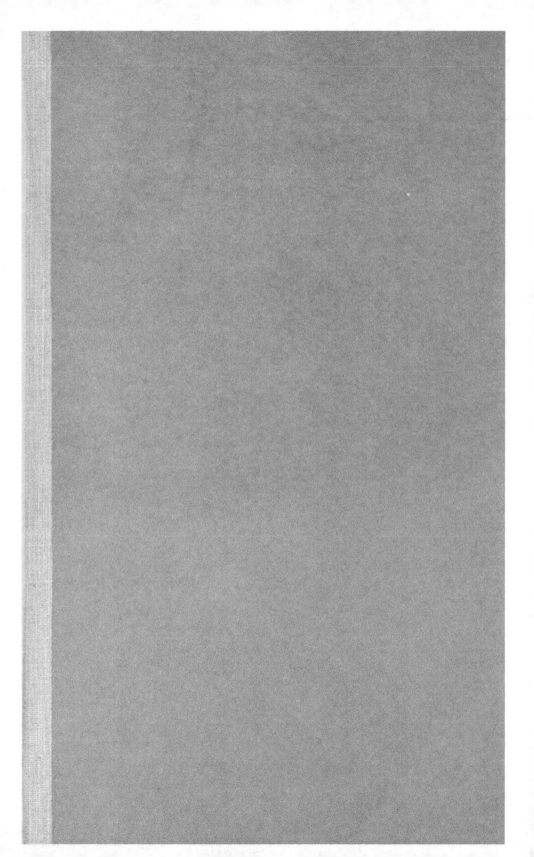

Check Out More Titles From HardPress Classics Series In this collection we are offering thousands of classic and hard to find books. This series spans a vast array of subjects – so you are bound to find something of interest to enjoy reading and learning about.

Subjects:
Architecture
Art
Biography & Autobiography
Body, Mind &Spirit
Children & Young Adult
Dramas
Education
Fiction
History
Language Arts & Disciplines
Law
Literary Collections
Music
Poetry
Psychology
Science
…and many more.

Visit us at www.hardpress.net

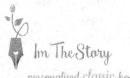